MW00528569

The Wonderful and Surprising History of Sweeney Todd

Kingston upon Hull City Libraries

WITHDRAWN

FROM STOCK

FOR SALE

Also available from Continuum

Backstage Stories
Edited by Barbara Baker

Musical Theatre
By John Kenrick

Seven Basic Plots
By Christopher Booker

The Bedside, Bathtub & Armchair Companion to Agatha Christie
By Dick Riley and Pam McAllister

The Bedside, Bathtub & Armchair Companion to Sherlock Holmes
By Dick Riley and Pam McAllister

The Wonderful and Surprising History of Sweeney Todd

The Life and Times of an Urban Legend

Robert L. Mack

continuum

Continuum
The Tower Building
11 York Road
London SE1 7NX
www.continuumbooks.com

80 Maiden Lane, Suite 704
New York
NY 10038

© Robert L. Mack 2007
All rights reserved. No part of this publication may be reproduced or transmitted in any form or by any means, electronic or mechanical, including photocopying, recording, or any information storage or retrieval system, without prior permission in writing from the publishers.

Robert L. Mack has asserted his right under the Copyright, Designs and Patents Act, 1988, to be identified as Author of this work.

First published 2007

British Library Cataloguing-in-Publication Data
A catalogue record for this book is available from the British Library.

ISBN: 978-0-8264-9791-8

Library of Congress Cataloging-in-Publication Data
A catalog record for this book is available from the Library of Congress.

Typeset by Fakenham Photosetting Ltd, Fakenham, Norfolk NR21 8NN
Printed and bound in Great Britain by MPG Books Ltd, Bodmin, Cornwall

For Roger Short
(who first thought of it)

HULL LIBRARIES	
0127~~7216~~ 310 789	
Bertrams	23.01.08
398.22	£25.00

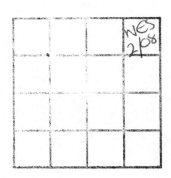

v

Contents

Acknowledgements

I would like to take this opportunity to thank the following groups and individuals for their generous assistance in completing this project:

My colleagues in the Department of English in the School of Arts, Languages, and Literatures at the University of Exeter, especially Anthony Fothergill, Regenia Gagnier, Adeline Johns-Putra, Bob Lawson-Peebles, Angelique Richardson, Rick Rylance, Jane Spencer and Paul Young; and a special thanks to Julia Davey. I am indebted to the resources made available to me by the Library and Information Services provided by the University of Exeter, including online databases such as the Times Digital Archive and the Eighteenth Century Collections Online.

I would like to extend my very particular thanks to Mr Stephen Sondheim for his comments on earlier drafts of some of the material contained in these pages, and for the unusually generous support and interest he showed in my book in progress. All quotations from Mr Sondheim's work are reported here by kind permission of the author; direct quotations from his 'musical thriller' *Sweeney Todd, The Demon Barber of Fleet Street*; more particularly, are © 1978, 1979 by Revelation Publishing Corp. and Rilting Music.

I am also grateful for the assistance on this particular project of John Adcock; Bill Blackbeard; Lynne Chapman (Administrator, The Stephen Sondheim Society); Dr Dick Collins; John Chadwick-Healey and John Copley (Royal Opera House, Covent Garden); Mike Dash; Margaret Anne Doody; Michael Dixon (Honorary Archivist, British Puppet and Model Theatre Guild); James Durston (The Barber Shop; Exeter Guildhall); Rachel Hassall (Assistant Keeper, University of Bristol Theatre Collection); Steve Holland; Michael Holmes; Catherine Howell and Noreen Marshall (The Museum of Childhood, Bethnal Green); David Orme. Michael Zulli generously allowed me to reproduce material from his own original 'Sweeney Todd' project in the illustrations.

I owe special thanks to my unfailingly enthusiastic and helpful Research Assistant, Ms Margaret (Peggy) Yoon, and to Justin Gilbert, who generously offered to share both his unparalleled knowledge of and material relating to the early history of *The String of Pearls* and the Sweeney Todd story as a 'penny blood'. I must emphasise that any errors that remain in the work are my own.

A much abbreviated version of the Chronology that ends the present volume was included in my edition of the original text of *The String of Pearls*, published as *Sweeney Todd, The Demon Barber of Fleet Street* (Oxford: Oxford University Press, 2007), xxxi–xxxvii.

Finally, I owe a special debt of gratitude to my fellow Manhattanite Louise Crocoll, who suggested one Saturday afternoon in 1979 that we might enjoy the matinee performance of Stephen Sondheim's *Sweeney Todd* at the Uris Theater in New York. She was right.

List of Illustrations

Hoc etiam quod scribo, pendet plerumque ex aliorum
sentatia et auctoritate; nec ipse forsan insanio, sed
insanientes sequor.

[I write for the most part to satisfy the taste and
judgement of others; I am not mad myself, but I follow
those who are.]
(Catullus)*

If thou were a pie I would eat thee.
(traditional English saying)

Friends help you move. Good friends help you
move bodies.
(Anonymous)

*   Catullus, as quoted in Robert Burton, *The Anatomy of Melancholy*, Pt. 3, Sec. 1, Mem.
1, Subs. 1. Introduction by William H. Gass (New York: New York Review Books,
2001), 8.

Preface

It isn't the pleasantest thing in the world to sit for an hour or two looking at murders.
(Thomas W. Erle, *Letters from a Theatrical Scene-Painter*)[1]

Contrary to the seemingly commonsensical view expressed by Thomas W. Erle in the passage quoted as an epigraph above, theatre-goers on both sides of the Atlantic (and, indeed, throughout the entire English-speaking world) would appear for well over 150 years to have found the activities that were supposed to have taken place in Sweeney Todd's notorious tonsorial parlour in London's Fleet Street to provide not only 'pleasant' but positively compulsive viewing. Todd and his casually opportunistic accomplice – the no less infamous pie-maker, Mrs Lovett – have entertained generations of audiences within the varying frames of a narrative that is (to put it mildly) not exactly the stuff of which such dreams are normally made.[2]

Some readers, as the chronicler and historian of boys' magazines, E.S. Turner once emphasized, have gone so far as to credit Sweeney Todd with having brought a perfectly suitable word describing his trade into eternal disrepute.[3] 'Sweeney Todd, both on stage and in print,' wrote one Leader Writer in the *Times Literary Supplement* in March 1941, 'was considered so vulgar that the word "barber" was considered vulgar too. An old-fashioned schoolmaster once commanded his boys never, never to use such a word, and always say "hairdresser"'.[4] The writer may in fact, in this instance, have been recalling the admonition of Charles Dickens: 'I would suggest', as one of the novelist's characters opined in *Master Humphrey's Clock* (1840), 'that *barbers* is not exactly the kind of language which is agreeable and soothing to our feelings; I believe there is such a word in the dictionary as *hairdressers*'.[5] In a later Dickens periodical, *All the Year Round* (1876), a customer in a barber's shop who is requested by the shop's owner to take a seat and amuse himself with a newspaper for five minutes begins quickly to entertain the notion that he has placed himself in 'a ticklish situation'. 'There was once a barber', the recently arrived customer muses with anxious concern,

Sweeney Todd by name, if I rightly remember, who kept a shop in Fleet-street, ostensibly for cutting hair and mowing beards, but whose real business was the cutting of human throats. There was a trap-door in the floor of Sweeney's shop on which the victim's chair was placed, and after he had been lathered, Mr. Todd would say, 'Just tilt your head a little farther back, sir, so that I may get at the underneath part!' And then – slish! and in a jiffy the body was robbed, the bolt that held the trap withdrawn, a splash was heard in the turbulent flowing Fleet-ditch below, and a mop and a handful of sawdust made the shop clean and tidy for the next customer. Might not this be the fate in store for me, the villainous haircutter's suavity being a mere blind? I need not be shaved, at all events. I would merely have my hair brushed and my whiskers trimmed. An assault with a pair of scissors might be painful; but it was hardly likely that the first snick would do my business, and in a tussle I felt pretty confident who would get the best of it. So I sat down and opened out the newspaper, before carelessly observing that I was in no hurry; at the same time resolved to diligently watch and listen.[6]

The customer does his best to prevent such thoughts from overwhelming him, however, and soon admits to himself: 'now that I came to observe the barber more attentively, he was not in the least like the cross-eyed, goblin-visaged, person Sweeney Todd was represented as being; on the contrary, he was rather a pleasant-looking little man'.[7]

Regardless of any of its other possible claims on our attention, the story of Sweeney Todd – even if encountered only once – possesses the rare, narrative power forever to transform our perceptions, awareness and responses to an otherwise innocuous event, and to haunt the imaginations of entire generations. Few people who have watched Alfred Hitchcock's *Psycho* (1960) ever feel quite the same about closing their eyes whilst taking a shower again; few of those who have read Peter Benchley's *Jaws* (1974) or have seen Steven Spielberg's film of the same name (1975) can ever swim in the ocean without the apprehension – however absurd or unrealistic – of being attacked by a shark. Fortunately for us, the invention and manufacture of a safety razor with disposable blades by King Camp Gillette in 1903 rendered the use of straight razors generally obsolete, but anyone who has perforce submitted themselves to the hirsute ministrations of a barber wielding such a 'cut-throat' razor is likely to have tended, like the gentleman in the anecdote quoted above, 'diligently' to have kept at least one eye open at all times.

For many, the name of Sweeney Todd has remained as close to synonymous with his profession as that of any practitioner could ever be. When a proposed Hairdressers' Bill came under discussion in Parliament in July 1949 (it would have required all barbers to be registered with a 'hairdressers' council') the Labour member for Norwich, John Paton, objected to the feeble leniency of its provisions, suggesting that under the bill's terms Sweeney Todd 'the Demon Barber of Fleet Street, could go on for the rest of his life not only shaving throats, but cutting them, provided he always remember to pay his annual 5s. registration fee'.[8] Writing in the pages of *The Times* in 1973, the columnist Philip Howard observed that even in the late twentieth century (by which time the trade had of course almost entirely relinquished the custom of shaving its male clients) the hairdressers of London yet possessed their great predecessor's unrivalled ability to 'alarm' their paying customers in any number of ways:

> When they get you in their chair, they will do more than cut your hair. For instance, they will make your scalp crawl with allegations of dandruff and receding hair, then sell you a bottle of 'honey and flowers' as a potion for eternal hairiness.
>
> The barbers of London were recognized as craftsmen distinct from surgeons only in 1745; and some of the morose clippers and gashers beneath the metropolitan railway stations still practise their craft as if they longed for the good old Sweeney Todd days, when a sharp man could make ear pie on the side in his basement.[9]

In 1982 the *New York Times* columnist William Safire continued to link Todd's name with the tendency for contemporary haircutters to replace the designation of 'barber' with more palatable euphemisms. 'Barbers', Safire contended, 'have snipped the word out of their vocabulary, much as marketers sold salesmen, administrative assistants shredded gal Fridays, and funeral directors buried the morticians who had previously interred the undertakers'. Thanks to the likes of tonsorial gangsters such as Sweeney Todd, Safire suggested, 'the word barber has been rubbed out'.[10]

However much he may be perceived by some to have discredited his profession, the figure of Sweeney Todd himself would appear not only to have proven to be a perennially popular draw at box offices around the world, but also to have staked a solid claim – alongside such figures as Brutus (the legendary founder of the city), Richard or 'Dick' Whittington, Samuel Pepys, Samuel Johnson, 'Jack the Ripper', or even Dickens himself – to being one of the most famous Londoners of all time.[11] Even those who maintain a healthy scepticism regarding the facts of the barber's history seem willing to be converted when confronted with the slightest bit of anecdotal or circumstantial evidence. A property manager by the name of Mr A. Waller, at work on a building (No. 154) on the north side of Fleet Street, opposite Bouverie Street, in 1947, for a long time professed, like many Londoners, to have 'no strong opinion on the matter'; his discovery, in the course of his demolition of the structure then occupying those premises, not only of 'a fanlight and some pieces of wood which were buried below plaster, all bearing the Demon Barber's name', but also 'signs of trap-doors, and a cellar with a manhole which [led] to a sewer' transformed him at once into a true believer. (Mr Waller may forever have remained unaware that a pre-War barber operating out of the neighbouring property of No. 153, whose name appeared in the *London Directory* in 1939, had adopted the name 'as an attraction to his customers'.)[12] For other Londoners, Sweeney Todd was simply a fact of city life, and likely to manifest himself as such in any number of ways. It is recorded that no less a figure than Sir William Treloar, Lord Mayor of the City of London in 1907, who had been born and raised in his family's famous carpet shop on Ludgate Hill, recalled that when he was a child, he and a group of playfellows 'delighted in going into a barber shop that stood at the corner of Fleet Street and Fetter Lane, with a doorway in each. At a concerted signal they would rush through the front door one after the other and, shouting "Sweeney Todd" as they went, dash out of the Fetter Lane door.' 'There was a rush', he would confess, 'as the last one ran a risk of being caught'.[13]

Todd's story has been told by many different people and in many different forms, but the essential outline of his narrative is straightforward enough. Driven by motives ranging from simple greed in most early versions, to a complex scenario of carefully exacted revenge in subsequent retellings, Todd is a barber who routinely murders the patrons of his Fleet Street shop – on some occasions slitting their throats, on others stabbing, strangling, or bludgeoning them to death with his bare hands, but almost always making use of his ingeniously constructed barber's chair in the process. After dramatically hurtling his chosen victims head-over-heels into the dank and inescapable basement of his Fleet Street shop, he then disposes of their bodies by transferring them to the nearby premises of Mrs Lovett, who turns the fresh corpses into succulent meat pies (veal, her customers are often told). The clothes, possessions and unusable body parts of Todd's former customers are hidden both within the barber's house and within the increasingly noisome and overcrowded vaults of the neighbouring church of St Dunstan's in the West, also on Fleet Street. Todd and Lovett are eventually brought to justice, in most versions of the story through the efforts of an enterprising pair of star-crossed young lovers, usually named Mark Ingestrie and Johanna Oakley.

The relatively simple frame provided by Todd's history has not only presented an unusually wide variety of writers and artists with the opportunity to offer (each in his or her own fashion) a gruesomely compelling piece of gothic horror and melodrama, but has demonstrated itself to be peculiarly resonant; each successive generation has been compelled to use the mythic and metaphorical elements inherent in the tale of Sweeney Todd – the themes of avarice, ambition, love, desire, appetite, vanity, atonement, retribution, justice and cannibalism in all its many forms – effectively to mirror its own concerns, both as individuals and as members of society at large. A closer examination of the various manifestation of the many 'lives' of Sweeney Todd yields considerable insight into some of the most compelling mythical and metaphorical elements inherent in modern city life, and in the experience of human 'civilization' and the civilizing process, generally. The ghosts of Sweeney Todd and Mrs Lovett, though subject to some radical transformations in time, linger in our traditions of popular representation. Any investigation into the historical conditions that have given rise to this resonance offers a glimpse into the trauma related to the real and imagined landscapes of the modern urban environment.

*

> *Let me know fully therefore the effect*
> *Of this thy dismal preparation,*
> *This talk, fit for a charnel.*
> (John Webster, *The Duchess of Malfi*)[14]

The present volume is divided into three main sections. In the first part ('Contexts, Themes and Background') my central purpose has been to provide a leisurely introduction to some of the larger cultural concerns that are raised by the story of Sweeney Todd. These pages offer what might best be described as a paratactic, inductive examination of the nature and function of the cultural information and urban mythology that underlies the barber's story. When, in Charles Dickens's *Martin Chuzzlewit* (1843–4), the character of Tom Pinch is compelled to seek his fortune in London, the author feigns some surprise that such a guileless country man is not within minutes of his arrival 'led into the dens of any of those preparers of cannibalic pastry, who are represented in many standard country legends as doing a lively retail business in the Metropolis'.[15] Although, as we will see, written just before the earliest documented appearance of Sweeney Todd as a figure in England's criminal or literary history in 1846, Dickens's aside makes it clear that the possibility that some unscrupulous pie-makers were contravening the Trade Descriptions Acts of their day was entertained well before any single 'textual' version of Mrs Lovett's activities in Bell Yard was ever put to paper. The first part of this book undertakes to survey in a pointedly casual manner the general background against which the specific story of Sweeney Todd originally emerged, and against which it has, in its many versions, continued to play itself out; the aim of its enlargement is to render Todd's history more understandable than if it were presented at once to the reader in a merely straightforward or dryly factual manner.

The second part of the book ('Text and Sources') is focused more tightly on the origins and literary history of the specific narrative of Sweeney Todd. This section examines in some detail the barber's earliest appearance in English fiction in the anonymously authored serial *The String of Pearls*, which first appeared in the pages of Edward Lloyd's *The People's Periodical and Family Library* in 1846–7. It also traces both the specific textual precedents as well as some of the mythic analogues and narrative prototypes that led to the creation of that same tale. The story of Sweeney Todd, as we shall see, was in actual fact cobbled together from a curious and complicated amalgam of sources. Some elements of the story were taken from urban myths that had circulated both in England and on the continent for literally hundreds of years. Others had been drawn from more recent sources in the popular and periodical press. Still others, finally, would appear to have been extracted from or somehow inspired by contemporary fictions being written throughout the mid-nineteenth century. The true originality of *The String of Pearls* lay more in its own uniquely innovative and effective conjunction of a number of tales that had already been widely available as independent stories and motifs. Its central strength, in other words, was the simple novelty of its narrative conceit.

The third section of the present volume ('Visions and Revisions') – when taken together with the more comprehensive Chronology that follows the main body of the text here – explores just some of the many manifestations of Todd's story subsequent to its initial appearance in 1846–7. The scope of the Chronology itself has been extended so as to offer the modern reader some indication of the range of those particular texts and sources – both within the British tradition and within a wider European context, more generally – that might legitimately be situated as the possible narrative precedents and proto-myths for the very specific tale of Sweeney Todd, as the barber's story was first published in the form of a serial fiction, and then dramatized as a stage melodrama in England in the mid-nineteenth century. The main purpose of the Chronology is to provide both a summary and a convenient point of reference for information regarding the most significant of the many versions of the Sweeney Todd story, and to note the various ways in which that same story has periodically urged itself into the consciousness of the nation, appearing in print, on stage, on cinema screens and within a range of other media through, even, to the opening decade of the twenty-first century. Presented from 1847 in theatres either as *Sweeney Todd* or *The String of Pearls*, the barber's narrative retained its enormous popularity as a stage melodrama for many years. George Dibdin Pitt and, later, Frederick Hazleton drama- tized the story in the nineteenth century; the work of the former was being performed by the company at the Britannia Theatre, in Hoxton, even before the original serial narrative had reached its own conclusion within the pages of *The People's Periodical*. Sadly, the Britannia Theatre itself was destroyed in the Blitz, but a number of contemporary sources combine effectively to recreate the atmosphere of Dibdin Pitt's original production. *Sweeney Todd* continued to be regarded a quintessential example of the Victorian melodrama well into the twentieth century. This section looks at the contexts within which some of the productions in Britain that purported to be based on Dibdin Pitt's seminal drama were originally staged; it also examines an early silent film adaptation from 1928, featuring Moore Marriot, as well as the more widely known film adaptation (starring Tod Slaughter) in 1936, and several later film versions. Throughout the twentieth century, 'revised' stage versions, such as that by Christopher Bond in 1973, were also presented to the public; each of these versions and variations to some extent expanded the reach of Todd's story as a vehicle for social commentary, satire and reform. Bond's work in particular raised the possibility that Todd's narrative could be re-presented as a national and domestic tragedy of almost Shakespearean proportions, and led eventually to the creation of a work that would soon be recognized as constituting a defining moment in the already long and eventful life of Sweeney Todd – the epochal event of Stephen Sondheim's 'musical thriller' based on the story in 1979.

Part Three moves on eventually to consider the central achievement of Sondheim's work, and briefly traces some of the debate that has surrounded the cultural status of his *Sweeney Todd* – a debate that finds a great many critics identifying the work as occupying a crucial moment in the inter-twining histories of musical theatre, opera and light opera. (Sondheim's *Todd* is now regularly performed by many of the most respected houses in the world, Covent Garden, Sydney and the Chicago Lyric among them.) Finally, some of the other, even more peculiar manifestations of Sweeney Todd (e.g. in the form of a surprisingly popular series of puppet plays, ballets and graphic novels) are also selectively considered in this section.

PART ONE

Contexts, Themes and Background

KINGSTON UPON HULL
CITY LIBRARIES

Chapter 1

Du Côté de Chez Todd: Man Eating, Meat Pies and the Macabre

*Potted meats. What is home without Plumtree's potted meat? Incomplete. What a stupid
ad! Under the obituary notices they stuck it. ... Lord knows what concoction.*
(James Joyce, *Ulysses*)[1]

In February 2004, police investigating charges against accused Canadian
serial killer Robert Pickton approached provincial health officials in British
Columbia with what they were careful to characterize at the time as a purely
'hypothetical question'.[2] Pickton, then 53, was already awaiting trial for the
killings of 20 young women. The Canadian authorities in fact suspected that
Pickton had actually been involved in the murder of more than 60 women,
many of them local Vancouver prostitutes. Most of the victims had disappeared from the streets of the city's notoriously seedy 'Downtown Eastside'
neighbourhood within the previous ten years or more. The police believed
that the often homeless street-workers (many of whom were addicted to
drugs) had been picked up by Pickton in the district; he appears then to have
driven them back to his dilapidated, small-scale farm just outside Vancouver.
Once there, authorities alleged, he assaulted and then killed them.

Although quick to single out Pickton as a prime suspect in the disappearances, local officials were slow to awaken to some of the more grotesque
implications of his arrest. The rural Port Coquitlam farm where Pickton
was apprehended also served as home to his part-time 'occupation' as a
processor and distributor of pork products. Police were aware from the
beginning of the investigation that the suspect raised and slaughtered pigs
on the property. The farm – today a muddy and desolate wasteland marked
only by patches of wild grass and heaps of concrete rubble – lay some 40
minutes south-east of downtown Vancouver. The police were eager to point
out that the farm's pig-slaughtering operation was 'not officially licensed';

3

they emphasized that neither the accused himself nor members of his family were any longer serious commercial farmers 'professionally' in the business of selling processed meat to wider retail outlets. The authorities were rather less keen to acknowledge that Pickton had nevertheless continued regularly to sell and distribute 'processed meat products' among his friends and acquaintances. He was known more particularly to have supplied pork to be grilled and roasted at the region's local party hall – a venue which, as chance would have it, just happened to be owned and operated by his brother, David.

David Francis Pickton's so-called party hall, the 'Piggy Palace', was in actual fact little more than a converted farm property. A run-down if reasonably capacious barn-like structure covered by a tin roof, the 'Palace' was best known among Port Coquitlam locals for hosting wild and unruly (and often, it was rumoured, drug-fuelled) parties and late evening barbeques. Despite its decidedly working-class appearance and reputation for attracting a raunchy crowd of rough and (in the words of one patron) 'bad-ass' night-time regulars, the hall served as home to the 'Piggy Palace Good Times Society' and was therefore officially registered as part of a non-profit charitable organization. As such, it was just as likely to function by default within the relatively small community as a legitimate venue for money-raising events sponsored by sports teams and other 'respectable' civic bodies. The 'Palace' had in its recent past hosted dances, 'concerts' and a variety of other recreations for local groups. These same organizations were said to have included among their members representatives of the city council, prominent regional politicians and area business men, the neighbourhood's 'ice hockey moms', and even elementary schoolchildren.

Given the nature of the charges being levelled against Pickton, health officials were soon reporting reluctantly to have concluded that the probabilities of what they delicately described as 'cross-contamination' within the triangle that connected the farm with the nightclub and then linked both to Pickton's other neighbours, suggested that human remains had *possibly* found their way into or otherwise 'contaminated' an untold amount of the pork meat at the Port Coquitlam properties. The authorities did their best to play down the gruesome chain of circumstantial evidence linking the murders alleged to have been committed on Pickton's land with any of the meat products that might have made their way to his friends or to the food served at his brother's social hall. 'There is no evidence', Captain Catherine Gulliford of the Royal Canadian Mounted Police was careful initially to stress, 'that we are dealing with anything other than a very specific localized issue, with a number of local people.' As the investigation widened, however, both police and health officials began reluctantly to concede that a great many more individuals were likely to have received meat from Pickton in some form or another than they had originally been led to believe. To make matters worse, an increasing body of evidence further suggested that other, assorted remains traceable to Pickton's meat-processing operation – remains that would in any case have been deemed 'unsuitable for human consumption' in any form – had nevertheless managed covertly to be made available to an even wider range of consumers.

The original police warrant for Pickton's arrest had been served in February 2002; subsequent charges were added in May and October of that same year. As the months passed, the unspoken implications of the peculiarly evasive language used by officers early in their investigations became increasingly clear. Local headlines began to alert readers to the ghoulish possibility that Pickton's friends and neighbours might very well have unsuspectingly consumed significant portions of his victims, in the form of their seemingly inoffensive breakfast sausages and fried pork patties. News agencies around the world were soon reporting to shocked and incredulous readers and listeners that there could be little doubt but that the meat products distributed from the murderer's farm 'contained human remains'. Workers for local agencies involved in the case – among them one Elaine Allen, the former coordinator at a drop-in centre for sex workers in precisely the area within which Pickton had habitually picked up most of his victims – were both sickened and yet at the same time anxiously frustrated in their investigations by the fact that police had still, nevertheless, found 'no whole bodies at the pig farm'. Pickton, in other words, appeared to have managed almost completely to have destroyed any of the vital physical evidence that might have been used against him by disposing of the remains of his victims with such ruthless efficiency. In fact, there was now little reason to doubt that – thanks to the killer's association with his brother's meeting place and frequented night-spot – not only Pickton's friends but a significant portion of the town's entire population had been feeding for some time either on the meat of his victims themselves, or on the flesh of animals that had in turn consumed the better part of those same human remains. Pickton was suspected in many cases simply to have dismembered the bodies, possibly before feeding them piece by piece into a wood chipper on the farm. Much of what would have been left over might then have been mixed with other food by-products and likewise eventually thrown to the hogs.

To add one final and almost inconceivably bizarre twist to what was already a grim scenario, the otherwise 'unusable' remains of the very same slaughtered pigs that had fed on the flesh of the murdered women – bones, nerve tissue, and other gore – would appear with economic diligence to have been carried off to a local rendering plant, where they too had eventually contributed to the base ingredients used in a range of personal beauty and grooming products. These products included such commonplace items as lipstick, soap, perfume and hair shampoo. The use, in any form, of human body parts in the constitution of common household toiletries that were most often sold to consumers precisely for their abilities to enhance physical appearance and excite sexual allure was not merely shocking, but almost inconceivably unpalatable.

The possibility that a significant number of the town's population – among them friends and relatives of the missing women – had actually feasted on the bodies of the murdered victims in the guise of roast pork or other meat products was unthinkable. How, after all, was a small and relatively tightly connected community of just over 35,000 rural and semi-suburban inhabitants possibly meant to respond to such revelations? Or was there even such a thing as a proper mode or even a precedent for any kind of response at all? As a stunned family member of one of Pickton's many victims was reduced to admitting with blunt if close to catatonic under-statement when interviewed on a local radio programme: 'I'm not eating dinner tonight.'[3]

*

From childhood we eat pies – from girlhood and boyhood we eat pies – from middle age to old age we eat pies – in fact, pies in England may be considered as one of our best companions du voyage through life. It is we who leave them behind, not they who leave us; for our children and grandchildren will be as fond of pies as we have been.
(Alexis Soyer, *A Shilling Cookery for the People*)[4]

The passage quoted immediately above is taken from the work of one of the most famous innovators in the history of British cooking: Alexis Benoit Soyer (1809–58).[5] Born in the French village of Meaux-en-Brie, Soyer served his apprenticeship in the kitchens in and around Versailles, where he worked at one point for the reactionary Prince de Polignac, the Prime Minister of the revolutionary Charles X. Crossing the Channel shortly after the revolution of 1830, he soon established his reputation in London serving up elaborate banquets in the households of the country's elite. In 1837 Soyer was appointed Head Chef at the Reform Club. He would occupy the position until 1850 (a version of his 'Lamb Cutlets Reform' remains on the Club menus to this day). In 1851 he opened his own restaurant. Considered by many food historians to be among the first of such establishments in London, Soyer's 'Universal Symposium to All Nations' stood just opposite the Great Exhibition in Kensington Gardens. The press launch for the venue was attended by Karl Marx, who was duly chastised by his recent collaborator Friedrich Engels for regaling himself at the opening celebrations with champagne and *hommards à la Washington*.[6]

In marked contrast to some of his even more celebrated rivals (Antonin Carême, for example, who worked for both Napoleon I and the Tsar Alexander I before being lured to the Royal Palace at Brighton to cook for the Prince Regent, or Charles Elmé Francatelli, who served as personal chef to Queen Victoria), Alexis Soyer himself grew in time to be just as comfortable within the indigenous traditions of English cooking as he was among the rather more rarefied practices of continental haute cuisine. Although his

6

specially designed kitchens in the Reform's new Pall Mall clubhouse (1841) soon gained a reputation as one of the 'must-see' sights of London in their own right, and although he would never be behindhand in cultivating aristo-cratic patronage, Soyer himself was arguably the most genuinely enthusiastic of the great male chefs of the period. He was also among the first to realize the practical advantages to be gained by condescending to listen to and learn from his female contemporaries. The substantial, accumulated heritage of English cooking was – even at the time that chefs such as Soyer were importing new Parisian ideas into the kitchens of the British aristocracy – being preserved for the nation's culinary history in the more practical recipe books of native cooks such as Maria Rundell, Eliza Acton and Mrs Isabella Beeton (although the latter, as her recent biographer Kathryn Hughes points out, did not hesitate to repay any such compliment by plundering shame-lessly from Soyer's own published works).[7]

An aristocratic household throughout the eighteenth and nineteenth centuries would have been expected to employ – under the authority of the steward and housekeeper – not only a head chef, but also a clerk of the kitchen, to say nothing of innumerable kitchen maids and scullions. The extended period admittedly witnessed a number of debates regarding the range of domestic duties that were normally to be expected of the proper, aristocratic woman. Such debates were to some extent connected to the larger concerns manifested throughout British culture in the period that pitted the 'private' against the 'public', and that had begun in the closing decades of the eighteenth century to bring out into the open the nature of a woman's place in the so-called 'domestic sphere'. Some women considered it beneath their situation to know all that much about exactly what went on in their own kitchens, perhaps because such matters would have been consigned to the office of the household's male chef – an individual who in most cases would in any event, of course, have been hired not by the titular female head of the house, but by her husband. The social historian Rosemary Baird reminds us that in the mid-eighteenth century the wealthy brewer and friend of Samuel Johnson, Henry Thrale, maintained that his own wife's place was 'either in the drawing room or the bedchamber'. '*His* wife', the fastidious Thrale is said to have pronounced emphatically, 'was not to *think of the kitchen*.'[8]

Yet popular fiction throughout the eighteenth and nineteenth centuries seemed increasingly to reflect the country's growing interest in cooks and cooking. Jane Austen's Mrs Bennett, in *Pride and Prejudice* (1813), may airily dismiss the making of pies and kitchen work in general as occupations with which 'her daughters had nothing to do', but her fellow country-women were typically less snobbish and socially self-obsessed.[9] Novels throughout the period frequently focused on the weight such culinary skills could carry in the marriage market. The heroine of Eliza Haywood's hugely influential *The History of Miss Betsy Thoughtless* (1751) had been criticized by the father of one of her more eligible suitors for her lack of practical skills in the kitchen.

'I'll be hanged if she knows how to make a pye [sic] or a pudding,' the father – a city alderman – complains of the young Miss Betsy, doubting that she would even be capable of '[teaching] her maid to do it'.[10] The 'gentlefolks of Cranford', in Elizabeth Gaskell's volume devoted to the inhabitants of that village, published some 100 years after Haywood's novel (in 1851–3), were said still, typically, to pride themselves on practising an 'elegant economy' when it came to matters in the kitchen; in a similar vein, however much the mistress of a Cranford household might pretend 'not to know what cakes were set up' when her neighbours came to call, 'she knew, and she knew that [they] knew, and [they] knew that she knew that [they] knew, she had been busy all the morning making tea-bread and sponge-cakes'.[11]

Food, eating and consumption were inescapably universal concerns; the self-conscious 'universality' of Soyer's own 'Symposium' constitutes something of an acknowledgement of that fact. Then, as now, food and food preparation were almost always, if not acceptable domestic *activities*, then at the very least agreeable topics of conversation. Recounting the details of a Holland House dinner on the evening of 13 August 1832 in a letter to his sisters, the historian Thomas Babington Macaulay – whose fellow guests at the party that evening included the Prime Minister, Lord Grey, the chancellor, Lord Palmerston, and Luttrell – devoted less attention to the momentous events of the day (the parliamentary sessions had ended and the Reform Bill had been passed) than to the household management of Lady Holland herself. 'The dinner was not as good as usual', Macaulay confided, 'for the cook was ill, and her ladyship kept up a continual lamentation during the whole repast.' 'It was a comfort for me', he wrote dryly, 'to find no rank was exempted from these afflictions.'[12] Increasingly throughout the nineteenth century, there was nothing at all disrespectable about being thought to be a good cook; *employing* a good cook was doubtlessly a more comfortable option, although not every home could afford to keep its own male chef on the premises.

One of the more striking characteristics of Alexis Soyer, as both his recent biographers and modern food historians such as Mark Kurlansky have emphasized, was his commitment to the notion that his own personal interest in cuisine should form only part of a greater concern with 'taking part in the world's nutritional problems and in ending hunger'. Moreover, as Kurlansky further observes of Soyer, 'he did more than write about [his] ideas'.[13] Indeed, far from catering only to the most discriminating tastes in his Kensington eatery, Soyer famously opened a relief kitchen in Dublin for the benefit of victims of the Irish potato famine in 1846 (his recipes, one historian of the blight observed, would have seemed 'relatively luxurious' to the 'soupers' fortunate enough to taste them).[14] From 1855 to 1857 he served in the capacity of what we would today recognize as a 'nutritional adviser' to the British army in the Crimea, where he revolutionized the practices of hospital catering (it was the revelation that a soldier's typical daily diet in the Crimean War was less nutritious than the food served to English prisoners at home that provoked Soyer's intervention). He ran an improvized battlefront field kitchen (innovative 'Soyer stoves' were still being used by the British army in the first Gulf War of 1990), and became an associate of Florence Nightingale's at Scutari.[15] Soyer's well-circulated writings on gastronomy and dietary reform notably included *The Gastronomic Regenerator* (1846), *A Shilling Cookery for the People* (1855) – one of very few such recipe books to influence both middle-class readers as well as the cooks in more affluent households – as well as his earlier and more ambitious *Pantropheon, or, History of Food, and its Preparation* (1853). To whatever extent Soyer may have served (as some critics have contended) as one of the models for the satirist William Makepeace Thackeray's memorable caricature of the flamboyant society chef Monsieur Alcide Mirobolant in his 1848–50 novel *Pendennis*, at least one London newspaper had been prescient enough to observe with no little respect of the high-profile cook several years earlier: 'The impression grows on us that the man of this age is neither Sir Robert Peel, nor Sir John Russell, [nor] even Ibrahim Pasha, but Alexis Soyer.'[16] Even in the mid-nineteenth century, it seems, celebrity chefs could at their most out-spoken be counted on easily to out-distance politicians (and certainly entertainers or athletes of any sort) in the celebrity stakes. After all, however much individual reputations might rise and fall, the basis of their work could always be counted on to remain supremely relevant. As Soyer had himself predicted of posterity in the passage quoted above, 'our children and grandchildren will be as fond of pies as we have been'.

It is perhaps Soyer's unapologetic and emotionally genuine affection for the great British art of pie-making in particular, as expressed in his comfortable testament to the multi-generational appeal of these 'best *companions du voyage* through life' in those same lines, that somehow renders him unusually endearing to a modern audience. The appeal and the oddly intimate vision of his statement rest in the simple fact that he so comfortably confirms the status of the English meat pie as one of the most quintessential and symbolic products of the island's culinary heritage. Soyer's sentimental vision of an unbroken line of infants, children, adults and grandparents, all linked to each another across the centuries in a grand, patriotic chain of meat pastries, stands as one master cook's close to prophetic testament to his adopted country's seemingly irrepressible fondness for the manifold traditions of what Mr Alfred Jingle succinctly and appetisingly jumbled together in Dickens's *Pickwick Papers* (1836–7) as 'fowls and pies, and all that sort of thing'.[17] The native birds and blossoms in the mind of the poet Robert Browning when abroad notwithstanding, the home thoughts of most Englishmen when confronted in moments of crisis or high emotion with the national idea seem to have turned instinctively to the business of food and eating. When the Duke of Wellington first caught sight of the White Cliffs of Dover upon returning home from the continental victories of 1814, he was claimed to have been heard to mutter with muted passion, 'Buttered toast, buttered toast'. More often than not at such times, however, meat and the meat pies of England had a vital role to play in the patriotic visions of the best and most stalwart of men. The venerable Roast Beef of old England – the national significance of which had been so memorably captured in Hogarth's 1748 painting of the same name – was valued none the less for being minced and baked into a pie, or married with the virtues of veal or kidney. Foreigners seemed often to look upon hot meat pies as – in the words of of two twenty-first-century food historians – 'preternaturally British'. 'When des Essientes, the hero of the decadent novel À Rebours [Against the Grain] (1884) visited an English restaurant in Paris', they point out, 'he passed a table of women "who were unaccompanied, were dining together, facing each other, hearty English women who had boyish faces, teeth as broad as shovels, apple-coloured cheeks, with long hands and feet. They were making violent assaults on a beef-steak pie, which contained hot meat cooked in a mushroom sauce and covered in a crust like a paté".'[18] It is just possible that when Prime Minister William Pitt died unexpectedly in office shortly after Napoleon's victory at Austerlitz in 1806, his awareness of the tenuous position in which he left the nation's interest was indeed summed up – as some would have had it believed – in a final, anxious exclamation of, 'Oh, my country! How I leave my country!'; popular tradition, however, was rather more willing to credit the exhausted Pitt with having whispered suggestively in the ear of his valet: 'I think I could eat one of Bellamy's veal pies.'[19] The latter valediction, certainly, would in any case appear suitably to have betrayed sentiments no less loyal or reverential to his native land than the former. (Even the 'Bellamy' referred to in the anecdote appears, with appropriate standing, actually to have been a courier in the House of Commons.) If the 46-year-old Pitt was dismally unaware of the proximity of his own imminent demise – as one modern food commentator wryly observed of the Minister's famous last words – he should nevertheless be commended for having remained, unto the last, 'very sensible of where his priorities lay'.[20]

All this is not to say that the English, as Soyer would himself have been the first to acknowledge, were at all unique in their long-standing affection for sculptured combinations of 'manipulated' pie-crusts and meat pastries. Meat pies in some shape or form were almost certainly as ancient as European civilization itself. As early as the first century AD the Roman writer Petronius referred in his famous (or infamous) description of Trimalchio's Feast in his *Satyricon* to the appearance of meat pies and 'pastries as tall as buildings'.[21] Throughout the Middle Ages similar meat and pastry constructions – sometimes known as 'subtleties' because of the intricate artistry of their design – graced the banqueting tables of the southern continent's fashionable elite. When, a little later, in the sixteenth century, influential arbiters of taste such as Catherine de Medici began to import the changing manners and culinary styles of Italy to the kitchens of the French court and beyond, the homely puddings and dressed meats of England found themselves being transformed into rather more spectacular 'Batalia', savoury Olio Marrow pies, and in time (though in such rarefied forms often without any great indigenous enthusiasm among even English gourmands themselves) close to unrecognizable *vol-au-vents*, timbales and croustades.

The indigenous culture of a people possesses a peculiar staying power, however. The essential and idiosyncratic nature of the meat pies of England managed in spite of all such foreign impositions somehow not only to endure, but to flourish. The culinary changes within which such creations continued to prosper were of no little consequence, particularly because the shifting conventions relating to the preparation and presentation of various meats were almost always likely to reflect the imperatives of greater and very often more socially consequential cultural practices. In the case of trends in food and eating habits, official laws and dictates frequently underscored important social distinctions. In England, as has often been pointed out, the equal distribution of the meat being served among the various and frequently diverse social constituents of any group of people gathered together in the early modern period was commonly interpreted as an expression of egalitarian ideals. The actual process of mincing and quite literally re-forming different pieces of meat into the shape of an homogeneous pie filling (as opposed to the hierarchical or meritocratic allocation of various cuts or quantities of fare among different, socially stratified guests) underscored a perceived or desired sense of unity among the group that consumed the final product.[22] For some, such equality perhaps savoured of a democratic ideal. In a related manner, the restriction for sale by butchers at certain periods in the country's history of offal and organ meats to the lower classes of society could similarly reflect shifting social practice at any given period by emphasizing the various fluctuations in the value and desirability of different kinds of meat. The devaluation of innards, for example – portions that had at certain times been highly valued – could for any number of economic or cultural reasons simply be an indication of what was 'acceptable' and what was not. Some may wish to emphasize the fact that, as in so many aspects of human social interaction, the consumption of meat was a matter not merely of scarcity or availability, but of straightforward 'fashion'. We need to remind ourselves, however, that even the seemingly ephemeral and often whimsical dictates of fashion can have important things to tell us about ourselves. 'Fashions' and the ever-changeable perception of that which is either valued as 'fashionable' or dismissed as 'unfashionable', as the case may be at any given moment in history, have the potential to expose with real candour the fundamental assumptions and beliefs of a community. In terms of history, they tell us a great deal about the manner in which the constituent members of a society perceived the material world in which they lived, and of the ways in which they made sense of and prioritized their own experience and representation as human subjects. In England, for example, organs such as livers and kidneys (however odd it may seem to some of today's readers) almost always carried with them very specific if widely variable meanings or significations. An old collective term for the viscera of an animal – 'numbles' or 'umbles' – was employed in the late nineteenth century to suggest that any individual whose status compelled them to sustain themselves primarily on such organs was said to live on or to eat 'humble pie'. The phrase and traces of its original connotations remain a part of our language to this day. At different points in time, on the other hand, the very same fare was among the most valued and desirable portions of any slaughtered animal, and was often reserved only for the most respectable of guests.

If cuts and portions were a matter of consequence, so too, of course, was quality. In England, consumers of meat pies baked in public were protected with unusual care and precision from at least as early as 1378, when – in the reign of Richard II – an order set out the prices that pie-makers were permitted to charge for their products. The sale, price and distribution of 'made' foods among the cook-shops that had long been clustered together in certain streets and neighbourhoods of London were almost always carefully regulated. Ordinances throughout the fourteenth and fifteenth centuries continued protectively to regulate precisely what *could* and could *not* be sold to the public as a meat pie, much in the same way that legislation such as Food Regulations Acts still govern similar matters in England. Woe betide the English pie-maker who today offers for sale to his countrymen a product advertised to consumers as a cooked meat pie containing anything less than 19 per cent meat (not, one must admit, a very encouraging proportion; Richard II and subsequent monarchs would probably have had something to say about such a standard). In any event, these specific distinctions, regulations and early attempts at 'quality control' made for at least some standard of reliability, and ostensibly protected both purchasers and producers alike. Popular chroniclers of London life such as Peter Ackroyd note that by the late eighteenth century, competition from the city suburbs prevented the Worshipful Company of Butchers from enforcing such regulations. 'Every kind of shoddy or mouldy flesh could be purchased', Ackroyd observes of the period, so that the 'unchecked reign of commerce' involved with the sale of meat became itself a kind of 'symbol of city life'.[23] Inevitably, some disputes relating to what we might now think of as product promotion or regard as 'false advertising' resisted all attempts at arbitration. The native makers of the traditional pork pies of Melton Mowbray in Leicestershire, a pie that features distinctive, hand-raised crusts (or 'coffins', as they are called) and chunky lumps of pork, and one that was said originally to have been prepared for local fox hunters using jelly so as specifically to prevent the pies from being shaken and falling to pieces when roughly carried in the course of the chase, appear to be engaged in an ongoing dispute with meat pie-makers elsewhere in the country for the right exclusively to market their product under its fiercely protected 'original' name. Indignant rivals in counties throughout England's 'pork pie belt', which stretches from Nottingham, in the east, all the way to the border of Wales, routinely disparage the town's specifically local claims to the recipe and its designation as, at best, spurious and, at worst, positively illegal. At the very least, the vehemence of such ongoing disputes testifies to the fact that the social, cultural, provincial and commercial significations of meat pies seem still to have the power to incite disagreement and even heated controversy. The closely related question of exactly who has the right to make and vend 'Cornish' meat pasties under that similarly specific, regional designation is an issue that is probably best for the sake of personal safety not raised anywhere west of the Tamar, the river that inexorably separates Cornwall from its neighbouring county of Devon, to the east.

Alexis Soyer's own indignation in the nineteenth century when confronted with the seeming disrespect with which some of the nation's cooks appeared casually to disregard the peculiar traditions and virtues of the indigenous meat pies and meat pastries of England – virtues that had only over a long period of time and with a considerable degree of careful attention transformed a common and generally unremarkable commodity into a veritable national treasure – would appear, after all is said and done, merely to have reflected his own sensitivity to the long and distinguished history of the Great British Pie. The fact of the matter is that Soyer was far from alone in his protestations and complaints regarding the devaluation of the meat pie. Eliza Acton had also championed the benefits of the scrupulously careful making of pies. In her well-known volume *Modern Cookery for Private Families* (1845), Acton commented that the pretence of serving 'home cooked' dishes to guests, when those dishes had in fact been prepared at a local bake-house, though popular, was a fault far too prevalent among certain classes any longer to be tolerated. 'Great disadvantages attend to the sending to the public oven,' Acton wrote of such baked dishes, 'and it is very discouraging to a servant to have [her reputation as a pie-maker] injured by the negligence of other persons.'[24] Meat pies, in other words, were to be taken seriously, even personally. Pies had something significant to say about who you were, how you managed your household, how you valued and protected your status, and where your priorities lay. Like Acton, Soyer took grave offence when confronted with careless or unworthy attempts at all such hasty crusts and pastries; he would have had nothing but contempt for those who approached with indifference such matters as precisely which ingredients properly belonged in an acceptable meat pie. He was more than likely to have been personally insulted by those who remained unconcerned about the manner in which such fillings should then be prepared for the oven. Such inattention or lack of skill was a source of disgust. The very sight of a poorly made meat pie was enough to fill Soyer with righteous indignation. 'Believe me,' Soyer confided to readers of one of his early cookery books with genuine warmth, 'I am not jesting, but if all the spoilt pies made in London on one single Sunday were to be exhibited in a row beside a railroad line, it would take an hour by special train to pass in review of these culinary victims.'[25]

Suitably in keeping with the frustration expressed by Soyer in such funereal passages, the pages that follow will at various points necessarily deal specifically with the meat pies of London, and with some of the many bakers who made them. We will have occasion to venture into at least one of the penny pie shops that had begun increasingly to flourish in the city throughout the late eighteenth and early nineteenth centuries, even as the itinerant street-dealers still plied their ancient trade selling their own hot pies from Greenwich, in the east, as far as Hyde Park Corner, the traditional entrance to London from the west. The customs, methods and merchandizing of meat pies will be of no little importance to our story. The central focus of this narrative, however, will remain to a necessary degree on an altogether different kind of 'culinary victim' than those excoriated in Soyer's cookery book: the kind so gruesomely highlighted in the opening pages of this section. They were the sorts of victims that we more often encounter today only in the literature of terror or in horror films; the kind that we tend still to be disinclined to talk about with any degree of comfort or candour. They were, in fact, the culinary victims who were baked into the famous meat pies of Mrs Lovett, and who had been supplied to her with regular dispatch, if not with loving care, by the hand and the razor of Sweeney Todd, the legendary 'Demon Barber of Fleet Street'.

*

This looked like some new scheme of villainy.

(Bram Stoker, *Dracula*)[26]

Quintessentially representative in so many ways both of the extended period in which they were supposed to have flourished (*c.*1785–1801) and of the era in which their story first achieved its solid currency in popular culture (*c.*1846–80), London's famous Sweeney Todd of Fleet Street and his pie-making accomplice Mrs Lovett of Bell Yard were in other respects oddly ahead of their time. Street-smart and savvy business partners – prescient and entrepreneurial predators in the modern urban jungle – they spoke to contemporary preoccupations with appetite, consumption, consumerism and luxury, no less forcefully than they gave voice to some of the anxieties of a new period of growth and development. The expansion of London and its wealth, a phenomenon that was to see its full flowering in the mid-nineteenth century, had been gaining momentum for many decades. Between 1688 and 1800 the city had more than doubled in physical size, and throughout that extended period, as R.W. Harris put it, the metropolis had 'constantly sucked in people from the countryside'.[27] A crisis of sorts was reached by the middle years of the nineteenth century. Writing of the 1840s generally, Raymond Williams observed:

> We can see [the decade] as the decisive period in which the consciousness of a new phase of civilization was being formed and expressed. The radical transfor-

14

mation of life in Britain, by the extended development of the first Industrial Revolution, by the transformation from a predominantly rural to a predominantly urban society, and by the consequent political struggle for representative political democracy and [both] for and against the emergence of an organized working class, was then in its most disturbed and creative phase.... . What comes through most decisively in the novels [of the period] is the consciousness of this transforming, liberating, and threatening time.[28]

The most striking feature of Williams's description of the period in this passage is the volatile combination of creative possibility, on the one hand, with anxious trepidation and disorientation, on the other – the simple fact that the period was perceived somehow to have fostered an unusually tense atmosphere that offered, as Williams's language would have it, the 'threat' of 'liberation'.

To be sure, however luxurious it could be, London throughout the eighteenth and nineteenth centuries was still in many ways just as much a jungle as any other growing metropolitan city of the period, if not more so. Contemplating the capital's 'immense Number of Lanes, Alleys, Courts, and Bye-places', the magistrate and novelist Henry Fielding had suggested as early as the mid-eighteenth century that any observer unfamiliar with the environment of the city might be forgiven for supposing the whole of London to be 'a vast wood or Forest, in which a Thief may harbour with as great Security as wild Beasts do in the deserts of Africa or Arabia'.[29] Fielding was far from alone in imagining the city to be a kind of labyrinthine wilderness into which any self-respecting criminal could disappear with ease. 'Wood', 'forest', 'desert', 'maze', 'wilderness', 'jungle': these were the words that, somewhat paradoxically (considering the material fabric of the urban landscape), first leapt to the minds of many Englishmen when attempting to describe London from the earliest years of the Hanoverian period onward. For quite some time before the closing decades of the eighteenth century, much less by the time Alexis Soyer came to write his best-selling cookery books in the early and middle years of Victoria's reign (and well before Mrs Beeton's volume became a fixture in almost every British household), not even the most enthusiastic advocates of the indigenous possibilities of England's metropolis, gastronomic or otherwise, would ever have been so bold as to have promoted the capital as a peaceful or calming place – or as any stranger, for that matter, to often violent acts of crime. Soyer's 'Universal Symposium' may have been able, as an altogether new kind of establishment, to count on causing a brief sensation in Kensington but, as one City Marshall had written several years earlier, others were still compelled very much to contend with 'the general complaint of the taverns, the coffee-houses [and] the shop-keepers [that] their customers are afraid when it is dark to come out of their houses and shops for fear that their wigs would be snatched from their heads or their swords taken from their sides, or that they may be blinded, knocked down, cut or stabbed'.[30] For many readers, the images of London's darkened courtyards and alleys, cobwebbed doorways, and the murky, gothic horror of the dark urban scene are most readily conjured by Victorian or Edwardian evocations of the city; yet for a great many years prior to the end of the nineteenth century itself, in fact, the city was no less typically characterized by the criminal activities of a darkly mysterious and sinister underworld – an underworld of footpads, highwaymen, pick-pockets and racketeers – than it was by the more virile if often equally venal ambitions of its increasingly powerful champions of empire. One modern chronicler of the London under-world reminds us that by 1720 there were estimated to be no fewer than 10,000 criminals active in the capital; by 1805, the Middlesex magistrate and pioneer criminologist Patrick Colquhoun could assert with no small degree of confidence, in his *Treatise on the Police of the Metropolis*, that '115,000 persons in London were regularly engaged in criminal pursuits'.[31] To a very real degree, when it came to the underworld of London's criminal activity, the Victorian era only reaped the foul harvest of the preceding century. Indeed, some of the most popular novels published in the early decades of the nineteenth century – novels such as William Harrison Ainsworth's *Rookwood* (1824) and *Jack Sheppard* (1839) – self-consciously and even nostalgically treated the thieves and highwaymen of the preceding era as the romantic forerunners of their own criminal age.

The enormous popularity of the so-called 'Newgate novels' of Ainsworth and others demonstrated the extent to which certain historical and increas-ingly mythologized events and individuals had stimulated the public's seemingly ever-present but always expanding appetite for lurid accounts of both social and traditional crime. The famous highwaymen and figures of organized crime in the early eighteenth century, the criminalization of rights that had previously been customary under the Black Acts of 1723, the murders and mischief in London instigated by the activities of John Wilkes and the anti-Catholic Gordon Riots of 1780: all these things reminded nineteenth-century audiences – much as they tend still to emphasize for the modern reader – of the fact that urban life could, throughout its history, generally be relied upon to be particularly vicious and unknowable. Throughout the later decades of the Hanoverian era and well into the even more expansive years that followed, the city's crime rate rose constantly. Instances of casual violence (and many no doubt went unreported) also continued to increase. Certainly, by modern standards, rural outsiders and foreign visitors alike tended to regard London from as early as the beginning of the eighteenth century as an extraordinarily dangerous and unpredictable place. Cities – as the country mouse in the satire (II.vii) of the great Roman poet Horace could have told his cousin close to 2,000 years earlier – were always bound to be thought by any outsider to be risky places in which to spend one's time. The perception and representation of criminal activity could be subject to slight if significant changes, however. Highwaymen and footpads such as Claude

Duval, Tom King, Dick Turpin, Jack Sheppard, James Maclaine and 'Spring Heeled Jack' may all have had their predecessors on the high roads and in the alleys of the Rome of Juvenal or Domitian (the former had described the 'drunken bullies' ready eagerly to attack any 'lonely pedestrian trudging home by moonlight') but the murderers and criminal heroes to be found in a mushrooming, early modern metropolis such as London would appear to have had something new to offer in the way of purely bloodthirsty appeal.[32]

The literature of crime and criminals had long enjoyed a wide circulation, even among the most 'respectable' class of readers. If chap-book writers, ballad sellers and the writers of sensational biographies of footpads and highwaymen had glamorized the life of crime for the mass market, their supposedly more literate and fastidious betters were no less captivated by salacious and romantic narratives of terrible murders and tales of horror.[33] From the 1780s and 90s onward, England – and London in particular – was to be increasingly obsessed with narratives of terror. The popular fiction of the late eighteenth and early nineteenth centuries, as E.S. Turner summarized:

> was steeped in darkness and diablerie: spectres gliding in green phosphorescence, hags picking over the bones of charnel houses, deathsheads in closets, heirs to great estates chained in dungeons, forests stuffed with robbers and werewolves, graves creaking open in the moonlight to let the vampires out – these were the stock-in-trade of the Gothic, and bogus Gothic, novelist. The vogue for these romantic horrors had been set by Horace Walpole (*The Castle of Otranto* [1765]), Ann Radcliffe (*The Mysteries of Udolpho* [1794]) and Matthew Gregory Lewis (*The Monk* [1796]); and there were plenty of pens ready to imitate, translate, paraphrase, and purloin for the benefit of the literate fringe of the working classes. In rising spate, and at ever cheaper cost, came romances set in clammy castles in the German forests or in convents ruled by degenerate nuns who wielded the knout [sic] upon their novices. The atmosphere of all of them was oppressive. Neither indoors nor outdoors was there a stirring of fresh air. In the turrets of castles censers smoked before unholy alters; no one opened a window, unless to jump from it. Out of doors the air was foul with the reek of gibbets.[34]

Moreover, however much the so-called 'gothic' fictions of popular novelists such as Walpole, Lewis and Radcliffe may have framed their narratives in the past, they betrayed fears that were very much felt in the present. 'Terror', as one historian of the gothic has put it, 'had an overwhelming political significance in the period,' and gothic images of destruction proliferated in an era of anxious political and social change.[35] The recent blood-letting of the French Revolution ensured that the spectre of the guillotine and the fear of the violent and uncontrollable energy that fuels an unruly mob were never far from the minds of that country's insular neighbours, and every urban encounter was fraught with new and sneaking kinds of disruptive potential. Late Hanoverian and early Victorian England was to witness and encourage scenes of explosively violent political, commercial and bodily appetite.

17

Even more disconcerting for many by the earliest years of the Victorian period, however, was the fact that particularly macabre and brutal crimes seemed to many to have begun to attain a disturbingly morbid degree of media attention and even celebrity. The emergence and prevalence of 'true crime' writing or reportage, accounts of criminal trials and street ballads pretending to relate the stories of 'popular' crimes and the trials that followed them (in publications such as the *Select Trials at the Old Bailey* (1772) and the *New Newgate Calendar* (1795)), had since the early 1700s encouraged entirely new genres and subgenres of narratives, and so gave rise in time to new kinds of narrative conventions. Stories of criminals originally retailed in publications such as the *Newgate Calendar* were told in a novel manner – with new and hitherto unemphasized characters and detail of incident – and to a new and rapidly growing audience. The initially broad hints of titillation and sexual scandal that lurked within the popular commentaries on and accounts of criminal trials – and that seemed to grow even more explicit – sought eagerly to emphasize the wider and ever-present threats and lurking social horrors of a genuinely melodramatic urban life. At the increasingly dark heart of the mysterious world of London, throughout much of the eighteenth and nineteenth centuries, it may well have seemed to many that only some extraordinarily gifted and intelligent individual – only a figure who we would now recognize to possess the abilities of an Inspector Bucket, a Sergeant Cuff, or (more certainly) a Sherlock Holmes and, later, those with the talents of a Father Brown or a Philip Trent – could ever hope to follow the line of their own deductive reasoning, and thus uncover the degrees of physical evidence that so spectacularly revealed the acts of London's criminals. Parisians had already, by the early decades of the nineteenth century, benefited from the crime-fighting efforts of masterful turncoats such Eugene-François Vidocq – the model for Balzac's Vautrin, Victor Hugo's Javert and even Edgar Allen Poe's Auguste Dupin. As head of the secret police, Vidocq reduced the crime rate in Paris by 40 per cent; he subsequently formed what was probably the world's first private detective agency. It seemed that London, however, would have to wait. The great detectives in England, each of whom were to follow the admirable paths of their own unique, evidential reasoning, were all to come much later.[36] Things were different in the recently remembered decades of the passing era and the dubious promise of the new century. One particular series of events seemed for many in the waning years of the Hanoverian era all too accurately to anticipate the shape of things to come. They were all the more frightening because they were true. And, to make matters even worse, they seemed with a kind of dreadful inevitability to herald the gruesome possibilities of a century still young and ripe with potential.

*

18

My homicidal maniac is of a peculiar kind. I shall have to invent a new classification for him.... What he desires is to absorb as many lives as he can, and he has laid himself out to achieve it in a cumulative way.

(Bram Stoker, *Dracula*)[37]

In the Big City large and sudden things happen. The City is a sprightly youngster, and you are red paint upon its toy, and you get licked off.

(O'Henry (William Sydney Porter), 'Squaring the Circle')[38]

In the winter of 1811, two families living in London's thriving if increasingly over-burdened East End were discovered murdered in their homes.[39] The uncharacteristically brutal attacks, although clearly connected, took place on two separate occasions. The first incident happened on the night of 11 December. A maid who had been serving in the household of one Mr Marr, a draper who had set up his business not far from the new Commercial Road in Ratcliff, was sent by her employer just before midnight to purchase some oysters from a nearby coster or street trader; a request of this sort, made so seemingly late in the evening, would not in fact have been at all out of keeping with the lengthy and often erratic working hours of many labourers in the area.

When the maid returned to Marr's shop shortly afterwards, she was surprised to find herself unable to gain entry as usual through the premise's ground-floor shop. A local watchman was summoned for assistance, but it was thanks largely to the efforts of one of the draper's more agile neighbours that the three managed finally to find a way into the building. Inside, both Mr Marr and his young apprentice were discovered in the ground-floor workspace. The bodies of the two men lay sprawled out across the shop floorboards; large pools of blood seeped from devastating head wounds and had begun to stain their surroundings crimson. The walls and areas surrounding the men's bodies had been spectacularly splattered with gore. The pair had obviously been attacked by an intruder who (it would later be established) had made ruthlessly efficient use of a maul and ripping chisel or sailor's knife to both batter and stab the men to death.

Anxiously mounting the stairs to the upper storeys of the building, they encountered an even more horrific scene. The lifeless bodies of the draper's wife and young child were found in the premise's living quarters. Both had been set upon in a manner almost precisely like that which appeared to have claimed the lives of the two men downstairs. Marr's wife and child had been battered to death in much the same way by someone who was obviously capable of wielding such everyday working tools as weapons not only with extreme strength, but with unusually callous brutality. Again, blood seeped everywhere from the wounds. Just for good measure, the intruder appeared gratuitously to have slit the throat of the couple's infant – who was found still lying in its cradle – from ear to ear.

Such events were shocking, but there was very little time for the locals to recover. The second of the East End attacks followed hard upon the first. Only days after the discovery of the first four murders, a partially clothed individual was spotted scrambling from an upper-storey window of the nearby King's Arms tavern. The half-naked man was heard frantically screaming to anyone within hearing distance: 'They are murdering the people in the house!' When the district police managed to make their way to the tavern's second floor, they came upon the bodies of the publican, his wife and the family's female servant. All three had been butchered in a manner similar to that of the victims in the draper's household. Once again, the bodies bore multiple wounds, and the fractured skulls of those who had been attacked were shattered quite literally to pieces by a series of extraordinarily violent blows to the head. On this occasion, the throat of the serving girl had been slashed so deeply that she appeared by many who saw the body to have been almost completely decapitated. There was no obvious reason for the degree of savagery involved in what appeared merely to be a sort of signature touch on the part of the intruder.

The unprecedented and ruthless ferocity of the December 1811 attacks – a 'double event' in its own right that was soon known among the locals as the Ratcliff Highway Murders – caused a tremendous sensation in Stepney, Wapping and, indeed, throughout much of the East End. The brutality of the assaults and the subsequent, perceived incompetence of the local forces in handling the case stimulated a degree of volatile public unrest that had not been seen anywhere within London since the Gordon Riots just over 30 years earlier. Widespread panic gripped the thriving, working-class districts surrounding the London Docks. One local shopkeeper claimed to have sold some 300 alarm rattles (roughly the citizen's equivalent of a policeman's alert whistle) within only ten hours. In their understandable impatience to apprehend the murderer (or murderers), the police had within days arrested no fewer than 40 men as suspects in the case.

Not much time was allowed to pass, however, before the authorities decided to bring in a sailor by the name of John Williams. Williams had recently been staying at a nearby public house. Although a great many questions regarding his guilt or innocence were to remain unanswered, Williams was immediately accused of the crimes both by the authorities and by the public. He anticipated the certain death sentence he would have received for the attacks by hanging himself from a rafter whilst still in police custody – even, in fact, before committal proceedings had begun. The immediate aftermath of the killings was in some respects no less dramatic than the murders themselves. All the serving watchmen in Shadwell were discharged from their duties, and a new, armed police force was assembled to patrol the area. In a decidedly gruesome twist to the whole affair, Williams's body – still dressed in its original clothing and wearing around its neck the 'kerchief with which he had hung himself – was trundled through the streets of Stepney and Wapping, protected by a convoy of some 300 police, and surrounded by even greater numbers of agitated locals – a crowd that resented having been deprived the spectacle of a conviction and its ensuing public vengeance. The corpse was hastily covered by a thin layer of soil at the corner of Cable Street and Cannon Street Road. Before perfunctorily dumping the body in its shallow grave, the residents of Stepney hammered a stake through Williams's heart. An age-old privilege, perhaps, but one that vividly anticipates the crowd's perception of the killer as a kind of monster – a criminal 'vampire' just barely ahead of his time.

The Ratcliff Highway Murders would be remembered for years by many Londoners primarily for the changes and reforms they helped to effect in the ongoing reorganization of the metropolitan police force. Yet the inexplicably violent manner in which the murderer's seven victims had been so savagely slaughtered was to linger no less powerfully in the popular imagination. The killings were regarded as examples of a new, extreme and grotesque *kind* of violence, the frightful enigma of which served as a premonition of future attacks. Admittedly, the phenomenon of such a callous act of crime was by no means altogether new. Eighteenth-century thieves and highwaymen such as those already mentioned – Dick Turpin, Jack Sheppard and James Maclaine, for example – had all achieved a certain degree of notoriety and even celebrity among the general populace in their day for the supposedly glamorous nature of their passage from the prison to Tyburn, where most felons were executed for their crimes. Then, even as now, to a certain extent, the stories of darkly handsome and (supposedly) justifiably angry and rebellious young men could exert a romantic and almost erotic fascination on the public consciousness. The offences of earlier generations of felons had been brutal enough, to be sure, yet there had been very few precedents for such daring and grotesquely bloody acts of violence as seemed to be increasingly common in the final years of the Hanoverian era.

Other strange incidents had begun also to attract an unusual degree of attention. The bizarre assaults supposedly perpetrated by Rhynwick Williams – the so-called 'London Monster', who was alleged to have attacked or terrorized as many as 50 women on the city streets from the spring of 1788 through to the early summer of 1790 – had briefly captured the metropolitan imagination at a time when, thanks again in large part to certain events then taking place across the Channel, people were already exceptionally anxious regarding any possible threat to public order.[40] Yet with the exception of the narrative of William Corder's murder of Maria Marten in the famous 'Red Barn' at Polstead in Suffolk in 1828, nothing vaguely approaching the Ratcliff Highway Murders would be the subject of such widespread discussion, or certainly of such obsessive media attention. Throughout the century, the very mention of any violent death, or any reference to the perverse presence of human evil in modern urban society, would inevitably have brought to the mind of almost any Londoner the East End Murders of December 1811. Only the inaugural appearance of Jack the Ripper on the streets of Whitechapel toward the end of the century would change all that; and even the Ripper would find himself competing in the long term with figures such as Sweeney Todd. 'The new world may have its Charles Mansons,' a *Times* reviewer would write in 1973, 'but it is raw, neon-lit stuff compared to Sweeney Todd, the demon barber of Fleet Street and the ghastly Ripper; they are the veritable Oxford and Cambridge ivied walls of murder.'[41]

*

My Lord, you are aware that at this moment, the public feeling is strongly excited against the perpetrators of the late foul and cold blooded murders that have taken place in the very centre of a populous and civilized city. . . . Your Lordship is aware, that in all civilized nations, blood calls for blood.
('Letter to the Lord Advocate . . . by the Echo of Surgeons' Square')[42]

Why don't they stick to murder and leave art to us?
(Sir Jacob Epstein, British sculptor)[43]

If the bloodthirsty nature of the Ratcliff Highway crimes was looked upon later in the period as having all too accurately anticipated the 'new types' of killers that were to emerge even more spectacularly in the final decades of the century, some of the circumstances relating to the crimes achieved a different but no less sustained degree of notoriety in fashionable literary society. Thomas De Quincey was to make the Ratcliff Highway assaults the focus of his memorable essay 'On Murder Considered as One of the Fine Arts'. De Quincey published his essay in two parts in *Blackwell's Magazine* in 1827, and added a significant postscript to the piece in 1854. (Curiously enough, the original year in which De Quincey's essay appeared would also witness the first appearance of what some critics regard to be the earliest genuine English 'murder mystery', *Richmond: Scenes in the Life of a Bow Street Runner*.) In his own essay on the art of murder, De Quincey displays, among other things, a simultaneously mocking and genuinely fascinated interest in the public's increasing obsession with the workings of the criminal mind. The piece takes the form of a formal address to a supposed meeting of the 'Society for the Encouragement of Murder'.[44] The speaker seems dispassionately and with an almost clinical, scholarly detachment to address the history and methods of murder as an aesthetic or artistically significant event. De Quincey's speaker expresses his disapproval of the manner in which contemporary society's increasing desensitization to violence (a process which, he claims, has 'blunted the discriminating powers of the mind') had reduced the act of murder to the level of such mundane crimes as could lead the perpetrator to other, more ironically reprehensible vices – vices that De Quincey declares with mock horror to be as indecent as, say, incivility, or even procrastination.

The more serious effect of De Quincey's Swiftian satiric tone in the essay serves to warn his readers of the ways in which 'the savage forces of contemporary life can appropriate and destroy the civilized ones'.[45] Here, as in much the same way he was to do in certain passages of his *Confessions of an English Opium-Eater* (1821; 1856), De Quincey adroitly draws his readers' attention to the disturbing proximity that exists between 'normal' human behaviour – between the qualities of the innocent or charitable mind – and the depraved thoughts of the most savage of murderers. Aboriginal chaos and perils, as he was to put it in his 1856 revision of the *Confessions*, exist 'in the ambush of midnight solitude, brooding around the beds of sleeping nations; perils from even worse forms of darkness shrouded within the recesses of blind human hearts; perils from temptations weaving unseen snares for our footing; perils from the limitations of our own misleading knowledge'.[46] In other words, not only do we all live within the jungle, it is we ourselves who constitute the most appalling potentials of its dangers. Simply put: we are our own worst enemies.

De Quincey's macabre if effective manner of addressing his subject and alerting readers to the myriad evils that not only surround us, but that we are incapable even of perceiving, was naturally to influence subsequent writing related to the topic. George Orwell's much shorter yet even better-known essay on the 'Decline of the English Murder', first published in 1946, sardonically laments that the British reading public's habit of immersing itself in the comfortably warm and reassuring pleasures provided by a good narrative of slaughter and carnage had sadly declined, if only in terms of standards. The quality of such narratives had fallen dramatically since the sanguinary period of those killings that Orwell himself christened as having constituted 'our Elizabethan period, so to speak' – the great era of inspired savagery from about 1850 to 1925, the era that most famously included figures such as Jack the Ripper, Dr Palmer of Rugeley, Madame Caillaux, Mary Pearcey and Dr Crippen, some of whom Orwell mentions by name.[47] Orwell's standards for such 'perfect' murders – a set of criteria that are close to Aristotelian in their tendency to judge the quality of any murder tale most accurately by its *effect*, its capability for inspiring emotions such as pity, drama and excitement – are themselves set out with seemingly genial warmth. 'It is difficult to believe that any recent English crime', Orwell opined with apparent regret at the time, 'will be remembered so long and so intimately [as such former incidents], and not only because the violence of external events has made murder seem unimportant, but because the prevalent type of crime seems to be changing.'[48] It is not so much that European civilization had just experienced the global slaughter of tens of millions of people in the unprecedented carnage of the Second World War that has changed the nature in which we perceive and read about more local or dramatic murders, Orwell suggests; it is simply that folks here in England seem to have lost the knowledge of just how to go about the 'general pattern' of such murders with any degree of style or flair. Murderers appear to have lost their touch. Orwell's essay is permeated by a bizarre and incommensurate sense of loss and disappointment. Gone with the 'stable society' of the world as it had existed before the war was the 'all-prevailing hypocrisy' that had at least ensured that comfortable, domestic murders had 'strong emotions behind them'.[49] It was not so much the tastes of the public had changed all that much; rather, such change was the indication of a decline in standards of the world itself.

As Orwell would have it, the average Englishman, on the typical Sunday afternoon – having first enjoyed a solid lunch of roast beef and Yorkshire pudding, his wife already napping, and himself lying at length with his feet stretched out on the cushioned sofa – is still at his happiest and most content with the pages of newspapers such as the *News of the World* spread open before him. 'In [such] blissful circumstances,' Orwell asks innocently, 'what is it you want to read about? Naturally, about a murder.'[50] For Orwell, the contrast between – and the possibly sudden and violent intrusion within – the comfortable suburban setting of domestic respectability by an act of carefully planned, impassioned, and yet ruthlessly determined murder made for (many, if not most) English readers a close to perfect form of entertainment. (Orwell, incidentally, had already dwelt on this supposed taste or proclivity in his 1938 novel *Coming Up for Air*.) Narratives including episodes of domestic poisoning were particularly delightful to read about, although Orwell incidentally took the time to suggest that the well-calculated employment of 'romantic' poisons such as arsenic or strychnine between jealous wives and lovers seemed sadly to have fallen out of use. Likewise, if a supposedly fine domestic murder does not bring with it the spectacle of moral weakness or social disgrace, what then is the use of it?

Revisiting much the same topic not very long ago, in the months following the distressingly genuine abduction and subsequent murder of a young girl in England that had attracted an enormous amount of national attention, award-winning journalist Neil Mackay was nevertheless able still similarly to point out that the distinctions drawn by Orwell between the crimes of the Victorian and Edwardian 'golden age' killers, on the one hand, and those of stereotypical post-war murderers, on the other – at least in terms of their dramatic or histrionic and social qualities – may well in their strangely prophetic way have been all too valid. By the opening decade of the twenty-first century, contemporary killings had come to be described typically in the press as more 'random' and 'plotless' than ever. They are not infrequently even described as 'dull' or pedestrian. Mackay, rather more sympathetically than the other admittedly more creative writers before him, once again usefully charted the connections between the manner in which certain individuals 'at the extremes of humanity' seem to be driven to kill by the nature of the impoverished societies and the slime of the dead-end cultures from which they have only barely managed to emerge. Of such killers, Mackay wrote perceptively, 'they are not *like* us, but they *speak* to us of the complete loss and abandonment that goes hand in hand with the way we live – or just how fragile the veneer of civilization and society can be'.[51] Thomas De Quincey could hardly have said it any better himself.

For De Quincey, for Orwell and for a modern journalist such as Mackay, then, the more 'interesting' murders of earlier years – the compelling and captivating killings of Orwell's Golden Age – almost always involved some aspect of class and social aspiration. So-called 'crimes of passion' may indeed take place in this world, but they are usually executed by uneducated fools or farcical dupes who are either in the grip of angry despair and rage, or (far too often) simply drunk. Likewise, only negligible thieves and petty criminals get killed or murdered with little comment on the circumstances surrounding their cases. (Presidents and heads of state, as the playwrights John Weidman and Stephen Sondheim allow a major character to observe in one of their more controversial stage collaborations, are not so much 'killed' or even 'murdered'; they are, rather, 'assassinated' – a shift in terminology that the playwrights suggest marks a profoundly consequential distinction in status: 'Adulterers and shopkeepers get murdered . . .', sneers the character of John Wilkes Booth, defending the supposed nobility of his actions; only people of consequence are 'assassinated'.)[52] In any event, even apart from occasional political assassinations or the spectacularly professional 'hits' of organized crime, the best shockers still look to shake the system to its core, as it were – to violate the mundane patterns of diurnal life with a deviousness that borders on a peculiar brand of mysterious and malicious genius.

*

Q. Are human beings fundamentally nice or nasty?
A. Nice, on the whole, though the last one I ate was too salty for my taste.
('Questions Answered', in The Times)[53]

The conjunction of cannibalism, grooming, culinary commercial enterprise, appetite and (of all things) love and desire, as brought together in such narratives as Sweeney Todd's, might seem at first to constitute a strangely limited topic. Yet the connections between such apparently diverse elements run deeper than one might expect. The performance of desire, the erotics of the body, the cultivation of physical appearance, and the appetite of the consuming subject are all inextricably linked with one another. Even our living language itself remains to an extraordinary degree permeated with the signs, the symbols and the lingering rumours of what is sometimes characterized as 'lustful cannibalism' – a common rhetoric of erotic possession and physical consumption. Lovers, for example, still typically call each other by pet names such as 'honey', 'honey bun', 'sweetie', 'sweetie-pie', 'cookie' and 'sweetheart'. Objects of sexual desire, both male and female, can be referred to in popular slang as 'hot tomatoes' or – on occasion, in America – 'hot tamales'; they are described not only as looking 'hot', but often 'luscious' and 'good enough to eat'. 'I could eat you up,' the beloved may very well be told by his or her 'lip-smacking' admirer. A similar rhetoric of peculiarly edible behaviour pervades a great many other related aspects of our social lives as well. Some sit and 'chew the fat', whilst in disputes and arguments people are said to 'chew' each other out, to 'snap' at their opponents, or to make 'biting' and 'bitter' remarks when 'mouthing off' or 'biting back'. Adversaries might offer enemies a 'taste' of their prowess, or claim to be powerful enough to 'swallow them whole', to 'chew them up' and then 'spit them out'. 'Don't bite my head off!' we cry when someone appears to yell at us. Similarly, we 'chew over' matters or, more explicitly, 'ruminate' when making difficult decisions; we 'digest' opinions or ideas that are difficult to 'swallow' or 'stomach', or offer others a 'taste' of some innovative approach. We 'sink our teeth' into 'choice' or 'meaty' subjects that might provide 'food' for thought, and – when feeling unusually adventurous – we are perhaps encouraged to 'take a bite' out of life. More recent slang simultaneously taunts and contemptuously reduces potential antagonists by dismissing their own cannibalistic prowess as negligible: 'Bite me'.

In a manner closely related to the use of such language in our everyday lives, the pre-eminent folklorists and story-collectors Iona and Peter Opie were able to trace a number of lyrics and phrases used by schoolchildren well into the twentieth century when referring to food such as school dinners as – if not *explicitly* cannibalistic – then certainly intimately related to the subject. A meat pie served in a shop or institution was 'cat's meat' or (in Manchester) 'growler' – a designation signifying that the meat used therein was supposed to have originated from local dogs (hence the area's similar reference to the mince used in such pies as 'hound pudding').[54] Closer to our specific subject is the descriptive yet subtly obscure Mancunian designation of cottage pie as 'resurrection pie'. One hesitates to ask precisely *who* has been resurrected, in this particular instance. And, perhaps, just how recently?

. The fate of the physical human body and its appurtenances with cannibalism are further intertwined by the bizarre and ancient tradition of lore that has gathered around the notion of 'cannibal rags' – the wearing by those living of clothes that have already been worn by the dead. In his short ghost story 'A Romance of Certain Old Clothes' (1868), Henry James wrote of a young bride distressed by the fact that the remarkably fashionable wardrobe of her suddenly departed sister had been left unused and unworn in a chest. 'Was it not a pity', the narrator asks, 'that so much finery should be lost, for lost it would be, what with colours fading, and moths eating it up, and the change of fashions?'[55] Needless to say, the results of the young woman's attempt to revive her sister's clothing, as it were, are predictably disastrous. (Strikingly, the figure of Dracula, in Bram Stoker's 1897 novel, first 'cannibalizes' Jonathan Harker's clothing before moving on to Harker's fiancée Mina and his other victims; 'it was a new shock to me', Harker writes in his journal after a nocturnal glimpse of Dracula while immured in the Count's Carpathian Castle, 'to find that he had on the suit of clothes which I had worn whilst travelling here'.)[56] Yet the supposedly supernatural power of human garments has in fact been thought to be such that those who wear the clothing of dead people are suspected not only to bring the concept of death much closer to themselves than is in any way comfortable or desirable, but also extends to the notion that the clothes of the deceased will rot and decay simultaneously along with the decomposing corpse. More particularly, if there are knots of any sort in the clothing, the current wearer's own good fortune in life is liable likewise to rot away forever.[57] It's something to think about the next time you have a look at the bargain garments in your local charity shop, at least.

Of course, despite this sustained predilection for metaphors and turns of phrase that are obsessed with oral-erotic consumption – the constant use of language that relies explicitly on acts of cannibalizing others – the actual practice of man-eating tends reassuringly to be extremely rare. The desire to consume human flesh is typically classified in modern Western society as the aberrant manifestation of an extreme psychosexual disorder that is seldom deliberately acted upon.[58] Odd and extremely uncommon individuals, perhaps provoked or motivated in some way by unspeakable social or psychological conditions, may be attracted to or can even resort to such pathological behaviour. But the sheer inhumanity and current, fundamental irrationality of cannibalism as a physical and psychological act render it a mercifully rare phenomenon. When it comes to the subject of cannibalism, in other words, it would appear that however much we still like to talk the talk, as it were – and so retain something of the posture of cannibalism's threat of brutal and painstakingly thorough annihilation – we seem at the same time successfully to avoid walking the walk; we seem to have suppressed the atavistic impulse to follow through on such possibly instinctive behaviour in any grotesquely consequential way. So it is, again, that the idea of human bodies eating other human bodies is today more often than not perceived and addressed as a matter more of anxious symbolism and cultural distinction than it is of any actual reality.[59] As we shall have cause to mention, however, there yet remains some fetishistic impulse even in the most 'normal' of human responses to the phenomenon of cannibalism – a compelling, lingering, sadistic fascination in the very act of witnessing (or more typically reading or hearing tales of) this supreme act of 'the power of the gaze' as it is wielded over and against another human being. We may be compelled to refrain from acting on it, but we are just as likely to remain closeted, scopophilic cannibals deep down inside.

And yet – accidents *will* happen. If inadvertently eating human remains would for most if not all of us constitute an almost inconceivable misfortune, the idea of *knowingly* eating the flesh of another human being, we have often been told, is and always has been one of the deepest and most ancient taboos of European culture. Even more disconcerting, perhaps, is the growing body of evidence that suggests that – far from being revolted by the prospect of taking the occasional bite out of one another now and again – our communal ancestors may very well have engaged in acts of deliberate cannibalism as a matter of course. Analyses of the patterns of cut marks on broken bones and cracked skulls unearthed by Neolithic archaeologists in the late twentieth century can be argued to prove that, in the words of culinary historian Margaret Visser, 'our Stone Age ancestors relished human brains and sucked [human] bone marrow when they could get at it'.[60] As still another student of the overpowering human 'instinct' towards cannibalism has argued, modern anthropologists have increasingly 'turned up masses of evidence to show that as soon as man was able to walk upright he indulged freely in carnivorous activity and cannibalism was widespread'.[61] The precise reasons behind such activity, cultural historians have observed, could of course vary wildly. 'There was cannibalism resorted to in times of famine', writer Moira Martingale notes, 'or as the preferred form of protein.' It was practised for magical, mystical and religious reasons. It was a form of revenge against enemies. 'And finally', Martingale concludes, 'then, as now, inevitably there would likely be a scattering of deviant individuals who obtained sexual gratification from acts of sadism and cannibalism.'[62] The obvious conclusion would be that there has never really been any need to look as far afield as Papua New Guinea, sub-Saharan Africa, or the South American rainforests for evidence of cannibalistic activity among humans; there has never really been a need, in fact, to look very far beyond our own familiar surroundings in the first place. The answer, all the time, lay in our own backyards. A 1987 dig at a cave near Cheddar Gorge in Somerset was only one of several excavations in Europe to have turned up a large number of bones that suggest the practice may have been very close to commonplace in Stone Age Britain as well as elsewhere throughout Europe.

Speculation of this sort regarding the conjectured universality of cannibal activity – and, even more particularly, generalizations about Western assumptions regarding the routine practice of cannibalism in areas such as Africa, Oceania, Central America, and elsewhere outside of Europe – has of course been vociferously challenged. The supposed absence of any *thoroughly* incontrovertible evidence that can be examined with reference to *actual* cannibal activities is likely to leave the matter open to debate for quite some time to come, and this particular disagreement has on occasion turned particularly nasty. It is best briefly to state the position of those who have contested the existence of cannibalism as openly and clearly as possible. The central trope of what many critics in the late twentieth century insisted on characterizing as the imperial 'myth' of savagery, cannibalism (it has been claimed since the early 1980s) is in fact nothing more than the behaviour most stereotypically used by the European West strategically to define all that is *not* civilized – all that exists in mystery beyond the comfortable borders of one's own culture and society. According to such arguments, the stigmatized and 'primitive' man who partakes of human flesh is merely the central symbol of the unrecognized or unidentified *presence* in colonial discourse – the 'absolute sign of the Other' in imperial thought.[63] The activity of cannibalism consequently is 'and always has been', in the words of modern critics such as Laurence R. Goldman, 'a quintessential symbol of alterity, an entrenched metaphor of cultural xenophobia'.[64] Such a theory would thus contend, for example, that Spanish assertions that the Aztecs first encountered by Conquistadors in Central America had regularly engaged in large-scale human sacrifices and other rituals that called for routine acts of cannibalism were quite simply fabrications made up by the Spanish themselves. The controversial anthropologist William Arens, who published his influential and provocative (if now seriously discredited) study *The Man-Eating Myth* in 1979, went so far as to insist that customary cannibalism among non-European cultures remained 'unobserved and undocumented', and contended that 'the cannibal complex' as it was defined and understood by European anthropologists was 'more plausibly interpreted as a mythic dimension of cultural world views (especially in the West) than a conclusion of proper empirical observation'.[65] Cannibalism, in other words, existed almost exclusively in the minds of such Western subjects who have looked always to define themselves as essentially different from – and demonstrably superior to – quite literally everybody else in the world.

Contentions such as those of Arens would be rather more convincing, again, were it not for the growing body of evidence that strongly suggests that cannibalism was routinely practised by an immensely wide and culturally diverse range of ancient societies – practised, moreover, not merely as part of communal religious rituals, but also during times of siege, famine, natural disaster, and even prison overcrowding. In fact, rather than existing exclusively as an oppressive and decidedly European cultural construction, Arens's followers must have noted that cannibalism had been recognized in the West itself thousands of years earlier to be merely one of a set of many cultural practices that was only naturally treated in different ways by different societies. One of the earliest recorded accounts, for example, of the manner in which attitudes towards cannibalism were expected only naturally to vary from one society to another was included by the wonderfully inclusive, cosmopolitan traveller Herodotus in his *Histories* (*c.*470 BC). Herodotus neither praised nor condemned the practices he found. Rather, the earliest of Greek historians assumed a non-judgemental stance that echoes other passages in his work that value cultural relativism at the expense of any narrow-minded Hellenic provincialism. 'When Darius was king of Persia', Herodotus reminded his readers to illustrate his point,

> he summoned the Greeks who happened to be present at his court, and asked them what they would take to eat the dead bodies of their fathers. They replied

that they would not do it for any money in the world. Later, in the presence of the Greeks, and through an interpreter, so that they could understand what was said, he asked some Indians of the tribe called Callatiae, who in fact eat their parents' dead bodies, what they would take to burn them. They uttered a cry of horror and forbade him to mention such a dreadful thing.[66]

'Everyone without exception', Herodotus concluded without any apparent bias or judgement in this instance, 'believes his own native customs, and the religion he was brought up in, to be the best.' To whatever extent some of the historian's larger issues of veracity or credulity may still remain open to question, it is remarkable that even when it came to the question of human cannibalism, Herodotus could hardly be accused of having exercised any very significant or even perceptible degree of cultural xenophobia. It is simply something that *they* do, the historian implies – and something that *we* do not.

The assertion that attributions of cannibalism in popular belief both within and outside of Western institutions were strictly mythical or metaphorical has consequently been more or less completely re-evaluated – if not resolved. Arens and many of his followers, it soon became increasingly clear, had tended unjustifiably to ignore or blithely to dismiss the increasing body of irrefutable archaeological evidence that indicated that remarkably few places in the world – Europe certainly not excluded – had been untouched in their histories by *some* form of genuine cannibalism. The casual eating of human flesh may indeed have begun most quickly to disappear as a cultural practice in Europe because its inhabitants surrendered their activities as hunter-gatherers rather earlier than most. And although the move towards the domestication of animals and the cultivation of the soil in all likelihood encouraged Europeans to cease the practice of feeding on their own species relatively early in their history, it is not surprising that the collective cultural memory of the patterns and rituals of cannibalism proved to be remarkably resilient. In recent years, a great many ethnographers and anthropologists have weighed in on the side of those who – strange as it may seem – regard anthropophagy (literally, the 'consumption of men') as less of an aberration than a typical human practice, and not one, in fact, that was inherently repugnant to mankind. As Margaret Visser put it when attempting finally to refute those who would still argue that cannibalism was an imperial cultural myth, however much we would like to convince or to reassure ourselves that the actual practice of cannibalism was little more than a disparaging ideological and culturally generated myth, the 'rather attractive idea – that people have never really eaten each other – [has] had to be abandoned'.[67]

Anticipating the observations of a generation of later scholars such as those referred to above, the great if often controversial anthropologist James Frazer famously commented that the rationale for consuming the body of another human being was, on the face of it at least, 'simple enough'. He was even among the first to give practical reasons for doing so. No enemy to diversity himself, Frazer argued in his hugely influential *The Golden Bough* (1890–1915) at great and increasing length that, 'the savage commonly believes that by eating the flesh of [a man], he acquires not only the physical, but also the moral and intellectual qualities of that ... man'. Pointing anecdotally to the manner in which certain African tribes were thought ritually to consume the livers of their enemies (supposedly the seat of valour) to acquire bravery, or to the way that the Ashantees and other tribes were rumoured similarly to cut out and eat the heart of any brave man killed in battle, Frazer anticipated the conclusions of many later students of the phenomenon when he observed that 'the flesh and blood of dead men are commonly eaten and drunk to inspire bravery, wisdom, or other qualities for which the men themselves were remarkable, or which are supposed to have their special seat in the particular part eaten'.[68] Cannibalism, he concluded, was a recognized and eminently sensible means of acquiring the valuable qualities even of one's most fearsome enemies.

*

All we have to go upon are traditions and superstitions ... Yet must we be satisfied; in the first place, because we have to be – no other means is at our control – and secondly, because, after all, these things – tradition and superstition – are everything.
(Bram Stoker, *Dracula*)[69]

For all the rancour it may have inspired, the dubious anthropology of Arens's often wayward and ideologically blinkered followers succeeded in yielding some genuine cultural insights. The debate initiated by the labelling of cannibalism as a myth has thrown up some important issues relating to everything from morality and folklore tradition, to political and economic commerce. Literary critics were quick to get in on the act by linking cannibalism to issues of cultural 'difference', consumption and concepts of the body. Anecdotes relating to the topic of man-eaters continue to evoke a morbid fascination among modern readers quite as strong – if not stronger – than any preliminary responses of antipathy or disgust. On the more positive side, too, accounts of cannibalistic activity can at least be argued to serve a useful purpose, insofar as they highlight the possible hazards of cross-cultural misinterpretation and miscommunication of all kinds. Admittedly, such insight is more likely than not to take the form of humorous representation and discourse. The masked cannibal standing beside his oddly oversized and anachronistic, cast-iron cooking pot, thanks in large part to classic images popularized by cartoonists such as Charles Addams, Peter Arno and others, even today remains one of the most fixed and endurable of graphic caricatures in contemporary newspapers and magazines. Laughter – nervous or otherwise – is one of the most consistent features to punctuate the contemporary discourse of cannibalism. Contemporary anecdotes relating to man-eating almost always include at least *some* element of macabre humour. When visiting the mountain village of Nabutautau (or Navatusila) in Fiji in 1867, as one frequently repeated story would have it, the Wesleyan Methodist minister Thomas Baker, serving with the London Missionary Society, removed a comb from the hair of a local chief, unaware that touching the head of the chief was strictly forbidden by local custom; he was immediately butchered and eaten by the locals, who apparently consumed everything but his boots, which were thought to be too tough. The bizarre incongruity of those who would find it easier to swallow a Methodist preacher himself than to waste valuable time on the stubborn mastication of his more sensibly minded footwear inevitably provokes at least a smile, if not outright laughter.

Not everyone is inclined to see the funny side of such events, however. In 2003, the island natives of Nabutautau themselves offered a formal apology to Baker's descendents for the missionary's murder at the hands of their cannibal ancestors. Members of the tribe (it was reported) believed themselves still to be the victims of an age-old curse relating to the incident. They had already offered a similar apology seven years earlier, when they were said to have gone so far as officially to present the Methodist Church in Fiji with Baker's 'overcooked and slightly chewed boots'.[70] In a similar vein, parodying modern debates about man-eating in his short story '99' – and perfectly capturing the unflinchingly self-righteous posturing of many contemporary academics – the writer James Hynes included the character of a keynote speaker at a conference in the late 1990s devoted to 'Captains and Cannibals' delivering an address entitled, 'Eat Me: Captain Cook and the Ingestion of the Other'.[71]

A measured degree of levity is by no means out of place in what remains for many reasons a highly volatile topic. Finally, and at their most productive, the more recent scientific and academic investigations into the topic of cannibalism – although backing away from claims regarding the completely mythical nature of such activity – have also instigated an unusually lively debate concerning the deployment of the man-eater as a cultural symbol, and have prompted us with renewed interest to analyse the place of such a symbol within the history of colonial encounters. A number of central, historical events seem invariably to constitute the focus of these analyses. Preceded only by the so-called 'million lies' of the Venetian traveller Marco Polo (who had his own admittedly dubious tales to tell of cannibals in the course of his travels throughout Central Asia in the thirteenth century), Christopher Columbus was naturally among the first European explorers to offer any 'first-hand' accounts of such behaviour in the New World. Contrary to much popular public belief, Columbus tended personally to dismiss the earliest reports of cannibalism that came to his attention as unlikely, much in the same manner that he would have dismissed any other fantastical superstition. Documenting one early encounter in 1492 with some Arawak natives on the coast of what is now Haiti (Hispaniola), the explorer noted that two of the men he encountered 'had lost some chunks of flesh from their bodies and said that the Canibales had bitten out the pieces'. He then added succinctly to the log: 'I do not believe this.'[72] Columbus had been similarly disinclined to credit earlier rumours of cannibalism among tribes encountered in the New World. 'They say that the cannibals eat people and are well armed,' he wrote of some local tribesmen in his log not long after landfall in the Caribbean,

> I believe there is some truth in this, although if they are armed they must be an intelligent people. Perhaps these people may have captured some of the other Indians; when the captives did not return to their own country, it was said that they were eaten.[73]

It was only with great reluctance that Columbus came eventually to accept the possibility that such behaviour was not only conceivable but possibly verifiable as fact. Anthropologists still labouring under the influence of Arens, on the other hand, would contend that Columbus was in this early instance merely the dupe of what was, in effect, anti-Carib tribal propaganda; 'the word for man-eater is now cannibal and not "arawakibal"', Arens himself had argued, 'because Columbus first encountered the latter, who were eager to fill him in on their gossip about their enemies to the south'.[74]

There would be plenty of other historical encounters with cannibals – many of them far more celebrated than Columbus's own. The great eighteenth-century explorer Captain Cook would perhaps most notoriously claim to bear witness to cannibalistic behaviour in November 1773, when his ship the *Resolution* was anchored off the New Zealand coast for repairs. On that occasion, some of Cook's officers took advantage of the opportunity to go ashore to – as Cook himself put it – 'amuse themselves among the natives'. About a mile from the ship, Cook's party came across what appeared to be the remains of a recent cannibal feast. The heart and entrails of one victim were lying 'quite fresh upon the ground'. Nearby, a severed head was displayed on the top of a forked stick at the end of a canoe. The lieutenant in charge, Richard Pickersgill, made the unusual decision to carry the remains back to the *Resolution*, purchasing the head from local natives at the price of two nails. Following their return to the ship, Pickersgill and the other officers were visited by another group of New Zealand Maoris, some of whom were said to have taken to eyeing the head 'very wistfully'. 'As I was standing by it', another one of Cook's lieutenants, Charles Clerke, wrote in his journal shortly afterwards, they 'begged [him] to give it to them.' As Clerke described what followed,

> I questioned them why they wanted it? They answered to eat. I then asked one of them if he would eat a piece there directly, to which he very readily and cheerfully assented. I then carried it to the fire by his desire, gave it a

little broil on the gridiron and delivered it to him. He caught it in rapture, devoured it most ravenously, and licked his finger half a score times after it.[75]

It was at this point that the Captain himself returned to the *Resolution*. Although Cook professed to be horrified by the spectacle taking place on the quarter-deck, he later claimed to have been too intrigued by the situation to bring the proceedings to a halt. Cook watched in fascination as Clerke cut a second 'steak' for his newfound 'friend', who grilled it and then ate it happily, in the presence of the Captain and almost the entire ship's company. Afterwards, Cook and William Wales (one of two astronomers on the voyage by agreement with the Royal Society) debated the possible atavistic impulse behind such behaviour. 'Few consider what a savage man is in his original state', Cook wrote in his journal later that evening,

> and even after he is in some degree civilized; the New Zealanders are certainly in a state of civilization, their behaviour to us has been Manly and Mild, shewing allways a readiness to oblige us; they have some arts among them which they execute with great judgement and unwearied patience. ... This custom of eating their enemies slain in battle (for I firmly believe they eat the flesh of no others) has undoubtedly been handed down to them from the earliest times and we know that it is not an easy matter to break a nation of its ancient customs let them be ever so inhuman and savage.[76]

Cook's defenders have argued that in most cases he went out of his way to understand the natives he encountered in his explorations. Certainly, any Rousseau-esque preconceptions he might possibly have entertained about the happy 'natural state' of man would have been sorely tested by episodes such as this one. His more recent critics, however, have continued to argue that it was the very British discourse on cannibalism that itself 'produced' the Maori practice of cannibalism; that on this occasion, as one cultural historian has put it, 'the British fascination with and horror of cannibalism was perceived by the Maori, who responded by admitting to and exaggerating their own cannibalism, sometimes in play as part of a dialogue with the Europeans, sometimes for real as a weapon of terror, one of the few weapons they possessed in an unequal contest'.[77] What you see, as it were – and just what it is you *want* to see – is what you get.

By the time popular authors such as R.M. Ballantyne got around to retelling Cook's adventures for an audience of younger readers in lurid tales, 'Robinsoniads', and boy's adventure stories such as his *The Cannibal Isles* (1869), the perspective had unquestionably been skewed to present the antipodeans as savage 'others'. 'It was long before people in the civilised world would give credit to stories such as that just related,' Ballantyne was to write of his own recapitulation of Cook's adventures among the cannibals, transforming much of the impact of the incident as an incentive to zealous missionary work, and even now there may be some who doubt the truth of them. But the number and the characters of the travellers who have visited these islands since the days of Cook, and who have brought home similar reports, put the matter beyond question. Men ought neither to doubt these shocking details because they seem incredible, nor turn away from them because they are disgusting. Like the surgeon who calmly and steadily examines the most hideous of wounds or sores that can affect the human body, so ought the Christian and the philanthropist to know and consider in detail the horrible deeds that are done by our fellow-men in the Cannibal Islands. It is good for us to be made acquainted with the truth in order that we may be filled with strong pity for the degraded savages, and in order, also, that our hearts and hands may be opened towards those noble missionaries who venture themselves into the midst of such awful scenes for the sake of souls, and in the name of Jesus Christ.[78]

Of course, there always had been – and there always would be – room for misrepresentation or hypocrisy, as well as genuine moral and cultural confusion. Any European who professed instinctively to feel a stomach-churning horror at the very thought of customary cannibalism would need to contend first with the brutally frank and famous assessment of the French essayist Michel de Montaigne. Writing only a century after the voyages of Columbus, and well before Cook's more rigorously (if still questionably) documented expedition, Montaigne had influentially commended not only the apparently uncorrupted virtue but also the comparative happiness of the primitive societies then being encountered by New World explorers. His indictment of what he effectively saw to be European double standards was fierce. 'I am not sorry we notice the barbarous horrors of such acts', Montaigne wrote so memorably of supposed instances of actual cannibalism,

> but I am heartily sorry that, judging their faults rightly, we should be so blind to our own. I think there is more barbarity in eating a man alive than in eating him dead; and in tearing by tortures and the rack a body still full of feeling, in roasting a man bit by bit, in having him bitten and mangled by dogs and swine (as we have not only read but seen within fresh memory, not among ancient enemies, but among neighbours and fellow citizens and what is worse, on the pretext of piety and religion), than in roasting and eating him after he is dead.[79]

The various atrocities that had been perpetrated by all sides in the religious wars of the sixteenth century, Montaigne effectively cautioned his readers, left no room for European complacency. His ironic assessment of the degree to which the cannibals' Old World counterparts had so efficiently and in so sophisticated a manner complimented the ironically crude literalism of their newly discovered cousins put paid to the supposed horrors of so-called 'uncivilized nations'. As Montaigne reasoned when considering the ethical implications of cannibalism in his essay (much like Herodotus before him), 'each man calls barbarism whatever is not his own practice; for indeed it seems we have no other test of truth and reason than the examples and pattern of the opinions and customs of the country we live in'.[80]

*

The laws of nature do indeed tell us to kill our neighbour, and that is the way people behave throughout the world. If we ourselves do not exercise our right to eat our neighbour, that's because we've got better things to eat.

(Voltaire, *Candide*)[81]

Is it progress if a cannibal uses knife and fork?

(Stanislaw Lec, *Unkempt Thoughts*)[82]

And what of actual instances of cannibalism among modern or even contemporary Europeans themselves? Such acts may have been considered unspeakable, but rumours of soldiers, sailors and merchants who had been driven to atrocities in extreme circumstances had long circulated among the seafaring community in Great Britain, at least. Whispered accounts had for years told of men who had been set adrift in the waters of uncharted oceans – men who had been lost or left for dead deep within the deserts and jungles of the New World – and who had been forced to turn upon their companions in the struggle for survival. Even if one conceded that other cultures routinely participated in acts of cannibalism as different forms of 'social practice', under what possible circumstances might cannibalism ever have become 'routine' amongst civilized Europeans themselves? Desperate times, it was often said, called for desperate measures.

The subject – although quite literally unpalatable – had been openly broached in the past. Herodotus, as we have already seen, could hardly have been accused of having shied away from the topic. The famous Roman orator, Marcus Tullius Cicero, was even more memorably to consider the issue in his treatise *De officiis* ('On Duties'), when he pondered the related question of whose survival should take precedence in the event of a shipwreck. If it were necessary to jettison something or someone in the event of a perilous and stormy sea, Cicero began by asking, which should be the first to be thrown overboard – the 'expensive horse' or the 'cheap and worthless' slave? Should a contest arise for the possession of a life-saving plank of wood large enough to support only one individual, would the life of the wise man take precedence over that of the fool? Or would the life of the ship's owner count for something more than that of, say, a mere passenger? Cicero came closest to confronting the issue of cannibalism outright when he asked: if two men of the same worth, intelligence and value – if equals, in other words, were to find themselves in a situation in which it was necessary for one to sacrifice his life for the survival of the other, by what method should the choice between

36

them be made? Cicero's conclusion that the point would best be 'decided by lot or by a game of chance' is among the earliest associations of the concept of a random lottery or draw with the possibilities of what would in time become more conventionally known as an act of 'survival cannibalism'.[83]

By the eighteenth century, cannibalism among sailors in such situations had come to be regarded within the nautical community in England, at least, as one of many regrettable but practically unavoidable 'customs of the sea'. Broadsheets, penny ballads and humorous poems (W.S. Gilbert's 'Yarn of the Nancy Bell' being perhaps the best known) would all address the issue, not infrequently in a darkly comedic manner. The narrative tropes of the castaway and – by extension – the cannibal 'survivor' would eventually enter the larger culture from sometimes odd and curious angles, in the form of fictional works such as Defoe's 1719 *Robinson Crusoe*, or indirectly in the works of poets such as William Cowper later in the century. Putatively historical accounts recalling the fate of vessels such as the *Admiral* in the late sixteenth century or the *Nottingham Galley* in 1710, and of individuals such as Pedro de Serano and Alexander Selkirk (still thought by many to have been the model for Daniel Defoe's *Robinson Crusoe*) all presented readers with tales of real-life survival in desperate situations. The connection between the British Navy and cannibalism was to be further reinforced by the sometimes peculiar derivations of maritime slang. In 1867, a nine-year-old girl named Fanny Adams from Alton in Hampshire was murdered by a solicitor's clerk by the name of Frederick Baker. After he had cut up and disembowelled his victim, Baker distributed the body parts in various locations, and apparently some portion of Fanny eventually turned up in the Navy's Victualling Yard at Deptford. Shortly afterwards, a sailor was said to have discovered a button in his ration of tinned mutton – a product that had only recently been introduced as an article of diet for members of the Royal Navy – and the descriptive term 'Fanny Adams' to refer to tinned meat quickly became lower deck slang (the used tins would subsequently be used by sailors as articles of mess gear, and 'fanny' is still, among other things, naval slang for a cooking pot).

It took the startling events relating to the wreck of the *Mignonette* – which in turn resulted in the case of *The Queen v. Dudley and Stephens* late in the nineteenth century – finally to compel the British public at large openly if belatedly to confront the issue of cannibalism at sea. What is perhaps most striking to modern students of the case is the extent to which contemporary debate focused less on the harsh realities of survival cannibalism itself than it did – in Ciceronian fashion – on the rationale behind deciding precisely who, in such situations, was justifiably to be sacrificed in the interests of others, and by what method they were to be chosen. (It has been pointed out that the law as an institution appears typically to be more concerned with the precise *manner* in which a cannibalistic meal has been obtained – i.e. murder, manslaughter, suicide etc. – than it is with the substance of the meal itself.

Such scrupulous precision in English law has resulted in the anomalous situation whereby the only meat that one is absolutely forbidden to consume is swan – which remains, as ever, the property of the Crown.)

The details of the case against Dudley and Stephens were undeniably compelling. The small English yacht *Mignonette* had departed from Southampton for Sydney on 19 May 1884. The vessel, which was being delivered to its new owner in Australia, was captained by 31-year-old Thomas Dudley. Accompanying Dudley were a mate, Edwin Stephens, 36, an ordinary seaman by the name of Ned Brooks, 38, and a 17-year-old cabin boy, Richard Parker. When the ship foundered in bad weather on 5 July in a storm on the high seas some 1,600 miles north of the Cape of Good Hope, the crew took refuge in a 13-foot dinghy. The only provisions they were able to rescue from the *Mignonette* before she disappeared beneath the waves were two one-pound tins of turnips. On their fourth day adrift, they caught a sea-turtle, and managed to consume some of its flesh. From the twelfth day of their voyage in the dinghy they had nothing left to eat at all. Dudley later recounted what happened next:

> I proposed to Stephens and Brooks that we should cast lots who should die for the maintenance of the others, but they not agreeing to that, I then said to Stephens 'How many children have you?' He said 'Five and a wife.' I said 'I have three and a wife, and would it not be better that we should kill the boy Parker in order that three lives might be saved?' Dudley then said 'If there is no vessel by to-morrow morning I think we had better kill the lad.' No vessel appearing on the following morning, I made signs to Stephens and Brooks. 'We had better do it,' but they seemed to have no heart to do it, so I went to the boy.[84]

Dudley murdered the delirious and only semi-conscious Parker himself, 'stabbing' him in the throat. For just over three days, the survivors fed upon the flesh of the body. On the fourth day, before Parker's remains had been entirely consumed, the surviving crew-members of the *Mignonette* were picked up by a passing vessel and taken to Falmouth, where Dudley and Stephens were committed by the local Magistrates for trial on charges of 'the wilful murder of Richard Parker on the high seas' (Brooks having been made a witness of the Crown).[85] They had made no secret of the events that had taken place in the dinghy. Reporting the guilty verdict passed upon the two men by the Court at Exeter later that year, the columnist for *The Times* wrote that the situation was 'terribly trying'. 'But', he continued:

> we protest against the notion that in the extremity of hunger or thirst men are to be considered as released from all duties towards each other. It is an abuse of words to speak of the time as due to necessity .... In the annals of our seamen are plenty of instances of their overcoming impulses as strong as those to which Dudley and Stephens succumbed. Our columns in 1836 contained

DU CÔTÉ DE CHEZ TODD

an account of the perils of a shipwrecked crew who suffered hardships as cruel as befell the survivors of the *Mignonette*. But no one among them suggested the idea of killing any of their number, and the dead, we are told, were cast overboard lest the living should be tempted to forget themselves and seek relief from their misery in a horrible repast. Miners who are walled up in a subterranean gallery with no food or water devour, in the agony of their hunger, candle ends, and even the soles of their boots, and then die heroically; and the records of war are rarely tarnished with horrors such as those of which the crew of the *Mignonette* were guilty.[86]

To acquit Dudley and Stephens or to qualify their actions by applying a doctrine of necessary homicide to the situation could only lead to 'deplorable' results. The *Times* correspondent found himself asking much the same questions as those first raised by Cicero many hundreds of years earlier. 'If too many are in a boat which has the survivors of a shipwrecked crew on board', the reporter queried,

> must the weakest be thrown overboard in order to lighten it? If food is insuf-
> ficient for the sustenance of all, are the women and children, as the weaker,
> to be deprived of their fair allowances in order that the rest may live? Or, to
> take a case more probable, on the occasion of a shipwreck or fire at sea, are the
> strong men to cast aside all restraints and do as they please so that they may
> save their lives?[87]

Yet the judgement that declared the pair to be guilty, which was returned by the jury after a very short period of deliberation, was in actual fact a 'special verdict', to which had been added a strong expression of 'sympathy and compassion for the sufferings the prisoners had undergone'. The sentence of death pronounced upon the two was a simple formality. Both were free men in a mere matter of months.

In a very short period of time, the subject and even the open discussion of cannibalism in a much wider variety of situations and within a surprisingly more inclusive range of forums was to become almost commonplace. Mary Kingsley, niece to the novelist Charles Kingsley, travelled twice to West Africa. On her second journey to the area, in 1895, she stayed among the Fang tribe (in present-day Gabon), a group that remained among the most notorious and persistent cannibals in the region. Although having witnessed evidence of cannibalism herself, Kingsley insisted on staying in the huts of the local tribes; much to her credit, she remained a committed advocate of a more humane colonial government in the area, and refrained from any counterproductive acts of overtly missionary zeal.

*

They want to eat others, and at the same time they're afraid that other people are going

39

to eat them. That's why they're always watching with such suspicious looks in their eyes.

(Lu Xun, *'Diary of a Madman'*)[89]

The case of the Crown against Dudley and Stephens, not surprisingly, remains a significant landmark in any discussion of man-eating activities. The pages of *The Times* – and other metropolitan newspapers, for that matter – appear always to have been genially disposed to debate the propriety of cannibalism among gentlemen. When the publisher of *The New York Herald*, James Gordon Bennett, mounted the African expedition of Henry M. Stanley to locate the whereabouts of the Scottish missionary David Livingstone in 1869, the newspapers seem to have been as interested in making as much of the explorers' supposed contact with tribes of cannibals around Lake Tanganyika as they were in any more substantial developments relating to the hunt for the missing Livingstone.

The popular predisposition already to associate the most famous of the British Imperial adventurers with cannibalism had received a further boost a few years earlier when Livingstone's predecessor, the eccentric Richard Francis Burton, christened the Anthropological Society's London dining club 'the Cannibal Club'. The mace belonging to the Club's chairman was decorated with a carving of an African figure gnawing on a human thigh-bone. The explorer's close friend, the poet Charles Algernon Swinburne – a self-confessed admirer of the Marquis de Sade on whom the periodical *Punch* would bestow the nickname of 'Swine-born' for his sexually saturated celebration of acts of cannibalism in poems such as 'Anactoria' and 'Dolores' – composed a charter for the society that he dubbed the 'Cannibal catechism', and that was then read out loud at meetings.[89] Burton himself assembled documents relating to cannibalism in South America and maintained a life-long interest in the subject; he claimed later in life to regret the fact that he had never had the privilege of witnessing cannibalistic behaviour at first hand.

Burton was not alone, although there were arguably an equally impressive number of those who, perhaps titillated by the academic idea of cannibalism, were rather loath to confront the brutal realities of the act itself, particularly when such realities were associated with the most noble-minded of British Imperial endeavours. Some revisionist accounts of Captain Robert Falcon Scott's doomed Antarctic expedition of 1911, for example, have gone so far as to suggest that the surviving team of Scott, Oates and Bowers are very likely toward the end of their ordeal to have resorted to cannibalism. The absence of any photographic record of their actual fate – the absence of any 'deathbed' photographs of the polar heroes – represents a curious lacuna in the otherwise meticulous valedictory record of photographs taken by Surgeon Atkinson of the Relief Party; the historian Max Jones has suggested that the Edwardian era was still far from ready to be confronted with the possibly gruesome display of dismembered and partially devoured corpses

40

in what was otherwise 'the most filmed and photographed [expedition] in history'.[90] Still others remain unconvinced by such speculation. In his own highly readable biography of the explorer, Sir Ranulph Fiennes disdained even to countenance such suspicions with regard to Scott and his colleagues, although he did not shy away from the fact that indications of cannibalism 'which the British Public found it difficult to accept' had inevitably attached themselves to the findings of those explorers who preceded Scott, including, of course, those who had gone in search of Sir John Franklin's vanished expedition to find the fabled North-West Passage to the Indies in 1845.[91] Recent authors such as Michael Smith have argued from documents such as the journal kept by Sir James Wordie, chief scientist on the ship *Endurance*, that those members of Sir Ernest Shackleton's failed polar expedition of 1914 who were left to await the arrival of their leader's rescue team were deeply troubled by the seeming inevitability of resorting to cannibalism. It was one of the most 'delicate subjects' among the men, Smith comments, taking note that one of the rumours circulating immediately prior to their rescue involved a plot to kill an unpopular crew member and eat him.[92] At the very least, cannibalism – it is hardly surprising to learn – can still be counted on to sell newspapers, and even books, and is a matter for endless speculation.

Other crimes and criminals have attained a grim sort of glamour by their mere association with cannibalism. Also famous by proximity, as it were, is the frequently related crime that is sometimes more euphemistically described as the intentional 'misappropriation' of human remains. Just what happens to one's body after death was a question that occupied cannibals, grave-robbers, and eventually (although in far more practical terms) Sweeney Todd and Mrs Lovett as well. It is, after all, a question to which we have all probably given at least *some* thought ourselves. 'Resurrection men', 'lifters', 'resurgam homos', 'grabs' and 'sack-'em up men': the sordid body-snatchers of the late eighteenth and early nineteenth centuries were all the more sinister for the 'unnatural' use to which they put their depredations – and the simple fact that they made money from them. The 'Edinburgh Horrors' perpetrated by the pair of William Burke and William Hare in 1828 had alerted the populace to the possibilities of killing-for-dissection. (Together, Burke and Hare had, in the course of the 1820s, murdered some 15 people, selling the fresh bodies to Dr Knox's School for Anatomy at a going rate of £8–£14 a-piece.) The phenomenon resurfaced in an even more gruesome guise in 1831, when three more 'Burkers' were accused of the murder of the street urchin Carlo Ferrari in London's Bethnal Green.[93] Such activities could inspire panics close to hysterical. An acquaintance of the poet John Clare had been told at about the same time that unwary walkers in the great metropolis routinely disappeared into trap-doors connected to a subterranean network of tunnels, where they were 'robbed and murdered and thrown into boiling cauldrons ... [their] bones sold to the doctors'.[94]

And yet the notion that particular areas of London did indeed conceal an underground maze of tunnels was not all that fantastical; the sewers of the metropolis played host to a particular breed of human scavengers – 'sewer hunters' – who survived by desperately retrieving anything that had quite literally fallen through the cracks of society. 'D'you recollect hearing of the man', one scrounger responded to questioning, 'as was found in the sewers about twelve years ago – oh, you must; the rats ate every bit of him, and left nothink but his bones.' 'I knowed him well,' the sewer hunter reminisced with fondness, 'he was a regular down there.'[95] As the social historian Sarah Wise has noted of such fears in the period, 'the notion of boiling, cooking, and consuming had become intermingled with the notion of dissection and anatomy'.[95] Dickens would memorably depict grave robbing as the night-time pastime of the character Jerry Cruncher in *A Tale of Two Cities* (1859), but the body-snatchers had by then been engaged in such practices for years. (Cannibalism and body-snatching likewise turn up in a peculiarly wide range of fiction aimed at younger readers, ranging from Mark Twain's *The Adventures of Tom Sawyer* (1876), to L.M. Montgomery's *Anne of Windy Willows* (1936), in her Avonlea series.) Most such body-snatchers sold their exhumations for cash to surgical schools as specimens for dissection. Corpses of various sorts, shapes and sizes, only naturally and according to fluctuations in the demands of the market commanded different prices. A meeting of the parish churchwardens of central London in July 1795 was appalled to learn not only that the prices set by gravediggers for recently interred corpses were agreed at a market rate (an adult at two guineas and a crown, and those underage 'six shillings for the first foot, and nine pence per inch for all it measured more in length'), but that some of the bodies thus procured were used not only for dissection, but also shipped to various parts of the kingdom ('with the flesh on'). The costs of local exhumations borne by legitimate local authorities could amount to considerably more and might well include a substantial amount for sundry expenses extending to several bottles of whiskey to fortify the undertakers in their task. Human skulls were said to have been used as nail boxes, and human flesh rendered into candles and soap. One man testified that he had given his own daughter the skeleton of a child to play with in place of a doll.[97]

Some nineteenth-century coffin makers were said to have begun making heavy, cast-iron coffins in their efforts to discourage body-snatchers. It was assumed that those who had taken to exhuming bodies from burial grounds were unlikely to make the extra effort of dragging up such heavy and unwieldy hauls. City authorities were no more supportive than the grave robbers, though for different reasons; most were rather less than enthusiastic about the prospect of their already overcrowded cemeteries being filled with non-biodegradable caskets in a period when the sought-after accommodation in the London churchyard soil was routinely turned over to make room for newer occupants.

Still stranger stories abound. Following the burial of the novelist Laurence

Sterne in a small churchyard near Tyburn, a widely credited rumour circulated that his corpse had been stolen by body-snatchers; the body was said to have turned up on the dissecting table of Charles Collignon, an anatomist at Sterne's own university. One individual present at the commencement of the dissection is said to have 'recognized Sterne's face the moment he saw the body'. The anatomy lesson went ahead as planned, it seems, but at least Sterne enjoyed enough of a reputation to ensure that the body was returned to its original London resting place and quietly reburied.[98] Sterne's pointed characterization of himself in his own work as 'Yorick' rather qualifies the veracity of the anecdote although, again, it has often been repeated, and was believed by many at the time to be true.

Surprisingly, even the activities of body-snatchers, though invariably bizarre, were not always entirely unwelcome. In April 1824, one John Macintire, who had been suffering from a long and lingering fever, awoke to consciousness to find himself incapable of any physical movement; he heard the nurse who had been watching at his bedside tearfully declare, 'He is dead.' 'My father drew his hand over my face and closed my eyelids,' Macintire later recalled: 'I heard my friends speak in low accents, and felt myself placed in the coffin and borne away.'[99] His body was lowered into the grave, and he heard the sound of the churchyard soil scatter across the coffin lid and then slowly bury him. Not much time passed, however, before he again began to hear the murmurings of 'rough' voices above him, and felt the coffin tremble as it was rudely hauled to the surface and carried off to the dissecting chamber. Still unable to move, Macintire eventually heard the sound of the doctors, nurses and students who gathered for his anatomization. 'When all was ready', he wrote, 'the Demonstrator took his knife and pierced my breast; I felt a dreadful cracking throughout my whole frame; a convulsive shudder of my body instantly followed, and a shriek of horror arose from all present. My terrible trance was ended; the utmost exertions were made to restore me, and in the course of an hour I was in full possession of all my faculties.'[100] One is left to speculate about the long-term effects of such an experience on Macintire's subsequent state of mind. Hopefully he was spared the experience of reading in the newspapers only four years after his own ordeal of the city surgeon who was arrested for disinterring and carrying off the corpse of his own mother from her grave in Hendon in north-west London, and then – with a seemingly gratuitous and unfilial *coup de grace* – beheading her. The surgeon claimed at his trial that his family suffered under the continued shadow of an hereditary disease, to which his parent had succumbed. He pleaded before a suitably astonished court that he had hoped that by dissecting his mother's head he could learn more about the nature of the illness, and perhaps discover a cure for it. Again, one wonders whether the mother in question would have regarded her own capital disfigurement at the hands of her son as an act of commendable if strangely dispassionate filial devotion, or, rather, as a brutal instance of rude and supremely self-interested corporeal vandalism.

*

Fine fellows – cannibals – in their place.
(Joseph Conrad, *The Heart of Darkness*)[101]

Such macabre tales of flesh, bones and body parts were naturally of a piece with the gossip related to similar stories of unspeakable desecrations in the heart of an increasingly mythologized London after dark – a London of gas-lit, yellow streets, and deep, impenetrable fog. The so-called 'gaslight ghouls' of the Victorian era, at least, appear to have been all the more ghoulish when they confessed to feeling a bit peckish. The otherwise familiar, diurnal landscapes of the ordinary metropolitan citizen gained an added *frisson* of terror when confounded with the murky, nocturnal activities of the beastly 'savage'. When, as late as 1891, General William Booth ventured to compare the squalid environs of Whitechapel, where the spectacular murders of Jack the Ripper had only three years earlier caused such a sensation, to the 'barbarous' conditions one might expect to find only in 'darkest Africa', he was simply making use of what had already begun to feel like a familiar trope. 'May we not find a parallel at our own doors', Booth asked his readers, comparing indigenous conditions to those of the supposedly unprecedented barbarity encountered abroad, 'and discover within a stone's throw of our cathedrals and palaces similar horrors to those which Stanley has found existing in the great Equatorial forest?'[102] 'They have no institutions of their own to speak of,' wrote Walter Besant of East London's 'obscure' and 'wild' residents in 1882, 'no public buildings of any importance, no municipality, no gentry, no carriages, no soldiers, no picture galleries, no theatres, no opera – they have nothing.' 'No one', he wrote in sum, 'wants to see the place.'[103] In a similar vein, T.H. Huxley commented more succinctly that the most primitive Polynesian 'was not half so savage, so unclean, so irreclaimable as the tenant of any East London slum'.[104] Certainly in October 1890, when Mrs Phoebe Hogg and her 18-month-old child were discovered to have been savagely murdered in Hampstead, with related evidence turning up not very far away in the streets of neat, Victorian Finchley, it was assumed at once by many that the Ripper had indeed resumed his activities. He was supposed on this occasion merely to have chosen to do so amidst rather more genteel and respectable middle-class surroundings. There had already been a great deal of speculation that the Ripper may very well have engaged in acts of cannibalism himself. The 'Jack the Ripper' who subscribed his name to the famous letter 'from hell', within which was wrapped a piece of kidney, and which was sent to George Lusk of the Whitechapel Vigilance Committee at the height of the Ripper's activity, claimed to have eaten the rest of that same organ; 'it was very nice', he remarked. By the time Joseph Conrad's fictional alter-ego Marlowe acknowledged, when contemplating the prospect of the Thames estuary in the opening pages of his *Heart of Darkness* in 1899, that London too had been 'one of the dark places of the earth', the ironic association of the supposedly 'civilized' world of the great city with the most outrageous practices of the most savage and atavistic of tribal primitives would have been close to inescapable.[105]

Londoners themselves, in fact, would appear always to have been peculiarly fascinated by the idea of cannibalism. As we shall see, cultural and historical circumstances combined to render this same attraction very close to unavoidable – and perhaps even inevitable. To a certain extent it could be argued that the comparative abundance of meat available as food in modern society stimulates our curiosity regarding the metaphorical connotations of the acts of violence that underlie our need to consume other animals; or perhaps we are intrigued by the relative proximity of the practice of slaughtering animals to be consumed as meat, and the possibility of killing one another or being consumed ourselves. These are questions of basic social practice all the world over, admittedly, but Europe – and England in particular – would appear to constitute a peculiar case. Writing of the social rituals of communal eating in the West in the late twentieth century, food historian Margaret Visser commented: 'it has been rare in the history of humankind to eat as much meat as we [the English] do'.[106] Sound husbandry and scarcity alone dictated that the killing of animals for food was a practice reserved in most cultures for ceremonial and festive occasions (the culturally devalued status of women further suggested that the eating of any sort of meat by the female sex was frowned upon). Still, as one might expect, they managed these things differently in England. Veal, ham, lamb, and pork pies formed a no less integral part of the main, distinctive traditions of English cookery than those of, say, poultry and game. The English fondness for meat dishes (extending even to the establishment of the unruly Sublime Society of Beefsteaks that met in Covent Garden Theatre) was remarkable. The 'Roast Beef of England' of Hogarth's famous engraving became a potent national symbol (notwithstanding the fact that the artist himself ironically died very soon after he had finished eating a steak); in time roast beef became, in the words of the social historian Roy Porter, 'the Englishman's sacramental meal'.[107]

The identification of an abundance of meat with John Bull was hardly likely to pass unnoticed by visitors from other countries. 'Food', Ben Rogers has pointed out, is, after language, 'the most important bearer of national identity'. As Rogers noted in his study *Beef and Liberty*:

> This is particularly true of meat, which is, as anthropologists remind us, the most prized of foods and the one most deeply invested in metaphor. Blood, after all, is the essence of meat, and blood has rich symbolic power. It is the seat of the soul, the root of sexual and violent passions, the special unifying character of race and nation.[108]

Among the French, the English are even today occasionally referred to (disparagingly) as *les rosbifs*. As early as the seventeenth and eighteenth centuries foreign travellers in London were already given to commenting on the unusually carnivorous nature of the culture of the metropolis. When the young Sophie von La Roche arrived in the capital from the continent in 1786 and attended a performance at Sadler's Wells, she was clearly no less impressed by the astonishing quantity of meat pies and pasties provided for the patrons than she was by the 'delightful' setting of the playhouse and gardens themselves.[109] Some few years later, yet another German visitor to the city wrote home of a similar astonishment at the rate of consumption at both private and public events, and confessed that his own countrymen would be 'surprised to see what flesh eaters the English are'. 'He will be struck by the sight of an enormous piece of beef,' the traveller predicted of anyone unfamiliar with the dietary habits even of the less affluent of the city's citizens, 'such, perhaps, as he never in his life placed before him on the table.'[110]

If the country was indeed to be famous for being a nation of 'beefeaters', it was only fitting that London itself should naturally be famed as the home of many 'beef houses', 'pie shops', 'chop houses' and, a little later, seemingly innumerable 'ordinaries' and cook shops that were to be the forerunners of the nineteenth-century dining hall, and of the modern restaurants. Meat was everywhere. And, far from being sacrificed in an atmosphere of solemnity as in many other cultures, or surrounded by some degree of religious ceremony, the animals were killed with a brutal dispatch that would probably have horrified the members of almost any other world culture. Butcher shops were themselves – by any standard – ghastly places; moreover, many other sorts of vending shops could offer meat for sale, and the means of transport provided for animals brought to market and slaughtered were indisputably harsh. Bullocks were driven along the streets in stampeding herds to Smithfield Market, where they were then brutally slaughtered, pole-axed just below the horn to shatter the brain before their spinal chords were roughly broken; the streets around the slaughterhouses ran thick with blood; any dung, blood, bones, unusable offal and entrails were dumped straight along the open drainage channels to communal cesspools. Describing the streets of Smithfield in *Oliver Twist* (1837), Dickens wrote: 'The ground was covered nearly ankle deep with filth and mire; a thick steam perpetually rising from the reeking bodies of the cattle, and mingling with the fog.... The whistling of drovers, the barking of dogs, the bellowing and plunging of oxen, the bleating of sheep, the grunting and squeaking of pigs ... rendered it a stunning and bewildering scene.'[111] Practical preservation of meat products for any of the city's poorer inhabitants was practically unheard of. Throughout the eighteenth and nineteenth centuries, the carcasses of poultry and cuts of rank meat were hung by vendors outside their shops, and were frequently left to fester unpleasantly in the open air.[112] Salted and tinned meat products were first introduced to the public marketplace in 1847, but were regarded with some legitimate degree of suspicion, and were slow to find a place in the typical household. Londoners, and the English in general, were more than happy to subscribe to the notion that being a regular eater of freshly slaughtered meat perfectly exemplified the national myth and character.

Yet even those who might acknowledge the possible connection between the voracious eating of red meat, on the one hand, and suppressed and atavistic impulses towards cannibalism, on the other, might have been puzzled by the eagerness with which the topic of man-eating, once made explicit, was embraced. Once acquainted with the general notion of cannibalism in the urban world, at any rate, hardened denizens of the capital lost no time in laying claim to man-eaters of a peculiarly home-grown and sanguinary kind. The cultural circumstances that worked to join the increasingly refined and often exquisite tastes of the new cosmopolitan environment with the uninhibited energy of the country's larger imperial ambitions – the historical moment that mixed the heady scent of mercantile acquisition with appetites of the rankest greed – were made manifest in a cultural moment that witnessed a significant awakening to the possibilities of an unprecedented sense of urban anonymity, and then linked a sophisticated awareness regarding representations of the self (or of self-effacement and erasure) with an ever-increasing sense of pride in the boundless, seafaring mentality of the world's greatest port city. The dynamic and irrepressible combinations of this new London wherein the *forbidden* was so closely bound up with the *possible* converged in the later eighteenth and early nineteenth centuries to forge one of the most potent urban myths in the city's long history. As such, it was and remains a myth that dramatizes the human cost of the self-devouring and all-consuming drive of the modern urban environment. Sweeney Todd and Mrs Lovett emerge from the dark recesses and move within the dynamic chaos of the moving city's increasing anonymity to earn their reputations as the definitive personifications of the urban appetite. In the growing body of folklore that would come in time to surround the figures of London's demon barber and his pie-making accomplice, their story's sensational exploration of transgressive desire achieved something beyond mere cultural staying-power – it achieved the vital force of living history itself.

*

Some people have a foolish way of not minding, or pretending not to mind, what they eat. For my part, I mind my belly very studiously, and very carefully; for I look upon it, that he who does not mind his belly will hardly mind anything else.
(Samuel Johnson in Boswell's *Life of Johnson*)[113]

The itinerant trade in pies is one of the most ancient of the street callings of London. The pies are made of beef or mutton ... Summer fairs and races are the best place for the pieman. In London the best times are during any grand sight or holiday-making, such as a review in Hyde-park, the Lord Mayor's show, the opening of Parliament,

Greenwich fair, &c. . . . The pie dealers usually make the pies themselves. The meat is bought in 'pieces', of the same part as the sausage-makers purchase – the 'stickings' – at about 3d. the pound. 'People, when I go into houses', said one man, 'often begin crying "Mee-yow", or "Bow-wow-wow!" at me; but there's nothing of that kind now. Meat, you see, is so cheap'.

(Henry Mayhew, *London Labour and the London Poor*)[114]

The meat of wandering cats and dogs may indeed – by the time Mayhew's records and transcriptions of London street life, quoted immediately above, were published between 1851 and 1862 – no longer have formed a staple ingredient of the products being sold even by the least reputable of the itinerant pie-makers of London. Even so, Sam Weller's anecdote of having once shared a house with a pie-man ('reg'lar clever chap, too – make pies out o' anything') who, as Sam informed his master with no little admiration, trapped and seasoned the local felines 'for beefsteak, veal, or kidney, 'cordin to the demand' had been all too credibly included in Dickens's *Pickwick Papers* not very many years earlier.[115] Any hot pie, in mid-Victorian England, was consumed at one's own peril and was probably best eaten only, as Sam sagely advised his employer, 'when you know the lady as made it, and is quite sure it ain't kitten'.[116] Even twenty-first-century food authors and reviewers have been known to write: 'Never buy a pie unless its maker tells you its story.'[117] As we turn toward the specific legends and narratives related to the Sweeney Todd tradition, it is appropriate to end this section with two last, related anecdotes regarding the unforeseeable dangers of the meat pies of England.

The first is brief. In May 1718, a tremendous meat pie – four feet in diameter with a circumference of over 12 feet – was drawn by a group of Londoners (on six asses) up Fish Hill Street, which was at that time the central thoroughfare leading towards London Bridge and the Tower.[118] Before the prize had made any great progress towards its final destination, however, it was set upon by ravenous locals. 'The escort was routed', one contemporary reported, and the pie 'taken and devoured'. 'Its smell', the same observer noted with a peculiar combination of sympathy and disapproval 'was too much for the gluttony of the Londoners.'[119] However much the savoury steam of the greasy cooked meats emanating from the city's many pie stalls may have 'turned the stomachs' of visitors to the city such as the novelist Tobias Smollett, the same noise and stench that emanated from places like Smithfield Market and from the many successors to Cock Lane's famous 'Pie Corner' clearly held a decided appeal for the less fastidious and perpetually hungry bone-grubbers of another class of native city-dwellers.[120]

Yet the greater English fascination with meat pies could lead to real disaster. The public appetite for such patriotic fare was to have considerably more dire consequences elsewhere in the country than those experienced by the ravenous mob on Fish Hill Street in 1718. Not to be outdone by their southern cousins, the tiny village of Denby Vale near Huddersfield in South

Yorkshire has long had a tradition of marking memorable events by baking rather extraordinary meat pies.[121] The earliest Denby pies, baked in the ovens of local pubs and mills and divided among the villagers in the open fields nearby, were made to celebrate such occasions as the anticipated recovery of King George III in 1788 and the Duke of Wellington's victory at the Battle of Waterloo in 1815, and had been modest enough. Disaster struck on the third of the great Denby pie celebrations – the repeal of the Corn Laws in 1846. The villagers aimed to mark the success of the Anti-Corn Laws League with a pie of almost eight feet in diameter and 22 inches deep. A special stage was prepared for its reception, and the pie – having been drawn through the village on a wagon pulled by 13 horses – was placed first on display for public consumption. When the time came to cut the mammoth pie, however, the platform on which it had been placed collapsed under its own weight and the weight of the many spectators. The crowd of 15,000 that surged forward in its efforts to grab a piece of the pie ended up trampling one another, and the offering, under foot. Rumours of sabotage spread like wildfire: a neighbouring village had deliberately undermined the platform; the speeches on the occasion were so long-winded that local men had kicked out the supports out of sheer boredom; the Denbyites were victims of a Tory plot to spoil the Liberal celebrations. Whatever the cause, the fields of Denby lay thick with spoiled pastry, poultry and beef.

But even worse was yet to come. The fourth of the great Denby pies was intended to honour the Golden Jubilee of Queen Victoria in 1887. A special oven was constructed behind the village's White Hart pub. Alongside the oven was placed an 80-gallon stewing boiler that had also been specially built for the occasion by a local blacksmith. This time, a village committee decreed that the meat was to be stewed prior to being placed in the pie dish, and a special chef was brought in from London to act as an adviser to a professional team of bakers.

The contents of the Jubilee pie were to be truly colossal: close to 940 lbs of beef and 160 lbs of veal, 160 lbs each of both lamb and mutton, 309 lbs of pork, 45 rabbits, 34 hares, 49 pigeons, 12 grouse, 8 ducks, 4 plovers, over 100 specimens of small game bird, and 42-stone worth of potatoes. So many and various were the ingredients that those in charge decided to undertake the cooking in phases over the course of several days. One batch of meat was added to the pie dish even as another was being stewed; subsequent new and piping hot batches were then added to the contents of the dish, which had of course already begun to grow cold. To complicate matters even further, the uncooked game birds were ringed around the side of the dish, with the intention that they would be sufficiently cooked when the pie was placed in the oven to bake. The pie that finally entered the oven at Denby that afternoon weighed close to one-and-a-half tonnes.

As in the past, the cooked pie was ceremoniously paraded among the villagers, and eventually set down to be divided into portions in a local park.

The moment the pie was cut, however, the celebrants must have realized that something had gone horribly wrong. A rank and nauseating smell immediately filled the air, and the villagers turned away in disgust at the veritable mountain of putrefying meat. The pie was rotten through and through. So strong was the stench that hounds a far as ten miles distant from Denby were said to have been attracted by the smell.

The following day, the festering remains of the pie were hauled to nearby Toby Wood, where they were buried in a pit of quicklime. Formal, black-bordered funeral cards mourning the loss of the pie were circulated among local residents. The verse on the card read:

Tho' lost to sight, yet still to memory dear,
We smell it yet as though it still was here;
Tho' short its life and quick was its decay,
We thought it best to bury it without the least delay.[122]

Denby's reputation as a pie-making town would eventually be redeemed, but it would take many, many years to live down the disaster of 1887.[123] Today's visitors to the village of Denby are encouraged to take a walking tour that encompasses the town's Pie Hall (holding a large collection of 'pie memorabilia') as well as two of the mammoth pie dishes used in the past (one now serving as a giant planter, the other the unlikely home to a butterfly garden). A special moment should be saved, however, for a respectful visit to the final resting place of the 1887 pie, buried on August 27 of that same year, aged three days. The spot remains an ambivalent testament to the country's long-standing love affair with meat pies and their makers.

Now then, on to some other – in the words of Alexis Soyer – 'culinary victims'.

Chapter 2

Aren't There Butchers Enough?: The Roots of Myth and Meaning in the Tale of Sweeney Todd

If you love someone, set them free. If they return to you, put several 8-inch blades into their head. If they return again, then run ... just run.

(Anonymous)

The complex origins of the actual story of Sweeney Todd either as an urban myth or as a genuine and verifiable historical event will be examined as we move through the narrative itself a little later in this book. What *can* be said from the start, however, is that stories obviously related in some way to the tale of the demon barber have long been familiar to us in many forms. Some of these stories are as old as civilization itself. Cannibalism is of significant thematic importance in the famous heroic narratives of antiquity; it features prominently both in Homer's works (especially in *The Odyssey*, in which the cannibalism of the Cyclops Polyphemus is a sure sign of his generally inhospitable nature) and in *Gilgamesh* (c. 2500–1300 BC), in which the hero slays the terrible giant Humbaba in the great Cedar Forest in the Country of the Living.[1] It is also central to the later Greek and Hellenic mythic tradition, which would include the cannibalism of Kronos (Saturn), as well as the story of the House of Atreus; it was to appear and reappear as a narrative motif in the works of Ovid (*Metamorphoses*), Seneca (*Thyestes*) and – much later, of course – Shakespeare (*Timon of Athens*).

Cannibal narratives often take the shape of traditional folklore and fairy tales. 'Hansel and Gretel', for example, reflects at least in part age-old cultural fears of the young or vulnerable being dismembered and devoured not only by ghouls, ogres and other monsters, but by their stronger and more powerful neighbours as well. Likewise the story of 'Bluebeard' and his bloody chamber (eventually captured in written versions by Charles Perrault and the Brothers

Grimm) may explicitly present itself as a warning against the dangers of female curiosity, but the images that have lingered in the minds of countless generations of children are those of bloodied basins and dismembered bodies in hidden chambers. Fairy tales, folktales, and all those kinds of often improvised and culturally inherited narratives that one tends to imagine being told within the necessarily comforting glow of the hearth, or by the security of a household fireside on cold winter nights (tales such as the memorably terrifying nursery stories about 'Captain Murderer' told by Mary Weller to the young Charles Dickens, which will be considered later in these pages) are in fact filled with stories warning of the threat of consumption that reflect the social realities of a peasant culture's very real fear of starvation; but, as Maria Tatar observes, 'the peasants of folktales may have to worry about famines, but children in fairy tales live under the double threat of starvation *and cannibalism*'.[2] The prominent folklorist and critic Marina Warner has pointed to the great many fairy tales that feature the 'male appetite for babies', noting that 'only four stories by Perrault do *not* feature cannibalism as such [and] in the Grimm brothers' later, seminal anthology, the tally can't be made, as stories of ogres and flesh eating witches are so numerous, and many of them overlap. Yet these collections are the foundation of nursery literature in the West.'[3]

We should always keep in mind that the very peculiar kind of fearful anxiety expressed in such narratives – an anxiety that links the treatment of physical violence to the body with a state of psychological and often explicitly sexual uncertainty – also makes its presence felt just beneath the surface of rather more recent artefacts of popular culture. Well-known gothic suspense films such as Alfred Hitchcock's *Rebecca* (1940), George Cukor's *Gaslight* (1944) and Fritz Lang's *Secret Beyond the Door* (1948), for example – to say nothing of a seemingly inexhaustible number of less accomplished if dramatically more graphic 'spatter' films – can all be connected thematically with the fears embedded in stories such as 'Bluebeard'. 'Nearly every thriller we see', Northrop Frye once observed, 'is a variant of Bluebeard'; although, he continued, 'it is seldom explained why even the greatest writers are interested in such tales'. Offering his own explanation for such recurrent and comprehensive patterns of narrative, Frye suggested:

> Writers are interested in folk tales for the same reason that painters are interested in still life arrangements: because they illustrate essential principles of storytelling. The writer who uses them then has the technical problem of making them sufficiently plausible or credible to a sophisticated audience. When he succeeds, he produces, not realism, but a distortion of realism in the interest of structure. Such distortion is the literary equivalent of the tendency in painting to assimilate subject-matter to geometrical forms, which we see both in primitive painting and in the sophisticated primitivism of, say, Léger or Modigliani .... Myth is a special type of story, seldom located in history, but

rather above ordinary time. Like folk-tale it provides an abstract story-pattern, but it differs from folk-tale in that it engages special categories of seriousness, as if they really happened in ritual or life. Folk-tale is more local, repetitive. Myths stick together to build larger structures.[4]

Even more to our own particular purpose, such myths and narratives form the bases of the innumerable and specifically *urban myths* that would appear now, as in the past, constantly and with a capacity for infinite mutability to circulate worldwide, retelling gruesome stories of disappearance, abduction and cannibalism both in the modern urban environment and in the creation of that environment.[5] At its most comprehensive, Sweeney Todd's is a story that makes use of some of the darkest myths of human culture to comment on everything from the exploitative nature of capitalist enterprise, to the arguably more essential and seductive powers and appetites of love, sex and desire.

Some other and even more unusual traditions of tales and folklore lie behind the Todd story, on occasion having made their way to the final narrative by some odd and circuitous routes. One such story can serve as a representative example of the manner in which these sorts of tales can, over the years, pick up many of the smaller incidental details and tropes of many stories over a significant period of time, and subtly transform and include them within the frames of thematically or even mythically related narrative traditions. The famous Italian dramatist Carlo Goldoni (1703–93), for example, had throughout his life written dramas not only for the legitimate stage, but for the flourishing toy puppet theatres of eighteenth-century Venice as well. One such play – *La Favola de' Tre Gobbi* or 'The Tale of the Three Hunchbacks' – was part of the repertory of the character of Pulcinella (our English Punch), and was based on one of the stories that had almost always been included in the collection of oriental tales known in English as the *Arabian Nights*, which was first translated from Arabic into French (and thence almost immediately into Italian and English) beginning in 1704.

Briefly, in Goldoni's version of one of these tales, three hunchbacks – identical triplets named Babekan, Ibad and Sibad – all live together. Only the first of the brothers, Babekan, is married, and he employs his siblings to work in his eatery. Ibad and Sibad are over-worked by their eldest brother, however, and receive some relief only by means of Babekan's wife, who allows them to enter the cellar of the shop, where they can eat their fill of pies and biscuits and drink as much wine as they please. So much do they consume, however, that they both pass out on the cellar floor and fall into comas. The proprietress thinks them both dead. She decides that – rather than confront her husband with the self-indulgent mortality of both his brothers – she will tell him that she does not know where they have gone, and will dispose of the bodies in his absence by dumping them in the nearby Tigris. It is the character of Pulcinella, the simple-minded porter, on whom she calls to haul the two bodies away, one by one; she appeases any curiosity Pulcinella might have regarding the identity of the bodies in question by telling him only that, in each case, the sack contains the remains of a customer who has unexpectedly died in the shop. The unquestioning Pulcinella dutifully dumps the sack with the first of the unconscious bodies into the river, but when he returns to be paid for his work, he is merely chastised by the wife for having done nothing at all. Pulcinella stares in amazement at the sight of the body of the second of the three brothers; naturally, he mistakes it in appearance for the very same corpse that he has just thrown in the river. On the way back to the café, having now tossed the second body into the Tigris with the first, he is stunned to meet up with the eldest brother himself, whom Pulcinella now assumes to be the ghost of the body he has (twice, now, already) dropped into the flood. Exclaiming, 'This is the last time you'll do it!', he slams Babekan over the head, knocks him unconscious, shoves him into a sack much like the one into which he had deposited his brothers, and throws him in the river to join his floundering siblings. A little later, all three brothers are pulled out of the river by a fisherman, and restored to life by a Cailif, who happens to be passing by with his Vizier.

Although the Goldoni narrative may seem at first to have little to do with any recognizable English version of the Sweeney Todd story, elements or tropes of the final narrative are already present here in some form or other (and so, given the age of the stories in the *Nights*, literally thousands of years old). Among those motifs already present that would find a place in later versions of the Sweeney Todd story, for example, one could identify the satire on appetite or overindulgence (in this instance, merely men who have overeaten themselves into a comatose state) within an enterprise run mutually by a man and woman (here, married); the freedom allowed a subterranean captive to indulge in a seeming superabundance of otherwise hard-to-come-by food; the surreptitious disposal by clever means of seemingly multiple corpses (although not yet reconstituted to provide still further food for others); the use of an imperceptive dupe unknowingly to carry out the final stages of the killing and/or disposal of victims; and (finally) the mistaken identity of an individual who is yet alive for one already dead.

Professional folklorists would be able to adopt a scientific approach of cross-referencing such tropes, using any number of categories so as effectively to connect and hopefully to illuminate the reappearance and reuse of the themes and motifs of thousands of stories from different countries and cultures. Most such categories are based in some way on those first developed by the pioneering folklorist Sabine Baring-Gould in the late nineteenth century, who suggested that certain common themes or 'story radicals' circulated throughout time on a massively complex international level. If a reader were to consult Stith Thompson's highly complicated, six-volume *Motif-Index of Folk-Literature* (1955–8), for example, an encyclopaedic collection that is essentially an elaboration of Baring-Gould's original system of taxonomies, one might note that all stories or folk tales involving cannibalism would be subcategorized within the general category G (Ogres), and that those from G.10 to G.99 further differentiated between types or kinds of 'cannibals and cannibalism'.[6] G.10–G.49 categorize with even greater specificity the habits of 'regular cannibalism', and take note of the fables and stories of all kinds that present a narrative in which human flesh is consumed. Further, more specific examples within the categories G.50–G.79 ('Occasional Cannibalism') would then be listed as, for example:

G.60: Human flesh eaten unwittingly.
G.61.1: Girl recognizes relative's flesh while it is served to be eaten.
G.62: Murderer caused to eat victim's flesh unwittingly, or, [...]
G.70: Occasional Cannibalism – deliberate.

In such a manner, at least, would a modern folklorist perhaps attempt to bring some sense of order to the complex diversity of folk motifs that have intruded and then made themselves at home throughout the story-telling traditions of the world, with little regard for any traditional or nationally sanctioned cultural boundaries.

*

Eating human flesh is the same thing as assimilating yourself to the body you are eating.

(Shu Kishida, Japanese psychologist)[7]

Fairy tales and their motifs may be one thing, but just how do genuine incidents of modern cannibalism relate to narratives such as Sweeney Todd? Interest in such incidents, although thought by many to be prurient or morbid, or even dangerous to our mental hygiene, is incontestably reflected in the public's sustained appetite for stories relating to – for example – the grisly end of the ill-fated Donner Party among the Sierra Nevada Mountains of America in 1846, or the only slightly less celebrated activities of the Colorado mountain guide Alfred Packer just 30 years later. Many American readers will recognize Packer as the gold prospector who offered his services as a guide from the Great Salt Lake into the San Juan Mountains to other parties looking to stake claims in California. He apparently ate his first employers in the course of a long and particularly cold winter in the Rockies, and subsequently turned into a 'mad dog' of a cannibal in the course of later and even more thoroughly gruesome attacks. When finally brought to justice and sentenced to 40 years' hard labour for his crimes, Packer was memorably chastised by the bench: 'There were only seven Democrats in Hinsdale County, and you ate five of them, you depraved Republican son of a bitch!'[8]

Discomfiting stories and dramas relating to modern-day cannibalistic serial killers such as Albert Fish, Edward Gein, Arthur Shawcross, Andrei Chikatilo and Jeffrey Dahmer command worryingly large audiences.[9] The concurrence of cannibalism and necrophilia attracts particular interest – an interest by no means limited to psychologists and criminal profilers. The specifics of such crimes can often quite easily be manipulated to stand as indictments of the particular societies and cultures – and of the historical circumstances – that supposedly produced them. The missionary serial killer and cannibal Arthur Shawcross, who in 1972 began routinely to kill prostitutes in and around Rochester, New York, claimed that his predilection for sexually abusing and then cannibalizing his victims was the result of learned behaviour that he had acquired only after having served as a soldier in Vietnam, where he had begun eating from the bodies of dead babies and children.[10] The Nevada murderer Edward Cole preferred to target 'loose women' whose lives, his plea suggested, were not only expendable, but positively detrimental to the community. In performing such a social service, in essence, he was (at least to his own mind) simply doing the rest of us a favour.

Verifiable modern instances of genuine 'survival cannibalism' attract even more general (and not infrequently sympathetic) interest. The journalist Piers Paul Reid's best-selling *Alive* told the story of a team of 16 young Uruguayan rugby players and their friends who resorted to eating the frozen corpses of their fellows when their airplane crashed in the remote heights of the Andes on the way to Chile in 1972. The story of their ordeal was hugely popular both as a narrative account and, later, as a film. In his study *Meat: A Natural Symbol*, Nick Fiddes contended that what was 'most significant about the aircraft crash in the Andes is not that a few survivors were willing to resort to cannibalism but that several would *not* do so, so strong was their aversion, and perished as a result'.[11] Yet, just as arguably, the particular appeal of the aircraft survivors' story was the result of the unusual detail with which the survivors' individual accounts of their response and behaviour could be corroborated and compared with one another, and the startling similarity of some of their reactions. Whereas some readers and reporters were fascinated by the long-term psychic damage suffered by some of the crash victims, just as many were riveted by the macabre responses of those who claimed in the course of their 70-day struggle either to have developed a taste for particular organs and 'cuts' of meat, or by others who responded to the grim necessities of the ordeal by becoming completely numb to the specific details and reality of their activities. Such desensitization or apparent insensitivity resulted in behaviour that could only be incomprehensible to the outside world. As Reay Tannahill recalls of one such incongruous response: 'When the rescuers at last arrived, they were horrified when one survivor, trying to identify what remained of the bodies, tossed a skull to another and said cheerfully: "You should know who this guy is, you ate his brains."'[12] Further complicating the case of the Andes survivors was their subsequent justification of their actions not on the plausible basis of nutritional necessity (they needed the protein), but rather on theological and ethical grounds. They explained their behaviour by means of a religious analogy. 'If Jesus, in the Last Supper,' as one calmly put it, 'offered his body and blood to all his disciples, he was giving us to understand that we were to do the same.'[13] A representative of the Church in Rome supported such a view, reasoning that the Catholic piety behind their circumstances and right to survive justified the desecration of the frozen bodies, and so deprived their actions 'of any negative element'.[14]

Finally, explicitly fictional creations such as the novelist Richard Harris's 'Hannibal Lecter' and the award-winning film versions of his narratives, or director Richard Fleischer's 1973 cult film *Soylent Green* (based in turn on Harry Harrison's 1966 science fiction novel *Make Room! Make Room!*), testify to a similarly sustained if macabre public fascination with the subject that has endured for generations. Innumerable Gothic novels, as well as tales of werewolves, vampires, ghouls, traditional natural and ethnic myths, and elements, again, of age-old story collections such as the *Arabian Nights* and Homer's *Odyssey* all include episodes of cannibalism, although readers tend often to overlook their significance. However strongly we may wish to deny it, we seem as a culture to welcome and more often than not positively to *enjoy* stories of gruesome mystery that include the element of cannibalism. Perhaps more disturbingly, we relish them all the more when they stubbornly stake their claims and testify to their own veracity – when, that is, they claim to be true.

*

They were crude enough, those old melodramas, but they at least gave people a vision of a world in which right and wrong were never confused, and in which sorrow was in the end alleviated, cruelty overthrown, virtue honoured, and courage rewarded. . . . Was it such a bad world to offer for the admirations of simple people?
('Blood and Thunder', in *The Times*, 1942)[15]

It would be easy enough, on the face of it, to ascribe the fascination with the story of Sweeney Todd and Mrs Lovett – and so to account for the sustained popularity of the celebrated demon barber himself – to the sensational thrill of melodrama, pure and simple. Although routinely dismissed as a mode shamelessly void of any genuine artistic merit – a form that caters to the basest of its audience's tastes and expectations – melodrama remains for almost every one of us a kind of guilty pleasure. It is rarely if ever truly out of fashion. We tend to revel, however strongly we might wish to deny it, in the slightly strange conjunction of sensational trials and triumphs of both murder and sentimental romance. As readers and audiences, we are inclined to be fascinated by tales that are, quite simply, totally outrageous in their narratives, and brazen in their unapologetic manipulation of such basic (and Aristotelian) emotions of pity and horror. The element of what is often referred to as dark or 'black' humour in such stories is not unconnected with this melodramatic appeal; we enjoy our illicit engagement with material that we know ought more properly to be treated with greater seriousness, or perhaps not treated at all. However, as Herman Melville observed in his *Pierre* (1852): 'If fit opportunity offer in the hour of unusual affliction, minds of a certain temperament find a strange, hysterical relief in a wild, perverse humorousness, the more alluring from its entire unsuitableness to the occasion.'[16]

The popular melodrama of the nineteenth century both in print and on the stage was sensational. Moreover, it was often sordid, suggestive and thrilling entertainment. Yet the element of transgressive humour inherent in the 'type' likewise forms a considerable element of the appeal of the melodramatic fiction, romance and theatre of the very late eighteenth and nineteenth centuries. We are strangely delighted by the element of illicit comedy or laughter attached to subjects that remain traditionally sacrosanct. We respond with a seemingly physical, reflexive gesture of near hilarity to representations that would in any other circumstance be considered completely beyond the bounds of the acceptable or the civilized. We enjoy the breaking of taboos and the dramatic enactment of forbidden pathologies, but we seem to enjoy them all the more when they are accompanied by the sound of sardonic laughter.

Although rarely respected as a literary genre in any of its forms, representations of crimes, criminal trials and subsequent punishments can simultaneously reaffirm and undermine the apparatus of state or social control. The details of most Newgate-style narratives ring true, while remaining at the same time oddly conventional and limited. But just what is it that the 'true' stories of these 'historical' figures mean to accomplish or achieve? In what ways do they differ from narratives of the period labelled more straightforwardly as novels or romances? The reaction of most viewers or listeners unfamiliar with the work of the American composer Stephen Sondheim, when told that his own 1979 version of the tale of Sweeney Todd is most accurately classified as a work of *musical comedy*, tends even today to be one of disbelief. Yet the very essence of such exercises in 'black' humour (the fiendish delight of which has always been a part of the Todd story) is the sense of there being in such efforts, as one writer put it, 'a comic element utterly at odds with the horror of the scene'.[17] Sweeney Todd is a story of the macabre in which, as the critic Philip Thompson notes, 'the strange comic tinge is used to increase sensitivity to gruesomeness, which presented unadulterated in large doses, may dull our responses'.[18] The horror of Sweeney Todd, as we will see, is related intimately at times to the designedly compact and graphic terror of Grand Guignol in twentieth-century drama, a tradition in which short pieces of a horrific kind are usually played successively to an intimate and inescapably involved audience. The bizarre conventions of the Grand Guignol – a dramatic format that takes its name from an actual theatre in Pigalle that from 1872 to 1962 offered its audiences visually shocking plays with titles such as *A Crime in the Madhouse*, *The Castle of Slow Death* and *To Hell With You* – further connect Todd explicitly, by name at least, with the violent Punch and Judy characters of English and continental puppet theatre, and so by extension with the traditions of the *commedia dell'arte* as noted in the work of Goldoni, above.[19] 'Guignol' is even today the specific French name for a particularly violent 'Punch' puppet; puppet versions of the Todd story, as we shall see, have been far more widespread than one might at first suspect, and the connections between the characters of Sweeney Todd and Mrs Lovett and the ancient figures of Punch and Judy can carry deep significance. Relating yet another brief but bizarre anecdote possibly connecting the role of Punch ('Pulcinella') to Todd in early eighteenth-century Italy, the puppet historian Michael Byrom noted that 'it is reliably reported that in Rome, at least, executions were performed as one of the Carnival attractions in the Piazza del Popolo by men dressed as *pulcinelli*, so that the last earthly sounds heard by the unfortunate victims were the obscene jests and derisive laughter of their grotesque executioners'.[20] In many versions of Todd's story the barber himself is represented as a gruesome yet curiously compelling figure of darkness – a bizarre executioner operating under a system of laws all his own. There in fact exists in Todd's theatrical personality what might be described as a convergence of the traditional pantomime clown and the more ominous 'villain' of melodrama. Sweeney Todd may at one and the same time be both playful and subversive, yet he is also desperately and dangerously malicious – a beater, a punisher, a casual torturer and (of course) a killer who takes *delight* in his acts of violence. However much we may find the representation of his activities entertaining, we forget at our peril that the famous 'demon barber' of the Todd story is quite literally a *'dæmon'* – in the etymologically precise sense that he is a *skilled* and *deathly* agent of destiny. It may be masked within the mundane or hidden by the secret and insidious betrayal of familiar things and objects, yet the archetypal villainy of Sweeney Todd is nevertheless capable of carrying with it the power of a darksome, cosmic force of fate.

There would of course have been other and more obvious reasons for Sweeney Todd's earliest popularity among nineteenth-century readers and audiences. Publications such as the ever-expanding *Newgate Calendar* and the frequently reprinted ordinarys' accounts of thieves and robbers, mentioned earlier, as much as the dramatic representations of authors such as John Gay and George Lillo in the eighteenth century, had for years developed a taste for literature dealing with the criminal underworld, and with the seedy side of what is often now called 'Hogarthian' London life.[21] The public had for some time succumbed to the dubious allure of Tyburn, and to the inescapable histrionics of the 'theatre of the scaffold'. An increasing number of scholarly and historical studies have emphasized the continued appeal of the genre of the criminal biography beyond the eighteenth and early nineteenth centuries, and characters such as Dick Turpin, Jack Sheppard, Claude Duval and Paul Clifford assumed a vital role in the life of the English theatre.[22] As Jonathan Keates has noted of the tradition of representation associated with the famous highwayman Dick Turpin: 'Crime is a species of performance art .... However much we proclaim our hatred of the sinner, his sinfulness nourishes our less respectable dreams and fantasies. Thus the agents of havoc are easily metamorphosed into folk heroes, loved, envied, and applauded even at the foot of the gallows.'[23] The traditions of the hugely popular Newgate novels of the 1830s and the later, related 'sensation' novel as practised by writers such as William Harrison Ainsworth, Edward Bulwer-Lytton, Wilkie Collins, Mary Elizabeth Braddon and even Dickens himself, in the nineteenth century kept the appeal of such 'performance art' very much alive. The heroes of such 'gallows-school' novels were often captivating rogues whose criminal activity tended to be the result not of personal inclination or weakness, but inescapable social injustice. Nevertheless we take just as much pleasure in the spectacle of their punishment as we do in their successes; we remain peculiarly eager to witness the spectacle both of their own fall and subjugation, the punishment of those who do *not* buy into the modern culture of purchasing and consumption – the careless rejection of health and industry. Even more practically, and quite apart from the large number of dramatic representations that were frequently being performed in London theatres, the appetite for writing and circulating such stories by mass-circulation newspapers and tabloids was to increase tremendously throughout the second half of the nineteenth century. Eric Hobsbawm has noted that whereas in 1871 only 2,148 claimed as their profession (for tax purposes) to be authors, editors, or other journalists, by 1914 that number had risen to over 14,000 people.[24]

Looking beyond the strictly literary environment of such transgressive figures, one could also make an historical connection between the emergence of the Sweeney Todd narrative in a definitive or at least consistently recognizable dramatic form in the middle of the nineteenth century, and the end of the actual spectacle of execution at Tyburn and elsewhere. In his hugely influential work *Discipline and Punish: The Birth of the Prison* (1977), the French theorist Michel Foucault argued controversially that the feudal spectacle of brutal corporal punishment – the 'society of the spectacle' – was succeeded in the late modern era by an altogether more sinister form of discipline and control: the institutional manifestation of the modern prison. Instead of seeing the elimination of judicial punishment and the rituals of public torture and execution as a healthy step forward in the development of a more humane form of social justice, as one might expect, Foucault instead crafted a sophisticated argument suggesting that the elimination of such state-sanctioned atrocities led to a series of professed reforms that only added to the powers of 'totalitarian' oppressors – to the control of what Foucault called the '*société disciplinaire*'. 'In the totally ordered, hierocritized [sic] space of the nineteenth century prison', Foucault maintained, 'the prisoner is put under constant surveillance, discipline, and education, in order to transform him into what power as now organized in society demands that *everyone* become: docile, productive, hard-working, self-regulating, conscience-ridden, in a word "normal" in every way.'[25] State-sanctioned torture was merely replaced, according to Foucault, by a more efficient system of internal self-policing.

If one chooses to accept such a paradigm, it could be argued that Todd's staged narrative helps to occupy what might be described as a dramatic or performative 'gap' at such a particular historical moment. From the 1780s onward, rather than witnessing a central, carnivalesque display of 'real' social justice in action – an open display in which vengeance was enacted upon the individual by the state in a traditional public space – spectators in the theatre were permitted in its place to witness a dramatic representation of an earlier 'discourse on criminality' – the rehearsal of a satisfying and classically cathartic but now-displaced concept of deviancy. The narrative of Sweeney Todd – who is not only executed but serves as a self-appointed executioner himself – emerges in its historically identifiable form as drama and fiction at about just the same moment that public executions as theatrical spectacles were themselves finally being eliminated altogether from social life.

One need not entirely accept the precise logic of Foucault's own narrative chronology of spectacle and surveillance to find compelling explanations for the convergence of various popular folktale and narrative elements in the form of Todd's story in the late eighteenth and nineteenth centuries. An equally intriguing way of situating the appearance of the Sweeney Todd narrative in its precise form at this historical point in time might seek to link the story with such phenomena as the emergence of the modern police force in the course of eighteenth- and nineteenth-century London development. The unique triumph of modern London as the centre of world capitalism and its accompanying growth as Britain's biggest port would entail radical changes in the manner in which the city tackled the threat of criminal activity. 'As towns became cities and as cities grew in size', as urban historian Witold Rybczynski has observed of such transformations, 'social control would have to become explicit. The informal familial and personal mechanisms for exercising authority of miscreants no longer sufficed.'[26] The early eighteenth-century system of professional 'thief takers' – by which self-appointed men captured known criminals and delivered them up to authority – was itself a rather crude development of the medieval notion of the *posse comitatus*, whereby the entire social community had been held responsible for apprehending wrong-doers and bringing them to justice. Professional thief-taking was in actual practice open to gross corruption, however, and the blurring of the lines between burglars, highwaymen, informants and law enforcers led to the pre-eminence of figures such as Jonathan Wild, who manipulated conditions to establish even greater control of the activities of the criminal underworld. The famous reforms of Henry Fielding and his blind half-brother Sir John Fielding led to the formation of a small group of paid and generally reliable constables (originally six, then seven – one for each local parish). This group eventually evolved into the celebrated 'Bow Street Runners', an organization that was to play a prominent role in almost all versions of the Sweeney Todd story. The establishment of the Bow Street police office was perceived to effect a genuine change in the detection and suppression of crime in London, and by the end of the century the officers of the Bow Street Runners numbered above 70.[27] The year 1763 saw the establishment of a mounted horse patrol; a similar foot patrol to detect criminal activity was established in 1780; other districts of London began forming similar organizations and police patrols at about the same time. The centralized, professionally paid police force proposed by Sir Robert Peel and finally established in Great Scotland Yard in 1829 did away with the old system of rewards for the apprehension of criminals, and only slowly gained the authority necessary to serve as an effective metropolitan force. As Critchley has noted:

> After the turn of the eighteenth century ... under the influence of Jeremy Bentham (1748–1832) the two movements [Bow Street and the police reformers] began to draw together once more. A man of catholic learning, liberal principles and incalculable influence in many branches of public affairs, Bentham had early been impressed by the work of the Italian Marquis Beccaria, whose *Essay on Crime and Punishments*, with a commentary by Voltaire, had been published in an English translation in 1767. Beccaria, in a passage which, in Professor Radzinowicz's words, had all the force of a new concept, wrote: 'It is better to prevent crimes than to punish them. This is the chief aim of every good system of legislation, which is the art of leading men to the greatest possible happiness or to the least possible misery, according to the calculation of all the goods and evils of society'.[28]

Given such developments in the organization and implementation of criminal investigation and control, it could be argued that – rather than illuminating merely one aspect of Foucault's formulation of a paradigm shift in early modern conceptions of social justice – Todd's story could also be read as a commentary on the replacement of the system of criminal apprehension and justice under the Bow Street Runners by that of the modern police force. Many of the earliest versions of Sweeney Todd's story, as we shall see, argue for the efficiency of the Runners, who in some versions of the tale slyly out-manoeuvre Todd and his accomplices, while just as many seem to view the possibilities of such control as threatening and dangerous to traditional English liberties. ('All forms of melodrama', Northrop Frye observed, 'were advance propaganda for the police state, in so far as that represents the regularising of mob violence.')[29]

More conservative critics might likewise suggest that Todd's narrative is just as concerned with the possible threat involved in Britain's imperial enterprise to the country's own sense of identity as it is with the potentially tyrannical developments of internal structures of authority and surveillance. If the wealth of the world was to make its way up the Thames estuary and into the great global emporium of London, the disquieting and increasingly visible presence of cultural and racial 'invasion' reminded citizens of the metropolis that they were not only importing the material wealth of nations into their own environments, but opening themselves up to the concomitant importation of alien ideas, habits, languages, manners, faiths and modes of social and domestic organization. The threat of 'reverse colonization', entailing the corruption of British traditions and the possibilities of racial decay, were to become an increasing obsession in the novels of the nineteenth century; many versions of the Todd story depict scenes set in colonial Africa, and dwell on the very subject of just what happens when the otherwise profitable inter-exchange between the foreign and the indigenous becomes so porous that it is perceived to pose a threat. Conversely, the economic expansion and increasing urbanization of the period, and the trading ships that returned to British ports with goods such as tea, coffee, spices and sugar, could be said to have encouraged the global exchange of ideas, and created environments within which the values of indigenous cultural traditions were themselves subject to scrutiny.

Marxist critics, on the other hand, would argue rather that the focus of the story is on the exploitative structures of capitalism itself, and the manner in which such structures lead to the creation of policing agents – to the investment of despotic and arbitrary powers in agents of the government, the ideological function of which was to manage any potential disruption to its calculated and manipulative system. The Bow Street Runners and other agents who act as police *seem* to be upholding the authority of law in most versions of the story, but is that their true purpose? One could argue that the imaginative investment both of those who have produced and consumed Todd's story lies in a narrative subtext that belies the tale's ostensible participation in romance. Those who tell us the tale of Sweeney Todd appear often, as it were, to be saying: 'Look! This is the real nature of such a society and its institutions.' In such an attack on the administration of justice and equity, the world depicted is one of mad houses and scenes of isolated and intensely claustrophobic confinement. Just beneath the surface of its churches (which literally stink) lies a subterranean and honeycombed hollowness. In such versions of Todd's story, the satiric ethos is clearly against the accumulation of capital and the supposed 'progress' of a mercantile society – against the settled bourgeois existence of families such as the Oakleys; against the lawyers who 'eat people up' with their endless litigation; against the vigilance and policing of the runners and the magistrates; against, in fact, the *idea* of the city itself. London is the ironic 'embodiment' of a world in which people are willingly sacrificed, and Sweeney Todd himself is only a more laudably honest version of merchants and retailers such as Oakley (in several later versions of the story, Oakley is said to be not a spectacle-maker, but a ship-owner directly involved in colonial expansion). The interior space of Todd's barber shop can in turn be seen as functioning to some degree as offering an ironic commentary on the increasing mechanization of the period – the replacement in the course of the eighteenth century of the production of goods by individual artisans in their own homes or in small, independent workshops by the mass production of goods in larger factories – in short, the Industrial Revolution. Todd's own trade was not historically affected by such changes, perhaps, but in the narrative, his shop becomes one of those gathering places for the spread of new ideas; industrialization and the construction of global markets is a phenomenon from which he, too, is clearly benefiting. His customers are mostly sailors returning home with the riches they have acquired abroad, or wealthier farmers come to market who have similarly profited from increased sophistication of agricultural methods. His ingenious chair can be seen as a parodic representation of the entire procedure of mass production and its efficiency – a mechanical device that allows him swiftly to deliver the products that will allow Lovett to make her pies in batches of hundreds. In the pie shop, we even witness the division of labour between the supplier (Todd), those who prepare the 'meat' (Lovett), those who bake the pies (Jarvis Williams and her other 'cooks'), and Lovett, again, as the vendor.

Aspects of Todd's story also appeal to readers and audiences on far deeper, psychological levels. The predatory and boastfully incisive nature of Sweeney Todd's invasive conquests ('it stung a little but not for long', Sondheim's musical chorus observes of Todd's delicate touch with a razor) speaks rather obviously to our deepest fears concerning sexuality, and to the role of the erotic perverse in the activities not only of sadists and sadistic killers, but in 'normal' sexual activity as well.[30] To be sure, the outlines of Todd's character to some extent anticipate the socio-pathic mentality of the sexual predator and modern serial-killer; hence the connections that have frequently been made between the fictional figure of Todd, on the one hand, and the historical Jack the Ripper and other sadistic killers and sexual cannibals, on the other. Yet for all the ambient potency of such connections, the identification of Todd's character with any particular psychosexual or fetish disorders is far less prominent a feature in most versions of the narrative than is his rather more simply obvious status as a loner – as a solitary exile from society, an outsider. The barber is in almost all versions of the tale a character who either sees himself unjustly as having been denied fair access to that which has been made available to others, or as having been deprived access to what is rightfully his own. In most cases he has been denied any sense of social or personal belonging, and so, in the very act of grooming others for social presentation and desirability, reaches out for his own form of control. As more than one commentator on Britain's most prolific serial murderer of modern times, Dr Harold Shipman, has observed when trying to account for the motives behind that killer's activities, Shipman was himself obsessed not with the erotics of mortality per se, but with the act of inducing death and *controlling* the moment of death. 'We need relationships with other human beings', one psychologist noted of Shipman's singularity, and 'if we don't have them, we don't progress as human beings'.[31] Even more fundamental to our psychological health than a sexual self is a sense of *any* self in relation to others at all. As the social shell inside of which the inadequate individual needs to reinvent himself grows every day more hollow and frail, so too do the very things they can control grow fewer and, strangely, more precious. The remarks offered by the psychologist on Shipman's motives, above, recall nothing so much as the sentiments of the notorious French writer Donatien-Alphonse-François de Sade, who not only experienced a similar sense of isolation or 'apartness from the feelings of his fellow-men', but, in a series of erotically explicit novels published in the 1790s, argued that such 'apartness' was to be cultivated for the benefit of genuine human progress. For de Sade, 'the whole history of civilized humanity was a mistake, and one had to revert to the condition of holy nature. Nature taught destruction, murder, [and] sexual promiscuity.'[32] As the critic Mario Praz has written, in the work of de Sade the period saw the *reductio ad absurdum* of the idea of a return to holy Nature, 'because all the progress of man had consisted in getting further and further away from Nature, in creating an artificial ethical state, creating a new standard of values, as artificial as a city is artificial in comparison with the swamp which originally occupied the site.'[33] A century after de Sade, Max W. Nordau was to pick up the idea of such an atavistic impulse towards nature, but would apply its implications to rather different effect. Nordau's influential work *Degeneracy* (1892) applied popular theories of physical degeneration to the intellectual aspect of man's existence, and argued that there is evidence in art and literature, as in social evolution, of decadence and hysteria. Nordau also said that there were detectable criminal types, and that man's animal nature could at any time resurface without warning. The notion that greatness was near allied to madness was of course nothing new (Oscar Wilde observed of Nordau's suggestion that all men of genius were insane, 'but Dr Nordau forgets that all sane people are idiots'[34]), but his work voiced a peculiar *fin-de-siècle* fear that the Victorian era had witnessed the appearance of a new kind of moral, political, sexual and personal degeneracy. Andrew Smith has argued that such ideas about degeneration were reflected in characters such as Count Dracula, Jekyll and Hyde, the Elephant Man, and Jack the Ripper.[35] One might very well add Sweeney Todd to any list of this sort.

Today, of course, most of us would probably agree that fictional characters such as Todd, along with the frighteningly real Shipman and a host of other media figures, have been and, indeed, *must* be represented and so understood as psychologically 'damaged'. If, as criminal psychologists have argued, the act of modern cannibalism in many individual instances arises from a sense of self-inadequacy and an accompanying fear of total isolation and abandonment, then it seems logical to argue that the only way to save one's self from being abandoned entirely is to consume – quite literally to ingest – those who would otherwise leave one apart and alone. Although Sweeney Todd and Mrs Lovett do not themselves, in most of the narratives devoted to their story, consume the meat pies that are made from the flesh of their victims, each of them nevertheless appears to fit the psychological profile of the cannibal. Both are isolated loners, both hide in intricately compartmentalized dwellings and work-spaces that betray an underlying vacancy and emptiness of soul, and both tend in almost every version of the narrative to hold captives in the form of 'employees' or apprentices who they ritually abuse and kill. In many versions, both are disinclined if not incapable of displaying any overt or normal degree of sexuality or even affection. Todd arguably dispatches his many victims not merely because he is greedy for their material wealth, but because by killing them he jealously eliminates from view the possibilities of any sort of healthy sexuality, and so protects himself from those who demonstrate an active and transformative love. If, in some retellings of the story, the barber's murderous spree is related to the experience of sexual arousal achieved in the killing (and in certain versions, such as the well-known stage and screen performances of Tod Slaughter, the gleefully sardonic butcher is presented in precisely such a state of arousal), Todd's story is arguably the narrative of an obsessive erotic madness that spins completely out of control; the extreme violence of his typical end is reminiscent of nothing so much as the spectacular bloodbath in Miller's Court that brought Jack the Ripper's East End reign of terror to its abrupt and inconclusive end in the grim and chilly November of 1889.

Finally and most importantly, the story of Sweeney Todd is clearly in some respects an emphatically pastoral, *anti-urban* myth. It is a story that finds its earliest origins in the kinds of tales told round the fireside in country cottages throughout Europe, and, indeed, throughout the civilized world. It is the cautionary folktale told by a rural narrator to a rustic audience about the alien city that quite literally consumes those foolish or gullible enough to fall victim to its allures – an admonitory parable to anyone who would be led astray by the *ignis fatuus* of the fabled 'Lights o' London'. It is the story told by wary seamen at the expense of those who would unadventurously but foolishly confine their lives to dry land – seamen such as Ransome in Robert Louis Stevenson's *Kidnapped* (1886), who is said, whenever he finds himself in the unfamiliar terrestrial environment of a town or city, to '[think] every second person a decoy, and every third house a place in which seamen would be drugged and murdered'.[36] It offers an archetypal and mythic image of the single individual who stands alienated from and frozen with fear in the face of an unknown and seemingly unknowable environment. Such anxious attitudes find their precedents in the ancient world's depiction of the dangers of Rome itself (as in the epistles of Horace); they would witness their prolific legacy in the vast range of fictions (including those of American writers such as Richard Yates and John Cheever) and films (Neil Simon's *The Out-of-Towners*, or Ira Levin's *The Stepford Wives*) that pit the rural outsider against the threatening anonymity of the city and the suffocation of its undifferentiated, ever-encroaching suburbs – those appetitive and vaguely entomological extremities of urban angst. 'Most horror stories change with time', Nina Auerbach has commented, noting that '*Dracula* has shed and assumed more skins than any vampire deserves to have.'[37] The threat of being eaten up by the sprawling urban monster has proven itself capable of similar transformations. Todd's final aim in almost all the narratives devoted to his story is not only to dispatch the individual victims in his barber's chair, but to see the whole of Fleet Street and even Greater London destroyed in a cataclysmic conflagration. Todd may be representative of the centrifugal, consuming force of the City – of civilization itself – yet he is also, paradoxically, a force the sheer atavistic anarchy of which, when creatively channelled, gives rise to such cities in the first place.

Marx would famously argue that capitalist profiteering generated a gothic sensorium involving demonic presences and the supernatural – a commodity fetish that simultaneously located and drew attention away from systemized exploitation. The marketplace is not a scene of sympathetic fellow-feeling and natural rationalism, but a space in which gothic and sensational conventions and performances inscribe and mask socially coercive encounters, both urban and national: the blood sacrifice of civilization itself. Strikingly, Todd's signature 'sound' in most prose versions of the story is the unnatural laugh of a hyena: Christopher Bond, in his twentieth-century dramatic adaptation later used by Sondheim, gives the barber's original surname, not inappropriately, as 'Barker'. Sweeney Todd barks, growls and snaps his way through his own story. What Mario Praz said finally of de Sade's dubious achievement might also be said of nearly all representations of the character of Todd himself: 'He has recorded and made articulate for us the voice of the cave man, that extinct species that still lingers at the bottom of our souls, and not infrequently ... comes up to the surface.'[38]

*

In the beginning when the world was young there were a great many thoughts but no such thing as a truth. Man made the truths himself and each truth was a composite of a great many vague thoughts. All about the world were the truths, and they were all beautiful.... And then the people came along. Each as he appeared snatched up one of the truths, and some who were quite strong snatched up a dozen of them. It was the truths that made the people grotesque.

(Sherwood Anderson, *Winesburg, Ohio*)[39]

In his unfailingly thought-provoking *Anatomy of Criticism* (1957), the Canadian critic Northrop Frye suggested that the central myths of human culture constantly recur throughout our literary history.[40] Their precise contours and narrative details may change across time – they may, for various reasons, in some eras be more realistic or 'plausible' than in others – but such changes never really affect the fundamental insights to which such archetypes ultimately give shape and expression. 'Myths of gods merge into legends of heroes,' Frye maintained:

> legends of heroes merge into plots of tragedies and comedies; plots of tragedies and comedies merge into plots of more or less realistic fiction. But these are changes of social context rather than of literary form, and the constructive principles of story-telling remain constant through time.[41]

These archetypes, in other words, effectively work as the constantly recurrent symbols of our literary universe. As such, they can be thought of as inhabiting the conceptual space within which the human imagination is liberated. A theoretically coherent literary methodology should aim properly at tracing the role and meaning of such symbols in accomplishing the human project of understanding, as it has been expressed in our literary universe. Literature enlivens archetypes, and archetypes are in their own way ritualistic expressions of the pattern both of the fulfilment and the inhibition or 'blocking' of human desire – a desire, as Frye sees it, that is the restless force at work behind the construction of civilization itself. It is no disservice to the achievement of individual literary works to suggest that, when looked at in perspective, they are to some extent historically and culturally specific manifestations of the 'outworking' of this same, more fundamental impulse or desire.

All myths or stories, Frye further contended, participate to a greater or lesser degree in what he saw to be the central human myth of the 'quest'. Some of the more obvious, recurrent elements of this comprehensive, mythic paradigm include some sort of basic conflict between protagonist or hero and a monstrous foe, the disappearance and – not infrequently – the apparent death of the hero in the action of a tremendous encounter, and, finally, the reappearance of this (often still mysterious) hero, around whose figure a new societal order arises. One central form that this quest romance has often taken in the Western tradition has been the theme of the dragon-slayer; within the basic pattern of such a tale, certain narrative elements constantly recur or are in some manner displaced: the beast or dragon typically inhabits an underground labyrinth; the dragon or beast that the hero confronts is destroyed in a violent contest; victims thought to have been killed or (very often) consumed are, remarkably, rescued alive and whole at the end of the tale; and the hero emerges from the underworld lair of the monster to establish a new community.[42]

Although such a brief summary obviously does a grave disservice even to the simplest of Frye's ideas, one need not agree with all the aspects of Frye's schema of modes, genres and *mythoi*, to recognize the insight it can offer into man as creature who has largely been shaped and defined by his ability to tell stories about himself and his world. One might certainly entertain the possibility that at the core of a story such as Sweeney Todd (indeed, at the centre of all such basic folk and fairy tales that offer both their tellers as well as their listeners or readers some more comprehensible sense of the nature of the journey undertaken by all human beings through the darkness of this world) lies a mythic vision that looks to reconcile the individual both with his or her own participation in the larger project of human civilization and identity, on the one hand, and with the ultimate loss of that same sense of individuality or 'selfhood' in the annihilation of death, on the other. More specifically, Sweeney Todd can be seen as participating in the systemic cultural memory of all such folk stories – Tom Thumb, Red Riding Hood, Hansel and Gretel, Collodi's *Pinocchio*, the *Alice* books of Lewis Carroll – that make use of eating and food, consumption and ingestion as a means of making sense of the most atavistic of human impulses and emotions, desires and destinies. Writing with specific reference to such tales, one modern critic observed:

> When Perrault closes his tale with Red Riding Hood and grandmother still inside the wolf's belly, he communicates a basic human fear, one which the cannibalistic art and the return to a quasi-womb symbolize: the loss of one's identity, of one's self. Both child and crone are totally incorporated within the furred beast, and there they remain. He is the maw of annihilation, the cavity of death from which no huntsman can rescue us.[43]

These same narrative patterns that relate to issues of human identity and human mortality – of selfhood and otherness, isolation and community – can quite often be of significant relevance to Todd's particular story, as well. 'When the child is devoured,' The same critic continues,

> the witch baked, the act embodies in an exaggerated, extreme manner the oral concerns with which the tale has played all along. Eating may well be the 'basic metaphor' representing all the ways in which we daily incorporate and assimilate the world around us. We ingest reality through our senses and faculties while also experiencing literal foodstuffs as tangible metaphors for comfort, security, and love. The tales' concern with eating and food *per se* may constitute their major appeal... .[44]

An even more ancient and decidedly more sinister catalogue of cannibalistic 'monsters' – Croesus, Tantalus and Pelops, Procne and Tereus, the self-consuming Erycicthous, and the foolish Lykaon – loom large in those foundational myths that set out to define the nature of human limitations and boundaries – that set out to explore the penalties of transgression. Very possibly, like the Minotaur who lurks at the heart of the immense labyrinth of King Minos, Sweeney Todd represents a force also lying in wait, ready to destroy all those who might put their faith in any over-ingenious Daedalus foolish enough to think he can easily outwit him.

Chapter 3

Maybe It's Because I'm a Londoner: True Lies and the Life of an Urban Legend

Though buried in the country, I was made for a London life; the very air of the metropolis intoxicates me.

(Wilkie Collins, *Armadale*)[1]

Shaving one's throat in a mirror with a naked blade required skill and not a little courage. Even practiced users set aside a half an hour for the procedure, while barbers did a brisk business shaving those who had never mastered the art. At the end of the 19th century fathers taught their sons to shave. This was a necessity, since the implement of choice was still the open straight razor, a potentially hazardous article of toiletry which enjoyed a nice sideline as a murder weapon.

(Tim Dowling, 'Bare-Faced Chic')[2]

Fact and fiction – history and myth – have a disconcerting way of getting mixed up. A recent survey of some 2,000 young adults suggested that a staggering number of Britons were deeply confused about some of the most important events and personalities in their country's history. Half of those surveyed were convinced beyond question that King Arthur was undoubtedly a real – and not possibly a mythical or semi-legendary – figure. Conversely, as many as one in ten thought that Adolf Hitler had *not,* in fact, been a 'real' person, whereas one in 20 adults confirmed that the comic-book character 'Conan the Barbarian' had been a genuine figure in history; almost half of the respondents were willing to extend the same privilege to Robin Hood, to say nothing of his genial band of merry men. 'There has always been myth and legend in history', observed media historian Tristram Hunt with reference to the survey's worrying conflation of fantasy and reality; but, he added with a note of caution, 'these findings show that there is a real need for clear understanding'.[3]

71

Yet clear understanding of any such sort, as historians such as Hunt would be among the first to admit, is notoriously hard to come by. Had the same newspaper poll gone on to question Londoners, in particular, regarding the truth or error involved in any number of the myths and popular beliefs that surround their city's heritage, they might very well have thrown up their hands in despair. Even those who would claim to be intimately familiar with the urban environment and its history would be hard pushed to judge the validity of a great many tales that have been perpetuated throughout the years regarding London lore and mythology. What is the truth about Richard Whittington and his cat? Where, exactly, was Shakespeare's London residence located? Was there ever any truth to all the stories about the Cock Lane Ghost? Can one still visit the original shop upon which Charles Dickens modelled his 'Old Curiosity Shop'? Is it true that Jack the Ripper was actually a member of the royal family, or one so closely connected to Queen Victoria and her children that his identity was concealed by the government for fear of the outcry such a revelation would cause? Almost all of these questions and a great many others concerning London history and topography can be answered with little if any equivocation. Even so, as Sydney Cockrell once observed in the *Times Literary Supplement*: 'Errors and perversions once served up can never perish. In spite of their exposure they will go on being rehashed often and with new flavourings for ever and ever.'[4] Todd's activities are no less relished for all their ghoulish eccentricity than those of the metropolitan area's other legendary killers: William Corder, who in 1827 slaughtered Maria Marten in the notorious 'Red Barn' in Surrey, Dr Hawley Harvey Crippen, who murdered and dismembered his wife at 39 Hilldrop Crescent in 1910, the 'Charing Cross Trunk Murder' committed by John Robinson in May 1927, and even the ghastly attacks of Jack the Ripper himself from the months of August to November 1888 in the Whitechapel area of East London.[5]

Few today, certainly, would contest the claim that particular criminal cases – as the investigative analyst John Douglas, for example, has argued – can, in time, assume an unassailable life of their own. It might be argued that we tend to remain fascinated in such instances not so much by the more essential circumstances of a given act or acts of violence, but by the various narratives, motives, characters and details that we, ourselves, are likely somehow to have imposed upon the individuals involved – that we are, in other words, obsessed by the narratives that we have re-imagined into and so re-inscribed within our own, idiosyncratic understanding of events. Consequently, we are transfixed by the depth and extent of our own imaginative investment in such crimes – captured and horrified by our perception of a private and frankly gruesome sense of complicity, and held with strange fascination by a 'privileged' partnership into which we have entered with those who would so spectacularly transgress within that shared space of humanity, the very possibilities of which form societies, and make civilization possible. We permit ourselves vicariously to participate in the kinds of extreme expressions of human behaviour that are otherwise proscribed and that remain – for almost all of us – not merely forbidden, but frankly unthinkable. In short, it is not the facts or the actualities of such crimes that are of deepest interest to us; indeed, we tend, when presented in such cases with the 'facts' alone, to look upon them not merely as sordid or unsightly, but distinctly mundane. We are captivated, rather, by the immense possibilities of the boundless if fatal form of freedom they seem to afford.

Alternatively, the earliest impetus that prompts our initial fascination with extraordinarily compelling crimes can sometimes be explained away as the result simply of the particular personalities involved – as the result, that is, of an arguably 'normal' interest in the highly unusual and aberrant human pathologies that are exposed in the very manifestation of such behaviour. Such an interest might be motivated by the instincts of a primal and primitive human curiosity that recognizes in such events and within such personalities the metaphysical shadow of what many, even today, would yet simply describe as Evil. Such an essential idea of evil is still believed by many somehow to inform, to motivate, or even actually to *constitute* such crimes. Those who would acknowledge such an entity suggest that it betrays itself in a barely perceptible awareness of the unspeakable and diabolic presence that inhabits such brutal acts of violation and transgression. More problematically, the simple fact of our own curiosity regarding such cases can itself be read as an expression of lingering atavistic impulses within our own personalities – impulses which, if unchecked, might possibly move us to commit such crimes ourselves.

Finally – as is arguable in the case of Sweeney Todd – we could more particularly be responding to the mythic resonance of the story's symbolic evocation and conjunction of blood, appetite and desire. If we allow ourselves to entertain this last possibility, we can perhaps see how and why Todd's narrative possesses or exerts much the same element of haunting fascination that has attached itself in the criminal lore of American culture, for example, to the ferocious axe murders of Lizzie Borden, or to the circumstances of the Lindburgh kidnapping, in 1931. Sweeney Todd has exercised a no less compelling pull on the collective imagination of Londoners – and of so many visitors to London – for hundreds of years. The 'London Dungeon' – a successful if otherwise generally unimaginative tourist attraction in London's Southwark (and one that might sufficiently stand as the latter-day equivalent of an earlier era's wax museum) – periodically boasts a special display devoted entirely to a seemingly non-fictional and 'historic' Sweeney Todd. Given the apparent nature of our unfortunate but ineradicably human propensity towards the dynamics of evil itself, the barber's place in the demonic pantheon of evil-doers, villains, and murderers can be counted on safely to remain – even well into the far-foreseeable future – more than reasonably secure.

Londoners themselves, it is not all that surprising to learn, have always had something of a soft spot for Sweeney Todd and Mrs Lovett. Few, certainly, would wish to deny the pair a legitimate and well-earned place in the city's criminal history. London may well have been for many throughout the eighteenth and nineteenth centuries – as Henry Mayhew so famously observed in his *London Labour and the London Poor* (1861) – 'the focus of modern civilization ... a city of palaces, adorned with parks, ennobled with triumphal arches, grand statues and stately monuments'; but London in that same period was also for a far greater number of its less fortunate inhabitants a city of 'narrow lanes and musty counting houses, with tall chimneys vomiting black clouds, and huge masses of doors and warehouses with doors and cranes ranged one above another'. The capital could be, as Mayhew was to put it, a city 'of despair' and of 'the darkest crime'.[6] As the social historian Robert Shoemaker has more recently noticed, the 1700s were in fact the most riotous decades in English history. Included in the insurrections, of course, were the anti-Catholic Gordon Riots of 1780, a free-for-all in the course of which some 285 Londoners lost their lives.[7] One observer much earlier in the century had already noted – and with understandable anxiety – that by 1715 the country and particularly the capital had already witnessed 'more mobs and insurrections in Great Britain than [had] happened in all the reigns since the Conquest'. Shoemaker has argued convincingly that one of the central reasons for such mob violence and scenes of open, active dissent was the simple fact that the sheer size of London defied increasingly outmoded methods of civic organization and authority. Londoners, it was said, had taken to conducting their business – and to pursuing their mercantile disagreements as well as their personal quarrels – on the pavements and in the streets. Those boundaries that had for previous generations more clearly distinguished the interior from the exterior – the codes of expression and forms of behaviour that had separated and embodied society's attitudes regarding important notions of space and propriety – seemed for many to be teetering on the verge of collapse.

At the same time, however, a peculiar, residual sense of what could only be described as genuine fellowship and community worked to forestall the worst excesses and disruptions possible within the increasingly confusing environment of the city, and to mitigate the perceived threat to the status quo posed by the mentality of mob. Workable new rules arose to replace older ones. Throughout the eighteenth and early nineteenth centuries, as has already been mentioned, the spectacle of punishment was a public and carefully ritualized event. Some of the changes in the methods of law enforcement contributed to the dramatic decline in such anarchic public events and mob activity in the decades following 1800; historians such as Shoemaker contend that as the city grew even more populous and anonymous, the spirit of such socially coherent public-spiritedness was replaced by an increasing need for privacy and a growing middle-class sense of individualism. 'Private associations and clubs', as Andrew Holgate has commented on one of the central arguments of Shoemaker's work, 'replaced public assemblies; the world moved indoors.'[8] And as the world of the city moved indoors, so too did its people, along with the formerly more public concerns of their business. Despite the advent of considerably brighter and more effective street-lighting in large parts of London by the mid-nineteenth century, the world of the city had in many respects grown a darker place. Ford Madox Ford later wrote perceptively:

> An awakened sense of observation is in London bewildering and nerve-shattering, because there are so many things to see and because these things flicker by so quickly. We drop the search very soon. And these great crowds chill out of us the spirit of altruism itself, or make of that spirit a curse to us. Living in a small community we know each member of it. We can hope to help, or to be interested in, each man and woman that we meet on the roads, or we can at least pay to each one the tribute of a dislike. But that, in London, is hopeless.[9]

But it is a commonplace of both narrative and cultural history, of course, that even the darkest or most potentially violent and dangerous places – the haunts of beasts, dangerous wolves, wild men and vengeful witches – are of course the very environments within which the stuff of myths, folklore and fairy tales have been created and have flourished. Village girls get eaten by wolves or trapped by misshapen old crones; naïve young men are waylaid into lives as captives or even slaves; parents may try to warn their children of the perils and possibilities of this dangerous world, but they often do so to little or no avail. The typical environment of such transformations and revelations for young children (at least) is the wood or forest – a labyrinthine and uncharted world of sinuously leafy rural enchantment. 'The forest', as Bruno Bettelheim famously observed, 'symbolizes the place in which inner darkness is confronted and worked through; where uncertainty is resolved about who one is; and where one begins to understand who one wants to be.'[10] Stephen Sondheim and James Lapine's 1987 musical *Into the Woods* explored the symbolism commented on by Bettelheim, and in many ways attempted thoroughly to disassemble or decon-struct it, but the frequently treacherous and certainly deceptive green-world of our ancient, pastoral mythology is likely always to remain the quintessential environment of discovery, disillusionment and (rarely enough) contentment. The myths associated with the maze of such a world, in other words, can reasonably be assured to remain with us for a particularly long period of time. 'Believe me,' Sir John Malcolm cautioned his readers in the early nineteenth century, 'he who desires to be well acquainted with a people, will not reject their popular stories or local superstitions'.[11]

These stories and superstitions must by this point in time include the legends and the mythologies of the urban world as well. A great many of our people now live within the boundaries of cities and vast areas of urban sprawl. The shade of trees has in many instances given way to the shadows of skyscrapers; the threats of the wolves and the witches, perhaps only in a less fantastic shape but in a form no less dangerous or deceptively recognizable, remain all too familiar to us all. The romance and terror of the world of the mythical forests of folklore have in a great many respects given way only to the even more overwhelming threats and confusion of the city. Like the woods and the forests of folklore, the dark and mysterious places of the modern urban city have long cultivated and perpetuated their own peculiar myths and legends. Indeed, the story of Sweeney Todd and Mrs Lovett significantly takes place as close to the centre of the great metropolis as possible, in the very location of Fleet Street that the city's popular press would for generations call home. Here, Londoners of every possible social standing kept close quarters with those very same writers and newspaper journalists; clerics on their way to St Paul's or to the other ancient and famous local churches passed men of business hurrying to and from their city offices; farmers, vendors, butchers and retailers passed through on their way to their nearby markets; prostitutes worked their trade at every hour of the day and night; lawyers scurried in and out of the Temple and the law courts; socialites of every standing headed in the direction of the nearby West End and its popular clubs and theatres; manual labourers typically returned in the evenings to their dwellings in the city's East End – all crossed one another's paths at this very heart of London. 'The area [around Fleet Street] was, in point of fact,' as Gregory Dart has commented, 'a labyrinth, a Bermuda Triangle, a place of grotesque spectacles, class collisions, and sudden and mysterious disappearances.'[12] And like any dark wood or forest of mythical transformation, this urban jungle similarly demanded its rightful share of myths, traditions and convincing spectres of malevolence.

In July 1939, M. Willson Disher contributed a column to *The Times* headlined simply, 'On the Trail of a Legend'. In the column, Disher attempted to trace the possible historical reality behind the stories surrounding the figure of Sweeney Todd – a figure who had by that date become the subject of a seemingly endless succession of theatrical melodramas and serialized novels; Todd was a figure who the majority of citizens (then as now) simply assumed *must* have been a genuine historical figure. As Disher put the matter:

> Many people believe that there once lived in Fleet Street a demon barber called Sweeney Todd. So firmly is this opinion held, that his career of crime is taken for granted. Were not Dick Turpin, Jack Sheppard, and Maria Marten actual persons? Then, it seems to be argued, so must he have been. In Fleet Street his shop can still be pointed out, yet no evidence admissible in a court of law has ever been found even to hint at Sweeney Todd's existence, either under his own name or any other, at any time in this country. No sins resembling his have ever been recorded in the Newgate Calendar. . . . Then when and where, and by

whom, was he invented? This is an exacting age, and even a ruffian suffused in glamour must finally be brought to book.[13]

If some historical Sweeney Todd *had* managed somehow to escape judgement at the bar of the Old Bailey in the late eighteenth or early nineteenth centuries, modern readers, Disher made clear, would settle for nothing less than an unequivocal conviction, or a clear acquittal. Some of the journalist's own private speculations regarding the possible origins of the Todd myth will be addressed later. What is most startling about his article in terms of the privilege and sustained popularity of the Todd narrative, however, is the speed with which his dismissal of Todd as a character who existed solely in the world of the theatre and in the eyes of its insatiable audiences prompted a response. Manifesting their discontent in allowing even a single day to pass with Todd being denied his status as a Londoner, born and bred, the newspaper's editors inserted in the very same issue their own mock 'Affirmation of Sweeney Todd'. 'On another page this morning', the paper's defence began,

> a writer hitherto deserving of confidence and respect strikes a shattering blow at a very popular figure in London tradition. Mr. Willson Disher, usually so anxious to preserve the slightest fragment of past London life, suddenly turns iconoclast, and with savage swipe on swipe knocks into nothingness an image which has been, if not exactly venerated, at any rate cherished with awe and wonder for a century and more. Many people, he writes, believe there once lived in Fleet Street a barber named Sweeney Todd. That is putting it – obviously for the sake of his fell purpose – very mildly. Thousands of people know for a fact that Sweeney Todd, the demon barber, lived in Fleet Street; they know where he lived, between St. Dunstan's Church and Fetter Lane; and they know that he used to cut the throats of his customers while he was shaving them, and drop their bodies down a trap door into the cellar, whence the pieman [sic] who lived next door transferred the edible portions of them to his kitchen.[14]

Unconvinced by Disher's 'anti-Sweenian' sentiments, the editorial went on to make quick work of his commonsensical arguments, comparing Todd to some of the other larger-than-life figures in London history:

> On certain persons and certain subjects we do not need to practise – in the too familiar tag from Coleridge – a 'willing suspension of disbelief'. Given the moment and the stimulus we believe to the roots of our being, and the belief remains a habit. It is useless for learned sceptics to maintain that Sweeney Todd or Robin Hood or Little John or Blondel cannot be proved to have ever existed or can be proved *never* to have existed. We cannot get on without them. The most effective retort would be an immediate production of a Sweeney Todd play in London, the city where Sweeney Todd lived and wielded his razor. Such a production would stoutly affirm the pubic belief in Sweeney Todd, the demon barber of Fleet Street.[15]

The heightened reality of the activities of Sweeney Todd and his accomplice itself provided the very proof for their existence as 'real' figures in London history; the demon barber is a figure of unshakeable 'historical solidity' precisely *because* he is larger than life. Disher's own verdict on Todd is dismissed no less swiftly than one of Todd's own victims might have been as nothing more than a mean-spirited and cut-throat raid on the unshakeable strength of the public's Sweenian faith.

Figures of such stature, as we have already noted, are rare enough in any metropolitan or national culture. Sweeney Todd may well be, as we shall see, a specific creation of the early modern imagination, but the degree to which Londoners have for centuries extended to him the historically verifiable privilege of their own birthright merits few comparisons. Few indeed are the fictional creatures who are apotheosized into the confused material world of our lives in this way. Disher himself draws comparisons to such familiar (and genuinely historical) figures such as Jack Sheppard and Dick Turpin, and *The Times*'s own evocation of Robin Hood, Little John and the troubadour Blondel underscores the exclusivity of any such society. Todd's reality is in some respects even more solidly attested to than that of these earlier national heroes and anti-heroes. Well into the twentieth century, there was no shortage of residents who could be called upon to point out the precise address of Todd's tonsorial parlour (Nos. 69, 153, 154, 184, 186 and 187 Fleet Street have all variously contended for the honour; the discovery of human remains scattered within the vaults of St Dunstan's when the church was being rebuilt lent further credence to the legend). Some could point out the exact location of his accomplice Mrs Lovett's infamous pie shop in Bell Yard, near Chancery Lane, while still others could testify to the hidden network of vaults and tunnels that extended beneath St Dunstan's and under Fleet Street that connected the two establishments. In any event, the names of individual victims and of witnesses were a matter of public record, were they not?

Almost any spectator who attends a contemporary performance of, say, Sondheim's 1979 *Sweeney Todd*, or perhaps a revival of the original stage adaptations of the story by George Dibdin Pitt or Frederick Hazleton from the mid-nineteenth century, or even any one of the several more recent versions of the drama, is likely to be offered an account in their programme notes of the 'life and times' of Sweeney Todd. Some very few of these informative histories reluctantly acknowledge the fact that Todd is a figure who appears to '[haunt] the boundary between myth and true story'.[16] Writing in a short essay included in the programme for a 2004 production of Sondheim's work at Covent Garden, Gregory Dart seemed similarly to admit only grudgingly that 'no conclusive proof has ever been found of Sweeney Todd's existence'.[17] A surprising number of such guides, however, not only go so far as to assert that Todd was a genuine historical figure, but even offer a detailed biography of his life, and a complete account of his trial in 1801, as it was supposedly compiled from the original transcripts included in the *Newgate Calendar*. The story goes something like this.[18]

*

Now all is ready for your initiation into the mysteries of the razor ... (Ah! I see you wince a little at the lather: it tickles the outying limits of the nose, I admit.)

(George Eliot, *Romola*)[19]

'Yes,' he said, 'let us go into the Chamber of Horrors; that's a good idea, Miss Bunting. I've always wanted to see the Chamber of Horrors.'

(Marie Belloc Lowndes, *The Lodger*)[20]

According to most such accounts, Sweeney Todd was born on 26 October 1756 into the family of a poor weaver living in Stepney. As a child, he spent whatever spare time he had visiting the nearby Tower of London, just to the west, where he took particular interest in the collection of grotesque instruments of torture, and enjoyed watching the wardens feed the ravenous lions housed within the fortress on bones and large chunks of raw meat. In the bitter winter of 1768, when the young Todd was just 12 years old, his parents unaccountably disappeared from their Brick Lane dwelling, either perishing from the cold, or simply abandoning their son to the city streets. Todd managed to find refuge as an apprentice to a cutler, one John Crook, who ran a shop in Holborn; it was in Crook's workshop that he first learned that facility with razors and other sharp instruments that was to serve him so profitably later in life. After working two years as an apprentice to Crook, he was arrested on a charge of petty theft, and sentenced to five years in Newgate Prison. In the course of his imprisonment, he began to serve as a 'soap boy' or assistant to the prison's resident barber.

Following his release from Newgate in the autumn of 1775, he joined the ranks of London's so-called 'flying barbers' – itinerant shavers and hair-cutters who set up moveable, temporary premises on suitable street corners, and served their customers where and as they could find them. Todd eventually established his own premises somewhere in the area of Hyde Park Corner, where he remained until the end of 1784. It was here, later chroniclers of his story would claim, that he probably committed the first of his murders; a brief notice in the *Annual Register* for 1 December 1784, in any event, did indeed relate that an enraged barber had killed an unsuspecting customer at that location. 'In the height of the frenzy', the newspaper is said to have reported, the barber 'cut the gentleman's throat from ear to ear and absconded'.

The early months of 1785 found Todd, still undetected, established in a new barber's shop just next to the church of St Dunstan in the West, on Fleet Street. Much like any barber-surgeon of the period, Todd not only attended to shaving and hairdressing his customers and preparing wigs carried to his shop for that purpose, but would probably have been expected to extract teeth and perform minor surgery. Although Todd's most famous neighbour on Fleet Street was Mrs Salmon and her museum of waxworks (a verifiable establishment of the period), the barber soon struck up a closer acquaintance with Margery (or Sarah) Lovett, who owned and operated a pie shop in nearby Bell Yard that was enormously popular with the legal students of the nearby Temple.

The Fleet Street area around St Dunstan's was riddled with a labyrinth of underground passageways so dark and ancient as to be virtually uncharted. Bricked up and often only barely passable tunnels led through crypts and vaults for untold distances, and to unknown or unremembered destinations. Some time very soon after discovering these subterranean tunnels, Todd and Lovett embarked on their ingenious enterprise, whereby Todd murdered his customers – typically farmers, drovers, and other unsuspecting country-men come to market – and so supplied the raw material for his near-neighbour's savoury meat pies. After killing his victims, usually by hurtling them from his cleverly constructed barber's chair to the sharp stones of the caverns deep below, though not infrequently 'polishing them off' by dextrously slicing their throats, Todd stripped them first of their clothes and valuables, and then of their flesh. He then dismembered their bodies. He hauled the fresh meat off to Mrs Lovett's cookhouse, before concealing the heads, bones and any other unusable portions of the corpses that remained deep within the vaults of nearby St Dunstan's Church.

Matters went on like this for a considerable length of time; in the course of about five years both Todd and his accomplice accumulated a considerable amount of money and jewellery, reputedly amounting in some accounts to tens of thousands of pounds. Eventually, rumours of the unaccountable disappearances of several of the barber's customers, and complaints of an unusually strong and unpleasant stench emanating from the crypt of St Dunstan's, led to investigations by the local Bow Street Runners and the magistrate in charge of the area, Sir Richard Blunt. It was not very long before Blunt and his assistants discovered the ghastly, partial remains of hundreds of corpses literally crammed into the old church vaults. Even more strikingly, they traced a trail of bloody footsteps that connected the premises of Todd's shop to the basements and storerooms of Mrs Lovett's Bell Yard bake-house. They also discovered the personal possessions of seemingly countless individuals – clothing, hats, buckles, watches, swords – hidden in the rooms and cupboards of the upper floors in Todd's Fleet Street building.

The accumulated evidence was enough for the Runners to arrest both Todd and his accomplice, and the two criminals were brought before the judge at the Old Bailey in December 1801. Mrs Lovett – who upon being captured barely escaped being torn limb from limb by an outraged mob – confessed to her role in the murderous operation, but evaded further hostility and the ignominy of a public trial and conviction by swallowing poison in her cell. Todd, although charged specifically with the singular murder of one Francis Thornhill, was suspected actually to have been responsible for the deaths of at least 160 individuals, and probably many more. The jury in the case returned a verdict of guilty after deliberating for less than five minutes. Todd was executed at 8am in the morning of Tuesday, 25 January 1802, aged 46.

*

He happened to have been sharpening his razors, which were lying open in a row, while a huge strop dangled from the wall. Glancing at these preparations, Mr. Bailey stroked his chin, and a thought appeared to occur to him. 'Poll,' he said, 'I ain't as neat as I could wish about the gills. Being here, I may as well have a shave, and get trimmed close.'

(Charles Dickens, *Martin Chuzzlewit*)[21]

All very grimly fascinating, to be sure. But not a word of it is true. Surprisingly, the inclination openly to question the veracity of Sweeney Todd's story began only in the earliest years of the twentieth century; even then, such questioning was more likely to be met with scepticism and even scorn. To what purpose, after all, would one begin to undermine the testimony of seemingly generations of Londoners, and the (supposed) legal records that dealt with the case? A lengthy series of exchanges in the journal of scholars and academics *Notes & Queries* in the early years of the twentieth century testified to the irresistible desire to invest the story with historical truth, even while other and close to simultaneous entries disputed the authorship of demonstrably fictional versions of the story, or traced the possible continental precedents of what some were already labelling a 'myth' or a 'legend'. One contributor, signing himself only as 'Gnomen', protested that he was 'acquainted with the story in print before 1840'.[22] More tellingly, he insisted that he knew of the Fleet Street location where, as he wrote,

> *to my personal knowledge* a penny pie shop carried on its business in the forties of the last century on the very site attributed to it in the tale under discussion. Whether the adjacent house (at that date thriving as a cook-shop, conspicuous for that succulent kind of Yorkshire pudding described by Dickens in [*David Copperfield*] under the name of 'spotted covey' from the raisins liberally adorning its greasy surface) was a barber's shop once I do not know.... These two apparently very ancient houses stood about the centre of the group extending from the east corner of St. Dunstan's Churchyard to the south-west corner of Fetter's Lane. Many readers will remember them, for they were demolished but a very few years ago, their upper stories were of wood, and they were surrounded by a peculiar wooden parapet or balustrade Gallery overlooking the busy thoroughfare below. When the pie-shop discontinued purveying its special

comestibles (and I have, as a boy, many times sampled its excellent wares), it was carried on as a bookseller's business.[23]

In his anecdotal history of the London theatre world in the nineteenth century, *A Playgoer's Memories*, H.G. Hibbert wrote similarly of Todd's shop as a verifiable memory:

> When I was a young Londoner, *I was shown in Fleet Street the very shop of the demon barber* – and shuddered to think that meat pies are still on sale there. And I read that an enterprising Tradesman has again, by way of advertisement, labelled the new building erected on its site as the authenticated abode of the wretch.[24]

'Other anecdotes', Hibbert observed, were even 'more long-lived and more specific'. In 1956 *The Story Collector* included an item relating to Todd, describing an account published in the middle of the eighteenth century. The contributor, Charles W. Daniels, wrote:

> While an empty shop in Fleet Street was undergoing repairs the workmen discovered several bodies buried beneath the cellar flooring. The man who had occupied the premises had recently died. He was a barber named Todd.[25]

Historically reliable works testify at least to the accuracy of such recollections with respect to the situation and architecture of Todd's vanished Fleet Street environs. The historian E. Beresford Chancellor noted that St Dunstan's was 'notable for the number of shops that clung barnacle-like to its south side and east front'. 'These shops harboured all sorts of trades,' he added, 'there were many passages running underground through which thieves used to escape after ill-using their victims'.[26] The detail and seeming precision of the memories of those who would claim to be no more than one or two distances removed from the world of the 'real' Sweeney Todd continues to exert a certain fascination. The Fleet Street journalist and story-collector Peter Haining, who would appear determined against all his better judgement and instincts as a reporter to believe in an historical Todd, clearly spent days wandering through and around the network of streets that still reflects the courtyards and alleyways of the barber's vanished city.[27] The tight-knit topography of the Sweeney Todd narrative seems determined to draw attention to its transparent veracity.

The modern novelist Neil Gaiman, who with Michael Zulli in the early 1990s contemplated an ambitious illustrated novel devoted to Todd's story, to be published as an ongoing 'work-in-progress', reiterated in a 1997 interview that while he was at times frustrated and confused by the many different versions of the myth that had been handed down to modern Londoners, the peculiar specificity of place that always made itself felt in the narrative exerted a sustained fascination. 'I kept reading version after version of Sweeney Todd', Gaiman confessed,

Here is a couple of Victorian plays, over here would be some Penny Dreadfuls, here's something from the 1930s. It was like watching a cheap road company, going through the motions of the play in which one thing was always the same, but every character with the exception of Sweeney was allowed to go off stage and come back ... they'd throw dice to see who came in as a good guy or a bad guy. A hero of one would be killed in Act One of the next. There is no consistency. There is a sort of cast of about six people who always seem to be in it. There's always Mr Fogg in his lunatic asylum, there's always Toby Ragg, there's normally a sailor. There's always Mrs Lovett, there's always Sweeney Todd, there's always a judge. But after that it becomes so amazingly fluid, and I think that was what attracted me. Also what attracted me was very much the location .... What started fascinating me was that all the old Penny Dreadfuls and plays were very location specific. His barber shop is built into the structure of St Dunstan's church, and connected by an underground passage to Mrs Lovett's pie shop in Bell Yard down the road. It's just next to Temple Bar, across the road from the temple where the Knights Templar were. It seemed a beautiful way of talking about Fleet Street, about London, about the nature of London.[28]

Gaiman's comments underscore a particularly perceptive point here. Any readers who make their way through the many versions of Sweeney Todd – the penny bloods, the melodramas, the novelizations, the films – cannot help but be struck by the bewildering variety of narratives within which Todd's central story has been made a vehicle. Given the extent to which many of the earliest prose versions of the tale appear to have been lost to us over time, such diversity of narrative incident is all the more impressive. Retaining, as Gaiman notes, a consistent if skeletal cast of central characters, the actual events of Todd and Lovett's criminal career are subject to a wild variety of narrative possibilities. Theatrical versions of the story in the later half of the nineteenth century were no less convoluted and subject to variation (the scene-painter Thomas Erle, writing of the productions he had witnessed at the Britannia Theatre in Hoxton in the 1870s, added that the limited resources of smaller dramatic companies could lead to further complications; 'half the dramatic personae', he wrote, 'have to be played by the other half').[29] Any survey of Todd's story that pretends to be thorough or in any way 'complete' in fact resembles nothing so much as a summation of one of the more popular Hellenic myths; to make sense of the tale, the scattered and frequently irreconcilable elements of any number of lesser-known variants would need to be gathered together at the conclusion. As Richard Buxton has written of such myths: 'There was no single, canonical, orthodox version of a tale which all its tellers had to repeat. Rather, each teller remade tradition according to the requirements of the particular social and artistic context.'[30] The same is true of Todd. His ghost lingers in storybooks, novels, plays, works of musical theatre, and collections of local legends that possess an astounding, subsequent resonance. Spurious connections such as that which link the demon barber via cockney rhyming slang with members of the London Metropolitan

'A View of Dunstan's Church, Fleet Street' (No. 38 of Rudolph Ackerman's *Respository of Arts* ...), showing the church and Temple Bar as they would have appeared in the late eighteenth and early nineteenth centuries.

Police Flying Squad (a.k.a. 'the Sweeney') further help to keep the Fleet Street legend alive in our popular language and imagination; the reference is actually to John Sweeney, the Irishman who first organized the unit.[31]

*

London was hideous, vicious, cruel, and above all overwhelming; whether or not she was 'careful of the type', she was as indifferent as Nature herself to the single life.... It appeared to me that I would rather remain dinnerless, rather even starve, than sally forth into the infernal town, where the natural fate of an obscure stranger would be trampled to death in Piccadilly and have his carcass thrown into the Thames.
(Henry James, 'London', 1888)[32]

The Londoner bites off from his town a piece large enough for his own chewing.
(Ford Madox Ford, *The Soul of London*)[33]

The second of Gaiman's observations in the interview quoted above, concerning the consistency of the setting of the story, is in some respects even more germane, although its significance may only become obvious after we have undertaken a closer look at the original version of the Todd story. The many narratives relating to Sweeney Todd are, for all their diversity, oddly obsessed not merely with the urban environment – with London itself – but with the exceptionally heightened and narrow representation of physical space.

Featuring as the pulsing jugular vein of the narrative, the arc of Fleet Street itself functions within Todd's story as a central embodiment of the many roads along which, proverbially, all that belongs to life and to the living will, in time, necessarily pass; it stand for all those wider paths of experience that work their way with curiosity and with confidence through a bustling and potentially profitable world of social engagement. Fleet Street's close proximity to and even (in the form of The Strand) its very physical extension into and within the busy area of Charing Cross suggests its near-alliance to the teeming, universally inclusive ethos of social intercourse that Samuel Johnson so famously idenified as being best represented by the forum of the latter place. Fleet Street, of course, already carried with it an enormous amount of even more specific symbolic meaning as well. As Peter Ackroyd put it: 'Fleet Street is an example of the city's topographical imperative, whereby the same activity takes place over hundreds of years in the same small area.'[34] And the traditional business of Fleet Street, of course, was the business of newspapers and journalism. Of the close to 300 newspapers, journals and periodicals that were being published in the city by the end of the eighteenth century, almost every one of them was the product of Fleet Street, the Strand and its adjoining streets and courtyards. News readership in the period was forever growing. By the time Queen Victoria came to the throne in 1837, an astonishing 30 million people read Fleet Street's newspapers each day, and the figure was to rise even higher throughout the century. It would be no overstatement to say that this concentration of London's journalistic enterprise in and around the relatively small area made Fleet Street the global epicentre not only of national news and the reporting of significant foreign affairs, but a street into which all the gossip and hearsay of the wider world seemed inevitably to tend. Whatever was novel, whatever was passé, who was 'in', or who was 'out': such intelligence, admittedly, might first still, by necessity, be compelled only slowly to make its way up the Thames estuary from abroad; yet even as the several landings and the many sets of stairs that met the City at the river's edge came into view of any approaching ship, those same items of intrigue, information, scandal, rumour and gossip which – then as now – constituted the very lifeblood of the city's ever-ravenous newspapers, journals and chapbooks, were likely already to have leapt from the vessel, and so begin to make the short sprint to Fleet Street, and thence to the rest of the country.

The nature of such an urban space, as several critics have pointed out, made the area and the labyrinthine series of courtyards and alleyways that spread so chaotically around it a space within which the members of different social classes mingled; classes, in other words, that would not normally have come into contact with each other in any vaguely social or companionable capacity did business with, and even socialized in this sphere as well. The area in and around Fleet Street was one in which the class divisions that elsewhere often rigorously separated and divided one group from another broke down; it was an area of unpredictable social contagion and collision.

Barber shops, in particular, would have invited precisely such an intermingling of different *kinds* of people. The democracy of the razor brought all men (and, for what it's worth, the wigs and headdresses of a great many women) together in the same place and, much like the coffee-houses of the late seventeenth and early eighteenth century one encounters in the stage comedies of the period, or in Addison and Steele's *Tatler* and *Spectator*, it functioned as the hub and the social resort of newsmongers, gossips and conversationalists of all types. 'Mankind have always taken great delight in knowing and descanting on the actions of others,' the novelist Henry Fielding observed in *Tom Jones* (1749),

> hence there have been, in all ages, and nations, certain places set apart for publick rendezvous, where the curious might meet, and satisfy their mutual curiosity. Among these, the barber shops have always borne the pre-eminence. Among the Greeks, barbers-news was a proverbial expression; and Horace, in one of his epistles, makes honourable mention of the Roman barbers in the same light.
>
> Those of England are known to be nowise inferior to their Greek or Roman predecessors. You there see foreign affairs discussed in a manner little inferior to that which they are handled in the coffee-houses....[35]

'Barber shops, you know,' Parson Brown similarly reminds his patron Mr Grooby in Robert Bage's 1796 novel *Hermsprong*, 'are receptacles of scandal'

– places where people 'prate', and where the talk is comprised of rumours, neighbourhood gossip, and character assassination.[36] As one columnist would write in editorial pages of *The Times* over 150 years later: 'Notoriously, the barber's shop is a pleasant place, where all the gossip is known; and the barber, too, is a pleasant man, full of not too unkind tales of his neighbours.'[37] 'Barbers', the same editor contended, 'do not often attract much attention outside the shop'; inside that shop, however, they performed something of the function of a master of ceremonies. They helped to inspire a strange sort of intimacy between apprentices, tradesmen, city merchants, and their social superiors. The further, long-standing association of barber-surgeons not only with difficult straight-edged razors, but with the tasks of blood-letting and other surgical practices, could possible have made the shops of barbers even more likely to be only naturally associated, in some respects, with the sight of blood, and the close to casual shedding of blood.[38] Since at least the fourteenth century, barbers had typically performed minor surgical procedures, as well as tooth-drawing, and in time had begun to take on even more demanding or difficult surgical tasks – Italian barber-surgeons carried out actual dissections under the casual administration of an attendant physician. In England, a government Act of 1540 specifically permitted barber-surgeons to administer to 'all outward hurts and tokens of disease', although they were prohibited from administering any medicine for specifically 'internal complaints'; they were even designated to perform amputations. The legal implications of such professional overlapping remained vague and the source of increasing dispute among various practitioners. Barbers blooded customers and administered enemas. By 1843, Queen Victoria's government had more effectively than ever before disassociated the practices of authorized surgeons from those of barbers, but professional distinctions between the work of barbers, surgeons, apothecaries, druggists and other irregular practitioners (quacks) could well have remained confused in the popular mind. Medicine and surgery, on the one hand, and the activities of barbers, on the other, only very slowly emerged as fully separate skills and identities. To this day, almost any person would recognize the striped signification of the traditional barber's pole (in an age when almost all other such professional symbols have disappeared completely). Most associate the red of the pole with the blood possibly shed, and the white with the gauze or bandage used to staunch any cuts or wounds. It is rather more likely that the staff that stands outside the shop exterior itself is a symbol of the actual, physical staff the barber-surgeon would have had his patient grasp whilst being bled (or perhaps whilst some more painful procedure was performed); red, black, or blue bands may well have marked the colour of the actual covering with which the 'customer' was patched up and bandaged. Other researchers, both ancient and modern, have come up with very similar and sometimes even more detailed explanations. One Comenius, a seventeenth-century Moravian bishop, wrote in his 1658 volume, known in England under the title of *The Visible World*, with some authority:

The barber's pole has been the subject of many conjectures, some conceiving it to have originated from the world poll or head, with several other conceits as far-fetched and as unmeaning; but the true intention of the party coloured staff was to show that the master of the shop practiced surgery and could breathe a vein as well as mow a beard: such a staff to this day being by every village practitioner put in the hand of the patient undergoing the operation of phlebotomy. The white band, which encompasses the staff, was meant to represent the fillet thus elegantly wound about it.[39]

Still others versified the history of the barber's pole with an almost close-to-mythical accuracy befitting Albion's legendary history. In 1708 the *British Apollo* (a typical, early Fleet Street production) included the lines:

In ancient Rome, when men lov'd fighting,
And wounds and scars took much delight in,
Man-menders then had noble pay,
Which we call surgeons to this day.
'Twas ordered that a huge long pole,
With bason decked should grace the hole,
To guide the wounded, who unlopt
Could walk, on stumps the other hopt;
But, when they ended all their wars,
And men grew out of love with scars,
Their trade decaying, to keep swimming
They joyn'd the other trade of trimming,
And on their poles to publish either,
They twisted both their trades together.[40]

Yet if the association of the actual barber's pole with its history of blood and surgery emphasizes the shop location as a suitable venue for Todd's narrative, it serves too as a constant reminder of what Gregory Dart has described as a 'collective invention, a figment of popular nightmare'. In his historical-geographical notes to a recent production of Sondheim's 1979 *Sweeney Todd* at London's Covent Garden Opera House, Dart noted the narrative's inclusion of Western fears regarding cannibalism and consumption, and concluded with brilliant accuracy: 'But', he points out,

they also tap into a network of more historically specific anxieties, which have to do with labour, commodity, and the industrial revolution. One of the scariest things about Sweeney, aside from the famous squint, is his efficiency: the fact that he manages to turn murder and the recycling of human flesh into a highly efficient cottage industry. Specifically, in using his special chair to dispatch his victims, and then 'reprocessing' them underground, he drama-tizes the mysterious, alchemical power of 19th-century factory production, its extraordinary capacity for effecting unseen transformations. In this way, Sweeney and Mrs Lovett's split-site enterprise offers a neat parody of modern capitalism, with its talent for suppressing the link between production and consumption, untreated raw material, and final, pristine commodity.[41]

Dart's comments capture the essence of much of the story's mythical force and sustainability. But although Todd may well be specifically designated as the demon barber 'of Fleet Street', one soon notices that his sphere of action – and to an even greater extent the domain of Mrs Lovett – is even more carefully and precisely designated than that. All of the Todd narratives and theatrical adaptations noticeably present a highly actualized depiction of an extraordinarily and unusually delimited urban area – one that is far from extending the length of Fleet Street all the way to the Strand. This specific stretch in fact extends along Fleet Street from just beyond Chancery Lane in the west, to Fetter Lane in the east, and encompassing Temple Bar, St Dunstan's, Bell Yard, and the Precincts of the Inner Temple to Temple Stairs on the river. There are very few parallels in nineteenth-century fiction for such a scrupulously focused and circumscribed presentation of narrative environment. The tendency of the narrative to remain fixed within such a proscribed and historically resonant locale is further reinforced by the equally obsessive return to a small handful of very precise and particular images and references. Most significantly, the reader is constantly returned to the church of St Dunstan's, and the image of the church is itself most frequently located by a return to its best-known feature – the famous bracket clock, with its giants striking the hours with clubs. This emphasis on physical space is important because it creates an overpowering sense of claustrophobia and confinement; it helps also to give the story a tremendous degree of credibility, but even more significantly, the precision of the description, when combined with the intimate labyrinth of passages, shop fronts, cellars, cells and storm rooms that connect Todd's barber shop with Mrs Lovett's bake-house, reflects a cultural impulse that leads to the re-imagining of a complex nexus of human dynamics. In this focused cityscape, people who should feel themselves to be individuals are instead trapped and dis-empowered by their presence in an expanding and exploitative urban society. The satisfaction or fulfilment that might otherwise have been rooted more healthily in relationships of meaning and value is looked for instead in the pursuit of vanity and appetite. Personal vanity may be a universal human characteristic, but it is hardly the enduring foundation upon which any stable personal identity should be shaped. The trauma of Sweeney Todd's tale, as critics such as Dart have pointed out, is embedded in both the actual and imagined landscape of Fleet Street just as much as it is in the historical conditions that gave rise to his continually mutating myth.

The significance of St Dunstan's Church and its famous clock is on closer examination one of the most striking and memorable features of almost every version of Todd's story; this meaning and its significance needs to be pointed out before we examine Todd's first appearance in an extended fiction of his

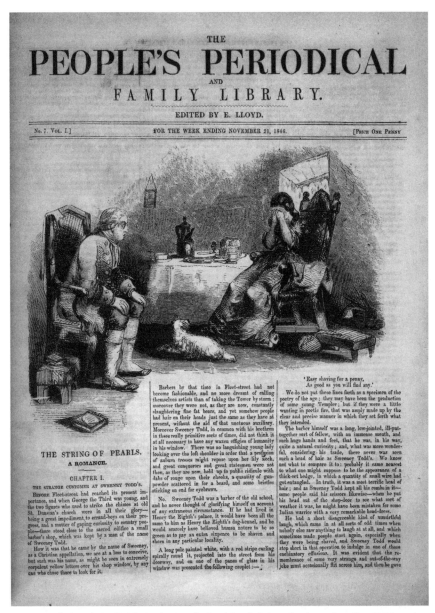

First page of Edward Lloyd's *The People's Periodical and Family Library* for the week ending 21 November 1846.

own in the mid-nineteenth century. The clock and its figures at St Dunstan's had been a famous London landmark since 1671. It had been commissioned shortly after the Great Fire to mark the structure's having been spared in the conflagration. Describing the church in the *New Records of London* in 1732, the Company of Parish Clerks had drawn attention to the clock on the south side, 'here being two figures of Savages or wild men ... each with a Knotty Club in his Hand, whereby they strike the quarters'. 'They are more admired', the entry added, 'by the populace on Sundays, than the most elegant Preacher in the Pulpit.'[42] Oliver Goldsmith mentions it in *The Vicar of Wakefield* (1766).[43] When the hero of *David Copperfield* escorts Peggotty through the city streets in Dickens's 1849–50 novel, the two dutifully pause outside a Fleet Street shop to see the giants of St Dunstan's ring the bells – 'we had timed our going', Copperfield remarks, 'so as to catch them at it, at twelve o'clock'.[44] Dickens had earlier referred in *Barnaby Rudge* to the tolling of 'St Dunstan's Giants'. The poet William Cowper, no doubt recalling his own residence in both the Middle and Inner Temple as a young man, compared the clock-work regularity of the figures to the metrical predictability of poorly written verse:

When labour and when dullness, club in hand,
Like the two figures at St Dunstan's stand,
Beating alternately, in measured time,
The clockwork tintinnabulum of rhyme,
Exact and regular the sounds will be,
But such mere quarter-strokes are not for me.[45]

In Lloyd's original 1846–7 version of the Sweeney Todd story, the demon barber frequently sends his apprentice Tobias off to check the time against the clock. Significantly, the first of Todd's victims to whom the reader is introduced on a personal level, Mr Thornhill, is initially glimpsed standing in the driving rain near the barber's shop, where he is pointedly watching and commenting on the figures from the pavement. 'Run out and see what o'clock by St. Dunstan's', Todd had advised Tobias; once there, the boy notes Thornhill and others:

There was a small crowd collected opposite the church, for the figures were about to strike three-quarters past six; and among that crowd was one man who gazed with as much curiosity as anybody at the exhibition. 'Now for it,' he said, 'they are about to begin; well, that is ingenious. Look at the fellow lifting up his club, and down it comes bang upon the old bell.' The three-quarters were struck by the figures; and then the people who had loitered to see it done, many of whom had day by day looked at the same exhibition for years past, walked away, with the exception of the man who seemed so deeply interested.[46]

Todd's establishment is in almost all versions of the story said to be 'just opposite' or 'a few steps' from the church clock, and the scene of passers-by observing the clock-work figures is reiterated with minor variations in subsequent retellings of the story. The enormity of Todd and Lovett's crimes is specifically 'a secret that will never be forgotten in connections with old St Dunstan's church, while it is in existence; it is bound up with the history of the church and its timepiece'.[47] Appropriately enough, the historical St Dunstan (AD 909–88) was himself reputed to have been a craftsman. He remains to this day the patron saint of locksmiths, jewellers, goldsmiths and other skilled labourers adept with precision tools; several bells are claimed to be his work. He is a figure whose past had been associated with the study of black magic and superstition. In his *Child's History of England* (1851–3), Dickens told younger readers:

> [Dunstan] was an ingenious Smith and worked at a forge in a little cell ... he used to tell the most extraordinary lies about demons and spirits who, he said, came there to persecute him. For instance, he related one day while he was at work the devil looked in at a little window, and tried to tempt him with a life of pleasure; whereupon, having his pincers in the fire, red hot, he seized the devil by the nose and put him to such pain, that his bellowings were heard for miles and miles.[48]

A saint intimately connected to English mythical and historical identity, who is said to have come from Glastonbury in Somerset, and who later designed the coronation crown for Edgar, King of Northumbria and Mercia, Dunstan was the country's most popular saint prior to being eclipsed by Thomas Becket. For readers of Sweeney Todd, the association of St Dunstan with craftsmanship in a small shop, a forge like a hell-mouth, and with jewellery and precious gems is of some significance. (The other saint whose hagiography bears some relation to the story is of course Saint Nicholas of Myra, also known as Nicholas of Bari. In one famous episode from Nicholas's life, the saint rescued and resurrected three young men who were – depending upon which version one reads – pickled or turned into meat pies by an innkeeper and his wife in a time of famine.)

The London historian John Strype, writing in 1720, identified the figures on the Fleet Street clock only as 'two savages of Hercules'; iconic tradition, however, links them more firmly to Gog and Magog. They are thus connected to the mythology surrounding the sometimes confused pre-history of the city of London itself. According to legend, Gogmagog was an ancient giant of folklore who was slain by the Trojan Corineus when the latter arrived on the shores of Albion in about 1000 BC, and who founded his capital city of Troynovant or New Troy. Over time, Corineus' name dropped completely from the legend, and that of his antagonist was divided in two to serve for them both. The giants who strike the hours at St Dunstan's are representations therefore of the same Gog and Magog of London's Guildhall. They are of the breed of mythical English giants who in legend ate the flesh and drank the blood of their enemies – the primitive dolmen-builders of the island's country legends who survive to this day in children's tales and household folklore as beings of extraordinary size who grind men's bones to make their bread, devour little children, or who force reluctant travellers to eat human flesh. They are the legacy and the remnants of the ancient tales and prehistoric narratives associated with a specific place and with the growth of civilization itself. If, as was mentioned earlier, cannibalism was at an early stage of civilization part of a ritual among those who would consume the flesh and blood of their enemies so as to acquire their strength and vigour, the stories of forcing human flesh on those reluctant to eat it, as Sabine Baring-Gould pointed out some time ago, 'may carry us back to an earlier period when cannibalism was not done away with, but when the conscience had begun to revolt against the practice'.[49] Or, as another commentator has written: 'man emerged from the slime, passed through aeons of blood-filled ritual ruled by primal instincts like cannibalism and blood-drinking, and now we imagine we have reached the pinnacle of evolutionary sophistication and civilization'; the giants of our own past remain with and within us, however, related to the remorseless passage of time and the primal, rhythmic coursing of blood and life through our veins.[50] Although it may represent the lowest point on the imagined scale of erotic desire and behaviour, the orgiastic cannibalism – the symbolic representation of time and death in such figures of Gog and Magog – grounds us in the blood lust and sexual hunger of our atavistic ancestors. As one critic has observed: 'The scent of terror and blood seems to excite and move a greater proportion of "civilized" Westerners than we may wish to imagine or admit.'[51]

To a very real extent, the giants of St Dunstan's stand at the very heart of London's history and sense of identity. In *Nicholas Nickleby*, Dickens refers to Gogmagog as 'the guardian genius of London', and the magazine that was eventually to be called *Master Humphrey's Clock* was intended originally to have featured a series of 'Arabian Nights tales by Gog and Magog, the Giants in the Guildhall'.[52] When another clock manufacturer in nearby Cheapside set up images of the giants above his shop in the early eighteenth century, as the city's historian Peter Ackroyd has observed, the owner 'was expressing a general truth. These tutelary deities of London were used to strike the hour, confirming the identity of time and the city.' 'For a city based upon work and labour,' as Ackroyd further commented, 'upon power and commerce, time becomes an aspect of mercantilism.'[53] Connected so intimately to the tolling of the city's hours at St Dunstan's, Sweeney Todd's tonsorial parlour and Mrs Lovett's pie shop also stand within the symbolic nexus of the city's relationship to time and power. The persistent reiteration of Todd's narrative throughout the nineteenth and twentieth centuries demonstrates its deeper symbolic importance as a tangible representation of an ongoing struggle that exists deep within the heart of modern urban civilization – a struggle that pits strong against weak, rich against poor, authority against subservience or submission, and greed and avarice against the imperatives of simple human charity. The dark side of the increasing anonymity afforded by the rapidly expanding city environment provided the basis for a narrative of mythic significance. Todd himself stands as a representation of the force of all that is dangerous, dehumanizing and ultimately deadly in the new Londons of the world; Mrs Lovett stands as the (at best) morally ambivalent representation of a profit-driven society that caters to the basest of human appetites, and in the end winds up consuming itself. Driven by a malevolent greed that is almost motiveless in its will towards greater acquisition, capital and consumption, such a society engages in a self-destructive orgy of anthropophagy forestalled only by an equally spectacular act of self-destruction.

The French sociologist Véronique Campion-Vincent, examining the evolution and reception of urban myths and legends, has remarked upon this possible connection between key moments of industrial expansion and narratives of involuntary cannibalism:

> [The theme of] cannibalism is no less evident in accounts that detail the motif [or urban myth] of 'the body in the cistern'. Typically in such tales it is only long after all of the wine contained in such a cistern or vat has been sold and distributed among customers that the owners discover a dead body at the bottom of the container.
>
> [This trope typically] drives indictments of negligence in the food-processing industry. Upton Sinclair's *The Jungle* (1906) denounced in its pages the story of the unregulated capitalism in the slaughter houses and meat-processing plants of Chicago, and testified – repeating as it did so traditions of oral myth – to the existence of frequent industrial accidents in the course of which the bodies of factory workers fell into processing vats and eventually ended up being served in the form of sausages or pies.
>
> In cities throughout Europe such charges of traffic in human flesh, arising not by means of industrial negligence, but rather by the deliberate acts of criminals, are quite old. Barbers and butchers figure as partners in crime, the one choking his customers, and the other turning the bodies into delicious meat pies that are praised by patrons until the horrible disclosure of the couple's villainy. Typical representations one could cite include, in London, Sweeney Todd and his accomplice the baker Mrs. Lovett, who dispatches his victims with the help of an ingenious, tipping barber's chair, and in Paris the barber and baker of the rue des Marmousets. Stories of this sort have continued to circulate in twentieth-century Germany (the crimes of the 'Butcher of Hanover' have helped to give them a certain degree of verisimilitude) as in the stereotypical anecdotes and tales of survival cannibalism that were said to have taken place in 1946 Berlin. Today, however, they function among us as urban myths. Such is not the case in the sprawling urban mega-cities of the third world, shaken at regular intervals by accounts of traffic in human remains set amidst a scene continually rocked by confusion and riots.[54]

The peculiar and timely Englishness of Todd's fable of the potential criminality and corruption inherent in the nation's mercantile enterprise is encoded further in most versions of the story within the very names of its characters, and in the precision of its original setting. Todd's place in the late-Hanoverian era is pointedly positioned between events such as the Gordon Riots of 1780 and the American War for Independence, on the one hand, and the continental upheavals that followed in the wake of the beginning of the French Revolution in 1789, on the other. The story of Todd's own reign of terror on Fleet Street is set in a time of rebellion and revolution – a time that was also one of deep concern with the possibilities of human commodification. The names of the central characters in the earliest versions of the story seem on occasion to have been drawn from the satiric traditions of the beast fable. The surname 'Todd', for example, can mean 'fox' (from Middle English dialect) or a 'crafty' person likened to a fox, while 'Sweeney' metaphorically connotes 'pride' (a figurative usage derived from the equine, physical disease that atrophies the shoulders of a horse); the Revd Lupin's name obviously signifies, from the Latin, 'wolf'. Other names appear almost crudely symbolic of appetite and specifically erotic desire. The name Lovett is deliberately redolent of the sexually rapacious females of Restoration comedy, such as George Etherege's Mrs Lovett (in his *The Man of Mode* (1676)), and William Congreve's Lady Wishfort in his *The Way of the World* (1700). Mark Ingestrie's decidedly unusual Scots surname clearly connotes 'ingest' or 'ingestion', where others are indications of social status and poverty (Ragg). Admittedly, the author of the original narrative seems to have been so heavily indebted to the contemporary works of Charles Dickens that he almost certainly, if unwittingly, echoed the names included in that novelist's work in his own writings. The name 'Sweeney Todd' itself might to some degree, after all, simply be an unconsciously reversed recollection and slightly jumbled reformulation, in its assonance, of *Martin Chuzzlewit*'s 'Poll Sweedlepipe'. Sweedlepipe, whose services as 'an easy shaver ... and a fashionable hairdresser, also' are available to his clients in his shop at Kingsgate Street, High Holborn, figures prominently in the latter half of Dickens's novel, and (particularly as he serves as landlord to the unforgettable Sarah Gamp) would still have been fresh in the public's imagination.[55] Moreover, the memorable illustration for Chapter 19 of Dickens's novel by Hablot Knight Browne ('Phiz') that features Sweedlepipe's Kingsgate Street premises not only includes an advertisement announcing his services ('Easy Shaving') as standing prominently in his shop window, but his business and residence is pictured as being located next door to an establishment designated by an equally large sign as 'The Original Mutton Pie Depot'; a second such advertisement – an oversized replica of a meat pie with words 'Mutton Pies' on it – stands above the shop.[56] It is close to inconceivable that the author of the original Sweeney Todd narrative did not, in some way, pick up on the possibilities suggested by such a depiction. Be that as it may, the individuals who, as we shall see, combine with the

Bow Street Runners finally to overcome the purveyors of cannibalic meat pies on Fleet Street are peculiarly British in their symbolic status (Oakley), honest and straightforward (Blunt), or simple, native-bred and strong (Big Ben, suggestive of the famous boxer of the period, 'Big Ben' Brain); the bell of the clock in the Palace of Westminster was named after the Minister of Works, Sir Benjamin Hall, in 1859). The only vaguely central individual to fall victim to Todd's razor – Thornhill – is even a man whose very name, although similarly reminiscent of the allegorical designations of eighteenth-century novels and stage comedies, manages still to suggest a figure of martyred eminence and sacrifice (although Thornhill's name, in Todd's narrative, like that of Arabella Wilmot, seems to find its precise source and inspiration in Goldsmith's *The Vicar of Wakefield*). Many of the names used in the original narrative may well have been taken no less casually or unconsciously from far more local or pedestrian sources. The working *Memoranda* or notebook that Dickens began keeping in January 1855, for example, reveals the extent to which even a novelist possessing Dickens's imaginative powers assembled extensive lists of 'Available Names' variously plucked from anywhere he happened first to notice them.[57] The name 'Todd' itself, alternatively, may have lingered in our author's own mind as a recollection of 'Mr Todd's young man' who figures prominently as the baker's assistant in Dickens's own early *Sketches by Boz* (1834). The surname was also widely available from John Galt's popular 1830 novel *Laurie Todd; or, The Settlers in the Woods*. One 'Stuart Todd' even worked out of a Fleet Street premises in the period as a pearl stringer. Sweeney was also the singular stage-name of a popular banjo player who enjoyed a vogue in the London theatres in the 1830s.

The themes and concerns noted above have made Sweeney Todd a permanent fixture of the urban landscape. Some literary critics have made use of the term 'troping' to describe the use of a fictional figure in a sense not necessarily proper to it – the manipulation and remodelling within different cultural environments of a familiar or recognizable character to convey different social or ideological meanings. Whether they are being positively 'assimilated' and 'reproduced', or less faithfully 'expropriated' and 'exploited', such figures carry with them a potentially enormous amount of 'tropic baggage'.[58] Sweeney Todd would certainly qualify as one such figure.

Even when not in his native guise, Todd can often be found haunting twentieth-century authors. Evelyn Waugh's 1934 *A Handful of Dust* (conceived originally as a short story entitled 'The Man Who Liked Dickens') is an excellent case in point. The close of Waugh's novel finds its central character in a distinctly unenviable position. The appropriately named Tony Last, having lost his wife, his son and his beloved ancestral home in England, embarks on an expedition in search of a fabled lost city among the Pie-wie Indians deep within the jungles of South America. This city of popular legend – rumoured among the natives to be a 'shining' and 'glittering' place – is supposed to have existed in a kind of splendid isolation for over 500 years. The satire of Waugh's previous pages had relentlessly targeted the decline of values and stability in an age increasingly given over to fads, surfaces and – at best – a vulgar materialism. Tony Last is driven insane by a world the madness of which seems to shriek about his ears. His final attempt to escape this moral chaos by searching for an elusive Eldorado culminates in a scene of grotesque absurdity when he finds himself lost in the darkest and most inaccessible reaches of the Amazon. Waugh's earlier, shorter version of the episode had emphasized the centrality of the connection between food and sustenance, and urban civilization, observing that his hero 'had always believed that the jungle was a place full of food, that there was danger of snakes and savages and wild beasts, but not of starvation'. 'But now', Waugh comments wryly, 'he observed that this was far from being the case.'[59] In the finished novel, Tony Last finds himself trapped, endlessly reading and re-reading the novels of Charles Dickens to a madman. The name of the madman is Mr Todd.

Waugh's decision to invoke the figure of Sweeney Todd at the end of his satire of the civilized urban world of the twentieth century is the stroke of a master. His Mr Todd, very possibly though not explicitly a cannibal himself, consoles himself in his ironic exile with endless wanderings in the labyrinth of the Dickensian metropolis so redolent of cannibalic pastries. Seeking to find a world of order, light and community, Waugh's hero stumbles instead on the inhuman personification of all our urban nightmares. 'Sweeney Todd and Mrs Lovett between them', as Gaiman has commented, 'embody two basic human needs. The need to look good and the need to eat.'[60] Unfortunately, the two are intimately connected. Locked in the heart of London or in the heart of the Amazon, the beast in the jungle of the civilized world reveals himself to be the razor-bearing barber of our deepest heart's vanity and our darkest night's fears – a primal mythic presence – equally at home in both.

PART TWO
Text and Sources

Chapter 4

Fiends in Human Shape:
The String of Pearls *and*
the Earliest Histories of Fleet
Street's 'Cannibalic Pastries'

Horrors that would the sternest minds amaze,
Horrors that demons might be proud to raise.
(George Crabbe, 'Peter Grimes' in The Borough)[1]

Don't laugh at me – I'm not a lunatic! – but I understand that researches have shown
that even in some of the most astounding of the ancient legends there was some substratum
of fact.
(Richard Marsh, The Beetle)[2]

The character of Sweeney Todd, the infamous 'Demon Barber of Fleet Street', made his first formal appearance in English fiction in November 1846. The narrative within which Todd was introduced to the public did not, however, bear his name on its original title page. Rather, the issue of the publisher and newspaper proprietor Edward Lloyd's *The People's Periodical and Family Library* for the week ending 21 November (price one penny), included the first instalment of an anonymously written story entitled simply *The String of Pearls. A Romance.* And it was within the serialized chapters of this same 'romance' that Sweeney Todd would eventually come to play such a prominent role. The narrative concluded in March of the following year after a total run of 39 chapters (issued in 18 weekly instalments, within issues nos. 7 to 24 of Lloyd's publication).[3] The final narrative of *The String of Pearls* as it originally appeared in *The People's Periodical* ran to a total of just some 100,000 words. Even so, it nevertheless succeeded, as the chronicler of halfpenny boys' magazines and 'penny dreadfuls', E.S. Turner, would later put it, in '[setting] the general pattern for all Sweeney Todd stories' that followed.[4] Lloyd's *The String of Pearls*, in other words, indelibly established in the popular imagination those narrative tropes and incidents that would memorably characterize almost every subsequent version of the barber's murderous career. From this point on (at least in its English incarnations), as Turner further observed of the narrative:

> Todd usually had a terrified assistant whom he ill-used, and sent out of the shop on some errand when a likely customer was about to be dispatched. The chair was dropped through the floor by the pulling of a bolt in the back room. Victims were usually strangers to the town, wealthy drovers who boasted of their profits at market, or seafarers back from, or setting out on, long voyages. The proprietor of the pie shop was always a woman, and the actual pie-maker was a wretch imprisoned in the basement. There was commonly a hat found in the shop when the customer had departed, and of course a dog which sat outside the shop and howled.[5]

Subsequent re-printings based on this original version of the tale would in time swell to a much greater size. Lloyd himself began printing an extravagantly expanded version of the original narrative less than three years after its first appearance in his *People's Periodical*; the bound, single-volume edition of this extended version of 1850 currently in the British Library runs to 732 pages, and is comprised of no fewer than 92 separate, eight-page instalments. Publisher Charles Fox's 1880 version of the story was to fill 576 two-columned pages, having grown in the retelling to an admittedly rambling and frequently repetitive narrative of above 800,000 words. Although both the names of Sweeney Todd and of Mrs Lovett the pie-maker appear in some of the individual chapter headings of the original 1846–7 version of the tale (the 39 chapters of which, again, were published within a period just short of four months), the title of that first version of the story was to remain *The String of Pearls* throughout the entirety of its initial run. Following the week ending 5 December, the narrative, having apparently already 'hooked' its audience and established its readership as intended, was, as might be expected, displaced from the illustrated front pages of the periodical to make room for its successor (yet another serialized romance narrative), and unapologetically relegated – in the middle of its eighth chapter – to the inside pages of the publication. Exceptions to this 'demotion' of sorts were made in the first (2 January) and third (16 January) weeks of January 1847, when the story returned to the front pages of Lloyd's publication, complete with suitable sequential vignette covers or illustrations in the manner of George Cruickshank and later cartoonists in the early and mid-Victorian period, such as George Cattermole, W.L. Emmett, Frederick Gilbert, Robert Prowse, Marcus Stone and *Vanity Fair*'s 'Spy'. (The exact artist who illustrated *The String of Pearls* for Lloyd's publication remains unidentified.) All of the instalments subsequent to that of the first week of December were to be found interspersed among the periodical's other material, which consisted of a highly eclectic mix of other short fiction (e.g. 'Riding on a Night-mare', 'Ayesha, the Maid of Kars'), sentimental poems (e.g. 'Home', 'The Sick Child'), moralized and sometimes comic anecdotes (e.g. 'The Death-Bed of an Infidel', 'Knowledge for the Poor. – Why are Oysters the greatest anomalies in nature?'), medical advice ('Remedy for a Sprain'), and personal notices and advertisements of various sorts. Although the weekly serialization of *The String of Pearls* obviously lent itself to the creation of narrative suspense in the manner of other, contemporary publications, the publisher Edward Lloyd appears to have done little to encourage his author to whet the appetites of his readers towards the end of each instalment. Individual chapters were broken up with seemingly little regard to the narrative action itself, and the story was fragmented in such a way as can only be described as utilitarian, at best. Despite the inherently suspenseful nature of the story being related, there was little if any attempt to create the feel of what today's readers would recognize as 'cliff-hangers' (or what Kathleen Tillotson characterized as 'the grosser kinds of suspense'), by means of which each episode ends in a desperate and often seemingly irresolvable situation.[6] Of the five, front-page illustrations that accompanied the publication of the original narrative, only one – that which was produced for the cover of the issue for the week ending November 28 – contained a clear representation of Sweeney Todd himself (although one other number – for the week ending 2 January 1847 – included a shadowy and indistinct image of an individual that appears to be Todd moving toward the foreground of the picture). At no point would *The People's Periodical* include any picture depicting Mrs Lovett or her pie shop (although the cover illustration for the issue of 2 January 1847, noted above, had also depicted the subterranean bake-house and ovens of Lovett's establishment in Bell Yard). Most of the vignette cover illustrations in fact attempted in some way to represent not the villains of the piece, but rather the situation of the romantic hero and heroine of the story.

Yet the famous 'Demon Barber of Fleet Street' is a character who, even from the moment of his first appearance within the pages of English fiction, appears to have been possessed of a truly cannibal nature – he is a character who takes over and devours what was intended originally to have been the stories and narratives of others. Both he and Mrs Lovett are *generically* transgressive and appropriative as well – macabre, imaginative creations who from their earliest incarnations suitably consume the narrative substance of what was fundamentally meant to be a 'romance', transforming it generically in the very process of their appropriation into a primordial tale of terror, or even into the more basic stuff of horror fiction. As a designation of a literary type or genre, the term 'romance' is a notoriously difficult one; it has little if anything to do, certainly, with what today's reader might conceive of as 'romantic'. Since William Congreve first drew a distinction between the 'novel' and the

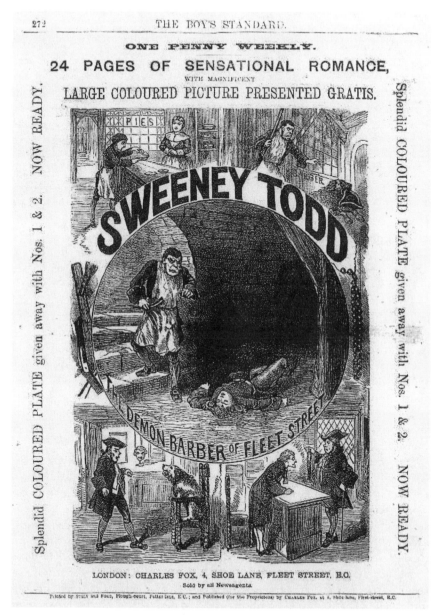

Illustrated advertisement for publisher Charles Fox's enlarged 1878–80 version of *Sweeney Todd*.

PORTRAIT OF SWEENEY TODD, FROM THE ORIGINAL IN THE BRITISH MUSEUM.

'Portrait of Sweeney Todd; from the original in the British Library', reprinted here from a copy of Harry Hagel's 1852–3 'adaptation' of Lloyd's original, entitled *Sweeney Todd: or the Ruffian Barber*.

'romance' in the preface to his 1692 fiction *Incognita*, writers have generally used the latter term to refer to works of fiction that are – as the eighteenth-century author Clara Reeve was to put it in her own *The Progress of Romance* (1785) – told in 'lofty and elevated language' and describe 'what has never happened nor is likely to'; the typical novel, on the other hand, presented to readers 'a picture of real life and manners, and of the times in which it was written'.[7] By the early and middle years of the nineteenth century, however, a work of fiction might acceptably be designated a 'romance' simply if it told a story of exciting and exotic events, or dealt in some way with mysterious or supernatural experiences of some kind. David Masson, who was Professor of English Literature at University College, London, gave a series of lectures entitled 'British Novelists and Their Styles' to the Philosophical Institution in Edinburgh in March and April 1858, in which he attempted to render the generic distinctions implied by the long-established terms of some greater use to his contemporaries. Of the differences between 'novels' and 'romances' in the mid-nineteenth century, Masson observed:

> I have not hitherto recognized this distinction, nor do I care to recognize it very distinctly, because, after all, it is one more of popular convenience than of invariable fitness. A Romance originally meant anything in prose or in verse written in any Romance language; a Novel meant a new tale, a tale of fresh interest. It was convenient, however, seeing that the two words existed, to appropriate them to separate uses; and hence, now, when we speak of a Romance, we generally mean 'a fictitious narrative, in prose or verse, the interest of which turns on marvellous or uncommon incidents;' and when we speak of a Novel, we generally mean 'a fictitious narrative differing from the Romance, insomuch as the incidents are accommodated to the ordinary train of events, and the modern state of society.' If we adopt this distinction, we make the prose Romance and the Novel the two higher varieties of prose fiction, and we allow in the prose Romance a greater ideality of incident than in the Novel. In other words, where we find a certain degree of ideality of incident, we call the work a Romance.[8]

The appeal of *The String of Pearls* as a 'romance', therefore, was intended to lie in the 'ideality of incident' in its representation of characters and events that were somehow set apart from the diurnal and mundane provenance of 'realism' – in its depiction of incidents that were, to use Masson's terms, 'marvellous or uncommon'.

The String of Pearls is a title that would within only a short matter of months be diminished, and would finally be severed altogether from any substantial connection to subsequent versions of the 'Todd' story; it would effectively be lost to narrative history. Further complicating both the history of the barber's earliest appearance by name in fiction and the very notion of such narrative appropriation or cannibalism is the fact that even before the final number of Lloyd's story had appeared in print on 20 March 1847, a dramatized version of the tale, adapted for the stage by George Dibdin Pitt, was being performed at the Britannia Theatre in the High Street, Hoxton, from 22 February of that year – performed, in other words, more than three weeks *before* the 'original' narrative in *The People's Periodical* had even had the opportunity to bring the story to its own conclusion. So it is that the conclusions even of the earliest known stage and prose versions of Todd's narrative differ in a number of significant respects. The barber and his accomplice arrive at their fates on stage in the several dramatic versions of the story in a manner substantially different than they eventually do in Lloyd's *The String of Pearls* simply because Dibdin Pitt himself would probably have had little if any idea as to the manner in which the original, anonymous author of the story had decided to conclude his own tale. (Such rapid appropriation for the stage of a piece of contemporary fiction that was still a work-in-progress, it should be noted, was not at all unusual in the period.)

Edward Lloyd, again, was within a year or so of the stage production to begin publishing his own, much expanded, penny-part serialization of the Sweeney Todd story. Consequently, if (as it would certainly appear) Dibdin Pitt initially took the central idea for his popular stage version of the barber's story from Lloyd's periodical, the latter may very well have paid the dramatist back in kind, as it were, by incorporating elements of Dibdin Pitt's own characterization of Todd within his subsequent, more elaborate versions of the story. The cross-fertilization that began with the narrative exchanges between the publisher Edward Lloyd and the dramatist George Dibdin Pitt was to become something of a recurrent motif in Todd's history. His very story is rapacious and appetitive, forever consuming whatever material it might happen to deem suitable to its own purpose.

The circumstances surrounding the dramatizations of both Dibdin Pitt and of some of his immediate followers – most prominently among them Frederick Hazleton (*c.*1865) – will be discussed briefly in the section that follows. Before turning any attention to Sweeney Todd's phenomenal popularity in the sensational theatre of the day and to his subsequent career on cinema screens in the twentieth century, however, we need to look closely at the plot of his story as it was first outlined in the earliest prose version published by Lloyd in 1846–7. This, after all, was the story that would form the basis for all succeeding versions of Todd's narrative. The original creator of Sweeney Todd, as it first appeared in English, told his story as follows.

*

You have called an uncreated being out of the void. How much more godlike that is than if you had only ferreted out the mere facts! Indeed, the mere facts are rather comic and commonplace by comparison.

(G.K. Chesterton, 'The Absence of Mr Glass', 1913)[9]

The opening pages of *The String of Pearls* firmly set the scene nostalgi-cally in the Fleet Street that had existed 'when George the Third was young' (the year is only a few paragraphs later specified more precisely to be 1785, by which date the long-lived Hanoverian king, just turned 47, had in fact already been on the throne for 25 years).[10] The story opens with the two figures of old St Dunstan's Church – 'in all their glory' – striking the chimes of the hours, impeding the progress of passing errand boys, and offering those country people who were strangers to the city 'a matter of gaping curiosity' (*PP* 97). In the shadow of this 'sacred edifice' on Fleet Street stands the barber shop of Sweeney Todd. The shop is advertised to passers-by by a sign over the front window bearing the barber's name, 'as it may be seen, in extremely corpulent yellow letters', and by 'a long pole painted white, with a red stripe curling spirally around it' (*PP* 97). Todd's shop is a simple place, the product of an earlier era; the barber advertises, as a notice in the otherwise plain shop-window boasts:

> Easy shaving for a penny,
> As good as you will find any.

The shop may be well stocked with combs, razors and scissors of various kinds, but unlike the more fashionable establishments of the mid-nineteenth century, which attempted to entice clients into their increasingly luxurious premises by the ornamented wig blocks and 'waxen effigies of humanity' in their windows, or by the more seductive image of a 'languishing young lady looking over the left shoulder in order that a profusion of auburn tresses might repose upon her lily neck', Todd's barber shop is comparatively bare (*PP* 97). Lying to hand for waiting customers are the various weekly and daily news-sheets of the day (the author specifically mentions a copy of one journal, *The Courier*, by name).

Sweeney Todd himself is rather more noteworthy. He is first described as 'a long, low-jointed, ill put-together sort of fellow, with an immense mouth, and such huge hands and feet, that he was, in his way, quite a natural curiosity' (*PP* 97). His hair is said to resemble a 'thick-set hedge, in which a quantity of small wire had got entangled'. 'In truth', the description continues,

> it was a most terrific head of hair; and as Sweeney Todd kept all his combs in it – some people said his scissors likewise – when he put his head out of the shop door to see what sort of weather it was, he might have been mistaken for some Indian warrior with a very remarkable head-dress. (*PP* 97)

Also distinctly characteristic of Todd is his habitual squint, and a 'short disagreeable kind of unmirthful laugh, which came in at all sorts of odd times when nobody saw anything to laugh at at all, and which sometimes

made people start again' (*PP* 97). Todd's laugh, as readers are led to
hear it in their imaginations, is peculiarly and designedly bestial. The
barber's inhuman outbursts seem to form the atavistic and unpredictable
complement to the civilized regularity of the comfortably predictable
and measured tolling of the church bells of St Dunstan's, outside. Todd's
'cachinnatory effusions' (*PP* 97), as the writer describes them, sound the
bark of the essential primitive that lurks in the shadow of the 'sacred' and
ecclesiastically sanctioned progress of Christian time, defying the reassuring
teleology of the divine comedy with a glimpse of the dark, anarchic chaos
of the abyss. Todd's tourette-like outbursts are in fact specifically described
as 'hyena-like'. 'But', the writer continues, such explosions are typically
'so short, so sudden, striking upon the ear for a moment, and then gone,
that people have been known to leap to the ceiling, and on the floor, and
all round them, to know from whence it had come, scarcely supposing it
possible, that it proceeded from mortal lips' (*PP* 98). Other novels and tales
from the period may feature characters of a dark or sardonic appearance, but
few contain a figure capable of terrifying other individuals merely by means
of their laughter (the nearest creature with whom one might compare Todd
in this respect is perhaps Dickens's grotesquely evil Daniel Quilp, in his *The
Old Curiosity Shop* (1840–1)).

A great many contemporary readers would probably have recognized the
writer's description of the demon barber as having possibly been influenced
by the acceptance of those ideas regarding physiognomy that had been
popularized by the likes of Johann Lavater in the late eighteenth century –
ideas that suggested that the nature of the mind was clearly and recognizably
reflected in the form of the body and face.[11] The 'curiosity' of Todd's simian
or ape-like appearance, with its 'immense mouth' and its oversized hands
and feet, would seem obviously to signal his animal nature; the comparison
of the barber's hair to a 'thick-set hedge' uncertainly pierced by combs and
the threatening points of scissors no less effectively suggests his affinity with
the many 'wild men' of folklore tradition, and the uneasy taming and accommodation of a hostile nature within the bounds of the civilized grooming of
the human world (*PP* 97). Yet Sweeney Todd, as we first glimpse him, also
bears a striking resemblance to the Edinburgh body-snatcher, William Hare,
as described by Professor John Wilson, shortly after his arrest, in *Blackwood's
Edinburgh Magazine* in March 1829:

His dull, dead, blackish eyes, wide apart, one rather higher up than the other;
his large, thick, or rather coarse-lipped mouth; his high broad cheekbones
and sunken cheeks, each of which when he laughed – which he did often –
collapsed into a perpendicular hollow, shooting up ghastlily [sic] from chin
to cheek bone ... inspired not fear, for the aspect was scarcely ferocious,
but disgust and abhorrence, so utterly loathsome was the whole look of the
reptile.[12]

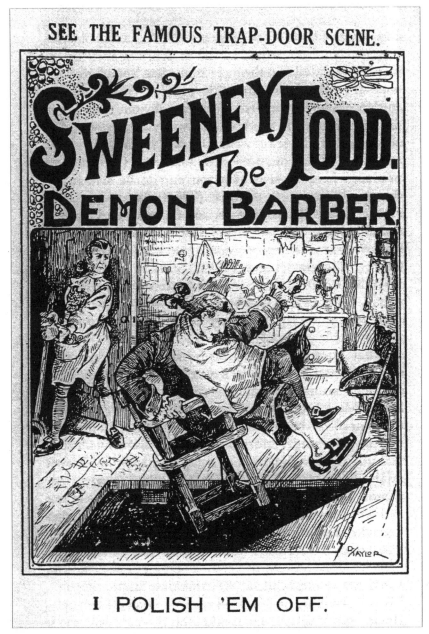

Illustration commonly used throughout the late nineteenth and early twentieth centuries to advertise both dramatic performances and prose adaptations of *Sweeney Todd*.

Much like the body-snatcher William Hare, Sweeney Todd inspires in his unsuspecting customers a sensation not so much of fear, but one that is more akin to an instinctive animal repugnance or aversion. His oversized ugliness is a distorted reflection of something within the human presence that is better left unacknowledged – something, rather like the 'lethal side of man', the evil of which is written 'broadly and plainly' on the face of Doctor Jekyll's alter-ego, Mr Hyde, in Robert Louis Stevenson's famous gothic tale – something that is better hidden or left behind.[13]

Surprisingly, in spite of this grotesque physical appearance, Todd is said to run a successful business. Easily accessible to the young law students in the Temple, who are among his most regular patrons, Todd's shop would appear to be open all hours of the day and night. He is thought by many of his neighbours to be a 'thriving' man, although his often peculiar behaviour and the barren emptiness of much of his substantial property (the upper storeys of the building he occupies, we soon learn, appear to remain completely untenanted) occasionally attract the comments of others. Even so, as the author concludes on an almost sympathetic note, 'when they came to consider what a great crime and misdemeanour it is in this world to be odd, we should not be surprised at the ill-dour in which Todd was held' (PP 98).

When we first meet Todd for ourselves, as it were, he is reiterating the terms on which he has taken on a new apprentice, the young Tobias or 'Toby' Ragg, who cowers in a posture of 'trembling subjection' in front of him (PP 98). Ragg's mother works as a 'laundress' or cleaner in Paper Buildings – one of a cluster of buildings in the nearby law courts of the Temple (the chambers of Sir John Chester, in Barnaby Rudge, had also been located in Paper Buildings). Mrs Ragg is said to have offered Tobias as an apprentice to Todd because she fears that 'a little weakness of the head-piece' has left him unqualified to pursue his legal studies (PP 98). From the very beginning of the story, the proprietary nature of the barber's peculiar vigilance is emphasized. 'I'll cut your throat from ear to ear', Todd growls at the boy threateningly, 'if you repeat one word of what passes in this shop, or dare to make any supposition, or draw any conclusion from anything you see or hear. Now you understand me – I'll cut your throat from ear to ear – do you understand me?' (PP 98). When Tobias reassures Todd that he would just as soon be 'turned into veal pies at Lovett's in Bell-yard' if he betrays so much as a word of the shop's activities, Todd's reaction is remarkable:

> Sweeney Todd rose from his seat; and opening his huge mouth, he looked at the boy for a minute or two in silence, as if he fully intended swallowing him, but had not quite made up his mind where to begin. (PP 98)

It is again worth noting that well before the central action of the story has even begun, the opening paragraphs of The String of Pearls immediately confront the reader with images of primitive savagery and violence – 'gaping' mouths, the threat of being 'swallowed' piece by piece, and the promise of throat-slitting brutality and reprisals. The metaphorical language of cannibalism will be heard throughout the narrative. These early pages, with their repeated references to the towering proximity of the tolling clock of St Dunstan's, will also make a point of emphasizing the commemorative passing of time and approaching death, all within the swirling and seemingly relentlessly vital and thriving commercial activity at the heart of London's Fleet Street.

In the drizzling rain outside of Todd's shop, one Lieutenant Thornhill, only just returned from a voyage to the East Indies, has momentarily paused with his faithful dog Hector by his side; standing in Fleet Street, Thornhill watches the figures on St Dunstan's clock strike the quarters of the hour before proceeding in his search to locate a Miss Johanna Oakley, the daughter of a spectacle-maker whom he knows operates an establishment on Fore Street, in Moorfields. Thornhill's errand is not a happy one. It has fallen to him to inform the young Johanna that her professed lover, one Mark Ingestrie, who had promised to return to her on this very date two years earlier, has disappeared. Thornhill believes Ingestrie to have been killed when his ship caught fire and foundered in the seas off the eastern coast of Africa, near Madagascar. Said to have been a handsome if 'wild' and head-strong young man, Ingestrie had rebelled against the wishes of his only guardian – an uncle, Mr Grant – when the latter had attempted, against his nephew's will, to make a lawyer out of him. Ingestrie had instead, like so many young men possessed of a wide imagination and the resilience of youth, pursued his dream of 'going to sea'. More specifically, he had embarked as a sea-faring adventurer on a voyage to discover the precise location of a river on one of the islands in the Indian Ocean that was rumoured, like some modern Pactolus, to accumulate enormous deposits of gold dust in its progress to the ocean. Ingestrie's ship, the *Star*, was thought to be in the immediate vicinity of this sought-after destination when it was encountered by another vessel then journeying homeward from India, called the *Neptune*. Shortly after making contact with the *Star*, the travellers on the *Neptune* watched in horror as the former ship was set ablaze by lightning, and foundered in the wake of a storm that had lashed both vessels for almost three days. Turning about to come to the aid of the *Star*, the crew of the *Neptune* found only a single piece of wreckage floating on the seas, to which was clinging the lone human survivor of the disaster – Lieutenant Thornhill – along with his dog Hector, who managed to stay alongside his master 'with all the energy of desperation' (*PP* 131). In the course of a lengthy return voyage back to England, Thornhill had slowly recovered from his ordeal, and was befriended by another young man on the journey, Colonel Jeffrey, a member of the British army then serving in India. The two men eventually formed a strong bond with each another, and Thornhill confided to Jeffrey the story of his fellow-adventurer on board the *Star* – Johanna's lover Mark Ingestrie – who, even as their vessel was about to be swamped, could speak only of his devotion to Johanna Oakley, in London. Feeling a strong presentiment of his own immediate death in the shipwreck, Ingestrie had passed on to Thornhill a string of 20 pearls – a piece of immense value. Minutes before the *Star* was destroyed, Mark asked his friend to promise that in the event of his own death, Thornhill would present the pearls to Johanna in his name; if, that is, Thornhill himself chanced ever to make it safely back to England. Thornhill considered the trust to be a sacred one, and had accordingly, at the very first opportunity following the *Neptune*'s arrival in the Thames estuary, made his way into the city to locate the whereabouts of Johanna Oakley.

Unfortunately, just as he prepares to move on into the City after pausing to watch the figures on St Dunstan's, Thornhill succumbs to the momentary impulse to make himself somewhat more 'tidy' and presentable to the company of a young lady after such a lengthy voyage, and steps across the road and into the barber's shop nestled close beneath the church tower to be shaved (*PP* 99). He has no way of knowing that it has for some time been the practice of Sweeney Todd particularly to attract the custom of those who were strangers to the town – sailors just returned from lengthy trips abroad or drovers and country farmers, unfamiliar with the city, who had driven their goods to the nearby markets. Both sorts of men tended often to be newly paid or flush with the profits of a recent sale, and were less likely than others to be traced to Todd's door should anyone eventually come looking for them. Once inside the shop and seated in Todd's barber's chair, the unsuspecting patrons would have no time even to realize what was happening to them before the barber – having disappeared into an adjacent room on the pretence of searching for a misplaced strop or razor – pulled on a secret bolt hidden just within the room next door that flipped his specially constructed chair completely upside down, through the floor, and hurled the 'customers' to their deaths on the rough and jagged stones of the storerooms and basement vaults that lay deep below the Fleet Street shop. Those few victims who managed somehow to survive the drop were dispatched in their helpless and unconscious state by Todd himself, who, drawing his razor deftly across their throats, had no problems with thus 'polishing them off' for good. Having carried on this practice for some years now, Todd had accumulated an impressive amount of gold, silver, gems and other jewellery.

On this occasion, Lieutenant Thornhill falls an easy prey to Todd's designs. Once the terrified and already suspicious apprentice Toby has been sent out on a typically pointless errand (he is almost always sent out to find something to *eat*), the newly returned traveller has disappeared from Fleet Street forever. The persistence of Thornhill's dog Hector in howling for his master and refusing to leave the shop door attracts some unwanted attention, but the string of pearls that Mark Ingestrie had intended for Johanna Oakley – shortly to be valued at over £10,000 – would seem already to have become a particularly valuable addition to the barber's 'collection'.

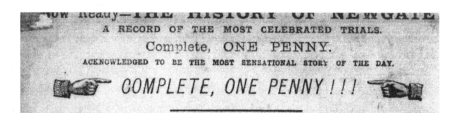

Early cover (c. 1892) for A. Ritchie's abbreviated version of *Sweeney Todd*.

FIENDS IN HUMAN SHAPE

*

Now demons, whatever else they may be, are full of interest.
(Lytton Strachey, 'Life of Florence Nightingale')[14]

It may be useful to pause at this point to observe that if, as was noted in Part One, Sweeney's name may recall for some modern readers the figure of the mad king 'Sweeney' of the *Buile Suibhne* of Celtic legend, such a nominal recollection is in many ways, when supplemented by some of the details of Todd's own narrative, strikingly appropriate for this otherwise unrelated nineteenth-century tale. In the version of the original Irish legend first recorded in the seventeenth century and most recently translated for the modern reader into English by the award-winning poet Seamus Heaney, a bishop by the name of Ronan Finn establishes a church within the boundaries of Sweeney's kingdom. King Sweeney is angered most by the tolling of Ronan's church bell, which the bishop wears around his neck, and which he rings as he marks and measures out the boundaries of his church lands. The enraged Sweeney rushes from his home 'to hunt the cleric from his church', and would certainly have killed him, but for the arrival of a summons calling him immediately away and into battle. In the confusion of the ensuing conflict, Sweeney slays one of Bishop Ronan Finn's eight psalmists with a spear; he throws another spear at the bishop himself, which, missing its intended target, instead strikes the very bell that hangs from Ronan's chest, and pierces it. For this act, Bishop Ronan curses the king:

> My curse fall on Sweeney
> for his great offence.
> His smooth spear profaned
> my bell's holiness,
>
> cracked bell hoarding grace
> since the first saint rang it –
> it will curse you to the trees,
> bird-brain among branches.
>
> Just as the spear-shaft broke
> and sprang into the air
> may the mad spasms strike
> you, Sweeney, forever.[15]

Bishop Ronan's curse entails that, just as the church bell had been broken by the king's shaft, so too will Sweeney himself in future be 'broken' or driven to madness by any sharp, tintinnabular sound. Strikingly, in the romance of *The String of Pearls*, as first retailed in Edward Lloyd's *The People's Periodical*, there is on almost every occasion a synchronicity between the ringing of the

115

bells of the church of St Dunstan's, just above Todd's shop, and the barber's quasi-ritual acts of slaughter. The passing of the hours as signalled by the bells of St Dunstan's appear to constitute the campanological catalyst – or at least an auricular cue to the reader – for outbreaks of madness and murder. Struck as they are by the figures of the foundational giants of London's history – Gog and Magog – the bells seems to conjure something close to primeval from the depths that stretched beneath the thin veneer of the civilization of the city streets.

Strangely enough, the resonance surrounding a myriad other ancient myths and legends lies surprisingly close to the surface here as well. Much in the fashion of Homer's *Odyssey*, the 'romance' of *The String of Pearls* to some extent participates in the traditions of the ancient νοστοι or '*nostoi*' – it is the story of a 'homecoming', or even the story of several, interrelated homecomings. In this instance, however, the *nostoi* tend (like Agamemnon's) to go horribly wrong. Like Odysseus, Lieutenant Thornhill, too, is a weary traveller who has returned home from the sea; unlike Odysseus, who in his wanderings manages to escape from the clutches of the cannibal Lystragonians and the man-eating giant Polyphemus, Thornhill *does* fall victim to the murderers, predators and cannibals (however unwitting they may be) who beset him. The telling irony for Thornhill lies in the fact that, despite his promiscuous travels among supposedly dangerous tribes of man-eating savages in Africa, it is in this very heart of London that he finally encounters the anthropopophagists who will devour him; the sacrificial blood that is shed upon the occasion of his homecoming, like the memory of an ancient ritual, is his own. Thornhill's fate raises the possibility that while the potential dangers posed by and within the new worlds of empire may be considerable, they are at the very least matched at home by the consuming energies of the city itself, and by the motivating desire and appetite that initiate and sustain those energies.

Mark Ingestrie is similarly posited as a model of the sailor-adventurer (possessed of Odysseus' curiosity, if not the canny trickery that would apparently allow him to survive) who would appear to have been destined not to return home safely, but to disappear in the course of his own misguided, appetitive wanderings, consumed by the sea. We are led to believe that the young man who has undertaken his voyage out to 'ingest' the world (as his very name suggests) has, like Thornhill, somehow been 'ingested' himself – he appears at the story's beginning to have been consigned to the waves like one of Odysseus' ill-fated crew-members. Even Johanna Oakley, Mark's intended bride, can be looked upon as something of a modern-day, mercantile-era Penelope, who – in the manner of her ancient predecessor, though yet unwed – in the absence of her proper partner very soon finds herself engaged in a multitude of wily matrimonial games, attempting on the one hand to discover both the fate of her lover and the true identity of the missing Lieutenant Thornhill, while on the other fending off the persistent advances of unwanted suitors, including in this case, as we shall see, the sympathetic Colonel Jeffrey, the unctuous evangelical Reverend Lupin, and her father's clownish apprentice, Sam Bolt. Like so many other figures in the traditions of classical mythology, too, Johanna appears to have been confronted with a choice of irreconcilable destinies. She can have either love or riches, but not both. As Colonel Jeffrey will later suggest when considering her situation, 'if she cannot be Mark Ingestrie's wife in this world, she shall be rich and happy, poor young thing, while she stays in it, that is, as happy as she can be: and she must look forward to meeting him aloft, where there are no squalls or tempests' (*PP* 131). Also, and much like the heroine of the mythical tale of Ceyx and Alcyone as retold by Ovid in his *Metamorphoses*, Johanna will experience terrific, visionary nightmares in which she believes she witnesses the destruction of her lover's vessel in a storm at sea.

Mark Ingestrie's own narrative is no less reminiscent of other classical legends, resembling as it does the trials of a typical hero of myth and folklore; he is early in the story dismissed by Johanna's father as a young man who has not yet earned the right to his daughter's affections. 'My dear,' Oakley consoles his daughter when she first suspects that Mark has not kept his promise to return to her, 'one would have thought that if Mark Ingestrie had really loved you, and found that he might make you his wife, and acquire an honourable subsistence both for you and himself – it seems a very wonderful thing to me that he did not do so' (*PP* 100). Oakley's own name is itself suggestive of his solid and substantially home-grown wealth, but the subsequent narrative suggests that even he can also, in certain matters, be as thick and as impenetrable as an oak himself; he is one of many such archetypal spectacle-makers who is incapable actually of seeing things properly. Johanna's father is further placed in a fairy-tale situation in which he is harassed by a shrewish and misguided wife (we soon see that Mrs Oakley is under the thumb of psalm-singing, hypocritical Parson Lupin). Like many a romance hero, Mark Ingestrie will nevertheless need to prove his worth and value within this same domestic unit. In his own particular case, he will be compelled to physical labour (like some unhappy version of the young Ferdinand in Shakespeare's *The Tempest*) in the stygian darkness of Margery Lovett's bake-house to demonstrate the extent of his despair, and the true value of his devotion to Johanna.

Mr Oakley is also, early in the story, the spokesman for a work ethic that appears with surprising suddenness to have become old-fashioned and out-dated – a work ethic of an England that is itself a thing of the past. 'The lad is a good enough looking lad,' Oakley says of Ingestrie when attempting to console Johanna when she first fears that her lover has been lost at sea, 'and has, I believe, a good ability, if he would put it to some useful purpose; but if he goes scampering about the world in an unsettled manner, you are well rid of him' (*PP* 100). Oakley's stay-at-home dedication is well enough in its way, but it is emphatically *not* the way of the new age of empire and imperial conquest and expansion. He is the face of *old* business, whereas Thornhill and Mark are to some extent the face of the new and rather more obviously dangerous commercial energy finally coming to strength and age in the mid-nineteenth century. The nature of the period as a time of conflict and expansion – and the need for individuals possessing Mark's particular brand of strength and even fool-hardy determination – is made clear from the beginning of the narrative. The description of the *Neptune* – the ship from which Thornhill disembarks in search of Johanna – is, tellingly, one of the most quietly detailed in the narrative:

> A man-of-war, which had been the convoy of the fleet of merchantmen through the channel, fired a gun as the first glimpse of the morning sun fell upon her tapering masts. Then from a battery in the neighbourhood came another booming report, and that was answered by another farther off, and then another, until the whole chain of batteries that girded the coast, for it was a time of war, had proclaimed the dawn of another day.
>
> The effect was very fine, in the stillness of the early morn, of these successions of technical reports; and as they died away in the distance like mimic thunder, some order was given on board the man-of-war, and, in a moment, the masts and cordage seemed perfectly alive with human beings clinging to them in various directions. Then, as if by magic, or as if the ship had been a living thing itself, and had possessed wings, which, at the mere instigation of a wish, could be spread out far and wide, there fluttered out such sheets of canvas as was wonderful to see; and, as they caught the morning light, and the ship moved from the slight breeze that sprang from the shore, she looked, indeed, as if she
>
> *'Walk'd the waters like a thing of life'.*
>
> The various crew of the merchantmen stood on the decks of their respective vessels, gazing after the ship of war, as she proceeded on another mission similar to the one she had just performed in protecting the commerce of the country. (*PP* 101)

It is the prospect of 'protecting the commerce of the country' that sparks the landscape of the Thames estuary to life. The mission of the merchantmen under protection of the Royal Navy's man-of-war constitutes an act of heroic endeavour evocative of the primal and fatal force of the dark hero of Byron's 'Corsair' (1814), from which poem the line quoted above has been taken. The unique national impulse that prompts this instantaneous vitality, lest the reader miss the point, is explicitly delineated in the passage that follows:

> It was a proud and a delightful sight – such a sight as none but an Englishman can thoroughly enjoy – to see that vessel so proudly stemming the waste of waters. We say none but an Englishman can enjoy it, because no other nation has ever attempted to achieve a great maritime existence without being most

signally defeated, and leaving us still, as we shall ever be, masters of the seas.
(*PP* 101)

Of all individuals to constitute the sacrificial victim – the male Iphigeneia –
by means of which such voyages and the wealth of such a glorious enterprise is
to be so easily purchased, Thornhill falls the peculiarly appropriate candidate.
Having once himself, as a young man, attained the rank of lieutenant in the
navy, the appropriately named Thornhill had been cashiered 'for fighting a
duel with his superior officer'; such an insurrection against authority stripped
him of his rank and status. 'A braver man never stepped, nor a better officer;'
the captain of the *Neptune* confides in Colonel Jeffrey early in the tale, 'but
you see they have certain rules in the service, and everything is sacrificed to
maintain them' (*PP* 101).

If, as noted in passing in the previous section, Thornhill's name itself
suggests the gratuitously imposed pain and martyrdom ('thorn') and altered
eminence ('hill') of this sacrificial victim's particularly commercial and pedestrian Calvary, a certain mythic resonance plays no less certainly about that of
his dog, Hector, as well. The name of Thornhill's faithful canine companion
automatically associates the dog in the minds of readers with an ethic of
unswerving if doomed and slightly mournful Trojan bravery. When taken
together with the similarly Homeric echoes awakened by the *nostoi* of the
returning travellers already noted, the presence of the protective Hector also
evokes the similarly unswerving fidelity of Argos, the long-suffering dog of
Odysseus, who lives just long enough to welcome his master home to Ithaka
in the *Odyssey* before promptly expiring at his feet. Within such a scheme of
mythic recollection in the narrative, Sweeney Todd himself assumes another
guise, and constitutes something akin to an inevitable force of destiny or
retribution, his efficient razor resembling nothing so much as the termi-
nating forfex of Atropos – the third of the three parthenogenous daughters
of the Great Goddess Necessity – who in Hellenic mythology snips (with a
pair of scissors, of course) the thread of mortal life, which has been spun on
her sister Clotho's spindle, and measured by the rod of their sibling, Lachesis.
Todd, as his earliest description has already indicated, certainly appears to
constitute a supernatural force of nature – a force that both the more intuitive
natures of Tobias Ragg and the dog Hector sense at once to be unusually
dangerous. Strikingly, the term 'barber's chair' was commonly used in the
period as vulgar slang for a prostitute, because of the manner in which both
might well be made 'use' of by almost everybody (e.g. 'she's as common as
a barber's chair, in which the whole parish sits to be trimmed'), and hence,
by extension, was redolent of a common fate – a shared mortality.[16] Readers
can trace other mythic tropes in the relation of incidents as slight as Todd's
reaction to his apprentice Tobias's early, unanticipated return to the barber
shop immediately following the murder of Thornhill. Toby's untimely return
recollects innumerable archetypal incidents in which figures of classical

119

mythology see the unseeable, or otherwise witness a scene the sight of which they have been forbidden – and so recalls a range of mythical incidents extending from Perseus' encounter with the Gorgon Medusa to Psyche's transgression against the nocturnal privacy of her lover Cupid (an encounter of course brought to life in the early modern period in tales such as 'Beauty and the Beast').

Another possible gesture towards a symbolic structure in the narrative can be glimpsed in the peculiar way in which the sequence detailing Thornhill's early visit to Todd comes to an end. Almost immediately after Todd has dispatched Thornhill to the cellar and pocketed the eponymous string of pearls, Mark Ingestrie's uncle Mr Grant enters the shop. While preparing to shave Grant, Todd engages him in some seemingly inconsequential conversation about the weather. Just a few pages earlier in the narrative, the day had been described as being 'drizzling' and dull. Yet when Mr Grant asks the barber if there has been 'any news' to speak of, Todd replies: 'No, sir, nothing stirring. Everything very quiet, sir, except the high wind. They say that it blew the king's hat off yesterday. And he borrowed Lord North's. Trade is dull, too, sir. I'm afraid people won't come out to be cleaned and dressed in the misling rain' (*PP* 99). The strikingly odd self-contradiction of Todd's report (how, exactly, can a period of 'high' and boisterous wind be described in the same breath as 'drizzling' and 'dull'?) arguably constitutes a small but tellingly significant slip on the part of a hasty author – an author whose subconscious was engrossed in the narrative's deeper substance as a tale obsessed with unstable 'heads' of all sorts, and a society in which even the suitable headpieces of monarchs are replaced with dangerous dispatch by those more appropriate to ministers; a society in which the traditional loyalties and deferential hierarchies of the Oakleys of the world are open to swift disruption and displacement; a society in which the sway of kings can abruptly give way to the more arbitrary dominion of government ministers and trade. The 'string of pearls' of the story's title is itself in many respects a classic type of misleading symbol, exhibiting as it does all the hallmarks of what the film director Alfred Hitchcock memorably denominated a 'Mcguffin' – a device or object that seems at first glance to drive the plot forward, and around which all the action of the narrative appears to centre, but one that functions finally only to lead us astray. The string of pearls, as we shall see, constitutes precisely this type of narrative 'sleight of hand', as it were. It is no doubt important to keep in mind that the reader is kept in a state of narrative suspense – and will *remain* in suspense – throughout the entire tale. Not only are we led to believe that the string of pearls will itself figure prominently in the 'solution' to the mystery of Thornhill's disappearance – we will, to some extent, throughout the serial narrative remain as much in the dark as Johanna with regard to the ultimate fate and identity of Lieutenant Thornhill, to say nothing of the exact nature of Todd's business practices. Unlike a dramatist such as Shakespeare, who in almost all his comedies takes special care (usually by means of theatrically effective techniques of 'discrepant awareness') always to reassure his audience very early on in the action of the play that all will, indeed, end well, the earliest readers of *The String of Pearls* are offered no such privileged or even vaguely reassuring information.

*

> *We, who are thieves without a license, are at open war with another sort of men who are thieves according to law.*
>
> (William Godwin, *Caleb Williams*)[17]

Lieutenant Thornhill's disappearance from the *Neptune* does not pass unmarked. Gazing across the river estuary at the splendid fleet of vessels lying below Sheerness, Thornhill's friend Colonel Jeffrey and the ship's captain are startled to see the dog Hector swimming towards them with his master's hat in his mouth. Once on board the ship, Hector appears to betray his anxiety regarding his master. Jeffrey and the captain at once decide to follow in Thornhill's footsteps and, with the eager assistance of Hector, soon trace his path to the Fleet Street entrance of Todd's shop. Although the barber confirms that he had earlier that day shaved a customer who answered to Thornhill's description, he claims that the gentleman in question had left the shop without incident, having announced his intention to seek out Oakley's residence in Fore Street. The two men can get no more information from Todd, although Hector's violent reluctance still to leave the entrance of the barber's shop leaves them suspicious as to exactly what has taken place there. The captain is due to depart with his ship for Liverpool, but Colonel Jeffrey, refusing simply to accept that the trail has run cold, plans to remain in London and enlist the help of another one of his city friends, one Captain Rathbone, in pursuing Thornhill's disappearance further. He decides first, however, to seek out Johanna Oakley for himself.

Meanwhile, in Fore Street, Johanna Oakley has grown increasingly distraught by the failure of Mark Ingestrie to make his promised appearance. Johanna's father is sympathetic to her situation, although he warns her that she should not expect too much from a fiancé who felt it necessary to travel abroad to make his fortune, rather than demonstrating the patience or dedication necessary to 'be respectable' and stay at home. Johanna's continued distress only makes the family's domestic situation worse. The foolishly susceptible Mrs Oakley has for some time opened her home to the evangelical clergyman, the Revd Lupin, a hypocritical and lecherous drunkard whose designs against Johanna are frustrated by her father's towering cousin, Big Ben. Ben is one of the upstanding beefeaters stationed at the nearby Tower of London, although his antipathy to Lupin results in his being described by Mrs Oakley as a 'good-for-nothing lump of carrion' (*PP* 154). Mr Oakley's own resentful and clumsy shop-boy, Sam Bolt, further aggravates the situation in the Oakley household by stubbornly insisting on his own claims to the hand of his master's daughter: 'Didn't I tell you, more than three weeks ago, that you was the object of my infections,' he asks Johanna, confessing in solitude after she has left him in disgust, 'I am ready to gnaw my head off that ever I consented to come here' (PP 101). (The strands of the plots or subplots that are begun with reference to characters such as Lupin, Big Ben and Sam Bolt are never adequately followed through in the initial version of The String of Pearls; in fact, they are dropped abruptly and without explanation. They would be picked up by subsequent authors who were to take up – to no great effect, it must be admitted – Lloyd's initial version of the tale, and would be elaborated at much greater length in the expansions of 1850 and 1880.)

Colonel Jeffrey eventually manages to get a message through to Johanna. She agrees to meet with him in the Temple Gardens, the very place where she had taken leave of Mark Ingestrie exactly two years earlier, and a garden location redolent both of Johanna's own vaguely prelapsarian innocence, and of the romantic naïveté of the two young lovers. (In the concluding chapters of Dickens's Martin Chuzzlewit, the last double number of which had only just been published in July 1844, the Temple Gardens and Fountain Court had figured prominently as the scene of the courtship of a similar young couple, John Westlock and Ruth Pinch.)[18] There, Jeffrey reluctantly informs Johanna what he knows about the fate of Mark Ingestrie; he also tells her as much as he can about Thornhill's mysterious disappearance following the last known sighting of him in Sweeney Todd's shop. Jeffrey promises to pursue the matter, although he also makes it clear to Johanna that the expedition on which Mark had originally set out had probably been a fraudulent one. 'There came to London,' Jeffrey recalls to Johanna, 'a man with a well authenticated and extremely well put together report, that there have been discovered, in one of the small islands near the Indian seas, a river which deposited an enormous quantity of gold dust in its progress to the ocean.' He told his story so well, 'and seemed to be such a perfect master of all the circumstances connected with it, that there was scarcely room for a doubt upon the subject'. 'And Mark Ingestrie, I am told,' Jeffrey persists,

> was the most hopeful man on board. Already in imagination he could fancy himself homeward-bound with the vessel, ballasted and crammed with the rich produce of that shining river.
> Already he fancied what he could do with his abundant wealth, and I have not a doubt but that, in common with many who went on that adventure, he enjoyed to the full the spending of the wealth he should obtain in imagination – perhaps, indeed, more than if he had obtained it in reality. (PP 131)

Thus 'tempted' by an idea that had 'seized completely hold of his imagination', Mark had eagerly joined the crew of a vessel – the Star – that had been 'duly chartered and manned for the purpose of proceeding to the Indian seas in search of the treasure, which was reported to be there for the first adventurer who had the boldness to seek it' (*PP* 131). Interestingly, although Jeffrey (and, of course, the author) casts substantial doubt on the authenticity of the reports of riches that had served to draw Mark Ingestrie to the East Indies in the first place, no explanation is ever given anywhere in the narrative as to where or how Mark obtained the valuable piece of jewellery that is the immediate cause of all his subsequent misadventures.

Colonel Jeffrey goes on to inform Johanna more fully of the destruction of the *Star* and of the sole survival among the wreckage of Thornhill, who had befriended Ingestrie on the voyage. Perhaps predictably, Johanna exonerates the ambitions of her lover, and displaces the blame both for his own misfortunes and for Thornhill's subsequent disappearance onto the temptations afforded by the lure of the actual 'string of pearls'. Jeffrey seems to understand her desire to shift any burden of responsibility from the individual to the object itself. He tells Johanna:

> I much fear that those precious pearls he had have been seen by some one who has not scrupled to obtain possession of them by his death [to which she responds:] Yes, it would seem so to me; but what are pearls to me. Oh! Would that they had sunk to the bottom of the India sea, from whence they had been plucked. Alas, alas! It has been their search for gain that has produced all these evils. We might have been poor here, but we should have been happy. Rich, we ought to have been in contentment; but now all I lost, and the world can present to me nothing that is to be desired, but one small spot, large enough to be my grave. (*PP* 131)

Johanna reluctantly places her trust in Jeffrey's own plans to uncover the immediate mystery of Thornhill's disappearance. The subsequent attempt of Jeffrey and his friend Captain Rathbone together to visit Todd's shop in the search for some sort of evidence, however, comes to nothing. Alive to the possibilities of detection by such suspiciously easy 'marks', Todd shaves the pair (who have rather ostentatiously posed as jewellery merchants) promptly and efficiently, and allows them to go on their way unmolested:

> They had no recource but to leave the shop; and when they had gone, Sweeney Todd, as he stropped the razor he had been using upon his hand, gave a most diabolical grin, muttering, –
> 'Clever – very ingenious – but it wouldn't do. Oh dear no, not at all! I am not so easily taken in – diamond merchants, ah! ah! And no objection, of course, to deal in pearls – a good jest that, truly, a capital jest. If I had been accustomed to be so easily defeated, I had not now been here a living man.' (*PP* 163)

*

In both Macbeth and Lady Macbeth the germ of crime was latent; they wanted only favourable circumstances to convert them into one of those criminal couples who are the more dangerous for the fact that the temptation to crime has come to each spontaneously and grown and been fostered by mutual understanding, an elective affinity for evil. Such couples are frequent in the history of Crime.

(H.B Irving, *A Book of Remarkable Criminals*)[19]

Only in the fourth chapter of *The String of Pearls* are readers introduced to Mrs Margery Lovett and her pie shop. Mrs Lovett's business is operated from premises in Bell Yard, one of the many streets that angled their way north of the main thoroughfare of Fleet Street, just within the ancient boundaries of the city, past Temple Bar. The first appearance of the woman whose status as Todd's murderous accomplice will be revealed only much later in the narrative, is again – much like the barber's own introduction – announced by the tolling of the bells of St Dunstan's. As the noon-day chimes of the church giants ring out across Fleet Street, customers rush from all sides into Lovett's Bell Yard shop:

Is it a fire? Is it a fight? Or anything else sufficiently alarming and extraordinary to excite the junior members of the legal profession to such a species of madness? No, it is none of these, nor is there a fat cause to be run for, which, in the hands of some clever practitioner, might become quite a vested interest. No, the enjoyment is one of a purely physical character, and all the pacing and racing – all this turmoil and trouble – all this pushing, jostling, laughing, and shouting, is to see who will get first to Lovett's pie shop.

Yes, on the left-hand side of Bell-yard, going down from Carey Street, was, at the time we write of, one of the most celebrated shops for the sale of veal and pork pies that London ever produced. High and low, rich and poor resorted to it; its fame had spread far and wide; and it was because the first batch of these pies came up at twelve-o'clock that there was such a rush of the legal profession to obtain them.

Their fame had spread even to great distances, and many of them carried them to the suburbs of the city as quite a treat to friends and relations there residing. And well did they deserve their reputation, those delicious pies! There was about them a flavour never surpassed, and rarely equalled; the paste was of a most delicate construction, and impregnated with the aroma of a delicious gravy that defies description. Then the small portions of meat that they contained were so tender, and the fat and the lean so artistically mixed up, that to eat one of Lovett's pies was such a provocation to eat another, that many persons who came to lunch stayed to dine, wasting more than an hour, perhaps, of precious time, and endangering – who knows to the contrary? – the success of some law-suit thereby. (*PP* 115)

The connections that link the 'fat causes' for which the young lawyers ought more properly (at least in their burgeoning, professional capacities as 'clever practitioners') to be running both with the succulent or even addictive meat pies, on the one hand, and with the passing of 'precious time' and the chaotic impulses of accumulation and acquisition, on the other, all stand spectacularly revealed even in this early passage. Lovett's shop exerts a magnetic, centripetal pull on anyone who happens to be close to it; yet it also exercises a no less compelling, centrifugal impulse that throws its allure *outward* into the city; the mysteriously enticing aroma of her baking draws customers to Lovett's shop, even while other patrons carry her pies to the suburbs, and so fling the infection emanating from Bell Yard far and wide across the sprawling urban landscape.

The appeal of Lovett's famous shop, however, would appear to be difficult for anyone to withstand. Her premises seem even to function as an informal social centre around which the lives of the young barristers and solicitors in training are focused:

> The counter in Lovett's shop was in the shape of a horseshoe, and it was the custom of the young bloods from the Temple and Lincoln's Inn to sit in a row upon its edge, while they partook of the delicious pies, and chatted gaily about one concern or another.
>
> Many an appointment for the evening was made at Lovett's pie shop, and many a piece of gossiping scandal was there first circulated. The din of tongues was prodigious. The ringing laugh of the boy who looked upon the quarter of an hour he spent at Lovett's as the brightest of the whole twenty-four, mingled gaily with the more boisterous mirth of his seniors; and, oh! With what rapidity the pies disappeared!
>
> They were brought up on large trays, each of which contained about a hundred, and from these trays they were so speedily transferred to the mouths of Mrs. Lovett's customers that it looked quite like a work of magic. (*PP* 115)

Even before we learn anything at all relating to the ingredients in Mrs Lovett's pies, the description of the shop's prodigious 'din of tongues' transforms the scene of her shop into a sort of Babel of vicious and even vaguely criminal activity – a scene in which scandalous rumours are not only circulated but given their earliest spur, a location wherein dubious assignations are both set and met. The speed with which the pies themselves are consumed is said to smack of 'magic' and enchantment. The Bell Yard pie shop is a venue that is at once part of yet also distinctly set apart from the more typically staid and sober law courts and chambers that surround it; it is a place of noise, speed and appetitive transformation in the midst of a diurnally plodding environment that more readily accommodates the stubborn and often sleepy intractability of the legal world.

Mrs Lovett is herself said to be one of the main attractions of the shop, as the grasping impulses of material, oral and erotic consumption become entwined with one another. 'For what', the reader is asked, but a female hand, and that female buxom, young, and good-looking, could have ventured upon the production of those pies. Yes, Mrs. Lovett was all that; and every enamoured young scion of the law, as he devoured his pie, pleased himself with the idea that the charming Mrs. Lovett had made that pie especially for him, and that fate or predestination had placed it in his hands.

And it was astonishing to see with what impartiality and what tact the fair pastry-cook bestowed her smiles upon her admirers, so that none could say he was neglected, while it was extremely difficult for anyone to say he was preferred. [Some] declared that her smile was cold and uncomfortable – that it was upon her lips, but had no place in her heart – that it was the set smile of a ballet dancer, which is about one of the most unmirthful things in existence.

Then there were some who went even beyond this, and while they admitted the excellence of her pies, and went every day to partake of them, swore that Mrs. Lovett had quite a sinister aspect, and that they could see what a merely superficial affair her blandishments were, and that there was

'a lurking devil in her eye'

that, if once roused, would be capable of achieving some serious things, and might not be so easily quelled again. (*PP* 115)

The otherwise unattributed phrase isolated by reason of its prominent quotation in this passage – 'a lurking devil in her eye' (vaguely redolent for some readers, perhaps, of lines from 'romantic' works such as Byron's 1817 *Mazeppa*) – would in time become something of a favourite of writers of gothic fiction (it shows up in Arthur Conan Doyle's *The Hound of the Baskervilles* (1901–2), for example, and its language had already been evoked in Washington Irving's 1820 'The Legend of Sleepy Hollow'). Much like Todd himself, Mrs Lovett is a figure who inspires a divided response amongst those who encounter her. Although 'buxom', 'young' and 'good-looking', Lovett possesses the set and inflexible smile of the manikin or effigy – a demonic grin that puts the more discerning of her young customers on their guard. The passage containing her earliest description is no less noteworthy, however, for the manner in which the possibly sinister aspects that lurk just beneath the 'superficial ... blandishments' of her physical appearance are linked to the achievement of appetite and desire. In a short scene subsequent to the description of Mrs Lovett's presence in the shop, in which she considers the desperate application of a 'half-famished, miserable-looking man' for employment in her bake-house, the reader glimpses the 'strange' expression on her countenance and first notes the 'low tone' in which she confesses even to herself, mysteriously, that a new cook – one that 'will suit for a few months' – will indeed soon be required (*PP* 164).

Todd, meanwhile, has attempted to dispose of the string of pearls, taking it to 'one of the most celebrated lapidaries in London' (*PP* 132). The jeweller, who maintains a small shop in Moorfields (not all that far from the residence of Johanna Oakley), is not above attempting to convince the barber that the jewels – which, in an initial moment of astonishment, he in fact acknowledges to be worth a small fortune of £12,000 – are fakes; he offers Todd a paltry £50 for the necklace, awkwardly and unconvincingly claiming that the pearls are counterfeits. Todd, not one to be taken in by any such clumsy attempt at deception, moves as if to leave the shop, at which point the jeweller sends up a loud cry of 'Stop thief!', obviously calculating that any authorities thus summoned would believe that it was Todd who had been attempting to rob the string of pearls from the jeweller himself to begin with. Hotly pursued both by the jeweller and by the mob that had been hastily roused by the hue and cry, Todd stumbles into a local thieves' den. The atmosphere described in the subsequent passage, coloured as it is by the sorts of details and language that readers would readily have associated with highwaymen, cutpurses and the criminal underworld of the city ('looby', 'tip-top man', 'swag of tin' etc.), is written in rather obvious imitation of similar sequences in works such as Dickens's *Barnaby Rudge* and the Newgate novels of Ainsworth and others, and to some extent merely caters to the popular taste for descriptions of dens of thievery in the literature of crime; yet the author manages also to exploit the dangerous situation in which Todd has so suddenly and unexpectedly found himself so as to emphasize the pervasive atmosphere of surveillance, and the fear that such omnipresent watchfulness entails. 'There is something awful in seeing a human being thus hunted by his fellows,' we are told,

> and although we can have no sympathy with such a man as Sweeney Todd, because, from all that has happened, we begin to have some very horrible suspicion concerning him, still, as a general principle, it does not reduce the fact that it is a dreadful thing to see a human being hunted through the streets. (*PP* 132)

The sympathetic insight that seems on one level only reluctantly to be extended to Todd in passages such as this one aspires to the kind of general social commentary of which Dickens would prove himself to be such a master. Even as it stands, however, the reader cannot help but be struck by the manner in which the dark and unknowable streets and alleys of the city at night turn even on a figure such as Todd himself – by the manner in which the pursuer or the hunter can so easily and so suddenly within such an environment become the hunted and the pursued. Writing on the element of the 'macabre' in Dickens's early novels, Humphrey House observed that even the most irremediably and intractably villainous of that novelist's grotesque characters – Sikes, Fagin, Daniel Quilp, Jonas Chuzzlewit – tend often and unexpectedly to reveal, if not a streak of good, then at least 'an immense depth of intricate, confused, and pitiable humanity'. 'Suddenly', House commented of Dickens's characters at such moments, 'their awakened sense of guilt, their fears, remorse, regrets, and above all their terrible loneliness strike out like lightning ...'.[20] Something of the empathy of which Dickens was himself capable can arguably be glimpsed in the author's gesture of understanding in passages such as this one.

There are soon several schemes afoot to discover for certain just what it is that takes place in Todd's barber shop, and just what has happened to those of his customers who would otherwise appear to have vanished into thin air. In addition to the combined attempts of Colonel Jeffrey and his friend Rathbone, Johanna Oakley has decided to take matters into her own hands. The young heroine is encouraged by her close friend Arabella Wilmot (whose name, again, has been taken straight out of Oliver Goldsmith's 1764 sentimental novel *The Vicar of Wakefield*, and who is the victim of having read one too many romantic novels herself) to disguise herself as a man and enter Todd's shop on her own. Johanna – already troubled at home by the undesirable attention of her mother's Revd Lupin, which her cousin Ben, the beefeater at the nearby Tower of London, takes it upon himself actively to discourage – decides to act on her own; when she once again meets with Colonel Jeffrey in the Temple Gardens, she keeps her plans to herself.

Todd makes a second attempt to exchange the string of pearls for some ready cash, this time embarking on a more elaborate plan – one that involves his assuming the unlikely disguise of a fashionable member of the royal court – and travelling east, to Uxbridge, to deal with a well-known money-lender and usurer by the name of John Mundel. Todd succeeds in deceiving Mundel into believing that in temporarily pawning the string of pearls for £8,000, he is acting on the authority of the Queen herself. 'He did not suppose for one moment that it was the Queen who wanted the money', we are told of Mundel, 'but his view of the case was, that she had lent the pearls to this nobleman to meet some exigency of his own, and that of course they would be redeemed very shortly' (*PP* 217). In the absence of his master, Tobias takes the risk of exploring the entirety of the Fleet Street shop, and is horrified by his discovery of a locked cupboard containing 'hats of all sorts and descriptions', and later, upstairs, a similar cache of walking-sticks, as well as innumerable numbers of umbrellas, swords and scabbards, boots and shoes, and piles of such personal items as watches, gold chains, snuff boxes, shoe-buckles and brooches. 'How could Sweeney Todd come by these articles', he asks himself in shock, 'except by the murder of their owners?' (*PP* 197). As the bells of St Dunstan's clock strike the hour and jar him out of his momentary paralysis, Toby decides instantly to flee the shop. His intention is to return briefly to his mother's small set of rooms, so that he can at least let her know of his own decision to escape the immediate threat of his situation by going to sea (a resolution that of course echoes the similar resolve of Mark Ingestrie).

Before he has the opportunity to effect any such plan, however, Tobias is kidnapped by Todd, who has returned home to his shop to be confronted by the evidence of his apprentice's discoveries. Todd instantly carries the boy off to Peckham Rye, where he plans to incarcerate him in the 'private' lunatic asylum of one Mr Fogg; it is a solution that he has obviously employed before. The unfortunate Tobias is fated to endure some grim treatment at the hands of Mr Fogg and his lumbering assistant, Mr Watson, before eventually escaping from Fogg's premises, and making his way back to his mother's home in London. The episode in Fogg's asylum permits the author to introduce the separate, inset narrative of another victim of the misuses to which contemporary laws regarding sanity and property could be put.

Colonel Jeffrey and his friend Rathbone, meanwhile, have watched yet another one of Todd's customers seemingly disappear within his shop before finally contacting a local magistrate by the name of Sir Richard Blunt. Blunt has already entertained a good number of his own suspicions with regard to Todd's activities. As he immediately recalls when Colonel Jeffrey tells him of his concern:

> A lady once in the street took a fancy to a pair of shoe-buckles of imitation diamonds that Todd had on, when he was going out to see some entertainment; she screamed out, and declared that they had belonged to her husband, who had gone out one morning, from his house in Fetter Lane, to get shaved. The case came before me, but the buckles were of too common a kind to enable the lady to persevere in her statement; and Todd, who preserved the most imperturbable coolness throughout the affair, was of course discharged. (*PP* 313)

With the help of his laconic and street-wise assistant, Crotchet, Sir Richard begins to make the connections that will eventually lead to Todd's capture. The introduction of Crotchet – 'as rough a specimen of humanity as the world has ever produced' – is among the more successful of the author's attempts to introduce humorous characters in the manner of Dickens. 'He was tall and stout', we are told of Sir Richard's assistant, 'and his face looked as if, by repeated injuries, it had been knocked out of all shape, for the features were most strangely jumbled together indeed, and an obliquity of vision, which rendered it a matter of doubt who or what he was looking at, by nice means added to his personal charms' (*PP* 313). The introduction of Sir Richard and Crotchet as the team whose detective work will effectively displace the rather less effective methods of Colonel Jeffrey and Rathbone likewise allows the author to indulge in the kind of comic exchanges that, at their best, similarly recall the idiolects of his Dickensian prototypes:

> 'Well, Crotchet' [asks Blunt], what do you think of all that? What does Sweeney Todd do with his customers?'
> Mr. Crotchet gave a singular and peculiar kind of grin, as he said, still looking apparently out of the window, although his eyes were really fixed upon the magistrate, –
> 'He *smugs* 'em.'
> 'What?'

'Uses 'em up, yer worship; it's as clear to me as mud in a wine glass, that it is. Lor' bless you, I've been thinking he does that 'ere sort of thing a deuce of a while, but I didn't like to interfere too soon, you see.' (PP 313)

In one of the most effective and memorable passages in the entire novel, Sir Richard is led by the local parish beadle and the churchwardens of St Dunstan's into the vaults that stretch in a series of maze-like caverns beneath the decaying fabric of the church. Well aware that the catacombs have not been used for the internment of bodies for many years, the church officials are shocked by the horrible stench that reaches them when the paving stones are removed, and the passage into the lower reaches of the structure revealed. Sir Richard descends into the vaults by the timid light of a single torch; as the link boy moves cautiously in front of him, the magistrate holds a handkerchief to his face and makes his way across the rugged flagstones:

> There was a death-like stillness in the place, and a few crumbling coffins which were in niches in the walls were, with their tenants evidently too old to give forth that frightful odour of animal decomposition which pervaded the place.
> 'You will see, Sir Richard,' said the churchwarden, producing a piece of paper, 'that according to the plans of the vaults I have here, this one opens into a passage that runs half-way round the church, and from that passage opens a number of vaults, not one of which has been used for many years past.'
> 'I see the door is open.'
> 'Yes, it is as you say. That's odd, Sir Richard, ain't it? Oh! Gracious! – just put your head out into the passage, and won't you smell it then!'
> They all tried the experiment, and found, indeed, that the smell was horrible. Sir Richard took a torch from one of the constables, and advanced into the passage. He could see nothing but the door of some of the vaults open: he crossed the threshold of one of them, and was away about a minute; after which he came back, saying. –
> 'I think we will retire now: we have seen enough to convince us all about it.'
> 'All about it,' said the churchwarden, 'what about it?'
> 'Exactly, that will do: – follow me, my man.'
> The officers, without the slightest questions or remarks, followed Sir Richard, and he began rapidly, with them at his heels, to ascend the stone staircase into the church again. (PP 346)

Passages such as this (readers had already been treated to a description of the stench emanating from the subterranean vaults, and the disgusted reactions of a visiting bishop and other church authorities in the serial's nineteenth chapter) are written in obvious emulation of some of the similarly 'gothic' scenes in novels such as William Harrison Ainsworth's splendidly spooky (and hugely successful) *Rookwood*. Like Ainsworth at his early best, the author is sure to retain that element of suspense that raises the worst suspicions of the reader, even as he only just falls short of the revelations that would confirm them.

At this point, however, the novel begins to pick up the narrative momentum that will carry it relentlessly towards its spectacular closing scenes. Johanna, disguised as one 'Charley Green' – a young orphan from Oxford, professing himself to be unfamiliar with London – is taken on in the absence of Toby as Todd's new apprentice. (The bells of St Dunstan's once again have a significant role to play here; Todd is convinced of the authenticity of Johanna's account only when she pretends, as Charley, not even to know where the church of St Dunstan's is to be found. Sir Richard Blunt, aware of Johanna's dangerous disguise, manages to let her know that he and his men are now keeping both Todd and his shop under constant watch, and alert her to be ready to act when the watch-word – 'St Dunstan's' – is given.)

It is only at this late point in the story that the reader actually sees Sweeney Todd and Mrs Lovett together in the same scene. Todd makes known his plans for shutting up his barber shop, and reveals his decision to leave England for Holland; he has also decided that it will be necessary to poison Mrs Lovett before he departs, so that she will have no opportunity of betraying him to the authorities. 'I must dispose of one whose implacable disposition I know well', he considers, 'and who would hunt me to the farthest corner of the earth, if she were not at peace in the grave. Yes, the peace of the grave must do for her. I can think of no other mode of silencing such a claim' (*PP* 346). Conveniently for Todd, Lovett writes to him regarding the growing despair of the young cook whom she had hired towards the beginning of the story (he has been the most troublesome cook she has had, 'because the most educated'). Had Lovett (who is herself no less eager than Todd to bring their partnership to an end) bothered to look closely, she would no doubt have recognized that 'the mysterious bond of union that held her and the barber together was not in that blooming state that it had been' (*PP* 362).

Sir Richard Blunt enters Todd's shop disguised as a wealthy farmer from Braintree, in Essex. The barber's final arrest is accomplished swiftly and with surprisingly little difficulty. 'The moment his back was turned', the narrator writes of Todd,

> the seeming farmer who has made such a good thing of his beasts, sprang from the shaving chair as if he had been electrified; and yet he did not do it with any appearance of fright, nor did he make any noise. It was only astonishingly quick, and then he placed himself close to the window, and waited patiently with his eyes fixed upon the chair, to see what would happen next.
>
> In the space of about a quarter of a minute, there came from the next room, a sound like the rapid drawing back of a heavy bolt, and then in an instant, the shaving chair disappeared beneath the floor; and the circumstances by which Sweeney Todd's customers disappeared was evident.
>
> There was a piece of the flooring turning upon a centre, and the weight of the chair when a bolt was withdrawn, by means of simple leverage from the inner room, weighed down one end of the top, which, by a little apparatus,

was to swing completely round, there being another chair on the undersurface, which thus became the upper, exactly resembling the one in which the unhappy customer was supposed to be 'polished off'.

Hence was it, that in one moment, as if by magic, Sweeney Todd's visitors disappeared, and there was the empty chair. No doubt, he trusted to a fall of about twenty feet below, on to a stone floor, to be the death of them, or, at any events, to stun them until he could go down to finish the murder, and – *to cut them up for Mrs. Lovett's pies!* after robbing them of all money and valuables they might have about them. (*PP* 381)

After believing himself to have dispatched his Essex farmer to the basement, Todd returns to the shop, where he is, much to his own horror, confronted by the form of Sir Richard:

When he got round [the chair] and saw his customer calmly waiting with the lather upon his face, the cry of horror that came gurgling and gushing from his throat was horrible to hear.

'Why, what's the matter,?' said Sir Richard.

'O God, the dead! The dead!,' cried Todd, 'this is the beginning of my punishment. Have mercy heaven! Oh, do not look upon me with those dead eyes.'

'Murderer!' shouted Sir Richard, in a voice that rung like the blast of a trumpet through the house.

In an instant he sprang upon Sweeney Todd, and grappled him by the throat. There was a short struggle, and they were down upon the floor together, but Todd's wrists were suddenly laid hold of, and a pair of handcuffs most scientifically put upon him by the officer[s], who, at the word 'murderer', that being a preconcerted signal, came from the cupboard where they had been concealed.

'Secure him well, my men,' said the magistrate, 'and don't let him lay violent hands upon himself. Ah! Miss Oakley, you are in time. This man is a murderer. I found out all the secret about the chair last night, after twelve, by exploring the vaults under the old church. Thank God we have stopped his career.' (*PP* 381)

The final scenes of the novel, in which the revelations follow hard upon one another, are exciting ones, and – as one might by now have expected – the action is signalled by the tolling of the giants of St Dunstan's:

One, two, three, four, five, six, seven, eight, nine! Yes, it is nine at last. It strikes by old St. Dunstan's church clock, and in weaker strains the chrono-metrical machine at the pie shop echoes the sound. What excitement there is now to get at the pies when they shall come! Mrs. Lovett lets down the square, moveable platform that goes upon pullies in the cellar; some machinery, which only requires a handle to be turned, brings up a hundred pies in a tray. These are eagerly seized by parties that have previously paid, and such a smacking of lips ensues as was never known. (*PP* 381)

The final batch of pies seems particularly heavy, yet still Mrs Lovett refuses any offers of assistance in hauling them to the shop floor:

> How the waggish young lawyers laughed as they smacked their lips, and sucked in all the golopshious gravy of the pies which, by-the-by, appeared to be all delicious veal that time, and Mrs. Lovett worked the handle of the machine all the more vigorously that she was a little angry at the officious stranger. What an unusual trouble it seemed to be to wind up those forth-coming hundred pies! How she toiled, and how she waited; but at length there came up the savoury steam, and then the tops of the pies were visible.
>
> They came up upon a large tray, about six feet square, and the moment Mrs. Lovett ceased turning the handle, and let a catch fall that prevented the platform from receding again, to the astonishment and terror of everyone, away flew all the pies, tray and all, across the counter, and a man, who was lying crouched down in an exceedingly flat state under the tray sprang to his feet.
>
> Mrs. Lovett shrieked, as well she might, and then she stood trembling and looking as pale as death itself. It was the doomed cook from the cellars, who had adopted this mode of escape.
>
> The throng of persons in the shop looked petrified, and after Mrs. Lovett's shriek, there was an awful stillness about a minute, and then the young man who officiated as cook spoke.
>
> 'Ladies and Gentlemen, – I fear that what I am going to say will spoil your appetites; but the truth is beautiful at all times, and I have to state that Mrs. Lovett's pies are made of *human flesh!*'
>
> How the throng of persons recoiled – what a roar of agony and dismay there was! How frightfully sick became about forty lawyer's clerks all at once, and how they spat out the gelatinous clinging portions of the rich pies they had been devouring. 'Good gracious! – oh, the pies! – confound it!' (*PP* 382)

All has now been revealed. Mrs Lovett manages to disappear briefly within the chaotic scene that follows these revelations, but her escape from justice is short-lived; her body is recovered shortly thereafter, Todd himself having poisoned the brandy for which he knew she would reach in her anxiety or despair. The barber, we are told, was promptly sent to Newgate. 'In due time', the author further and succinctly informs his readers, 'a swinging corpse was all that remained of the barber of Fleet Street' (*PP* 382). Mr Fogg's private lunatic asylum in Peckham Rye was broken up shortly thereafter, and Fogg himself was transported for his crimes. Mark, having misconstrued the significance of Johanna's meetings with Colonel Jeffrey and who in his romantic despair then passed himself off as Jarvis Williams in the service of Mrs Lovett, is finally reunited with Johanna, and a restored Tobias is eventually taken into Mark's service.

The narrative concludes with a reflection on the former patrons of Lovett's pie shop that simultaneously distances the reader from the activities that took place beneath Fleet Street and Bell Yard, whilst at the same time bringing those same activities home with the *frisson* of a vibrant, visceral memory – a memory which, even across such a distance in time, has lost none of its power to disturb the supposed 'sole survivor' of such outrages:

The youths who visited Lovett's pie-shop, and there luxuriated upon those delicacies, are youths no longer. Indeed, the grave has closed over all but one, and he is very, very old, but even now, as he thinks of how many pies he ate, and how he enjoyed the flavour of the 'veal', he shudders and has to take a drop of brandy. (*PP* 382)

The final passage of the novel returns its readers to the precise point from which they had first set out; we are left to contemplate the untold extent of the barber's activities, as if within the very shadows of the Fleet Street church that would appear so passively and imperturbably to have presided over Todd and Lovett's horrors:

Beneath the old church of St. Dunstan were found the heads and bones of Todd's victims. As little as possible was said by the authorities about it; but it was supposed that some hundreds of persons must have perished in the frightful manner we have detailed. (*PP* 382)

'As little as possible was said by the authorities about it': the supposedly official policy of reticence and even obfuscation on all matters relating to Todd's activities – the allegation, in fact, of an early nineteenth-century 'cover up' – in the end, paradoxically worked only to lend credence to the story. The facts relating to the barber's murderous spree and the suggestion of widespread cannibalism, it might have been argued, posed a genuinely dangerous threat to public safety and to the necessary maintenance of civic order and authority. The fear that public rioting would result should the specifics of Todd's crimes and the alleged number of victims who had fallen prey to his razor ('it was supposed', the closing lines of the story reminded its readers, 'that some hundreds of persons must have perished in the frightful manner we have detailed') provided a legitimate and all-too-believable excuse for any such recourse to a policy of official censorship. Readers familiar with the narrative of the Gordon Riots as it was related in the many reprintings of the *Newgate Calendar* throughout the late eighteenth and early nineteenth centuries would recall that the circulation of volatile rumours could easily lead to a situation wherein the constituted authorities would be 'held in terror'. 'The very existence of the City', as the *Calendar* reminded its readers of the dark days of June 1780, 'depended for some days on the caprice of an uncurbed multitude.'[21] Who could tell how the citizenry of London would respond were the gruesome details of Todd and Lovett's partnership revealed? The notion that the story was simply too volatile for public consumption at the time likewise lent some credence to the argument that it was only after a matter of many years – and within the pages of such publications as made a point of ferreting out the 'true' stories that would otherwise have been denied any public airing at all – that the narrative of Sweeney Todd could finally be told.

Chapter 5

I Shall Have to Polish Him Off:
Proto-Myths and Precedents

Beyond this there is nothing but prodigies and fictions, the only inhabitants are the poets and inventors of fables; there is no credit or certainty any further.
(Plutarch, 'Theseus' in *The Lives of the Noble Grecians and Romans*)[1]

The derogatory terms 'penny blood' and its successor 'penny dreadful' have – in our own day – become exceptionally vague and confused; one is often interchanged for the other, and their original meanings have been almost hopelessly obscured. Protesting the decision of the National Book Foundation in the United States to present an award for 'lifetime achievement' to the enormously popular novelist Stephen King in 2003, for example, the well-known academic Harold Bloom spluttered that King – a writer of gothic thrillers who has sold more books than any other writer in the history of publishing, and whose novels have earned him advances well in excess of $30 million – was undeserving of such an honour. Bloom appeared to cinch his argument with his dismissal of King as nothing more than 'a writer of penny dreadfuls'. 'But perhaps even that is too kind', Bloom reconsidered, adding of King: 'He shares nothing with Edgar Allen Poe.'[2] The fact that a critic of Bloom's stature and perception could himself muddle the generic characteristics of the 'penny dreadful' both with King's peculiar brand of fantasy and horror fiction, on the one hand, and with the gothic and romantic symbolism of Poe's demonic tales of mystery and imagination, on the other, is a striking testament to the extent of our contemporary confusion.

The term 'penny blood', as it was first used to describe a popular genre of literature in English that began in the first half of the nineteenth century, itself originated as a term of derision. The 'bloods', as one would expect, generally retailed for the affordable price of one penny. They offered inexpensive serial narratives to an emerging audience of (mostly) young readers for whom even the least expensive of the many novels being sold by booksellers would still have been considered something of a luxury. In the period of which we are speaking, the pound (£) was divided into 20 shillings (s.); each shilling (or 'bob') was in turn divided into 12 pence (d.), and each penny (or 'copper') was further subdivided into two halfpennies or ha'pence, or four farthings.[3] Although the highest paid, skilled workmen of the mid-Victorian period might expect to earn as much as 80 or 90s. per week, unskilled or agricultural labourers typically earned no more than 10s. a week; women could often expect as little as 6s. for performing much the same tasks. (It is extraordinarily difficult to estimate the 'actual' value that a pound or shilling would have held for the early and mid-Victorians since, as Daniel Pool has commented, 'we don't buy the same goods and don't have the same economic needs, [and this] makes the purchasing power of the two currencies fundamentally incommensurable'; some critics would value the pound early in the nineteenth century to be as much as £25 to £50 – or even £100 – today.[4]) Early in the nineteenth century, novels were often published in three or (occasionally) four volumes. Three-volume novels (or 'triple-deckers' or 'three-deckers' as they were commonly known) regularly sold for as much as 31s. 6d. (a guinea and a half for all three volumes) or £1.11s.6d., and so were available for direct purchase only to readers in upper-middle-class households or above. Novels published in two volumes usually cost about 18 shillings. Single-volume novels (typically cheap reprints of earlier publications, or religious novels or tales intended to appeal to very young or very old readers) could cost as little as one to five shillings. The price of purchasing fiction was so high that a common complaint of the period from publishers was that the British were 'not a book buying people'.[5] First editions generally numbered not in thousands but rather hundreds of copies, rather like the print runs of many scholarly or 'academic' titles today. 'Very few people', Kathleen Tillotson wrote of the period in the mid-twentieth century, '*bought* new fiction in volume form, and of these, fewer still would feel inclined to buy an unknown writer. ... But after reading early reviews of [a novel such as] *Jane Eyre*, the reader would probably order a copy from the circulating library. By the eighteen-forties the circulating library was everywhere – ...'.[6] A standard subscription to circulating libraries like Charles Mudie's – at a cost of one guinea or 21s. a year – was squarely aimed at a genteel audience of modestly aspirational middle-class readers. It is now commonly acknowledged that lending libraries such as Mudie's own 'had important effects upon the economics of publishing, for his manner of buying books in quantity in effect subsidized publishers, often making it easier for new authors to enter print – as long, that is, as they conformed to the demands of Mudie's and its audience'.[7]

Advances in education, such as Forster's Education Act of 1855, would eventually go some way towards ensuring the development of a larger and more comprehensively literate reading public. Those emerging generations of children who were fortunate enough to receive regular schooling throughout the century gradually benefited from the increased emphasis on a basic education in reading and writing. Industrial advances such as the development of the rotary steam printing press, type-setting machines, the use of new types of paper from Spanish 'esparto' grass, the possibilities of the paper-making machine patented by John Gamble as early as 1801, and (eventually) the abolition of the stamp tax on newspapers in 1855 and the duty on paper in 1861, also led, in time, to the introduction of new outlets for writers.[8] As Louis James noted in his important study *Fiction for the Working Man*, which was first published in 1963, 'the combination of cheap paper and mechanical printing was the greatest step forward in book production since [William] Caxton. It was also to have profound social and political effects.'[9] Simply put, from about 1830 it became increasingly possible for workers – for those still set apart from the emerging middle class – regularly to purchase and to read 'literature' and fiction of whatever sort they chose.

It was in this period, of course, that the serialization of novels became a popular form of publishing fiction. Originally, in the earliest years of the nineteenth century, older works – 'standard' novels – were those most likely to appear reprinted in the form of serial publications. Publisher John Harrison had to some extent led the way with his hugely popular *The Novelist's Magazine*, which ran from 1780 to 1788, but later innovators, such as William Emans and George MacGowan, began in the earliest decades of the nineteenth century to sell fiction in cheap parts of 16 pages or so to a new audience of workers, craftsmen and artisans.[10] Eventually, serialized novels were to be published in three forms: in newspapers, within weekly or monthly magazines, or (in the form pioneered by publishers such as Emans and MacGowan) in weekly or monthly 'parts'. Part issues in loose covers were widely popularized by Charles Dickens early in the period (although his early contemporary William Harrison Ainsworth disdained the form as too 'low'), but these separate 'parts' gradually gave way to magazine serialization as the century progressed (Dickens's first great success, *The Pickwick Papers*, had originally been published in 18 monthly parts at 1*s*. with a final double number at 2*s*., in 1836–7; the single-volume Cheap Edition of the same novel first published in 1847 retailed at 4*s*. 6*d*., or in cloth at 5*s*.; by the end of Dickens's career the first edition in monthly parts of his final, unfinished novel, *Edwin Drood*, was published in six numbers, still at the price of 1*s*. each; an 1873 bound edition cost 8*s*.)[11] Monthly serials, which generally ran for about 20 numbers, not only encouraged a taste among readers for the tension and suspense entailed by the form, but allowed authors the opportunity to respond to the emerging criticisms of readers even as they wrote their fictions.[12] Again, publication in separate monthly parts gradually gave way in the mid-century to serial publication within the pages of larger family and literary magazines, the most prestigious of which included Dickens's own *Household Words* (beginning in 1850) which was eventually

– in 1859 – incorporated into its successor, *All The Year Round*, which the novelist continued to edit until his death in 1870. Also popular was William Thackeray's *Cornhill Magazine*, which began publication in 1865, and which included within its pages novels by (among many other) Anthony Trollope, Elizabeth Gaskell, George Eliot and Thomas Hardy.

Serializing fiction in newspapers had always been the least reputable of the three options available to writers. Trollope himself had poked fun at newspaper publishing in his early novel *The Three Clerks* (1857), in which one of the title characters, Charley Tudor, reads aloud from his own novel – the parodically entitled *Crinoline and Macassar; or, My Aunt's Will* – which he has misguidedly allowed to be published in the pages of the no less satirically designated newspaper, the *Daily Delight*.[13] Trollope mocked the pretensions of such news-sheets to educate 'the British female public', and 'always to hold up a career of virtue for the lower orders as the thing that pays'.[14] Just one year later, Dickens's sometime collaborator, Wilkie Collins, writing in *Household Words*, went one step further, and lamented the standard of writing not merely in the newspapers, but in those journals supposedly dedicated to fiction, as well. 'The future of English fiction', Collins warned, 'may rest with the Unknown Public, which is now waiting to be taught the difference between a good book and a bad book. It is probably a question of time only. The largest audience for periodical literature, in this age of periodicals, must obey the universal law of progress, and must sooner or later learn to discriminate.'[15] But, as Graham Law has pointed out, 'the emergence of the Unknown Public tended in many respects to diminish rather than to multiply the demand for literary fiction, since it coincided with the gradual opening up of the divide between the serious and popular markets'.[16]

This widening 'divide' that separated exactly what the increasingly literate public *wanted* to read – as opposed to what its self-designated moral and aesthetic guardians felt that it *should* read – was a matter of considerable concern. No small amount of distress was voiced by the larger, established literary community that this new and rapidly expanding 'Unknown Public' tended to display what was almost universally regarded as an unwholesome taste for the literature of crime and the underworld. Yet the affinity of London writers for crime literature, it might be argued, could hardly be looked upon as something altogether *new*. As early as the sixteenth century, relatively popular writers such as Thomas Dekker and Robert Greene seemed to delight most in exploring the habits and features of the city's under-world; they tried as much as possible to employ the 'cant' or low language of thieves themselves, and openly depicted criminal practices, ranging from detailed descriptions of robberies and various forms of 'cheating law', to descriptions of the manner in which (for example) certain hidden trap-doors opening onto Fleet Ditch afforded 'easy means of getting rid of bodies'.[17] The sustained appetite among Londoners for apparently realistic depictions of the very real criminality that surrounded them would continue to manifest itself throughout the eighteenth century in works ranging from the fictions of Henry Fielding and the drama of George Lillo, to the earliest versions of what was eventually to become the *Newgate Calendar*. Alarmists early in the nineteenth century looked with horror on the representational excesses of the so-called 'Newgate novel' – those fictions mentioned earlier that took as their heroes criminals and highwaymen, and a type that flowered briefly in the 1830s in the works of William Harrison Ainsworth and Edward Bulwer-Lytton; mid-century critics were no less alive to the potential dangers posed by the 'sensation' novels by the likes of Wilkie Collins, Charles Reade and Mary Elizabeth Braddon; yet from where else did these same literary modes or subgenres arise, if not from the now respectable gothic fictions and novels of sentiment and sensibility that had flourished in the latter part of the eighteenth century? It became increasingly difficult for the moral and aesthetic guardians of the period to distinguish just what was acceptable from what was not.

Side by side with these subgenres of novelistic fiction grew the even more popular periodical narratives of the 'penny bloods'. The bloods were often dismissed by critics for their supposedly black-and-white characterization, and for their highly improbable melodramatic plots. Even today, a great many critics still confuse the bloods, however, with the distinctly different literary type that followed them – the 'penny dreadful'. The latter term was coined only in the last quarter of the nineteenth century, and – although, admittedly, originally used by some almost synonymously with 'penny blood' as a catch-all designation for any and all cheap literature designed for a juvenile or adolescent audience – was intended more specifically to designate stories such as those produced by supposedly 'reformed' publishers such as Edwin J. Brett, W.L. Emmett and Charles Fox from the late 1860s onward; these same publishers aimed squarely at a juvenile (and primarily male) readership. The reaction against the 'penny bloods' led eventually to the publication of magazines such as *Boys of England* (1866), the *Boy's Standard* (1875) and the *Boy's Own Paper*, the latter of which was published by the Religious Tract Society beginning in 1879. Penny bloods earlier in the century, by contrast, had tended to target a much wider audience which, though largely made up of the poorer members of the reading public, was by no means limited to the working classes. The form's exaggerated presentation of thrilling and bloodthirsty narratives – often of a specifically criminal nature, frequently 'historical' in subject, and almost always set within a pseudo-gothic landscape of dungeons, prison cells, castles, and wild, abandoned heaths – brought together elements of the earlier traditions of the 'gothic' novel with features of the morally ambivalent sensation novels, and appealed to a wider audience than would ever openly have acknowledged a stomach for such broadly 'sensational' material. These narratives tended to be written in what has sometimes been characterized as a short-breath, 'short-sentenced' style. They were frequently repetitious, and the central narrative was more often than not unapologetically padded with material only marginally related to its ostensible subject, so as to fill literally hundreds of columns. As E.S. Turner wrote of the prose style of bloods:

> There was no attempt to make an instalment end at a logical point in the narrative. Nor was there any attempt to build up a climax, in order to stimulate the reader to buy the next number.... It was by no means rare for the illustrations to refer to a previous part, or to a future part; occasionally they bore no relation to the story whatever. Spelling mistakes were nearly as copious as grammatical mistakes, and they were legion. Few of the writers of penny parts seemed to be happy about their moods and tenses. Any entry into the field of the conditional or the subjunctive was usually doomed to failure. Gradually extreme simplicity of style came to be cultivated ... Each paragraph consisted but of a single sentence, and five out of six sentences were strangled at birth. Quite a number of sentences, indeed, contained one noun, one verb, and nothing more. Sometimes they did not contain even a verb. All affectations like colons and semi-colons were ruthlessly purged, but exclamation marks were used profusely. Simplification – presumably for the benefit of the only-just-literate public and not (as some averred) for the convenience of the only-just-literate authors – was carried to a pitch never seen before or since.[18]

Until Louis James's 1963 study, noted above, the 'bloods' had never really been permitted to play any significant role in – or had never been perceived even as having contributed in some way to determining the directions of – what might be characterized as the 'mainstream' traditions of canonical English literature. Even today, such periodical literature is often admitted only with great reluctance to have formed an important strand of the narrative traditions in English prose. Although some of this critical neglect can be legitimately attributed to the comparative rarity of many of the original publications themselves (it is thanks largely to the efforts and enthusiasm of a single individual, 'Barry Ono' or Frederick Valentine Harrison, that a great many of these works survive in any form at all), or from the fact that the 'bloods' when taken as a literary kind constitute a truly gargantuan body of work, the tendency of literary critics to dismiss the form as morally degrading, debilitating and positively criminal in itself has been far more damaging to its reputation. As the commentator David Oswell has observed: 'The mix of sensational narrative, relatively low price, and large working class readership gave the established English middle-class cause for concern.... . The penny dreadful and its readership was regularly castigated in the middle class periodicals of the time.'[19] Oswell's assertions can be amply supported by reference to debates on the subject throughout the nineteenth century; the pages of *The Times*, certainly, have often testified to contemporary concerns with regard to the pernicious effects of such 'literature'. In November 1888, the following article appeared under the headline 'Criminal Literature', for example, detailing some of the questions that had been raised in the House about the possible connections that explicitly linked the reading of penny bloods to the confessions of actual criminals:

> Mr. Channing, for Mr. S. Smith, asked the Secretary of State for the Home Department whether his attention had been drawn to the report that the two boys now waiting their trial for murder in Maidstone Gaol had been addicted by their own confession to the reading of such books as 'Dick Turpin' and 'Varney the Vampire: or, the Feast of Blood' and 'Sweeney Todd' and that one of them had told a correspondent of the Tunbridge Wells Advertiser that he was prepared for his fate now he had made his name known; whether he was aware that there was an enormous circulation of criminal literature among the young, and that about 25 English newspapers had been publishing the lives of Charles Peace, William Palmer, the Rugeley Poisoner, and the murders of Burke and Hare; whether he was aware that those stories attractively written were widely circulated and read by enormous numbers of children, and instigated many of them to the commission of crimes.[20]

Today's readers have of course grown familiar with those arguments that would insist on a direct, causal connection between the deleterious effects of 'subversive literature', on the one hand, and the development of a criminal mentality and of patterns of criminal behaviour, on the other. Most attempts to curb the youthful consumption of 'attractively written' crime and horror stories, however, have failed miserably. Campaigners in the mid-twentieth century would themselves be no less alarmed than their Victorian counterparts had once been by penny bloods by the supposed threat posed by American horror comics such as EC's (i.e. 'Entertaining Comics') *The Haunt of Fear*, *The Vault of Horror*, *Tales from the Crypt*, and *Crime SuspenStories*. In early 1954, Frederic Wertham, then a prominent liberal psychiatrist and the director of the 'mental hygiene' clinic at New York's Bellevue Hospital, published his provocatively titled *Seduction of the Innocent*. Wertham's study – which presented 'scientific evidence' of the wanton damage supposedly inflicted on young minds by violent comics – led to considerable public alarm, and eventually to Hearings before the Sub-committee to Investigate Juvenile Delinquency of the Committee on the Judiciary House, which was opened at the Foley Square Court House in Manhattan. By the summer of 1954, the call to eliminate comic books had become international. An exhibit of horror and crime comics, prominently labelled 'Made in the USA', even toured Great Britain; although Winston Churchill himself, on seeing the exhibit in the House of Commons, is said to have requested, 'Pass them over. I should like to read some horror comics,' hardly anyone dared speak up in their defence.[21] Wertham's campaign was perceived to have been a success at the time (a Comics Code Authority was officially established to regulate the industry in America in September 1954, and EC comics folded), but its long-term effects were negligible, at best. Subsequent campaigns against the often violent and explicitly sexual representations contained in popular song lyrics, video games and many of today's movies and DVDs have been similarly vocal and high-profile – and more often than not similarly ineffectual.

Yet all is not lost. It is more than likely that however dangerous, tasteless, or simply shocking such material may appear at the time, all such allegedly 'subversive' literature – whether it takes the form of penny bloods, horror novels, graphic comic books, obscene lyrics, or explicitly violent media of any sort – seems very quickly, in retrospect, to appear tame and even innocuous. One tends always to wonder what 'all the fuss' was about in the first place and – more often than not – sneer at the supposed prudery of preceding generations. Few would argue, certainly, that out-and-out censorship is ever a legitimate or effective response to such perceived threats; draconian tactics are rarely in order. 'Research funded by the BBC', critics such as Oswell insist, 'has supposedly shown that children not only want television programmes specifically for themselves, but also that they are more "moralistic" – in their assessment of suitable stories for themselves – than television producers'.[22] The rediscovery and reappropriation of the penny blood by popular children's authors such as Philip Pullman in the very late twentieth and early twenty-first centuries (in works such as the 'Sally Lockhart quartet', including *The Ruby in the Smoke*, *The Tiger in the Well* etc.) may, if anything, signal the re-emergence and incorporation of the once dreaded form of the blood as part of the 'respectable' tradition of literature for children. Pullman has even resurrected one of the specific 'stars' of the early blood, 'Spring-Heeled' Jack, in his own 1989 fiction of the same name. A legendary criminal more frequently associated with Jack the Ripper and Sweeney Todd himself, 'Spring-Heeled' Jack was suddenly being described by Pullman as 'a character from Victorian penny dreadfuls [sic] who was a sort of early Batman who dressed up as the devil to scare evil-doers'.[23] One need only wait long enough, it would seem, before even the most dastardly villains and highwaymen will somehow be made safe for even the youngest of audiences.

The most famous and arguably the most influential publisher of penny bloods throughout the mid-nineteenth century was Edward Lloyd (1815–90). Working consistently with a small handful of tremendously prolific if poorly paid writers, Lloyd was among the first to recognize and fully to exploit the extent of the new reading public's taste for narratives of crime and criminals. As a young man, Lloyd had worked in a solicitor's office and had excelled in the study of shorthand at the London Mechanics' Institution in Chancery Lane. By the time he was 18, he had already published a volume explaining what he presented to the public as his own system of stenography or shorthand. His *Lloyd's Stenography* (1833) was in actual fact a pirated copy of *Pitman's Shorthand*; Lloyd simply stole the text of the original, put his own name on the cover, and undersold his competitor. As a newsagent, Lloyd had soon opened a number of shops in the capital that specialized in the sale of comic valentines, theatrical 'portraits' and penny story books.[24] As Lloyd's most recent biographer, Rohan McWilliam, observed of the publisher's early career:

> Lloyd launched himself into a career as a leading publisher of cheap and mostly sensational literature aimed at the working class. Among these were a series of plagiarisms of the work of Charles Dickens that included *Nikelas Nickelbery* (1838), *Oliver Twiss* (1838–9), and *The Penny Pickwick* (1837–9); the latter apparently enjoyed sales of 50,000 copies. He also started a series of periodicals mainly containing popular fiction which included Lloyd's *Penny Weekly Miscellany* (1842–7) and *Lloyd's Penny Atlas* (1842–5). In addition, he published songbooks and treatises on domestic economy. In September 1843 he moved his offices to 12 Salisbury Square, near Fleet Street, which became the centre of his 'penny dreadful' publishing industry.[25]

Lloyd's plagiarisms of Dickens appeared under the pseudonym 'Bos', in obvious imitation of Dickens's own early pen-name, Boz (the publisher's original intention to ascribe the piracies to 'Boaz' had been ruled out only because it was deemed to be 'too Biblical').[26] As McWilliam notes, because of the location of Lloyd's printing offices among the cluster of alleys and warehouses just off Fleet Street, at 12 Salisbury Square, Lloyd and his stable of writers were soon dubbed the 'Salisbury Square School'. Ironically, it was in Salisbury Square (then called Salisbury Court) that Samuel Richardson had first set up as a printer in about 1724, and it was there that he had written much of his celebrated 1740 bestseller *Pamela*, as well as significant portions of his later novels *Clarissa* (1747–8) and *Sir Charles Grandison* (1754). Salisbury Court had played host to such figures as William Hogarth and Samuel Johnson, and Oliver Goldsmith had spent some time correcting proofs there in 1756–7. It is rather striking that the same physical location might be regarded as the birthplace both of those works that were in time to form the foundational, textual basis for the 'classic' and canonical tradition of English fiction, as well as those 'bloods' and 'shockers' that would no less assuredly be looked upon as its alternative and disreputable (bastard) cousin.

Much of Lloyd's success in the earliest years of Victoria's reign was due to the fact that he was unapologetic about stealing his material from the most popular writers of the day. The Copyright Act of 1842 made such plagiarisms more difficult, but Lloyd continued to lift much of his copy from older works such as the *Newgate Calendar*. He had also scored a major hit in 1836, when he issued the first of what would prove in time to be many editions of his *History and Lives of the Most Notorious Pirates of All Nations*; he followed this with *The History of and Lives of the Most Notorious Highwaymen, Footpads ... and Robbers of Every Description* (1836–7). (Lloyd was not – as has often been asserted – the publisher of 1835's *Calendar of Horrors*; that work would later be attributed to him largely on the basis of his reputation as the most prominent publisher of penny bloods.)

Throughout the 1840s, Lloyd continued to publish several series of 'penny-a-week Gothic shockers', historical romances and melodramatic domestic tragedies in his weekly newspapers.[27] Indeed, it is estimated that he produced no fewer than 200 separate serial fictions in the years between 1836 to 1856 alone. 'Lloyd also', as McWilliam notes, 'moved into journalism, publishing *Lloyd's Illustrated London Newspaper* for a penny in September 1842 as a rival to the *Illustrated London News*.' The paper was originally unstamped but was compelled by the stamp office to pay the duty, as the paper contained news. It was then re-launched on 27 November price 2*d*. In 1843 the paper became *Lloyd's Weekly London Newspaper*; it was to continue under this title until 1931, 'one of the most successful newspapers of the Victorian period and the first of the cheap Sunday newspapers aimed at the working class'.[28] Lloyd's short-lived *The People's Periodical and Family Library* began publication in 1846, and contained primarily periodical literature (as opposed to news items); each issue comprised 16 pages, with an engraving on the front page. The actual text in *The People's Periodical* was presented to readers in three tightly printed columns. Lloyd would later in his career attempt to distance himself from the alleged disrepute of his earliest publications, although he would never quite lose his flare for self-promotion. As McWilliam writes of the publisher's later projects:

> Lloyd became increasingly concerned about the respectability of his publica-
> tions, a move signalled by his abandonment of 'penny dreadfuls' in the early
> 1850s and the appointment in 1852 of the popular writer Douglas Jerrold
> (1803–1857) as editor of *Lloyd's Weekly Newspaper*. Circulation rose thereafter.
> By 1853 the paper was selling 90,000 copies to a lower-middle-class and
> working-class readership, particularly in London, although the paper was
> distributed throughout the country and abroad; it enjoyed a strong following
> among women and small property owners. The abolition of the stamp and
> paper duties allowed for a reduction in price to 1*d*. in 1861. By 1872 the paper
> was selling half a million copies. Lloyd was devoted to publicity, scouring the
> country for hoardings to advertise his paper. At one time, he paid his staff with
> coins on which his newspaper's name was embossed so that they would enter
> the currency; he was only stopped by government intervention.[29]

Edward Lloyd may have been its publisher, but exactly who was it, then, who actually wrote *The String of Pearls* and introduced Sweeney Todd to the English reading public? Which individual member of the 'Salisbury School' is to be credited with his creation? Unfortunately, the 'invention' and writing of penny bloods was an extremely casual matter. Attributions of authorship are bound to be – in the words of one recent historian of the form, Helen R. Smith – 'haphazard and accidental'.[30] As an earlier chronicler of 'bloods', W.O. Lofts, had put it, 'the whole history of ... [Lloyd's 'penny bloods'] seems to be riddled with misleading statements, incorrect data, and pure guesswork'.[31]

In her detailed bibliographical survey of the authors of the original penny stories, published in 2002, Smith herself attempted to put to rest the long-disputed question as to precisely who among Lloyd's team or 'stable' of authors had been responsible for the conception and actual writing of *The String of Pearls* as it had first appeared in 1846–7.[32] Noting that earlier studies and surveys referred to the subject – including Montague Summers's mammoth *Gothic Bibliography* (1940) – had long been recognized to contain numerous errors, Smith attempted to make use of such material as the advertisements for Lloyd's publications so as convincingly to narrow down the possible attribution to a contest between two main contenders: Thomas Peckett Prest and James Malcolm Rymer.

Prest had in fact long been credited with being the author of the tale, and many sources continue to attribute the authorship of *The String of Pearls* solely to him. Prest – whose name begins to be associated with Lloyd in about 1835–6 – was born in May 1810 in Marylebone, London.[33] By his early 20s, he appears already to have achieved some reputation as a song-writer and performer in local saloons and singing clubs, and he soon became a hack writer for the unstamped periodical press. In the late 1830s, Prest also began writing melodramas for the Pavilion Theatre. As Louis James and Helen R. Smith note of Prest's early career, it was at this point that his work became inextricably connected to Lloyd's own, and to some of the titles already mentioned above:

> [Prest's] quest for new material drew him to the work of Dickens, and in 1836 Edward Lloyd, then a minor publisher of ephemera, issued Prest's *The Sketch Book*, by 'Bos' in penny numbers. In April 1837, a year after Dickens (Boz) had begun *Pickwick Papers* (1836–7) in monthly shilling parts, Prest began writing a penny weekly serial, *The Posthumous Notes of the Pickwick Club, or, The Penny Pickwick*, by 'Bos' (1837–8). Prest's version freely adapted and expanded Dickens's work for a working-class readership. Aided by spirited woodcuts by the popular cartoonist C. J. Grant, 'this disgraceful fabrication', as G. A. Sala noted, 'had an immense sale'.... At over 850 pages it was considerably longer, and at the time probably sold more copies, than Dickens's original. Prest followed this success with other adaptations, including *Oliver Twiss* (1838), *Nickelas Nicklebery* (1838), *Pickwick in America!* (1839), *A Legend of the Tower of London* (1840) by 'J. H. Hainsforth' after the novel by W. H. Ainsworth, and a plagiarism of Henry Cockton's *Valentine Vox, The Adventures of Valentine Vaux* by Timothy Portwine (1840).[34]

Early in Prest's career many of his works were published under his own name, although it seems that as time wore on he began increasingly to produce a great deal of material for Lloyd that was then published anonymously. 'Prest's most popular single work, the gypsy romance *Ela, the Outcast* (1839–40),' it is noted,

was followed by over sixty 'bloods' written for Lloyd in the 1840s. These showed a remarkable versatility in adapting literary genres – historical fiction after Scott in *The Hebrew Maiden* (1840), naval in *Gallant Tom* (1840), Gothic in *The Death Grasp* (1841), and domestic in *Emily Fitzormond* (1841), while a novel like *The Death Ship, or, The Pirate's Bride and the Maniac of the Deep* (1846) combines them all. Possibly as a result of ill health his fiction output decreased in the 1850s, and his last major novel was *Grace Walton, or, The Wanderers of the Heath* (1857). He continued to write melodramas, notably *The Miser of Shoreditch* (the Standard Theatre, 1854) and *Lucy Wentworth* (prize-winning play, the City of London Theatre, 1857).[35]

Prest's later life was complicated by his worsening alcoholism. He eventually died penniless, at his home in Islington, in June 1859, at the age of 49. 'Although not possessing a major creative talent', his biographers concede, 'Prest wrote vigorous, stylised prose that popularised penny fiction at the moment when an increasingly literate working-class public were tiring of political and educational reading and looking for entertainment. With his knowledge of popular taste and in particular melodrama he adapted middle-class writing for a popular audience, facilitating a significant stage in the development of literature for the masses.'[36]

James Malcolm Rymer (1814–84) has been described as 'a more retiring writer' than Prest, but he, too, was by any measure extraordinarily hard-working and productive. He was said at one point in his career (by his contemporary Thomas Catling) to have been working on no fewer than ten serials or stories simultaneously.[37] Curiously, Rymer never published under his own proper name, 'choosing instead to employ a number of pseudonyms, the most common of which were M. J. Errym and Malcolm J. Merry, but which also included Marianne Blimber, Nelson Percival, J. D. Conroy, Septimus R. Urban, Bertha Thorne Bishop, and Captain Merry USN'.[38] His near-contemporary, George Augustus Sala, who wrote about Rymer in his 1894 volume *London Up to Date* (1894), noted that the author had in his youth worked as an illustrator for Lloyd before moving on to writing his own fiction, and Louis James pointed out that 'some of [Rymer's] own fiction was illustrated by woodcuts with distinctive quality and panache, probably indicating the hand of the author'. His most popular pieces included the penny blood *Ada, the Betrayed* (*c*.1843; reprinted 1846), and *Varney the Vampyre*. Sala referred dismissively to Rymer as a 'penny-a-liner', but towards the end of his life his financial situation appears to have become more secure and, unlike Prest, he died reasonably secure in 1884, leaving an estate of close to £8,000.

Smith's central point regarding the contest between Prest and Rymer for the authorship of *The String of Pearls* is that reading the story as it was first published in *The People's Periodical*, it simply 'does not feel like a work by Prest'.[39] The attribution of the 1846–7 serial to Prest had been made by almost every researcher on the subject subsequent to the initial 1963 publication of Louis James's *Fiction and the Working Man* (James, who had discovered a portion of *The String of Pearls* in Rymer's handwriting, had in fact written in his own volume that 'the version [of the Sweeney Todd story] known in England *may* have originated when Thomas Peckett Prest was looking through back numbers of *The Tell-Tale* for usable material).[40] Others had insisted that Prest had merely taken over the authorship of a tale that had been set going by another bloods author, George Macfarren, whose sight or poor health had prevented him from continuing work on the story himself. The confusion over the authorship of the story had, again, been compounded by writers and researchers earlier in the twentieth century who had likewise mistakenly placed George Dibdin Pitt's February 1847 version of the story, written for the Britannia Theatre, Hoxton, in 1842 on the stage before the appearance of the 1846–7 serial itself.[41] Most significantly for Smith's argument, however, was the simple fact that the story had been advertised for sale by Edward Lloyd himself as the product of Rymer, not Prest. Moreover, the attribution of an early American edition of the work *c.*1853 credits the work to one 'Captain Merry' – an obvious anagram of 'Rymer'. 'So far', Smith wrote in 2002, 'my research [suggests] a considerable reassignment of authorship, supported by more confident ascriptions from title page and advertisement evidence and some consideration of style.' While admitting that much work remained to be done on the lives and circumstances of both Prest and Rymer, Smith nevertheless convincingly reattributed the tale to James Malcolm Rymer, noting that the same author's *A Mystery in Scarlet* had delighted the author Robert Louis Stevenson; she suggested too that Rymer was an author who 'now deserved proper reassessment as a writer'.[42]

Dick Collins has subsequently questioned Smith's claims in favour of Rymer, noting that on the basis of Smith's evidence alone, 'we cannot simply hand it over to Rymer'. 'What Smith failed to note', Collins pointed out,

> was that the advertisement referred, unequivocally, not to the 1847 version but to the second, larger and inferior 1850 version. The 1847 version was always referred to simply as *The String of Pearls: A Romance*, and by no other title; the subtitle *A Sailor's Gift* refers to the 1850 version only. Given the similarity between the expansions to [*Varney the Vampire*] and those to *The String of Pearls*, it is quite possible that a third (fourth?) hack was brought into the already composite work. Both text and advertisement support this theory.[43]

Smith's reattribution of *The String of Pearls* to Rymer, Collins concludes, 'cannot be taken as fact'. In attempting himself to answer the question of who was the first author of the serial narrative, Collins conceded that the writer's identity remains a matter of pure guesswork. He nevertheless felt confident in suggesting two further candidates for the honour. The first of these, E.P. Hingston, was a dilettante writer who lived in Paris, and financed his life by writing pieces for Lloyd. The second – Albert Richard Smith – was throughout the 1840s a regular contributor to *Bentley's Miscellany* and served as the regular drama critic of the *Illustrated London News*; Smith was the author of nearly 30 novels, including an account of the career of a French poisoner in *The Marchioness of Brinvilliers* (1846).[44] 'To sum up the problem of authorship', Collins concluded,

> Lloyd accepted and bought a story from someone unknown, and gave it to a staff-writer, probably Prest, to bring in line with Lloyd's idea of a good Penny Dreadful. Three years later, he decided to reissue it on its own, and asked someone else, probably Rymer, to expand it for as long as people kept buying it. And this is all we can say on the matter. *The String of Pearls* remains anonymous until further notice.[45]

Whether or not one accepts Smith's assertion of the very real possibility that James Malcolm Rymer deserves to be credited as the 'author' of *The String of Pearls* as it was first published by Edward Lloyd in 1846–7 and – consequently – that he deserves recognition likewise for being *the* creator of the character of Sweeney Todd himself, or whether one decides rather to rest with the more judicious scepticism of Collins, the twenty-first-century reader finds him or herself having advanced only part of the way towards establishing the origins of the tale itself. How did Rymer (or Prest, Hingston Smith, etc.) first come to think of the story? How was it *conceived*? Was it – as so many over the years have insisted on believing – based to any degree in actual historical fact? Or was Rymer himself simply the writer who happened fortuitously to pull together, in print, the strands of several narratives and narrative traditions that had already existed in some shape or form for many years?

We have already had cause to note that such myths and legends relating to the phenomenon of urban cannibalism had been circulating for many generations and in many different countries – indeed, many of them continue to do so to this day. These same myths had, again, most prominently featured in Dickens's 1843–4 novel *Martin Chuzzlewit*. The major, seemingly proleptic or anticipatory references in that same novel to the activities of Sweeney Todd and Mrs Lovett (although they are not, of course, referred to by name) are all associated with the sweet-tempered and gentle character of Tom Pinch. In Dickens's novel, Tom is the devoted admirer and long-suffering 'assistant' to the monumentally hypocritical figure of the Wiltshire-based architect and surveyor, Seth Pecksniff. After Tom's eyes have finally been opened to the extent of his patron's self-serving cant and hypocrisy in Chapter 31 of the novel, he journeys from just outside Salisbury to the capital, where he eventually sets up housekeeping with his sister Ruth (who has been similarly exploited and abused in her position in the city as a governess). Tom's departure from the country and his arrival in London are recounted by the author in the fourteenth monthly 'part' of the novel (of an eventual 19 parts), which comprises Chapters 36 to 38 in any complete edition of the work;

this instalment originally appeared in February 1844.[46] Upon his arrival in London, the stunned and giddy Tom is quite literally clueless (or clew-less). The city itself appears to him to be one vast and incomprehensible labyrinth of 'countless turnings' and 'countless mazy ways'.[47] He first seeks out his old friend John Westlock, whom he knows to occupy a set of rooms in Furnivall's Inn, High Holborn; once together, the two men head out in search of Tom's sister Ruth. Tom knows that the household to which his sister is attached is that of 'a wealthy brass-and-copper founder's' in Camberwell.[48] Westlock, having accompanied his old friend to that same neighborhood, and feeling confident that he has 'put him beyond the possibility of mistaking' his way, leaves him to handle the situation for himself. Tom's friend would appear to have been less than completely observant with regard to his companion's true state of mind, however. As Dickens tells the readers, Pinch is far from certain as to his surroundings:

> So many years had passed since Tom was last in London, and he had known so little of it then, that his interest in all he saw was very great. He was particularly anxious, among other notorious localities, to have those streets pointed out to him which were appropriated to the slaughter of countrymen; and was quite disappointed to find, after a half-an-hour's walking, that he hadn't had his pocket picked.[49]

Tom soon 'rescues' his sister from her unhappy situation, and the siblings immediately begin searching for lodgings in the neighborhood of Islington. So happy is he once again to be in the company of his sister, and so caught up is he in their search for somewhere they might live together in a 'cheap neighborhood ... not too far from London', that Tom completely forgets his earlier promise to return to Westlock at Furnivall's Inn; he finally recalls the appointment with some alarm, and hurries to meet him:

> 'Upon my word', thought Tom, quickening his pace, 'I don't know what John will think has become of me. He'll begin to be afraid I've strayed into one of those streets where the countrymen are murdered, and that I have been made meat pies of, or some such horrible thing'.[50]

Dickens immediately reassures his readers, however, that:

> Tom's evil genius did not lead him into the dens of any of those preparers of cannibalic pastry, who are represented in many standard country legends as doing a lively retails business in the Metropolis.[51]

Peter Haining, writing in 1993, commented of these two passages: 'Although these are clearly references to Sweeney Todd, Dickens may well have refrained from being more specific because of the possibility that some among his readers might have lost friends or relatives in the infamous barber's shop a little over forty years earlier.'[52] Such speculation is of course absolute nonsense. The 'preparer of cannibalic pastry' had yet to be incarnated as Mrs Lovett, and Sweeney Todd himself had still to be granted a local habitation and a name. Dickens's fiction merely confirms the fact that those cautionary urban or rural myths, which suggested that 'countrymen' who journeyed to the city risked disappearing entirely or being 'gobbled up' by the vast metropolis, had already been circulating throughout England for some time (hence the reference to the seeming multitude of 'standard' or well-established folk rumours). Although – to use the terminology of folklore scholars such as Jan Harold Brunvald – the basic motifs or 'proto-legends' that came eventually to constitute Todd's narrative had already passed through a phase of widespread 'communal recreation' (i.e. 'the process by which oral folklore varies as it is passed from person to person in a folk group'), they had yet to be consolidated into any *single* narrative fiction.[53] If anything, Dickens's own language suggests that they were still manifesting themselves in the more traditional forms of oral performance and transmission.

Be that as it may, the near synchronicity of Dickens's fragmentary allusions to urban cannibalism in *Martin Chuzzlewit* and the full-blown appearance of Sweeney Todd and Mrs Lovett in Lloyd's *String of Pearls* – separated as they are by just a little over two years – would appear to insist that the imaginative nexus that linked the explosive growth of London and its rapacity, on the one hand, with the anxieties that characterize the threat of anonymity and disappearance within the brooding metropolitan environment, on the other, were an extraordinarily forceful part of the urban zeitgeist in the early 1840s. In fact, the two explicit references to the proto-Sweeney-esque legends of cannibalism in *Martin Chuzzlewit* are merely the most obvious examples of a pervasive fear of the city that is present throughout Dickens's novel – a novel elsewhere marked by recurring references to the 'maze' of the urban landscape and the threat of consumption, and also by reassuring images of domestic comfort, order, precision and accountability that alone help to insulate the individual against the onslaught of the city, and the complete breakdown between those boundaries that separate the public from the private world. (Dickens himself seems to have shared Tom's obsession with the very idea of 'order'. With the help of his sister Ruth, Tom sets about turning their new home into 'a paradise of neatness and precision'; the critic John Carey observed that although Ruth later 'protests to her husband [John Westlock] that she wants to be something much worthier than a doll in a doll house, it's plain that Dickens finds her most delicious simply as that'.)[54]

Dickens's vision is not an entirely pessimistic one. Tom's own intrepid negotiation and eventual conquest of the maze of London is represented by the snug success of his domestic establishment with his sister Ruth. In the novel's fifteenth 'part' (at the beginning of Chapter 39), and following her initial, modest success in preparing chops for the siblings' evening meal, Ruth Pinch famously proposes making a beef-steak pudding. The 'pudding' stands in some respects as the Pinchs' defiant, culinary gesture against the mysterious forces of the metropolis that would have had them turned into puddings and pies themselves. '"In the whole catalogue of cookery, there is nothing I should like so much as a beef-steak pudding!" cried Tom: slapping his leg to give the greater force to his reply.'[55] Strikingly, Tom further responds to his sister's initial hesitation in undertaking such a comparatively ambitious meal by facetiously observing that her own intimation that she isn't certain exactly how the dish will turn out only adds further zest to the dish. '"Why", said Tom, "this is capital. It gives us a new, and quite uncommon interest in the dinner. We put in a lottery for a beef-steak pudding, and it is impossible to say what we may get. We may make some wonderful discovery, perhaps, and produce such a dinner as never was known before." '[56] Within the easy space of only three chapters (or one monthly part), Tom has moved from the position of being a wary and suspicious potential victim – from possibly constituting the ingredients of a meat pie himself – to being complicitous in the dubious mysteries of their very creation. The figurative language and imagery of the novel that posits the comfort of homemade products – domestic cookery – against the morbid uncertainty and unreliability of urban consumption, generally, is further highlighted when Ruth subsequently confesses to both her brother and John Westlock to having substituted one ingredient called for in the recipe – beef suet – with an improvised succedaneum – flour and eggs. Tom's response to this modest revelation verges on hysteria:

> 'Oh good gracious!' cried Tom. 'Ours was made with flour and eggs, was it? Ha, ha, ha! A beefsteak pudding made with flour and eggs! Why anybody knows better than that! *I* know better than that! Ha, ha, ha!'
>
> It is unnecessary to say that Tom had been present at the making of the pudding, and had been a devoted believer in it all through, and was tickled to that degree of having found her out, that he stopped in Temple Bar to laugh; and it was no more to Tom, that he was anathematised and knocked about by the surly passengers than it would have been to a post; for he continued to exclaim with unabated good humour, 'flour and eggs! A beefsteak pudding made with flour and eggs!' until John Westlock and his sister fairly ran away from him, and left him to have his laugh out by himself, which he had; and then came dodging across the crowded street to them, with such sweet temper and tenderness (it was quite a tender joke of Tom's) beaming in his face, God bless it, that it might have purified the air, though Temple Bar had been, as in golden days gone by, embellished with a row of rotting human heads.[57]

It is almost impossible, when reading this passage in close conjunction with the similar descriptions of Temple Bar in *The String of Pearls*, not to interpret Tom's laughter as a delayed response of nervous anxiety. The conjunction of so many of the details here with the later descriptions in Lloyd's narrative – the jostling of the passers-by on the busy thoroughfare, the echoing of loud and peculiar laughter along Fleet Street, the evocation of 'golden days gone by' (which immediately brings with it the recollection of the stench of rotting flesh), the concern with the mysterious 'ingredients' properly belonging to meat pies or puddings – may be serendipitous, but at the very least it suggests something about the climate in which both fictions were produced. It should be noted, as well, that the threat of being killed by having one's throat slit by a razor is a possibility that is made quite explicit elsewhere in *Martin Chuzzlewit*. Late in the story, the murderer Jonas Chuzzlewit picks up a case of his associate Doctor John Jobling's 'lancets':

> Jonas had opened one of the shining little instruments; and was scrutinising it with a look as sharp and eager as its own bright edge.
> 'Good steel, doctor. Good steel. Eh?'
> 'Ye-es,' replied the doctor, with the faltering modesty of ownership. 'One might open a vein pretty dextrously with that, Mr Chuzzlewit.'
> 'It has opened a good many in its time, I suppose?' said Jonas, looking at it with growing interest.
> 'Not a few, my dear sir, not a few. It has been engaged in a – in a pretty good practice, I believe I may say,' said the doctor, coughing as if the matter-of-fact were so very dry and literal that he couldn't help it. 'In a pretty good practice,' said the doctor, putting another glass of wine to his lips.
> 'Now, could you cut a man's throat with such a thing as this?' demanded Jonas.
> 'Oh certainly, certainly, if you took him in the right place,' returned the doctor. 'It all depends on that.'[58]

A little later in the novel, Jonas lures his enemy – the adventurer Montague Tigg – to a secluded wood near Salisbury and kills him in precisely such a manner.

It is useful to note that if Dickens's portrayal of Tom Pinch's anxieties and the urban threat symbolized by the figures of Todd and Lovett do indeed spring to some degree from the shared impulse of a particular historical moment in the city's history, Tom's own notions of what the city itself is actually like are noted to be quaint and out-of-date. Dickens makes a point of emphasizing the extent to which Tom's own fears are compounded by the fact that the capital is changing at such a rate that he hardly recognizes it. Although still a relatively young man himself, Tom lives an un-self-consciously nostalgic existence; even the word 'countrymen' in the passage focusing on his fears of being killed and eaten (i.e. 'one of those streets where countrymen are murdered') would appear to be used specifically in its original sense of 'one who lives in the country or rural parts and follows a rural occupation; a husbandman'.[59] The term emphasizes the 'countryman' as one who is the antithesis of all that is urban and urbane; he is not just *from* the country, he is *of* the country – one for whom the city is an altogether different and alien world. When attempting to find a home for himself and his sister Ruth, Dickens is careful to let us know that the neighborhood Tom chooses –

Islington – is arbitrarily settled upon by the nostalgic country figure of Tom himself: 'It used to be called Merry Islington, once upon a time,' he muses aloud to his sister, 'Perhaps it's merry now.'[60] Tom is recalling a phrase from the poet William Cowper's popular 'The Diverting History of John Gilpen' (1785), which notes of Gilpen's wild horse, as he makes his own way from Cheapside to Edmonton:

> Thus all through merry Islington,
> These gambols he did play,
> And till he came unto the Wash
> Of Edmonton so gay.[61]

Such, at least, are Tom's conscious thoughts; in actual fact he seems really to be recalling that same poet's wariness of the city in his *The Task* (1785 – *The Task* and 'John Gilpen' were published in a single volume). The antithesis between 'town' and 'country' features as one of the central polarities in Cowper's poem (especially in Books I and IV), and the poet voices his concern that what were once the city's problems have in time become everyone's problems. 'The town has tinged the country', as Cowper writes:

> The course of human things from good to ill,
> From ill to worse, is fatal, never fails.
> Increase of pow'r begets increase of wealth,
> Wealth luxury, and luxury excess;
> Excess, the scrupulous and itchy plague
> That seizes first the opulent, descends
> To the next rank contagious, and in time
> Taints downward all the graduated scale
> Of order, from the chariot to the plough.[62]

If anything, the sheltered tranquillity of Tom's eventual domestic existence in Islington recalls the famous description of Cowper's own retreat at Olney, and his sketch of a cozy front parlour – with its 'shutters fast' and the 'bubbling and loud-hissing urn' brewing tea – as a place of safety where he and his companions can 'welcome peaceful evening in'.[63]

Passages such as those included in *Martin Chuzzlewit* are proof that although the constituent elements that would in a very short time coalesce to form the central narrative of *The String of Pearls* were 'in the air', as it were, the barber himself had not yet officially taken up residence in Fleet Street; Mrs Lovett had not yet opened for business in Bell Yard. It has already been noted in Part One that Dickens's own depiction of 'Poll Sweedlepipe' in that same novel – when taken together with Phiz's illustration that situates Sweedlepipe's property alongside a famous meat pie shop – may have sparked the imagination of the author of *The String of Pearls* to some degree. There would seem to be no escaping the fact that Dickens's work was generally a determining component in the imaginative creation that shaped the later story. If *The String of Pearls* was, as critics such as Smith and James have recently argued, written by James Malcolm Rymer, then one of course remembers that he had himself begun his own career by plagiarizing Dickens's work at length. It would have been only natural for him still to have looked to the popular novelists for 'inspiration'. Dickens remained, in any event, inescapable throughout the 1840s, and dominated the popular reading market like no other novelist before or since.

Readers of Dickens's own work cannot help but be struck by his own keen interest in matters relating to appetite, food, cannibalism, and of course the compelling power of the city, generally. It has often been noted that Dickens 'had had since childhood, a strong horrified fascination with the subject of cannibalism'; the very notion of eating the otherwise inedible exerted a powerful pull on his imagination.[64] It would eventually, in the 1850s, become an issue that he would be compelled to confront explicitly, in his attempts to defend the reputation of the explorer Sir John Franklin (1786–1847), the fate of whose polar expedition was the subject of many official and private rescue missions, and of much public speculation. Even so, cannibalism had already been a prevalent theme in Dickens's fiction since as early as *The Pickwick Papers*, in which it shows up repeatedly, particularly in the comments of Sam Weller and the tendencies of the Fat Boy. Characters throughout Dickens's novels – Hugh in *Barnaby Rudge*, Vholes in *Bleak House*, Magwitch in *Great Expectations* – display a verbal or actual inclination towards cannibalism, or are otherwise described through cannibalistic imagery of some kind. To Dickens's way of thinking, as John Carey put it, cannibalism was even 'more amusing' than another one of his favourite subjects, capital punishment, and we can as readers 'see [Dickens's] thoughts straying to it on several occasions'.[65]

The most significant earlier source for the novelist's lifelong obsession with cannibalism and with the dark humour associated with anthropophagy were the tales that had been recounted to him as a very young child by his nurse, Mary Weller. Among her tales, Dickens claimed most vividly in later years to recall the adventures of a certain 'Captain Blood'. (Dickens refers on several occasions to the influence that Mary Weller's stories exercised upon his young imagination, and claimed that he recalled being told such tales from about the age of six (*c.*1817). He later incorporated the story of 'Captain Murderer' within an autobiographical fragment originally published in the periodical *All The Year Round*, which was subsequently included in the collection of essays and sketches that comprised his *The Uncommercial Traveller* (1860–8). In the sketch, entitled simply *Nurse's Stories*, he recounted Mary Weller's grim narrative. 'The first diabolical character who intruded himself on my peaceful youth', he recalled, '... was a certain Captain Murderer':

> This wretch must have been an offshoot of the Blue Beard family, but I had no suspicion of the consanguinity in those times.... . Captain Murderer's

mission was matrimony, and the gratification of a cannibal appetite with
tender brides. On his marriage morning, he always caused both sides of the
way to church to be planted with curious flowers; and when his bride said,
'Dear Captain Murderer, I never saw flowers like these before: what are they
called?' he answered, 'They are called Garnish for house-lamb,' and laughed at
his ferocious practical joke in a horrid manner, disquieting the minds of the
noble bridal company with a very sharp row of teeth, then displayed for the
first time. He made love in a coach and six, and married in a coach and twelve,
and all his horses were milk-white horses with one red spot on the back which
he caused to be hidden by the harness. For, the spot *would* come there, though
every horse was milk-white when Captain Murderer bought him. And the
spot was the young bride's blood. (To this terrific point I am indebted to my
first personal experience of a shudder and cold beads on the forehead.) When
Captain Murderer had made an end of feasting and revelry, and had dismissed
the noble guests, and was alone with his wife on the day month after their
marriage, it was his whimsical custom to produce a golden rolling-pin and a
silver pie-board. Now, there was this special feature in the Captain's courtships,
that he always asked if the young lady could make pie-crust; and if she couldn't
by nature or education, she was taught. Well. When the bride saw Captain
Murderer produce the golden rolling-pin and silver pie-board, she remembered this, and turned up her laced-silk sleeves to make a pie. The Captain
brought out a silver pie-dish of immense capacity, and the Captain brought
out flour and butter, and eggs and all things needful, except the inside of the
pie; of materials for the staple of the pie itself, the Captain brought out none.
Then said the lovely bride, 'Dear Captain Murderer, what pie is this to be?' He
replied, 'A meat pie.' Then said the lovely bride, 'Dear Captain Murderer, I see
no meat.' The Captain humorously retorted, 'Look in the glass.' She looked in
the glass, and still she saw no meat, and then the Captain roared with laughter,
and suddenly frowning and drawing his sword, bade her roll out the crust. She
rolled out the crust, dropping large tears upon it all the time because he was so
cross, and when she had lined the dish with crust, and cut the crust all ready to
fit the top, the Captain called out, '*I* see the meat in the glass!' And the bride
looked up in the glass, just in time to see the Captain cutting her head off; and
he chopped her in pieces, and peppered her, and salted her, and put her in the
pie, and sent it to the baker's, and ate it all, and picked the bones.

The villain makes his way through an unreasonable number of brides
although, as the listener might expect, the Captain finally encounters one
young woman who – albeit still to her own cost – outsmarts him:

[B]efore she began to roll out the paste she had taken a deadly poison of
a most awful character, distilled from toads' eyes and spiders' knees; and
Captain Murderer had hardly picked her last bone, when he began to swell,
and turn to blue, and to be all over spots, and to scream. And he went on
swelling and turning bluer, and being more all over spots and screaming,
until he reached from floor to ceiling and from wall to wall; and then, at
one o'clock in the morning, he blew up with a loud explosion. At the sound

of it, all the milk-white horses in the stables broke their halters and went mad, and then they galloped over everybody in Captain Murderer's house (beginning with the family blacksmith who had filed his teeth) until the whole were dead, and then they galloped away.[66]

Mary Weller's horrific fictions were by no means the only possible source for Dickens's later obsession with cannibalism. Anthropophagy turns out to be a remarkably frequent trope in nearly all those popular novels that he claimed himself to have 'devoured' as a very young boy, including, of course, Defoe's *Robinson Crusoe* (1719), Smollett's *Peregrine Pickle* (1751) and the *Arabian Nights* (particularly in 'The Story of Sidi Nonman' included as part of 'The Adventures of the Caliph Haroun Alraschid'), to all of which the novelist would often subsequently refer in his own work. Some critics have suggested that – try as he might – Dickens was so impressed (and, indeed, so terrified) by Mary Weller's relation of this story that he would never be able completely to 'exclude from his work the morbidity of temperament which was so deeply stirred by stories like [Captain Murderer]'. Such early tales of physical violence, although present only in an 'evasive and inchoate form' in Dickens's earliest novels (where they are offered 'without any artistic assimilation') would only much later in the novelist's career be more fully incorporated within his larger artistic vision.[67] Critics such as Carey would even argue that the tale's anti-hero eventually provided the template for some of his later villains, suggesting even more specifically that Captain Murderer himself could be looked upon as 'an early version of Krook in *Bleak House*'.[68]

*

I fell at last into the hands of the miscreants that are nourished with human blood.
(William Godwin, *Caleb Williams*)[69]

The widespread taste for conspiracy theories of all sorts, coupled as it seems to be in the earliest decades of the twenty-first century with a prevailing conviction (in academic circles, at least) that certain, established ideological constructs will seek always to occlude or otherwise to conceal their often fragile structures of power and 'hegemonic meaning', has served only to encourage those readers – and there remains a surprisingly large number of them – who would yet insist that, even so, and despite any and all such specific narrative or broadly mythological precedents, the story of Sweeney Todd *must* be based on *some* incident of actual and verifiable historical *fact*. When journalist Peter Haining began his own search for the 'earliest of all the stories that have been claimed to be the inspiration' for the English versions of Todd's narrative in the late 1970s and early 1980s, he came across a relatively recent version of what he reported to be a medieval ballad originally written in French. 'The ballad', Haining observed in his 1993 survey of the story, 'was apparently

sung by Parisian mothers as a warning to recalcitrant offspring.'[70] The lyric
– in which the barber was thus posited as having long served in the capacity
of some sort of continental equivalent to the spectre of 'Old Boney', with
whose sinister vigilance English mothers would, in turn, regularly terrorize
their own children into domestic submission well into the twentieth century
– had been discovered by Haining (or so he claimed) in an otherwise elusive
collection of French ballads edited by one 'M. Laurine' in 1845. Reprinted in
his own volume under the unlikely title 'Le Jeune Homme Emoisonne [sic]',
the mid-nineteenth-century English text of what Haining no doubt intended
at least to have designated as 'Le Jeune Homme Empoisonné' or 'The Young
Man Who Was Poisoned' appeared as follows:

Towards the end of the fourteenth century
There lived a sort of demon barber
Who slit his clients [sic] throats at 24 rue des Marmouzets

He carried on this horrible trade
And nobody could resist him,
In his cellar he polished them off
His accomplice a villainous pie merchant next door.

> *CHORUS: With a pie – with a mer – with a chant,*
> *With a pie – mer – chant, Ha! Ha!*

This horrid tale also tells us
That he worked with a ferocious female
Fiercer than the fiercest bailiff.

For all the poor devils he killed
His partner converted into pork pies!
And he said of his customers when they were defunct,
They are gone – pork creatures!

> *CHORUS: With a pork – with a cre – with a ture*
> *With a pork creature. Ha! Ha!*[71]

Haining's transcription in this instance poses any number of problems, not
least of which is the omission of some form of reliable source documentation
for the text in question, or – even more fundamentally – the absence of any
narrative element in the lines that might even vaguely have served their
conjectural purpose as a 'cautionary tale' aimed specifically at an audience
of small children, precious few of whom could ever have been directly
threatened by the prospect of having their throats slit whilst being shaved.
Moreover, although dramatic dialogue ballads or 'murder ballads' in which
a young lover is poisoned by drink or food, as the critic Sophie Jewett has

commented in one study of continental balladry, 'belong in [their] most central themes to ancient and persistent romance' (indeed, versions of one such popular work, 'Lord Randal', are still routinely included in popular teaching anthologies of English poetry), the verses reprinted by Haining manifestly do not even belong within such a tradition in the first place.[72] The title given to these lines by Haining – albeit in itself a valid variation on a traditional formulation that focuses on the poisoning of a romantic lover – bears no relation whatsoever to the actual narrative substance of the song itself. The 'demon barber' may in this instance as in others slit the throats of the 'poor creatures' who are his customers, but nowhere, certainly, is he accused of having poisoned them.

H. Chance Newton included the lines of the original French version of the ballad in his volume *Crime and the Drama: or, Dark Deeds Dramatised* (1927); the rough English translation that follows the original is my own:

> Ça remonte au moyen âge,
> C'était en l'an douze cents.
> Un merlan vrai sauvage
> Coupait le cou de ses clients.
> Rue des Marmousets vingt-quatre
> Il faisait son noir traffic,
> Inutile de se débattre,
> Dans son cave – on faisait conic
> Il avait ce perriquier,
> Pour complice un pâtissier,
> > Pour complice un pa –
> > Un ti – un sier –
> > Un pâtissier.
> > > Ah! Ah!

> Cette legende atroce,
> Ajoute que le pâtissier,
> Était un femme féroce,
> Plus féroce qu'un hussier!
> Avec tous les pauvres diables
> Qu'ils égorgeaient nom d'em nom,
> Ces monsters abominable
> Faisaient des pâtés des jambons!
> Et dans tout ça voila ce que c'est
> C'est le client qui patissait
> > C'est le client qui pa –
> > Qui ti – qui sait –
> > Qui patissait![73]

[As far back as the Middle Ages,
In the year twelve-hundred,

A truly savage barber
Slit the throats of his clients
At 24 rue des Marmousets
He carried on his sinister business,
He was truly irresistible
He polished them off in his cellar!
For his accomplice he had a pastry-cook
     For his accomplice he had pastry –
     A cook – a pastry-cook! Ah! Ah!

This terrible tale adds
That the pastry-cook was a ferocious female,
Fiercer than a freebooter!
And all the poor souls
Whose throats they slit and sent to hell,
These abominable monsters
Turned them into pork pies!
And all that could be said was that
The clients were the pies –
     The meat – the meat pies! Ah! Ah!]

Many years after this ballad was published by Newton, M. Willson Disher wryly observed in the pages of *The Times* (26 July 1939) that as the first line of the ballad began 'Ça remonte au moyen âge' (roughly 'This tale dates back to the Middle Ages'), it was 'plainly not as old as those critics who date it to the fourteenth century would have us believe'.[74] Disher himself dismissed the ballad as, at best, a thematically relevant antecedent, but not a source, and asserted that the popular drama in fact found its origins in the early nineteenth century. 'The first English account of the Demon Barber', he wrote confidently, 'was published under the title of "A Terrific Story of the Rue de la Harpe", in a periodical of 1824 called "The Tell-Tale".'

The story to which Disher referred had indeed appeared in publisher Henry Fisher's monthly magazine, *The Tell-Tale*, in 1824. Its provenance seems first to have been noted by Brighton resident Henry C. Porter in a letter published in *Notes & Queries* on 3 May 1902. The account that was included in *The Tell-Tale* in 1824 and then reprinted elsewhere in the earliest decades of the nineteenth century read, in full, as follows:

In the Rue-de-la-Harpe, which is a long dismal street in the fauxbourg of St. Marcell, is a space or gap in the line of buildings upon which formerly stood two dwelling houses, instead of which now stands a melancholy memorial, signifying, that upon this spot no human habitation shall ever be erected, no human being ever must reside!

    Curiosity will of course greatly be excited to ascertain what it was that rendered the devoted spot so obnoxious to humanity, and yet so interesting to history.

159

Two attached and opulent neighbours, residing in some province, not very remote from the French capital, having occasion to go to town on certain money transactions, agreed to travel thence and to return together, which was to be done with as much expedition as possible. They were on foot, a very common way even at present, for persons of much respectability to travel in France, and were attended, as most pedestrians are, by a faithful dog.

Upon their arrival at the Rue-de-la-Harpe, they stepped into the shop of a perruquier to be shaved, before they would proceed on business, or enter into the more fashionable streets. So limited was their time, and peremptory was their return, that the first man who was shaved, proposed to his companion, that while he was undergoing the operation of the razor, he who was already shaven would run and execute a small commission in the neighbourhood, promising that he would be back before the other would be ready to move. For this purpose he left the shop of the barber.

On returning, to his great surprise and vexation, he was informed that his friend was gone; but as the dog, which was the dog of the absentee, was sitting outside of the door, the other presumed he was only gone out for the moment, perhaps in pursuit of him; so expecting him back every moment, he chatted to the barber whilst he waited his return.

Such a considerable time elapsed that the stranger now became quite impatient, he went in and out, up and down the street, still the dog remained stationed at the door. 'Did he leave no message?' 'No.' All the barber knew was, that when he was shaved he went away. 'It was certainly very odd.'

The dog remaining stationary at the door was to the traveller conclusive evidence that his master was not far off; he went in and out, up and down the street again. Still no signs of him whatever.

Impatience now became alarm; alarm became sympathetic. The poor animal exhibited marks of restlessness in yelps and howlings, which so affected the sensibility of the stranger, that he threw out some insinuations not much to the credit of the barber, who indignantly ordered him to quit his boutique.

Upon quitting the shop he found it impossible to remove the dog from the door. No whistling, no calling, no patting would do, stir he would not.

In his agony, the afflicted man raised a crowd about the door, to whom he told his lamentable story. The dog became an object of universal interest, and of close attention. He shivered and howled, but no seduction, no caressing, no experiment, could make him desert his post.

By some of the populace it was proposed to send for the police, by others it was proposed a remedy more summary, namely to force in and search the house, which was immediately done. The crowd burst in, every apartment was searched, but in vain. There was no trace whatsoever of the countryman.

During this investigation, the dog still remained sentinel at the shop door, which was bolted within to keep out the crowd, which was immense outside.

After a fruitless search and much altercation, the barber, who had prevailed upon those who had forced in to quit his house, came to the door, and was haranguing the populace, declaring most solemnly his innocence, when the dog suddenly sprang upon him, flew at his throat in such a state of terrific exasperation, that his victim fainted, and was with the utmost difficulty

rescued from being torn to pieces. The dog seemed to be in a state of intellectual agony and fury.

It was now proposed to give the animal his way, to see what course he
would pursue. The moment he was let loose, he flew through the shop, darted
down stairs into a dark cellar, where he set up the most dismal howlings and
lamentations.

Lights being procured, an aperture was discovered in the wall communi-
cating to the next house, which was immediately surrounded, in the cellar
whereof was found the body of the unfortunate man who had been missing.
The person who kept this shop was a patissier.

It is unnecessary to say that those miscreants were brought to trial and
executed. The facts that appeared upon their trial, and afterwards upon their
confession, were these: –

Those incautious travellers, whilst in the shop of this fiend, unhappily
talked of the money they had about them, and the wretch, who was a robber
and murderer by profession, as soon as the one turned his back, drew his razor
across the throat of the other and plundered him.

The remainder of the story is almost too horrible for human ears, but it is
not upon that account the less credible.

The pastry cook, whose shop was so remarkable for savory [sic] patties that
they were sent for to the Rue-de-la-Harpe, from the most distant parts of
Paris, was the partner of this perruquier, and those who were murdered by the
razor of the one were concealed by the knife of the other in those very identical
patties [sic], by which, independently of his partnership in those frequent
robberies, he had made his fortune.

This case was of so terrific a nature, it was made part of the sentence of the
law, that besides the execution of the monsters upon the rack, the houses in
which they perpetrated those infernal deeds, should be pulled down, and that
the spot on which they stood should be marked out to posterity with horror
and execration.[75]

M. Willson Disher's attempt to set the record straight by suggesting that the
mystery of the story's original appearance in English could thus succinctly be
dealt with by pointing to the pages of the 1824 *Tell-Tale*, rather surprisingly,
elicited a response from an Oxford-based correspondent within only days of
its publication in the pages of *The Times*. Elizabeth Nitchie, an American
academic then living in England, wrote of a strangely fortuitous discovery.
'It so happens', Nitchie wrote,

> that I can cite an earlier published account of the demon barber than that
> referred to by Mr. Disher in his article... . Yesterday, in the course of
> examining the early nineteenth-century periodicals for a quite different
> purpose, I chanced to see in the *Tickler Magazine* for February 1, 1822, under
> 'Correspondence' a 'Terrific Story of the Rue de la Harpe at Paris.'
> This is the tale of the barber and his neighbour and accomplice, the pastry
> cook. The discovery of their crimes was made through the agency of a dog
> which belonged to two travellers, one of whom had been murdered. The

villains were executed upon the rack, their houses were pulled down, and a memorial was erected saying that on that spot no human habitation must ever be built.

The *Tickler*'s correspondent, 'B. of Cecil-street,' refuses to vouch for the truth of the story, especially as he has 'looked in vain through all the French Tourists who have ransacked Paris, since the abdication of Napoleon, for the "Rue de la Harpe."' In a post-script he adds that, although murders may not be any more numerous in France than in England, murders on the Continent are generally attended with more horrible circumstances.[76]

Nor was this to be the end of the exchange. Writing on 1 August, Ernest J. Parry, while admitting that the details relating to the French story published in *The Tell-Tale* and in the columns of *The Tickler Magazine* as recollected by Elizabeth Nitchie were accurate as far as they went, nevertheless insisted that the tale found its basis in an earlier 'French legend' that had obviously been in circulation for many years prior to the nineteenth century. The earlier magazine's correspondent may have 'looked in vain through [the accounts of] all the French Tourists who [had] ransacked Paris since the abdication of Napoleon', but even so, Parry pointed out, similar versions of the same story could be found in any one of a number of 'various old histories of Paris'.[77] Antoine Nicolas Béraud and Pierre Joseph Spiridon Dufey, he noted, were among those who had recorded very precisely, in their two-volume *Dictionnaire historique de Paris* of 1828, that since at least 1206 a house that passed by the name of the 'Marmousets' (the word roughly translates as 'a small grotesque figure') had existed in the Île de la Cité, near what was now the street of that same name. A barber was said to have lived there, although the exact dates of his occupancy were not recorded. It was told that after his own arrest and execution, and of that of his patissier accomplice (the nature of their crimes often goes without saying), the house itself had been pulled down, and a memorial in the form of a 'pyramid' or obelisk was erected on its foundations in memory of those who had been killed. The shop of the patissier, Parry added, had been situated on the corner of the Rue des Deux Hermites. The remainder of the Marmousets lot remained vacant for over 100 years; few had any desire to inhabit a space, it was said, that had witnessed such horrors. In 1536, however, Francis I granted permission to one Pierre Belut to build a house on the site.

It remains unclear at what point the story that appears initially to have been associated with the Rue des Marmousets was transferred to the Rue de la Harpe. However, one of the original French accounts as printed in an early edition of Béraud and Dufey's *Dictionaire historique de Paris* (1832) notes the details relating to the Rue des Marmousets as follows:

Marmousets-en-la-Cité (rue des); elle commence rues de la *Colombe* et *Chanoinesse*, et finit rues de la *Lanterne* et de la *Juiverie*, 9e arrond., Q. de la Cité; le dernier n° impair est 35; le dernier pair, 40. Une maison, dite des *Marmousets*, existait dans cette rue en 1206. Faut-il mettre au rang des contes populaires l'association d'un barbier et d'un pâtissier, dont l'un assassinait les gens qu'il livrait à l'autre pour en faire des pâtés qui eurent une vogue extraordinaire? Le barbier et son complice auraient été contamnés à mort et exécutés, la maison où se commetaient leurs crimes, rasée, et une pyramide érigée sur son emplacement. Il est certain que pendant plus de cent ans il resta un terrain vacant dans cette rue. François 1er permit en 1536, à Pierre Belut, conseiller au parlement de Paris, de bâtir une maison sur ce terrain, nonobstante le prétendu arrêt qui defendait d'y faire aucune construction.[78]

[The street of 'Marmousets-en-la-Cité' starts at the junction of the Rue de la Colombe and the Rue de la Chanoinesse, and ends at the Rue de la Lanterne and the Rue de la Juiverie, in the ninth arrondisement, Q. de la Cité. The last odd-numbered dwelling is numbered 35; the last even-numbered residence is number 40. A house, which was called 'Marmousets' ['grotesques'] stood on this street since 1206. Could this possibly be a candidate [for that house] known in popular stories because of the association of a barber and a pastry-cook, of whom the first killed his customers and then delivered them into the hands of the other to turn them into meat pies – meat pies that had enjoyed an extraordinary popularity? The barber and his accomplice were condemned to death and executed [and] the house in which they had committed their crimes was razed to the ground, and a [monument in the shape of] a pyramid was erected in its place. It is certain that the site of the house [on this street] remained vacant for over one hundred years. In 1536, François the first gave permission for Pierre Belut, an adviser to the parliament in Paris, to construct a house on this land, notwithstanding the supposed order that forbid anyone to build on the site.]

A considerably earlier French source for this same story is Jacques du Breuil's *Le Théâtre des Antiquités de Paris* (1612), in which a portion of the account reads:

De la maison des Marmousets.

C'est de temps immemorial, que le bruit a couru qu'il y avait en la Cité de Paris, rue des Marmousets, un patissier meurtrier, lequel ayant occis en sa maison un homme, aidé à ce par un sien voisin Barbier, saignant raser le barbe: de la chair d'ici lui faisoit des pastez qui se trouvient meilleurs que les autres, d'autant que la chair de l'homme est plus délicate, à cause de la nourriture, que celle des autres animaux. Et que celà ayant esté décovuert, la Cour de Parlement ordonna qu'oultre la punition du Pâtissier, sa maison seroit razée, & outre ce une pyramide ou colomne érigée audict lieu, en mémoire ignomin-ieuse de ce détestable faict: de la quelle reste encores part & portion en ladicte rue des Marmousets.[79]

[Since time out of mind, it has been rumoured abroad that there was once in the city of Paris, on the Rue des Marmousets, a murderous pastry-cook who killed a certain man in his house; he was helped in doing so by a neighbour of his – a barber – who slit the man's throat whilst shaving him. From the flesh of this man they made meat pies that were found to be better than all others, insofar as human flesh is more tender, because of its diet, than that of other animals. And the murder having been discovered, the parliamentary court ordered that in addition to the punishment of the pastry-cook, his house be razed to the ground, and also that a pyramid or pillar be built on the site in its place, in shameful memory of this disgraceful fact – a part of which aforesaid memorial stands to this day in the rue des Marmousets.]

The Paris street, thanks largely to this association, became something of a by-word for urban squalor. Ernest Parry noted in passing that the well-known water-colourist and chromolithographist Thomas Shotter Boys had issued a lithograph of the Rue des Marmousets as part of his 1839 series of *Views of the Picturesque Architecture in Paris, Ghent, Antwerp, and Rouen*; Parry observed that the illustration was subsequently included by 'Mr Chancellor' in his volume along with details about the barber.[80] It is worth noting that the native French painter, designer and engraver Maxime Lalanne (1827–86) also produced an etching of the *Rue des Marmousets (Vieux Paris)*, which shows a nineteenth-century view of the street as a close and claustrophobic alley of narrow, tottering tenements. Such graphic representations added to the notion that the street and the area immediately adjacent to it had always been noisome and unpleasant; the Rue des Marmousets was also noted in several other works of fiction dating from the mid- to late eighteenth century to have been a particularly insalubrious location. These included Charles Antoine Guillaume Pigault De L'Epiney Lebrun's (1753–1835) gothic tale *L'Enfant du Carnaval* (1792), which had been translated into English in 1797 as *The shrove-tide child; or, the son of a monk*. A description of the Rue des Marmousets was also to be included in the second chapter of Balzac's *The Brotherhood of Consolation* (1809).[81] For many years, again, the Rue des Marmousets preserved its reputation as one of the more unwholesome and unsavoury passages in the older part of the city. Even as late as 1865 (October 30), *The Times*, announcing the news that the new hôtel Dieu or hospital was to be built on the site, reported: 'The Rue des Marmousets is greatly deficient in light and air, and it will be a blessing to the inhabitants to have it removed'.[82]

In her 2002 study, Helen R. Smith had attempted to set the record straight on the possible influence that such French sources – the murderers associated with the Rue des Marmousets and the Rue de la Harpe, respectively – might have had on the English writer of *The String of Pearls*. Smith noted that two additional appearances of the supposed sole source of this tale in *The Tell-Tale*, 1824, as 'A terrific story of the Rue del la Harpe, at Paris', had been identified since the debate regarding the possible continental origins of the Todd legend had flourished in the pages of journals such as

Notes & Queries 100 years earlier. Significantly, *The Tell-Tale* had been reissued in 1841, much closer in time to the penny blood version of *The String of Pearls*. There was also another previously unrecorded verbatim printing of the episode, excluding the surrounding framework device of a letter to the editor that questions its truth, as the first item in *The New Wonderful and Entertaining Magazine* in 1825, where it was given the title *The Murderous Barber*. This reprinting 'draws more attention to a likely subject of a dramatic tale'.[83] To confuse matters even further, however, Smith had also discovered an intermediate variation on, or 'version' of the supposed French source in the fully fledged 'blood' contained in *Lloyd's Penny Atlas* (September or October 1844); this was the anonymous *Joddrel the Barber; or Mystery unravelled*. In this tale, the barber Lewis Joddrel – of French and Irish parentage – has been transferred to London, and now plies his trade in Bishopsgate, not Fleet Street. His neighbours begin to grow suspicious when his customers seem continually to disappear without a trace. Eventually, a number of bodies are discovered in a cupboard by Joddrel's curious neighbours; the missing customers are found with wooden stakes driven through their skulls. 'There are no cellars or pies', Smith admitted of this possible precedent, but noted a further connection to *The String of Pearls*, insofar as 'an earlier story in the same periodical [i.e. *Lloyd's Penny Atlas*] features a mysterious descending bed made for unwary travellers'.[84]

Smith is almost certainly correct in suggesting that the narratives that appeared in *The Tell-Tale* (both as published in 1824 and again in 1841) as well as the story of *Joddrel the Barber* in *Lloyd's Penny Atlas* (1844) thus provided some of the immediate textual cues for the author of *The String of Pearls*. It is worth noting, however, that there were still other legends of murder and cannibalism 'in the air', as it were, in the 1840s; some of them were French, some were not. The substance of these legends suggests that there may have been other manifestations of the 'murderous barber' that have since been lost to us. Charles Dupressoir's *Drames judiciaires: Scenes correction-alles. Causes celebres des tous les peuples* (Paris: Librarie ethnographique, 1848–9), for example, which was published only slightly after Lloyd's original serial publication appears, tells the story of one Bernabe Cabard, whom some have dubbed 'the French "Sweeney Todd" '.[85] The serially published *Drames judiciaires* retails highly dramatized and often very detailed (and thoroughly illustrated) accounts of infamous French trials for murder and other criminal and political cases. The case of 'Pierre Miquelon and Barnabe Cabard' tells the story of two students from Spain who visited the French capital in 1415. They decided to stay at a Parisian hostelry 'Les Trois Rois', the proprietor of which, Bernabe Cabard, supplemented his income as an innkeeper by serving as the local barber. Pierre Miquelon was a relatively well-to-do investor who shared in the profits from the inn; he was also a baker. Dupressoir notes that he

> avait aussi acquis une grande célébrité; ses pâtés etaient tellement succulents

que tout Paris affluait chez le pâtissier du mont Saint-Hilaire. En vain ses
confrères cherchaient a découvrir son secret ... cette saveur qui faisaient en
même temps la gloire de Miquelon et le désespoir de ses rivaux.[86]

[had also acquired considerable celebrity; his meat pies were so delicious that
all of Paris flocked to his pastry shop on Mont Saint Hilaire. In vain did his
competitors try to discover the secret of his success – this flavour [in his pies]
that was at one and the same time the triumph of Miquelon and the despair
of his rivals!]

Bernabe Cabard's shop contained a barber's chair much like the one that
Todd would use to even greater effect, by means of which he had murdered
the two Spanish students. His crime was discovered by authorities who
had been alerted to the disappearance of the two young men in question.
Searching Cabard's cellar, they were said to have found a number of partially
cut up cadavers of some of the innkeeper's other unfortunate clients. Acting
together, Cabard and Miquelon were said to have been responsible for the
death of as many as 143 individuals. One of the two illustrations printed in
Dupressoir's account depicts the corpses that were said to have been found
hanging in Cabard's basement; the second shows the barber actually slitting
the throat of a customer in his chair.

Other, vaguely similar stories that were in some cases only beginning to
be written down suggested that narratives of this sort had long formed part
of oral story-telling traditions on the continent; they were connected to a
larger body of tales and folklore that dwelt on the threat posed to children by
'monsters', ogres and night visitors of all kinds. In 1598 a tailor of Châlons
was sentenced by the Parliament of Paris to be burned alive for lycanthropy.
'This wretched man had decoyed children into his shop, or attacked them in
the gloaming when they strayed in the woods, had torn them with his teeth
and killed them, after which he had dressed their flesh as ordinary meat, and
to have eaten it with a great relish. The number of little innocents whom
he destroyed is unknown. A whole cask full of bones was discovered in his
house.'[87] Many years later, in about 1850, a beggar in the village of Polomyia,
in Galicia, was proved to have killed and eaten 14 children. In this story, a
house had one day caught fire and burned to the ground, roasting one of the
inmates, who was unable to escape. The beggar passed by soon after, and, as
he was suffering from excessive hunger, could not resist the temptation of
making a meal of the charred body. From that moment he was tormented by a
craving for human flesh. He met a little orphan girl about nine years old, and
giving her a little ring told her to search for others like it under a tree in the
neighbouring wood. She was slain, carried to the beggar's hovel, and eaten. In
the course of three years 13 other children mysteriously disappeared, but no
one knew whom to suspect. At last an innkeeper missed a pair of ducks, and
having no good opinion of this beggar's honesty, went unexpectedly into his

cabin, burst suddenly in at the door, and to his horror, found him in the act of hiding under his cloak a severed head; a bowl of fresh blood stood under the oven, and pieces of a thigh were cooking over the fire.[88]

Other such tales pushed the possible date of the 'incidents' in question further back in time, depending on just how scrupulous one wished to be regarding the details. Some versions of the early French stories relating to barbers, pie-makers and cannibalism insisted that the events had taken place *outside* of Paris. In 1691, the Swedish artist, cartographer and engineer Peter Mårtensson Lindeström, who had in 1654 travelled from Gothenburg to what was then New Sweden (on the Middle-Atlantic coast of North America), left on his death a manuscript account of his journey to the New World. Lindeström's manuscript – although not translated into English or published until 1925, when it appeared under the title *Geographia Americæ. With an Account of the Delaware Indians Based on Surveys and Notes Made 1654--56* – contained a detailed account of a story that he claimed to have been current in (and to have taken place in) Calais, in France, when he passed through that port city on his journey in 1654. The story then being circulated told of the collusion of a resident barber and a pastry-maker of the same town in a series of murders. Lindeström's written version of the tale anticipated the details of Sweeney Todd and Mrs Lovett's narrative in almost every significant respect, including even the use of a specially made chair and trap-door that dropped the victims into a secret cellar below the barber's shop. Although, again, Lindeström's account was not published in any form until 1925, the story he recounted – and which he apparently heard from the merchants and residents of the town themselves – suggests that the archetypal tale of a barber who murdered his customers in league with an entrepreneurial pie-maker had already enjoyed a wide circulation in Calais and elsewhere in France since at least the middle of the seventeenth century.

Again, Peter Lindeström sailed for the New World in 1654. On his trip, the ship on which he was travelling from Gothenburg, the *Ohrn*, was forced by 'violent storms and ... the dark and obscure' weather conditions to put in at Calais:

> At that time, here in Cales [sic], many delicious, palatable and rare pies were baked, which were widely cried out [for sale]. [I] will relate a story which happened then in Cales, concerning an affair between a barber and a pie-baker, which took place thus: The barber had a front chamber in his house in front of his [own] room. Below that chamber-floor he had made for himself a secret cellar and above the floor was a square trap-door, so nicely made that one who did not look for it closely could not see where it was joined, and the said trap-door shut so hard that a person could sit on a chair on it and [it] did not go down by it. But when one stamped once hard on it with the foot, it fell down immediately. Now when any traveler [sic], who was of a foreign nation, came to this barber to be shaved, then he took him into this said chamber, placed a chair on the aforesaid trap-door for him to sit upon, while he was to

shave him. The stranger did thus. When now the barber began to shave him and came to shave him under his chin, he cut his throat, stamped thus while he cut him on the said trap-door with his foot, by which the trap-door with the man and chair fell down into the cellar and immediately thereafter he robbed him. And because the said barber and pie baker were in company and council together in this [affair], the former sold the human flesh to the latter of which he baked the above mentioned rare pies. These were at last betrayed and discovered in this manner, namely: Two travelling [sic] students from a foreign country arrived there, and in going along the street came right before the barber's [house]. Then one companion said to the other: 'Brother, go and engage good lodgings for us somewhere, where you can find some good people. I will in the meantime, go into this barber and get shaved, where I will wait for you so long, until you return here to me again'. However, the barber did away with him, after his usual aforesaid manner and custom with others. Now finally the other one returned and asked the barber after his companion. He answered that he went his way immediately after he had been shaved. But this companion of his did not believe it, rather [he] considered his companion's word to be more creditable, upon which he relied, but did not [yet] know what he should do. Nor would he risk to accuse the barber right away, although he might have his suspicions, but went away at first everywhere about the city and sought for him, but did not find him. He therefore went back to the same barber again and began to quarrel with him, telling him that he must produce his companion, 'for here in the house I must have him again,' he said. At this the barber waxed angry and wanted to treat him with striking and beating. The other [one] then made a complaint before a magistrate of the city, stating the nature of the case of his comrade, with the request that he might get some good men to go with him to search the barber's house for his companion, which was granted him. Now when those were arrived there, who were ordered to search [the barber's house], they searched everywhere, but did not find him. Finally they came into the said chamber, where the sergeant stepped on the trap-door, saying, 'According to the word and account of this comrade of his, we must really find the man here in the house,' and with this he stamped on the trap door. Thereby the sergeant fell down into the cellar on the comrade of the other, who had not yet been undressed. Here the cellar was as full of skulls and skeletons as a charnel house in a churchyard. Thus both the barber and the pie-maker were arrested and locked up and soon afterwards received as a reward a miserable departure [from this life]. This account is written with the object of [instructing] him who intends to travel and gain experience.... .[89]

A footnote to this translation of Lindeström's account notes: 'This story is told in a number of variations. Human flesh is relished by many tribes, and the basis for Lindström's story, told by some seamen, may have had a foundation of truth.'[90]

In England, meanwhile, all such gruesome accounts of the apparent continental and particularly Gallic predilection for such activities were relished, even if they went no further than telling the story of a murderous barber of *some* kind. One account reprinted in the 'Law' columns of *The Times*, beneath the headline 'Horrible Murder', in August 1824, for example, ran:

> The Court of Assizes at Rouen has been occupied with the trial of a barber of that town, named Veilliere, for the murder of his wife, on the 28th of April last. The principal facts, as detailed in evidence, were as follows:
>
> On the day above-mentioned, Veilliere, whose wife had been living separate from him, in consequence of the cruelty and depravity of his conduct, called at the house of a Madame Padais, where his wife happened to be, and insisted on seeing her. He affected a calm and penitent air, and entreated his wife to be reconciled to him. This, however, she refused, but without, however, using any irritating expressions; she endeavoured to leave the apartment, but was prevented by her husband, who still continued talking to Madame Padais. All of a sudden, and without the slightest word or look that could have intimated his intention, he drew his hands from his pocket, where he had held them since his entrance, and rushing upon his wife, seized her by the hair of the head, dragged her into a corner of the room, and stabbed her twice with a knife in the neck. At her cries, Madame Padais ran towards them, seized Veilliere and tore him from his victim, but not until he inflicted another wound upon her. Madame Padais and he then struggled for a long time, until they both fell, when he escaped from her grasp, leaving the skirt of his coat behind. With redoubled fury, he returned to his expiring wife, and taking the blade of the knife, for the handle had been broken off in the struggle, he plunged it into her belly, in which he made a circular incision, of four or five inches in diameter. Some women who had been present at the commencement of this horrid scene, fled away, terrified, and crying out for help. Their cries brought the other lodgers in the house to the scene, and, as they were about to seize Veilliere, he gave himself several stabs with the knife, exclaiming, 'I wish to die with her.'[91]

Veilliere did not succeed in this last attempt. When, after an 'examination' to establish his mental state, the barber was tried in Rouen, the jury needed only a few minutes' deliberation unanimously to declare him guilty of murder. No less delightfully shocking to readers of *The Times* than the actual events of the murder, to be sure, would have been the account of the manner in which the condemned man faced his sentence several weeks later. 'He had an inordinate passion for gambling', the correspondent wrote of Veilliere,

> which was the primary source of his depravity and ruin. To get his fellow-prisoners to play with him, he used to threaten, when they refused, to haunt them after his death. The day before his execution, the cards were never out of his hands till he went to bed, when he slept soundly. Next morning, after breakfasting heartily, he renewed his card playing, and did not leave off till the fatal moment came for him to go to the chapel, on his way to the scaffold.[92]

*

While I am at home in England, I am in Venice abroad indeed.
(Charles Dickens, in a letter to John Hullah, 1835)[93]

In his brief account of the origins of Sweeney Todd mentioned earlier in this section, M. Willson Disher had referred in passing to the existence of a source for the narrative that has long remained unidentified and for the most part uninvestigated. In his letter to *The Times* in July 1939, Disher had noted one possible source for Todd's story as having come from 'Delpini, one of the Italian clowns who exerted a strong influence on the stage towards the end of the eighteenth century' in Anthony Pasquin's 1793 *The Life of the Late Earl of Barrymore*. The 'Delpini' here referred to was Carlo Antonio Delpini (*c*.1740–1808). Born in Rome, and once a pupil of the famous musician and pantomimist Nicolini, Delpini was an actor and stage manager, who would come to be best known in England for his talents as a pantomimist and *commedia dell'arte* clown. Delpini in fact distinguished himself on a number of levels in the arts. He began his career in England in 1774, performing with David Garrick's company at Drury Lane as a traditional 'Pierrot' or harlequin figure. He was a modestly popular favourite on the London stage throughout the last three decades of the eighteenth century, performing both at Covent Garden and the Haymarket, as well as Drury Lane, from his first arrival in England in 1774 until his death in 1828. Delpini is perhaps best remembered by subsequent students of the theatre as the author of *Don Juan; or the libertine Destroyed* (1790), an original pantomime version of *Bluebeard; or, the flight of the Harlequin* (1791), and an earlier, revised version of *Robinson Crusoe, or Harlequin's Friday*.[94] Delpini's anarchic comic talent introduced him into some rather privileged if slightly disreputable circles of young London society, and he eventually became something of a favourite of the Prince Regent, performing original masquerades and pantomimes both in London and at the Royal Pavilion in Brighton.[95]

Earlier in his career, Delpini had been intimate within the fast-living set that gathered around Richard, 7th Earl of Barrymore, the eldest son of the 6th Earl and more commonly known by his nickname of 'Hellgate'. The Earl, who was to die from an accidental gun-shot wound through his eye at the age of only 24, devoted much of his short life to fashionable pursuits such as horse-racing and prize-fighting; he was an accomplished pugilist, known for 'polishing off' his opponents (the phrase originally comes from the boxing ring). He was no less vigorous in his fondness for acting and the drama. He built his own private theatre in the small village of Wargrave, just outside London, where he persuaded personalities such as Delpini and others to join him in his amatuer productions. Their performances were only rarely opened to a public audience. A notice in *The Times* on 12 April 1791, for example, noted that both Lord Barrymore and Delpini would be among those participating in the following evening's productions of Sheridan's *The Rivals*, Delpini's *Robinson Crusoe* and his *Bluebeard*, as well as 'a Divertisement, by

Lord Barrymore and Mr Delpini, in the characters of Pluto and Proserpine, in Shades below'.[96] In 1793, just after Barrymore's death, a short account of his life was published by Anthony Pasquin, who praised Barrymore's restless vitality, and related a number of anecdotes relating to the dramas staged at Walgrave, and to the proposed subjects for future efforts. Buried in the pages of Pasquin's brief life is an anecdote that may stand among the earliest references to the story in English that eventually became the core narrative of Sweeney Todd. 'Delpini told us a Venetian story', Pasquin recalls,

> which he affected to be literally true, and which Lord Barrymore meant particularly to introduce into a pantomime. – the events were these. In the neighborhood of St. Mark's there lived a pastry-cook, who became very rich in consequence of selling small meat pies, the flavour and crust of which were uncommonly gratifying; they were sought for so eagerly through the republic, that the man could not find material to make a number adequate to the general demand. Various were the conjectures as to the contents of those pies; some thought they were veal, some ortolans, and others imagined there might be a mixture of both; every baker endeavoured to make similar luxuries, but all failed. During the progress of this man's culinary fame, it was observed that many children had been lost in the city; it was a matter, at last, of public consternation; the police did all they could to discover their retreat, but in vaine, and the streets were crouded with bewailing mothers. At length, it pleased Heaven to unravel the mysterious evil. One of these pies being opened at the table of a senator, the joint of a child's finger was found amidst the pastry. The discovery created a common horror; and the idea instantly occurred, that the baker was the monster who had trapped and destroyed the missing infants; a party of soldiers were immediately ordered to examine the premises, when, after a long search by torch-light, they could find no other proof to justify the presumed guilt, and were on the eve of departure; when suddenly one of their party disappeared and they could not find where, until they seized the baker by the throat and threatened him with instant death if he did not shew them where their companion was enveloped. The wretch complied, and led them to a sliding trap-door, which covered a deep and gloomy vault, upon which he had heedlessly stepped, and been swallowed up; they descended by means of a bucket, and found the soldier, stretched upon the bodies of various dead children recently massacred. Upon this unnerving testimony of diabolism, savageness, and enormity of the cook and his family, the senator ordered the doors and windows of the house to be chained and barred, and surrounded with the army; who joyfully set fire to the building which, with all in it, was consumed to the ground, and an obelisk raised upon the ashes, significant of the atrocity and conflagration.[97]

As is so often the case with such stories, there is no evidence, apart from this singular anecdote of Delpini's as related by Pasquin, that any such events actually took place. Certainly, no such obelisk or memorial pillar of any kind now stands relating to such an event in 'the area of St. Marks'. Obviously,

Delpini's story is in some significant respects similar to the accounts relating to both the Rue des Marmousets and the Rue de la Harpe, in Paris; the events are simply said to have taken place elsewhere. Even so, one might discern a possible but still very broad pattern emerging with regard to the general *movement* of the narrative – a kind of perverse parody of the notion of a 'westward expansion of empire', whereby urban myths and stories concerned with tales of unsuspecting cannibalism also move to the west, as Mediterranean civilization extends its boarders, and as the centres of focus in the great business of trade and mercantile expansion themselves similarly shift and jostle with one another for prominence. From the ancient legend and folklore of the Near East and the Hellenic world in mythology, to the turbulent, commercial centre of early modern Venice; thence from Italy – exported like so much else in the late Medieval period and the Renaissance – to Paris, an emerging city at the heart of an increasingly unified and powerful France – and then, finally, to the epicentre of the greatest cosmopolitan city of them all, London, at the precise historical moments when Britain herself was awakening to her status as the greatest of world empires. Perhaps; stranger things have happened, after all.

*

You are not a cannibal if you eat art.

(Marco Evarissti, Chilean artist)[98]

The persistent search for the 'genuine' historical incidents that inspired the narrative of Sweeney Todd suggest that on at least some level there is a part of our collective psyche that actually *wants* or even *needs* his story to be true; to have it reduced to a mere fiction among other fictions would somehow detract from its aura. Yet as an alternative to turning (as we have just been doing) to possible continental sources or prototypes – sources that might conceivably distance and so diminish the *frisson* of threat posed by his crimes – many traditional critics and readers of penny bloods have looked to find traces of Todd's activity if not in London, then at least a little closer to home, and in Great Britain generally.

Among the most noteworthy of these indigenous narrative 'precedents', were the events that surrounded the printing of a small pamphlet by the broadsheet publisher James Catnach (1792–1841) on 1 June 1818. Catnach, who had inherited not only a business but an actual wooden printing press of his father in 1813, worked out of cramped quarters at No. 2 Monmouth Court, in the notoriously squalid neighborhood of Seven Dials. He had also inherited from his parent a considerable stock-in-trade, including the original blocks of many fine woodcuts that had been executed by the masterful Thomas Bewick (1753–1828) at the height of his powers towards the end of the eighteenth century. Catnach was said to have collected original ballads from the many singers and 'patterers' who performed in the city taverns, and throughout the country. Although many of Catnach's duodecimo chapbooks and broadsheets (single sheets of verse or prose, printed on very cheap paper and sold for a penny) would arguably play an important and even positive role in preserving an entire tradition of native British nursery rhymes and fairy tales for posterity, they tended also, and increasingly in the earliest decade of the century, to feature sensational incidents of crime, often including (fraudulent) accounts of criminal trials and 'dying confessions'. These execution broadsheets were typically illustrated by crude woodcuts (no longer did Catnach's products contain images of Bewick's standards), and were sold cheaply and often in tremendous quantities by itinerant hawkers. Catnach's version of the confession and execution of the notorious William Corder (for the murder of Maria Marten), it has been asserted in the twentieth century, sold no fewer than 1,116,000 copies.[99]

On at least one occasion, however, Catnach went too far. In June 1818, he published a broadsheet alledging that a butcher by the name of Thomas Pizzey, of Clare Market, London, had been selling human flesh to his customers in the form of pork sausages. The opening lines of the sheet incited its readers into a state of hysteria:

> Another dreadful discovery! Being an account of a number of Human Bodies found in the Shop of a Pork Butcher. We have just been informed of a most dreadful and horrible discovery revolting to every feeling of humanity and calculated to inspire sentiments of horror and disgust in the minds of every individual. On Saturday night last, the wife of a Journeyman Taylor went into the Shop of a Butcher in the neighborhood of [Drury Lane] to buy a piece of Pork. At the time the Master was serving a Man came into the Shop carrying a Sack. The woman thought by the appearance of the Man that he was a Body Snatcher and when she left the shop she communicated her suspicions to an acquaintance she met with; the news of this soon spread abroad and two officers went and searched the house and to their inexpressible horror found two dead bodies wrapped up in a sack. Great flocks of people were assembled from all parts of the town at Marlborough Street in expectation of the offender having a hearing.[100]

The bewildered and soon terrified Pizzey found himself and his shop at the centre of a riot, as crowds of readers who had been stirred into a frenzy by the unscrupulous publisher immediately besieged his premises. As *The Times* reported the events of 1 and 2 June 1818:

> A riotous mob assembled on Monday and yesterday in front of a pork-butcher's shop in Clare-market, and could scarcely be restrained by a numerous police from destroying the shop and its tenant. The cause of this disturbance was an atrocious handbill, circulated by one Catnach, a printer, in which in was stated that the pork-butcher cut up human bodies into sausages; Catnach, at Bow

Street, yesterday confessed that there was no foundation for the rumour, and
that he had published it merely by way of his trade, as a retail and marvellous
treat to the vulgar. He was ordered to circulate a printed contradiction.[101]

'Two of the rioters were committed for want of bail', *The Times* account
further reported, 'but it does not appear that Catnach was committed,
though his libel certainly *tended* to break the peace.' Pizzey later successfully sued the publisher for malicious libel, and at least had the satisfaction
of seeing Catnach spend some time in prison. Catnach eventually retired in
1839 (with a supposed fortune of some £10,000) at the early age of 46, only
to die of jaundice while revisiting his Seven Dials shop less than two years
later.[102]

Another London incident often mentioned with relation to Todd is an
article recorded in the *Annual Register* for 1784–5, which was a reprint of a
murder first reported in the *London Chronicle* (2 December 1784):

A most remarkable murder was perpetrated in the following manner, by a
journeyman barber that lives near Hyde Park Corner, who had been for a long
time past jealous of his wife, but could in no way bring it home to her: a young
gentleman by chance coming into his master's shop to be shaved and dressed;
and, being in liquor, mentioned his having seen a fine girl home to Hamilton-
Street, from whom he had certain favours the night before, at the same time
describing her person; the barber, concluding it to be his wife, in the height of
his frenzy cut the gentleman's throat from ear to ear, and absconded.[103]

Still another possible (if general) source for Todd's story, not mentioned
by previous critics, is both recounted in the Proceedings of the Old Bailey
Sessions for 26 February 1724, and reprinted in a slightly different version
in John Villette's four-volume *Annals of Newgate*, published in 1776.[104]
According to both accounts, Lewis Hussart was a French barber who had
been living for some years in London, and who in March 1724 was brought
before the court on the charge of murdering his wife 'by cutting her throat
with a razor'.[105] She lived apart from him in Shoreditch. They had been
married six years earlier, but the relationship had not been a successful one.
Hussart was apprehended at the home of his second wife, shortly after the
discovery of his victim's body, and there confronted with the constable. 'He
set up a barracks laugh' the account reported, 'and bid us look in his face, to
see if there was anything in his countenance that should induce us to believe
he would be guilty of such an action.' The constable found a razor in the
pocket of the white coat associated with his profession that Hussart had been
wearing on that day. Eventually, Hussart was found not guilty on the charge
of murder because of insufficient evidence; he would later that same year be
prosecuted and convicted for bigamy.

Yet perhaps the most popular candidate for being the 'real life' Sweeney
Todd throughout the twentieth century was the so-called 'Man-Eater of

Scotland', Sawney Beane. An actual connection between Beane and Sweeney Todd appears first to have been suggested in 1901 by the regular contributor to *Notes & Queries* (already mentioned in Part One) who signed himself merely 'Gnomen'; the deputy epithet seems in this instance to indicate the superficial similarity between the names 'Sawney' and 'Sweeney' to have been an obvious point of comparison. 'I have always been under the impression', 'Gnomen' opined,

> that the legend of 'The Demon Barber of Fleet Street' was suggested by the 'penny shocker' of the eighteen-thirties by incidents of the *cause célèbre* in Scotland of the sixteenth century, the revolting trial of Sawney Beane and his associates, introduced by Mr. S.R. Crockett in his powerful romance of *The Grey Man of Auchinleck*, the scene in Sawney Beane transferred to London and Fleet Street, where, to my personal knowledge, a penny-pie shop carried on its business in the forties of the last century on the very site attributed to it [i.e. 186 Fleet Street] in the tale under discussion.[106]

Sawney Beane's own narrative – which had been published many times and in various versions as an historical account throughout the eighteenth and nineteenth century before being incorporated by S.R. Crockett into the novel mentioned by 'Gnomen' here (about which more in a moment) – was intriguing enough in its own right. Like many others who have written on Todd, Peter Haining hoped somehow to make use of 'Gnomen's' suggestion to link the barber's story to that of his northern predecessor, but even he (for once) was compelled to admit that he found the connection between the two killers 'tenuous in the extreme'.[107] Nevertheless, Sawney Beane is to this day the name most often connected to Todd's own; even the most recent (2002) entry in the *Oxford Dictionary of National Biography* notes that he 'may have been the original of the Todd legend'.[108]

A native of East Lothian, some eight miles east of Edinburgh, Sawney Beane was said to have lived in the reign of James VI of Scotland. Described in most accounts as 'naturally idle and vicious', Sawney at an early age found a female companion who matched his indolent temperament with her own.[109] The pair retired to 'the desarts of Galloway', where they took up residence in a deep, sea-side cave. The cave, which extended for at least a mile in length and was of a labyrinthine complexity, was close enough to the shore so that the high tide penetrated about 200 yards into its entrance. Together, the pair began robbing and murdering passing travellers in the area; they took to dragging the remains of their victims back to their lair, where the bodies were then quartered, salted and pickled, and dried for later provisions. (Their criminal activity continued for such an extended period, that when finally discovered they were found to have together raised no fewer than eight sons, six daughters, 18 grandsons and 14 granddaughters, all of whom seem to have become involved in a grotesque, incestuous entanglement of relations with one another.) Sawney's tribe prospered for many years, until one day a man and his wife who were returning to their home after visiting a nearby market fair were attacked. The man managed to survive the assault and escape, but not before looking on in horror as the attackers not only slaughtered but ripped the entrails from his wife. With difficulty, he made his way back to the site of the fair, and returned to the location accompanied by a group of 20 to 30 men. The search party had no luck in tracing the attackers that night, but together they insisted that the man go to Glasgow to tell his tale to the chief magistrate, who then wrote to the king himself for advice. The king himself was said to have accompanied a team of 400 men to scour the area, and eventually bloodhounds sniffed the trail of the attackers to the outlet of the cave. They entered it and there discovered a scene the account of which had been so often reprinted in the criminal literature of the eighteenth and nineteenth centuries:

> Legs, arms, thighs, hands, and feet of men, women, and children, were suspended in rows like dried beef. Some limbs and other members were soaked in pickle; while a great mass of money, both of gold and silver, watches, rings, pistols, cloths, both woollen and linen, with an innumerable quantity of other articles, were either thrown together in heaps, or suspended upon the sides of the caves.[110]

The men who made this gruesome discovery buried the flesh in the sand of the cave, and carried the bulk of the goods back to Edinburgh, with the prisoners in tow. There, Sawney and his brood were confined in the Tollbooth (the term in Scottish signals the town jail) under a strong and heavily armed guard. There were said to be a total of 27 men and 21 women. All were eventually executed at the common place of execution in Leith Walk, without benefit of a formal trial. The men were further punished by having their 'privy members' severed from their bodies and thrown into the fire; their hands and legs were also severed from their bodies, and they were allowed to bleed to death. The women were cast into three separate fires to be burnt to death. (In some versions of the capture and execution, the prisoners were said to have been taken in a body to Leith, and executed there.)

There are any number of reasons for disqualifying the story from being authentic, much less from having exerted any real influence on Todd's narrative. While some of the details recounted in the various versions of the story perhaps 'ring true', others clearly do not. No real evidence for the assault, the capture, or the executions was ever to be forthcoming, and the many accounts offer a variety of conflicting dates and questionable details. Bloodhounds, for example, may indeed for many years have been used in the mountainous regions of Scotland for tracking because of their keen sense of smell; Scottish raiders were known to use them (so-called 'slough dogs') in forays against English border towns. But the use of bloodhounds as tracker dogs for criminals (a modern breed developed by crossing several strains) was a much later development. Indeed, the practical use of bloodhounds in such a manner was still to be a major issue in the hunt for Jack the Ripper in 1888.[111] Moreover, although the area that was said to have been the Beane clan's hunting ground may indeed have been a dangerous one for travellers, there are no official contemporary accounts recording any such sustained incidents of robbery, assault or abduction. There is more than one parallel legend to that of Sawney Beane in Scotland, as well. Local traditions told of one family that was rumoured to have inhabited a cave near St Vigeans, in Forfarshire, and who were said to live off the bodies of passing travellers. There was also the story of 'Christie o' the Creek', who ate his victims after dragging them from their ponies with a hooked axe.[112] Scotland in general, in fact, could be said to be something of a hotbed for tales and legends of cannibalism. The invasion of Roman Britain *c.*AD 367 by the Saxons and the Franks was said to have been assisted by the local Attacotti, a cannibal tribe from Argyllshire. The later mosstroopers or freebooters of the borders were reputed to drink the blood and eat the flesh of their victims, and it was said that they had boiled one Lord de Soules alive and then supped on the resulting broth.[113] The young St Jerome, visiting Gaul in about 393–7, speculated: 'I may have seen the Attacotti, a British people who live on human flesh; and when they find herds of pigs, droves of cattle, or flocks of sheep in the woods, they cut off the haunches of the men and breasts of the women, and these they regard as great dainties'; as the eighteenth-century historian Edward Gibbon later put it, when the Attacotti hunted, 'they attacked the shepherd rather than his flock'. 'If in the neighborhood of the commercial and literary town of Glasgow', Gibbon observed with a peculiar mixture of scepticism and hope in his *Decline and Fall of the Roman Empire*, 'a race of cannibals has really existed, we may contemplate, in the period of the Scottish history, the opposite extremes of savage and civilized life. Such reflections tend to enlarge the circle of our ideas, and to encourage the pleasing hope that New Zealand may produce in future ages, the Hume of the Southern hemisphere.'[114]

Other accounts seemed to parallel the story of Sawney Beane even more carefully. One Nichol Brown, said to have come from roughly the same area as Beane, was executed for killing and eating his wife in the mid-eighteenth century. The activity appears to have been nothing out of the ordinary for him. He bragged to his captors that on one occasion he had told some drinking companions that he would go to the gibbet where a man had been hanged a week earlier and return with a piece of the body and eat it in front of them; he accordingly returned with a piece of the thigh of the dead man, one Norman Ross, cooked it, and ate it before their eyes.[115] Robert Lindsay of Pitscottie, in his *Chronicles of Scotland*, gave a full account of the case of a robber and his daughter in the fifteenth century that had also been noted by 'Boethius' in his *History of Scotland*. 'About this time [c.1460]', he wrote, there was ane brigand ta'en with his haill family, who haunted a place in Angus. This mischievous man had ane execrable fashion to take all young men and children he could steal away quietly, or tak' away without knowledge, and eat them, and the younger they were, esteemed them the mair tender and delicious. For the whilk cause and damnable abuse, he with his wife and bairns were all burnt, except ane young wench of a year old who was saved and brought to Dandee [sic], where she was brought up and fostered; and when she came to a women's years, she was condemned and burnt quick for that crime. It was said that when she was coming to the place of execution, there gathered ane huge multitude of people, and specially of women, cursing her that she was so unhappy to commit so damnable deeds. To whom she turned about with an ireful countenance, saying: – 'Wherefore chide ye with me, as if I had commited ane unworthy act? Give me credence and trow me, if ye had experience of eating men and women's flesh, ye wold think it so delicious that ye wold never forbear it again.' So, but for any sign of repentance, this unhappy traitor died in the sight of the people.[116]

For those who might be inclined immediately to discredit Sawney Beane's own tale, the modern writer on cannibalism Moira Martingale has countered: 'the tale has been very well documented in its claim to be factual, [and] it must be noted that unlike ... mythological night monsters, there are no elements of magical or even devilish dimensions to Sawney Beane. There is danger, too, in falsely believing that because a person's crimes are so unspeakably shocking as to defy the laws of humanity, they could not possibly have taken place in reality.'[117]

The original suggestion of 'Gnomen' in 1901, it will be recalled, had been that a 'penny shocker' based on the legend of Sawney Beane had led his story once again to re-enter the imagination of contemporary popular culture. This was the sensation novel *Sawney Bean: the Man-Eater of Midlothian* (1844). 'Gnomen' also noted the later publication of S.R. Crockett's *The Grey Man* (1896); Crockett's novel was to allow the story a much larger circulation than it had ever before enjoyed. In the relevant sections of Crockett's *The Grey Man*, the novel's hero, Sir Launcelot Kennedy, finds himself trapped with his companions in Sawney's cave, when he begins to hear some noise. Crockett's description of Sawney's crew is worthy of a penny dreadful itself:

[T]he horrid brabblement filled all the cave, and sounded louder and more outrageous, being heard in darkness. Suddenly, however, the murky gloom was shot through with beams of light, and a rout of savages, wild and bloody, filled the wide cave beneath us. Some of them carried rude torches, and others had various sorts of back-burdens, which they cast down in the corners. I gat a gliff in one of these, and those in battle I had often seen things grim and butcherly, my heart now sprang to my mouth, so that I had well-nigh fainted with loathing.... . Then I knew that these execrable hell-hounds must be the hideous crew who called [Sawney Beane] lord and master. They were of both sexes and all ages, mostly running naked, the more stalwart of them armed

178

with knives and whingers, or with knotted pieces of tree in which a ragged stone had been thrust and tied with sinew or tags of rope. The very tottering children were striking at one another, or biting like young wolves, till the blood flowed.... Then the red climbing flame went upward. The wood smoke filled the cave, acrid and tickling, which, getting into our throats, might have worked us infinite danger, had it not been that the clamour of the savages was so great that it never stilled for a moment.[118]

[...]

All this was horrid enough, but that was not the worst of it, and I own that I hesitate to write that which I saw. Yet, for the sake of truth, I must and will. The cavern was very high in the midst, but at the sides not so high – rather like the sloping roof of an attic which slants quickly down from the roof-tree. But that which took my eye amid the smoke were certain vague shapes, as it had been of the limbs of human beings, shrunk and blackened, which hung in rows on either side of the cave. At first it seemed that my eyes must certainly deceive me, for the reek drifted hither and thither, and made the rheum flow from them with its bitterness. But after a little study of these wall adornments I could make nothing else of it than that these poor relics, which hung in rows from the roof of the cave like hams and black puddings set to dry in the smoke, were indeed not other than the parched arms and legs of men and women who had once walked the upper earth, but who by misfortune had fallen into the power of this hideous, inconceivable gang of monstrous man eaters.[119]

Kennedy's experiences are about to get even worse, however.

The fire on the floor flickered upward and filled the place with light. I felt something touch my cheek. Speedily I turned and, lo! it was a little babe's hand that swung by a cord. The wind had caught it, so light it was, and it had rubbed my cheek. By the lord, it was enough and more than enough![120]

As in the reputed 'historical' account of the legend, so too in Crockett's novel are an unrepentant Sawney Beane and his family brought to rough justice at the hands of their Scottish captors. As Sandy Hobbs and David Cornwell have observed:

Crockett's *The Grey Man* (1896) is an early example of a Scottish writer taking the Sawney Bean [sic] story and using it to his own literary ends. Sawney is a secondary character in this historical novel. However, a particular point of interest is that Crockett has him living in a cave near Bennane Head in the region of South Ayrshire called Carrick, not in Galloway as in earlier texts. Bennane is near Galloway, but definitely not in it.... It is our belief that Crockett used his author's license to make this change, which fitted the mechanics of his plot. However, once made, this relocation took hold to the extent that the cave at Bennane is widely regarded as Sawney Bean's cave, and Crockett's literary device is treated as history, or at the very least 'tradition'. C.H. Dick says there is a Carrick tradition that Sawney Bean lived in the cave.

James Gracie (1994) told the Sawney Bean story as a 'Carrick legend' without even mentioning Galloway.[121]

Hobbs and Cornwell's essential argument is that 'although [the story of the Scottish cannibal] may now be regarded as a popular legend, it originated in eighteenth-century English commercial publishing. Its survival is aided by the fact that it is a "good story" to tell to tourists.'[122]

Several other possible, indirect 'sources' that were ultimately to feed into Todd's narrative must also, finally, be taken into account. These include those thematic strands in the story of which contemporary readers are likely already to have been aware – generally familiar narrative elements that could be said to carry with them a powerful cluster of what we might today call 'intertextual significance'. One might include here the many stories then in circulation regarding the casual abuse of apprentices. Such abuse had been fictionalized in verse in the well-known story of 'Peter Grimes' included as part of George Crabbe's *The Borough* (1810). Crabbe's poem dwells on the easy availability of a veritable 'slave-shop' of young boys effectively to be sold to their masters:

> Peter had heard there were in London then, –
> Still have they being! – workhouse-clearing men,
> Who, undisturbed by feelings just or kind,
> Would parish-boys to needy tradesmen bind:
> They in their want a trifling sum would take,
> And toiling slaves of piteous orphans make.[123]

The condition of the apprentices is very close to that of Tobias in Todd's story:

> Pinn'd, beaten, cold, pinch'd, threaten'd, and abused –
> His efforts punish'd and his food refused, –
> Awake tormented, – soon aroused from sleep, –
> Struck if he wept, and yet compell'd to weep,
> The trembling boy dropp'd down and strove to pray,
> Received a blow, and trembling turn'd away,
> Or sobb'd and hid his piteous face; – while he,
> The savage master, grinned in horrid glee;
> He'd now the power he ever loved to show,
> A feeling being subject to his blow.[124]

Peter Grimes, in Crabbe's poem, after murdering three of his boys, is driven mad with visions of their ghosts. He shows remorse, and is in time (although dying) in some way reconciled within the community.

Even more certainly, any mention of the mistreatment of apprentices or young servants and shop-boys was very likely still to have called to the minds of many Londoners the notorious case of Elizabeth Brownrigg, who had been executed in September 1767. Bronwrigg was a plumber's wife who had lived just off Fleet Street, and who had practised midwifery for St Dunstan's parish. She took in several orphans to work for her as apprentices from the Foundling Hospital and elsewhere, most of whom she appears to have treated with 'the most savage barbarity'. She was finally convicted for starving and beating one girl to death, after having subjected her to abuse as a servant.[125] As the *Newgate Calender* commented:

> The long and excruciating torture in which this inhuman woman kept the innocent object of her remorseless cruelty, before she finished the long-premeditated murder, more engaged the attention and roused the indignation of all ranks, than any criminal in the whole course of our melancholy narratives.[126]

Yet three distinct strands of the narrative in *The String of Pearls* are likely to have stood out for the narrative's original audience more emphatically than others. These include: (i) the representation of overcrowded graveyards and cemeteries that emit a repulsive smell; (ii) the narrative motif of the 'faithful hound', and, finally; (iii) the use of an ingenious murder device that turns on its hinges to hurl the victim to his death.

*

In looking one day at Roque's plan of London (1742–5) I noticed how many burial grounds and churchyards were marked upon it which no longer existed. I made a table of them, and traced their destiny.
(Mrs Basil Holmes, *The London Burial Grounds*, 1897)[127]

The author's source for the conceit of signalling the growing awareness that all is not as it should be in the vicinity of Todd's shop by depicting the churchwardens of St Dunstan's as being overwhelmed by the 'horrid charnel-house sort of smell' inside and around the church seems almost certainly to find its origins in the many accounts that had only very recently been published in the contemporary press relating to the appalling state of London's cemeteries. Hand-in-hand with the construction throughout the mid-nineteenth century of affordable working-class housing, road improvements and significant advances in metropolitan sanitary facilities, medical provisions and water supply were the problems posed by addressing the condition of the numerous 'congregations of the dead' in Inner London. 'By the early nineteenth century, squalid and noxious,' as the city historian David Piper writes, 'they had become a public scandal, and recognized as a danger against the health of the living.'[128] Sir Edwin Chadwick (whose comprehensive *Sanitary Conditions of the Labouring Population of Great Britain* of 1842 was eventually to provide the massive and irrefutable evidence that led to effecting necessary reforms in almost every area of public health and safety) was already, throughout the 1830s, calling attention to the state of the city's cemeteries. 'On spaces of ground which do not exceed 203 acres,' Chadwick observed, 'closely surrounded by the abodes of the living, 20,000 adults and nearly 30,000 youths and children are every year imperfectly interred.'[129]

The overcrowding and rapidly deteriorating condition of London's traditional burial grounds soon became a cause for growing concern. As campaigners like Chadwick observed, old grave sites were increasingly being disturbed to make room for the interment of the newly dead. Subsequent campaigners such as George Frederick Carden successfully petitioned the Commons for the establishment of new graveyards only just beyond what were then the residential suburbs of the metropolis, removed at what was thought to be a healthy distance from the city centre.[130] 'Most of the [traditional] parish grounds', as David Orme writes, 'were closed after the passing of the burial act of 1852 and large cemeteries were opened much further out – even as far out as Brookwood, Surrey, which was served by its own train service from the London Necropolis station at Waterloo. Over the next few years some grounds were built on, while others were simply left to fill up with rubbish.'[131]

Yet the earliest readers of *The String of Pearls* in 1846–7 would still have been going about their daily lives in a very different environment indeed. The account included in David Bartlett's 1852 volume *London by Day and Night, or Men and Things in the Great Metropolis*, written before the government reforms of the 1850s had begun to take effect, is wonderfully representative of precisely the sorts of sensational accounts that were typically included in the 'Shock-Horror' literature of the period. Bartlett whets his readers' appetites with some gruesomely exact statistics before treating them to what remained perhaps the best-known story circulating in the period:

> St Martin's Church, measuring 295 feet by 379, in the course of ten years received 14,000 bodies! St Mary's, in the region of the Strand, and covering only half an acre, has by fair comparison during fifty years received 20,000 bodies. Was ever anything heard of more frightful? But hear this: two men built, as mere speculation, a Methodist Church in New Kent Road, and in a mammoth vault, beneath the floor of that church, 40 yards long, 25 wide, and 20 high, 2000 bodies were found, *not buried*, but piled up in coffins one upon the other. This in all conscience is horrible enough, but seems quite tolerable in comparison with another case.
>
> A church, called Enon Chapel, was built some twenty years ago, by a minister, as a speculation, in Clement's Lane in the Strand, close on to that busiest throroughfare in the world. He opened the upper part for worship of God, and devoted the lower – separated from the upper merely by a board floor – to the burial of the dead. *In this place, 60 feet by 29 and 6 deep, 12,000 bodies have been interred*! It was dangerous to sit in the church; faintings occurred every day in it, and sickness, and for some distance about it, life was not safe.

And yet people not really knowing the state of things, never thought of laying anything to the vault under the chapel.

But perhaps the reader will exercise the arithmetical powers, and say that it would be impossible to bury 12,000 persons in so small a space, within 20 years. He does not understand the manner in which the speculating parson managed his affairs. It came out before the Committee of the House of Commons, that sixty loads of 'mingled dirt and human remains' were carted away from the vault at different times, and thrown into the Thames, the other side of Waterloo Bridge. Once a portion of a load fell off in the street, and the crowd picked up out of it a human skull.

W. Chamberlain, grave-digger at St Clement's, testified that the ground was so full of bodies that he could not make a new grave 'without coming into other graves'. He said 'We have come to bodies quite perfect, and we have cut parts away with choppers and pickaxes. We have opened the lids of coffins, and the bodies have been so perfect that we could distinguish males from females; and all those have been chopped and cut up. During the time I was at this work, the flesh has been cut up in pieces and thrown up behind the boards which are placed to keep the ground up where the mourners are standing, and when the mourners are gone this flesh has been thrown in and jammed down, and the coffins taken away and burnt.'

An assistant grave-digger testified that, happening to see his companion one day chopping off the head of a coffin, he saw that it was his own father's! Another digger testified that bodies were often cut through when they had been buried only three weeks. Another testified to things more horrible than ever Dante saw in hell. He says: 'One day I was trying the length of a grave to see if it was long and wide enough, and while I was there the ground gave away, and a body turned right over, and two arms came and clasped me round the neck!'[132]

'We beg the pardon of the reader for relating such horrible facts', Bartlett pauses to note, '– but they occurred *in London.*' Much of the information that we have regarding Enon Chapel comes from eyewitness accounts contained in the work of George Alfred Walker (1807–84). Walker was a physician and sanitary reformer whose own interest in the subject of interment is said to have been awakened 'when, as a boy in Nottingham, he had witnessed shocking mutilations and upturning of human remains in the overcrowded graveyards of the town'.[133] A licentiate of the Society of Apothecaries since 1829, and a member of the Royal College of Surgeons since 1831, Walker had in 1835 studied at St Bartholomew's Hospital, and the following year at the Hôtel Dieu in Paris. Whilst staying in the French capital, he made a point of visiting the city's great cemeteries – Montmartre in the north, Montparnasse in the south, Pere Lachaise in the east – which had recently been established (in the earliest decades of the nineteenth century) outside the city boundaries. Returning to London in 1837, Walker set up his own medical practice at 101 Drury Lane, within a short distance both of Enon Chapel in St Clement's Lane, and Green Ground in nearby Portugal Street – 'two of the most overcrowded and pestilential graveyards in London'.

'A believer in the miasmic theory of disease,' as the reformer's biographer, John Pinfold, notes,

> Walker was convinced that the smell emanating from these overcrowded grave-yards was poisonous and could ruin the health of those who lived nearby.
>
> In *Gatherings from Graveyards* (1839) he exposed the appalling state of urban graveyards and, drawing on his extensive knowledge of health, sanitation, and mortality, sought to prove the connection between disease and burial. His solution was to propose the prohibition of intramural interment and the establishment of new cemeteries outside the towns. This was the first of a series of publications on the subject which was instrumental in securing the appointment in 1842 of the parliamentary select committee on intramural interments.[134]

The refusal of the man who was then home secretary, Sir James Graham (1841–6), to act on the report that was eventually to be produced by this committee, and the continued complacency of many of the medical and ecclesiastical authorities (who, as Pinfold notes, made a tidy bit of money from burial fees), prevented campaigners such as Walker from closing the metropolitan graveyards altogether. Walker was to continue his campaigning for reform, however. In 1845 he established the National Society for the Abolition of Burials in Towns, and he continued to write at length on the subject, publishing *Interment and Disinterment* (1843), *Burial Ground Incendiarism* (1846) and *A Series of Lectures on the Actual Conditions of Metropolitan Graveyards* (1847). 'Some time in 1846–7', Pinfold notes, 'Walker purchased or leased Enon Chapel, with the intention of removing the remains. At his own expense, he arranged for these to be reburied at Norwood cemetery, and 6000 people witnessed their removal in four van loads.'[135] (Excavations for new building in the area undertaken in the mid-1970s revealed human remains still on the site.) Enon Chapel itself remained in existence until the 1890s, by which time it had been renamed the Clare Market Chapel; its location is clearly visible on the 1872 ordnance survey map of the area, close to the site of the law courts, which were then under construction.[136]

An altogether different strand of Todd's narrative – the depiction of the dog Hector's ill-fated fidelity to his master, Lieutenant Thornhill – although clearly featured as part of the Rue-de-la-Harpe story as retold in *The Tell-Tale*, also connects the story with the traditions of still another popular legend that frequently exercised the imagination of Charles Dickens. The original French tale, generally known under the title 'The Dog of Montargis', is set in the fourteenth century (*c*.1371). The legend told of the murder of one Aubrey de Montdidier, a courtier at the court of the Emperor Charles V. According to legend, Montdidier had been murdered in the forest of Bondy, near Montargis, by one Robert Macaire (or Marcaire). The fidelity of the victim's dog to his master and his sustained animosity to Macaire was so great that the dog managed actually to hunt down his master's killer. The Emperor, witnessing the dog's hostility to Macaire and suspecting the circumstances of his inflexible devotion to his dead master, ordered the latter to face the hound in a formal 'combat'. Although Macaire was armed with a cudgel, the dog managed to pin him to the ground; Macaire's full confession to Montdidier's murder resulted in his hanging. In some dramatic and extended prose fiction versions of the story, Macaire was depicted as having come to an even more violent end. In one such retelling he is said to have been pursued by the dog until he was compelled suicidally to jump from a cliff; in another, Montdidier's dog, managing with his mouth somehow to manipulate a gun, even fires a shot at Macaire and kills him.

The most popular and generally available textual and dramatic source for the story was a French melodrama by René-Charles Guilbert de Pixérécourt (1773–1844), *Le Chien de Montargis*. An English version of Pixérécourt's stage play was first produced in London, at Drury Lane, in 1814. The legend continued to furnish the plot for a number of popular melodramas throughout the 1830s and 1840s, variations often presented to the public under the name *The Forest of Bondy, or the Dog of Montargis*. The performance of a trained dog on stage (in some English versions given the name of 'Tiger' or 'Dragon') is said frequently to have caused a sensation. Dickens, again, knew the legend of 'The Dog of Montargis' well; he made use of the tale in 'Our School' (originally published in 1836) and later in both *Dombey and Son* (1846–8) and 'A Christmas Tree', included in *Household Words* (1850).[137]

Tales such as 'The Dog of Montargis' would appear to some extent to have served as a counterbalance of sorts to the negative designation and dismissal of dogs – and of the canine, generally – in much widespread cultural and language imagery (e.g. 'hounds', 'curs' etc.). On closer examination, one is likely to find that traditional stories that make some use of the 'faithful dog' motif are to be found in almost every national culture in Europe, and in nearly every era. The Welsh legend of 'The Dog Gellert', for example, in which the faithful Gellert is slain by his own master, Llewellyn, who has been deceived into believing that the dog has devoured his infant son, is a close narrative cousin to a nearly identical German tale, in which the name of the hound has been changed to 'Sultan'. Another French story of the same type – 'Folliculus and his Dog' – can be found in French collections of *fabliaux* that were first compiled by the likes of Le Grand d'Aussy and Edéléstand du Méril, the substance of which was in turn popularized throughout the continent in the medieval collection *Gesta Romanorum* or 'Deeds of the Romans' (*c.*1300). The French essayist Montaigne, certainly, as part of an extended discussion comparing the behaviour of men and animals included in his *Apology for Raymond Sebond*, remarked that there was no shortage of 'histories [that] tell of the keen pursuit that some dogs have made after the murderers of their masters', and included anecdotes relating to King Pyrrhus, Hesiod and Plutarch among his examples of such behaviour.[138] Some have even suggested that the notion that intelligent animals such as dogs were capable of maintaining this sort of harmonious relationship with their masters belonged to a 'twilight stage' of human intelligence, in which primitive man has not yet established the extent of his innate superiority to such animals.[139] Ultimately, such stories can usually be traced in some form as far back as Sanskrit collections of tales.[140]

Finally, a possible, very early source for one of the more peculiar features of the Sweeney Todd narrative that has been overlooked by almost all previous writers on the subject is the remarkable product of a late sixteenth-century writer of popular poems and romances by the name of Thomas Deloney (c.1543–c.1602).[141] (It is worth pointing out at once that, in this particular instance, *The String of Pearls* may very well share a significant aspect of its textual ancestry with no less illustrious a cousin than William Shakespeare's *Macbeth*.)[142]

The author of three ballads celebrating the defeat of the Spanish Armada in 1588, Deloney, who was by trade a silk-weaver and pedlar, also wrote a number of pieces of prose fiction that subsequently earned him some reputation, along with his rather more celebrated contemporary Thomas Nashe (1567–1601), as one of the earliest writers of realistic 'novels' in English. Among the most popular of Deloney's fictions was the rather inaptly named *Pleasant History of Thomas of Reading*, which was first entered in the *Stationer's Register* in 1602, and survives in a fourth edition published in 1612.[143] Deloney's prose narratives typically dealt with the activities of the urban tradesmen, factory workers and 'industrious apprentices' with whom he would have had contact in his everyday world; it was in Deloney, as the historian of the novel Walter Allen observed some time ago, that London tradesmen of the era 'found their spokesman'; behind Deloney's work it is possible even today to 'feel a whole tradition of humble popular tales'.[144] Insofar as he was obviously captivated by the 'underworld' literature of his day, Deloney was to find companions and successors in such like-minded figures as the poet and playwright Ben Jonson – a writer who would similarly be drawn against his more decorous impulses to the emerging criminal literature of the rapidly expanding metropolis. Deloney's writing is also to some extent closely connected to the so-called 'coney-catching' pamphlets of authors such as Robert Greene (c.1560–92), and the Kentish magistrate Thomas Harmon (fl.1560). 'Coney catching' was a phrase commonly used in the underworld writing of the sixteenth and seventeenth centuries to describe the deception of innocents by those who might today be called 'con artists'; such Elizabethan rogue literature 'is often vividly descriptive and often confessional, providing an important source for our knowledge of everyday common life and its language, as well as for the canting [i.e. slang] terms of thieves and beggars'.[145]

Deloney's *Thomas of Reading* is most noteworthy for including the anecdotal account of an innkeeper and his wife who routinely murder those unfortunate guests who stop to spend the night with them as they journey up to London from the country. Aware that the eponymous Thomas of Reading 'having every time he came thither great store of his money to lay up', the couple 'appointed him the next fat pig that should be killed'. 'For it is to be understood,' as Deloney relates with no small degree of relish, intended no doubt to send a chill of horror through his readers, 'that when they plotted the murder of any man, this was always their terme, the man to his wife & the woman to her husband, Wife, there is now a fat pig to be had if you want one. Whereupon she would answere thus, I pray you put him in the hogstie till to morrow. This was, when any man came thither alone without others in his company, and they saw he had great store of money.'[146]

The couple's avarice and low cunning in their manner of thus waylaying their unwary and trusting guests – even their use of an obscenely humorous and cannibalistically coded language – would appear at first glance merely to be an early, written version in English of many such tales in which stranded or quite literally benighted travellers are 'done in' by their seemingly generous but unctuously duplicitous hosts. Arguably, Deloney is particularly adept at capturing something of the casual and unaffected diction that might well have been used by his characters. Episodes of this sort, long something of a fixture in local folk and fairy tale traditions throughout Europe, would in time be incorporated within lengthier or more substantial narrative fictions, much in the manner that, for instance, Matthew Lewis would draw upon sources such as Lorenz Flammenberg's *Der Geisterbanner* ('The Necromancer' (1792)) in the 'History of Don Raymond' included in his sensational gothic novel *The Monk* (1796).[147] Dramatists roughly contemporaneous with Deloney, such as the anonymous author of the Elizabethan domestic tragedy *Arden of Feversham* (1592), which had itself been based on a notorious murder that had occurred in February 1551 – a prose account of which had even been included in a 1557 edition of Holinshed's *Chronicles* – had already made use of similar stories, and other such 'lugubrious' cautionary tales would continue to prove popular with theatre audiences in England well into the eighteenth century.[148] George Lillo's 1736 tragedy, *Guilt its own Punishment; or, Fatal Curiosity*, was to be based in turn on a crime reported in a pamphlet, *Newes from Perin in Cornwall of A most Bloody and un-exampled Murther ...* (1618); Lillo's drama, in which an elderly married couple living on the Cornish coast, 'tired with [their] woes and hopeless of relief', unwittingly murder their own long-lost son in their attempt to steal his possessions, would draw for much of its thrill on its supposed veracity (the story had been included in the reputable histories of William Sanderson (1656) and in the popular *Frankland's Annals* (1681), although Austrian, Bohemian, German, Italian, Corsican, Bulgarian, Polish and even Chinese analogues were already in circulation).[149] It is no coincidence that Lillo had himself planned to present his own version of *Arden of Feversham* before his death in 1739.

What memorably sets Deloney's narrative apart from its possible precedents and analogues in English, however, is the manner in which his scheming couple actually set about killing their victims. The pair would invite the traveller into their home and show him into a bedroom.

> This man would be then layd in the chamber right over the kitchin, which was a faire chamber, and better set out than any other in the house; the best bedstead therein, though it were little and low, yet was it most cunningly carved, and faire to the eye: the feet of whereof were fast naild to the chamber floore, in such sort, that it could not in any wise fall, the bed that lay therein was fast joined to the sides of the bedsted: Moreover, that part of the chamber whereupon this bed and bedsted stoode, was made in such sort that by the pulling out of two yron pinnes below in the kitchin, it was to be let downe and taken up by a drawbridge, as in manner of a trappe doore: moreover, in the kitchin, directly under the place should fall, was a mighty great caldron, wherein they used to seethe their liquor when they went to brewing. Now, the men appointed for this slaughter, were laid in this bed, and in the dead time of the night when they were found asleep by plucking out the foresaid iron pinns, downe the man would fall out of his bed into the boyling caldron, and all the cloathes that were upon him: where being suddenly scalded and drowned, he was never able to cry or speak one word.[150]

Having thus so efficiently done away with their chosen victim in this brutal manner, the murderous couple would then set about disposing of the body and of any circumstantial evidence that might connect them to the crime:

> Then had they a little ladder ever standing in the kitchin, by the which they presently mounted into the sayd chamber, and there closely tooke away the mans apparell, as also his money, in his male or capcase: and then lifting up the sayd falling floore which hung by hinges, they made it fast as before. The dead body would they then take out of the Caldron and throw it down the river, which ran nere unto their house, whereby they escaped all danger.[151]

On the occasion of their murder of Thomas of Reading, the husband, having kept a careful eye on the traveller, betrays some unwonted anxiety, and appears to be beset by second thoughts; he is spurred on by his more grimly resolute partner (hence the possible connections to *Macbeth*):

> [The] host and hostesse, that all this while noted his troubled mind, began to commune betwixt themselves thereof. And the man said, he knew not what were best to be done. By my consent (quoth he) the matter would passe, for I thinke it is not best to meddle on him. What man (quoth she) faint you now? Have you done so many, and do you shrinke at this? When shewing him a great deale of gold which Cole had left with her, she said, Would it not grieve a bodies heart to loose this? Hang the old churle, what would he do living any longer? He hath too much, and we have too little: tut husband, let the thing be done and then this is our owne.[152]

Unfortunately for Thomas, the husband submits to his wife's persuasions:

> Her wicked counsell was followed, and when they had listened at his chamber doore, they heard the man sound asleep. All is safe, quoth they, and downe into the kitchin they goe, their servants being all in bedde, and pulling out the yron pinnes, downe fel the bed, and the man dropt out into the boyling caldron. He being dead, they betwixt them cast his body into the river, his clothes they hid away, and made all things as it should be.[153]

The murder of Thomas of Reading proves to be the couple's final outrage, however. In having thus so brutally killed a well-known merchant who was, moreover, employed 'in a great office under his Majesty', the two had over-reached their ambitions, and were punished accordingly. Yet even the execution of Thomas's murderers was not enough to satisfy the royal authority:

> When the king heard of this murder, he was for the space of [several] days so sorrowful and heavy that he would not heare any suite, giving also commaundement, that the house should quite be consumed with fire wherein [Thomas] Cole was murdered, and that no man should ever build upon that cursed ground.... And some say, that the river whereinto Cole was cast, did ever since carry the name Cole, being called, The river of Cole, and the towne of Colebrooke.[154]

Professing thus merely to provide a rudimentary, etiological myth for the name of a local river and the foundation of a provincial English town, Deloney's tale of course left a far more influential legacy in the form of the narrative substance that it may well have provided for the specific motivations of Shakespeare's own unspeakable regicides. It remains of considerable interest to followers of the Sweeney Todd myth, of course, for its detailed inclusion and description of a mechanical device remarkably similar to the barber's famous revolving chair. A number of later retellings of Todd's story attribute the invention of his 'ingenious' chair (which, as an infallibly effective piece of dramatic business, was almost always to figure prominently in subsequent dramatic versions of the story), to the knowledge the barber had gained in his early training as a cutler. Still others, as we will see, include the representation of an accomplice mechanic (e.g. 'Ezekial Smith') whose efforts on Todd's behalf are ill-repaid when he falls an early victim to his own device. The details described by Deloney in his account of the trap-door, hinges, ladder and iron pins involved in the treacherous device of the Colebrooke murderers certainly warrant some consideration that the writer of *The String of Pearls* may very well have been explicitly aware of his predecessor's narrative, or, at the very least, that this most unusual feature of the tale of *Thomas of Reading* remained an element of the narrative yet in oral circulation in the early and mid-nineteenth century.

*

Hell is a city much like London.

(Percy Bysshe Shelley, *Peter Bell the Third*)[155]

Whenever and however it was that the original author of *The String of Pearls* first conceived of the essential plot of his story, he would have been aware of the fact that many of the most significant narrative and thematic elements that were eventually to play some sort of role in his final tale had already been scattered fairly widely throughout narrative and (perhaps) actual European history. In no other *single* written narrative, however, had these otherwise diverse and often 'free-standing' elements been drawn together so as to form a unified and organic whole. The central achievement of *The String of Pearls* as it was first articulated in Lloyd's 1846–7 publication was to pull together these various analogues and precedents – the murderous barber, the purveyor of 'cannibalic pastries', the basis of their criminal partnership, the 'faithful hound', the spectacle of unsanitary and overcharged cemeteries, rural fears of the city, metropolitan notions of the 'country' etc. – and to give them expression within the conceit of a combined melodramatic plot. The many components of the story of *The String of Pearls* otherwise appear in forms so diverse and dispersed that it would be fruitless to look any further – as so many have attempted over the years – for any one, single historical incident upon which the serial was based, or to speculate as to *precisely* how and when they came to be united in the mind and imagination of the tale's anonymous author. This diversity of origins is perhaps reflected in the manner in which the story itself has rather perversely refused ever since to assume any single or definitive form – it is known to some as a myth or a novel, to others as a melodrama or a play, and to still others (as we shall see) as a film, a musical, an opera or even a ballet. It remains deeply significant, however, that the created elements of myth that were given voice through the story became a part of the mythic structure of the city itself; the story of Sweeney Todd seems increasingly to have functioned as a kind of imaginative nexus that connected the experience of urban enterprise and of speculators in urban goods and merchandise, with the exploitation and consumption of the human frame itself. The 'soaring ascent' of the City of London as a 'whole earth emporium' for the entire world, as David Kynaston has put it, is one the grandest and most intriguing spectacles of nineteenth-century European history; the story of 'Sweeney Todd' is the myth of dark foreboding that captures the grim and cautionary warnings of the dangers inherent within the otherwise astounding rise of metropolitan and cosmopolitan civilization. If Victorian London was in many ways 'a world of its own', then it was a city that had captured and articulated a myth that could likewise, in time, be looked upon as something 'all its own', as well.[156]

The preceding section made note of the observation of the twentieth-century novelist Neil Gaiman that part of the sustained appeal of Todd's story for modern readers appears to lie in its inescapable *relevance*. 'Sweeney Todd and Mrs. Lovett between them', Gaiman commented, again, 'embody two basic human needs. The need to look good and the need to eat.' Appetite and appearances will always be important to us; but of these two, it is appetite that is a paramount human *need*; furthermore, of the objects of our two primary appetites – sexual and nutritional – it could be argued that while we may be able to *live* without the first (however inconvenient that might prove to be for some), we can hardly be expected to disregard the second entirely. The very notion of 'appetite' as expressed in Todd's story again, however, links the expression of needful desire to the figurative language of the city. As Peter Ackroyd notes, one of the predominant images of the urban landscape is that of 'the body'. London is 'fleshy and voracious, grown fat upon its appetite for people and for food, for goods and for drink; it consumes and it excretes, maintained within a continual state of greed and desire'; it is commonly portrayed in nineteenth- and twentieth-century fiction 'in monstrous form, a swollen and dropsical giant which kills more than it breeds'.[157] Moreover, just as appetite concerns itself ultimately with a combination of a desire for satiety on the one hand, and a more fundamental human impulse toward survival, on the other, Todd's story is one that will in all its forms (as suggested by the original's recurring obsession with the passage of time as marked by the hands of the clock at St Dunstan's) concern itself closely with approaching time and mortality, and with the twin human emotions of curiosity and simple fear (a remarkable number of characters in the story – even Todd himself – live their lives in a perpetual state of wakefulness and anxiety). As the critic of one of Sweeney Todd's most immediate descendants – Bram Stoker's *Dracula* – Marjorie Howes, has commented of that later novel:

> *Dracula's* dominant emotion is ambivalence: an intimate complex combination of desire and fear. Desire for what, or whom? Fear of what, or whom? ... In many respects the novel is crushingly conventional, and the forces of good and evil seem ranged against each other unambiguously. The text champions a number of standard Victorian values; sexual restraint, especially in women, rigidly defined gender roles, the superiority of West over East, and the triumph of science and reason over superstition and madness. At the same time, however, *Dracula* undermines all these principles, and threatens to blur the boundaries between things that the Victorians wanted to think of as opposites: life and death, good and evil, reason and madness, men and women, desire and fear.[158]

Much the same sort of deconstructive reading that Howes suggests here with references to *Dracula* – a reading that sees the conscious priorities of a supposed series of binary oppositions that are set out within the text collapse upon themselves when the components of those same oppositions are traced and examined with any degree of care – could be applied successfully to Todd's story. (Much like Stoker's *Dracula*, certainly, 'Sweeney Todd' is arguably far more important to our culture when it is considered in light of its status as 'a sensory shocker' than as a literary text.)[159] Although the ostensible heroes or 'good guys' of the piece are Sir Richard Blunt, Colonel Jeffrey and Mark Ingestrie and his young fiancée Johanna Oakley, readers are obviously intrigued more by the demonic and disruptive 'anti-heroic' activities of Todd and Lovett themselves. The necessary maintenance of certain values involving cleanliness, hygiene and appearance – not only with regard to the individual (i.e. shaving), but with reference to society and civilization generally (e.g. burial, food preparation, the protection of the food supply etc.) is, at best, re-inscribed only perilously. Contemporary distinctions between 'us' and 'them' – anxieties of societal self-definition that surrounded the dangers inherent in the imperial enterprise – are spectacularly collapsed through images of reverse colonialism that will be increasingly exploited in subsequent versions of the story. It is not the activity of the supposed savages and 'cannibals' of Africa or the East Indies that Londoners should be worried about; it is the activity of their own near neighbours – the increasingly prosperous lawyers and merchants of Fleet Street and the Temple. The astounding amount of movement and interaction brought about by the rise of commerce brings with it both the fear of societal 'pollution' from abroad, at the same time that it seems to awaken the atavistic impulses that lay buried under a veneer of civilized behaviour increasingly stretched thin (like the crust of a pastry?), and fast approaching its breaking point.

Many readers of Lloyd's original fiction are taken by the fact that the actual spectacle of cannibalism seems to be minimized in the text. At no point in the story is the reader offered any depiction of the grim activities that would have been involved in severing, dissecting and preparing the human carcasses that disappear through Todd's oubliette for consumption; the shelves of Mrs Lovett's are simply described as being 'always ... well stocked with meat' (*PP* 249). Indeed, the author seems more obviously concerned to represent Lovett's cook as an example of the worker alienated from his own labour: 'I cannot be made to be a mere machine for the manufacture of pies,' he cries at one point: 'I cannot, and I will not endure it – it is past all bearing' (*PP* 230). The text appears to be more interested in representing a general *atmosphere* of horror and exploitation, than it is in any graphic descriptions; unlike many of the supposedly more sophisticated gothic novelists that preceded him in the traditions of English fiction, his method is terror by insinuation, rather than by graphic depiction (compare the story's prose, for example, to that of Matthew Lewis's *The Monk*, or even to the admittedly restrained descriptions of physicality in Mary Shelley's *Frankenstein*). Suspicions are raised many times – by Toby, by Sir Richard, by Johanna and by 'Jarvis Williams' – before their conclusions are ever given full voice, and the 'horrific' revelations of the story are delayed until the very end of the tale. It is left to the readers themselves – complicitous, therefore, in the very horrors they might claim to find repulsive – to recreate scenarios of actual murder and cannibalism in their own minds. We constitute and form the very stuff of our fears.

Many modern readers are struck, too, by what might best be described as the degree of cultural and temporal self-awareness that the story seems to betray. *The String of Pearls* is a narrative very conscious of the fact that it is offering its readers a depiction of a society in flux – a snapshot image of a world experiencing constant transformation. To put it another way, it is a fiction that is aware of and seems often to foreground the simple and inescapable *fact* of the metamorphosis of the urban landscape. Like almost all fictions of the 1840s, it is a novel that betrays a startling degree of self-knowledge in its awareness of change – in its perception of the displacement of older age by one that is younger, newer and strikingly more disruptive and dynamic. Yet if the environments, the individuals and the now charming habits and customs of that previous era seem so suddenly to have disappeared, *The String of Pearls* itself appears to dwell not so much on any feeling of nostalgia for what has been lost (as do, for example, the early novels of Dickens himself), as it does on the more sinister aspect of the present and contemporary. The past is irretrievably gone. (If we are – in fact – meant on some level to recollect the figure of 'Suibne' or 'Sweeney' of the historical cycle of Irish legend as a character whose cursed wanderings among the forest madmen had originally been symbolic of Celtic exile, it may be intended also that we recall the era when the *filidh* or poets passed on poems relating to such heroes also as one long gone and now inaccessible. Part of the story's emphasis on 'growth' and change is to suggest that in the very act of expansion, one inevitably leaves the heroes of one's ancient traditions in the past – or at least gravely diminished – as well.) Even the descriptions of the modern Fleet Street with which the story opens – descriptions that *do*, to some extent, emphasize the slower pace of life in the past – move swiftly to dwell at greater length with the 'busy-ness' and conspicuous consumption of the 'modern' Fleet Street of the 1840s. The world of the past – as embodied in the Temple's ancient foundations of law, precedent, accountability – has been abruptly displaced by the hungry young solicitors eager to plead 'fat causes'. The comparative placidity of the 'knowable' has been exchanged for a new age of frantic consumption. 'It has been their thirst for gain that has produced all these evils,' Colonel Jeffrey says of the presumed fates of Thornhill and Mark Ingestrie in his early conversation with Johanna in the Temple Gardens (*PP* 131), and, indeed, the entire world of the narrative is one driven nearly to madness by a collective 'thirst for gain'.

Sweeney Todd himself remains throughout the narrative a creature of deepest paradox – a symbolic representation of the conflicting impulses of the era from which he emerges with his history and his name. He is, of course, a great literary villain, as is Mrs Lovett, but he is one of those villains for whom we tend to cultivate a bizarre and deeply irrational kind of affection. Todd stands himself as the embodiment of an imaginative force that is far too powerful to be confined within the ostensible moral of the tale in which he takes part. While he obviously refuses to accept the dictates of contemporary society, his transgressions are to some extent mitigated by the fact that his superb and absolute egotism reflects the expansive and appetitive spirit of the age, as well. Sweeney Todd is the perfect epitome of the thrusting individualism and aggressive self-determination of the new capitalism. For much of the story he outwits his pursuers and foils the slow-paced attempts of Colonel Jeffrey, Johanna and the forces of Sir Richard Blunt to apprehend him. Our sympathy for Todd's disruptive saturnalian impulses raises the larger social problem of precisely how any form of coercive power can prevail against the potential of such transgression and anarchy. Throughout much of the narrative of Sweeney Todd, the appointed representatives of the law are his most public enemies, and the barber has for years been successful in his attempt to outwit all comers – lesser thieves, detectives and money-lenders among them.

Todd is an atavistic force that is itself reacting against the combined, traditional authorities of social control: the state (in the form of the magistrate and his Bow Street runners), religion (in his 'practical' use of the sacred space of St Dunstan's, and his casual disregard for the supposed sanctity of human life) and even the domestic authority of the family (in the possible union in marriage with Mrs Lovett, or his disruption of Oakley's power over his own household). Arguably, Todd transcends the impulses of mere greed to become the representative figure of those who would utterly reject the social values of his society; he represents that darker aspect of human nature that disregards morality and mortality, yet one, too, who is free from the hypocrisy that plagues and pervades the rest of the world.

PART THREE
Visions and Revisions

Chapter 6

The Way of All Flesh: Sweeney Todd, Melodrama and the Theatre

> *Victorian melodrama may be a bit strong for some squeamish modern palates, but it has the supreme merit of gripping the attention and keeping the interest of the reader on tenter-hooks until villainy is at the end suitably rewarded.*
> (Anonymous, Preface, *Sweeney Todd, the Demon Barber,* 1936)[1]

In a letter sent to the Welsh playwright Eric Jones Evans in May 1961, the actor-manager and stage director Malcolm Morley – who throughout his long professional life maintained a thoroughgoing interest in dramatic adaptations of the work of Charles Dickens, and who was to remain fascinated by the novelist's life-long involvement in the world of the theatre, generally – announced with no small degree of excitement that he had managed finally to discover what he believed to be a substantial connection between Dickens's own writings and the 'Sweeney Todd' story. 'Did you know', he confided to Evans,

> that some of the Madman's speech in *The Pickwick Papers* (the story called The 'Madman's Manuscript') is part of the text of a 'Sweeney Todd' play? It is actually printed in what is called the Traditional Version – I have the versions by [George Dibdin] Pitt and [Frederick] Hazleton which have none of it. Have you any other versions? I want to track this madman down & make an article for the *Dickensian.*[2]

The material to which Morley was referring in this passage would indeed seem to have been well suited to Todd's own tale. The 'Madman' in question is the narrator of the clergyman's story recounted as one of the several darker tales or vignettes that are set within the larger comic narrative of *The Pickwick Papers*; it is read by the character of Pickwick himself, when he is possessed by a fit of insomnia at Dingley Dell, in Chapter 11; it would therefore originally have appeared in Part IV (Chapters 9–11) of the serial, which was

197

first published in July 1836. The secretive tone of still-anxious anticipation and curiosity in Morley's letter suggests that he himself, at least, was eager to entertain the possibility that Dickens had had some hand in the creation of *Sweeney Todd*, or in its earliest expressions. If some portion of the text of Todd's story – however small – that had appeared in what was asserted to be nothing less than a 'traditional' acting version of the play could be traced directly to the hand of the novelist, then Dickens's involvement with some early expression of the story became a distinct possibility. The passage identified by Morley, it should be remembered, pre-dated the first appearance of the work as a prose narrative in Lloyd's periodical by just over a decade.

Morley himself suggested that he owed his newfound awareness of the possible connection between Dickens and Todd to the experience of a friend, the actor John Greaves, who (he claimed) had several months earlier attended a revival of *Sweeney Todd* at the Richmond Theatre. 'Towards the end of the drama', as Morley recounted the anecdote, '[if] his ears did not deceive him, he found himself listening to lines he had himself uttered in his own Dickens Recitals.'[3] In a scene towards the end of the play that was not present in the original prose version of the story, Todd was presented as having escaped the hands of justice; he fled from Fleet Street and Ludgate Hill, with his pursuers hot on his trail. The actor playing Todd that night in the Richmond revival then paused in his flight and soliloquized:

> Straight and swift I ran, and no one dared to stop me. I heard the noise of feet behind, and redoubled my speed. It grew fainter and fainter in the distance, and at length died away altogether: but on I bounded, through marsh and rivulet, over fence and wall, with a wild shout that was taken up by the strange beings that flocked around me on every side, and swelled the sound, till it pierced the air. I was borne upon the arms of demons who swept along upon the wind, and bore down bank and hedge before them, and spun me round and round with a rustle and a speed that made my head swim, until at last they threw me from them with a violent shock, and I fell heavily upon the earth. When I woke I found myself here ... .[4]

The fragment quoted here had indeed been lifted verbatim from Dickens's own text; Morley had discovered the same passage in Montague Slater's 1928 edition of what was described in its title as a 'Traditional Acting Version' of *Sweeney Todd*. 'Easily available,' Morley asserted, 'this is the version generally performed by Repertory Companies for their supporters to cheer or boo in a spirit of mockery and fun.'[5] Slater himself had been rather more qualified in his assumptions. 'Later drama houses [in the nineteenth century] were wont to play Sweeney Todd each in its own version', he wrote in the Introduction to his edition, 'and the text used here follows one of these. It is hopelessly corrupt.'[6] '*Sweeney Todd*,' as Slater elsewhere commented, '*in one or another of its many adaptations*, was frequently played in London and throughout the provinces.'[7] Slater acknowledged that play-texts of Todd's story could vary tremendously not only from company to company and from place to place, but even from one performance to the next. Special adaptations such as the decidedly comedic turn of *Mr Todd of London* – written by the popular music-hall artist John Lawson, who was even to spend several years touring as far afield as South Africa and America – would only complicate matters further for anyone searching for an authoritative edition of the play-text.

Morley's subsequent researches into the matter would eventually compel him to admit that the insertion of the fragment of Dickens's 'Madman's Manuscript' in the particular *Sweeney Todd* play-text reprinted in 1928 by Slater was a simple matter of the frequently opportunistic circumstances that had so often governed the writing and construction of plays throughout the nineteenth century. The many repertory companies of the period routinely tailored their dramatic presentations so as specifically to suit the strengths and weaknesses of their own, particular members (the more innovative playwrights of the period were endlessly baffled, as Michael Booth has written, by the fact that they were 'stuck with actors that could play one typed part and nothing else'). As any reader familiar with the company of Vincent Crummles, as presented by Dickens himself in *Nicholas Nickleby*, would have been aware, the melodramatic play-texts of the period could more accurately be described as a series of pastiches, translations, plagiarisms and palimpsests than as works with any claim to originality. Establishing 'definitive' or even reliable versions of those dramas constructed specifically for the penny gaffs and travelling fit-ups of the period, as opposed to the great patent houses of the West End, was a hopeless endeavour.[8] Not only could roles and characters vary from production to production; they could often disappear entirely. As Morley observed of the early history of *Sweeney Todd* on the stage:

> In [the] first dramatisation of [Thomas Peckton Prest's] story was an effer-
> vescing young woman, Cecily Maybush, a character enacted by the manageress
> of the Britannia, the [renowned] Sarah Lane. The lively Cecily afterwards
> vanished from the 'terrible tale' as did others of the dramatis personae from
> the numerous dramas that spread themselves over the Minor Theatres. Ben
> Bluffhead, Bully Grayson, Sneaking Joe, and Tom Cutaway were all discarded
> in the course of time.[9]

'It is quite possible', Morley speculated, when he finally got around to writing the material up for publication,

> that, at some time or other, an actor playing Sweeney thought to build up
> his part with the descriptive wording of Dickens. It had a literary flavour
> and, in a version where Todd is shown in flight from the officers of the law,
> could be made applicable. The text of the old melodrama was not considered
> sacrosanct. Speeches often travelled from one play to another, particularly
> when the lines were apropos of a stereotyped situation. Actors looked for what

they termed 'bits of fat'; rhetorical outbursts which they embellished with their favourite flourishes. In one of the Sweeney plays of comparatively recent vintage, the leading man revelled in an oration from *The Silver King* [1882] of Henry Arthur Jones. Dickens was thus not the only author to contribute anonymously to *Sweeney Todd*.[10]

Both the general interest and the more precise literary detective work necessary to speculations such as Morley's are worth dwelling on, if only because they highlight the unusually persistent belief that *Sweeney Todd* – when admitted to be a work of fiction in the first place – is the product of the world of the theatre, as opposed to that of popular prose fiction (however 'coarse' and popular) or the printed page; many individuals over the years, that is, have continued in the face of all the evidence to assert that Todd *originated* not as a serial narrative in the periodical press, but as a drama. Montague Slater seems unfortunately to have made an incalculable contri-bution to such sustained misunderstanding when – in precisely the 1928 edition referred to by Morley, above – he dated the earliest dramatic version of the story from 1842 (thus pre-dating the serial in *The People's Periodical* by as much as four years), rather than (as was correct) 1847.

George Dibdin Pitt's stage version of the play was, indeed, the first of many such dramatizations of the barber's story and the theatre would, no doubt, be perhaps the primary medium through which *Sweeney Todd* was to be transmitted to subsequent generations. As much influence as it was to enjoy, however, readers must always remind themselves that Dibdin Pitt's was *not* the first version of the story to reach the public. Before tracing something of the early history of his stage adaptation, it might be convenient here to mention something about the man himself.

*

I must say the Barber was well played and as dramatic impressions are so strong with me, I should not go out of my way to get my hair cut in Fleet Street just at present.
(Thomas W. Erle, *Letters from a Theatrical Scene-Painter*)[11]

Some time in 1767, the well-known actor, composer and writer Charles Dibdin the Elder (1745–1814) left his wife to live with his mistress, a Covent Garden dancer by the name of Harriet Pitt (*c.*1748–1814); Harriet was herself the daughter of Ann Pitt (*c.*1720–99), who had been one of the most celebrated comic actresses of her day (she had played opposite Garrick at Drury Lane, before moving on to a long and successful career at Covent Garden).[12] By the time Charles Dibdin and Harriet Pitt began living together, Harriet had already borne two children – Harriet and Cecil – to the actor George Mattocks. Eventually she was to give birth to another two sons – Charles and Thomas – before being abandoned by Dibdin in about 1775.

Harriet's eldest son, Cecil Pitt, in time became a musician, and it was he who was father to the playwright George Dibdin Pitt (1799–1855). George – who thus stood in neither a natural nor a legal relationship with regards to his grandmother's one-time lover – would appear therefore to have taken on the 'Dibdin' name merely as a matter of professional expediency. Surrounded as he had always been by brothers, sisters, cousins, parents and grandparents who had themselves been musicians, actors, actresses and playwrights, there would seem to have been little possibility of his ever pursuing a livelihood anywhere outside the world of the theatre himself.

The first play recorded as being attributed to George Dibdin Pitt – *My Own Blue Bell* – was performed at the Surrey theatre in 1831; it is assumed by many that he was already by that date the theatre's 'resident dramatist'. By 1835, George had taken on the duties of stage manager at the Pavilion Theatre, Mile End, and very soon thereafter assumed the role of stock author to the Britannia Theatre in Hoxton. He was to remain at the Britannia until his death in 1855.[13] Although he may have been, as one critic of the period's melodrama put it, 'a hack writer of the most rough and ready kind', George Dibdin Pitt was by any standard remarkably reliable and prolific.[14] Whilst working at the Britannia in 1845, he staged no fewer than 16 of his own pieces, and enjoyed seeing another nine of his works performed at other theatres throughout London; just two years later, no fewer than 21 of his plays were performed at his home theatre, and five staged elsewhere in the capital. Among Dibdin Pitt's credits was a hugely popular adaptation of William Harrison Ainsworth's *Rookwood* (1840) – which the playwright produced as a 'horse-drama' – and one of the era's most famous monster-melodramas, *The Eddystone Elf*, first staged at Sadler's Wells in 1834. Like so many of the other authors who wrote to provide a steady stream of popular material for the crowds that patronized the cheap theatres of the capital, Pitt often turned to journals such as those published by Edward Lloyd for his material; not infrequently, he might lift entire plots and even specific and often extended sequences of dialogue from these same sources. The absence of any copyright laws to prevent such easy appropriation only helped to render what might otherwise have been deemed to be an act of wholesale 'piracy' entirely permissible. The twentieth-century editor Michael Kilgariff, attempting to describe the manner in which Dibdin Pitt produced his plays as 'pieces to order with conveyor-belt regularity', quoted his predecessor H. Chance Newton when describing the working methods of Colin Hazlewood, a stock writer who eventually followed in Dibdin Pitt's own footsteps at the Britannia. 'When I say that Hazlewood "wrote" these plays', Newton observed,

> of course it was hardly to be expected that he would be able to sit down and work out such new dramas in any pronounced literary fashion for such a weekly wage.

He had a very good method, however. He used to take in the popular periodicals of the time, such as *The London Journal*, *The London Reader*, *Reynold's Miscellany*, *The Welcome Guest*, and other such publications, alas! long defunct. To these Hazlewood added all the penny bloods of his young days, such as *The Boys of England*, *The Young Men of England*, and all the highwaymen stories and similar cheap books.

Hazlewood, or one of us working with him, would run through these periodicals, jotting down the main incidents in the stories thereof, and scissoring out here and there sundry axioms, aphorisms, and moral sentiments, and so forth. These were docketed alphabetically, and when Colin (a dear old fellow) was engaged in writing, or sticking down, a new play for the [Britannia], etc., he or his assistants would take down from the shelf sundry envelopes containing these aphorisms, such as 'Ambitions is', etc., or 'Kindness of heart', etc. and so forth, and would pop these moral, patriotic, and other reflections into the play-script then under way.[15]

Some critics have suggested that the writers of the 'Salisbury School' – aware of the fact that it would only be a matter of time (sometimes only weeks) before their own prose fictions could be counted on to show up on the boards of the capital's cheap theatres – entered into some sort of relationship with the theatre owners themselves, whereby they offered their services 'in the hope of getting a little financial recompense for their tales rather than stand by and see them stolen for nothing'.[16] Haining suggested that Thomas Peckett Prest, whom he believed to be the author of *The String of Pearls*, 'played a part in seeing [that work] transferred to the stage, perhaps even lending George Dibdin Pitt a hand in the actual dramatisation'.[17] 'The first stage presentation of *The String of Pearls*', Haining reminded readers, 'had opened at least *three weeks* before the serial reached its final episode in *The People's Periodical*; and although there are differences in the text of the serial and the play, the crucial closing episodes are much the same in both. These are surely developments that only Prest could have known and must have shared with Dibdin Pitt – if he did not actually write some of the drama itself.'[18] Haining also observed that Dibdin Pitt was to be credited with having produced no fewer than 26 plays in the course of 1847, 'a total that even in those prolific days it seems hard to believe he could have achieved without some form of assistance'. 'It therefore seems probable', he concluded, '… that Pitt and Prest pooled their talents on this occasion, too. The fact that the play is not specifically credited to Pitt – as most of his other works were – is also a factor not without significance.'[19]

Although Haining's last point (regarding the lack of attribution of the piece specifically to Dibdin Pitt on its earliest appearance) remains valid, his suggestion that Pitt and Prest joined forces to produce a version of the story for the stage is unlikely. Despite his assertion that 'the crucial closing episodes are much the same in both [the serial and the play]', it would be more accurate to state, as Dick Collins has in his recent edition of *The String of Pearls*, that 'the ending of the play is ludicrously wrong' when read in light of the printed, serial version of 1846–7.[20] In fact, the many subsequent adaptations of *Sweeney Todd* attributed to or based on George Dibdin Pitt's original 1847 version of *The String of Pearls* for the stage *do* tend to bear one thing at least in common: they are all remarkably *unlike* the prose version of the story first published by Lloyd. For one thing, they introduced a modified cast of characters into the story. One of the original playbills for the version of *The String of Pearls* attributed to Dibdin Pitt survives in the collection of the British Museum. It announces that *The String of Pearls; or, the Fiend of Fleet Street* has been 'taken from the much admired Tale of that name (founded on fact) in *Lloyd's Peoples* [sic] *Periodical*'. 'For Dramatic effect', the playbill continues, 'and to adapt the story to general taste, some alterations have been judiciously made, enhancing its interest.'[21] The playbill then gives the following cast for a performance at the Britannia Theatre, Hoxton, on 1 March 1847:

Colonel Jeffrey by Mr. J. Mordaunt
Captain Rathbone by Mr. Arthur
Mr Grant by Mr. Clements
Mr Oakley by Mr. Colwell
Rev Mr Lupin by Mr. F. Wilton
Sweeney Todd by Mr. M. Howard.
Tobias Ragg by Mrs. Hudson Kirby
Thornhill, alias Mark Ingestrie by Mr. Sawford
Mr Parmine by Mr. Cecil Pitt
Jarvis by Mr. J. Gardener
Hector by Mrs. Roby
Ben Bluffhead by Mr. Macarthy
Ruby by Mr. H. Pitt
Fogg by Mr. Roberts
Constable by Mr. Davidson
Johanna Oakley by Miss C. Braham
Mrs Oakley by Mrs. Colwell
Mrs Lovett by Miss Hamilton

Another cast list was printed in a published edition of the play in 1883, which differed in several significant respects from the original playbill. Later editors such as Kilgariff suggested that the play 'was probably altered in subsequent performances, and it is doubtless the improved version which was eventually published [in 1883]'. The second cast to be credited as having acted in the play 'as performed at the Britannia Theatre 1847' read as follows:

Sir William Brandon, a Judge, by Mr. C. Williams
Colonel Jeffrey, of the Indian Army, by Mr. J. Reynolds
Jasper Oakley, a Spectacle-maker, by Mr. Elliott
Mark Ingestrie, a Mariner, by Mr. S. Sawford
Sweeney Todd, the Barber of Fleet Street, by Mr. Mark Howard

Dr Aminadab Lupin, a Wolf in Sheep's Clothing, by Mr. J. Dunn
Jarvis Williams, a Lad with no small appetite, by Mr. W. Rogers
Jonas Fogg, a Keeper of a Mad-house, by Mr. C. Pitt
Jean Parmine, a Lapidary, by Mr. J. Pitt
Tobias Ragg, Sweeney Todd's Apprentice-boy, by Miss Burrows
Mrs Oakley, Jasper's wife, by Mrs. Newham
Johanna, her daughter, by Miss Colwell
Mrs Lovett, Sweeney Todd's Accomplice in Guilt, by Mrs. Atkinson

Mark Howard, noted in both cast lists here as having assumed the role of Todd, is the first of many minor actors to make something of a name for themselves by playing the role. Howard – who was later in his professional life nicknamed 'the Fiendish Figaro' – was to play the part of Todd several times throughout his stage career, and Haining suggested that he is to be credited with having originated some of the mannerisms that later came to be associated with the part. The actress Maria Hamilton, who is listed in the first of the two playbills as having originated the role of Mrs Lovett on the stage, appears soon afterwards to have turned over the part to a veteran actress in the melodrama of the day, Mrs Emma Atkinson. Tobias Ragg, it might be noted, is in both casts played by a young woman who cross-dressed as a boy, still a common enough practice at the time (similar roles, such as that of 'Smike' in early stage adaptations of *Nicholas Nickleby*, were likewise typically assigned to the diminutive actresses of a company).

Dibdin Pitt's dramatic adaptation of Todd's story was most frequently told within the space of two (or occasionally three) short acts – often less. The time in actual representation might run just over one-and-a-half hours. (In whatever version one encounters it, the play-text of the work is almost hopelessly confused; it comes as no surprise that many of those who have attempted to stage Dibdin Pitt's version in the twentieth century – Brian Burton (1962), Austin Rosser (1969), Christopher Bond (1973) – ended up rewriting the work almost entirely.) As the curtain rises on the scene of the interior of Todd's shop, the audience witnesses Sweeney Todd warning his servant Tobias not to be too inquisitive regarding what chanced to happen on the premises. As in the earliest prose versions of the story, Tobias's mention of veal pies in Bell Yard sparks the barber's suspicion that the boy may know more than he lets on. The young sailor Mark Ingestrie enters; newly arrived in London, he shows Todd the pearls he has brought back from the Far East. Mark inquires after Jasper Oakley of Fore Street, but before the young sailor can set out and find Johanna, Todd uses the excuse of having misplaced his leather strop in a next-door room to flip the barber's chair, and dump Mark into the basement. (Many versions of the play often thus dispose of the mystery surrounding Lieutenant Thornhill entirely, moving directly to the concerns of the central romantic couple.) Sweeney Todd returns to the stage with Mark's pearls in his hand, noting that its sum will complete the

£100,000 target he had set to attain for himself. His motives are articulated with inescapable clarity: 'When a boy', Todd tells the audience, 'the thirst of avarice was first awakened by the fair gift of a farthing; that farthing soon became a pound; the pound a hundred – so to a thousand'.[22] When Tobias tells Todd that the servant of a previous customer is inquiring after him, Todd notes that he will have to dispatch Tobias, who takes up the hat 'left behind' by the previous gentleman, as well.

Jean Parmine, a jeweller, then enters the barber shop. Todd asks him what kind of price the pearls might fetch. When Parmine first tries to swindle him and then questions the provenance of the pearls in question, Todd forces him into the chair and exclaims 'I've polished him off!' as he throws the jeweller to his death. Mark's former companion, Colonel Jeffrey, meanwhile, visits Johanna for himself. He tells her that both he and Mark had arrived in London on the same ship three days earlier, and Mark should have contacted Johanna by now. The troubled Johanna agrees to meet up with Jeffrey in a week's time. Dr Lupin, the comical but lecherous divine favoured by Mrs Oakley, arrives and attempts to seduce Johanna. He is frustrated when Colonel Jeffrey, in the company of some of Oakley's household servants, returns on the scene just in time to 'thump' him.

The scene then shifts to Mrs Lovett's establishment, where she is seen hiring the ragged Jarvis Williams to work in the bake-house. Lovett leaves Williams in her basement, with a pointed warning that if he is idle or neglects her orders he will, like the others before him, swiftly be dispatched to visit his 'old friends'. The ravenous Jarvis eats one of Lovett's meat pies, but is startled when he finds first a hair and then a button in the pie's filling. Williams begins to suspect that something is amiss, and soon realizes that the pies are made from human flesh. At that same moment, the jeweller Parmine, who had survived the typically fatal fall from Todd's chair into the cellar, hammers through one of the ancient, subterranean walls that separates the two properties. Parmine tells Williams that there are other hidden chambers and passageways in the cellars, and suggests that they use these passages in an attempt to find a way out. Sweeney, alone, enters and tells the audience that, in addition to ridding himself of Tobias, he will plan also to dispatch Mrs Lovett, who has outlasted her use to him and now stands in the way of his plans for the future. Todd decides to poison her. Lovett herself overhears Todd's musings, and confronts the barber to demand her share of the profits they have together accumulated over the years. The barber surprises her by suggesting that it is she who owes *him* money, for all the 'support' he has given her business. No sooner has Lovett drawn a knife, than Todd draws a gun and kills her, throwing her body into the bake-house oven.

As the second act opens, the bake-house cook Jarvis Williams enters in the company of Tobias; Williams claims that he has found the specific passage that connects the basement of Todd's barber shop to the cellar of Mrs Lovett's Bell Yard establishment. Tobias returns to the barber shop, where he is confronted by Todd, who claims that his power over his mother is due to his knowledge that she stole a silver candlestick from her previous employer, a lawyer in the Temple (such a crime would be punishable by death). Tobias threatens to denounce the barber himself for the crime. As Todd struggles with the boy, his barber's chair turns on its hinges and returns to its upright position in the shop, and the barber is confronted by the bloodied figure of Mark Ingestrie. Todd – thinking Mark to be an apparition – laughs hysterically.

As in the original story, Todd incarcerates Tobias in Jonas Fogg's Mad-house in Peckham, claiming that the boy is insane, and that he even thinks Todd himself to be a dangerous murderer. Tobias is rescued very soon after having been left in Fogg's care by Jarvis, who, having traced the boy to the asylum, rushes in and thumps Fogg and his men. Colonel Jeffrey, meanwhile, meets Johanna at the Temple Stairs as arranged in the first act; he tells her that he fears for Mark's safety, and also laments his misfortune to fall in love with someone who – committed as she is to another lover – cannot return his affection. Todd enters, mysteriously disguised in a cloak and mask, and tells Jeffrey he has some news for him and, as proof, hands him the pearls. Todd now thinks that suspicion for the theft of the pearls – and for Mark's subsequent disappearance – will attach itself to Jeffrey rather than to himself.

The closing scenes of the play are set in a courtroom. Jeffrey is presented as a prisoner before the bar. The judge suggests that Jeffrey's motive for removing Mark from the scene was so that he might gain access to Johanna for himself. The judge produces a mysterious letter that urges him to forbear pronouncing sentence upon Colonel Jeffrey just yet. Todd stands up to implicate the 'missing' Toby in the murder, at which point the barber once again sees the figure of Mark Ingestrie, arising to accuse him in the manner of Banquo's ghost. Todd's testimony becomes hysterical and incoherent in the presence of this bloody 'ghost'. Sweeney screams aloud a confession that it is he who is a murderer, and not Jeffrey. Mark ends the play with an affirmation of his survival and identity: 'Yes. Mark Ingestrie, who, preserved from death by a miracle, returns to confound the guilty and protect the innocent.'[23]

Theatre critics of the day would never have deemed the productions staged at theatres such as the Britannia worthy of their time and attention. Respectable citizens, it was assumed, would never venture so far east as Hoxton, and no press notices of any sort for the 'original' production of this *Sweeney Todd* survive (nor, indeed, are they likely even to have been written). We are, however, fortunate enough to possess several documents which, when taken together, shed considerable light on what the earliest productions of the drama might actually have looked like on the stage, and how they might have been received by their earliest audiences. The first two of these are from the hand of Charles Dickens himself. Although not offering an actual account of a production of *Sweeney Todd*, Dickens twice described the environment of the Britannia Theatre itself in his journalism. (The theatre is designated a 'saloon' in Dickens's piece and elsewhere; the term was used throughout the nineteenth century, as the theatrical historian Jim Davis notes, to describe those theatres where 'access was only possible to the theatre buildings through the taverns through which they were attached'.)[24] The first of Dickens's descriptions of the Britannia was included in his periodical *Household Words* on 13 April 1850. 'The Saloon in question', Dickens begins, of the Britannia:

is the largest in London (that which is known as the Eagle, in the City Road, should be excepted from the generic term, as not presenting by any means the same class of entertainment), and is situated not far from Shoreditch Church. It announces 'The People's Theatre' as its second name. The prices of admission are, to the boxes, a shilling; to the pit, sixpence; to the lower gallery, fourpence; to the upper gallery and back seats, threepence. There is no half-price.... .

The outer avenues and passages of the People's Theatre bore abundant testimony to the fact of its being frequented by very dirty people. Within, the atmosphere was far from odoriferous.

The place was crammed to excess, in all parts. Among the audience were a large number of boys and youths, and a great many very young girls grown into bold women before they had well ceased to be children. These last were the worst features of the whole crowd, and were more prominent there than in any other sort of public assembly that we know of, except a public execution. There was no drink supplied, beyond the contents of the porter-can (magnified in its dimensions, perhaps) which may usually be seen travelling the galleries of the largest Theatres as well as the least, and which was here seen every-where. Huge ham sandwiches, piled on trays like deals in a timber-yard were handed about for sale to the hungry; and there was no stint of oranges, cakes, brandy-balls, or other similar refreshments. The Theatre was capacious, with a very large capable stage, well lighted, well appointed, and managed in a business-like, orderly manner in all respects; the performances had begun so early as a quarter past six, and had been then in progress for three-quarters of an hour.

It was apparent here, as in the theatre we had previously visited [i.e. the Grecian Saloon, City Road, Hoxton, referred to above by its earlier name, the Eagle], that one of the reasons of its great attraction was its being directly addressed to the common people, in the provision made for their seeing and hearing. Instead of being put away in a dark gap of the roof of an immense building, as in our once National Theatres, they were here in the possession of eligible points of view, and thoroughly able to take in the whole performance. Instead of being at a great disadvantage in comparison with the mass of the audience, they were here *the* audience, for whose accommodation the place was made. We believe this to be one great cause of the success of these specula-tions. In whatever way the common people are addressed, whether in churches, chapels, schools, lecture-rooms, or theatres, to be successfully addressed they must be directly appealed to. No matter how good the feast, they will not come to it on mere sufferance. If, on looking round us, we find that the only things plainly addressed to them, from quack medicines upwards, be bad or very defective things, – so much the worse for them and for all of us, and so much the more unjust and absurd the system which has haughtily abandoned a strong ground to such occupation.

We will add that we believe these people have a right to be amused. A great deal that we consider to be unreasonable, is written and talked about not licensing these places of entertainment. We have already intimated that we believe a love of dramatic representations to be an inherent principle of human nature.... Ten thousand people, every week, all the year round, are estimated to attend this place of amusement. If it were closed tomorrow – if there were fifty such, and they were all closed tomorrow – the only result would be to cause that to be privately and evasively done which is now publicly done; to render the harm of it much greater, and to render the suppressive power of the law in an oppressive and partial light. The people who now resort here *will be* amused somewhere. It is of no use to blink that fact, or to make pretences to the contrary. We had far better apply ourselves to improving the character of their amusement. It would not be exacting much, or exacting anything difficult, to require that the pieces represented in these Theatres should have, at least, a good plain, healthy purpose in them.[25]

Dickens's emphasis in this description, obviously, was placed on the needful accessibility of the poor and lower classes to dramatic entertainment. 'It is interesting to note', as one of Dickens's recent editors has pointed out, 'that Dickens here attacks the system of official licensing of plays, not on the grounds of artistic freedom, but because it is connected with a royal official.'[26] Dickens's advocacy of the notion that 'people have a right to be amused', as Michael Slater also notes, looks forward to the similar argument, advanced in four years' time by the lisping words of Mr Sleary to Thomas Gradgrind in *Hard Times*: 'People must be amuthed, Thquire, thomehow ... Make the betht of uth; not the wortht.'[27]

Dickens later included a lengthier and even more valuable account of his impressions of the Britannia in his 'Two Views Of A Cheap Theatre', eventually published as Chapter 4 of *The Uncommercial Traveller* (1860). Having left his gloomy lodgings near Covent Garden, he tells the reader,

within half an hour I was in an immense theatre, capable of holding nearly five thousand people.

What Theatre? Her Majesty's? Far better. Royal Italian Opera? Far better. Infinitely superior to the latter for hearing in; infinitely superior to both, for seeing in. To every part of this Theatre, spacious fire-proof ways of ingress and egress. For every part of it, convenient places of refreshment and retiring rooms. Everything to eat and drink carefully supervised as to quality, and sold at an appointed price; respectable female attendants ready for the commonest women in the audience; a general air of consideration, decorum, and super-vision, most commendable; an unquestionably humanising influence in all the social arrangements of the place.

Surely a dear Theatre, then? Because there were in London (not very long ago) Theatres with entrance-prices up to half-a-guinea a head, whose arrangements were not half so civilised. Surely, therefore, a dear Theatre? Not very dear. A gallery at three-pence, another gallery at fourpence, a pit at sixpence, boxes and pit-stalls at a shilling, and a few private boxes at half-a-crown.

My uncommercial curiosity induced me to go into every nook of this great place, and among every class of the audience assembled in it – amounting that evening, as I calculated, to about two thousand and odd hundreds. Magnificently lighted by a firmament of sparkling chandeliers, the building was ventilated to perfection. My sense of smell, without being particularly delicate, has been so offended in some of the commoner places of public resort, that I have often been obliged to leave them when I have made an uncommercial journey expressly to look on. The air of this Theatre was fresh, cool, and wholesome. To help towards this end, very sensible precautions had been used, ingeniously combining the experience of hospitals and railway stations. Asphalt pavements substituted for wooden floors, honest bare walls of glazed brick and tile – even at the back of the boxes – for plaster and paper, no benches stuffed, and no carpeting or baize used; a cool material with a light glazed surface, being the covering of the seats.

[. . .]

As the spectators at this theatre, for a reason I will presently show, were the object of my journey, I entered on the play of the night as one of the two thousand and odd hundreds, by looking about me at my neighbours. We were a motley assemblage of people, and we had a good many boys and young men among us; we had also many girls and young women. To represent, however, that we did not include a very great number, and a very fair proportion of family groups, would be to make a gross mis-statement. Such groups were to be seen in all parts of the house; in the boxes and stalls particularly, they were composed of persons of very decent appearance, who had many children with them. Among our dresses there were most kinds of shabby and greasy wear, and much fustian and corduroy that was neither sound nor fragrant. The caps of our young men were mostly of a limp character, and we who wore them, slouched, high-shouldered, into our places with our hands in our pockets, and occasionally twisted our cravats about our necks like eels, and occasionally tied them down our breasts like links of sausages, and occasionally had a screw in our hair over each cheek-bone with a slight Thief-flavour in it. Besides prowlers and idlers, we were mechanics, dock-labourers, costermongers, petty tradesmen, small clerks, milliners, stay-makers, shoe-binders, slop-workers, poor workers in a hundred highways and byways. Many of us – on the whole, the majority – were not at all clean, and not at all choice in our lives or conversation. But we had all come together in a place where our convenience was well consulted, and where we were well looked after, to enjoy an evening's entertainment in common. We were not going to lose any part of what we had paid for through anybody's caprice, and as a community we had a character to lose. So, we were closely attentive, and kept excellent order; and let the man or boy who did otherwise instantly get out from this place, or we would put him out with the greatest expedition.[28]

Dickens's central point in so describing the audience and the environment at the Britannia was primarily to demonstrate the fact that the fashionable classes of the West End did not necessarily embody the entire theatre-going public of London. In the Britannia and theatres like it Dickens and other commentators marked, as Michael Booth observed, 'the huge and suffocating galleries packed with coatless youths who expressed approval and disappointment with shrill whistles, cheers, and unusual sound effects of massive volume; … the babies in the pit; the general spirit of enjoyment; the immense popularity of the stage favourites and comic songs; and the intense interest in the business of the stage'. As Booth concludes: 'Any account of the nineteenth-century London theatre audience and its tastes that confined its purview to the West End and omitted this very substantial audience would be seriously defective.'[29]

The third such document relating to the Britannia, however, is in many respects even more valuable to us than Dickens's descriptions of the theatre environment, insofar as it contains the only eyewitness account we have of an actual production of *Sweeney Todd* as it might have been performed at the Britannia at some point in the 1870s. The account was included in Thomas W. Erle's 1880 professional biography, *Letters from a Theatrical Scene-Painter*. 'An evening at the Britannia during the run of *The String of Pearls; or, the Barber Fiend of Fleet Street*', Erle recalled,

> was to sup full of horrors. In the vulgar tongue of Hoxton and elsewhere, a full supper is called a 'tightener'. The expression is coarse, no doubt, yet suggestive. Abominably so. Going to see *The Barber Fiend* was a 'tightener of horrors', like a visit to the small room [i.e. the Chamber of Horrors] at Madame Tussaud's.
>
> The plot was as follows. The Barber Fiend murders in succession all his customers who come to him to be shaved, and then, by way of utilising them to the utmost possible extent, as well as of conveniently disposing of their bodies, makes them into pies, upon which such of the characters as are left to carry through the business of the piece, are regaled. A series of effects is produced by successive discoveries in the pies of what may be called 'internal evidence' of the true nature of their ingredients. Thus, one of the customer finds in the first instance a woman's hair. This is not viewed as a circumstance of much gravity, since it is a matter of common experience that long hairs have an intrusive tendency which induces them to present themselves in combination with most alimentary substances. From buns, for example, they are as inseparable as grit. Lodging-house butter is usually fraught with them, and a marked affinity is developed in their constitution for London bread. Their frequent manifestation in mutton pies is natural enough, since it may so easily occur that the stumps of the horses' tails which supply the meat, may, on the occurrence of any press of business in the trade, be incompletely divested of them. This specific class of mutton is also distinguished by a wiry tenacity of fibre and sinew such as an advocate of 'muscular Christianity' might envy. It

is attributable to the fact that the particular kind of 'sheep' which supplies it forms the source of motive power in the cab system of the metropolis.

But to return to the Barber's pies. The discovery of the hair is followed by that of a thumb nail, which appears to give rise to some indistinct, but uneasy, misgivings in the breast of the consumer. He pursues his meal with reflective hesitation, and a zest which has now been obviously impaired by the operation of disquieting mental influences. The startling revelation of a brass button attached to a fragment of material substance of some kind or other which bears the aspect of having formed a constituent portion of somebody or other's leather breeches, proves what is called 'a staggerer', and brings the repast to an abrupt and uncomfortable conclusion. The terrors of the scene culminate in a full and detailed account of the whole matter set forth on the paper in which the pies had been wrapped. The narrative in question is accompanied by strictures on the conduct of the murderer, ably drawn up by his victims, and a free and explicit confession by himself is also appended to the document. At this point a torrent of fiddles is let loose, which rasp away for some moments with an energy worthy of the crisis.

The Barber is then taken into custody. But not by policemen. Not a bit of it! The R B management knows better than that. Police constables, no doubt, constitute a highly respectable and estimable body of men. Still, when they march in with the mechanical precision of automata, as stiff as a procession of animated lamp-posts, and with countenances fraught with utter unmeaningness, they present, it must be confessed, the essence of the unpicturesque in effect. And their plain, matter-of-fact truncheons are but silent and ineffective accessories to a situation. Now a party of supers rush in, attired in the uniforms in which they are accustomed to 'do' the Swedish army in Charles the Twelfth, and let off their muskets with signal intrepidity, firing earnestly upwards, as though anxious to hit some bird or other object which they must be supposed to have descried flitting about up among the gas patterns. This light fusillade, incidentally, brings about the desirable result of creating a strong smell of gunpowder, and the noise throws a collection of urchins at the door of the theatre, who cannot muster their sixpence for the gallery, into paroxysms of excitement to know what is going on inside. Of all the various sad forms of human destitutions, perhaps the most affecting to contemplate is that of small boys who hang night after night about the doors of theatres but can't afford to go in.

The apprehension of the wicked barber necessarily brings the drama to its conclusion, and at this point, therefore, all the murdered characters reappear. If it be objected that the supposition of his guilt is weakened by, not to say absolutely inconsistent with, the bodily presence of his victims – the *ipsissima corpora delictorum* – all as right and tight as can be, the answer is that the claims of the final tableau are paramount. The scene is then illuminated with red fire. An explanation of the propriety of this enrichment of the tableau is probably to be sought in the notion of its being in some degree typical of the subject-matter of the piece, since it is not within ordinary experience that the action of retributive justice is attended by any such meteoric phenomena. The whole of the characters then joined in a patriotic song, in which the invasion panic, and the discomfiture of the enemy by the Hoxton volunteers, together with any other point which might happen to be of general interest to the community at the particular moment, are very neatly and happily touched off.... Joking apart, I think that the representation of such a mass of unnatural and repulsive horrors is extremely wrong and pernicious, and the subsequent astonishing resuscitation of the victims does little to rectify it. If the Drama be 'holding the mirror up to nature', it should also be remembered that there is such a thing, and a very real thing too, as holding nature up to the mirror. For the contemplation, or vivid description, of an act of wickedness, frequently, as is perfectly well known, inoculates weak minds with an irresistible impulse to do the same kind of thing.[30]

Erle's apparent disdain for such representations of Todd were of little consequence to the audiences of the late nineteenth and early twentieth centuries. Dibdin Pitt's adaptation, as already noted, flourished in innumerable and constantly changing 'versions' for many decades. In a short essay rather coyly entitled 'Are You Being Served?: Cannibalism, Class, and Victorian Melodrama', Kristen Guest has argued plausibly that Victorian melodramatic versions of *Sweeney Todd* remain of genuine interest to us today primarily for the manner in which they engage in a pointed critique of the dominant cultural values of their time.[31] Hugely popular representations such as Dibdin Pitt's *Sweeney Todd*, Guest argued, evoked the colonial discourse of cannibalism – which, as noted in Part One, posited all such 'savagery' as existing in distinct contrast to the structures of civilized Western culture – to 'contain' the lower classes and the poor; yet the responses of those very same audiences that it was intended to dominate (as documented in texts such as Dickens and Erle) tended, in the end, to turn that same discourse against the dominant middle class itself. 'While earlier versions of the Sweeney Todd story reinforce the value of an existing political hierarchy', she observes, 'the Victorian play's use of cannibalism calls this hierarchy into question.'[32] Pointing to the scene included in some form in almost all existing versions of Dibdin Pitt's drama, in which Jarvis discovers first a hair, and then a fingernail (or worse) in the pie he is consuming, Guest comments:

> The sensationalistic effect of watching Jarvis discover that he has been duped into an act of cannibalism under discomfitingly familiar circumstances was undoubtedly the primary goal of the proprietors of the Hoxton Britannia Theatre. The process of reading the 'internal evidence' of the pies turns on the fact that we experience dawning knowledge along with the victim of the hoax and so relies, in effect, on our common experience of having ingested food products on faith.... By introducing cannibalism as an uncanny echo of a commonplace event, Pitt binds the audience's sympathies to the inadvertent cannibal who is also the victim of a vicious system of consumerism that knowingly sets out to deceive him. In this case it is not the cannibal consumer who poses a threat to civilization but rather the treacherous shopkeeper who values human life at so much the pound. Thus, through this reversal of the

mainstream view of the lower classes as threatening other, the designation of the poor as cannibalistic 'savages', is contested by the play's representation of unwitting 'cannibals' as *victims* of capitalistic greed.[33]

'Commonly evoked by the middle classes to define an ethnological other', Guest's study looks to emphasize, cannibalism is thus turned to completely different ends in *The String of Pearls*, where it appeals to the human body as the final indicator of where, on a visceral level, one may begin to define what 'common humanity' means'.[34]

Many other playwrights followed in Dibdin Pitt's footsteps. The second most influential and popular adaptation of Sweeney Todd's story was that of Frederick Hazleton (c.1825–90). His *Sweeney Todd the Barber of Fleet Street; or, the String of Pearls*, was first performed at the Old Bower Saloon, on Stangate Street, in Lambeth in 1865. As the century wore on, however, both versions of the story were subject to countless variations, and it soon became nearly impossible to distinguish any one such particular 'adaptation' from any other. Along with the theatrical variations, too, came an equally bewildering number of prose expansions. Lloyd's (poorly elaborated) version of 1850 ballooned in time into Charles Fox's massive 1880 retelling, which appeared ready tediously to extend the adventures of the barber until the public had had enough of him. Todd's story was pirated in America by one 'Captain Merry' (Harry Hazel) in the early 1850s. A. Ritchie, of Red Lion Court, London, likewise published his own version (bearing the subtitle *A Thrilling Story of the Old City of London. Founded on Fact*) in about 1892; the 'True Story' in question is thought by many enthusiasts of the penny blood to have been designed to serve as a spoiler for a much lengthier version of the tale. The barber even made an appearance as a character in an entirely different story, *The Link Boy of Old London* (c.1873). As E.S. Turner has commented of this distinctly substandard effort (which relies heavily on Dickens's *Oliver Twist*):

After a few chapters of old-fashioned Gothic, with a highwayman or two for good measure, the Demon Barber made his appearance. There were certain variations. Instead of the victims falling on their heads twenty feet below from the trap-door, as in Prest's story, this author had them falling down on to iron spikes. A suspicious constable was introduced. Failing to get any evidence on Todd, he would round the corner and solace himself with half a dozen pies from Mrs Darkman. Instead of having his assistant put away in a madhouse, the Barber knifed him in the back after a particularly crimson battle with two customers. Wiping his hands, at the end, Todd observes, 'Well, well, Mrs. Darkman can't complain of the supply tonight.' This barber was sufficient of a sentimentalist to fall in love with the wife of one of his customers. He dispatched the husband in the usual way, but knowing that he could not marry the widow unless he had proof of the husband's death, he forbore to have the corpse made into pies and arranged for it to be discovered mutilated in the street.

Illustrated 'print' in the manner of James Gillray and Thomas Rowlandson, used in George King's 1936 film version of *Sweeney Todd* featuring actor Tod Slaughter.

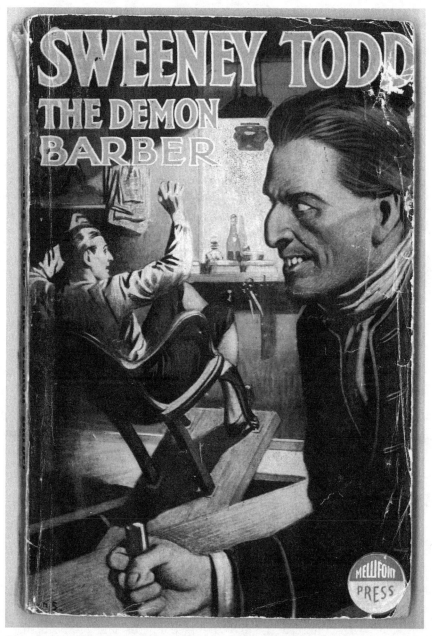

Cover of the Mellifont Edition of Sweeney Todd (c. 1936). The same cover illustration had been used for
the earlier prose version of the story published by the Pearson Press in 1929.

> In this version Todd was finally spitted through by a constable in a fight in the cellars of the shop. Mrs. Darkman died by poison. 'A good riddance of two wretches', said the head officer, 'for there is no death devised by law except burning which is bad enough for them'.[35]

As late as 1929, Todd's story was modified and retold in a new edition written for the Pearson Press (itself subsequently reprinted by Mellifont in 1936 as part of their 'Celebrated Crime Series').

One of the more unusual and still fondly remembered versions of Todd's story to appear in the twentieth century took the form of a music-hall monologue written by a composer of popular songs by the name of Robert Patrick Weston, who prepared the piece with his long-time collaborator, Bert Lee. Like most of the other song-monologues on historic themes composed by popular writers and composers such as Weston and Lee, the piece was written expressly for live performance – in this particular instance by the popular actor and entertainer Stanley Holloway (1890–1982). Holloway – who was prone to vary the pattern and delivery of such monologues when delivering them in London cabaret venues such as the Trocadaro, The Picadilly, and Chez Henri, in Long Acre – did not get around to recording it until 1957. The most authoritative printed version of the text begins as follows:

> In Fleet Street that's in London Town,
> When King Charlie wore the Crown,
> There lived a man of great renown,
> It was Sweeney Todd, the Barber.
>
> One shave from him and you'd want no more –
> You'd feel his razor sharp
> Then tumble wallop through the floor
> And wake up playing a harp
>
> – and singing
>
> Sweeney Todd, the Barber.
> Ba Goom, he were better than a play,
> Sweeney Todd, the Barber.
> 'I'll polish 'em off,' he used to say.[36]

Weston and Lee's monologue proceeds in comic fashion to tell of the customers who 'tumbled through' Todd's oubliette, and of the barber's profitable agreement with the obliging Mrs Lovett, nearby.

> His clients through the floor would slope,
> But he had no fear of the hangman's rope

Dead men can't talk with their mouths full of soap.
Said Sweeney Todd, the Barber.

Now underneath the shop it's true,
Where other bodies tumbled through,
There lived a little widow who
Loved Sweeney Todd the Barber.

She made her living by selling pies,
Her meat pies were a treat,
Chock full of meat and such a size
Cos she was getting the meat from

Mr Sweeney Todd, the Barber.[37]

Sweeney runs into trouble with the gentleman who proves to be his final 'customer', however, a bookmaker:

He went down straight away.
But what rotten luck – the darned trap went and stuck
For the hinge he'd forgotten to grease;
And a customer there started calling out 'Police',
Just as Sweeney was saying 'Next please'.

Yes, he ran to the door and he shouted 'Police',
He called 'Police' nine times or ten;
But no police arrived and a very good reason
police weren't invented by then.

But up came the brave Bow Street Runners – hurray!
And he had to let many a pie burn
While they dragged him to quad, [a]nd next day Sweeney Todd
Was condemned to be switched off at Tyburn.

And there on the gibbet he hangs in chains,
And they do say a little black crow
Made a sweet little nest in Old Sweeney Todd's whiskers
And sang as he swang to and fro,

Sweeney Todd, the Barber
Ba Goom, he were better than a play;
Sweeney Todd, the Barber
They buried him underneath the clay.

And Old Nick calls him from his grave
Shouting 'Wake up, Sweeney, I want a shave',
And Mrs. Nick wants a permanent wave
From, Sweeney Todd, the Barber.[38]

"Watson! Gregson! Grab his arm! Look out for that razor!"

Alfredo Alcala's illustration for Ken Greenwald's 'The Case of the Demon Barber' (based on the original radio play broadcast in January 1946 and written by Dennis Green and Anthony Boucher), included in Greenwald's *The Lost Adventures of Sherlock Holmes* (1988)

Holloway's stage persona – the essence of which (if not its precise, original, regional identity) was preserved in his portrayal of the philosophical dustman Alfred Dolittle in the film version of *My Fair Lady* (1964) – transformed Weston's admittedly light-weight comic monologue into a genuinely entertaining if deliberately 'colourful' performance (although, rather like the property of Lerner and Loewe's musical itself on that later occasion, as the film critic Andrew Sarris observed, Holloway's depiction was not so much 'adapted' for the screen as it was 'elegantly embalmed').[39] Holloway had in fact made something of a name for himself early in his career by introducing such broad comic monologues into his West End Variety performances at the Palladium and elsewhere; his greatest and most enduring successes in the form included those which featured the Yorkshire soldier character of 'Sam "pick oop tha musket" Small' (*c.*1927), and George Edgar's Hilaire Belloc-esque account of Albert Ramsbottom at Blackpool Zoo ('The Lion and Albert', based on an actual press item that reported the mauling of a small boy at the London Zoo, and first performed before the audience assembled for a Rugby League Dinner at the Grand Hotel, Newcastle, in 1932).[40]

The darkly humorous appeal of these and many other similar comic monologues relied to some extent on their being delivered in dialects appropriate and suited to their supposed speakers – a flat, unemotional Lancashire accent for the character of 'Sam Small', for example – which the performer took care to perfect over the years.[41] Holloway occasionally wrote his own material, although the monologues of Robert Patrick Weston (1878–1936), in particular, found the droll and deadpan manner of the performer's delivery particularly well suited to draw out the black humour of the macabre situations described. Weston's other comic monologues eventually sung by Holloway included 1934's 'With Her Head Tucked Underneath Her Arm' (again written with Bert Lee, about the ghost of Anne Boleyn); his earlier, 1910 collaboration with Fred Murray – 'I'm Henery the Eighth, I Am' – is still, thanks largely to a 1965 recording by Herman's Hermits, known to listeners even today. It is due in no small part to Holloway's interpretation of Weston's lines, however, that the characters presented in music-hall monologues such as 'Sweeney Todd the Barber' were further recognized and re-inscribed as (according to the *Times*) 'part of English folklore during the 1930s'.[42] Holloway himself, writing in later years, had anticipated such recognition when he wrote that he was proud to have captured in his work 'many of the virtues of all our Island race', and that it gave him a special pleasure to feel that the monologues and their characters had become 'part of the British way of life'.[43] Recorded versions of Holloway's monologues, originally marketed as 12" vinyl records, were priced for as much as six shillings. Weston's 'Sweeney Todd the Barber' was eventually included on the performer's 1956 LP for Columbia Records, *'Ere's 'Olloway*.[44]

Chapter 7

A Proper Artist With a Knife: Sweeney on Celluloid

And so did we welcome devils and their Death?
(Robert Browning, *The Ring and the Book*)[1]

The relatively sustained popularity of the various versions of both George Dibdin Pitt and Frederick Hazleton's stage adaptations of Todd's story throughout the late nineteen and very early twentieth centuries ensured that not much time would pass before the demon barber and his pie-making accomplice in Bell Yard made their debut on cinema screens across Great Britain. Despite the continued success enjoyed by the revivals of several 'sensational' plays staged at London venues such as the Elephant and Castle throughout the 1920s (and their close to unbroken longevity in the traditionally less savoury East End theatres such as the Britannia – as described above – the Effingham and the Pavilion), there would appear to have been a growing number of performers who had clearly begun to feel that, by the earliest decades of the twentieth century, stalwarts such as *Sweeney Todd*, *Maria Marten*, *East Lynne* and *Simon Lee* had at long last outgrown their welcome even in those theatres that specialized in domestic and criminal melodrama. A notice in April 1927, for example, that announced a special matinée performance in aid of the 'Sadler's Wells Fund', made a particular point of emphasizing the programme's title: 'Then and Now'. A new play written by Edgar Wallace and featuring Gerald du Maurier and Gladys Cooper was clearly meant to constitute the highlight of the contemporary representation – the 'Now' – to be included in the production; no less prominently showcased as the respectable centrepiece of the more nostalgic or retrospective portion of the evening's entertainment – the complimentary 'Then' to the earlier part of the afternoon – were appearances by Sybil Thorndike and Edith Evans in a scene from Shakespeare's *Twelfth Night*. The subsequent language with which the programme announced its plans also to

220

stage 'scenes from the old "thriller" *Sweeney Todd, the Demon Barber*, in which the audience will be able to take part', seemed to imply that the piece had been included on the bill not so much as a crowd-pleaser but as an after-thought; the manner of the performance also suggested (if only in its slightly grim warning of anticipated and even required audience participation) that *Sweeney Todd* was to be treated – and only as a matter of course – far more in the manner of a parody or burlesque than as a representative of the legitimate theatre.[2] The unspoken implication of those quotation marks that isolate and heighten the description of the piece as a 'thriller' is that although such pieces may have been effective enough in their own day, the fixed conventions and distinctive hallmarks of melodramatic acting – anguished facial expressions, wild laughs, oversized gestures and spasmodic, choking ejaculations – were, as we might put it today, long past their sell-by date.[3] Not only were such plays now to be treated as period pieces, they were unlikely to survive as viable theatrical curiosities much longer. Strikingly, when plans for the reconstruction of the Elephant and Castle itself were completed just one year later, in April 1928, the chairman of the new organization that governed the theatre, C.B. Cochran, announced with much fanfare of the new company: 'It is not proposed to depart to any great extent from the traditions of the theatre, although, at the same time, it is intended to provide all forms of dramatic entertainment.' 'I am desirous', Cochran added, 'of opening with a British "dramatic classic," either a production of a play by Shakespeare or a revival of some modern work, such as [George Bernard Shaw's] *Saint Joan.*' '*Sweeney Todd*', the same announcement concluded in an aside that looked ominous for the future of the melodrama, 'will end its run at the theatre on Saturday.'[4] In the brave new world of the twentieth-century theatre, any lingering taste for or even revival of those long-standing traditions of melodrama that had always reserved a space for *Sweeney Todd* seemed likely and suddenly to disappear altogether.

Yet those who were in any way inclined (or even eager) to dismiss the viability of sensation and crime melodrama on the stage as hopelessly out of both intellectual and popular fashion had little reckoned on the power of the yet-emerging medium of the cinema. Having swiftly passed through an early phase in which the simplest of physical movements, when captured for display on cabinet machines such as Edison's 'peepshow' Kinetoscope (e.g. short dances and vaudeville acts, boxing matches, a man sneezing etc.) had in themselves constituted enough of a novelty to entertain suitably astonished viewers, the nascent 'moving picture' industry in Britain was soon on the look-out for material suitable for their own 'photoplays'. Movie narratives and techniques – and movie audiences – grew sophisticated with a speed that was in many respects astonishing. Along with classical dramas and novels (many works by Shakespeare, Dickens, Charlotte Brontë and Thomas Hardy, for example, were among the very first items to be trans-lated to the British screen), the more recent stage successes – and more particularly, the popular melodramas – of an era that had only just begun to fade were among the most obvious sources to which the rapidly expanding medium could turn for suitable subject matter.[5] As Michael Booth has commented, a film aesthetic within which 'an idealized world of fast action and strong emotion, where character stereotypes and unchanging situations and settings are immediately familiar – and are loved for that reason' was itself perhaps 'the purest *form* of melodrama'.[6] What had so recently been dismissed as the form's primary weakness or drawback in the theatre – its familiarity – was transformed overnight into one of its most appealing and powerful selling points.

The earliest film version of 'Sweeney Todd' was a relatively short feature, now unfortunately lost, that is (somewhat unconvincingly) credited as having been based on the text of Dibdin Pitt's play. This *Sweeney Todd* was shown only to a select audience in 1926; it appears never to have been generally distributed to cinemas (at some 1,000 feet, the film would have run only a handful of minutes).[7] The movie was produced by P.L. Mannock and directed by George Dewhurst, with titles supplied by Lionel Collier. It featured in the starring role what was apparently to be the only screen performance of one G.A. Baughan, who, five years earlier, in 1921, had been credited with having provided the screenplay for Thomas Bentley's *The Adventures of Mr Pickwick* (it is impressive how once again Todd was being jumbled together in the collective mind of popular culture with Dickens). Director and cinematographer George Dewhurst, on the other hand – who, in addition to steering the 1926 *Sweeney Todd* through production, claimed a further credit as having served as one of the 'screenwriters' for the project – is today regarded as an important pioneer of the British film industry. He contributed to dozens of early features from 1905 until as late as 1948, having effected the often uneasy transition from silent films to talkies with an hour-long version of John le Breton's comedy *A Sister to Assist 'Er* in 1931 (Dewhurst had already directed a silent version of the same stage piece just three years earlier, and was in fact to release no fewer than four different film versions of the play in the course of his career). Of Dewhurst's many titles, only a handful survive. His greatest claim to fame is the fact that he is often credited with having 'discovered' the young Ronald Coleman, when he chanced to see the actor performing in an amateur stage play. Dewhurst subsequently featured Coleman in his early two-reelers, a 1917 comedy *Live Wires*, and 1919's *The Toilers* (a partial print of which still exists). Ronald Coleman would go on to make his American film debut just four years later, in *The White Sister* (1923). He rose to early fame when partnered with screen siren Vilma Banky by Samuel Goldwyn in 1925, and eventually became one of the most popular leading men in 1930s Hollywood, starring in such classic screen adaptations as *A Tale of Two Cities* (1935), *Lost Horizon* (1937) and *The Prisoner of Zenda* (1937).

Dewhurst's *Sweeney Todd*, described by its producers, New Era Productions, as 'a burlesque made for the Kinematograph Garden Party', appears in actual fact to have been a filmed spoof of what must already have been a dramatic version that relied only very informally on Dibdin Pitt's play. The 'Garden Party' for which the film was specifically made almost certainly formed part of the 'social arrangements' that were reported to conclude a joint meeting at Brighton in June 1926, of the Cinematograph Exhibitors Association and the Kinematograph Renters' Society. Those same two organizations were at that time in the midst of what had developed into an increasingly bitter dispute with their American counterparts over the issue of film distribution in Britain; in particular, the British organizations were fighting the implementation of a policy known as 'blind booking' (i.e. a commitment on the part of cinema proprietors to book films for screening in their theatres sight unseen, or without any previous selection on the basis of their merits). A 'burlesque' version of Todd's narrative would certainly have been deemed appropriate fare for that summer's audience of besieged industry representatives, many of whom felt that an agreement to any such distribution policy would result in their being force-fed a steady diet of American products without their consent. Much like the paying customers in Mrs Lovett's pie shop, they would never have any way of knowing precisely what it was they were on any occasion being compelled to consume.[8]

A second and considerably more substantial silent film version of the story was produced just two years after Dewhurst's burlesque.[9] This *Sweeney Todd* – a possibly unique (and for the most part remarkably pristine) copy of which is now held as part of the collection of the National Film Archive in London – was directed by Walter West (fresh from a similar adaptation of *Maria Marten*, earlier that same year), produced by Harry Rowson and distributed by Ideal Films Limited in 1928. The 'scenario', by J. Bertram Brown (already the experienced writer of a number of romances and crime dramas), was not only billed as having been 'adapted from the famous "Elephant and Castle" melodrama', but claimed at the same time, in what would appear to be a spirit of cheerfully unapologetic duplicity, to be 'based on authentic facts'. Starring as Sweeney on this occasion was the prolific actor Moore Marriott (1885–1949). Marriott, who claimed later in life to have made above 300 films, had begun his career on the stage as a very small child (his father had owned a theatre near London). By 1928, certainly, Marriott was already a well-established actor in the cinema, with several dozen films to his credit. He excelled in comic roles, although his rather oversized and often designedly threatening appearance (he tended to project a screen image that made him appear considerably older than he actually was) rendered him no less suitable for the part of the 'heavy' or villain in other features. One of his earliest leading roles, for example, was as the highwayman Dick Turpin in a 1908 film of that same name. That having been said, Marriott was capable of playing anything from a burglar or a convict, to a doorman, a lawyer, or even (on occasion) a king. The advent of sound (1928's *Sweeney Todd* was to be Marriott's last silent film) found him finally settling down and carving out a comfortable niche for himself as a character actor; he began, rather like the American 'Gabby' Hayes in the 1930s and 1940s, to specialize in roles that cast him as an old and avuncular rustic (variously 'Gaffer', 'Crabby', 'Old Man', 'Old Tom', or simply 'Oldest Inhabitant'). The carefully cultivated, countrified persona of Marriott's later career seemed to make him the ideal crotchety sidekick or cunning companion to a younger romantic lead. His later collaborations with the very successful, former music-hall performer, Will Hays, and the tubby Graham Moffat in popular and often surprisingly accomplished Gainsborough comedies such as *Oh, Mr Porter!* (1938), *Convict 99* (1938) and *Ask a Policeman* (1939) in precisely these sorts of character roles resulted in what remain perhaps his finest performances on film.

Although Marriott's portrayal of the title villain in Walter West's 1928 *Sweeney Todd* may thus have been destined eventually to be overshadowed both by his own, considerable if subsequently developed strengths as a character actor, as well as the rival claims of other performers who would soon look to claim the part as uniquely their own, his pioneering screen interpretation of the role holds up remarkably well. We should remember that any actor playing Sweeney Todd for this new breed of moviegoers would be facing a considerable, even daunting challenge. Audiences would only naturally have brought their own long acquaintance with and memories of Sweeney Todd – as they had each already encountered him (and in many cases on more than one occasion) on the stage – with them to the cinema. A first full-length, feature film version of the drama would, in its own day, have constituted something of an event for British cinema audiences, and Marriott needed somehow to fulfil the various and invariably conflicting expectations of a tremendous number of viewers in what might conceivably be looked upon as a definitive if still early interpretation of the role; Marriott's performance would instantly have acquired a rare kind of visual aura or 'permanence' that was, even as late as the 1920s, still something relatively new to theatre- and cinema-goers. No less than any contemporary actor who takes on the daunting task of playing a literary character who has already assumed a solid and unassailable shape in the minds of individual audience members (one immediately thinks, for example, of characters in the novels of Jane Austen or the Brontës), or one who attempts similarly to redefine for a new generation a role that would appear for all intents and purposes already to have been definitively interpreted on the screen (Rhett Butler and Scarlett O'Hara, perhaps, or, even more obviously, James Bond), any actor who committed himself to portraying Sweeney Todd needed both to convince the audience of the essential truth that lay at the heart of his performance, while at the same time – *somehow* – making the role his own.

The critics of the day, moreover, would have had little if any hesitation in judging the performance of any actor who took on such a familiar role by comparing him with his numerous predecessors on the stage. All 'Sweeney Todds' were effectively acting, at any given moment, against a host of memories, the dark shades of which had haunted most imaginations since early childhood. There were high expectations to be fulfilled, and high standards to maintain. Only months before Marriott's Todd first made his appearance on cinema screens throughout Britain, a production of the traditional stage version of the play, starring one Edwards Martin in the role of Todd, had been performed nightly (and including a further two weekday matinées) at the popular Elephant Theatre in Southwark. As one critic wrote at the time:

> One doubt assails us – is Mr. Martin's Sweeney quite large enough? This fellow is, after all, a monster of the theatre. He will cut a throat now and again, notably Mrs. Lovett's – for her throat is 'long and white' – an irresistible invitation to gore, and he does not scorn to crack a skull or two with a mallet as lesser men would crack an egg with a spoon. But his professional method of murder is to place his victims in a barber's chair which, swinging backwards, casts them into the vaults. How it swings! How they hurtle 'to perdition'! What a giant of crime he is, fiendishly chuckling, 'I'll polish 'em off!' Is Mr. Martin quite fiendish enough? There are moments when he seems to compromise his own convention, to chuckle a little, not at his victim, but at us, at himself. This is the sad way from melodrama to melodramatic burlesque, and it is not burlesque, unless we are very superior persons.[10]

Clearly (and despite the general perception voiced earlier in this section that the stage play had to some extent already begun to wear out its welcome on the stage) there remained critics – and probably a great many audience members, to judge from the confidence of the writer's tone in this passage – who demanded that their Sweeney Todd be played 'straight'. When they went to see Todd in the theatre, spectators wanted still to be genuinely frightened, and not simply titillated or amused. Any actor who misguidedly attempted a knowing interpretation of the role – anyone who betrayed what we might today describe as a 'meta-theatrical' awareness of the often heavy conventions of the part he had assumed – risked destroying the entire generic structure within which the dramatic illusion was maintained. We have long tended to look upon Victorian melodramas as hopelessly creaky and often patently ridiculous pantomimes that are best played for laughs; indeed, seldom do we even entertain the possibility that they can successfully be played in any other way at all. In so doing, we underestimate both the drama itself as well as the sophistication of its original audience, and we further put ourselves in danger of fundamentally misunderstanding the aesthetic impact and appeal of an entire era of theatrical entertainment in Britain. The critic in the passage quoted above draws an important distinction between melodrama proper, on the one hand, and 'melodramatic burlesque', on the other, that we would do well to keep firmly in mind. Sweeney Todd remained in the earliest decades of the new century a fiendish 'giant of crime' whose exploits were anything but simply diverting or 'entertaining'. His physical appearance alone – to say nothing of his maniacal laugh or propensity for casual brutality and violence – was enough to make one's skin crawl. His mere presence, so to speak, was tremendous.

Thus, Moore Marriott's turn as the demon barber made its appearance on cinema screens in Britain in 1928, less than one year after the unlucky Edwards Martin had rather unfortunately attracted the attention of *The Times* critic to his own stage performance at the Elephant. In central London, moviegoers in February 1929 would have been able to catch the new *Sweeney Todd* at the Capitol Picture Theatre, Haymarket, where it was billed as one of the main attractions in a continuous programme that also featured the American import *Captain Swagger* (1928) – a World War I drama from Pathé, pairing industry veteran Rod La Rocque with relative newcomer Sue Carol – and a Charlie Chaplin short. In many respects, the company shared by Todd on this occasion speaks volumes for the subsequent relative obscurity of the 1928 film; worse still – and for perhaps the only time in his long career – the barber's timing was badly off. Even as Moore Marriott's Sweeney Todd glared down from the Haymarket screen, other motion picture theatres throughout both Europe and America were already being hastily 'wired for sound'. Exhibitors very soon realized that, far from being a novelty attraction, 'talkies', which had only very recently arrived from the United States in the shape of the Warner Brothers' sensation *The Jazz Singer* (1927), were here to stay. The effects of the sound revolution were almost immediately to be no less obvious in Britain than they were in America. Director Alfred Hitchcock, already in the midst of filming his new feature *Blackmail* (1929) as a silent movie, switched in mid-production to sound. Tellingly, the very feature that topped the bill with *Sweeney Todd* at the Capitol, *Captain Swagger*, was essentially a silent movie to which synchronized music and sound effects had hastily been added just before its release. Long-time star Charlie Chaplin – who also shared the screen with Todd that winter, and who was singularly to refuse to make talking pictures himself – would effectively see his film career (if not his popularity in the long term) come to an end virtually overnight. Audiences in London were already thoroughly familiar with the silent little tramp with the cane, and were looking forward to the antics of a new and immediately more noisy comedian whose own star was on the rise, a close cousin to Chaplin by the name of Mickey Mouse. The time for a famous stage melodrama, certainly, to reach cinemas could not have been worse. Why pay to see – of all things – a silent Sweeney Todd, when everyone else on the screen seemed already to be talking, laughing and even singing as loudly as they possibly could?

The singularly poor timing of the release of Ideal Productions' version of Todd is perhaps to be regretted if only because Marriott's performance in the title role is far from disappointing. Here for all to see, at the very least, is the genuine shade of that same demonically grinning, hand-wringing and disconcertingly unctuous stage villain who had actually terrified theatre audiences throughout the better part of the nineteenth century. The film is rather more spectacularly let down – though it may just be likely to strike twenty-first century viewers as a cultural curiosity worthy of some scrutiny for the same reason – by its peculiarly transparent engagement with the possible combinations of oral and erotic appetite, and its unapologetically racist humour. Interestingly, the 1928 film appears to be the first version of the Todd narrative to make sustained use of a framing device; by means of this technique, the action of the drama is paradoxically both brought closer to audiences (in terms of its simple temporal proximity or cultural avail- ability), whilst at the same time, to some degree, safely being distanced from them (by positing the more dangerous or threatening aspects of the central narrative as being somehow 'contained' firmly in the past). The film opens in the 'present-day' era of a comparatively prosperous late-1920s Britain. A well-dressed and suited middle-class businessman (Moore Marriott) returns home from work to be welcomed into his pointedly modern (if still spare) urban flat by his wife, who is busy preparing the evening meal (the absence of any obvious household servants appears not so much as a sign of social class, but as a simple requirement of the narrative set-up). As his supper is not yet ready to be served, the husband settles comfortably into a chair and begins turning over the pages of the day's newspaper. His eyes pass over a notice advertising the sale of a barber's chair, as he falls asleep, and he begins to dream that he is himself that same barber who was 'the dirtiest dog ever' in London's history – Sweeney Todd. The conventional preparation for the dream-fantasy sequence triggered by immediate experience that follows (particularly as similar sequences would be used to such well-calculated and even stunning effect in later movies, most memorably MGM's 1939 *The Wizard of Oz*) naturally strikes the modern viewer as hackneyed. We must of course remember, however, that for the film's original audience, such a device would itself merely have been the first of what we shall eventually discover to be a surprising number of novel elements introduced into the film that would together have compelled its viewers to admit that they were now partici- pating in – and to some extent even colluding, in the capacity of privileged spectators, as willing accessories to – a decidedly new and innovative take on a familiar old favourite.

The structure of the dream frame may in fact have served as a relatively simple and straightforward – but perhaps, it was thought, increasingly *necessary* – means of induction into the main story (it is striking that English film critics had complained within the pages of *The Times* as early as 1920 that such narrative frames were already becoming an over-used device in the 'cinema'). No longer witnessing the crimes of a live Sweeney Todd, often in the very environments within which the Victorian melodrama had first come of age, twentieth-century audiences needed now, particularly with the advent of the newer medium, and often within new and unfamiliar venues, to be *drawn into* the action. More to the point, what had for some time continued to be presented to audiences as a relatively contemporary drama had suddenly become (and here, again, the cinema contributed to the shift) a play whose time and setting had slowly but surely become something set in the past. Simply put, *Sweeney Todd* had become a period piece. Consequently, there was little option but to emphasize rather than attempt to play down within the modern environment of the movie-theatre this element of temporal and cultural distance. Much of Todd's effectiveness in the environment of the older theatres had relied upon his threatening proximity – in more ways than one – as a villain; before the possibilities and unique strengths of the newer medium of the cinema had been fully developed (e.g. close ups, special effects, lighting effects etc.) film-makers tackling the subject seemed to have been very much aware that a two-dimensional Todd might not convincingly carry the impact of the 'real' thing.

Once having been so effortlessly inducted into the world of eighteenth-century London, the viewer finds that the business being carried on in Sweeney Todd's Fleet Street shop, at any event, is not quite business as usual. An earlier version of the film appears to have been submitted for the approval of the British censors in September 1928, but had been turned down. Only after a considerable amount of editing was undertaken was the film passed and allowed to be distributed. The editing entailed that any overt reference to the possibility that there were human remains in Mrs Lovett's meat pies be cut, and insisted that any scenes of graphic violence or depiction of murder likewise be excised.[11] Consequently, although practically every member of the British viewing audience could have been counted on already to have been familiar with the cannibalistic essentials of the traditional melodramatic plot, the lurid emphasis of the story was shifted elsewhere. In a decided 'twist' on the more traditional narrative, the dynamic between the two main characters and their respective enterprises was altered; in this film, it is the lure of the deeply sensual Mrs Lovett and that of her delicious pies that serves to draw customers to her shop first; only then are they sent on by the proprietress to be smartened up and shaved by Todd, who – on the surface level of the film's narrative, at least – is more often than not content simply to profit by the increased custom generated thereby. Marriott's Todd is still a murderer; yet he is rather more restrained than most. Somewhat peculiarly, therefore, the restrictions of the censors, in their efforts to excise the more gruesome aspects of appetite and cannibalism that had always driven the plot in the past, helped only to raise to a more explicit level of articulation the erotic machinations of the couple. This newly explicit emphasis on sexual and physical 'appetite' in the story was to bring with it a similarly novel awareness of some of the tale's latent implications regarding the subject of race and exploitation, as well.

'Business was brisk', one of the opening cards informs the audience of the activity in Todd's shop, and 'customers kept rolling in'. Todd's essential villainy is established early on with a new twist in the tale; it was Todd's own brother, we are informed, who had designed the machinery of his ingenious barber's chair, and who had then foolishly been the first to succumb to its dangers. The audience then watches as an unsuspecting farmer from Brentford enters the shop, commenting to the barber that his neighbour had curiously gone missing since the last market-day had brought him to London. Todd excuses himself from the room – to fetch a 'keener razor' – and spectators are treated to the full revolution of the shop's device in action. Descending to the cellar to make sure that the customer has been killed by the fall, Todd strips the body of its possessions and (pointedly) buries it. In a scene reminiscent of the final act of Shakespeare's *Richard III*, the barber is suddenly overcome by guilt, and is immediately confronted by the spectres of the Brentford farmer and his brother. The special effects employed so as to render this confrontation with Todd's visions of these semi-transparent ghosts would have emphasized one of the advantages of a screen as opposed to a stage Todd; as would so often come to be the case, the appeal of the former was based on its ability to deliver the sort of sophisticated and expert visual illusion that would remain simply unattainable within the world of the theatre.

Mrs Lovett, of course, is the attractive widow who owns the shop next door; and in this film version, at least, as played by Zoë Palmer, she *is* attractive. Her neighbour Todd invites her to join him as his business partner, although the precise terms of the deal entered upon by the two entrepreneurs remain unstated; 'Once they're next door', Todd simply tells her, 'you can leave them to me.' (Again, in this version, it is the pastry-maker who delivers the 'customers' to the barber, and not the other way around.) Business is soon booming, and Mrs Lovett is compelled to employ not one but two assistants, both of them, like herself, inviting and buxom young women. When the local parish beadle, Simon Podge (actor Judd Green), notes with lascivious pleasure that Lovett's pies have improved, she tells him simply that any such improvement must be chalked up to a new recipe she has introduced; it must remain, she further informs him coyly, 'a trade secret'. When some neighbours complain of the noise that the success of the new partnership has generated, the beadle cautions Todd, who tells Podge simply to mind his own business; he pours water from the upper storey window on the crowds that have gathered around both shops. All this circumlocution – extending, one notices, even to the necessary change in the nature of the local complaint – may have pleased the censors, but it makes for disappointingly obvious 'business'; thumping the local citizenry in the manner of Christopher Marlowe's Doctor Faustus is a poor substitute for the more substantial fare traditionally offered by Todd's narrative, and one can only assume that the film-makers relied on their audience's familiarity with the story to fill in any narrative gaps. When Ben Wigstaff, the sheriff's officer, arrives, the beadle singles out Todd for his particular notice, but tells him that there is 'no evidence against him'. Exactly what crime the beadle himself might expect the barber to have committed remains curiously vague.

Meanwhile, the good ship 'Star' has returned home to London from the South Seas; Mark Ingestrie disembarks 'hungry' for his native England, and for his anticipated reunion with Johanna. Mark is on this occasion accompanied by a new companion, one 'Sambo' (no name is given for the actor who played the role), who is described only as Mark's 'faithful companion in his adventures'. 'Sambo' (the name may have been lifted casually from the pages of Thackeray's *Vanity Fair* (1847–8)) is depicted as an African native in the outrageously caricatured manner familiar to the period in which the film was made. Tobias warns Mark away from Todd's shop, and he instead enters Mrs Lovett's in the company of Sambo. Mrs Lovett and Mark are in this version obviously old acquaintances, and she is keen that he lodge in her house. Ignoring the earlier advice of Tobias, Mark goes next-door for a shave, while Lovett prepares his room. Mark makes his usual mistake of showing Todd the rewards of his recent voyage, in this instance a handful of unstrung pearls. The underlying eroticism of the relationship that connects Todd to Lovett, and that here further fuels the predatory intentions of Lovett towards the rival Mark is emphasized by the manner in which those scenes that show the barber shaving young Ingestrie are intercut with extended images of Mrs Lovett making up a comfortable bed for her new lodger.

'Massa go get shave ...', Sambo succinctly and stereotypically informs Mrs Lovett when she returns to the shop premises in search of Mark. Lovett, however, loses no time in letting Todd know that she intends to keep Ingestrie (who has already been dropped through the barber's trap-door, and who now lies unconscious in the basement) all to herself: 'Hands off him Todd,' she says, 'he's mine'; she and Todd drag him across the barber's cellar floor and into her own basement, and then together carry him upstairs and place him in the bed that has already been prepared by Lovett. It is left to the audience to decide if Todd's ambiguous comment that Mark is 'as good as dead' is meant to refer to his own plans for the young hero, or to the fate to which his still somnolent body would appear to have been abandoned amidst the luxury of Lovett's bedroom. When Sambo (rather unfortunately taking on the role of the faithful dog 'Hector' in earlier versions of the story) enters Todd's shop in search of his 'master', Todd gratuitously (and rather lamely) reviles him as a 'black monkey face', before telling him that Mark has already left the premises. Sambo's response to this information is to settle comfortably in the dreaded barber's chair and begin eating his way through the several large pies he has purchased next-door. Todd attempts to drop him to the cellar, but Sambo does not fall from the chair; rather, he clings to the arms and rides its revolutions, as it is sent spinning in the manner of a thrill ride in a modern amusement park. He even cries for 'More', but is eventually hurtled to the space below. Unlike Todd's earlier victims he is not killed, nor is he even knocked unconscious; the entire scene is played completely for laughs, and Sambo's only response is to warn the barber jovially: 'You best be careful Massa Todd ... you go hurt someone, some day.'

Having thus spent an inordinate amount of time in setting out some of the basic exposition, the film progresses from this point in a manner that is only slightly more familiar. The action is radically condensed, and viewers are left to suppose that Johanna contrives to disguise herself as a boy and take the place of Tobias as Todd's apprentice even while Mark still lies unconscious in a room next door. Lovett is ultimately stabbed by an increasingly maniacal Todd, who believes she has somehow betrayed their partnership, while Johanna effectively alerts the staff of Lovett's pie shop to the dangers posed by their mistress. Most bizarre is the final confrontation between the barber and Mark, which takes place in the bedroom – and in fact upon the very bed – assigned to the latter for his recovery; the otherwise unarmed fight for masculine supremacy is won by the physically more fit and powerful Mark, and the end of the film sees Todd placed in his own barber's chair. There, he is confronted by the ghosts of his victims. The spectre of his brother pulls the chain that turns the chair upside down, and Todd falls to his own death. The film returns briefly to the frame narrative, and the comic denouement sees the modern-day wife preparing to serve her husband a meat pie for his dinner; the last visual gag in the film features a rather nice touch, as the final shot shows the husband tipping his own chair backwards and falling – into his wife's embrace.

Again, Marriott's creditable performance as Todd aside, the film remains a curiosity primarily because the thorough-going changes required by British censors of the period paradoxically resulted in a movie that may not have featured any graphic scenes of murder or cannibalism, but replaced them instead with the potentially more disturbing juxtaposition of scenes of a predatory sexual desire with images of a more mundane and familiar physical appetite. It would be nice to think that the film-makers had less difficulty than they might otherwise have had with the cuts demanded by the censors, if only because they realized that their audience's familiarity with the essential (if now somehow unspeakable) premise of the story freed them to pursue some of the tale's more sophisticated, subtextual elements. The inclusion of the character of 'Sambo', unfortunately, would itself be enough seriously to qualify a judgement of the film's ethos as in any way 'sophisticated'. (It remains curious that although the stereotypically cannibalistic 'Sambo' is alone of all the main characters seen ravenously enjoying Lovett's still dubious pies, he is likewise the only individual to survive the trial of Todd's chair completely unscathed.) Peter Haining, attempting to offer some rationale for the change in plot, suggested that the producers, Stoll Films, had been afraid that the subject matter might prove 'too revolting for the public who were just then getting over reading the horrific details over the arrest and trial of Fritz Hartman [Fritz Haarmann], a German homosexual killer, who had murdered some fifty young men and boys between 1918 and 1924 and sold their flesh for human consumption in his cooked meat shop'.[12] It is unlikely that such events had any effect whatsoever on the production and distribution of the 1928 movie.

Just seven years after Moore Marriott's early, silent interpretation of Sweeney Todd, actor Tod Slaughter stepped before the cameras for the producer George King, and began what would prove to be an astoundingly long run as the acknowledged master of the part. Indeed, Slaughter was to be identified with the barber for decades; he effectively 'owned' the role, and any other interpretations of Sweeney, whether on the stage or on the screen, were only naturally to be held up to his for comparison (and more often than not denigration, as well).[13] Sweeney Todd and Tod Slaughter soon became inseparable. When the actor died in February 1956, the headline of his *Times* obituary predictably identified him simply as the 'Demon Barber of the Stage'.[14]

Born Norman Carter Slaughter at Newcastle upon Tyne in March 1885, he began acting on the stage at the age of 20. His decision in 1912 to begin transferring recent West End hits to local variety theatres for twice-nightly performances led to a career that was, in reality, to be characterized as much by his canny abilities as a lessor and manager of companies such as the Richmond and Croydon Hippodrome and, later, both the Theatre Royal, Chatham and the Elephant and Castle, as it was by his acting style – a style typically described today as 'hammy', 'eye-rolling' or even 'scenery-chewing'.[15] Even at the time of his death, the writer of Slaughter's obituary observed: 'There was little subtlety in his work, but he never spared himself, and he was obviously disappointed if at the end of the evening his audience did not regard him as the greatest criminal to have escaped the gallows.'[16]

Slaughter – whose prominent features at once denied him the conventional good looks required for actors playing romantic leading roles, yet also ideally suited him for the part of the melodramatic villain – was regarded in his own day primarily as a stage performer. From 1935, however, he began transferring some of the more memorable of his theatrical triumphs to the screen in a series of horror films. Most of these movies were produced by George King at the recently established Shepperton Studios. In addition to *Sweeney Todd*, Slaughter was also to appear in movie versions of *Maria Marten, or Murder in the Red Barn* (1935); *The Crimes of Stephen Hawke* (1936); *The Ticket of Leave Man* (1937); *The Face at the Window* (1939) and *Crimes at the Dark House* (1940). *Sweeney Todd, the Demon Barber* (1936) was among Slaughter's earliest films.[17] Also directed by King, and featuring the actress Stella Rho in the role of Mrs Lovett, along with Eve Lister and Bruce Seeton as the pair of young lovers, the film was billed as nominally based on a version of Hazleton's text, with additional dialogue by 'H.F. Maltby'. The film's screenplay is in fact a radically simplified version of the story as dramatized by both Dibdin Pitt and Hazleton. The sequence of events taken from the stage originals has been simplified and rearranged; some episodes have been reworked, and many of the supporting characters in the drama have been eliminated. Interestingly, certain elements that helped to render the earlier, 1928 film memorable (i.e. the guilty Todd's haunting by the spectres of his several victims) are dispensed with completely. In this film as in its predecessor, it is left to the hero Mark Ingestrie and not (as in most versions of the play) the Bow Street magistrate Sir Richard Blunt to enter Todd's shop disguised as a farmer in order to trap him. 'But', as the film historian and critic Jeffrey Richards has observed, 'the familiar melodramatic elements of secret passages, disguises and star-crossed lovers are all there.'[18]

Once again, the film-makers chose first to situate Todd's story within a frame narrative. The 'flashback' method would again appear to have served its purposes by rendering the action more realistically proximate to its modern audience. 'Just as the melodramas ... [became] self-consciously historical', as Richards noted with reference to Slaughter's version of *Sweeney Todd*, 'they ... lost their specific contemporary relevance', and so needed to be brought closer to viewers.[19] A prosperous-looking gentleman wearing a top hat enters a barber shop in present-day (i.e. 1936) Fleet Street. The shop's proprietor – whose assistant's name, we overhear, is Toby – greets him with a broad grin, and begins immediately to draw attention to the wide range of dubious-looking products (hair tonics, oils promoting hair growth etc.) available for purchase; just as the name of 'Toby' suggests some sort of connection across time, the contemporary barber's slightly unctuous manner manages subtly to anticipate Todd's own particular brand of duplicitous greed. An old-fashioned print – an image of Sweeney Todd offering a 'general polish off' to one of his patrons, and engraved in what appears to be the manner of an original James Gillray or a Thomas Rowlandson – provokes a humorous quip from the customer, but the resident barber loses no time in letting the gentleman know that the particular print in question is not for sale; in fact, he tells him, it forms a valuable part of the shop's 100-year-old history. It is then, as he begins to shave the man, that the barber begins to tell him the tale that follows (of which the customer would appear to have been otherwise unaware). Set in the London of the 1800s, it is, the barber avows, with a peculiar sense of proprietary élan – 'the strangest story ever told in the days of sailing ships'.

Fleeing the 'narrow streets and dark alleys' of the late Hanoverian city, and already overheard by the skulking and sinister figure of the man whom the audience immediately identifies as Sweeney Todd, the young sailor Mark Ingestrie (played by the handsome Bruce Seeton with gentlemanly restraint) bids goodbye to his faithful Johanna (Eve Lister) on a bustling quayside near the Thames. Mark reassures Johanna of his own unfailing love for her, even though he is aware that her father – who in this version is not a spectacle-maker, but a well-to-do ship owner named Stephen Oakley – has forbidden the couple's engagement because of Mark's lack of any status or fortune. Determined to prove his worth to Johanna's father, Mark is to serve as a mate on board one of Oakley's own ships – the 'Golden Hope' – which is about to set sail for Africa and the East Indies. (Both of the romantic leads have been provided in this particular film with comic sidekicks – 'Pearley' (Jerry Verno) and 'Nan' (Davina Craig), respectively – whose parallel attachment is meant to provide some additional comic relief to the story's main action; the central conceit of their relationship, however, is based on little more than Pearley's constant muggings for the camera, and the fact that Johanna's personal maidservant, Nan, an 'adenoidal, open-mouthed, vacant-eyed lady's maid', is clearly the more dominant member of the pair.)[20]

A tip from the vigilant Todd – whose furtive and lascivious expressions quickly establish him as a rival for Johanna's hand, if not for her affections – leads Oakley to separate Johanna from Mark even as the latter prepares to board his vessel. The barber returns to his Fleet Street premises, where he receives his new apprentice, Tobias, and warns him not to speak to anyone regarding what passes in the shop. The scene between the two – as Todd gives the suitably quaking Tobias a penny to buy a pie from Mrs Lovett's shop next door – is filmed much as it would have been played for years on the stage, although Slaughter's Todd is markedly less physically violent towards the boy; the nature of Todd's true disposition towards and treatment of his apprentices is left to be inferred from the beadle's observation that Tobias is the seventh such boy he has handed over to the care of the barber in as many weeks. Mrs Lovett is introduced to the audience rather earlier in the film than in many other versions of the tale. Gone, however, is the sensual appeal that actress Zoë Palmer had brought to her 1928 interpretation of the role, which is replaced here instead by the Xantippe-like and shrewish characterization of Stella Rho. The aspect of pinched and perennial discontent that Rho brings to the part (combined with a vaguely sinister, continental accent) clearly situates her less as the alluring proprieties of the Bell-Yard pie shop, than as the hopeless rival to Johanna Oakley's good looks. The long-standing business partnership between her and Todd (whose personal relationship, although redolent of that between a stale and long-married couple, remains otherwise vague), the existence of the cellars that secretly connect their premises, the manner in which Todd uses his chair to kill hapless sailors and farmers and Lovett's increasing jealousy both of Todd's apparent squandering of the money they have accumulated and of the barber's desire to possess Johanna for himself: all these are economically set out for the film's audience within the space of just a few minutes.

The focus then shifts in a manner almost unprecedented in retellings of Todd's history to the story of Mark and the crew of Oakley's ship, the 'Golden Hope'. We catch up with the vessel not long after it has reached an obscure African trading outpost near the Cape of Good Hope; the jungle station is manned by a single Scottish resident-trader named Paterson (Aubrey Mallalieu) and his willing native servant who answers to the name of (and again the racial stereotyping will be astonishing to today's viewers) 'Snowball'. While members of the ship's crew are visiting Patterson's trading station, the outpost is attacked by a tribe of hostile natives. Snowball swims to the 'Golden Hope' to warn the ship of their Captain's danger. Both Patterson and the Captain are killed by hostile arrows in the course of the encounter that follows, leaving Mark, who had already proven his worth in the course of the voyage, to assume command as 'Acting Captain' of the 'Golden Hope' (the expiring trader, who had been inexpertly protected by Mark in the course of the attack, simultaneously bequeaths a handful of pearls to him). Meanwhile, back in London, we learn that it was Sweeney Todd himself who had financed the construction of Oakley's ship; the once-thriving Oakley has now suddenly been plunged into financial straits. The 'Golden Hope' is thought to have been lost, and the barber, rather than advancing the further £5,000 that Oakley needs to build an 'ambitious' new vessel, threatens him with ruin, and demands instead that Oakley at once repay the outstanding debt (a staggering £15,000) already owed to him with respect to the 'Golden Hope'. Oakley proves to be all-too-susceptible when Todd offers to wipe the slate clean in return for Joanna's hand in marriage. The embarrassed father introduces Johanna to Todd (who has resorted to dyeing his hair for the occasion) in his own home; the young girl is suitably disgusted by the barber's leering advances.

When the 'Golden Hope' returns unexpectedly to London with Mark as its Captain, newly covered in glory (not only has he proven his greater worth to Oakley, he is – even more importantly – now more than rich enough to marry Joanna), it is not his beloved but Todd who is waiting for him at the quayside. When the barber suggests that Mark could do with a shave before being reunited with the woman he can now with confidence refer to as his fiancée, the young man naturally proves susceptible. In the shop, Todd places Mark in his special barber's chair, and instantly drops his body down into the cellar. The jealous Mrs Lovett, however, who has taken to spying on Todd's movements, contrives to remove the young man's body from Todd's cellar and conceal him elsewhere in the cellars before the barber has had time to return to the basement to 'polish him off'. Todd himself has by now grown deeply suspicious of Lovett, but the pastry-maker protests her innocence and manages to convince him that Mark must have escaped of his own accord through some secret passageway. Todd is troubled but not unduly devastated by Mark's inexplicable disappearance, since, having stolen all of Mark's jewels and money, he knows that the young captain will once again be deemed too poor to pursue any plans to marry Oakley's daughter, and the girl will inevitably be pushed in his direction. Once Todd has left the cellar, Mrs Lovett helps Mark to effect his escape via one of the tunnels that leads towards nearby St Dunstan's.

Having already witnessed the barber in the act of killing an Indian nabob, one 'Findlay' (Norman Pierce), we watch as Todd dispatches yet another of his more regular customers – the 'fence' Parsons, a dealer in stolen goods who has foolishly attempted to blackmail him for £7,000, threatening to tell the authorities everything he knows about the means by which the barber has managed to amass such riches. A recovered Mark decides to effect Todd's exposure by disguising himself as a country farmer, and infiltrating the shop as a customer. The moment Mark arrives at Todd's shop, he sends Tobias to Johanna for his own protection. Tobias in turn informs Johanna that Mark is risking his life in Todd's chair; she decides to disguise herself in the usual manner as a boy apprentice, in order to gain entrance to the shop and assist Mark in his plan (there is also some comic cross-dressing business, in which Tobias is compelled by Nan to wear Johanna's clothes, presumably in an attempt to forestall any discovery of the latter's plans). Todd places Mark – who has metamorphosed into a bluff Devon farmer – in his special chair, and once again dispatches him through the trap-door and into the cellar. Prepared as he now is for the potentially deadly drop, Mark emerges completely unscathed; his friend Pearley, disguised as a monk, has been stationed nearby, and together the two men make their way through the rat-infested labyrinth towards the exit near the porch of St Dunstan's. For a second time, Todd descends to the cellar to find that his 'customer' has unaccountably vanished; now, feeling certain that Mrs Lovett has aided the potential victim's escape, he struggles with her, and eventually knocks her unconscious; we see Todd raise a large knife against her, and are led to assume that Todd either kills her then, or leaves her for dead on the cellar floor.

Johanna, disguised in the uniform of a charity boy, has by now arrived at the barber shop, where she tries to convince Todd to take her on as his new apprentice. The barber discovers that she is carrying a purse with a large amount of money, and knocks her unconscious in order to steal it. Hastily hiding her body in a convenient wardrobe, he then begins smashing the furniture of the shop, in order to set fire to the entire building, and so attempt to burn any evidence that might eventually link him to the disappearances and thefts. Mark and Pearley arrive on the scene, and Johanna's maid, Nan, informs Mark that her mistress must be trapped in the now burning building. Bursting into the blazing structure to save Johanna, Mark struggles with the fleeing Todd, who confronts him first with a blade and then a candlestick, but who is finally knocked unconscious as he collapses onto the special chair. The young lovers escape, and a burning beam of wood falls onto the secret lever that releases the chair, precipitating Todd to his just death in the cellar below. The narrative frame is quickly closed as, returning to the London of 1936, the shop's customer suspiciously asks the barber what he can smell cooking, only to be informed that the smell is emanating from the cooked meat shop situated just next door. The man leaps out of the chair in a panic, and flees down Fleet Street in the direction of Ludgate Hill.

The routine and arguably perfunctory achievement of the 1936 film is enlivened by Slaughter's performance, which justly established him for a generation or more as the screen's foremost Sweeney Todd. The movie has not stood the test of time at all well, however, and the film's famous catchphrases which, throughout his own lifetime, guaranteed the actor's continued reputation as one of the most dastardly screen villains – 'I polish them all off,' 'Beautiful throats. I love my work!', or even Mrs Lovett's own 'It's sad to be all alone in the world' – will invariably provoke not fright but incredulous laughter from twenty-first-century audiences. Be that as it may, Slaughter's performance in the film can be oddly compelling. As Jeffrey Richards notes:

> in all the Slaughter films the villain's role [was] built up to make him the centre of the action. Slaughter gives more or less the same performance in each film and it conforms exactly to [Peter] Brooks's definition of melodramatic acting, externalising emotions, expressing forbidden desires and rejoicing in his wickedness. It is a cinema of excess in which Slaughter is in his element, gleeful in his villainy, leering, cackling, eye-rolling, hand-rubbing, revelling in lechery and murder but doing it with such eye-twinkling relish that he makes the audience his accomplices. It is impossible not to warm to him... .[21]

Something of the sheer dramatic energy and over-the-top quality of Slaughter's performance remains captivating, but leers and grimaces that were once, both here and on the stage, a pardonable indulgence, appear to modern viewers hopelessly out-dated. As in the earlier silent film, all explicit reference to cannibalism and all direct representation of acts of physical violence have been omitted. It is *suggested* that Todd, stealthily approaching his victims with a grin and a raised straight razor, often finds it necessary to polish his victims off with some sort of *coup de grâce* in the cellar, but we never actually *see* him doing anything. (In fact, Todd on one occasion leaves the cellar – and the body of his latest victim – entirely in Lovett's care; the implication is that it is Lovett and not the barber who undertakes to do the 'dirty work' involved in their mutual enterprise.) Todd's motives are articulated with unprecedented clarity in the film; on the surface, at least, his own, insatiable appetite seems to be directed less towards the captivation and consumption of human flesh, as it is towards money, and the position wealth might bring him. This Sweeney Todd, confronted on all sides by a booming and entrepreneurial mercantile society that seems to be relentlessly upwardly aspirational and climbing, wishes himself to be thought a 'fine gentleman'; the film appears to wish to teach him a telling lesson in the necessary decorum of social mobility. The film manages to have it both ways, however. As Richards has observed of Slaughter's movies, generally:

> At the most obvious level [they] fulfil both [Michael] Booth's and Brooks's definitions of melodrama as demonstrating a morality that preferred good over evil and virtue over vice and ensured the punishment of wrongdoing. But the dominance of Slaughter's characters suggests another interpretation: a celebration of excess. At the same time when much of the main stream cinema was sexless, the keynote of Slaughter films was lechery, the shameless and gleeful pursuit of sex. It governed the actions of almost all of the Slaughter characters.[22]

The film of *Sweeney Todd* – with all its residual recollections of the original mythic foundations of the tale it has to tell – e.g. the ship rechristened allegorically as one of 'Hope', the faint survival of the narrative's original title in not only the (now unstrung) pearls for which Mark is dispatched, but in the name of his comic sidekick (Pearley) as well – wishes somehow to instil in its viewers the lesson that Todd's particular brand of acquisitiveness is somehow wrong, even while it sanctions the same appetitive desires – both sexual and monetary – when they are more fully integrated into the existing, acceptable structures of English society. There is a potentially fierce criticism of the essential hypocrisy of colonialism in the film; it is perfectly acceptable to kill in order to make a profit – Oakley, Mark, Pearley, and the entire crew of the British ship are all implicated in the suppression and exploitation of the film's African natives. What is *not* acceptable is to do so on your own doorstep. The manifest 'otherness' of the film's natives, regardless of their own possible striving towards an ethic of 'civilized' behaviour that aims for an identification with and assimilation within the hegemonic order of things (captured succinctly in all that is symbolized by a name such as 'Snowball') renders them fair game for imperial exploitation and consumption. In order to work properly, the mercantile ethic that regards the death and mistreatment of other human beings in the pursuit of profit as something that needs simply to be taken in stride demands always to be effectively mystified, or masked by a rhetoric that somehow obscures or distances the realities of its own rapaciousness.[23]

Finally, two other critical approaches would seem to make some sense of what Slaughter's film accomplishes on the level of social or cultural critique. The Anglo-American school of feminist criticism, towards the end of the twentieth century, memorably focused the attention of readers on the case of the so-called 'mad women' of Victorian literature (and there are – one has to admit – a remarkable number of them). Such critics observed that the labels of mental instability and illness – labels such as 'madness' and 'hysteria' – were routinely attached to the figure of the female who rejects the conventions of a repressive (and patriarchal) society. The transgressive female figure was – by very definition – not in her right mind. Taking such a critical stance into account, Slaughter's Todd himself, for all his seemingly straightforward heterosexual lechery, can be read as an oddly 'feminine' figure – one who acts as the agent of a subversion that is more typically manifest in 'madwomen' and those locked away as insane. Most viewers will agree that Todd can with some justice, as Richards makes a point of noting, 'be seen as an anti-hero like Margaret Lockwood's wicked ladies and James Mason's degenerate lords in the Gainsborough melodramas and Peter Cushing and Christopher Lee's aristocratic predators'.[24] Hand-in-hand with such a reading would be an interpretation of the film that sees it as a critique of Victorianism, more generally, and links its genealogy to that of a series of British films made throughout the 1940s and their 'heroes' and 'heroines' – Ingrid Bergman's 'Paula Alquist Anton' in *Gaslight* (1944), Robert Newton's 'James Brodie' in *Hatter's Castle* (1942), Googie Withers's 'Pearl Bond' in *Pink String and*

Sealing Wax (1946), Dennis Price's Louis Mazzini in *Kind Hearts and Coronets* (1949) – that constitute an implicit and devastating critique of Victorian patriarchy.[25] At heart, the film is sympathetic towards the 'outsider' who is to a very real extent victimized by a repressive and intolerant Victorian society. In these 1940s films, women (typically) are forced into marital liaisons against their will, or are denied by their fathers or guardians the right to marry the men they love; they are denied their legitimate rights over their own material possessions, excluded from all decisions of polity and isolated from the structures of law that might otherwise secure them. 'The films also consistently expose hypocrisy', it has also been observed, 'seen retrospectively as a cardinal Victorian vice, by showing "respectability" in the middle and upper classes to be a mask for evil-doing.'[26] Scratch the surface of any 'respectable' businessman or (certainly) any lawyer or politician, and you are all too likely to discover just another Sweeney Todd.

*

Tod Slaughter's inhabitation of the role of Sweeney Todd – much like Boris Karloff's comparable appropriation at about the same time of the figure of Frankenstein's monster in American cinema – was so complete that for many years few other actors would even consider attempting a rival interpretation on the screen. (Paradoxically, Slaughter's performance ensured that Todd remained one of the more popular figures in live theatre; throughout much of the twentieth century there was no dearth of amateur touring companies and professional 'barnstormers' for whom *Sweeney Todd* was among the most dependable of dramatic staples.)[27] A number of movies would in time be made that either referred to or otherwise referenced Todd's story – including Andy Milligan's *Bloodthirsty Butchers* (1970), Francesca Joseph's *Tomorrow La Scala!* (2002) and Kevin Smith's *Jersey Girl* (2004) – but no completely new film versions of the barber's tale were to be forthcoming for many years.

Radio and eventually television, however, offered options for airing alternative versions of the story, although these, too, proved oddly limited. Australian listeners had already (in 1932) been treated to J.P Quaine's radio play *Sweeny* [sic] *Todd, The Demon Barber of Fleet Street*, which was advertised as 'an entirely original version for the radio' and set 'in the Reign of George the Second'; the text of Quaine's play as broadcast was eventually printed in *The Collector's Miscellany*.[28] In January 1946, American audiences could tune into 'The Strange Case of the Demon Barber' – a half-hour long radio play written by Dennis Green and Anthony Boucher and based in part on an incident originally included in Arthur Conan Doyle's Holmes story 'The Yellow Face' (1893). The adventure featured an encounter between Sherlock Holmes and a performer in the theatre playing the role of Sweeney Todd who seems to be identifying rather too closely with his stage role. The broadcast was part of a series entitled 'The New Adventures of Sherlock Holmes',

No. 6. Vol 1.   April. 1947

SWEENEY TODD

— THE —

PUPPET MASTER

The Journal of

THE BRITISH PUPPET AND MODEL THEATRE GUILD

Edited by Arthur E. Peterson

279 NORTHGATE, COTTINGHAM, YORKS.

ENGLAND.

Copyright Reserved]   ONE SHILLING

Illustrated cover for the British Puppet and Model Theatre Guild's journal, *The Puppet Master*, for April 1947, depicting three of John Bickerlike's marionettes for a production of *Sweeney Todd*.

and the role of Sherlock Holmes was voiced by the popular British actor
Basil Rathbone, who had already, of course, secured for himself the screen
role of the famous detective no less thoroughly than Slaughter had made
Todd his own. (The actor Nigel Bruce, who in the movies always played Dr
Watson to Rathbone's Holmes, was likewise on board for the radio series.)
An expanded prose version of the text used for the original 1946 broadcast
(by Ken Greenwald, and based on the original script prepared by Green and
Boucher) was included in *The Lost Adventures of Sherlock Holmes*, published in
1989.[29]

Todd's appearances on television – apart from relatively regular screenings
of the 1936 film – were for many years of a similarly limited nature. In
February 1970 Robert Collin directed an adaptation of Dibdin Pitt's drama
(written for the small screen by Vincent Tilsley) as part of the British
anthology series 'Mystery and Imagination'. The ITV series had been on the
air since 1966, and was at that point nearing the end of its run (*Sweeney Todd*,
as it so turned out, was in fact to prove its penultimate episode). Yet having
previously dramatized works extending from the more obviously 'canonical'
classics of horror – e.g. *The Fall of the House of Usher* (February 1966),
Frankenstein (November 1968), *Dracula* (November 1968) – to a slightly
more esoteric range of titles – John Meade Falkner's *The Lost Stradivarius*
(January 1966) and M.R. James's *The Tractate Middoth* (February 1966) –
'Mystery and Imagination' at least placed the barber's story in rather eminent
company. The production was obviously made on a shoestring budget, but
the young Freddie Jones (fresh from early appearances in shows such as 'Z
Cars' and 'The Avengers') acquitted himself well enough as a Sweeney Todd
infatuated with Mrs Lovett, a role played by Heather Canning in one of her
first dramatic roles for television. Both Jones and Canning have long since
become familiar faces on British television, Jones enjoying lengthy runs in
soaps such as *Emmerdale* and *Heartbeat*, and Canning featuring in recent years
in dramatic series such as *Casualty* and *A Touch of Frost*.

In 1998 the British-born director John Schlesinger – who made his name
in the late 1960s and early 1970s directing such films as *Midnight Cowboy*
(1969) and *Sunday Bloody Sunday* (1971) – produced a full-length feature
version of Todd's story for the American television network 'Showtime'
entitled *The Tale of Sweeney Todd*. The adaptation was written by Peter
Shaw, who also served as executive producer to the project, and starred the
Academy Award-winning actor Ben Kingsley as Todd, and the popular (and
typically much more glamorous) Joanna Lumley in the role of Mrs Lovett.
Shaw's primary narrative innovation arrived in the form of an American
insurance investigator by the name of Ben Carlyle (played by Campell Scott),
who is on the trail of $50,000 worth of missing diamonds. Kingsley –
although receiving a nomination from the Screen Actor's Guild Awards for
'Outstanding Performance by a Male Actor in a TV movie or mini-series' for
his portrayal of Todd – turned in an oddly muted performance as the barber,

and Lumley failed fully to realize the potential of her opportunities as a Mrs Lovett who was at once both sinister and beguiling.

On 3 January 2006 the BBC – with considerable fanfare – aired a completely new adaptation of *Sweeney Todd*, one that had been written exclusively for the small screen by the television producer Joshua St Johnstone (*Sweeney Todd* was his first televised effort as a writer).[30] Although Johnstone freely admitted that he was inspired to tell his own version of the story only after having seen a production of Stephen Sondheim's stage musical based on the subject, he claimed nevertheless to have returned for inspiration to some of the earlier versions of Todd's narrative. This decision soon led him away from the tale as it had been retold in Sondheim's 1979 'musical thriller' – and, indeed, away from any of the previous cinematic adaptations with which his television audience might have been more familiar – and inspired him instead to envision something that was at once both markedly closer in narrative terms to the original serial of 1846–7, yet at the same time presented the character of Sweeney Todd as a recognizably modern and even contemporary figure. 'I wanted to try and write something that felt more like it could be a true story,' Johnstone explained. 'It's an attempt', he added of the methodology that lay behind his own adaptation, 'to apply a twenty-first century understanding of criminal psychology to an eighteenth-century serial killer.'[31] One of the first things Johnstone decided to do, in fact, was to return Todd's story to its original Hanoverian setting. He accordingly professed to have set about researching the history of the period, and confessed himself most surprised by the practical realities that would be entailed in attempting faithfully to recreate for his viewing audience the physical environments within which Todd would have flourished. 'The streets would have been filled with excrement, gin addicts, beggars, animal torture passing for entertainment, [and] dead babies,' he realized, adding, 'it's not a version of Georgian England that we're often exposed to'. 'From reading the histories', Johnstone continued:

> I learnt that in the 1760s the Bow Street Runners were in their infancy. It's a fascinating time, because the notion of a police force was unpopular for reasons of civil liberty.... It was a brutal and brutalising world, and [the reason] that we don't know of any real serial killers from that time might be more to do with the fact that murder was so easy to get away with, rather than that there weren't any. Maybe there really was a Sweeney Todd after all – he just never got caught.[32]

Johnstone clearly felt that a judiciously 'modernized' version of the tale – one that viewed Todd not as an inherently evil man, but rather more simply as a criminal who was the inevitable product of his environment, and one that likewise played up the possible curtailment of human rights and 'civil liberties' as a politically relevant issue in the first decade of the twenty-first century – could potentially speak to a wide popular audience. As Johnstone's producer, Gub Neal, further explained of the BBC's approach to the adaptation (misguidedly condescending, it would appear, to Sondheim's far more sophisticated work in so doing):

> This is no burlesque musical horror story. Sweeney is portrayed as a real man, someone whose own history was full of suffering and whose life becomes a kind of paradigm for the darkness of his age. Sweeney is portrayed as a man capable of great compassion and love, but whose only ability to exert power over the world was to murder.[33]

Unfortunately, Johnstone's 'researches' in early 2005 appear to have been anything but extensive; in fact, they seem to have led him only as far as Peter Haining's 1993 book on Todd, which of course presented the barber's story as entirely true. Researching the background of Todd's narrative with the help only of Haining's misrepresentation, Johnstone was compelled to admit that although he wanted people to believe the story to be true, he himself was increasingly sceptical. 'In the end it was only by visiting St Dunstan's Church, where Sweeney Todd was meant to have hidden the bits of the bodies that didn't go into the pies', he concluded, 'that I realised he probably didn't exist, as there was nothing there referring to it.'[34]

The BBC's promotional material neatly summarized the central narrative for viewers of the programme. Johnstone's *Sweeney Todd* is set in the harsh streets of London in 1765, a city in which 'life is not for the faint-hearted and only the fittest survive'.[35] Sweeney Todd now lives not near St Dunstan's Church, as in other versions, but rather in the very shadow of the fetid Newgate Prison, where he tries to insulate himself from the surrounding squalor, and carve out a quiet simple life as a barber. A chance encounter with Mrs Lovett, a local pie-maker, however, leaves the otherwise unsocial and unassuming barber besotted. Later, at a time of need, Mrs Lovett turns to Sweeney for help. He shows her nothing but kindness and compassion, and she begins to see him in a new light. It seems they are destined to fall in love. Lovett is unaware, however, that Todd was a child inmate at the infamous Newgate Prison himself, and that he suffered terrible wrongs during his incarceration. One afternoon the sadistic gaoler who had made his early life a living hell in Newgate happens by chance to enter his shop for a shave. Sweeney is repelled by the presence of his former abuser (the gaoler does not recognize the barber as a former prisoner) and takes revenge by slitting his throat with his razor. Initially appalled by what he has done, Sweeney waits for the law to come after him. But apart from an enquiry about the missing gaoler by Bow Street Runner Matthew Payne, no alarm is raised, and Todd soon returns to living his life as before.

After Sweeney's drunken father re-enters his life, however, Sweeney feels a compelling need to kill again. He seems on the verge of becoming a serial killer but his burgeoning relationship with Mrs Lovett pulls him back from the brink of his sanity. Sweeney hopes that she will bring him the love, solace and salvation he craves. Harbouring these hopes, he installs Mrs Lovett in the shop next to his, which she turns into a pie shop. One night, she makes a pass at him, and though he tries to respond, he is impotent. Shamed and angry, he starts to kill again. Now it is not the gaolers or officials of Newgate who feel his blade, but the lovers that Mrs Lovett takes to her bed. Soon, murder alone no longer provides the gratification Todd needs. In an even greater act of revenge, he begins to carve up the dead bodies of his 'customers' and hands Mrs Lovett the meat to serve in her pies. When Mrs Lovett falls seriously ill with the pox, Sweeney lovingly nurses her, and eventually confesses his terrible secret to her. Lovett is at first appalled by Todd's revelation, but after she recovers her health (though not her looks), the pair forge a complex and destructive partnership, and the barber's customers begin to disappear with alarming regularity. The pair are finally brought to justice through the efforts of Matthew Payne, the upstanding Bow Street Runner, who owes his life to Sweeney, and the magistrate John Fielding. When Fielding, at the end of the film, asks Todd why he has killed so many people, the barber's answer is both disarmingly simple and enigmatic: 'Because I could, and then I couldn't not.'

The well-known British film and television actor Ray Winstone, who played Todd in the 2006 adaptation, described his character to interviewers as a 'profoundly tortured' man. 'He spent 20 years in gaol for a crime he didn't commit,' Winstone explained, 'his brother was hung, and he was raped, and so Sweeney comes out completely tormented.... There is a scene where the dad comes back. Sweeney is desperate to give him a chance to redeem himself, but the self-pitying father doesn't take it. His dad is his blood and all Sweeney wants is for him to apologise. In that moment, everything might have been all right, but it isn't.' Winstone commented on the manner in which Sweeney's life was complicated even further by his confused yet intense relationship with Mrs Lovett. 'From the moment Sweeney sees Mrs Lovett,' Winstone said, 'he thinks of her as an angel. He falls in love with her, but she becomes like a prostitute and starts taking other lovers. He watches her with other men through a hole in the wall. That fuels his anger, and he starts to kill these men. He thinks what he's doing is alright because he's getting back at the people who run the world and they deserve it. It's fair to say that he's a pretty mixed up guy.' When it was suggested that the explicit violence of the television adaptation simply catered to a desire on the part of the audience for cheap thrills and sensations, Winstone protested,

> we are not glorifying murder in *Sweeney Todd*. These sort of things happen. We show it, and it isn't nice. But when people hit each other with chairs, they don't just get up again as though nothing has happened. The minute you start to compromise, you've lost it. What did Shakespeare write about? Exactly those subjects which are covered in this drama. The greatest dramas in the world are all about sex, violence and death.[36]

Winstone himself garnered relatively good reviews for his performance as the barber, although Johnstone's adaptation and Neal's production were less to the taste of many viewers. 'The imposing Ray Winstone always seems to pull off a mesmeric performance on the small screen,' wrote Terry Ramsey, the TV editor for London's *Evening Standard*, ' – and he does it once again in this bloody and gruesome version of the Sweeney Todd tale.' 'And it's a good job he does, too,' Ramsey continued,

> for there is precious little else in the story apart from the brooding, frightening presence of Todd. Yes, there are some important secondary characters – notably Mrs Lovett the pie-maker – but few actors other than Winstone could have shouldered the weight of the central character and not buckled under the sombre (sometimes even portentous) script.[37]

Chris Riley wrote similarly in the *Daily Telegraph*:

> Ray Winstone and the blood-spattered story of the demon barber of Fleet Street – a match made in a hellish sort of heaven. In lots of ways, this is exactly the type of high-end, one-off drama you'd imagine. The London of the 18th century has been evocatively, grimily realised (in Romania, but there you go). And, unlike many single dramas, the script, veined with resonant and provocative scenes, is aimed four-square at intelligent adult viewers. That's not to say there aren't elements which don't work so well.... Winstone's well-pitched Todd is given inner demons, a pre-Freudian profile (hung up on mum, mutilates his dad) and a vague socio-political agenda (like a kind of Georgian Equaliser) – all of which rather over-eggs the pudding.[38]

Writing in the *Sunday Times*, A.A. Gill was even less impressed with the entire production; his remarks, however casual, are typically insightful, and can serve aptly for our purposes as the final word on the 2006 television version.

> There are two ways to play Sweeney. You go either for black laughs or for gory horror, and casting Ray Winstone as the head boy, well, it could go either way.... Somewhere in the production process for this tuneless drama version, [the producers] decided it was really a psychological exploration of inner torment and abused childhood with rumpy-pumpy. Sort of Vidal Sassoon meets Fanny Cradock, directed by Luis Buñuel's less talented brother. It was a mess. Actually, it wasn't anything like enough of a mess. If there's no suspense, no horror, no laughs and little entertainment, what is there? Well, Winstone standing around being tortured and silent.... [T]here are internal actors and there are external actors. Ray Winstone is an external actor. If he's not emoting and being physical, then there's nothing going on. He doesn't do still and deeply pensive. His Christmas lights are all on the outside. I can't understand why you would cast an actor who is brilliantly good at being one thing and then direct him not to do it as hard and as thoroughly as he possibly could. I still rather wonder what the point of this expensive, full-fig costume drama was. What on earth was the audience supposed to come away with other than an itchy scalp and feeling a bit peckish?[39]

Chapter 8

Swing Your Razor Wide, Sweeney: Further Adventures of a Legend

There is something infinitely fascinating about those relics of the far-distant past which still live and breathe in our own times, their survival through the centuries the best evidence of their vitality.

(Tony Sarg, *Punch and Judy*)[1]

Visitors to London's Museum of Childhood – one of the more far-flung outposts of Knightsbridge's larger Victoria & Albert Museum, located in the unlikely neighborhood of Bethnal Green – are often surprised by the miniature Crystal Palace-like structure in which the institution is housed. First built in 1856, and the earliest home to the original South Kensington Museum (at which time it was situated on the Brompton Road), the actual building was taken apart and reconstructed some 15 years later in the East End. The original idea seemed to be that it could serve as a kind of local mini-museum for the borough. Dedicated initially as a resource for children and then as a permanent home to the V&A's ever-expanding collections of children's costumes, books, nursery items, toys and furniture in 1974, the museum reopened its doors in December 2006 after a closure of over two years, during which period it suffered a costly £4.7 million 'make-over' at the hands of the trendy architectural design firm of Caruso St John.

Some might question the very notion that a museum dedicated to such artefacts can ever truly succeed (or should even exist) in the first place. 'A toy in a box, or a toy in a glass case,' wrote one journalist shortly after the revamped Bethnal Green museum was reopened to the public, is no longer a toy; it becomes something less: 'an exhibit, a curio, an exercise in nostalgia or design history'.[2] Others, though not questioning the concept of such a museum, professed to be no less surprised by some of the particular items on display; the entire collection – only a small fraction of which, naturally, can ever be viewed at any one time – is nothing if not scrupulously thorough

246

and comprehensive. A museum that boasts (among its many other treasures) a representative selection of dolls containing everything from a wooden 'paddle' figure dating from as early as 1300 BC, on the one hand, to collections of the sorts of 'Masters of the Universe' character figurines so popular in the 1980s and 1990s and so complete as likely to render most amateur toy enthusiasts weak at the knees, on the other, does not exactly aim at simply providing its patrons – young and old alike – with the merely expected or the mundane. The qualification, too, that it is less a museum showcasing the material artefacts of children than it is a venue dedicated to the concept of 'childhood', generally, is an important one, and serves to draw the attention of visitors away from a collection of mere objects – and away from the simple changes effected by fashion or technology – and towards the gradual development and evolution of a far more consequential 'concept' – to what might accurately be described as a state of being that is itself the result of a frame of mind.

Prominently featured in one of the museum's galleries dedicated specifically to 'Moving Toys' is a selection of puppets. Hand (or glove) puppets and marionettes from all over Europe; shadow puppets from India, Greece and Turkey; traditional bunraku puppets from Japan: all are on display in the glass cases at Bethnal Green. Punch and Judy have perhaps only naturally traditionally received pride of place among their native fellows of the fairground, although even their well-deserved prominence and generally pervasive influence is not without its problems. The perennially feuding couple have tended to run afoul of many of the self-appointed censors and moral guardians of the late twentieth and early twenty-first centuries who – rather than reading the figures' ongoing, seditious rebellion against figures of authority as calculated acts of symbolic theatrical subversion – have earnestly insisted instead on a reductive interpretation of the most traditional play-texts for the puppets as pieces the most prominent features of which are dangerously uncomplicated representations of domestic and even sexual violence.[3] More to our present purpose, however, and generally to be found on display in the nearby 'Pushes and Pulls: Worked by Strings' section of the same gallery, are a set of three and occasionally four marionettes featuring that other famously unscrupulous and equally irrepressible English couple: Sweeney Todd and Mrs Lovett. The two marionettes (often presented here in the company of their own dramatic associates 'Captain [Mark] Ingestrie' and 'The Barber's Boy' [Tobias Ragg]), when one pauses to think about it, could hardly have found themselves in more perfect and compatible company at Bethnal Green. Who better, after all, to be paired with Punch and Judy than Sweeney Todd and Mrs Lovett? What more appropriate companions could there possibly be even in the world of the toy theatre than these two pairs of figures, both of whom – although routinely censured by the uninformed or simply ignorant for supposedly encouraging and glorifying 'acts of violence' – in fact participate in powerfully compelling, anti-authoritarian story-lines

247

that typically remain far more intelligently informed and morally aware than their would-be detractors? Some few of today's parents, overly anxious to 'protect' their children against what they already judge to be the unsuitably violent stories of puppets such as Punch (the politically incorrect Punch is a 'wife beater', 'demeans the police service' and is 'cruel to animals'), can occasionally be seen hurrying their offspring past the Sweeney Todd mario-nettes, in particular, no less nonplussed than they are by the sight of Punch and Judy, and hushing any questions among the younger members of their own parties as to just who they are, and just why they are there. Fortunately, most of the museum's visitors are themselves capable of perceiving that the venerable Punch and Judy narrative celebrates not physical violence, but the ecstatic and systematic victory of a recognizably human vitality over symbolic figures representing the forces of constraint, confinement, ignorance, social and politician restriction, and even, finally, over death and the devil himself. 'It may surely deserve consideration', as one historian of the puppet theatre in England, Tony Sarg, commented on the moral of Punch's performances as long ago as 1929, 'whether, wicked as Punch unquestionably is, the Devil is not the worse offender of the two, and, consequently, the more deserving of punishment. If so, poetical justice is satisfied.'[4] The triumph of Punch – 'the devil's butcher', as he was sometimes called – is the triumph of the life force itself. The subtext of Sweeney Todd's possible cautionary tale regarding the potential dangers of appetite and over-indulgence lurking within the ever-expanding consumer culture of the modern period may be less jubilantly obvious than Punch's comprehensive victory over the enemies of life and activity, but his ancient story, too, boasts a long and distinguished conti-nental lineage, and – much like Punch's own narrative – discovered its epic power to have been crystallized in some of its most articulate expressions in the late-Hanoverian and early- and mid-Victorian eras (John Payne Collier's classic 'Punch and Judy' play-text, illustrated by George Cruikshank, was published in 1828, not very long before the first appearance of Todd).[5] There is but a very short distance indeed between Punch's famous catchphrase, 'That's the way to do it!', and Todd's no less gleeful exclamation, 'I'll have to polish him off!' Each serves as a call to arms. Both invite gleeful complicity in an act of assertive violence that momentarily – in the age-old dramatic traditions of saturnalia and 'the world turned upside down' – symbolically liberates the individual in an ecstasy of subversive energy; both reify and eventually help to reassert the existing social order even as they so spectacu-larly defy it by acknowledging the atavistic power of those primal forces it necessarily constrains.

Many puppet versions of *Sweeney Todd* date from the end of the nineteenth century – more specifically, from the 1880s and early 1890s. The earliest marionettes used in these performances would have been to our eyes unusually large – many of them up to two and even three feet high. The troupes that performed plays such as *Sweeney Todd* routinely travelled throughout the country with their tents and carts; they carried with them, as they moved from town to town, tremendous amounts of scenery, equipment, musical instruments, portable seating, and sometimes hundreds of figures – the many wooden actors and actresses that featured in their dramas. Many also undertook regular tours throughout continental Europe. (British companies were the most highly regarded in the Western world; 'even French companies', as the great twentieth-century puppeteer Bill Baird has observed, 'found it advantageous to travel under English names'.)[6] Whereas their earliest predecessors in the eighteenth and early nineteenth centuries had most often performed material drawn from the deep traditions of old folk plays and popular ballads (usually in the manner of the knockabout satire that was eventually to survive, at least in England, almost exclusively in the rough-and-ready comedy of Punch and Judy), the itinerant troupes of the later nineteenth century had been deeply influenced – for better or worse – by the dramatic innovations that had gradually been introduced into the medium in England by the likes of Charlotte Charke, Madame de la Nash, Samuel Foote, Charles Dibdin and, most significantly, the Italian Fantoccini. The spectacles of the latter had first been presented in London by Mr Carlo Perico at the Great Room in Panton Street in October 1770. The Fantoccini (the word is simply Italian for 'marionettes') typically performed several light operas, mythological playlets and comedies by popular French authors in programmes variously interspersed with Italian airs and other musical pieces. The reception extended to the supposedly unprecedented sophistication and elegance of these continental performances was rapturous, and attendance at their performances soon became universally fashionable. The novel effects of the scenery and lighting were applauded, and the mechanical skill with which the puppets themselves were manipulated invited the highest admiration (and famously attracted the pathological jealousy of Oliver Goldsmith, who, when his companion Samuel Johnson voiced his delighted approval of the dextrous skill of the puppeteers, remarking 'How the little fellow brandishes his spontoon!', is said to have cried, 'There is nothing in it; I can do it as well myself,' and promptly injured himself trying). Interestingly, the original Fantoccini stage was purchased in March 1790 by no other than Lord Barrymore (mentioned earlier), who briefly altered the theatre to accommodate live human performers at Wargrave.[7]

The fashionable popularity of the Italian marionettes in London themselves was destined to be short-lived. Even so, as a phenomenon, their innovative and influential shows prompted some long-term changes with regard to the arts of puppetry in England, generally. Admittedly, the many native English adaptations to the continental traditions of Mr Punch (whose indigenous life is glimpsed in Dickens's *The Old Curiosity Shop* (1840–1), and whose story was to be captured in yet another version by Mayhew in the third volume of his *London Labour and London Poor* (1851)) continued to be the main fare provided by many itinerant performers who travelled up and down the country. Yet

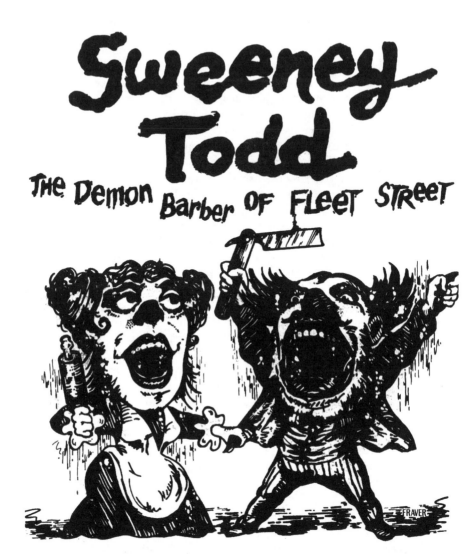

Poster art by Frank 'Fraver' Verlizzo for the original (1979) Broadway production of Stephen Sondheim's *Sweeney Todd: The Demon Barber of Fleet Street. A Musical Thriller.*

from the beginning of the nineteenth century onwards, the repertoires of the more famous touring companies aimed primarily to amaze and astound their viewers by spectacular effects; bills and brochures typically advertised the manner in which the company featured only the most modern and complicated 'machinery'. Their emphasis was less on plot than it was on properties. Such troupes guarded their professional secrets no less jealously than would an 'illusionist' or a latter-day magician. The most popular of all the Victorian puppeteers, Thomas Holden, was careful always to erect a canvas wall around the backstage area of his theatre, in order effectively to hide both from his audience and from his professional rivals the trade secrets of his own marionettes' construction and manipulation. Holden was rather more forthcoming when it came to letting others know just how much physical work and skill his job demanded. He boasted that his real talent lay in his ability

> to pull the strings, sometimes standing, sometimes kneeling and most often lying on one's stomach in positions often dangerous and always uncomfortable, sometimes hanging by a foot or clutching with an arm to an iron bar, rushing from right to left, up and down, singing, talking, shouting, according to the needs of the moment, without even time to take breath, changing one's voice according to the character presented to the public, and the whole time sweating as if in a Turkish Bath.[8]

It is worth reminding ourselves, lest we be at all inclined to suspect that Holden was exaggerating the physical demands of his profession in the manner one would only naturally expect from someone who came from a generations-old fairgrounds family, that the actual theatre in which he performed in the 1870s was eight feet high, as many feet deep and presented to its audience a proscenium arch no less than fourteen feet wide. These were not portable puppet 'booths', but nearly full-sized representational theatres.

The high-flown poetic tragedies and delicate dramas first introduced in the closing decades of the 1700s had invariably given way in the Regency and early Victorian period, however, first to romantic melodrama, and then to what some have distinguished as, rather, 'contemporary melodrama'.[9] 'It is now', as puppet historian George Speaight comments of the period, 'that we [in England] begin to get our Maria Martens, our Sweeny Todds {sic}, as well as our Oliver Twists.'[10] These original stage melodramas seem in fact with remarkable speed to have passed from the boards of the working-class theatres and penny gaffs into the possession of the puppeteers; those vehicles that were first seen by an audience when still the property of the regular theatres or of a company of strolling players, might very soon appear to have been taken over by the marionettes. Most of the puppet plays ostensibly based on George Dibdin Pitt's original dramatic adaptation of *Sweeney Todd* appear, again, to date from at least as early as the 1880s and 1890s, when a number of the country's best-known puppet showmen of the day (Harry

Wilding in the Midlands, Arthur Bolton in Yorkshire, Ambrose Tiller and Testo in Wales and elsewhere, and the long-established international troupe of the Middleton family) are on record as having performed *Sweeney* on numerous occasions, and as part of an established repertoire.[11] Here, Todd would have found himself in familiar company; some of the most popular of the other plays 'performed' by puppets at the time included versions of *Maria Marten, or the Murder at the Red Barn* (*c.*1860–90), *Spring-heeled Jack* (*c.*1860), *Dick Turpin* (*c.* 1880–90) and *Jack Sheppard* (*c.*1880–90). The companies that mounted these productions, like Thomas Holden's own, noted above, could by no means ever be dismissed as small-time operations. They tended often to be family concerns, and – also like Holden's operation – when travelling from fairs to villages, did so in substantial caravans. Ambrose Tiller's company is noted to have travelled in three wagons, the well-known Testo in five and Harry Wilding (who had taken over from his father) in no fewer than eleven wagons, all of which were needed to accommodate scenery and equipment, plus an additional five vehicles that served as living-vans for his performers and musicians.[12] Touring troupes on rural circuits might play to audiences of as many as 200 to 700 spectators in pitched tents at regional fairs, or – when visiting smaller towns and villages – stay anywhere from a few days to several weeks in one place, offering a different bill of fare in their portable pavilion each evening. Admission prices ranged from as little as a penny for matinées lasting 15 to 30 minutes, or 3*d.* to 1*s.* for regular performances of full-length bills in the evenings. It is important to stress that although selected performances, such as the matinees mentioned above, could be arranged more exclusively for audiences made up largely of children, the audiences for these puppet plays routinely expected to count amongst their number spectators of all ages. Even those related drawing-room entertainments of the period so often dismissed as 'Juvenile Drama' – whereby popular theatrical perform-ances were recreated in 'model theatres' featuring the figures of popular actors and actresses cut out from sheets of hand-coloured paper – were in the first instance the pastimes of sophisticated young men who were already fans of live theatrical performances, and not mere toys designed for children.[13]

Several of the actual *Sweeney Todd* marionettes in the collection of the Bethnal Green's Museum of Childhood were in fact designed and made in the mid-twentieth century by the master puppet craftsman John Bickerdike, probably some time in 1946–7. They are the product of a noteworthy revival of British puppetry that extended from 1925 through to the late 1940s, and that prospered under the general guidance of the British Puppet and Model Theatre Guild, an organization that for many years held annual exhibitions for the work of professionals and amateurs alike. Three of Bickerdike's *Sweeney Todd* marionettes (Todd, Mrs Lovett and Toby, the apprentice) featured in a photograph on the cover of the Guild's official publication, *The Puppet Master*, in April 1947. Mary Saunders offered some comments on the figures inside the journal itself:

In the picture on the cover are the three main characters from our version of 'The Demon Barber' – the over-ripe, time-worn, macabre and ever-interesting crime around which so many dramatic versions have been written in as many different periods. Sweeney Todd and Mrs Lovett (his horrid accomplice of the Bell Yard pieshop) confabulate together while the timid little 'prentice creeps near to hear what they are saying. Sweeney, the brutal conscienceless murderer, wears a red wig – as red as the blood that so often smears his razor, apron and hands. His velvet breeches are of deep maroon, his cotton shirt is grey, and his tucker and apron are (for the moment) spotless. The unspeakable, but not-quite-so-conscienceless Mrs Lovett wears a brown gown of thick shiny satin, and her fichu and mob-cap are of cream-coloured muslin edged with lace. Like Sweeney she has a discoloured face, but while his eyes are crossed and black, hers are hooded and yellow-brown. She is, like Sweeney, a figure of Guignol – one of the nightmares that will, someday soon, move across our small stage before a live audience, to thrill, to horrify, but (we hope!) to entertain.

Our very mellow drama will be presented in the manner of the Gillray-Rowlandson-Fuseli period, for we have tried to endow these puppets with the full red blood and somewhat cruel exaggerations and picturesqueness of those times.

We have, to be sure, taken certain liberties with the names of one or two of the lesser characters, but the two central figures remain unchanged. Our little country youth, at once so timid and so brave, wears a drab skirt-coat with brass buttons, and his hair is the colour of Devon butter. His face is pink and somewhat foolish, and he wears green buckles on plain shoes. There are other and more gracious figures in the cast, but these must wait upon the future to make their bow. To offset sin we have virtue, beauty, gallantry, and courage, and these, needless to say, triumph in the end, as, of course, they should.[14]

Writing as she was in a professional journal specifically dedicated to the art of puppetry, it was only natural for Saunders to comment in so detailed a manner on the design, costuming and colouring of the figures. Her observation that the production itself had been conceived, generally, 'in the manner of the Gillray-Rowlandson-Fuseli period' indicates the level of sophistication at which these craftsmen were still working, and provides a striking indication as well that, even as late as the mid-twentieth century, Todd's story was recognized by those who prepared and designed such productions themselves to be more appropriately set in the late Hanoverian – and not the early Victorian – era. The casual inclusion of Henry Fuseli's romantic vision as a suitable or even natural complement to the more traditionally 'cartoonish' graphic styles of Thomas Rowlandson and James Gillray suggests the production's easy marriage of the picturesque enchantment and gothicism of the early Romantic movement with the rather less pious, ebullient exaggeration of the engravers' caricatures. The precise details of the original costumes in which Bickerdike's marionettes had been dressed – bob and queue wigs, shoe-buckles, deep-cuffed skirt coats with knee-length hems, knee breeches, the frill of the 'tucker' that Todd wears around his neck and front, and the workaday negligée of the pie-maker's 'mob cap' – are scrupulously accurate with regard to the period setting (the puppeteers also typically provided 'special period furniture made to scale ... so that the melodrama shall not suffer from lack of genuine atmosphere').[15] Moreover, it is interesting to note the ease with which it is assumed that the journal's readers would be expected to take for granted that this yet-to-be-produced *Sweeney Todd* would allow itself naturally to adapt the dramatic material of the 'over-ripe' and 'time-worn' versions of the play already in existence; this new, marionette presentation of *Sweeney Todd* was permitted easily to participate in that aspect of its larger history as a melodrama, whereby no popular success was ever to be thought too sacred to be casually adapted to suit a particular occasion, or even parodied and burlesqued. The actual play-texts in such situations could be so variable – in the heat of an actual performance – as to verge on improvisation. The Ebor Marionettes (the company with which the craftsman Bickerdike was most closely associated) regularly performed productions of Shakespeare plays and musical *revues* as well as revivals of what they styled as 'new version[s] of the famous old melodrama[s]' in London theatres both before and after the Second World War.[16]

It is a further and particularly striking testimony to the versatility of the Sweeney Todd story as a dramatic narrative that in addition to the set of marionettes made by Bickerdike in 1946–7, the collection housed by the V&A also contains a similar (though incomplete) set of figures – including Todd, Mrs Lovett and the 'Barber's Boy' – in the slightly more familiar form of hand or glove puppets. Unfortunately, these figures are no longer on permanent public display, although they too date from roughly the same period as those discussed above (*c.*1938–45); they were made by the well-known English doll-maker Mary Bligh Bond. It is unusual for such established characters to exist simultaneously both as marionettes and as glove puppets (Punch and Judy, in their English manifestations, at least, are only very rarely if ever seen as 'string' puppets). Glove puppets, in which the performer's concealed hand manipulates the 'body' of the puppet from within, are by their very physical nature more restricted and forcefully erratic in their movements. Capable of swift exits and entrances, and of being extended physically beyond the limits of any proscenium arch (and therefore sometimes 'closer' to or more intimate with the audience), hand puppets are more suitable for violent rough-housing and knockabout comedy; hence the manifestation of Punch and Judy almost exclusively in the English tradition as glove puppets. Marionettes, by contrast, governed by often complicated guide wires and controls, lend themselves to more delicate manipulations, and their movements tend to possess a distinctly more ethereal and often even an exquisite, unearthly quality; the dextrous skill of a professional puppeteer can make such figures execute complex dance manoeuvres and, of course, if desired, go so far as to make them appear to fly.[17] The versions of *Sweeney Todd* written specifically for performance by glove puppets and marionettes, respectively, necessarily catered to the particular strengths and capabilities of the form of puppet used.

Those readers who find it unusual that Sweeney Todd and Mrs Lovett should have been at least as comfortable within the world of the juvenile theatre and the puppet stage as they were on the boards of the Britannia, the Bower, or the Elephant and Castle, will no doubt be even more surprised to learn about what perhaps remains their most remarkable – if not their most commercially or artistically successful – incarnation on the twentieth-century stage, as the subjects of a *ballet bouffe* or comic, narrative ballet. Choreographed by John Cranko with music provided by Malcolm Arnold, this ballet version of *Sweeney Todd* premiered as part of a special visit of the younger branch of the Royal Ballet to open the winter season at Stratford-upon-Avon on 10 December 1959. The South-African-born Cranko had scored his first major success as a choreographer in England some eight years earlier at Sadler's Wells with his *Pineapple Poll* (1951). That piece had made use of shreds and patches of the music of Sir Arthur Sullivan as rearranged by Charles Mackarras in a way that – as one critic would later comment – 'shocked Savoyards but delighted the rest of us'.[18] *Pineapple Poll*, as Nicholas Dromgoole has observed, signalled what was to become the major characteristic of much of Cranko's later work, insofar as it highlighted his 'willingness to refashion material well within his audience's theatregoing experience'.[19] His subsequent, generally well-received works from the mid-1950s, for example – *Harlequin in April* (1951), and the even better-known *Lady and the Fool* (1954) – both made use of traditional *commedia dell'arte* themes in ballets that similarly looked in some way to exoticize the otherwise familiar. The latter piece – in which Cranko once again worked with Mackarras, described on this occasion as performing 'plastic surgery' on fugitive fragments of Verdi's less familiar operas – attracted particular attention for Cranko's unique balletic idiom, described at the time as at once 'expressive', 'vivacious' and 'graceful'. Another successful work, *Bonne Bouche*, staged by the Sadler's Wells Ballet at Covent Garden in April 1952, anticipated the matter of *Sweeney Todd* somewhat more explicitly in its representation of a detective story about an Edwardian mother and daughter designed to serve as 'a cautionary tale'.[20]

In the context of Cranko's obvious desire in this earliest stage of his career to reinvent and reformulate material that had already been encountered by his audiences in other forms and media, his decision to turn his hand to such material as was provided by Todd's story not only makes sense, but begins even to appear inspired. No less splendidly appropriate was the decision on this occasion to choreograph the piece not to some overt pastiche of the work of an earlier musician, but to commission an entirely 'new' score from the hand of Malcolm Arnold. Arnold had by that date already demonstrated his incredible versatility as a composer; he was capable apparently of turning out operas, symphonies and concertos with as much ease as he was music for brass bands, musicals and film scores. In 1959 he was fresh from having only just the previous year won both the Ivor Novello Award and an Oscar for his still-memorable score to *Bridge on the River Kwai* (1958). His other major film scores from the same period would include *Inn of the Sixth Happiness* (1958) and *Whistle Down the Wind* (1961); such popular successes provided Arnold with the financial support necessary to pursue less commercially rewarding projects, although he was never much inclined (to his credit, many would say) to draw any hard and fast distinctions between his more 'serious' compositions and those that were intended rather for a wide and popular audience.

The premiere of Cranko and Arnold's collaboration at Stratford in December 1959 drew the following initial notice from the reviewer in *The Times*:

> It begins strongly with eerie music by Malcolm Arnold, a darkened stage, Sweeney in a pool of light fingering his razor and erupting in demoniacal laughter, then darkness again, and a squad of policemen blowing whistles and flashing torches at the audience. The parties of young people at this afternoon's *première* fell gratefully upon all this, noisily drawing in their breath, and giving shriek for participant shriek in the approved old manner.
>
> And then the tale begins: drunken Sergeant Lightfoot, with his lachrymose wife, and their heroine, Johanna, wooed by Mark the Sailor, Jeffrey the soldier, and Sweeney the sinister. Mrs Lovett allays every suspicion with the gift of a pie; Sweeney's apprentice puts in his thumb and pulls out two human appurtenances (it is difficult to identify them – an eye and a windpipe?). The gay, tuppence-coloured facades by Alix Stone fold back to show the *maison* Lightfoot, and the dread barber's shop with its *oubliette*.
>
> Cranko draws enthusiastically on music hall dance routines and acrobatics in general for his choreography. There is much knock-about comedy, some of his characteristic ingenuity, much of what may be called copper-bottomed burlesque and a little parody: the pace is fast, as Arnold's ebullient, allusive score demands, the timing and discipline as yet a little unsteady.
>
> Cranko's *Sweeney* stands or falls as dance theatre, and on these direct, unsophisticated terms it stands: it does not aspire to ballet, as *Pineapple Poll* and *Bonne Bouche* did, and in failing to do so it may seem to fall. But while aiming at robust entertainment it never sinks below the levels of the company's repertory, and for an audience that does not despise farce and a little vulgarity honestly presented it holds its own, not least because the dancers are clearly enjoying themselves hugely.
>
> The new ballet offers Mr Donald Britton a lively dramatic part as Todd, Mr Ian Hamilton a clever comedy role as the Colonel from Poona, and Miss Elizabeth Anderton some scope to deploy her grace and charm as a soubrette.[21]

Writing several months later, at the time of the ballet's London premiere at Covent Garden on 16 August 1960 (by which date the younger company had taken the production on tour throughout South Africa), the reviewer commented:

> As a kind of burlesque of Victorian melodrama the piece is an indisputable success, with its stock characters (including a bobbys' *corps de ballet*), its knock-about music hall antics and its penny dreadful sets (by Alix Stone). Moreover it is very much all of a piece with Arnold's clever, eclectic, and ebulliently vulgar score. In a review it would certainly rank as first-class entertainment. Whether or not it contained enough invention, in terms of pure dancing, to justify it a place in the repertory of the Royal Ballet is another matter. Certainly it was very well done, with witty thumb-nail sketches from Mr Donald Britton as the crazy barber himself, Mr Johaar Mosayal as the apprentice, Miss Margaret Knoesen as the crafty pie woman, Mr Desmond Doyle and Mr Ian Hamilton as navy and army types, and Miss Elizabeth Anderton as the generously inviting sailor's girl.[22]

The question posed in the first excerpt here as to whether or not the Cranko–Arnold collaboration in this instance qualified as a proper parody or (less demandingly) whether it even constituted 'copper-bottomed' entertainment (meaning, in this sense, work that was thoroughly 'sound' or 'authentic') seems to receive – for all the indulgence extended in both reviews – a negative answer; the successful status of its 'ebullient vulgarity' as burlesque is less open to question, although what or whom is being burlesqued remains unclear. Yet, as seems so often to have been the case both for performers and viewers of any vaguely innovative production or representation of Todd's story, the real problem seems very clearly to be one that centres around issues of genre or mode. Much of the reviewer's seeming hesitation to offer his wholehearted approval of the piece – his manifest unwillingness to extend to it the perceived privilege of being a 'genuine' ballet – stems from this sense of generic confusion. 'Music-hall dance', 'knock-about comedy', 'copper-bottomed burlesque', 'parody', 'dance theatre', 'ballet', 'entertainment', 'melodrama': just what *is* this *Sweeney Todd* supposed to be? In an era that was far less comfortable than our own in moving easily between forms of 'high' culture (e.g. ballet, opera, symphonies etc.) and 'low' culture (melodramas, music-hall entertainment, films, comics) – in an era that sought, rather, more often than not to reinforce the gap that separated the 'elite' or the privileged from the demotic as an aesthetically justifiable and socially necessary one – such a piece was bound to cause confusion. (The fact that the reviewer would appear to be unaware of those characters or elements that would normally have been expected to form part of any dramatization of Todd's story cannot have helped matters much.) What was required of any audience attending Cranko and Arnold's ballet: the vicarious thrill of emotional engagement, or the artistically perceptive chill of ironic detachment?

Whatever the calculated effect of Cranko's choreography, Arnold's score, at least, seems almost certainly to have aimed for a parodic resonance which

– although different from the variously modulated echoes of both opera and popular song later attained by Stephen Sondheim – looked in fragmented moments to conjure a number of different styles, and the peculiar originality of which seems largely to have gone unnoticed by the work's 1959 audiences. More familiar with the cues and signals of parodic reference in our own post post-modern era, it is perhaps easier for us today to hear the obviously deliberate manner in which recollections of, say, the soundtracks of horror movies are placed side-by-side with the stylings of the musical hall; unusual and often unexpected combinations and resituations of the familiar lurk just beneath the surface of Arnold's score to lend it the air of the uncanny. Many years after the work premiered as a ballet, in 1984, Arnold himself collaborated with David Ellis in transforming the original ballet score into a concert suite; this same suite was recorded finally in 1993, by the Royal Philharmonic Orchestra, conducted by Vernon Handley. Commenting on Handley's recording, Piers Burton-Page more clear-sightedly observed that originally, Cranko and Arnold had together

> produced a dance version of the familiar tale of the Demon Barber of Fleet Street that was largely good humoured, avoiding the note of tragedy that Stephen Sondheim was later to plumb in his very different score.... . [T]he suite is not above recourse to the stock-in-trade of film horror, with snarling semi-tones in the brass, screaming piccolo and flailing timpani in the opening. Periodically this mock-sinister mood returns, but it is interlaced with music of a better-humoured hue; a sequence of (mostly short) dance episodes overflowing with musical invention. For, despite the tongue-in-cheek flavour, this is a score from Arnold's richest and most prolific period. The numbers flow thick and fast, with a generosity of tunes and a characteristic humour, that can embrace at different moments a noisy polka, echoes of music-hall, and something suspiciously close to a parody of Tchaikovsky. At the end almost everything gets reprised, and the final impression is of a distinctly unthreatening Demon Barber![23]

Cranko and Arnold's combined efforts at Stratford in December 1959 perhaps attracted less critical attention than they might otherwise have been granted if only because their ballet precisely coincided with a more mainstream musical adaptation of the play then being produced in London. This rather less innovative or even traditional musical version of Todd had been announced earlier that same summer (on 20 July 1959) by J. Baxter Sommerville, who had recently purchased the Lyric Theatre in Hammersmith. 'The Demon Barber as the musical version will be called', The Times had then reported, 'will go into rehearsal in October under the direction of Mr. Colin Graham. The adaptation has been made by Mr. Donald Cotton. The music will be by Mr. Alan Langford.'[24] By the time the production was actually launched on 10 December (opening on exactly the same evening, again, as the Cranko–Arnold ballet) Langford's contribution had been replaced by that of Brian

Burke, and audiences were alerted only to the fact that 'the new musical version will be presented as a traditional melodrama'.[25] The director of the production, Colin Graham, had begun his long career as a stage director in close association with Benjamin Britten, and would later achieve considerable acclaim for his direction of the world premieres of such works as John Corigliano's *The Ghosts of Versailles* for the Metropolitan Opera in 1991.

This musical version was reviewed in *The Times* in the very same edition as Cranko's Stratford ballet; the judgement and even the language of the two reviews are strikingly similar:

> A well meant attempt is made by the production to revive the 'twopence coloured' glories of the toy theatre. Mr Disley Jones's scenery is bound to give nostalgic pleasure to all who have ever tried to work their own miniature stages. This, however, is a pleasure that wears thin before the evening is over. It is not so much that we tire of the scenery and the amusing little tricks that the producer plays with it. Rather it is that the lyrics and the general spirit of the production do not marry well with the scenery. The mockery of the old melodrama is carried out with so little comic finesse.... Robbed of its original grim-grotesque atmosphere [the plot] immediately takes on the meaningless absurdity of a pantomime story, with the victims passing through the mincing machine into pies which a wicked neighbour purveys to innocent customers. The Demon Barber himself, as played by Mr. Roy Godfrey, becomes a sort of Sam Weller who is resisting with good-humoured surprise the attempt to turn him into a sinister character.... Mr. Donald Cotton's lyrics are hearty rather than captivating, and much the same may be said of the singing. The Demon Barber stands or falls by its pictorial qualities.[26]

The review of the musical seems noticeably to echo some of the same confusion that greeted the Cranko–Arnold ballet. Perhaps the only central observation one can make with any confidence when discussing these long-vanished stage productions is that for all the possible virtues of the pieces in question, theatre-goers had by the mid-twentieth century grown uncertain as to precisely how they were meant to *react* to Todd's story. It is possible that for an immediate post-World War II audience, the notion of mass murder being conducted on a smoothly organized, industrial scale was at once both too familiar and simply too *real* to be dismissed as the stuff of simple melodrama, but (on the other hand) Todd's narrative was not yet available to be exploited as material for black comedy or used metaphorically. Any production that looked to provoke an increasingly old-fashioned, visceral feeling of 'terror' was likely to move too far in the direction of true 'horror'; any production that treated its material with a knowing or even comic awareness risked being labelled callous or – worse – simply tasteless.

*

'Now, master', he said, ... pressing the head gently further into the crotch of the chair,
'now master', and the steel glanced nigh the throat.

(Herman Melville, *Benito Cereno*)[27]

It has never exactly been easy to predict the directions in which the composer
and lyricist Stephen Sondheim has been prepared to lead the American
musical theatre. In the course of a professional career that has extended over
more than five decades, Sondheim – with a thoroughness that belies his
continued ability to surprise and even occasionally to shock his audiences
– seems to have turned his hand to close to everything. Having begun his
career writing lyrics for (now) classic Broadway shows such as *West Side Story*
(with Leonard Bernstein, in 1957) and *Gypsy* (with Jule Styne, in 1959)
Sondheim moved on in the 60s and 70s more fully to explore what might be
described as the darker side – often the more cynical side – of the relationships and romances inherent even in those earliest plays.

Born in New York City in 1930, Sondheim began playing piano – by ear
– when he was about four years old (although he later confessed that he took
lessons only because 'that's what every good Jewish boy in my circumstances
did'); as a teenager, he managed (initially to some extent, through the society
connections of his mother, who was a reasonably successful fashion designer
and interior decorator) to cultivate the acquaintance of the lyricist Oscar
Hammerstein. In spite of the obvious difference in age, the two became close –
Hammerstein is thought by some to have been something of a surrogate father
to Sondheim. The younger man would later in life offer a frequently retold
account of the ways in which Hammerstein encouraged him as a musician
when he was still a teenager. 'Oscar Hammerstein', Sondheim commented,

> gradually got me interested in the theater, and I suppose most of it happened
> one fateful or memorable afternoon. He had urged me to write a musical play
> for my school [George School, in Bucks County, Pennsylvania]. With two
> classmates I wrote a musical called *By George*, a thinly disguised version of
> campus life with the teachers' names changed by one vowel or consonant. I
> thought it was pretty terrific, so I asked Oscar to read it – and I was arrogant
> enough to say to him, 'will you read it as if it were just a musical that crossed
> your desk as a producer? Pretend you don't know me'. He said O.K., and I
> went home that night with visions of being the first 15-year-old to have a show
> on Broadway. I knew he was going to love it.
>
> Oscar called me in the next day and said, 'Now you really want me to
> treat this as if it were by somebody I didn't know?' and I said 'Yes, please',
> and he said, 'Well, in that case it's the worse thing I ever read in my life'.
> He must have seen my lower lip tremble, and he followed up with, 'I didn't
> say it wasn't talented, I said it was terrible, and if you want to know why it's
> terrible, I'll tell you'. He started with the first stage direction and went all
> the way through the show, for a whole afternoon, really treating it seriously.
> It was a seminar on the piece as though it were *Long Day's Journey Into Night*.

Detail by detail, he told me how to structure songs, how to build them with a beginning, a development, and an ending, according to his principles. I found out later there are other ways to write songs, but he taught me, according to his own principles how to, how to introduce characters, what relates a song to character, etc., etc. It was four hours of the most *packed* information. I dare say that I learned in that afternoon, more than most people learn about song-writing in a lifetime.[28]

Whatever it was that Sondheim *did* learn that afternoon, he appears to have learned exceedingly well. His work has at times been brilliantly successful and often controversial; few would contest the assessment of the former *New York Times* theatre critic Frank Rich, writing in 2000, that Sondheim has for some time now reigned as 'the greatest and perhaps best-known artist in American musical theatre'.[29]

Sondheim followed his earliest collaborations as a lyricist (while still young he worked also with Hammerstein's former partner, Richard Rogers) with the successful *A Funny Thing Happened on the Way to the Forum* in 1962. In the early 1970s he soon produced a trio of works – *Company* (1970), *Follies* (1971) and *A Little Night Music* (1973) – that together dissected the themes of isolation, non-conformity and sexual frustration that lay just beneath the surface of the mode; his work seemed relentlessly to focus on the ambiguous nature of seemingly all romantic – and even, for that matter, all *human* – attachments. *A Little Night Music* resulted in what remains today the most recognizable song of his career – what Rich characterized as 'the bittersweet cabaret turn' of 'Send in the Clowns'. In fact, Sondheim's work – while it has always attracted sustained and intelligent critical attention – has, with only very rare exceptions, never really been 'popular' in the manner of earlier Broadway composers. (Sondheim himself once described his own work, in the words of Shakespeare's *Hamlet*, as 'caviar to the general'.) Even those works that are now regarded as 'classics' would appear to have had a pretty tough time of it the first time round. The revolutionary and ground-breaking *Company*, for example, which opened on Broadway in April 1970, and which memorably featured actress Elaine Stritch's caustic rendition of 'The Ladies Who Lunch', was characterized by one reviewer, in *Variety,* as fit only for 'ladies' matinees, homos, and misogynists'. Other New York critics fortunately thought better of *Company*, sensing even in this relatively early musical both the theme of near existential loneliness and the confrontational quality that would come in time to pervade almost all of Sondheim's work; one such critic described *Company* as a musical that 'gets right down to brass tacks and brass knuckles without a moment's hesitation, staring contemporary society straight in the eye before spitting in it'. There have been a few box-office failures along the way, most notably the aggressively cynical *Anyone Can Whistle* (1963) – a musical about the mental patients at an institution called the Cookie Jar and a false miracle that ran for only nine performances in 1964 – and the original Broadway production of 1981's *Merrily We Roll Along*. Yet these shows, too, have in time assumed the status of favourites; several of the songs from both musicals have been regularly re-recorded, and the subsequent reincarnations of *Merrily We Roll Along* would alone be enough to demonstrate that the composer was more than capable of writing a stunningly memorable and intelligent 'conventional' Broadway score, when he chose to do so. Responding to the original failure of that same work on Broadway, Sondheim commented, 'I always wanted to have a smash, but I rather doubt that I ever will.... It's not that it's too good for people, it's just that it's too unexpected to sustain itself in the commercial theatre.' 'Half of my songs deal with ambivalence,' he noted succinctly, 'feeling two things at once.' Many of the composer's most compelling songs, as Sondheim acknowledged in his interview with Frank Rich, explore 'the aching, ambivalent, and often thwarted desire to connect with someone'.[30] On a more personal level, Sondheim's agent, Flora Roberts, once commented that she sometimes felt that the composer 'had a little list' – a list that allowed him to contemplate all the 'marvellous dark vengeful things to do with people who have done him in, but not go through with them'.[31] His biographer, Meryle Secrest, suggested of Sondheim that it seemed that 'his most poignant fear was of being at someone else's mercy'.[32] 'Perhaps it was just an interesting coincidence', she continued, 'that dramas about characters who controlled the fates of others were often found in Sondheim's lexicon; there was Madame Rose in *Gypsy*, the slave Pseudolus in *Forum*, and Robert in *Company*, to be eventually joined by Sweeney Todd, the homicidal barber, a galaxy of presidential assassins [in *Assassins* (1991)], and Fosca in *Passion* [1994], who used love as a weapon.'

But then again, perhaps not. This consistent focus on alienation, isolation, vengeance, and the depiction of naked yearning and desire that has occupied Sondheim's creative imagination seems in retrospect (as Secrest's brief enumeration above, demonstrates) not so much to render the story of Sweeney Todd a peculiar source for a musical, but a rather obvious one. Sondheim first came across Todd's story during a visit to London in 1973.[33] A reworking of Dibdin Pitt's original melodrama by Christopher G. Bond – a self-confessedly ambitious version of the story in which the young Liverpool playwright openly admitted to having 'cast [his] net wider than anyone else in "borrowing" from other authors' – was then playing to unusually responsive and enthusiastic audiences at Joan Littlewood's Theatre Workshop at the Theatre Royal, Stratford East.[34] (The Workshop found its origins in a radical, left-wing street theatre group in the north of England in the 1930s. In the post-war period – the Workshop itself was founded in 1945 – both its classical revivals and the contributions of contemporary playwrights such as Brendan Behan and Shelagh Delaney had earned it a reputation for being one of the best touring ensembles in Europe. Littlewood's guidance and leadership as a director produced over 150 productions that drew on Brechtian as well as music hall conventions. Her ultimate aim was to 'create a theatre to which the working classes would go with the same regularity and enthusiasm as to fun palaces and penny arcades'; once settled in the Theatre Royal, in East London, the company produced such acclaimed dramas of the period as *The Hostage* (1958), *A Taste of Honey* (1958) and *Oh! What a Lovely War!* (1963)).[35] Reviewing Bond's *Sweeney Todd* as it was produced in London by the Theatre Workshop in the pages of *The Times*, Irving Wardle observed that 'the story is horrible partly because of the idea of queues in Fleet Street gorging themselves on human flesh, and partly because Sweeney [in Bond's version] is not a true villain. He starts with all the right on his side.'[36] Maxwell Shaw, who directed the original London production of Bond's play, had been enthusiastic about some of the new possibilities presented by Bond's version of the story, noting that the author had not only taken traditional melodramatic material and revised it with 'real' plots and real characters, but that he had also (and for the first time in many years) given those characters 'something to say'.[37] Shaw was keen to acknowledge the effect of the cinema on the treatment of melodramas such as the original versions of *Todd*, and acknowledged that any contemporary attempt to reproduce Todd's story for the stage needed to be aware of its own place in theatrical history, and situate itself accordingly. 'The majority of Thriller/Melodramas, of which *Sweeney Todd* has always been one of the best-known,' Shaw observed,

> were written and performed with the express purpose of providing audiences with the thrills, horror and shocks which they have always, traditionally enjoyed. In recent years, however, the seemingly endless stream of Horror films produced by, in some cases, very brilliant film-makers have explored every conceivable means of doing this, and with far greater impact and realism than could ever be achieved in the Theatre.[38]

How might the theatre best respond to the more realistic effects achievable in such modern films? Not, Shaw suggested, by presenting plays of this type strictly for laughs, nor by inviting the audience itself to join in and poke fun at the deliberately exaggerated sentiment of the originals; allowing the cast and director the opportunity 'to indulge in a jolly romp, "hamming" the passion, and sending-up the romance and pathos' was *not* the answer.[39] What was needed instead was a genuinely innovative approach to such material. Bond, Shaw insisted, had in fact not so much rewritten an old and familiar melodrama as he had produced 'an entirely new play based on an original idea.... It struck me as a very positive comment on the fact that we have come to accept such things as violence, wholesale murder – and worse – as part of our everyday lives'. 'There was never any doubt in my mind,' Shaw concluded,

> about the style in which I would direct the play. The production, I decided, would be absolutely 'straight'. The sets, costumes and props must all be

authentic, not least of which 'The Chair' would have to be totally convincing. The cast would play for the truth of the situations, and leave the strength of the play – its drama, horror and comedy – to take care of itself. In the true style of melodrama, however, the actors would be encouraged to express their emotions freely and fully, with truth, but without 'over-acting'. In all the earlier versions of the play, the central character of Sweeney Todd has always been written and portrayed as a homicidal maniac, murdering his customers in order to rob them, and forcing others, through fear, to share in his crimes. But there was never any explanation or justification of this.[40]

And it was with reference to this crucial issue of motivation that Bond's text had finally provided a narrative background and answer that was both thematically satisfying and – more importantly – worked successfully as drama. For this first time in his many histories, Todd became 'an ordinary man whose initial motive is one of revenge for the wrongs committed against him and his family, but who soon succumbs to the fascination of the power of holding life and death in his hands'.[41] Bond, in his own preface to the printed play-text (published in 1974), reinforced the justice of Todd's righteous anger and vengeance by pointing out parallels in the action of the play to late Elizabethan and Jacobean drama (e.g. *The Spanish Tragedy* (1592) and *The Revenger's Tragedy* (1607)), and acknowledged that he had borrowed freely from works such as Alexandre Dumas' *The Count of Monte Cristo* (1844–6) to provide Todd himself with convincing 'motivation', while still allowing the production itself to revel in the ghoulish inclusivity and melodrama of the legend. Like the play's director, he, too, pointedly avoided any suggestion that he was in any way 'sending up' his sources. In a 1980 essay, Bond was even more straightforward regarding the changes he made to the original melodrama. 'I wrote it at top speed', he confessed of his own *Sweeney Todd*,

> to get the theatre I was acting in at the time out of a jam. (We'd announced we were doing *Sweeney Todd* and through one balls-up and another didn't get hold of the original 1847 script until a fortnight before we were due to start rehearsing it and then didn't like it when it finally arrived.) So I was asked to have a go at improving it. I kept the chair and Mrs. Lovett's meat pies, a couple of lines of Tobias Ragg, and the name Jonas Fogg which appealed to me, and invented the rest. Or rather I nicked bits and pieces out of my favourite stories, mostly *The Count of Monte Cristo* and *The Revenger's Tragedy*, added market patter I heard as a kid, odds and ends from Shakespeare, and bits and pieces off Brenda who kept the shop opposite where we lived. I finished it in nine days and my only sadness was that I don't think Brenda bothered to go and see it.[42]

Briefly, Bond's version of *Sweeney Todd* – which pointedly sets the tale in the earliest decades of the nineteenth century – tells the barber's story in two acts, as follows: Sweeney Todd arrives in London in the company of a young sailor by the name of Anthony Hope. When a passing Beggar Woman appears to recognize Todd, he moves as if to strike her and sends her scurrying away. Questioned by Anthony – who, we learn, had rescued the escaped prisoner Todd when he found him 'clinging to [a] makeshift raft, half-mad with thirst' at sea – as to why he should be so discomfited by a simple beggar, Todd finally permits himself to let the young man know something of his past (I.i). He tells Anthony that many years ago he had been falsely convicted on a charge of petty theft and transported for life by 'two upright men' – the corrupt Judge Turpin and a local beadle – who had set their sights on seducing his beautiful wife, Lucy; the pair – the sort of men 'who cannot look on beauty, and not defile it' – had trusted that with Todd safely out of the way, the virtuous Lucy would soon fall into their hands (I.i). A great many years have passed, but Todd now parts from Anthony in the hopes of finding out what became of her. The two agree to meet again the next day at 'St. Dunstan's market-place' at noon (I.i).

Todd quickly finds his way to his former residence, a room above Mrs Lovett's pie shop in Fleet Street. Lovett's business has lately been poor, and customers scarce. 'Mind you,' she sighs,

> you can't hardly blame them. There's no denying these are the most tasteless pies in London. I should know, I make 'em. (*She puts the pie on the table, then flicks a bit of dirt off the crust.*) Ugh! What's that? But can you wonder, with meat the price it is? I mean, I never thought I'd see the day when grown men and good cooks, too, would dribble over a dead dog like it was a round of beef. (I.ii)[43]

Lovett tells Todd that the rooms above her shop 'have been empty for years' (I.ii) – ever since the wife of the 'lovely' if 'foolish' barber who once lived there had been tricked and then raped by a corrupt judge and his accomplice, a beadle. After the barber's wife returned, distraught, to her Fleet Street room, Lovett continues, she poisoned both herself and her infant daughter, Johanna; when the latter survived, the judge took her in as his ward. Mrs Lovett soon recognizes that 'Sweeney Todd' is himself the woman's husband – the falsely convicted barber whose real name had been Benjamin Barker. Todd swears revenge for his 15-year imprisonment and his wife's fate. Hoping to provide a 'crumb of comfort', Lovett brings him his set of razors which she had saved in case he should ever return. 'I always had a fondness for you', she confesses to Todd, 'and hoped you might come back one day' (I.ii).

When Anthony meets Todd the following afternoon, the sailor describes how within just hours of his return to London he had glimpsed a beautiful young girl – with whom he instantly fell in love – at the casement window of the residence of one Judge Turpin. Todd immediately realizes that this must have been his own daughter, Johanna, and he invites Anthony to accompany him to Lovett's, where he has since reoccupied his old room. The pair also encounter a street mountebank, Alfredo Pirelli, and his assistant Tobias.

When Todd bests Pirelli in an impromptu competition in shaving and tooth-pulling, the latter graciously concedes defeat, but looks suspiciously at Todd's razors. He tells Todd he will stop by his shop the next day.

Johanna, at home, is horrified by her guardian's revelation that – now that she has come of age – he plans to marry her. She takes solace in the memory of having seen Anthony from her window earlier that day; 'I may again gaze from the window', she muses, 'in the hope that my love will come' (I.iv).[44] Todd, meanwhile, is anxious to take his revenge on the judge. He is almost revealed as 'Benjamin Barker' by Pirelli, who had recognized his distinctive silver razors, but Todd quickly strangles his rival, and then cuts his throat. (Pirelli's assistant Tobias is sent downstairs, where Mrs Lovett has soon won him over with the offer of a pie.) Anthony manages secretly to converse with Johanna, and they arrange to elope later that evening. At court, the beadle suggests to the judge that Johanna might be more responsive to his proposals if he looked somewhat smarter, and recommends that he immediately visit the adept new barber Sweeney Todd for a shave. The judge is in Todd's chair and Todd is about to wreak his long-deferred vengeance when Anthony bursts in, breathlessly blurting out his plans to elope with Johanna. The judge storms from the shop, leaving the barber furious with Anthony's youthful impetuousness. Todd seems to have missed the only opportunity he would ever have of killing the judge; even so, he seems to have achieved some sense of purpose. 'A second chance may come.... Until it does, I'll pass the time in practice on less honoured throats' (I.viii).[45] Mrs Lovett is at first confused by Todd's motives:

> I don't understand you. You let that Judge escape one minute, and the next you're on about slicing up any Tom, Dick or Harry. This revenge business don't half blow hot and cold, it don't. (I.viii)[46]

Wondering how they will dispose of Pirelli's body, however, Mrs Lovett offers a suggestion to their mutual benefit: she can use the meat in her pies. Tobias, meanwhile, can assist her in the pie house. Todd promises her, 'by my assistance, you shall never want for meat, Mrs. Lovett' (I.viii).

As the second act opens, Tobias drums up business for Mrs Lovett's now-thriving pie shop, troubled only by the peculiar questions and ominous but confused warnings of the Beggar Woman. Sweeney gets down to business himself, helped by means of his newly installed barber's chair, which tilts the bodies of his victims into the cellar of the bake-house below. Anthony has discovered that Johanna has been imprisoned by the judge in Jonas Fogg's lunatic asylum. When Anthony tells Todd where the judge has incarcerated Johanna, the barber realizes that, disguised as a wigmaker, the young man could easily gain access to the asylum, as it is from such places that the wigmakers of the city buy the hair for their wigs. Mrs Lovett patiently shows Tobias how to make the pies properly, and he is left to work the meat grinder on his own. Disgusted by the rank and 'nifty' smell that permeates the bake-house cellar itself, Tobias nevertheless soon yields to his hunger, and makes a familiar discovery:

> Cor, dear, I ain't never smelt nothing like it. Oh well. (*He holds his nose with one hand and takes a bite out of the pie*) Mmmmmmm. That's better. A bit of all right this is. (*Looking round*) These cellars aren't half big. Flaming huge, they are. I bet you can get yourself lost down there, unless you follow your nose. Never mind. (*He munches happily*) Hey, what's this? A hair! (*He finds a long hair in the pie*) Ycccc. That ain't very tasty, is it? (*He winds the hair round his finger*) Don't look like one of Mrs. L's. Oh well, must have been a hairy cow, or something. Don't know that I fancy that one no more, though. (*He pushes the pie aside, takes another one and inspects it*) Yea, that's a good'un. (*He bites into it*) Smashing! (*He chews ecstatically*) Aaaw! What's that? Come here, you little bleeder. Must be a bone or something. Funny shape for a bone. Here, it's a finger-nail – it's a whole bleedin' finger-nail. I don't think I like these pies no more. (II.v)[47]

Tobias discovers, however, that he has been locked in the bake-house by Mrs Lovett. The beadle arrives to search the premises of Todd and Lovett, having received complaints of the smell coming from the shop, but Todd is able to dispose of him by means of his mechanical chair.

The barber now writes a note to the judge, telling him that Anthony has abducted Johanna from the asylum, and will be bringing her to his shop that very night. Anthony rescues Johanna from Jonas Fogg's and brings her to Todd's shop; after Anthony leaves to find a coach in which they can effect their escape, Johanna is frightened by the appearance in the upstairs shop of the Beggar Woman, and hastily conceals herself within a chest, from within which she secretly observes the latter's peculiar response to her surroundings. Todd's rooms appear to bring back elusive memories to her, and when Todd enters, she again seems to recognize him. Todd hears the judge approaching to keep his assignation with Johanna, however, and, quickly cutting the woman's throat ('Curse her, she'll mar all. She must die' (II.x)), sends her body to the cellar. Telling Judge Turpin that Johanna yearns for his forgiveness, Todd convinces him to sit for a shave before he is reunited with her. Captive in the chair, the judge realizes the barber's identity just as Todd slits his throat. Todd then discovers the hidden Johanna in his shop, and is on the point of cutting her throat as well, when he hears a piercing scream from Mrs Lovett below. He rushes out, with his razor in his hand. Mrs Lovett had been dragging the body of the Beggar Woman to the oven as Todd enters; only as he moves to help her does he finally recognize the Beggar Woman for who she is – his own wife, Lucy. Todd is enraged that Lovett lied to him, but she insists that she told Todd only that his wife took poison, which she did – not that she had actually died. Feigning forgiveness, Todd clasps Lovett near enough to enable him to manoeuvre her towards the oven and fling her in. Tobias, driven to the point of insanity by his own realization that Mrs Lovett's pies were made from the corpses of the barber's victims, emerges from the cellar and, finding Todd's razor, takes it to the barber and then slits his throat; he is still turning the handle of the meat grinder when the members of the watch – accompanied by Anthony and Johanna, finally united – enter the bake-house and discover the play's final scene of carnage.

Audiences that saw the first London production of Bond's play were, again, clearly impressed by the extent to which the author had managed to breathe new life into what had become for most a familiar melodramatic property. This 'new' figure of Sweeney Todd, as *The Times* critic Irving Wardle stressed in his May 1973 notice for the show,

> starts with all the right on his side; returning from a false imprisonment to avenge himself on the legal vultures who destroyed his wife. The piece starts as one kind of melodrama, and turns into quite another kind when Sweeney discovers his taste for blood. 'With my assistance, Mrs. Lovett, you'll never want for meat.' It is still a spine chilling as well as comic line.
>
> With its scratch costumes, two-piece orchestra, and blundering lighting, Maxwell Shaw's production is a low-budget, rough-and-ready affair. But its tone is right, and so are the essential props. No expense, at any rate, has been spared on Sweeney's chair, which flushes the victims away like a regal water closet.... Mr. Murphy [actor Brian Murphy, who originated the role of Todd] is no heavyweight villain: a slight figure in auburn curls he plays Sweeney as an almost romantically haunted character, never wholly submerged in his terrible appetite. There are moments of complicity, as where he brandishes his first fistful of gore to the audience with a radiant smile. But generally, if the character prompts jokes, he leaves it to the audience to make them.[48]

Flora Roberts has been quoted as recalling that audience members were greeted as they stepped into the theatre by 'a piano player in the lobby and people drinking beer and eating meat pies'.[49] Sondheim himself later confessed that although he was immediately impressed by the vitality of the evening's performance, he only gradually awakened to the musical possibilities inherent in Bond's Todd. 'I had heard it was Grand Guignol', he commented,

> and it was something that just knocked me out. Bond's new version was a tiny play, still a melodrama, but also a legend, elegantly written, part in blank verse – which I didn't even recognize until I read the script. It had a weight to it, but I couldn't figure out how the language was so rich and thick without being fruity.... [Bond] was able to take all these disparate elements that had been in existence rather dully for a hundred and some-odd years and make them into a first-rate play.... It struck me as a piece that sings.[50]

Sondheim's reference to the traditions of the 'Grand Guignol' – the tiny Paris theatre that had from 1897 until as late as 1962 transformed the potential drawbacks posed by its relatively small performance space and its equally limited capacity to accommodate an audience of no more than 300 spectators to its advantage by staging short dramas of a strikingly naturalistic and often brutal kind – suggests the theatrical characteristics that featured most prominently in Bond's own *Sweeney Todd*, and that were in time intended to figure no less prominently in Sondheim's own further adaptation. Ideally, audiences were to be brought physically close to the action of the drama, which was unapologetically presented as a grisly spectacle. Of some of the more practical problems still to be resolved in any musical adaptation of Bond's original, Sondheim would later comment:

> I was only worried about how the audience would take the murders, whether they'd think them silly or not. And then, when Mrs Lovett gets the idea of making the meat pies, what would the audience's reaction be? In America [nobody had] ever heard of Sweeney Todd ... so they were seeing this wild plot for the first time, and there was a loud gasp at the first murder, which was staged very violently with a great swash of blood. Then when Mrs. Lovett got the idea for the pies and the audiences realised what was up, there was a satisfying laugh, the likes of which I've rarely heard.[51]

The British surrealist Roland Penrose once observed that although violence when met with in 'cold blood' can be 'particularly horrifying and intol-erable', the arts have the ability to avoid the brutal impact of the violent 'by their appeal to the emotions ... they warm us to its presence, turning terror into enjoyment and cruelty into compassion'. 'We participate in the act of violence', Penrose concluded, 'without suffering its evil consequences.'[52] Such an assessment of the transformative potential of the arts is perhaps as accurate a description of the effect of both Bond and Sondheim's *Sweeney Todd* on contemporary spectators as one could hope to find.

Stephen Sondheim is reported once to have described his own *Sweeney Todd* as his 'love letter to London' – an observation of which the theatre critic Charles Spencer, writing on the occasion of the first production of the work at the Royal Opera at Covent Garden, in 2004, aptly commented: 'reeling from the theatre after an orgy of mass murder, cannibalism, rape, insanity, and institutional corruption, one can only feverishly speculate as to what kind of letter Sondheim would write if he took a serious dislike to some-place or someone'.[53] It says something of the composer's depth of interest in the sheer musical and dramatic potential of the subject as it had been handled by Bond, however, that *Sweeney Todd* should stand as one of only two musicals Sondheim was ever to write that was to be entirely *his* idea – as opposed to the suggestion of one of his many other collaborators, directors, producers and friends (the other was 1994's *Passion*, based on a nineteenth-century epistolary novel by Iginio Ugo Tarchetti).[54]

It is also particularly interesting to note that if the director Maxwell Shaw had to some extent been drawn to Bond's original precisely because he saw in the play its potential to offer an effective and theatrically vital antidote to the kind of 'impact and realism' that contemporary horror films were so much more capable of delivering to modern audiences, Sondheim himself was to transform this same *Sweeney Todd* from a production based to some extent in a reaction *against* cinema to one that drew its own inspiration – at least in part – *from* the movies themselves. Sondheim had long been haunted by a particular film that he had first seen in a Times Square cinema as a very young man (and in the company of his friend Jimmy Hammerstein, the lyricist's son) called *Hangover Square* (1944).[55] Based only loosely on Patrick Hamilton's 1941 novel of the same name, *Hangover Square* (directed by John Brahm and distributed by Twentieth Century Fox) told the story of the young George Harvey Bone, who, already known as a 'distinguished composer' and listed in the 'British Catalogue of Music', is on the verge of a major professional breakthrough to real fame and fortune. His manic concentration on his work, however, leads him to experience what he can refer to only as 'moods' or 'lapses' – black periods in which, when they possess him, the composer seems to be taken over by some dark force, and in which he destroys anything and everything in his path. Once he returns to his senses, he can remember nothing of what has passed, or what he has done. Bone senses that these 'moods' are prompted or set off by discordant sounds (a sudden, high-pitched noise in his head), but he has committed himself to writing an important piano concerto; when a medical consultant suggests that he find some 'new emotional outlet' for himself, he can only say that 'music is the most important thing in the world for me', and refuses to take the consultant's advice. Torn not only between two love interests but between the appeal of writing music more suited to the popular taste and completing the more 'serious' work he has in hand, George commits a series of murders whilst in the grip of these 'moods'; in the film his own performance of what was to be the supreme achievement of his Concerto for Piano and Orchestra leads to a spectacular act of self-destruction. As the audience and the other members of the orchestra flee the auditorium, Bone manages to set fire to the concert hall; we see the composer still pounding the ominous chords of his own composition as the flames engulf him.

As an adaptation of Hamilton's novel, 1945's *Hangover Square* – which was in fact one of its studio's major releases for that year – is at best a qualified success.[56] Hamilton's original depiction of schizophrenia and sexual repression set in the grim realities of a depression-era Earl's Court is transformed into a highly atmospheric, Edwardian period piece; the psychological complexities of Hamilton's original character are swept aside to make way for what is in many respects an only slightly modified version of a familiar type – the gaslight ghoul as amnesiac. Richard Mallett, reviewing the film in *Punch*, suggested the film was 'a half-chewed collection of reminiscences of *Dr Jekyll and Mr. Hyde* and *The Lodger*' (the 1944 film version of which was to feature *Hangover Square*'s own Laird Cregar in the title role); the well-known *Sunday Times* critic James Agate rather more harshly dismissed it as 'the worst betrayal of a first-class novel [he] could remember'.[57] *Hangover Square* is arguably redeemed by two things, however. The first of these is its strong cast, which features fine performances from George Sanders and Linda Darnell, but which is dominated by the oddly compelling and genuinely haunted performance of Laird Cregar himself as Bone (tragically, it was to be the 28-year-old actor's last screen role; so desperate had the naturally large Cregar been to secure the part of the romantically seductive composer that he submitted himself to a crash diet that led to his death very soon after shooting on the film was completed). The second of the film's major strengths, however, is its wonderfully effective and evocative score, provided by the masterful Bernard Herrmann. Herrmann — who had already made a name for himself with (and earned his first Oscar for) his score for *Citizen Kane* in 1941, and who would later achieve perhaps his greatest fame for his contribution to Alfred Hitchcock films such as *Vertigo* (1958) and *North by Northwest* (1959) — used the opportunity of the screenplay's high melodrama to write a Lisztian concerto for the film's climax, and his sinister and percussive chords, with their strong, simultaneous recollections in particular both of Sergei Rachmaninoff and of Liszt's *Totentanz* (or 'Dance of Death', his 1849 symphonic piece for solo piano and orchestra), pound throughout the film with often diabolic intensity. Opera and music critic Eric Myers has written critically of Herrmann's score for *Hangover Square*, insisting with no small degree of truth that Bone's final concerto 'with its spooky, jagged dissonances tempered by surging themes of romantic longing, was far closer in tone to 1940s Hollywood than anything that would have been composed in Edwardian London'; 'it was', Myers complained of Herrmann's piece, 'very much a product of its time and place'.[58] Be that as it may, the piano concerto that Bone is supposed to have written plays on various elements in the film itself, and is in fact featured throughout the movie in a cleverly proleptic manner. 'The opening arresting theme', as Philip Lane has observed,

> pinpoints the end of each murder; the second is a cheap music-hall song he has written for the singer, Netta [Linda Darnell] with whom he becomes infatuated; while the central section is linked once again to the murders. The recapitulation returns to the earlier material, but is cut short as the orchestra falls silent 28 bars from the end. This mirrors the fact that in the film the composer, finally cornered by the authorities for his crimes, sets fire to the concert room, and completes the concerto alone, dying in the process.[59]

Sondheim told his biographer, Meryle Secrest, that after having first gone to the 7pm showing of the film with his friend, he then 'stayed for the 9pm so as to memorize the first six or eight bars of the score, the pages of which are seen for a matter of seconds. After playing the theme over and over he wrote a fan letter care of Twentieth Century Fox. Some three months later, he recalled, 'I got a reply back from Herrmann. It turned out he lived right around the corner from where I lived with my mother in New York. In tiny handwriting he said how rare it was that composers got fan letters.'[60] Herrmann, who died in 1975, was never to know just how influential he would prove to be in specifically influencing Sondheim's work on *Sweeney Todd* over 30 years later. 'It's an open secret', as Sondheim readily acknowledged, 'that the music for *Sweeney* is an homage to Herrmann's language.' 'I didn't consciously copy him', he paused to qualify, 'but it was *Hangover Square* that started that thought process in my head.' 'That snatch of score', as Secrest elaborated of the influence, 'that [Sondheim] had memorized in 1945 had surfaced more than thirty years later as a musical idea of such importance that it influenced Sondheim's most brilliant work. But George Harvey Bone, the gentle, kindly, socially correct composer with the guilty secret who feels compelled to kill without knowing why, has been replaced by the vengeful Todd, who is past all hope of redemption; his life has become a kind of witness to the annihilating power of vindictive revenge.'[61]

Sondheim's own vision of the dramatic and musical potential that Bond's reconceptualization of Sweeney Todd had liberated was profound; he perceived Bond to have effected a vital connection between a figure that had only recently been dismissed as the epitome of mere melodramatic excess, on the one hand, with possibly the grandest and most sophisticated Aristotelian traditions of the drama, on the other. 'For me', Sondheim had no difficulty in acknowledging, 'what the show is really about is obsession. I was using the story as a metaphor for any kind of obsession. Todd is a tragic hero in the classic sense that Oedipus is. He dies in the end because of a certain kind of fatal knowledge: he realizes what he has been doing. I find it terribly satisfying – much more so than any kind of accidental death, which often occurs in flimsy forms of melodrama.'[62] Director Hal Prince, who had worked on almost every major Sondheim production since *West Side Story*, and who was even at the time in the midst of collaborating with the composer on the tremendously ambitious *Pacific Overtures* (1976), was initially less enthusiastic about the possibilities of transforming Bond's play into a musical. '*Sweeney* was the one show I was reluctant about,' the director would later concede; 'I really didn't know what that play was.' As Prince admitted: 'It was only when I realized that the show was about revenge, that I knew how to do it. And then came the factory, and the class struggle – the terrible struggle to move out of the class in which you're born, and suddenly it became about the Industrial Age and the incursions of machinery on the spirit ... that was very important. It made it possible for me to conceive it.'[63] Hugh Wheeler, with whom Sondheim was to work on the show's 'book' (i.e. those spoken lines of the play that would not be set to music) weighed in with yet another vision of where the show was to find its focus. 'It's a wonderful story', Wheeler conceded, and I thought Bond's version was slightly better than the others, but from my point of view, even his version was that absolutely unreal, old melodrama where you boo the villain.... Whenever Sweeney would come in the audience would hiss and throw hot dogs. The version we wanted to do was a whole tone that was so difficult to get. We wanted to make it as nearly as we could into a sort of tragedy. I wrote it as a play, but I encouraged Steve to cannibalise it and make it nearly all music.... The hardest thing of all was how to make these two really disgusting people and write them in such a way that the audience can rather love them. And I think people did love Mrs. Lovett – yet she doesn't have a single redeeming feature.[64]

Such a startling lack of coherence – the absence of any unity of dramatic vision shared by composer, writer and director – would appear in retrospect not to have augured at all well for the final product. Nor did the disagreements as to what their own version of Todd was to be 'about' end there. 'I suppose people who are collaborating should be after the same thing,' Prince later added, 'but Steve and I were obviously not with *Sweeney*. I think it's also about impotence, and that's quite a different matter. The reason that the ensemble is used the way it is, the unifying emotion for the entire company, is shared impotence. Obviously, Sweeney's is the most dramatic, to justify all those murders. Impotence creates rage and rage is what is expressed most by Sweeney's behaviour.'[65] Obsession, revenge, tragedy, impotence: it seemed like the several creators who were together to produce this new Sweeney Todd for the stage would need eventually to make some difficult decisions. At the very least, they had their work cut out for them.

Towards the end of August 1976 – some eight months after the premiere of Sondheim and Weidman's 'Kabuki musical', *Pacific Overtures*, at New York's Winter Garden Theater, and hard upon the heels of that same show's closure (on 26 June) after a disappointing run of only 193 performances – an announcement appeared in the pages of the *New York Times* informing the public that the composer was already hard at work on his next project; Sondheim's adaptation of Bond's *Sweeney Todd*, the newspaper reported, was scheduled to open first in California in the spring of the following year before being brought to Broadway at some point in the summer or fall of 1977.[66] A number of previous commitments (including work on a film adaptation of *A Little Night Music*) prevented Sondheim from making any headway at all on the project until the summer of 1977. According to initial reports, Sondheim was not only to provide the music and lyrics, but was also to write the book for the musical. 'I started it', he would later write of those earliest weeks and months of solo work on *Sweeney*, 'trying to write everything myself because it was really all going to be sung ... it was going to be virtually an opera.' Realizing that the process of adaptation was proving to be too laborious ('I did the first twenty minutes', he recalled, 'and I realized I was only on page five of Bond's script'), Sondheim soon turned over the task of writing the book to Hugh Wheeler, with whom he had previously collaborated on the original stage version of *A Little Night Music* just four years earlier.[67]

Wheeler's participation had remarkably little effect on the composer's greater ambitions for the piece. The former's changes and additions to Bond's own text were in fact surprisingly limited, and for the most part *Sweeney* remained a work that was to be largely sung throughout. As John Dizikes was to note of the finished work: '*Sweeney Todd* is three quarters musical exposition, and Sondheim has perfected a form of contemporary recitative. The musical structure is complex – arias, duets, ensembles, motifs that recur in a way to sustain narrative in plotless stories.'[68] Sondheim would later argue that the musical structure of his *Sweeney Todd* was dictated not so much by any desire to move the form of the musical towards that of opera – to create some new hybrid kind of musical theatre that was a combination of the two – but that the shift was the result rather of his desire simply to create a sustained atmosphere of tension and suspense. 'One of the ways of making things creepy', he suggested,

> is to sing softly with very dry lyrics against a kind of rumble of 'Gee, what's going on? They're not saying terrible things on stage so why do I feel uncomfortable?' It's because something is *promised*. Hitchcock and all of the people who've ever done suspense used music that way. Music is what holds it together. That's why so much of *Sweeney Todd* is sung and underscored – not because I wanted to do an opera, but because I realized that the only way to sustain tension was to use music continually, not to let the heat out, so that even when they're talking, there's music going on in the pit.[69]

'Sondheim's plan for the score', Craig Zadan elaborated, 'was that the main characters would each have a basic musical theme, to serve as the starting point for his songs. Each of their songs would depend on the previous one, until the end, when the themes would collide.'[70] Actress Angela Lansbury – who was to originate the role of Mrs Lovett in Sondheim's piece, and who had just recently worked closely with the composer on the acclaimed 1974 revival of *Gypsy* – claimed that she sensed that Sondheim was on to something special from the moment she was first introduced to some of the musical's material. 'I felt it was going to be a very unique, rare piece of theatre,' Lansbury acknowledged. 'We sensed that Steve was breaking new ground that nobody's ever scratched. I certainly approached it with a good deal of seriousness of purpose, realizing that to be very funny, you sometimes have to be frightfully serious.'[71] 'But', the actress continued emphatically,

> I never, ever realized how put off people would be by the blood – and I'm a very squeamish person. I guess I never really addressed myself to what was really happening on stage. But from the very first of the previews, the gasps and the general reaction of the audience was stunning. They didn't like it. I

think they were awed by the presentation, which fascinated and interested them, but they didn't like what they were being asked to stomach.[72]

Len Cariou, who undertook the title role in the original Broadway production, recalled a similar feeling of generic uncertainty. 'I think most of our time', Cariou recalled, 'was spent discovering just how to walk that tightrope between broad farce and melodrama. I was mostly thankful that I had done Shakespeare because I needed that kind of energy for my performance.'[73]

Sondheim had originally intended the work to be a small chamber piece. The combination of the unresolved dissonances in the music redolent of Herrmann's movie scores and the persistent, fright-laden fragments that were to reappear as musical leitmotifs throughout the evening would arguably work best in an intimate theatrical environment. Scenically, he envisioned little more than a bare if atmospheric stage; 'just ... fog and a few street lamps'.[74] Sondheim again recalled the venue in which he had encountered Bond's production just a few years earlier:

> Stratford East is a workingman's theatre, attached to a pub; you can bring your beer back into the auditorium and during the interval there's lots of group singing and clunking of beer steins and stuff like that. A totally informal theatre with quite a small stage, where the play was done in an informal way but with professional actors and directed by a professional. I liked it a lot; it had a combination of charm and creepiness. I don't remember being particularly frightened.... But it must have scared me somewhat.[75]

Director Hal Prince, however, had other ideas about how this desired combination of 'charm and creepiness' was to be achieved. It so happened that their production, originally meant to be staged at the Shubert Organization's Broadway Theater, was eventually to be booked into the Uris (since renamed the Gershwin), which is one of the biggest Broadway theatres. Any performance that aimed at intimacy would be lost within its cavernous spaces; the productions that worked best at the Uris were those that were unapologetically huge, brassy, loud and oversized. Prince had no choice but to go directly against Sondheim's own wishes. 'I know what you want,' the director said. 'You want antimacassars and curtains parting. What I'll give you is an epic style. You'll lose on the scary part but you'll gain the size.'[76] Given the dimensions of the Uris, Sondheim had little choice but to concede; and with that concession came a shift of emphasis that transformed their *Sweeney Todd* decidedly from a drama about a single man and his struggle against authoritarian injustice, to one that became a depiction of the 'melodrama' of city life, generally – a kind of urban opera. 'The urban setting was largely Hal Prince's invention,' Sondheim later conceded:

> To me, Sweeney Todd was a story of personal obsession, and I really did not relate it very much to the milieu. I did a little bit, perhaps, when I referred to

the class structure, because Christopher Bond does that. But the sense of the city which is, in fact, a sense of the industrial revolution, machinery, steel, and all that, is very much Hal's approach to the material.

Hal Prince always likes to relate the work he does very strongly to the society from which the material springs. That is why most of his shows are what I call political shows. They are certainly social in that they relate very powerfully to the environment. All the time I was writing *Sweeney*, Hal was trying to find a way of relating to the material because the idea of the kernel itself – melodrama – did not appeal to him. He does not like pure farce or pure melodrama very much. What he likes is social context, and therefore he loves social melodrama, social farce, social anything, as long as it is related to the world around it, so that it doesn't feel tiny. Hal would always prefer to err on the epic side – and he's right.

Now Hal firmly believes that Sweeney Todd is a story about how society makes you impotent, and impotence leads to rage, and rage leads to murder – and, in fact, to the breaking down of society. Fine. In order to make the point, he had to show the society in action. When he grew excited about that idea, I started not so much to make reference to it but to soak it into the score. It's more than likely that I got the title for the song 'City on Fire' as a result of all that. And I'm a city boy myself; it's easy for me to relate to.[77]

Prince, as Sondheim elsewhere remarked, 'had a sense of a whole evening, a sense of an arc, a sense of design, of what an evening of theater is about'; the composer shrugged and decided, 'Someday it could be done small ... why not try it large?'[78]

And large it was. The stage of the Uris was transformed by Prince and the set designer Eugene Lee into an oversized industrial landscape. 'There was a peaked roof of grimy glass panes supported on steel trusses and rusty iron beams. Stairways and platforms filled the sides of the stage. The back wall was made of corrugated tin and rose to reveal a painted drop of nineteenth-century London. There was also a catwalk bridge suspended from a travelling girder and there were all sorts of moving parts that did little but create an atmosphere.'[79] Lee had managed to locate the wreckage of an old iron foundry in Rhode Island, and had it transported in its entirety to Broadway; the result was an apparent maze of pipes, beams, wheels, broken and filth-encrusted glass and inscrutable pieces of boilers. One of the beams eventually carried a sign identifying it as part of the 'London Iron Works, Ltd.' The theatrical backdrop against which this *Sweeney Todd* was to be performed took on the appearance – appropriate enough, given the material – of a gigantic and inhuman machine; it became a visual metaphor, as one New York reviewer was to put it, for the Industrial Revolution itself as something that dwarfed, degraded and dehumanized whatever it touched.[80]

The musical's narrative – certainly for the first half of the evening – was almost identical to that of Bond's 1973 drama; Sondheim often returned directly to Bond's original dialogue when writing his songs.[81] As the members of the audience slowly assembled and took their seats at the Uris Theater, they were immediately confronted by a banner that hung suspended from the ceiling of the curtainless stage, on which was emblazoned a large diagram of the 'British Beehive'. 'From top to bottom it depicted the royal family, the constitution, trial by jury, religious freedom, law and equity, figures representing the educated and commercial classes as well as tradesmen and labourers. The state, the church, and the social nexus that fuelled the industrial world of 19th-century England were displayed as a set of interlocking parts that dwarfed the individual.'[82] The banner was in fact an exact replica of the Victorian artist George Cruikshank's 1840 etching of the same name. Cruikshank's original print had used the familiar image of the beehive as a metaphor for social harmony within the industrial process; his image stressed the advancement that was possible within a society that recognized that a concept of industry and 'hard work' could achieve a kind of self-sustaining morality all its own. Inherent in such a highly stratified and classified vision was the enabling notion that an individual could – through a combination of hard work and moral integrity – move up the various rungs of the social ladder, i.e. a vision of positive social aspiration and mobility. Prince himself, however, used Cruikshank's original depiction only ironically – intending the stratified structure of Victorian order to act as a representation not of possible social improvement or amelioration, but as an image, rather, of the inescapable oppression and dehumanization of the individual by the processes of industrialization. (It was to stand as one of the few awkwardly heavy-handed and – oddly Victorian – moralistic features of the original production; subsequent revivals of the work have more often than not wisely dispensed with its grim didacticism.) Before the house lights had even begun to dim, two gravediggers made their way in a leisurely manner downstage, and began to dig what appeared to be a burial plot just in front of the banner. As the opening organ chords sounded a parodic recollection of the *Dies Irae* – from the Mass of the Dead in the Roman Catholic Church – the screech of a factory whistle pierced the air, and two workmen abruptly yanked down the banner of the British Beehive, metaphorically suggesting the imminent collapse of the social order it so neatly depicted. A chorus of workers emerged from the shadows of the stage wings to confront the audience with the prologue of 'The Ballad of Sweeney Todd'.

The ballad-prologue also echoes the *Dies Irae* (the motif is heard in the lines beginning 'Swing your razor wide, Sweeney!/ Hold it to the skies!'), but its main intention is to introduce the audience to the possibly unfamiliar story that is about to unfold:

MAN
Attend the tale of Sweeney Todd.
His skin was pale and his eye was odd.
He shaved the faces of gentlemen

Who never thereafter were heard of again.
He trod a path that few have trod,
Did Sweeney Todd,
The Demon Barber of Fleet Street.

ANOTHER MAN
He kept a shop in London town,
Of fancy clients and good renown.
And what if none of their souls were saved?
They went to their maker impeccably shaved
By Sweeney,
By Sweeney Todd,
The Demon Barber of Fleet Street.[83]

The barber himself emerges from the freshly dug grave to remind the audience that what they are about to see remains, after all, only a play; even so, to tell them any more of the narrative at this stage, he concedes rather coyly, would only spoil their possible entertainment.

As the main action of the drama begins, Anthony Hope sings of the youthful thrill of returning home in his positive *No Place Like London*, a sentiment to which Todd returns his own cynical vision of the city. 'You are young,' he informs Anthony laconically, 'Life has been kind to you. / You will learn.' The outline of Todd's own past as Benjamin Barker is economically recalled in response to Anthony's questions in Todd's trance-like *The Barber and his Wife*.

There was a barber and his wife,
And she was beautiful.
A foolish barber and his wife,
She was his reason and his life,
And she was beautiful.[84]

The two men go their separate ways and Todd, seeking out his former home, soon arrives at Nellie Lovett's Fleet Street pie shop. Sondheim offered Lovett's character (portrayed, again, in the original Broadway production by Angela Lansbury, for whom the part was intended) a tour-de-force introduction in the form of the first of the evening's show-stoppers, *The Worst Pies in London*. Lansbury subsequently described her character as 'the consummate cockney woman with an eye to the main chance – dishonest, lovable, cheery, typical of the 1850s'. When we first meet her, Mrs Lovett is bustling about her shop, attempting to fend off both vermin and her competitor (one Mrs Mooney) while still gamely trying to sell her pies. Bemoaning the circumstances that compel her to sell to her infrequent customers pies that she freely concedes to be 'revolting' and 'disgusting', she knowingly informs Todd that her competitor's wares may not be all they claim to be – although revealing at the same time that she is not beyond such strategies herself:

> Mrs Mooney has a pie shop,
> Does a business, but I notice something weird –
> Lately all her neighbors' cats have disappeared.
> Have to hand it to her –
> Wot I calls
> Enterprise,
> Popping pussies into pies.
> Wouldn't do in my shop –
> Just the thought of it's enough to make you sick.
> And I'm telling you them pussy cats is quick.[85]

When Todd asks her about the room above the pie shop, Nellie recounts the events of his own past in a variation on *The Barber and his Wife*, in which it is the barber himself who is described by Mrs Lovett as 'beautiful'. Questioned further by Todd, she tells him of the fate of his wife Lucy and daughter Johanna in *Poor Thing*. The barber is reunited with the set of razors Lovett has saved for him in *My Friends*, he holds the silver blade reverently, oblivious to a similar outpouring of affection for himself by Mrs Lovett.

Johanna is introduced at her window with the beautiful *Green Finch and Linnet Bird*, which reflects her own sense of imprisonment and captivity. Anthony responds with the rapturous *Ah, Miss*; when warned off by the judge and beadle, who threaten him, he voices his determination to win Johanna for himself in one of Sondheim's most explosively beautiful melodies, *Johanna*.

In St Dunstan's marketplace the next day, the encounter and competition with Pirelli is acted out in *Pirelli's Miracle Elixir* and *The Contest*. Back at the pie shop a day or two later, as the barber anxiously awaits the promised visit of the beadle to his shop, Nellie exhorts Todd to be patient (*Wait*); the arrival of Pirelli and Tobias is dealt with largely as in Bond's original. The plans of Anthony and Johanna to escape are transformed into the frantic duet *Kiss Me*, which is eventually joined to the beadle's suggestion that Judge Turpin visit Todd's shop to render him more appealing to the young girl, *Ladies in Their Sensitivities*. When the judge is finally in the barber's chair, the two join together to sing the praises of *Pretty Women*, accurately described by one of Sondheim's commentators as possessing 'an air of real beauty, lovingly harmonized by a masochist and a homicidal maniac'.[86] The first half of the drama comes to a tremendous conclusion with two musical numbers that follow hard upon each other. In the first, the astounding *Epiphany*, Todd's initial frustration by Anthony's interruption is transformed into a moment of maniacal insight – an insane man's vision of redemption. Reiterating the grim view of mankind he had voiced earlier in his response to Anthony's *No Place Like London*, Todd suggests that he has a change in store for its inhabitants. The crashing discord of his frustration gives way to chords possessed of a pounding, pseudo-industrial sense of purpose:

> They all deserve to die!
> Tell you why, Mrs. Lovett,
> Tell you why:
> Because in all of the whole human race, Mrs. Lovett,
> There are two kinds of men and only two.
> There's the one staying put
> In his proper place
> And the one with his foot
> In the other one's face –
> Look at me, Mrs. Lovett,
> Look at you![87]

Addressing the audience directly, Todd turns to face the members of the auditorium, asking:

> All right! You, sir,
> How about a shave?
> (Slashes twice)
> Come and visit
> Your good friend Sweeney –!
> You, sir, too, sir –
> Welcome to the grave!
> I will have vengeance,
> I will have salvation![88]

Todd's *Epiphany* ends with a near-schizophrenic recollection of his lost wife and child, whom he thinks he will now never live to see, and a strangely optimistic affirmation of his newly discovered mission, as he cries: 'But the work waits, / I'm alive at last / And I'm full of joy!'[89] As Todd's elation begins to subside, he is recalled to practicality by Mrs Lovett, who is already worried about how they are going to dispose of Pirelli's body. The comic relief offered by Lovett's own 'epiphany' as it is expressed in the first act's closing number, *A Little Priest*, is a stroke of genius, and allows the composer to defuse the possible tensions raised by Todd's agonized insight into the nature of mankind's shared mortality. Confronted with the body of Todd's competitor (and with the prospect of many more bodies to come), Mrs Lovett prods Todd gently but insistently towards her own purpose. The comic waltz that follows, and that closes the first half of the play, sees Todd and Mrs Lovett – both of them gleefully and enthusiastically murderous – enumerating the various types of 'clients' they will soon be serving, in more ways than one (priests, poets, bishops, lawyers, marines, grocers, actors etc.), and boasting that Mrs Lovett will be the only pastry-cook in town who will be in a position to promise her customers 'shepherd's pie peppered / With actual shepherd / On top'. As Todd cheerfully reminds Lovett as the curtain comes down on Act One, 'The history of the world, my sweet – / ... is who gets eaten and who gets to eat.'[90]

As the second half of the musical begins, Todd's special barber's chair – designed now to slide his clients directly into Lovett's basement – has arrived, and Mrs Lovett's business is so brisk that she and her new assistant, Tobias, can hardly keep up with the demand (*God, That's Good!*). Anthony, who has now set about London searching for the 'obscure retreat' in which Judge Turpin promised to incarcerate his ward, reprises his earlier *Johanna*, whilst Mrs Lovett's newfound prosperity sees her redecorating her little front parlour and planning excursions and possibly eventual retirement to the seaside with Todd (*By the Sea*). Following Anthony's discovery of Johanna in Fogg's asylum, the barber sets about transforming Anthony into a creditable wigmaker and baits his trap for the judge (*Wigmaker Sequence* and *The Letter*); Tobias voices his growing concern for Mrs Lovett's safety in the gentle and lyrical *Not While I'm Around*. The arrival of the beadle to have a look at the bake-house and to check with Mrs Lovett about the smell coming from her chimney sets off the *Final Sequence*, which rises to the same Grand Guignol climax as Bond's original. Having killed not only the beadle and the judge, but then his wife – in the guise of the Beggar Woman – and Mrs Lovett, Todd's anticlimactic moment of self-realization and recognition reveals him to have lost all sense of purpose. Before being slain (in an offhand and casually incidental manner) by Tobias, he can only reiterate some of the very first words the audience had heard him speak:

> There was a barber and his wife,
> And she was beautiful,
> A foolish barber and his wife,
> She was his reason and his life.
> And she was beautiful.
> And she was virtuous.
> And he was –
> > (*Shrugs*)
> Naïve.[91]

Once the melodrama has ended, the members of the cast appear one by one, and in a ghostly and impassive manner reprise the opening *Ballad of Sweeney Todd*, reminding the audience, as Robert Kimball has observed, 'that in a world full of Sweeneys revenge begets revenge'. Working only with the suggestions provided by Bond's original, Sondheim arguably transformed the stuff of melodrama into a theatrical spectacle that – on at least one level – has far more in common with Aeschylus' *Orestia* and Shakespeare's *Hamlet* than it could ever be said to have with *Maria Marten*.

*

One giant step for vegetarianism
(T.E. Kalem, reviewing Sondheim's *Sweeney Todd* in *Time* magazine)[92]

Sondheim's *Sweeney Todd* premiered at the Uris Theater in New York on 1 March 1979. Len Cariou and Angela Lansbury co-starred in the two main roles; also in the cast were Victor Garber as Anthony Hope, Sarah Rice as Johanna, Edmund Lyndeck as Judge Turpin, Merle Louise as the Beggar Woman, Ken Jennings as Tobias Ragg, Joaquín Romaguera as Pirelli, and Jack Eric Williams as the Beadle. The reviews for the Broadway production were overwhelmingly favourable and enthusiastic (Martin Gottfried notes that *Sweeney* 'arguably received the best reviews of any Prince-Sondheim musical'), although many focused on the degree to which Sondheim's work for the theatre seemed increasingly to have more in common with the opera than it did with the traditional form of the Broadway musical.[93] Jack Kroll, writing in the pages of the American weekly *Newsweek*, commented:

> In sheer ambition and size, there's never been a bigger musical on Broadway.... *Sweeney Todd* is brilliant, even sensationally so, but its effect is very much a barrage of brilliancies, like flares fired aloft that dazzle and fade into something cold and dark.... This 'musical thriller' about a homicidal barber, a tonsorial Jack the Ripper in Dickensian London, slashes at the jugular instead of touching the heart.... Sondheim has been inching closer and closer to pure opera and *Sweeney Todd* is the closest he's come yet.... The problem is one of concept and unity: *Sweeney Todd* [wants] to make the same fusion of popular and high culture that Brecht and Weill made in *The Threepenny Opera*. But the fusion is never really made.... Nevertheless as an exhibition of sheer theatrical talent, *Sweeney Todd* must be seen by anyone who cares about the gifts and risks of Broadway at its best.[94]

Richard Eder, in the the *New York Times*, similarly took exception to what he saw to be the show's generic ambitions, and further objected that – for all Prince's efforts to mount the production as one that offered its audience a clear social commentary – it lacked coherence. 'The musical,' Eder maintained,

> beautiful as it is, succeeds, in a sense, in making an intensity that is unacceptable. Furthermore, the effort to fuse this Grand Guignol with a Brechtian style of sardonic social commentary doesn't work. There is, in fact, no serious social message in *Sweeney*; and at the end, when the cast lines up on stage and points at us, singing that there are Sweeneys all about, the point is unproven.... These are defects, vital ones; but they are the failures of an extraordinary, fascinating, and often ravishingly lovely effort.[95]

But other reviewers were less qualified, and stressed both the achievement of

Sondheim's soaring, unforgettable romantic score and the skills that Prince brought to the project. Douglas Watt of the New York *Daily News* wrote:

> *Sweeney Todd* is a staggering theater spectacle and more fun than a graveyard on the night of the annual skeleton's ball.... Practically everybody connected with this wonderful enterprise [is] operating at the top of their form.... This is Sondheim's most playful score.... Harold Prince has staged the piece dazzlingly.... Lansbury is an endless delight as first the slatternly, then the gaudily splendid Mrs. Lovett. She is the grandest, funniest, most bewitching witch of a fairy tale sprite you are ever likely to encounter. And Cariou, hair parted in the middle and with the visage of deathly pallor, is a magnificently obsessed Todd.... So joy to the world, dear children! *Sweeney Todd* is here to enrich your nightmares. A triumphant occasion, indeed.[96]

Clive Barnes of the *New York Post* was perhaps the most prescient, and the most appreciative of Sondheim's achievement. 'I thought it was simply great,' he subsequently commented. 'The story is totally crazy but, in its macabre way, absolutely compelling, and the musical has been put together with unusual love, taste, and style.' Almost as if to counter the comments of Kroll in *Newsweek*, he added: 'Sondheim's score – the most distinguished to grace Broadway in years – owes more to Mahler, Alban Berg, and Benjamin Britten than Weill.'[97]

Nominated for nine Tony Awards, *Sweeney* nearly swept the boards when, in 1980, it picked up eight, including Best Musical, Best Score (Stephen Sondheim), Best Direction (Hal Prince), Best Actor in a Musical (Len Cariou), Best Actress in a Musical (Angela Lansbury) and Best Scenic Design (Eugene Lee). (Oddly, the show also won the Tony for Best Book, although Hugh Wheeler's contribution to a musical in which as much as 80 per cent of the material had been scored and written by Sondheim himself, and the rest based largely on Bond's original, was at best, minimal.) *Sweeney* settled in at the Uris for a run of 558 performances (closing on 19 June 1980). After completing a year with the show in New York, Cariou and Lansbury starred in the national tour of the production that was mounted in 1980 (the pair were replaced on the Broadway stage by veterans George Hearn and Dorothy Loudon); fortunately, the production – featuring many members of the original Broadway cast, including Angela Lansbury – was videotaped for posterity at the end of its national run, in Los Angeles. When broadcast on American television, this production garnered numerous 'Emmy' Awards, including once again, a nod to Lansbury (for 'Outstanding Individual Performance in a Variety or Musical Program'), and a similar distinction for Cariou's successor, George Hearn.

The London production of the musical, presented by the Robert Stigwood Organization, was announced in the pages of *The Times* on 12 March 1980, and the show opened at the Theatre Royal, Drury Lane on 2 July of that same year. The cast featured Denis Quilley in the title role, and Sheila Hancock as Mrs Lovett; also featured were Andrew C. Wadsworth as Anthony Hope, Mandy Moore as Johanna and Austin Kent as Judge Turpin. Key reviewers, such as Irving Wardle in *The Times*, were less enthusiastic than their New York counterparts. 'The word "camp"', Wardle sniffed,

> has often been applied to Broadway's re-tinted Victoria, but it will not do this time. The authors, Stephen Sondheim and Hugh Wheeler, and Harold Prince's production team have set about reincarnating the demon barber as seriously as Frankenstein. Their purpose is to rivet you to your seat, freeze your blood, and leave you with the feeling that Sweeney is alive and well and sitting all around you in Drury Lane.
>
> Those who believe, as I do, that the theatre is a place to which the spectator brings his independent attention and judgement, will strongly resist this kind of aesthetic bullying. . . . You might sum up the show's achievement by noting that all its elements assist in overcoming the essential problem of telling a simple unitary story in such a way as to take you constantly by surprise.[98]

On the merits of Sondheim's score, Wardle – if once again voicing the tiresome and frankly wrong-headed complaint that there was little about the music that was 'hummable' – was generally positive:

> 'Attend the tale of Sweeney Todd' runs the opening and closing ballad. And you do, thanks largely to the music. At this point it consists of terse melodic phrases backed with a whirring ostinato accompaniment suggesting the cogs of a deadly clock.
>
> There is nothing here or at the end to whistle as you go out. But if that has seemed a great weakness [in] Sondheim in the past, now it seems a deliberate choice. The score is full of broken-backed snatches of melody, broken off short.
>
> What gives the score its integrity are the motifs that return with ever increasing emphasis: a low string, two-note chromatic descent suggesting an anchor dragging the muddy Thames; sepulchral chords of the fifth in the bass organ register, punctuated with high-screaming brass interjections, which directly parallel the use of stabs of white light for moments of extreme horror.[99]

But ultimately, Wardle recoiled in the face of the deliberate generic confusion and the very resources of black comedy from which the show drew its greatest strength. 'What I cannot take', he concluded imperiously,

> are the passages where the grotesque is pushed over into black comedy, as in Lovett's pie-proffering number, 'Have a little Priest' [sic]. At such moments, the equation between Sweeney and his creators becomes altogether too close, and they seem to be going through the motions of a joke in which they really find nothing to laugh at.[100]

Cover art (by Michael Zulli) for Neil Guiman and Michael Zulli's proposed serial version of *Sweeney Todd* (published as *Taboo 6 – The Sweeney Todd Penny Dreadful*) (1992). Reproduced by kind permission of the artist. © Michael Zulli.

Disappointingly, and thanks in large parts to such comments, the first London production of *Sweeney Todd* closed in just four months, after only 157 performances.

Yet, as Martin Gottfried has noted, in effect, *Sweeney*'s run would, in the end, turn out to be much longer. 'Like *Porgy and Bess*, *Sweeney Todd* would become a repertory item, a staple of opera companies around the world, and an acknowledged classic. Had he composed nothing else, this show would have established Sondheim as a giant of the American stage.'[101] Meryle Secrest records an anecdote relating to the premiere of the original production at the Uris in 1979:

> Schuyler G. Chapin, commissioner for New York City's Department of Cultural Affairs and former general manager of the Metropolitan Opera, said that when he went to the opening night, Harold Clurman, then the dean of theater critics, 'came charging across the lobby at me and said, "Why didn't you put this on at the Met?" And I replied, "I would have put it on like a shot, if I'd had the opportunity." And I would have. There would have been screams and yells and I wouldn't have given a damn. Because it is an opera. A modern American opera.'[102]

If not exactly conceived as an opera to begin with, that is precisely what *Sweeney Todd* has become. Less than five years after it premiered on Broadway, *Sweeney Todd* was restaged by Hal Prince for the New York City Opera; this same 1984 production returned (with much acclaim) to the Lincoln Center in the 2003–4 season, starring the relatively young Mark Delevan in the title role, and the West End veteran Elaine Paige in her New York City opera debut. The Royal National Theatre first staged it with even more success in 1993. The Royal Opera House at Covent Garden arrived late on the scene, finally mounting a production – featuring Thomas Allen and Felicity Palmer – in December 2003. In actual fact, the Covent Garden Production had been produced in partnership with Chicago's Lyric Opera, which had already mounted the same production in 2003.

Sondheim's own comments on the generic status of his work remain qualified. On the one hand, as already noted, he claimed originally to have conceived the work as a chamber piece – one best suited to a small and intimate theatrical environment. Such a vision does not necessarily disqualify *Sweeney Todd* as an opera, however; we perhaps tend to think that all operas must of necessity be grand and tremendous affairs, if only to fill the ornate and often grandiose auditoriums of the world's great opera houses – Milan's La Scala, London's Covent Garden, or the Metropolitan Opera House in New York. Indeed, although Sondheim has rather notoriously claimed that he has 'never liked opera and ... never understood it', he has also admitted that his first instinct on seeing Bond's production suggested its suitability to the mode.[103] 'I remember thinking on my way home', he has written, that [Bond's drama] would make an opera, and I spoke to John Dexter, one of the directors of the Metropolitan Opera, who at that time was directing in the West End in London. In the course of our conversation I asked him if he thought that Sweeney Todd might make an opera, and he said absolutely and that encouraged me to look into the rights for it. That's how it all started.[104]

'It is precisely because *Sweeney* is clearly so much more than a musical comedy', as Sondheim commentator Christopher Hurrell has observed, 'that it has become a target for experiments in what has come to be described as "crossover" between popular contemporary musical theatre and opera.'[105] *Sweeney*'s many revivals — both in opera houses and in the more traditional confines of the musical theatre — have afforded the opportunity for many different directors and performers to offer their own visions of the work; it is a telling strength of Sondheim's score that it is only very rare indeed for the work to come off any the worse for wear. Of the co-production that reached the Royal Opera in early 2004, for example, critic John Olsen observed: 'this *Sweeney* [is] much less about social inequities in 19th-century London and more about deception, madness, revenge, and rage'; in order to convey this meaning, grids of heavy industrial piping were now used to present the entire stage less in the manner of a factory than as a cage, the confines of which conveyed to the audience 'the feeling of Sweeney's imprisonment in his own emotions'.[106] Director John Doyle's hugely successful revival at Berkshire's Watermill Playhouse (which eventually transferred both to the West End and to Broadway), on the other hand, aimed for something completely different. 'This', Doyle would insist of his own deliberately scaled-down version, in which the various characters themselves constituted the on-stage orchestra for the entire production 'was how Stephen Sondheim envisioned *Sweeney Todd* in its original production in New York: it would be in a small theatre, perhaps the Broadway, where Hal Prince had staged an environmental version of *Candide* a few years earlier. This time, it would be converted to London, with street lamps in the aisles and [in Sondheim's words] ' "the beggar woman would pop up behind you".' To create this effect, 'The theatre would be "like a coffin", all decked out in black — black seats, black drapes on the walls. When audiences entered, a man would be hunched over an organ playing "terrible funeral music". The organ would make a great crashing sound, and the audience would have no chance to get settled before the lights went out and the play began.'[107] The cavernous scale of the auditorium at the Uris had prevented Sondheim (and Prince) from ever seeing this effect achieved in its initial incarnation; needless to say, Sondheim has been hugely pleased by the fact that many of the revivals now stage *Sweeney* on precisely such a scale.

Ultimately, the situation in which *Sweeney Todd* finds itself at the end of the first decade of the twenty-first century was perhaps best summed up by music critic John Snelson; writing on the occasion of the work's premiere at Covent Garden in 2003, Snelson observed that Sondheim's insistence that

Sweeney Todd was a 'musical thriller' that functions the way 'old movie scores do' and 'is really an operetta [if only because] it requires operetta voices' in some ways held the key to understanding how the piece worked. Sondheim's multiple references to different genres, Snelson insisted,

> are a symptom of the problems we encounter when an individual work of art, formed from a gallimaufry of cultural influences, has to be squeezed into a limited set of predetermined pigeon-holes. And the more comfortable they fit into one of them, the better the work is so often judged to be. But such a process is a reverse of the order in which these things happen: whether the chicken came before the egg or not, both preceded the words for them. You need to write some musical comedies before you can categorize them, and you can't establish the difference between, say, the opera seria and bel canto repertoires until you have enough examples of both to be able to make the comparison. . . .
>
> Crucially, art forms develop, and consequently inherent within the idea of genre must be the concept of continual change. Over a period of time certain key works in any genre are thrown into prominence, they become established in the repertory and then form the pillars of that repertory: the canon. These canonic works in turn provide models of what good examples in a particular genre should be like, and we use them as yardsticks for other works in that genre, whether established or new. The paradox is that what we take as being the exemplars of a genre so often began life as its exceptions, and we forget to our cost that many works we take for granted as canonic today were met with ambiguous or downright hostile responses when first staged. Ultimately the new tends to win out in the face of the stagnation that results from avoiding change. Furthermore, a new work that can immediately be seen to follow whatever the current canonic precepts are will most probably be thought clichéd or derivative; we'll know what it's going to do and how it's going to do it before it does it, and that's not great for holding our attention.[108]

As Snelson emphasizes in conclusion, both musicals and operas today are 'the result of so many works over so much time that the palette of musico-dramatic characteristics that each can draw upon is daunting'.[109] Critics have debated whether or not Sondheim had been moving further and further away from the received idiom of the musical theatre he had inherited from the likes of Richard Rogers and Oscar Hammerstein and closer to that of opera even before *Sweeney Todd* was first staged in 1979 (the conductor André Previn memorably raised the issue in a 1977 interview with the composer). Critics such as John Rockwell and Carey Blyton maintained from the start that *Sweeney* was more opera than not; the latter even argued that the reason the work initially failed to find a public at Drury Lane was because 'it was heard by the wrong audience . . . it needs to be presented by an opera company like the English National Opera or the Welsh National Opera'.[110] Opera historian Fred Plotkin notes that works such as *Sweeney Todd*, along with *A Little Night Music*, are 'more operetta or even opera [than musicals], and have received numerous performances in opera houses'.[111] Even the most recent edition of Donald Jay Grout's standard volume, *A Short History of Opera*, singled out *Sweeney Todd* as one of those works that reveal 'the Broadway musical idiom to be a wellspring for the creation of American national opera'.[112] As Stephen Banfield, an astute analyst of Sondheim's work, finally observed: 'By no means just where Sondheim is concerned, distinctions between musicals and operas are becoming, or being, blurred.... One could argue that, instead, they need careful redefinition.'[113]

*

It is an amiable defect in the English public never to know when they have had enough of a good thing.

(Wilkie Collins, *No Name*)[114]

'Sweeney Todd' is among those rare proper names that have become a part of our language; the most recent (2002) edition of the *Oxford English Dictionary*, at least, glosses Todd's name simply as a generic term – '[a] (nickname for a) barber' – possessing neither necessarily positive nor negative connotations. The illustrative quotation offered by the dictionary to justify the entry, curiously enough, dates not from the heyday of Todd's career as a prominent figure of the Victorian melodrama and periodicals, but is an example of mid- to late-twentieth-century Scouse slang ('I'm goin' ter Sweeny ter 'ave me hur cut' (1966)). The peculiar persistence of Todd's odd, twilight existence between the realms of fact and fiction is even more bizarrely attested to by his formal entry in the 2004 edition of the *Oxford Dictionary of National Biography*, in which – in the understandable absence of exact birth and death dates – it is noted simply that he was a 'legendary murderer and barber' who was supposed to have flourished in about 1784.

Indeed, even had Sondheim never chanced upon Bond's own revision of the story of the murderous barber and his cannibalistic pie-making accomplice, and even had Tim Burton's more recent film production never been green-lit by Hollywood producers understandably wary of selling such a movie to middle-America's proverbial 'Mr and Mrs Front Porch', the seemingly slight and often spurious connections such as that which links the demon barber via cockney rhyming slang with members of the London Metropolitan Police Flying Squad (aka 'the Sweeney') would still have done much to keep the Fleet Street legend alive in English popular culture, at the very least.[115] Sweeney has always been hard at work somewhere within the British imagination, and (for all the truth of Sondheim's observation that until 1979 very few Americans 'had ever heard of Sweeney Todd') the barber's influence can in fact clearly be traced in now classic American horror stories such as Stanley Ellin's chilling 'Speciality of the House' (1948), and Charles Beaumont's 'Free Dirt' (1955).

Elsewhere, Sweeney took on the form of what might perhaps best be described as punning alter-egos. In March 1973, for example, the popular British comic magazine *Shiver and Shake* first chronicled the adventures of one 'Sweeny [sic] Toddler'. As conceived first by cartoonist Leo Baxendale and subsequently by Tom Paterson, this Sweeny was the ultimate manifestation of the 'terrible twos' – a manic and diabolic cousin to Dennis the Menace or even Bart Simpson. His later career as a graphic character was to be continued first in *Whoopee!* and subsequently (in 1985) *Whizzer and Chips*; in much the same manner as had been established over a century earlier by his nominal progenitors in the earliest nineteenth-century periodicals and stage adaptations, Sweeney cannibalized the substance of a strip that was supposedly meant to have featured a different character altogether.

Sweeney's legacy has also been busy elsewhere. In 1996 the mystery writer Frank Palmer produced the first of a series of best-selling detective thrillers featuring the character of one Phil 'Sweeney' Todd, and the enormously popular British comedy duo the Two Ronnies (Ronnie Barker and Ronnie Corbett) included a sketch featuring one 'Teeny Todd' (played by Corbett) in their late *Sketchbook* series, which first aired in March and April 2005. Modern purchasers of straight or 'cut throat' razors may be disconcerted to find such items not infrequently marketed as 'Sweeney Todd' blades; Sweeney's name is still being used in the first decade of the twenty-first century to market a brand of hair oil. There are both barber shops and restaurants that feature Todd's name – the latter often, prominently, on their menus to advertise a speciality in homemade meat pies. An Australian firm specializing in the safe removal of medical waste from hospitals and medical facilities has likewise been named after Todd (whose assumed, early proficiency in the profession could hardly have been bettered). Sweeney Todd – as the products of popular culture have little trouble acknowledging – still 'sells'.

Making use of a pun based on the recognizable familiarity of Todd's name in order to catch the eyes of potential readers is understandable enough. The decision of writer Cliff Edwards and illustrator Michael Strand to feature Todd as a central character in an educational text specifically designed to encourage literacy amongst younger readers was – at least when it was first published in 1981 – rather more unusual. Longman's 'Hair Raisers, Part 1, Sweeney Todd' combined conventional, comic-book-style graphics with graduated passages of prose texts and summaries to tell the story of a truant named 'Jacko'. As so often in the past, Todd's story is again 'contained' within an extended narrative frame. In this instance, the frame narrative tells the story of how Jacko and his friends become involved in a new youth club that has been organized at the 'Old Town Hall'. In the hall's musty cellar they discover an old magic lantern, which Jacko has soon set up in working order. The 'film' they then watch (Edwards is unfortunately less familiar than his story requires with regard to the actual visual capabilities of such early moving picture technology) is supposed to be an old version of Sweeney Todd

– a character the teenagers in the story immediately recognize. The images are frightening enough to scare the group out of the cellar entirely. Tellingly, by the narrative's end it is the former truant and troublemaker Jacko who is the one who calls the group to order.

Edwards and Strand apparently thought it necessary to reassure their young and impressionable readers at the end of their remedial retelling of the story that 'the terrible murder in the barber shop never happened', but was only 'a good murder story that [the Victorians] could see at the music hall, and it was very popular indeed'.[116] Offering a brief summary of what usually took place in Todd's barber shop, however, the writer and illustrator then effect a peculiar, rhetorical sleight of hand that almost works once again to bring Todd's murders back into the realm of historically verifiable experience:

> People talked about Sweeney Todd for a long time afterwards. Men tested the chairs in barbers' shops to see if they were safe to sit in. When people bought pies, they pretended to look for fingers in them.

Interestingly, the volume included in the Longman 'Hair Raisers' series would not be the only such text to have recourse to Todd's story in the interests of further education or practical classroom pedagogy. Yet another *Sweeney Todd*, published in 2002 and credited jointly to John Bilyard and the 'Basic Skills Agency', would be published by London's Hodder Murray as part of their 'Livewire' series of similarly remedial books aimed at teenage and adult-age readers with a reading level below age ten.[117] Still another work to adopt the barber as an unlikely but appropriately seductive poster-child for literacy had been Carey Blyton's *Sweeney Todd, The Barber* (which appeared at about the same time as Edwards and Strand's classroom 'text' in 1981, although apparently written some years earlier, in 1977). Blyton (1932–2002) was a nephew of popular children's writer Enid Blyton. He had also, like Colin Graham of the 1959 Hammersmith production, mentioned earlier, enjoyed a close relationship with the composer Benjamin Britten (serving as his personal editor). Blyton described his own piece as 'A Victorian Melodrama for Narrator, unison voices, and piano'. Rather like Edwards's more straight-forwardly didactic piece, above, Blyton's work was similarly aimed at an audience of older, school-age children and teenagers, and unapologetically billed as 'a fun piece for schools'. The lyrics provided for a series of seven songs with titles such as the apprentice Tobias's 'Today I Start My Working Life', Mark Ingestrie's 'Oh, I'm a Jolly Sailor' and Johanna Oakley's 'Mark, Mark, Where Are You Now?' could hardly be described as sophisticated (Mrs Lovett, in her own 'My Famous Pies Are Known to All', typically declares: 'Mister Sweeney Todd is helping me, a fortune make; And when I hear the trap-door drop, I know it's time to bake'), yet they rather gleefully delight in their own self-professed 'vulgarity', and are certainly no less accomplished in their way than any number of similar tunes that had traditionally accompanied the barber's story in various melodramas over the years. (Audiences, here, were openly encouraged to boo and hiss the stage villain etc.) When performed in full, Blyton's song-cycle runs some 17 minutes; an audio recording of the work (opus 79) was eventually released in June 2006.

Of an altogether different calibre is the use made of Todd's story by the award-winning author of children's books, Gillian Cross, in her 1982 thriller for younger readers, *The Dark Behind the Curtain*. A Londoner by birth and the author of over 100 novels, Cross has earned a particularly strong reputation as a writer in her native Britain. She was awarded the Library Association's Carnegie Medal in 1990, and the Whitbread Children's Novel Award in 1992. The series of six books that she began with the publication of 1982's *The Demon Headmaster* has proven to be perhaps her most popular creation, having inspired both a BBC television series and a published, musical version, first performed in London in 1998. 'I write because I love telling stories and finding out about things,' Cross has told her readers with unabashed enthusiasm. 'My stories don't have "messages", but I like to write about people in difficult and dangerous situations. I'm interested in how they cope and the decisions they make.'[118]

If Cross's *Demon Headmaster* series takes as its fundamental premise the threat posed by various sorts of insidious and invasive evils, then so too does *The Dark Behind the Curtain* represent her near-contemporary exploration of the possibility that certain manifestations of malice and cruelty can be so powerful as to exert a lingering and poisonous effect throughout society, and can even stretch their influence across time. Her book presents its readers with the eerie experiences of a group of grammar school students who have been set the task of putting on an unspecified dramatic version of *Sweeney Todd* as their school play (the text set for the performance would appear to be some highly edited version of Dibdin Pitt's original, although Cross herself invents any of the dialogue actually 'quoted' within the pages of her own book). The teacher who has been placed in charge of directing the play, Miss Lampeter, makes use of modern acting methods and practical exercises to conjure the emotions of fear and loathing that Todd's narrative would have inspired, and to evoke the 'feel' of his victims. So effective are these exercises, however, that the unprepared students actually succeed in bringing 'to life' the emotional resonance of their predecessors – of all those exploited and deprived children in whose lives they have been asked to immerse themselves. Sweeney Todd himself stands as the symbolic focus of their resentment, and the source of their collective misery. He is the embodiment, essentially, of all the human misery and exploitation of Victorian England. Discussing the uncanny phenomena they appear to be invoking, two of the book's central characters – the supposed troublemaker Jackus and the otherwise unpopular Ann, who has been cast in the role of Mrs Lovett – raise the possibility that they are dealing with actual 'ghosts' of some kind. 'Suppose', Ann speculates, that what causes ghosts is strong feelings. If you concentrate your energy into one kind of feeling, it might make a kind of print, that goes on after you're dead. Perhaps it stops you knowing you're dead even. The strength keeps on, even without a body. Then wouldn't it be terrible – '

She paused for a moment, as if what she was thinking was too horrible to say all at once.

'Yes?' Jackus prompted her.

'Well, don't you see what that would mean? It would mean that all those ghosts – and they were children, they must have been ... – all of them concentrated their energies into hunger. Hunger and fear. That was their *life*. Oh, imagine. How awful!'[119]

So frightening do their experiences become, that Jackus is compelled to ask Mr Garner, the school's headmaster:

'[T]his play we're doing, it's not true, is it? I mean, there never was a Sweeney Todd who killed people in a barber's shop and had them chopped up and made into pies?'

Mr. Garner shook his head. 'Not as far as I know.'

'But in another way it is true, isn't it? Then – in Victorian times – there were lots of people who were very cruel to other people, to make money out of them. Especially to children. There must have been lots of children who spent their lives being afraid and hungry and angry at the world. Mustn't there?'[120]

The framing narrative within which Cross situates the *Sweeney Todd* play that is being staged by the young students explores the relationship between the central character of Jackus (who has been assigned the role of 'Jarvis Williams', Mrs Lovett's assistant, as punishment for a supposed act of theft) and his nominal 'friend' and rival, Marshall, who is to play Todd. The two boys had already unavoidably been thrown together throughout their early lives by their mothers, who are the closest of friends, and who seem only naturally to wish that their own children will form a similarly close bond. The third character, Ann, is the smart but unattractive girl who plays Mrs Lovett, and who (as in the passage above) joins Jackus in attempting to discover the truth behind the ghostly phenomena that seem increasingly to haunt their production. Short excerpts from Ann's diary punctuate the omniscient narrator's tale of Jackus. Ann becomes so caught up in the 'misery' of the exploited children that she actually plots a revenge to kill Todd (i.e. Jackus) with his own razor (she replaces the stage prop with the genuine article) in their final scene together.

In the end, Cross manages cleverly to make use of the original Sweeney Todd story to address some of those issues that would be of genuine relevance to her younger readers – guilt, punishment, exploitation, recognizing the consequences of one's actions and the evil of objectifying and 'using' another human being in the pursuit of one's self-interest; she manages, in fact, within the necessarily limited range of a children's fiction ambitiously to alert her readers to some of the same issues of social injustice already implicit in the original penny bloods and melodramas and in Hal Prince's production of Sondheim's musical. In the best gothic tradition, seemingly supernatural phenomena are nicely reconciled with the conditions that govern the 'real' world.

Todd has not always been so fortunate. Whereas various forms of popular culture and entertainment have demonstrated themselves capable of carrying his legacy lightly, more self-consciously serious attention in the traditions of 'high' or avant-garde art tend to stumble, even when attempting to be most innovative. In 1973 the self-styled 'painter, collagist, and poet', Cozette de Charmoy, produced a 'collage novel' bearing the somewhat misleading title, *The True Life of Sweeney Todd*.[121] Charmoy later suggested that her familiarity with Todd – and, by extention, her subsequent exploitation of what she took to be the possibilities of his story – was the result of her own early life experience, and that the book itself was the product of an extended, imaginative gestation. 'The idea of Sweeney Todd', she would write,

> had possessed me for some years before I began his biography. I had grown up in London and his was a familiar name – more than that, the story of the Fleet Street barber was a legend, a horror story from the foggy Victorian past of London. Yet when I asked people what they really knew about him I found they knew surprisingly little.[122]

Charmoy – whom some might describe as an 'intermedial' artist, or perhaps a practitioner of 'visual poetics' – appropriated Todd's character to advance her own, somewhat ambiguous notion of 'romantic heroism'.[123] In Charmoy's work, Sweeney Todd becomes – in the words of one recent critic – 'the embodiment of the supreme social subversive'; or, as yet another commentator on the artist/writer's work put it: 'a brilliant dispassionate dissembler, capable of endless permutations in the pursuit of his art, [and one who] epitomises what Cozette de Charmoy demands from her [own] media'.[124] 'He was all things,' Charmoy herself wrote of her creation, 'mystic, resourceful inventor, dreamer, murderer; perfect criminal, superb lover, dedicated workman; a symbol, if you need a symbol, of the destructive energy of technology.' Unfortunately, the rhetorical gesture of that last clause is rather typical of the whiff of condescension that threatens often to render Charmoy's *True Life* little more than an extended exercise in overly mystified and self-indulgent *auto*biography; her product seems often to have little if anything, in fact, to do with the 'legend' by which she claims to have been so captivated, and more to do with a fanciful turn for self-regarding obscurantism.

In terms of its actual, visual appearance as an artistic 'object', the collage-pastiche of Charmoy's *True Life* is likely to strike today's reader at first glance as (at best) cleverly parodic, or (at worst) already, at the time of its publication, predictably derivative. Its originality might be said to lie in the manner in which it presents itself as something of an earnest, graphic melange of the more familiar work of artists extending from Heath Robinson or Rube Goldberg, on the one hand, to Edward Gorey and Ted Baxter, on the other: like the former pair, Charmoy delights in frequently industrial images of overcomplicated (and often highly politicized) 'machinery' of all kinds; like the latter, the world she presents is characterized most by its element of surreal and even absurdist incongruities. The actual 'text' itself is short and pointedly disjointed (words are inconsistently capitalized, there is little if any conventional punctuation, and the grammar and syntax is frequently fragmented, with only small bits of isolated writing often presented on the plane of each generously large facing, always moving in odd and irregular, unanticipated directions). Again, the primary aesthetic effect is likely to be one of parodic recollection – graphically of the more innovative and less self-consciously subversive collaborations of, say, Don Marquis and George Herriman, and the poetry of e.e. cummings, or of the work of more recent graphic artists such as Jay Cantor and Chris Ware. Overall, however, the look and feel of Charmoy's volume will inevitably recall for almost any twenty-first-century reader precisely the sorts of hand-crafted, cut-out animation sequences that Terry Gilliam had – by the time Charmoy's work was first printed in 1973 – been producing for *Monty Python's Flying Circus* for over four years (since 1969).

In Charmoy's retelling of *The True Life of Sweeney Todd*, the young Todd, though still said to have been raised amidst the slums of London, is in fact the son of an intelligent and curious man who went so far as to construct a laboratory in his attic. He was one of several children born to his parents; his favourite sister, Beth, had been left a cripple after a 'terrible encounter with an old man in the back garden' (it is in enigmatic or cryptic statements such as this that Charmoy's work most obviously and repeatedly recalls that of Edward Gorey).[125] An aunt who marries an embalmer moves to America; Todd later writes to her for some embalming fluid which, subsequently, 'his mother absent-mindedly added … to her husband's bath water. He swelled rapidly and died.' Following the eventual death of Todd's mother, he and his sisters write to the American aunt for money; with it they open a brothel. As a result of his sister Beth's unspecified sexual injury, 'there grew in Sweeney a great passion for women … an interest which led him to meet them in strange places; he spent rich and exhausting hours in their company, loving intensely'. Sweeney emigrates to America, where he becomes a student of his uncle by marriage (his aunt has since died), one 'Mr. F. A. Sullivan in New York, embalmer'. Returning to his sisters in London, Charmoy writes:

> Sweeney was relieved to see his sisters happy and secure. He wished to travel and see the world and better himself. He slit the throats of three rich customers at the brothel. From this he was not only in pocket, but discovered he enjoyed

slitting throats; it fulfilled some secret need in him. From then on he knew he had a special talent. Thirsty for adventure he went abroad. He wished to experience everything.[126]

Whilst in New York, Todd meets a Miss Rachel Rabinovitch, whom he marries. They travel across America before returning to England. 'Arriving in London he was delighted to learn his sisters' brothel was thriving and Beth had found a rich protector.'[127] Sweeney soon opens his own barber shop in Fleet Street, and he and his wife spend hours together 'making experiments'.[128] His wife becomes an expert maker of pies, and Todd devises many machines to help her in her labours, as well as constructing the trap-door in the barber shop.

> Sweeney's need to slit throats would be fulfilled. He was a man of enterprise and determination thinking of feeding the hungry doing a good business at the same time. Soon the barber shop had won a high reputation; he had to employ staff so that he could be alone for his special work. He gave them Saturdays off which made him admired as an enlightened employer, uncommon in those days.[129]

Rachel's pies soon become famous. It is at this point in her text – and specifically in her use of poetic repetition and epizeuxis – that Charmoy at once anticipates the specificity of Sondheim's lyrics in his own later version of Todd, whilst at the same time bringing to her work a notation of anatomy that is close to Homeric in its curiously dispassionate and clinical specificity:

> Keep your razor sharp
> Sweeney
> Keep your razor sharp
> Through skin
> Thyroid cartilage
> Sternohyoid
> Omohyoid
> Sternothyroid
> Innominate
> Internal Jugular
> Anterior Jugular
> External Jugular
> Lingual[130]

Sweeney's shop is visited by such famous customers as John Stuart Mill and Charles Dickens. The death of his sister Beth causes Sweeney to neglect the state of his machines, however, and a female customer raises the familiar complaint of having found a thumbnail in her pie. Police eventually search the premises and discover everything. At Sweeney's trial, Mrs Todd is called to the witness box but collapses, and has to 'be removed to an asylum, the London Lunatic Hospital. She never recovered; she spent the rest of her life in that institution.'[131] Todd is reliably reported to have been executed, but is then mysteriously said to have been spotted in America. 'Some travellers said they had seen him in the mountains; he passed one night in a Chinese opium den; an Indian fighter saw him with a wandering band of Sioux.'[132] 'The End' of the story is announced, abruptly and inconclusively with the turn of a page, in a manner that is otherwise vaguely cinematic.

Charmoy's work is, again, of some modest interest insofar as it antici-pates the irony and the more effective black comedy (as well as the satiric, social commentary) of later re-visitations to the story such as Sondheim's. Her images also highlight those elements of 'monstrous' sexuality that are elsewhere only latent in the barber's narrative. The explicit connections her collage effects between the fictional Todd and the historical Jack the Ripper (and the commercial exploitation of systemic prostitution of all kinds) are admittedly intriguing, as is the speculation that Todd would only naturally have looked to expand and carry on his enterprises in the New World. Charmoy effectively exploits the titillation of Todd's story as a never-to-be-solved mystery no less profitably than had the original version of the tale published by Edward Lloyd well over 100 years earlier. Of the actual visual or graphic 'style' of *The True Life of Sweeney Todd*, Charmoy would later insist:

> [T]he collages are not illustrations in the conventional sense. The images I collaged, using a raw material copperplate and wood engravings from nineteenth century [sic] English and American magazines, particularly from *The Graphic* and *The London Evening News*, are part of the story. I was gratified that some reviewers did understand this, and some saw the disturbance and perturbation. They saw that *The True Life* is not an entertainment and not just a comic turn which may frighten the children. It is a sort of moral tract for the time, if you don't mind morality.

Charmoy's argument for the integral and even organic function of her volume's 'illustrations' is fair enough; her simultaneous tactic of looking to emphasize the supposed profundity and insight of her own work at the expense of its more immediate (and less obviously self-conscious and self-obsessed) sources and predecessors, however, is unnecessarily denigratory, and perhaps betrays her own (understandable) anxiety that *The True Life* would fail to find its desired audience, or that it would even be completely misinterpreted. Quoting from a positive critical review of her own work in a further, brief commentary on the book published in 1980, Charmoy referred her readers to the observations of the arts critic Val Clery, of the Toronto *Globe and Mail*. 'Charmoy', Clery had written, 'rightly [emphasizes] Sweeney as the Industrial Revolutionary Hero, a near-Faustian materialist visionary who, implacable in his belief in progress and human perfectability, pursues it with his razor and ingenious barber's chair and monstrous human pie machine to the ultimate, the economic immortality [sic] of man eating man.'[133]

On the one hand, the essential notion here is the same as that which was more subtly implicit and embodied in the older versions of the story. If she had been working on the project a little later, Charmoy may have had less reason to be so self-conscious or even ashamed of its origins within mass popular culture ('*My* Sweeney', Charmoy had noted with proprietary segregation, 'is not a Victorian "demon barber".'). These days, she would have been less combative and defensive. Debra Kelly has observed that 'there are strategies of subversion at work in all of Charmoy's poetic and visual production' and that 'this questioning of conventional histories and of all forms of received wisdom is essential for an understanding of her project as a whole'.[134] Charmoy is an 'artist' operating in an era that would appear to insist (or, rather, to take it for granted) that *all* artists are by their very nature obliged to be politically subversive, as she herself would wish to be seen, of course, and that 'the artist versus society' is the defining aesthetic struggle in which they engage. In an age when everything is presented as subversive, Charmoy's work seems all too drearily familiar and banal.

Finally, one of the most promising of any such extended, graphic treatments of the Todd story was first proposed in the format of a mock 'penny dreadful' by Neil Gaiman and Michael Zulli in 1992. The larger project of which a 16-page pamphlet was intended originally to have formed only a small part would appear destined, sadly, never to be completed. It was worthy of note if only for the individuals involved in its conception. Gaiman has since emerged as one of the most successful science fiction and fantasy writers of his generation, and an author who has ably demonstrated himself capable of moving between modes and genres as diverse as prose fiction, poetry, children's stories, and screenplays. Zulli has similarly achieved considerable prominence not only as a comic-book artist, but as an illustrator whose best work achieves a delicate line of beauty that recollects the work of the Pre-Raphaelites. Both maintain frequently updated weblogs and journals devoted to their past and current work.[135]

The British-born Gaiman first rose to prominence in America when he scripted the popular *Sandman* comics. *Sandman* was partly the result of a resurgence of comic art, and one of the earlier manifestations of what some had already begun to call the 'graphic novel'; the mode rose to prominence in the wake of the successful resurrection and reconceptualization of an established generation of super-heroes, most notably Batman as *Batman: The Dark Night Returns* (1986). The same year had also witnessed the publication of Art Spiegelman's *Maus: A Survivor's Tale*. While the older traditions of comic art – represented in America since the 1930s by DC Comics and its rival, Marvel, and at least familiar to British audiences in the form of the *band desinée* such as *Tintin* and *Asterix* – had essentially been innocent and concerned primarily with simple entertainment, the illustrated 'novels' of the 1980s and 1990s were darker and more cynical than their predecessors; they were also better scripted and featured more inventive artistic styles – styles that broke the traditional frame in which the older comics had been set. The rebranding of the product was also important. 'In a sense', as Roger Sabin has written, 'the idea of the "graphic novel" was hype. It meant that publishers could sell adult comics to a wider public by giving them another name: specifically, by associating them with novels, and disassociating them with comics. They hoped that, even though the actual stories were about superheroes, people would buy them on the grounds that they represented a "new wave" of liter- ature. With a bit of careful media organization, it was even speculated that a whole new market could be opened up away from the fan shops.'[136] Critics of the form such as Sabin and Paul Gravett would emphasize the fact that the cultish aura of 'darkness' or edginess that supposedly characterized the new forms of the graphic novel had always lain just beneath the surface of more familiar comic strips and characters; for all their seeming innocence, even comics such as Charles Schulz's *Peanuts* – which began syndication in the 1950s – only barely concealed a world of 'inadequacy, disappointment, and melancholy'.[137] Other writers and artists participating in the form, however, would claim that the move from the older forms of illustrated stories to the modern graphic novels signalled a genuine shift in both moral and aesthetic values.

Gaiman's Sandman was an already existing creation that Gaiman resur- rected in 1988; he had first appeared as a member of the 1941 'Justice Society of America' as a character who could defeat his enemies by using sleeping gas (he wore a gas-mask to protect himself); Gaiman's character, however, was 'a pale-faced immortal who inhabits the realm of the unconscious, a mythical figure who is at once attractive and sinister'.[138] Gaiman, as Sabin notes, 'developed his own, sometimes very literary style. The stories would weave together elements from Greek mythology and European folklore, and were often designed to be read as complete graphic novels.... At the same time, it reflected many of the trends in contemporary horror novels and film: plot lines about demons and serial killers were often dealt with in an ironic, blackly humorous style, but could still be very shocking for their level of gore. Finally, there was not some unconnected New Age interest in states of the unconscious.'[139] The initial *Sandman* venture turned into a multi-million selling sequence of graphic novels, and Gaiman subsequently turned his attention to lengthier works of fiction. His interest in folklore and mythology surfaced most prominently in his 2001 novel *American Gods*, a work that takes as its premise the notion that the gods and demons that had been 'imported' from their original homelands to America by immigrants somehow live on in the modern world; some are found employed in the most mundane and prosaic – if still oddly appropriate – professions (the ancient Egyptian god Thoth, for example, operates a small, family-run funeral parlour under the name of 'Mister Ibis' in Cairo, Illinois; the novel also features an Irish leprechaun by the name of Mad Sweeney). Gaiman's well-grounded knowledge of London lore and topography had already been used to excellent effect in *Neverwhere* (1996), in which a young businessman accidentally comes into contact with a bizarre, subterranean, parallel world that exists beneath the city's streets, perpetuating its lost urban history and mythologies.

The delicate and often detailed realism of Zulli's style of illustration was well suited to the substance of Gaiman's several *Sandman* narratives. However, the 'penny dreadful' pamphlet that was published in 1992 as an earnest of their future collaboration on a version of *Sweeney Todd* revealed them to have been willing to take some considerable risks when embarking on a venture that would necessarily have carried with it a far greater burden of both textual and visual 'baggage', as it were. Zulli's published work relating to the Todd project (apart from one colour illustration intended originally to have served as a cover) consists almost entirely of deliberately rough pencil sketches rather than completed graphic work of narrative art.

It is more than likely that something of the mood and the neo-gothic sensibility that would doubtlessly have characterized any work that might otherwise have resulted from the proposed collaboration between Gaiman and Zulli will somehow make itself felt, albeit indirectly, in the scenic design and – even more generally – the overall 'look' and visual presentation of director Tim Burton's much anticipated, forthcoming film adaptation of Sondheim's *Sweeney Todd*, scheduled to reach cinema screens both in Britain and in America in January 2008. It is no surprise that rumours suggesting that Sondheim's 1979 theatrical venture was to be turned into a movie had circulated for some considerable time; such rumours, however, tended likewise – and no less surprisingly – to vary wildly in point of detail. Most speculated with occasionally inspired ingenuity regarding the prospects and problems any such adaptation would present. Who was to direct it? Who would feature in it? When and where was it to be filmed? Of course, too, there always remained that question which in every such instance is likely most to exercise the minds of producers, in particular: who will want to see it, and how much money will it make?

Certainly, the ever-increasing status of Sondheim's work over the course of the past two decades and more has fuelled the more recent buzz of rumours around *Sweeney Todd*, although, again, such speculation is as old as the musical itself. In a brief article included in the December 1979 issue of the New York theatre guide, *Playbill*, Frank Shanbaker – a private individual otherwise unconnected professionally with the entertainment industry or show business – wrote of his experiences as one of the financial backers of the original Broadway production of Sondheim's *Sweeney Todd*. Shanbaker's attention had been captured quite by accident two years earlier by an unusual advertisement that he chanced to encounter in the rather more typically sombre pages of the *New York Times*. The singular item – the solicitation of which managed at once to announce itself in terms that were utterly clear and unambiguous, while yet remaining tantalizingly cryptic in its possibilities – instantly grabbed his attention: 'NEW STEPHEN SONDHEIM MUSICAL OPEN FOR INVESTMENT'.[140] Shanbaker jumped at the chance to – as he put it – see his name 'in a limited partnership agreement along with those of Prince, Sondheim, Lansbury, and Cariou'.[141] It was, after all, the closest he was ever likely to come to seeing his name up in lights – and in lights on Broadway, at that.

In actual fact, Shanbaker appears to have been well aware that the romantic and sentimental fantasies that can seem so easily to attach themselves, at least in the minds of the uninitiated, to the world of 'the Theatre' – a world which, even a generation ago or more, had less to do with anything even vaguely resembling it in the real world, than it did with a vision conjured, perhaps, by the confused recollection of movies like *All About Eve* – remained precisely that: fantasies; he suffered no illusions when it came to the possibilities of making any money from such a venture. Not without reason was the New York backer cautious even as late as ten months subsequent to the musical's opening – and after the production had garnered its accolades from both the New York Drama Critics Circle and the Tony Awards – regarding any possible return on his investment. 'By the time it opened [in March 1979]', Shanbaker carefully recalled, '*Sweeney Todd* had lost $150,000 during previews and had gone over budget on its set to the tune of $200,000.' 'The reviews were mostly raves', he continued,

> but they didn't create any stampedes at the box office. As fond as I was of the show, I was convinced I'd been correct not to expect any return on my investment. I kept thinking, 'Look, the production was greeted with such critical hosannas as "Joy to the world – *Sweeney Todd* is here" (*N.Y Daily News*) and "You must see *Sweeney Todd*" (*N.Y. Post*). Isn't it enough to be associated with a *succès d'estime?*'[142]

As matters so turned out, for all its critical success, and after a 16-month run on Broadway, Sondheim's *Sweeney Todd* as first produced at the Uris Theater in 1979–80 still repaid only 59 per cent on its initial investment. As director Hal Prince reasoned some years after the show closed: 'I think if we were doing the show right now, we'd have a devil of a time getting it done on Broadway. Now, mind you, there is Steve and there is me, and maybe some good-hearted person would be willing to lose money. But it did lose money. It may have won every award in the book but it didn't pay back.'[143]

Non-professional financial supporters such a Shanbaker (known in the theatre business as 'angels') may never have lived to see any profit from the original Broadway production of the show, yet even as early as 1980 – and

301

at the post-Tony Awards height of its run at the Uris – Shanbaker's hopes had been buoyed somewhat by the fact that there had already been 'talk of a movie deal'.[144] Such 'talk' – as seems so often to be the case – in the short term led to nothing. The subsequent critical and popular success of film versions of stage musicals including *Evita* (1996) and *Chicago* (2002), however, began to alert Hollywood producers to the fact that there just might once again – after an exceptionally long dry spell, thanks in large part to such high-profile box-office disasters and now-legendary miscalculations as *Jesus Christ Superstar* (1973), *Mame* (1974), *Tommy* (1975), *Lisztomania* (1975), *Hair* (1979), *Xanadu* (1980), *Annie* (1982) and *A Chorus Line* (1985) – be an audience for such (non-animated) film musicals. After all, if director Alan Parker could transform Andrew Lloyd Weber and Tim Rice's politically confused and melodically tepid biography of an unscrupulous Argentinean prostitute-made-good into box-office gold (and could, in the process, make even Madonna look like something approaching a competent actress on the screen), then even a musical that revolved around the subject of cannibalism would at least seem to stand as good a chance as any of enjoying real success.

Rumours of a possible movie version of Sondheim's 'musical thriller' continued to circulate in trade publications and – later – on the internet for years. Initially, it had generally been assumed that any film version of the show would take advantage of the box-office appeal of Angela Lansbury as Mrs Lovett; the years immediately following her appearance in the role in both the Broadway production and throughout the subsequent, national touring company of *Sweeney Todd* had seen the veteran actress's appeal sky-rocket to new heights with the unprecedented success of her Sunday-night television series *Murder, She Wrote*, and for a period in the mid-1980s Lansbury topped opinion polls as one of the most beloved and 'trusted' women in America. The now historic videotaped performance that was recorded at the culmination of the national tour of *Sweeney Todd* at the Dorothy Chandler Pavilion in Los Angeles in 1982 (with Prince's staging directed for the small screen by Terry Hughes, and George Hearn in the title role of Todd), at least preserved Lansbury's interpretation of the role as a matter of record. A DVD edition of the performance was finally released in 2004, at which time one popular online reviewer commented:

> From a performance standpoint, the cast is superb. It is clear why Lansbury won the Tony Award for her performance; her Mrs. Lovett is everything the role demands—equal parts comic, calculating, and even a little crazy. George Hearn (who would later gain huge fame with the role of Albin in the musical version of *La Cage Aux Folles*) plays the title character with a mix of bluster and bitterness that accentuates Todd's homicidal tendencies. Although not the original Sweeney (sadly, Len Cariou's Tony-winning work in the role is left for memory to keep immortalized), Hearn never once hints that the character

is not his own invention. Everyone else, from Edmund Lyndeck's ominous Judge Turpin to Ken Jennings's endearing Tobias Ragg, is pitch-perfect and terrific. If you are not moved by the overlapping mania of 'God, That's Good' or touched by the haunting duet 'Pretty Women,' there is something wrong with your pleasure centres.[145]

In 2001, director Lonny Price (who had himself starred in Sondheim's brilliant but initially ill-fated follow-up to *Sweeney Todd* on Broadway, 1981's *Merrily We Roll Along*) offered yet another filmed 'concert' version of Sondheim's musical, produced this time with help of the San Francisco Symphony Orchestra, and once again featuring Hearn in the role of Todd, with Patti LuPone as Mrs Lovett (Lupone soon thereafter took up the role on stage in John Doyle's 2005 Broadway production).

Such video and DVD releases – along with its increasing incorporation, as already noted in the previous section, within the repertoires of some of the major opera houses across the world – have at the very least helped to keep Sondheim's *Sweeney Todd* very much in the public eye. The director Sam Mendes – shortly after his much-applauded success as the company director of London's Donmar Warehouse, with productions such as *The Glass Menagerie* (1995) and *Cabaret* (1998) and, more particularly, following his 1999 Academy-award winning film *American Beauty* – was rumoured by many to be taking on a full-scale film adaptation of Sondheim's musical as his next big project (Mendes's wife, the actress Kate Winslet, was said to be keen on the role of Mrs Lovett), but once again, as in the past, such rumours came to nothing.

Finally, in February 2007, DreamWorks Studio and Warner Bros. announced that director Tim Burton had begun co-production at Pinewood Studios, just outside greater London, on a film adaptation of Sondheim's *Sweeney Todd* (plans for the production had been formally announced by the two companies in August 2006). The cast was soon revealed as featuring the hugely popular actor Johnny Depp in the title role, and Helena Bonham Carter as Mrs Lovett. Also to be included in the film were Alan Rickman as Judge Turpin, Timothy Spall as Beadle Bamford, Sacha Baron Cohen as Signor Adolfo Pirelli, Jamie Campbell Bowen as Anthony Hope, Jayne Wisener as Johanna, and veteran actor Christopher Lee as 'The Gentleman Ghost'. The film was slated to be distributed in the United States by Paramount, and internationally by DreamWorks. 'I've always wanted to do a musical,' director Burton commented at the time of the studio's official announcement regarding the production, 'and *Sweeney Todd* is my favourite. Stephen's blend of humour, horror, and emotion is something that has always connected with me.' Sondheim, it was reported, joined the director in his enthusiasm. 'Sometimes a story or stage production has to wait a long time until the right people come together to turn it into a motion picture,' the composer observed: 'That's what has happened with *Sweeney Todd*, and I'm excited as well as confident that it will be a first-rate and startling movie.'[146] Sondheim had reason enough for some trepidation, however; his own stage musicals have tended to resist the transfer to the big screen, and he had been burned by Hollywood on more than one occasion before. Although he had of course shared to some extent in the surprising box-office success of Robert Wise's 1961 *West Side Story*, Mervyn Le Roy's subsequent adaptation of *Gypsy* (1962) was fatally flawed by the casting of Rosalind Russell in a role that patently belonged to Ethel Merman, and *A Funny Thing Happened on the Way to the Forum* – directed for the screen in 1966 by Melvin Frank – seemed to slight the very musical numbers that had made the show a comic hit on Broadway (the tightly scripted Plautine comedy also seemed generically adrift in the cinema; Pauline Kael wrote in *The New Yorker* that the film proceeded by fits and starts and left jokes suspended in mid-air, 'like coitus interruptus going on forever'[147]). *A Little Night Music*, filmed in Austria in 1977, while the composer was in the midst of writing *Sweeney Todd* for the stage, had also been musically eviscerated and dreadfully miscast (with Elizabeth Taylor taking the lead role away from Glynis Johns). Sondheim's attempts to write incidental music or individual numbers for film soundtracks had likewise been alternately muted if effective (*Stavisky*, 1974) or – through no fault of his own – disastrous (*The Birdcage*, 1996).

The news that Burton would once again be teaming up with Depp on the project (*Sweeney Todd* was to mark their sixth collaboration as entertainers) was initially greeted by dismay by some Sondheim devotees, who felt that the director was better equipped to deal with the decidedly more modest achievements of musicians such as Danny Elfman than with the veteran Broadway composer; most film commentators, at least, seemed to feel that Burton's own well-known feel for the macabre in popular culture would sit nicely with Sondheim's more rigorously intelligent parodic appropriation of Grand Guignol theatrical tradition. Depp's box-office popularity, certainly, had soared since he had decided to portray the character of 'Jack Sparrow' in Disney's *Pirates of the Caribbean* franchise in the manner of a buccaneering Keith Richards. Yet his cinematic partnerships with the persistently adolescent if often darkly picturesque palette of Burton's visual imagination had proven in the past to be somewhat hit-and-miss; the early success of *Edward Scissorhands* (1990) had not been followed up to any great effect in such films as the unremarkable remake of Roald Dahl's *Charlie and the Chocolate Factory* (2005), or in the disastrously incoherent *Sleepy Hollow* of 1999. Sondheim himself was thought to have left the actor slightly puzzled early in the planning stages of the film when he insisted that Depp take a voice test before being confirmed in the title role; as a spokesman for the then 76-year-old composer said, simply: 'he wants to make sure that all versions of his works are the best possible'.[148] (Sondheim could, again, be forgiven for not fully placing his trust in the abilities of contemporary film actors to handle the often notoriously difficult demands of his music; Madonna had recorded three of his songs for the film *Dick Tracy* in 1989, insisting on doing only two 'takes' of each number.)[149] Depp, for his own part, responded in a manner that seemed to suggest that he was worryingly unfamiliar with the depth of talent and professional training necessary convincingly to 'put over' such numbers as 'Epiphany' in Sondheim's *Sweeney Todd*. 'He finds it funny', one business associate of the actor was said to have remarked, 'that there are questions about his voice, as he has been singing all his life.'[150] 'Tim took a risk when he asked me to play Sweeney Todd,' Depp subsequently confessed as filming on the project neared its completion in May 2007,

> because neither he nor I knew if I could sing when I accepted it. I went into the recording studio with a friend of mine to see if I could do it. My singing's not unlike the mating call of a rutting stag. It's a strange sound, but I haven't been fired yet.[151]

With his worryingly persistent, post-production judgement and reiteration that the performance demanded of him had been 'a real challenge', Depp's voice remained for many fans of the film's score a genuine concern. (In the only other musical in which he had appeared – 1989's Cry Baby – the actor's vocal performance was eventually dubbed.) Yet another remark concerning the film attributed to Depp in the popular press shortly after filming had been completed, however – namely, his confused suggestion that it had helped him to conceive of the project as 'a silent film but with music' – was positively terrifying in its intimation of a possibly profound misapprehension regarding Sondheim's achievement. Be that as it may, when exclusive footage of a short scene (featuring the first act duet, 'My Friends') from the Burton film was previewed at the Venice film festival in September 2007, the response appeared to be generally welcoming. Moreover, in the brief passage of dialogue that was included in the sequence, some critics and journalists also appeared pleasantly surprised that Depp might just finally have mastered a convincing cockney accent – a bit of artistry that he had not exactly honed to perfection in the past.

All such concerns aside, expectations for the film throughout the summer and autumn of 2007 remained unusually high. Certainly, the cultural and artistic 'status' of Sondheim's original 1979 musical adaptation of *Sweeney Todd*, in particular, stands – at the current critical moment – higher and more secure than ever before; there is little if any reason to suggest that the perceived magnitude of Sondheim's achievement in that same work that will diminish rather than grow even stronger with the passing of time. Quite the contrary, Sondheim's version of Todd's story is a dramatic composition the original production of which is recognized now to stand as having marked a truly ground-breaking moment in the formal history of the American musical as a genre; *Sweeney Todd* constituted an event, moreover, that initiated the further development of entirely new and more ambitious strands of representation within the forms of music and in the aesthetics of the theatre, generally, even while tacitly asserting the incontrovertible legitimacy of its own claim to a place within the traditions of opera.

Finally, if the artistic and cultural significance of Sondheim's work, with which the film-makers have been entrusted, and which they choose (at their peril) to change or modify – remains assuredly secure, so too does the relevance of the most essential of the several myths that seem to express themselves within the barber's story. They are myths the many inflections of which, together, gesture towards a deeper and greater significance that is itself at once both curiously mercurial and unchanging. At the very least – and on some very basic level – the tale of Sweeney Todd can be interpreted as expressing a particular aspect of humanity, one that developed over time so far as to itself embody the spirit of an age. Todd's story encapsulates the most essential features and characteristics of the modern world – a world to which we ourselves stand as inheritors. Its greatest achievements have been borne of an impulse that has, at its best, expressed itself in the boundless exuberance and courage of its search for knowledge, and in its constant desire for some greater sense of understanding and self-definition. It is also, however, a world which, at its worst, has facilitated grotesque and unprecedented displays of appetite and greed, and so witnessed the devastation and destruction consequent upon such heedless and unfettered acts of consumption. The tale of Sweeney Todd is a story that not only enacts within its narrative the desires that are to be witnessed within the spectacle of our modern selves, but also depicts the cruelty of the technological processes and the dehumanizing effects of the industrial environments that have, in turn, been entailed by the very 'progress' to which our culture of enlightenment has aspired; and so, it is a story that highlights the culpability of that same industrial technology in the debasement of humanity itself, and in the dehumanization within the environment of those creatures who shaped it so as to take the form of desolation that it can now, alone, display. As a cautionary tale for our times, the tale of Sweeney Todd could hardly be bettered.

Notes

Preface

1   Thomas W. Erle, *Letters from a Theatrical Scene-Painter* (London: 1880); repr. in Michael Kilgariff, ed., *The Golden Age of Melodrama: Twelve 19th-Century Melodramas* (London: Wolfe Publishing Ltd, 1974), p. 267.

2   In the many versions that tell the barber's story in the English tradition, Sweeney Todd's name is occasionally spelled 'Sweeny Todd' or 'Sweeney Tod'. Mrs Lovett, likewise, occasionally appears as Mrs Lovatt; her given name is often Margery or some variation thereupon, although she also appears (as in, for example, the versions of the story written by Christopher Bond and Stephen Sondheim) as 'Nellie'. For the sake of uniformity, and unless otherwise indicated, the characters will be referred to as 'Sweeney Todd' and 'Mrs Lovett' throughout.

3   'A Leader Writer in *The Times* has advanced the interesting theory that it was the astonishing popularity of Sweeney Todd's legend in early and mid-Victorian times that caused a good old English word to lapse into disrepute among respectable people. In the late 'nineties "when the public sacrificed almost anything to be genteel, . . . *Sweeney Todd* was considered vulgar too".' See E.S. Turner, *Boys Will Be Boys: The Story of Sweeney Todd, Deadwood Dick, Sexton Blake, Billy Bunter, Dick Barton, et al.* (London: Michael Joseph, 1948), p. 37.

4   'Penny Dreadfuls' in *The Times Literary Supplement*, 15 March 1941. See also Turner, *Boys Will be Boys*, p. 37.

5   Charles Dickens, *Master Humphrey's Clock*; repr. in Charles Dickens, *American Notes, Master Humphrey's Clock, and 'Life of Dickens'* (London and Aylesbury: Hazell, Watson & Viney Ltd, n.d.), p. 289.

6   'Dog Worship' in *All The Year Round: A weekly journal conducted by Charles Dickens*, vol. 17, no. 412 (21 October 1876), pp. 130–1.

7   Ibid., p. 131.

8   '"Parliament" Section, "Hairdressers" Bill: Rejection by House of Commons' in *The Times* (Saturday, 2 July 1949), p. 2; Issue 51423; col. E. See also William Kent, *London Mystery & Mythology* (London and New York: Staples Press, 1952), p. 249.

9   Philip Howard, 'Master barbers are apt to alarm the unwary', in *The Times* (Wednesday, 3 January 1973), p. 3; Issue 58671; col. A.

10 William Safire, 'Snip, and another tradition is cut', reprinted from *The New York Times* in *The Times* (26 August 1982), p. 8; Issue 61321; col. F.

11 Of the several figures mentioned here, only Richard Whittington (d. 1423) and Samuel Pepys (1633–1703) were Londoners by birth. Samuel Johnson (1709–84) was a native of Lichfield; Dickens (1812–70) was born in Portsmouth. The identity and birthplace of Jack the Ripper, of course, remains unknown.

12 For the anecdote concerning the builder Mr Waller and the reconstruction of 153 Fleet Street following the Second World War, see Kent, *London Mystery & Mythology*, pp. 248–9.

13 Ibid., p. 250.

14 John Webster, *The Duchess of Malfi* (IV.ii.162–54) in John Webster, *Three Plays*, ed. David Gunby (London: Penguin, 1972), pp. 255–6.

15 Charles Dickens, *Martin Chuzzlewit*, ed P. N. Furbank (Harmondsworth, Middlesex: Penguin, 1968), p. 651.

Chapter 1

1 James Joyce, *Ulysses. The Corrected Text*, ed. Hans Walter Gabler with Wolfhard Steppe and Claus Melcher (London: Penguin Books, 1984), p. 140.

2 Quotations and many of the details regarding the Pickton case in the discussion that follows have been drawn from the wire report of the Reuters News Agency (11 March 2004). For an extended account of the circumstances surrounding the Pickton murders, see Charles Mudede, 'Death Farm: The Geography of Pig Farmer Robert Pickton, the Man Suspected of Having Killed Over 60 Vancouver, BC, Sex Workers' in *The Stranger.com*, vol. 13, no. 7 (5 November 2003), pp. 1–16. Additional reporting for the article was undertaken by Bess Lovejoy and Lesley Selcer, with further research contributed by Jane Berentson. See also *The New York Times* (Saturday, 23 November 2002).

3 As of January 2007, Pickton's trial was still ongoing. He had originally (in January 2006) pleaded not guilty to 27 charges of first-degree murder in the British Columbia Supreme Court. In March 2006 one of the counts was dropped, and again in August 2006 the charges were reduced from 27 to six counts, because the court felt that trying all remaining 26 counts at one time would place an unreasonable burden on any jury. A Media Publication Ban Order (21 November 2006) was placed on any further details from the trial until a jury had been chosen.

4 Alexis Soyer, *A Shilling Cookery for the People* (London: George Routledge and Co., 1855); quoted in Elizabeth Orsini, *The Book of Pies* (London: Pan, 1981), p. 70.

5 On the life and career of Alexis Soyer, see Ruth Brandon, *The People's Chef: Alexis Soyer, A Life in Seven Courses* (Chichester: Wiley, 2004). See also Lewis Jones, 'The Birth of the Restaurant' in *The Telegraph*, 'Arts' (22 May 2004), pp. 6–7; and Mark Kurlansky, *Choice Cuts: A Miscellany of Food Writing* (London: Vintage, 2002), pp. 118; 240. Note also Ruth Cowan, *Relish: The Extraordinary Life of Alexis Soyer, Victorian Celebrity Chef* (London: Weidenfeld and Nicolson, 2006).

6 Brandon, *The People's Chef*, p. 208.

7 Kathryn Hughes, *The Short Life and Long Times of Mrs Beeton* (London: Fourth Estate, 2005), pp. 201–2.

8 Rosemary Baird, *Mistress of the House: Great Ladies and Grand Houses, 1670–1830* (London: Weidenfeld and Nicolson, 2003), p. 43.

9   Jane Austen, *Pride and Prejudice*, ed. James Kinsley, intro. by Isobel Armstrong (Oxford: Oxford University Press, 1990), p. 58; see also Jane Austen, *Catherine and Other Writings*, eds. Margaret Anne Doody and Douglas Murray (Oxford: Oxford University Press, 1993), p. 338n.

10 Eliza Haywood, *The History of Miss Betsy Thoughtless*, ed. Christine Blouch (Peterborough, Ontario: Broadview Press, 1998), p. 52.

11 Elizabeth Gaskell, *Cranford*, ed. Elizabeth Porges Watson (Oxford: Oxford University Press, 1972), p. 3.

12 Thomas Macauley, Letter to his Sisters (August 13 1832).

13 Kurlansky, *Choice Cuts*, p. 118.

14 John Percival, *The Great Famine: The Irish Potato Famine, 1845–51* (London: BBC Books, 1995), pp. 75–6.

15 On the circumstances of Soyer's participation in the Crimean War, see A.N. Wilson, *The Victorians* (London: Random House, 2003), pp. 175–200. See also 'Marching on its Stomach' in *The Times* (19 August 2004), p. 11.

16 Originally from *The Globe* (1841); cited in Brandon, *The People's Chef*, p. xi.

17 Charles Dickens, *The Pickwick Papers*, ed. James Kinsley (Oxford: Clarendon Press, 1986), p. 106.

18 Laura Mason and Catherine Brown, *The Taste of Britain*. Foreward by Hugh Fearnley-Whittingstall (London: HarperCollins, 2006), p. 412.

19 See Earl Stanhope, *Life of the Rt. Hon. William Pitt* (1879), vol. 3, chap. 43, and G. Rose, *Diaries and Correspondence* (1860), vol. 2, p. 233 (entry for 23 January 1806).

20 See Orsini, *The Book of Pies*, p. 116.

21 Petronius, *The Satyricon*, trans. William Arrowsmith (New York: Signet/New American Library, 1959), p. 47.

22 See Margaret Visser, *Much Depends on Dinner* (London: Viking Penguin, 1991), *passim*.

23 Peter Ackroyd, *London: The Biography* (London: Vintage, 2000), p. 316.

24 Eliza Acton, *Modern Cookery for Private Families* (1845), with an Introduction by Elizabeth Ray (Lewes, East Sussex: Southover Press, 1993), p. 164.

25 Alexis Soyer, from *A Shilling Cookery for the People*, quoted in Orsini, p. 26.

26 Bram Stoker, *Dracula*, ed. Marjorie Howes (London: J.M. Dent/Everyman, 1993), p. 43.

27 R.W. Harris, *England in the Eighteenth Century: A Balanced Constitution and New Horizons* (London: Blanford Press, 1963), p. 5.

28 Raymond Williams, 'Introduction' to Charles Dickens's *Dombey and Son* (Harmondsworth, Middlesex: Penguin, 1970), pp. 11–12.

29 Henry Fielding, *An Inquiry into the Causes of the Late Increase of Robbers and Related Writings*, ed. Malvin R. Zirker (Oxford: Clarendon Press, 1988); see also Fergus Linnane, 'Introduction: The Wild Eighteenth Century' in *London's Underworld: Three Centuries of Vice and Crime* (London: Robson Books, 2003), pp. xi–xx.

30 Quoted in Linnane, *London's Underworld*, p. xii.

31 Linnane, *London's Underworld*, p. xiii.

32 Juvenal, Satire III, in *The Sixteen Satires*, trans. Peter Green (Harmondsworth, Middlesex: Penguin, 1967), p. 97.

33 For a general discussion of the convergence of the tastes for criminal fiction and gothic horror, and the manner in which the former anticipated many of the concerns

of the latter, see Lucy Moore, 'Introduction' to *Con Men and Cutpurses: Scenes from the Hogarthian Underworld* (London: Penguin, 2000), pp. ix–xxiv.

34 Turner, *Boys Will Be Boys*, p. 21.

35 See Fred Botting, *Gothic*, in *The New Critical Idiom* series (London and New York: Routledge, 1996), pp. 62–90.

36 On Vidocq, see James Morton, *The First Detective: The Life and Revolutionary Times of Eugene-François Vidocq, Criminal, Spy, and Private Eye* (London: Edbury, 2004).

37 Stoker, *Dracula*, p. 70.

38 From 'Squaring the Circle' in O'Henry [William Sydney Porter], *Selected Stories*, ed. Guy Davenport (London: Penguin, 1993), p. 138.

39 On the Ratcliff Highway Murders see, for example, 'Three East End Murders' in Steve Jones, *London, The Sinister Side* (Nottingham: Wicked Publications, 1986), p. 34; see also Ackroyd, *London*, pp. 274; 678. See also some of the original reportage regarding the murders: 'The Late Murders' in *The Times* (Friday, 13 December 1811); p. 3; Issue 8472; col. B; 'Interment of Mr and Mrs Marr, and Infant Son' in *The Times* (Monday, 16 December 1811); p. 3; Issue 8474; col. C.

40 See Jan Bondeson's rather odd and unsubstantiated account in *The London Monster: Terror in the Streets in 1790* (Stroud, Gloucestershire: Tempus, 2000).

41 Stanley Reynolds, Review of 'Jack the Ripper', BBC, in *The Times* (Saturday, 14 July 1973), p. 9; Issue 58834; col. F.

42 'Echo of Surgeons' Square', *Letter to the Lord Advocate, Disclosing the Accomplices, Secrets, and Other Facts Relative to the Murderers, etc.* (Edinburgh: Menzies, 1829), n.p.; see also Brian Bailey in *Burke and Hare: The Year of the Ghouls* (London and Edinburgh: Mainstream Publishing, 2002), pp. 135–43.

43 Sir Jacob Epstein, cited in *Oxford Dictionary of Quotations*, ed. Angela Partington (Oxford: Oxford University Press, 1992), p. 278: 5.

44 'On Murder Considered as One of the Fine Arts' in *The Posthumous Works of Thomas De Quincey*, ed. Alexander H. Japp, Volume I: *Suspiria de Profundis with Other Essays* (London: William Heinemann, 1891), pp. 77–84.

45 See the commentary of Marilyn Gaull, *English Romanticism: The Human Context* (London: W.W. Norton, 1988), p. 40.

46 Thomas De Quincey, *Confessions of an English Opium-Eater*, ed. Alethea Hayter (London: Penguin, 1987), p. 174.

47 George Orwell, 'Decline of the English Murder' in *Essays* (London: Penguin, 1994), p. 345.

48 Ibid.

49 Ibid., p. 348.

50 Ibid., p. 345.

51 Neil Mackay, 'The Decline and Fall of British Murder' in *Sunday Herald* (1 July 2001).

52 Stephen Sondheim and John Weidman, *Assassins* (New York: Theater Communications Group, 1991), Scene 16: 95.

53 'Query and Response from Wolverhampton', featured in 'Questions Answered' in *The Times* 'Register' (Wednesday, 25 August 2004), p. 54.

54 Iona and Peter Opie, *The Lore and Language of Schoolchildren* (Oxford: Oxford University Press, 1959; 1967), p. 163.

55 Henry James, 'A Romance of Certain Old Clothes' in Michael Cox and R.A. Gilbert, eds, *Victorian Ghost Stories* (Oxford: Oxford University Press, 1991), p. 97.

56 Stoker, *Dracula*, p. 44.

57 Peter Lorie, *Superstitions: A Book of Ancient Lore* (London: Simon and Schuster, 1992), p. 86.

58 Michael Pickering helpfully sums up six major classifications or approaches to cannibalism based on cultural and archaeological evidence in his 'Consuming Doubts: What Some People Ate? Or What Some People Swallowed?' in Laurence R. Goldman, ed., *The Anthropology of Cannibalism* (London: Bergin and Garvey, 1999), pp. 52–3.

59 See Peter J. Kitson, 'Sustaining the Romantic and Racial Self: Eating People in the '"South Seas"' in Timothy Martin, ed., *Cultures of Taste/Theories of Appetite – Eating Romanticism* (New York: Palgrave-Macmillan), pp. 77–96.

60 Margaret Visser, *The Rituals of Dinner: The Origins, Evolution, Eccentricities, and Meaning of Table Manners* (London: Penguin, 1991), p. 7.

61 Moira Martingale, *Cannibal Killers: The Impossible Monsters* (London: Robert Hale Limited, 1993), p. 2.

62 Ibid.

63 See, for example, Bill Ashcroft, 'Primitive and Wingless: The Colonial Subject as a Child' in Wendy S. Jacobson, ed., *Dickens and the Children of Empire* (London: Palgrave, 2000), p. 192.

64 Laurence R. Goldman, 'From Pot to Polemic: Uses and Abuses of Cannibalism' in L. Goldman, ed., *The Anthropology of Cannibalism* (London: Bergin & Garvey, 1999), p. 1.

65 William Arens, *The Man-Eating Myth: Anthropology and Anthropophagy* (Oxford: Oxford University Press, 1979), p. 18; Don Gardner, 'Anthropophagy, Myth, and the Subtle Ways of Ethnocentrism' in Goldman, ed., *The Anthropology of Cannibalism*, p. 28.

66 Herodotus, *The Histories*, trans. Aubrey de Selincourt, (London: Penguin, 1954), Book III.38, p. 298.

67 Visser, *The Rituals of Dinner*, p. 7.

68 James Frazer, *The Golden Bough: A Study in Magic and Religion* (London: Penguin Books, 1986), pp. 593–6.

69 Stoker, *Dracula*, pp. 235–6.

70 'Fijians Apologize for Cannibal Murder', *Associated Press* (Friday, 17 October 2003).

71 James Hynes, '99' in *Publish or Perish* (New York: Picador, 1997), p. 99.

72 Christopher Columbus, *The Log of Christopher Columbus*, trans. Robert H. Fuson, (Southampton: Ashford Press, 1987), p. 138.

73 Ibid., p. 115.

74 Arens, *The Man-Eating Myth*, p. 45.

75 Richard Hough, *Captain James Cook: A Biography* (London: Hodder and Stoughton, 1994), p. 278.

76 *The Journals of Captain Cook*, ed. Philip Edwards (London: Penguin, Penguin Classics, 1999), p. 320.

77 See Peter Hulme, 'Introduction: The Cannibal Scene' in Francis Barker, Peter Hulme and Margaret Iversen, eds., *Cultural Margins: Cannibalism and the Colonial World* (Cambridge: Cambridge University Press, 1999), p. 23; see also Gananath Obeyesekere, '"British Cannibals"': Contemplation of an Event in the Death and Resurrection of James Cook, Explorer', *Critical Inquiry* 18 (Summer 1998), 630–54.

78 R.M. Ballantyne, *The Cannibal Isles* (1869), from Chapter 9. http://www.athelstone.co.uk/ballanty/cannibal/canis09.htm.

79 Michel de Montaigne, 'Of Cannibals' (1578–80) in *The Complete Essays of Montaigne*, trans. Donald Frame (Stanford: Stanford University Press, 1957), p. 155.

80 Ibid.

81 Voltaire, *Candide and Other Stories,* trans. Roger Pearson (Oxford: Oxford University Press, 2006), p. 42.

82 Stanislaw Lec, *Unkempt Thoughts*, trans. Jacek Galazka (New York: St Martin's Press, 1962), p. 78.

83 Edward Leslie, *Desperate Journeys, Abandoned Souls: True Stories of Castaways and Other Survivors* (London: Macmillan, 1988), pp. 201–2.

84 'The Wreck of the Mignonette' in *The Times* (19 September 1884), p. 5; Issue 31243; col. A.

85 'The Mignonette Case' in *The Times* (7 November 1884), p. 11; Issue 31285; col. D.

86 'The Court of Queen's Bench' in *The Times* (10 December 1884), p. 9; Issue 31313; col. C.

87 Ibid.

88 Lu Xun, 'Diary of a Madman', trans. William Lyell, in Maynard Mack, gen. ed., *The Norton Anthology of World Masterpieces* (London and New York: Norton & Co., 1997), p. 2732.

89 Mary S. Lovell, *A Rage to Live: A Biography of Richard and Isabel Burton* (London: Little, Brown, and Company, 1998), p. 413.

90 Max Jones, *The Last Great Quest: Captain Scott's Antarctic Sacrifice* (Oxford: Oxford University Press, 2004). See also 'The Lost Boys' in *TLS* (21 May 2004), p. 32.

91 Sir Ranulph Fiennes, *Captain Scott* (London: Hodder and Stoughton, 2003), p. 9.

92 Michael Smith, *Sir James Wordie: Polar Crusader* (Edinburgh: Birlinn Ltd, 2004).

93 For a general account of this episode see Sarah Wise, *The Italian Boy: Murder and Grave-Robbery in 1830s London* (London: Jonathan Cape, 2004).

94 Ibid., p. 173.

95 Geoffrey Abbott, *A Macabre Miscellany: One Thousand Grisly and Unusual Facts from Around the World* (London: Virgin Books, 2004), pp. 163–4.

96 Wise, *The Italian Boy*, p. 173.

97 Extracts from Hackney Vestry Minutes, January 1795, Greater London Record Office P79/JN1/157; cited in Andrew Saint and Gillian Darley, eds., *The Chronicles of London* (London: Weidenfeld and Nicolson, 1994), pp. 160–1.

98 Ian Campbell Ross, *Laurence Sterne: A Life* (Oxford: Oxford University Press, 2001), p. 419.

99 Recounted in Abbott, *A Macabre Miscellany*, pp. 20–1.

100 Ibid.

101 Joseph Conrad, *The Heart of Darkness* (London: W.W. Norton, 1971), p. 35.

102 Gen. William Booth, *In Darkest England and the Way Out* (New York: Funk & Wagnalls, 1891), pp. 11–12.

103 Walter Besant, *All Sorts and Conditions of Men*, ed. Helen Small (Oxford: Oxford University Press, 1997), pp. 28–9.

104 Cited in Asa Briggs, *Victorian Cities* (London: Penguin, 1990), p. 315.

105 Conrad, *Heart of Darkness*, p. 5.

106 Visser, *The Rituals of Dinner*, p. 31.

107 Roy Porter, *English Society in the Eighteenth Century* (London: Penguin, 1982), p. 21.

108 Ben Rogers, *Beef and Liberty: Roast Beef, John Bull, and the English Nation* (London: Chatto & Windus, 2003), p. 3. See also Julia Twigg, 'Vegetarianism and the Meaning of Meat' in Anne Murcott, ed., *Sociology of Food and Eating* (Aldershot: Gower Publishing Company Ltd, 1983), *passim*.

109 *Sophie in London* (1786), trans. and ed. Clare Williams (London: Jonathan Cape, 1933), p. 132.

110 Reprinted in Ackroyd, *London*, p. 315.

111 Charles Dickens, *Oliver Twist*, ed. Angus Wilson (Harmondsworth, Middlesex: Penguin, 1966), p. 203.

112 See Steve Jones, *Wicked London* (Nottingham: Wicked Publications, 1989), p. 56; see also the same author's *London . . . The Sinister Side*, pp. 36–7.

113 James Boswell, *Life of Johnson*, ed. R.W. Chapman (Oxford: Oxford University Press, 1980), p. 331.

114 Henry Mayhew, *London Labour and the London Poor*, 4 vols (London: Frank Cass and Co., Ltd, 1967), I.9, pp.195–6.

115 Dickens, *The Pickwick Papers*, p. 278.

116 Ibid., p. 335.

117 Rose Prince, 'Taking the Lid Off the Great Pie Debate' in *Evening Standard* (16 May 2007).

118 Ackroyd, *London*, p. 315.

119 Cited in Ibid., p. 315.

120 Tobias Smollett, *The Expedition of Humphrey Clinker*, ed. Lewis M. Knapp (Oxford: Oxford University Press, 1984), p. 119.

121 For a general account of the Yorkshire pies see 'Monstrous Pies' in Ivor Smullen, *Yorkshire Pies: A Confection of Remarkable Tales from God's Own Country* (Glasgow: Fort Publishing, 2001), pp. 63–4.

122 'The Fourth and Fifth Pie: 1887 – Queen Victoria's Golden Jubilee'. Access date: 10 April 2006 www.denbydale.com.

123 Smullen, *Yorkshire Pies*, p. 64.

Chapter 2

1 See Mark Buchan, 'Food for Thought: Achilles and the Cyclops', in Kirsten Guest, ed., *Eating Their Words: Cannibalism and the Boundaries of Cultural Identity* (Albany, New York: State University of New York Press, 2001), pp. 11–34.

2 Maria Tatar, *The Classic Fairy Tales* (New York: W.W. Norton, 1999), p. 179.

3 Marina Warner, in *Cannibalism and the Colonial World*, eds Francis Barker, Peter Hulme and Margaret Iverson (Cambridge: Cambridge University Press, 1998), p. 160.

4 Northrop Frye, *Fables of Identity: Studies in Poetic Mythology* (New York: Harcourt, Brace & World, 1963), pp. 27–28; 30–31.

5 On some of the connections between the twentieth-century films mentioned and the story of 'Bluebeard', see Tatar, *The Classic Fairy Tales*, pp. 140–1.

6 Stith Thompson, *Motif-Index of Folk-Literature: A Classification of Narrative Elements in Folktales, Ballads, Myths, Fables, Mediaeval Romances, Exempla, Fabliaux, Jest-Books,*

and Local Legends (revised edn), 6 vols (Bloomington, Indiana, and London: Indiana University Press, 1955–8).

7 Shu Kishida, Japanese psychologist, quoted in Martingale, *Cannibal Killers*, p. 128.

8 Reay Tannahill, *Flesh and Blood: A History of the Cannibal Complex* (New York: Stein and Day, 1975), pp. 142–3.

9 On the activities of these figures see Martingale, *Cannibal Killers*; also Daniel Korn, Mark Radice and Charlie Hawes, *Cannibal: The History of the People-Eaters* (London: Pan-Macmillan, 2000).

10 See Korn, Radice and Howes, *Cannibal*, pp. 211–16; 242–5.

11 Nick Fiddes, *Meat: A Natural Symbol* (London: Routledge, 1991), p. 128.

12 Tannahill, *Flesh and Blood*, pp. 174–5.

13 'Cannibalism Admitted by Air Crash Survivors' in *The Times* (Saturday, 30 December 1972), p. 6; Issue 58668; col. B.

14 On the circumstances surrounding the Andes air crash see Tannahill, *Flesh and Blood*, pp. 174–6.

15 'Blood and Thunder' in *The Times* (Tuesday, 7 April 1942), p. 5; Issue 49203; col. D.

16 Herman Melville, *Pierre*, quoted in Leonard Feinberg, *The Satirist*, with a new Introduction by Brian A. Connery (London and New Brunswick, New Jersey: Transaction Publishers, 2006), p. 9.

17 Philip Thompson, *The Grotesque* (London: Methuen & Co, 1972), p. 57.

18 Ibid., p. 57.

19 See Frederick Witney, *Grand Guignol* (London: Constable, 1947).

20 Michael Byrom, *Punch in the Italian Puppet Theatre* (Fontwell: Centaur Press, 1983), p. 37.

21 For a wonderfully representative selection of such crime narratives see *Con Men and Cutpurses: Scenes from the Hogarthian Underworld*, ed. Lucy Moore (London: Penguin, 2001).

22 See Pieter Spierenburg, 'The Body and the State: Early Modern Europe' in Norval Morris and David J. Rothman, eds, *The Oxford History of the Prison: The Practice of Punishment in Western Society* (Oxford: Oxford University Press, 1995), pp. 55–61.

23 Note review of Dick Turpin (Jonathan Keates, rev. 'Dick Turpin: The Myth of the English Highwayman' by James Sharpe (Profile, 2004) in the *Spectator* 'Early Essex Man' (14 February 2004), pp. 38–9.

24 Eric Hobsbawm, *Industry and Empire: The Birth of the Industrial Revolution*, ed. Chris Wrigley (New York: The New Press, 1999), pp. 156–7.

25 Hayden White, on 'Foucault' in John Sturrock, ed., *Structuralism and Since* (Oxford: Oxford University Press, 1979), p. 106.

26 Witold Rybczynski, *City Life* (New York: Touchstone, 1996), p. 108.

27 See T.A. Critchley, *A History of Police in England and Wales* (London: Constable, 1978), pp. 34–5.

28 Ibid., p. 46.

29 Northrop Frye, *Anatomy of Criticism* (Princeton: Princeton University Press, 1957), p. 47.

30 See Stephen Sondheim and Hugh Wheeler, *Sweeney Todd, the Demon Barber of Fleet Street. A Musical Thriller* (New York: Dodd, Mead, and Co., 1979), p. 67.

31 'The Thrill of Killing Replaced Sex' in *Daily Telegraph* (14 January 2004).

32 Mario Praz, 'Introductory Essay' in Peter Fairelough, ed., *Three Gothic Novels* (London: Penguin Books, 1982), p. 12.

33 Ibid.

34 Quoted in Richard Ellman, *Oscar Wilde* (New York: Vintage Books, 1987), p. 550.

35 See Andrew Smith, *Victorian Demons: Medicine, Masculinity, and the Gothic at the fin-de-siècle* (Manchester: Manchester University Press, 2004).

36 Robert Louis Stevenson, *Kidnapped and Catriona*, ed. Emma Letley (Oxford: Oxford University Press, 1986), p. 42.

37 Nina Auerbach, 'A Hideous Skeleton, with Cries and Dismal Howlings', review of Judith Richardson's *Possessions: The History and Uses of Haunting in the Hudson Valley* in the *London Review of Books* 26/12 (24 June 2004), 25.

38 Praz, *Three Gothic Novels*, p. 13.

39 Sherwood Anderson, 'The Book of the Grotesque' in *Winesburg, Ohio* (London: Penguin Books, 1992), p. 23.

40 Frye, *Anatomy of Criticism*, esp. pp. 189–92.

41 Ibid., p. 192.

42 Ibid., pp. 189–92.

43 Joyce Thomas, *Inside the Wolf's Belly: Aspects of the Fairy Tale* (Sheffield: Sheffield Academic Press, 1989), p. 50.

44 Ibid., p. 50.

Chapter 3

1 Wilkie Collins, *Armadale*, ed. John Sutherland (London: Penguin Press, 1995), p. 338.

2 Tim Dowling, 'Bare-faced Chic' in *Telegraph Magazine* (17 July 2004), pp. 17–18.

3 Julie Henry, 'Hitler Wasn't Real, says one in ten historically challenged Britons' in *Sunday Telegraph* (14 April 2004), p. 5.

4 Quoted in William Kent, *London Mystery & Mythology* (London: Staples Press, Ltd., 1958), p. 19.

5 For succinct summaries of all these cases, see, for example: Brian Lane, *The Murder Guide to London: Detailed Accounts of the Capital's Most Gruesome and Bizarre Murders* (London: Magpie, 1992); Colin Wilson, *A Casebook of Murder* (London: Leslie Frewin, 1969); Tony Wilson, ed., *Murder and Mayhem* (London: Harmsworth, 1983).

6 Mayhew, *London Labour and the London Poor*. http://etext.virginia.edu/toc/modeng/public/MayLond.html.

7 See Robert Shoemaker, *The London Mob: Violence and Disorder in 18th-century England* (London and New York: London & Hambledon, 2004).

8 Andrew Holgate, review of Robert Shoemaker's *The London Mob*, in *Sunday Times*, 'Culture', p. 50.

9 Ford Madox Ford, *The Soul of London: A Survey of a Modern City*, ed. G. Hill (London: J.M. Dent, 1995), p. 96.

10 Bruno Bettelheim, *The Uses of Enchantment: The Meaning and Importance of Fairy Tales* (New York: Vintage Books, 1975; 1989), p. 93.

11 Sir John Malcolm, *Sketches of Persia*, ii.92, quoted in Thomas Keightley, *Tales and Popular Fictions: Their Resemblance and Transmission from Country to Country* (London: Whitaker and Co, rpt. New York: Norwood editions, 1972), pp. 8–9.

12 Gregory Dart, 'The Demon Barber and Fleet Street' in *Sweeney Todd, the Demon Barber of Fleet Street, a musical thriller*, by Stephen Sondheim, The Royal Opera, Covent Garden, Programme, p. 12.

13 M. Willson Disher, 'On the Trail of a Legend' in *The Times* (Wednesday, 26 July 1939), p. 12; Issue 48367; col. B.

14 'Affirmation of Sweeney Todd' in *The Times* (Wednesday, 26 July 1939), p. 12; Issue 48367; col. B.

15 Ibid.

16 Robert Viagas, 'Notes on Sweeney Todd', *Playbill*, The New York City Opera, (March 2004), pp. 28–33.

17 Dart, 'The Demon Barber and Fleet Street', p. 13.

18 For a thorough account of the narrative that follows see the several works of journalist Peter Haining, particularly *Sweeney Todd: The Real Story of the Demon Barber of Fleet Street* (London: Boxtree, 1993) and Haining, *The Mystery and Horrible Murders of Sweeney Todd: The Demon Barber of Fleet Street* (London: Frederick Muller, 1979); also Haining, ed., *The Penny Dreadful, Or, Strange, Horrid, and Sensational Tales!* (London: Victor Gollancz, 1975), pp. 13–29; 95–120. See also E.S. Turner, *Boys Will Be Boys* (London: Michael Joseph, 1948), pp. 37–47. Note also, for example, the programme notes to the Watermill, West Berkshire Playhouse 2004 production of Sondheim's *Sweeney Todd, The Demon Barber of Fleet Street*.

19 George Eliot, *Romola*, ed. and intro. Andrew Sanders (Harmondsworth, Middlesex: Penguin, 1980), p. 79.

20 Marie Belloc Lowndes, *The Lodger* (Oxford: Oxford University Press, 1996), p. 192.

21 Charles Dickens, *Martin Chuzzlewit*, pp. 529–30.

22 Exchange in *Notes & Queries*. Ninth Series, vol. VIII (July–Dec. 1901), p. 273.

23 *Notes & Queries*, Ninth Series, vol. VIII (26 October 1901), p. 348.

24 From H.G. Hibbert, *A Playgoer's Memories* (London: Grant Richards, 1920), quoted in Haining (1993), p. 5.

25 Ibid.

26 Quoted in Haining, *Sweeney Todd: The Real Story of the Demon Barber of Fleet Street*, p. 50.

27 See Peter Haining's 'edition' of Frederick Hazleton's *Sweeney Todd* (London: Redwood Burn Ltd, 1980), p. 7.

28 David Carroll, 'Master Shaper: An Interview with Neil Gaiman', first published in *Blood Songs*, 8 (1997); reprinted at http://www.tabula-rasa.info/AusComics/NeilGaiman.html.

29 Thomas W. Erle, *Letters from a Theatrical Scene-Painter* (1880); reprinted as 'A Reminiscence' in Michael Kilgareff, *The Golden Age of Melodrama: Twelve Nineteenth-Century Melodramas*, pp. 263–72.

30 Richard Buxton, *The Complete World of Greek Mythology* (London: Thames and Hudson, 2004), p. 14.

31 John Roberts Nash, *Dictionary of Crime* (London: Headline Books, 1992), s.v. 'sweeny'.

32 Henry James, 'London' (1888) in David Kynaston, ed., *London Stories and Other Writings*, (Padstow: Tabb House, 1989), pp. 241–5.

33 Ford, *The Soul of London*, p. 14.

34   Ackroyd, *London*, p. 401.
35   Henry Fielding, *Tom Jones*, eds John Bender and Simon Stern (Oxford: Oxford University Press, 1996), p. 76.
36   Robert Bage, *Hermsprong*, ed. Pamela Perkins (Peterborough, Ontario: Broadview Literary Texts, 2002), p. 61.
37   'Barbers at Oxford' in *The Times* (September 11 1948), p. 5; Issue 51174; col. D.
38   For information on the historical relationship between barbers and surgeons, see W.J. Bishop, *The Early History of Surgery* (London: Oldbourne, 1962).
39   William Andrews, *At the Sign of the Barber's Pole: Studies in Hirsute History* (Cottingham, Yorkshire: J.R. Tutin, 1904), p. 2.
40   *The British Apollo* (London, 1708); reprinted in Andrews, p. 6.
41   Dart, 'The Demon Barber and Fleet Street', p. 14.
42   *New Records of London* (London: 1732), p. 161.
43   Oliver Goldsmith, *The Vicar of Wakefield* ed. Robert L. Mack (Oxford: Oxford University Press, 2006), p. 34.
44   Charles Dickens, *David Copperfield*, ed. Trevor Blount (Harmondsworth, Middlesex: Penguin, 1966), p. 408.
45   William Cowper, *Poems of William Cowper, of the Inner Temple, Esquire* (London: 1782), pp. 27–8.
46   *The People's Periodical and Family Library* (London: Edward Lloyd, 1846), p. 98.
47   Ibid., p. 346.
48   Charles Dickens, *A Child's History of England* (London: Chapman and Hall, n. d.), pp. 18–19.
49   Sabine Baring-Gould, *A Book of Folklore* (London: Methuen, 1913; rpt. Pulborough: Praxis Books, 1993), p. 37.
50   Martingale, *Cannibal Killers*, p. 23.
51   Ibid.
52   Charles Dickens, *Nicholas Nickleby*, ed. Michael Slater (Harmonsdworth, Middlesex: Penguin, 1978), p. 195.
53   Ackroyd, *London*, p. 662.
54   Véronique Campion-Vincent, 'La véritable histoire de l'os de rat' in Claude Fischer, ed., *Manger magique: Aliments, sorciers, croyonies, comestibles* (Paris: Autrement, 1994), pp. 88–9.
55   Dickens, *Martin Chuzzlewit*, p. 376.
56   Ibid., p. 377; see also, on Brown's illustrations, *Phiz!: The Book Illustrations of Hablot Knight Brown*, by John Buchanan-Brown (Newton Abbot and London: David Charles, 1978).
57   *Charles Dickens's Book of Memoranda: A Photographic and Typographic Facsimile of the Notebook Begun in January 1855*, ed. Fred Kaplan (New York: The New York Public Library, 1981); see, for example: pp. 11–14; 22–5.
58   See, for example, Susan B. Iwanisziw, ed., *Troping 'Oronooko' from Behn to Bandele* (Aldershot: Ashgate, 2004). On some commentary on the relevant terminology see also Elizabeth Scott-Baumann's review of the same volume in *Times Literary Supplement* (14 May 2004), pp. 30–1.
59   Evelyn Waugh, 'The Man Who Liked Dickens', reprinted in Mary Danby, ed., *65 Great Tales of Horror* (London: Octopus Books Ltd., 1981), p. 613.
60   Neil Gaiman and Michael Zulli, *Taboo 6 – The Sweeney Todd Penny Dreadful* (n.p.: SpiderBaby Graphics, 1992).

Chapter 4

1 George Crabbe, 'Peter Grimes' in Howard Mills, ed., *The Borough*, in *Tales, 1812, and other selected poems* (Cambridge: Cambridge University Press, 1967), p. 111.

2 Richard Marsh, *The Beetle*, ed. Julian Wolfreys (Peterborough, Ontario: Broadview, 2004), p. 113.

3 The narrative of Sweeney Todd, again, was originally published under the title *The String of Pearls, A Romance* by Edward Lloyd in his *People's Periodical and Family Library* in 18 weekly instalments; the story appeared in the periodical's issues for the weeks ending Saturday, 21 November 1846 (issue 7) to Saturday, 20 March 1847 (issue 24). The chapters in the *People's Periodical* were twice incorrectly numbered in the course of their original appearance – on the first occasion subsequent to those included in the eighth number (Chapter 16), then again in the thirteenth number, following the (actual) Chapter 25. Consequently, the novel's 39 chapters totalled in the final number only 37. The actual chapter divisions and subdivisions of the part issue are as follows:

Number	Date (week ending)	Chapters
1	21 November (1846)	1–3(i)
2	28 November	3(ii)–5
3	5 December	6–8 (i)
4	12 December	8(ii)–10(i)
5	19 December	10(ii)–12(i)
6	26 December	12(ii)–13(i)
7	2 January (1847)	13(ii)–16(i)
8	9 January	16(ii)–19(i)
9	16 January	19(ii)–23(i)
10	23 January	23(ii)–25(i)
11	30 January	25(ii)
12	6 February	25(iii)–26(i)
13	13 February	26(ii)–28(i)
14	20 February	28(ii)–30(i)
15	27 February	30(ii)–31
16	6 March	32–34(i)
17	13 March	34(ii)–37(i)
18	20 March	37(ii)–39

4 Turner, *Boys Will Be Boys*, p. 39.

5 Ibid., pp. 39–40.

6 Kathleen Tillotson, *Novels of the Eighteen-Forties* (Oxford: Clarendon Press, 1954), p. 45.

7 See William Congreve, *Incognita: or, love and duty reconcil'd. A novel* (London: 1713), pp. 7–10; Clara Reeve, *The Progress of Romance, through times, countries and manners; . . . in a course of evening conversations. By C. R. author of the English Baron, . . .* ([Colchester], 1785), vol. 1, p. 111.

8 David Masson, *British Novelists and Their Styles: Being a Critical Sketch of the History of British Prose Fiction* (Cambridge: Macmillan, 1859), pp. 26–7; quoted by Andrew Sanders in 'Victorian Romance: Romance and Mystery' in Corinne Saunders, ed., *A Companion to Romance: From Classical to Contemporary* (Oxford: Blackwell Publishing, 2004), pp. 375–88.

9   G.K. Chesterton, 'The Absence of Mr Glass' in *The Penguin Complete Father Brown* (Harmondsworth, Middlesex: Penguin, 1981), p. 180.

10   *The String of Pearls: A Romance* in *The People's Periodical and Family Library*. ed. E. Lloyd. No. 7, vol. 1 (21 November 1846) – No. 24, vol. 1 (20 March 1847), p. 97. All references to *The String of Pearls* are taken from this original edition in Lloyd's publication, and will be cited parenthetically (as *PP*) in the text of this section.

11   See, for example, Johann Caspar Lavater, *Essays on physiognomy, designed to promote the knowledge and the love of mankind. … Illustrated by more than eight hundred engravings … Executed by, or under the inspection of, Thomas Holloway. Translated from the French by Henry Hunter.* 3 vols. (London: John Murray, 1789–98).

12   *Blackwood's Edinburgh Magazine*, March 1829; cited in Brian Bailey, *Burke and Hare: The Year of the Ghouls*, p. 33.

13   Robert Louis Stevenson, *The Strange Case of Doctor Jekyll and Mr Hyde*, ed. Roger Luckhurst (Oxford: Oxford University Press, 2006), p. 55.

14   Lytton Strachey, 'Life of Florence Nightingale' in *Eminent Victorians* (1918); rpt. (New York: Harcourt Brace, 1969), p. 135.

15   From *Sweeney Astray,* trans. Seamus Heaney (London: Faber & Faber, 1983), pp. 6–7.

16   See *Lexicon Balatronicum: A Dictionary of Buckish Slang, University Wit, and Pickpocket Eloquence* (London: 1811), reprinted as *The 1811 Dictionary of the Vulgar Tongue*, foreword by Max Harris (London: Senate, 1994), s.v. 'barber's chair'._

17   William Godwin, *Caleb Williams*, ed. Maurice Hindle (Harmondsworth, Middlesex: Penguin, 1988), p. 234.

18   See Charles Dickens, *Martin Chuzzlewit*, Chapters 50 and 53.

19   H.B. Irving, *A Book of Remarkable Criminals*, Part One (Oxford: Oxford University Press, 1918), p. 98.

20   Humphrey House, 'The Macabre Dickens' (1947) reprinted in Stephen Wall, ed., *Charles Dickens* (Penguin Critical Anthologies) (Harmondsworth, Middlesex: Penguin, 1970), p. 353.

21   George Theodore Wilkinson, ed., *The Newgate Calendar*, 3 vols. (St Albans: Granada Publishing, 1962), vol. 1, pp. 247–54.

Chapter 5

1   Plutarch, 'Theseus' in *The Lives of the Noble Grecians and Romans*, trans. John Dryden, edited and revised by Arthur Hugh Clough, 2 vols. (New York: Modern Library, 1992), vol. 1, p.1.

2   Bloom's criticisms are reprinted in John Sutherland, 'His Satanic Majesty' in *The Times*, Weekend Review (18 September 2004), pp. 8–9.

3   On a convenient summary of monetary values in the Victorian period generally see Richard Mullen and James Munson, eds., *The Penguin Complete Companion to Trollope* (Harmondsworth, Middlesex: Penguin, 1996), pp. 325–7. See also 'Currency' in Daniel Pool, *What Jane Austen Ate and Charles Dickens Knew*, pp. 19–21.

4   Daniel Pool, *What Jane Austen Ate and Charles Dickens Knew*, pp. 20–1.

5   George P. Landow, rev. of Guinevere L. Griest's *Mudie's Circulating Library and the Victorian Novel* (Bloomington and London: Indiana Univ. Press, 1970) in *Modern Philology* 69 (1972), 367–9.

6   Tillotson, *Novels of the Eighteen-Forties*, pp. 22–3.

7   Landow, rev. of Griest, p. 368.

8   On writing in the period see Richard D. Altick, *The English Common Reader: A Social History of the Mass Reading Public, 1800–1900* (Chicago: Chicago University Press, 1957), Chapters 13, 15; also Nigel Cross, *The Common Writer: Life in Nineteenth-Century Grub Street* (Cambridge: Cambridge University Press, 1985), Chapters 3, 6.

9   See Louis James, *Fiction for the Working Man* (Oxford: Oxford University Press, 1963), p. 12.

10 Ibid., pp. 10–11.

11 See James Kinsley, ed., 'Descriptive Note of Editions 1836–37' in Charles Dickens, *The Pickwick Papers* (Oxford: Clarendon Press, 1986), pp. lxxxvi–lixvi; Margaret Cardwell, ed., 'Descriptive List of Editions 1870–75' in Charles Dickens, *The Mystery of Edwin Drood* (Oxford: Clarendon Press, 1972), pp. li–liii.

12 See Michael Wheeler, *English Fiction of the Victorian Period*, 2nd edn (London: Longman, 1994), pp. 3–5; see also J.A. Sutherland, *Victorian Novelists and Their Publishers* (London: Athlone Press, 1976).

13 Anthony Trollope, *The Three Clerks*, ed. Graham Handley (Oxford: Oxford University Press, 1991), pp. 240–68.

14 Ibid., pp. 242; 250.

15 Wilkie Collins, 'The Unknown Public' in *Household Words* (1858), in *My Miscellanies*, vol. xx, p. 157.

16 Graham Law, 'Introduction' to Wilkie Collins, *The Evil Genius* (Peterborough, Ontario: Broadview Press, 1994), p. 20.

17 Peter Ackroyd, *London*, pp. 265–6.

18 E.S. Turner, *Boys Will be Boys*, pp. 33–4.

19 David Oswell, s.v. 'Children: Britain' in Derek James, ed., *Censorship: A World Encylopedia*, 4 vols (London: Fitzroy-Dearborn, 2001), vol. 1, p. 455.

20 In Report for the House of Commons, 13 November 1888, in *The Times* (Wednesday, 14 November 1888), p. 6; Issue 32543; col. B.

21 Maria Reidelbach, *Completely MAD: A History of the Comic Book and Magazine* (New York: Little, Brown, and Co., 1991), p. 30. Reidelbach's first and second chapters (pp. 2–41) contain an excellent discussion of the controversy surrounding crime and horror comics in the 1950s.

22 David Oswell, 'Children: Britain', vol. 1, p.455.

23 Pullman's description has been placed on his official website, www.philip-pullman.com, p. 16.

24 James, *Fiction and the Working Man*, pp. 28–9.

25 Rohan McWilliam, 'Edward Lloyd (1815–1890)' in *New Oxford Dictionary of National Biography*, vol. 34, p. 118.

26 Turner, *Boys Will Be Boys*, p. 23.

27 Ibid., p. 22.

28 McWilliam, 'Edward Lloyd', pp. 118–19.

29 Ibid.

30 Helen R. Smith, *New Light on Sweeney Todd, Thomas Peckett Prest, James Malcolm Ryder and Elizabeth Caroline Grey* (London, Bloomsbury: Jarndyce, 2002), p. 3.

31 Quoted in Smith, *New Light on Sweeney Todd*, p. 12.

32 Ibid., p. 13.

33 Louis James and Helen R. Smith, 'Thomas Peckett Prest' in *Oxford Dictionary of National Biography*, 45, pp. 251–2. Also Dick Collins, 'The Pirates of Salisbury Square: Two Dreadful Writers and an Appalling Publisher', accessed online at www.blooferland. com/drc/index.php?title= Bram_Stoker_%26_Dracula:_miscellaneous_articles.

34 Ibid., p. 252.

35 Ibid.

36 Ibid.

37 Smith, *New Light on Sweeney Todd*, p. 12.

38 Louis James, 'James Malcolm Rymer' in *DNB*, 48 (2004), p. 495.

39 Smith, *New Light on Sweeney Todd*, p. 24.

40 James, *Fiction and the Working Man*, p. 190.

41 Helen Smith confirmed authoritatively that 'the first appearance of the blood, in its earlier, shorter form was its serialization in eighteen instalments in *The People's Periodical* between November 1846 and March 1847, and the dramatized version by Dibdin Pitt was first performed at the Britannia Theatre, Hoxton, on 22nd February, 1847'. *New Light on Sweeney Todd*, p. 26.

42 Ibid., p. 23.

43 Dick Collins, 'Introduction', *The String of Pearls: The Original Tale of Sweeney Todd* (Ware, Hertfordshire: Wordsworth's Classics, 2005), p. viii.

44 Peter H. Hansen, 'Albert Richard Smith, 1816–1860' in the *New Oxford Dictionary of National Biography*, 51, pp. 29–30.

45 Collins, 'Introduction', p. viii.

46 On Dickens's number plans for *Martin Chuzzlewit*, see John Butt and Kathleen Tillotson, *Dickens at Work* (London and New York: Methuen, 1957), pp. 24–5; note also the useful Appendix ('The Number Divisions of Dickens's Novels') to Stephen Wall's *Charles Dickens: A Critical Anthology* (Penguin Critical Anthologies) (Harmondsworth, Middlesex: Penguin Books, 1970), esp. p. 531.

47 Dickens, *Martin Chuzzlewit*, p. 636.

48 Ibid., p. 642.

49 Ibid., p. 641.

50 Ibid., pp. 650–1.

51 Ibid., p. 651.

52 Peter Haining, *Sweeney Todd: The Real Story of the Demon Barber of Fleet Street*, p. 4.

53 Jan Harold Brunvand, *The Vanishing Hitchhiker: American Urban Legends and Their Meanings* (New York: W.W. Norton, 1981), pp. 193–5.

54 John Carey, *The Violent Effigy: a Study of Dickens's Imagination* (London: Faber & Faber, 1973), p. 34.

55 Dickens, *Martin Chuzzlewit*, p. 673.

56 Ibid.

57 Ibid., p. 766.

58 Ibid., p. 715.

59 See *OED*, s.v. 'countryman'; esp. illustrative reference for 1681, *Trial S. Colledge* 67 *Mr. Ser. Holl.*

60   Dickens, *Martin Chuzzlewit*, p. 649.

61   William Cowper, 'John Gilpen' in *The Task* (London: 1785), p. 351.

62   William Cowper, *The Task* (London: 1785), pp. 166–7.

63   Ibid., p. 139.

64   See Charles Dickens, 'The Lost Artic Voyagers, *Household Words*, 2 December 1854' in Slater, ed., p. 255.

65   Carey, *The Violent Effigy*, p. 23.

66   Charles Dickens, 'Nurse's Stories' originally printed in *All the Year Round*, and reprinted in *The Uncommercial Traveller*; reprinted in *Humourous Readings from Charles Dickens*, ed. Peter Haworth (London: Macmillan, 1939), pp. 320–4.

67   A.O.J. Cockshut, *The Imagination of Charles Dickens* (London: Collins, 1961), p. 93.

68   Carey, *The Violent Effigy*, pp. 22–3.

69   Godwin, *Caleb Williams*, p. 333.

70   Haining, *Sweeney Todd*, p. 9.

71   Quoted in Haining, *Sweeney Todd* (1993), pp. 9–10.

72   See Sophie Jewett, *Folk Ballads of Southern Europe, Translated into English Verse* (New York: G.P. Putnam's Sons, 1913), p. 7; for 'Lord Randal', see *The Norton Anthology of Poetry*, 3rd edn, ed. A.W. Allison et al. (New York and London: Norton, 1983), pp. 71–2.

73   H. Chance Newton, *Crime and the Drama; or, Dark Deeds Dramatised* (London: Stanley Paul & Co., 1927), pp. 81–2.

74   M. Willson Disher, 'On the Trail of a Legend' in *The Times*, July 26 1939.

75   From *The Tell-Tale* (1824), cols 509–12. The issue was printed at the Caxton Press, by Henry Fisher, and published at 38 Newgate Streeet, London. The engraved frontispiece is dated Jan. 1 1824. As noted, the 'Terrific Story of the Rue de la Harpe' was reprinted in 1841 in *The Terrific Record*.

76   Elizabeth Nitchie, 'Letters to the Editor' in *The Times* (28 July 1939), p. 15; Issue 48369; col. E.

77   Ernest J. Parry, *The Times* (Tuesday, 1 August 1939), p. 17; Issue 48372; col. D.

78   Antoine Béraud and Pierre Dufey, *Dictionnaire historique de Paris*, 2 vols (Paris: (Pierre Joseph Spiridion) Imprimerie de Casimir, Rue de la Vieille-Monnaie, no. 12, 1828; 1832), vol. 2, pp. 385–6. The final paragraph of this same account was reprinted in M. de Germain-François Poullain, *Essais historiques sur Paris, de Monsieur de Saintfoix*. Quatrième édition, revue, corrigée & augmentée. 5 vols (Paris: 1767), vol. 1, pp.173–4.

79   Jacques du Breuil, *Le Théâtre des Antiquités de Paris. Où est traité de la fondation des …glises et Chapelles de la Cité, Université, Ville, et Diocèse de Paris: comme aussi de l'institution du Parlement, fondation de l'Université et Collèges, et autres choses remarquables . . . .* (Paris: Claude de La Tour, 1612), i.110–13.

80   Ernest Parry, *The Times* (Tuesday, 1 August 1939), p. 17; Issue 48372; col. D.

81   Pigault Lebrun, *The shrove-tide child; or, the son of a monk.* (London: 1797), i.244.

82   *The Times* (Monday, 30 October 1865), p. 8; Issue 25329; col. A.

83   Smith, *New Light on Sweeney Todd*, p. 23.

84   Ibid.

85   Charles Dupressoir, *Drames judiciaries: Scenes correctional. Les causes célébres des tous les peuples* (Paris: Librarie ethnographique, 1848–9), pp. 149–54.

86   I owe the transcription of this text to Mr John Adcock.

87   On French werewolves and lycanthropy, see Reay Tannahill, *Flesh and Blood*, pp. 113–16.

88   John Fiske, *Myths and Myth Makers* (Boston: James R. Osgood and Co., 1873), pp. 81–2.

89   From Peter Lindeström, *Geographia Americae with an Account of the Delaware Indians*, trans. Amandis Johnson (Philadelphia: Swedish Colonial Society, 1925; reprinted New York: Arno Press, 1979), pp. 29–31.

90   Ibid., p. 31.

91   'Horrible Murder' in *The Times* (Thursday, 26 August 1824), p. 3; Issue 12427; col. E.

92   Ibid.

93   Charles Dickens to John Hullah (11 June 1835) in *Letters*, i.48; quoted in Edgar Johnson, *Charles Dickens, His Tragedy and Triumph*, 2 vols (New York: Simon and Schuster, 1952), i.108.

94   Antonio Delpini, *Don Juan; or, the libertine Destroyed: a grand pantomimic ballet, in two parts; first performed at the Theatre Royal, Drury Lane* (London: 1790); *The airs, glees, choruses, &c. in the new pantomime of Blue Beard; or, the flight of the Harlequin. As Performed at the Theatre-Royal, Covent Garden* (London: 1791). Delpini had earlier published *The Festival of Momus, a collection of comic songs, including the modern and a variety of originals* (London: 1780).

95   See s.v. 'Delpini, Carlo Antonio (*c.*1740–1828)' by Brenda Assael in the *New Oxford Dictionary of National Biography*, 15, pp. 747–8: 'pantomimist, was born in Rome, possibly in the parish of San Martino, and was a pupil of Nicolini. His first London engagement was apparently with David Garrick at Drury Lane in 1774, although two years later, on 26 December 1776 at Covent Garden, the playbills announced his 'first appearance on an English stage' when he performed in the pantomime *Harlequin's Frolics*, in the role of Pierrot. His attention then turned to behind-the-scenes work, particularly with respect to mechanical arrangements for the 1777–8 season at Covent Garden. However, he continued to act in pantomimes both there (1778–9, 1789, 1796–7, 1799–1800) and at various other London theatres, including the Haymarket (1780, 1784–5, 1788, 1794–5, 1795–6, 1806), Drury Lane (1779–80), and the Royal Theatre (1787–8, 1782), where his wife, whom he married in 1784, also acted. With his expertise in scenic invention and his stress on character acting, Delpini is credited with having invented the Regency pantomime. In 1788 he worked as acting manager at Hughes's Royal Circus, producing pantomimes alongside the entertainment provided by the theatre's horses, tigers, leopards, and other animals. In the following year he was seriously hurt in an accident at the Haymarket. He appeared in 1798 at Astley's Amphitheatre, the main rival of the Royal Circus, but the production was not well received. Delpini had failed to subscribe to a theatrical fund which acted as a friendly society providing for death and sickness; as a result, he lay on his sickbed in old age with no relief, except for the £200 granted to him by his patron, 'The Prince—his Present Majesty', George IV, for whom he had once organized a grand masquerade at the Pantheon and arranged entertainments at the Pavilion in Brighton. Delpini had a superstitious fear of the number eight and predicted that he would die in 1788; instead, he died early in 1828 at the age of eighty-eight, either on 20 January or on 13 February (according to different sources), in Lancaster Court, Strand, London.'

96   Notice for 'Wargrave' in *The Times* (12 April 1791), p. 3; Issue 1976; col. B.

97 Anthony Pasquin, *The Life of the Late Earl of Barrymore. Including a history of the Wargrave theatricals and original anecdotes of eminent persons. By Anthony Pasquin, esq. A new edition, corrected and much enlarged* (London: H.D. Symonds, 1793), pp. 52–4.

98 Artist Marco Evarissti as quoted in the *Santiago Times* (Chile), 12 January 2007; rpr. in 'Funny Old World', compiled by Victor Lewis-Smith, *Private Eye*, No. 1182 (13–26 April 2007), p. 17.

99 See the short piece entitled 'Martin or Marten' in *The Times* (Tuesday, 18 May 1943), p. 2; Issue 49548; col. E.

100 See Charles Hindley, *The Life and Times of James Catnach* (London: Reeves and Turner, 1878).

101 *The Times* (3 June 1818), p. 3; Issue 10373; col. F.

102 See Louis James on James Catnach, *New Oxford Dictionary of National Biography*, 10, p. 554.

103 *The Annual Register, or a View of the History, Politics, and Literature for the Years 1784 and 1785* (London: J. Dodsley, 1787), p. 208.

104 See John Villette, *The Annals of Newgate, or Malefactor's Register. Containing a Particular and Circumstantial account of the lives, transactions, and trials of the most notorious malefactors.* 4 vols (London: 1776), vol. 1, pp. 215–19.

105 Ibid., vol. 1, p. 215.

106 See *Notes & Queries*, Ninth Series, vol. VIII, 26 October 1901, p. 348.

107 Haining, *Sweeney Todd, the Real Story*, p. 12; for modern commentary see Tannahill, *Flesh and Blood*, pp. 103–5.

108 Matthew Kilburn, 'Sweeney Todd [*called* the Demon Barber of Fleet Street] (supp. *fl.*1784)' in *New Oxford Dictionary of National Biography*, 54, p. 888.

109 See 'The Life of Sawney Beane' in *The Lives and Adventures of the most Notorious Highway-waymen* [sic]*, Street Robbers, and Murderers* (London: 1759), pp. 70–6.

110 Ibid., p. 75.

111 Philip Sugden, *The Complete History of Jack the Ripper* (London: Robinson, 1995), pp. 136–7; 292–6.

112 Robert Lindsay of Pitscotti, *Chronicles of Scotland 1436–1603*, 2 vols, ed. J.G. Dalyell (Edinburgh: 1814), vol. 1, p. 163.

113 Denham tracts, Folklore Society, 2 vols (London: D. Nutt, 1892–5), vol. 1, p. 155.

114 Edward Gibbon, *Decline and Fall of the Roman Empire*, ed. and abridged by Dero A. Saunders (Harmondsworth, Middlesex: Penguin, 1985), p. 492.

115 Recounted in Moira Martingale, *Cannibal Killers*, pp. 5–6.

116 'Boethius' as quoted in Robert Lindsay, *Chronicles of Scotland* (Edinburgh: 1814), p. 163.

117 tingale., p. 5.

118 S.R. Crockett, *The Grey Man* (New York and London: Harper, Fisher, Unwin, and Brothers, 1896), p. 308.

119 Ibid., pp. 309–10.

120 Ibid., p. 310.

121 Sandy Hobbs and David Cornwell, 'Sawney Bean, the Scottish Cannibal' in *Folklore* 108 (1997), 52.

122 Ibid., p. 49.

123 George Crabbe, 'Peter Grimes' in *The Borough*, in *Tales, 1812, and other selected poems*, p. 107.
124 Ibid., p. 108.
125 Wilkinson, *The Newgate Calendar*, vol. 1, pp. 234–40.
126 Ibid., vol. 1, p.234.
127 Mrs Basil Holmes, *The London Burial Grounds* (London: 1857), as quoted on www londonburials.co.uk.
128 David Piper, *The Companion Guide to London* (London: Harper Collins, 1964), p. 401.
129 Sir Edwin Chadwick, quoted in Roy Porter, *London, A Social History* (Cambridge, Massachusetts: Harvard University Press, 1995), p. 273.
130 See Ben Weinrib and Christopher Hibbert, eds., *The London Encyclopedia* (London: Macmillan, 1983), pp. 132–4.
131 See David Orme, 'Introduction to site' at www.londonburials.co.uk.
132 David Bartlett, *London by Day and Night, or, Men and Things in the Great Metropolis* (London: 1852); see also Isabella M. Holmes, *The London Burial Grounds* (London: T.F. Unwin, 1896).
133 Orme, 'Introduction'.
134 Ibid.
135 Ibid. Walker's campaign was given a significant boost by the cholera epidemic of 1848, which convinced most people of a connection between disease and the state of public hygiene and sanitation. The Society for the Abolition of Burials in Towns campaigned vigorously in 1849; among the legislation that followed were measures forbidding any further burials in London's inner-city graveyards and prohibiting interment anywhere in the metropolis if such action were necessary for the protection of public health; the bodies were subsequently removed from most of these graveyards to the large new out-of-town cemeteries, as Walker had proposed. Also following Walker's proposals, burial inspectors were appointed.
136 See also Peter Jupp and Glennys Howarth, eds., *The Changing Face of Death: Historical Accounts of Death and Disposal* (Basingstoke: Macmillan, 1996). Also Catherine Arnold, *Necropolis: London and Its Dead* (London: Simon & Schuster, 2006).
137 Dickens, *'Gone Astray', and Other Papers*, p. 36; also *A Christmas Carol and Other Christmas Writings*, intro. and notes, Michael Slater (London: Penguin Classics, 2003), p. 277; Arthur L. Hayward, *The Dickens Encyclopedia* (London: George Routledge & Sons Ltd, 1924), p. 110.
138 Michel de Montaigne, *The Complete Essays of Montaigne*, p. 350.
139 Fiske, *Myth and Mythmakers*, p. 221.
140 S. Baring-Gould, *Curious Myths of the Middle Ages* (London: Rivington, 1872), pp. 134–44.
141 Kilburn, 'Sweeney Todd', 54, pp. 887–8.
142 On the possible connections between the two works, see Walter Allen, *The English Novel: A Short Critical History* (Harmondsworth, Middlesex: Penguin, 1954), p. 27.
143 See Paul Salzman, 'Deloney, Thomas (*d.* in or before 1600)', *Oxford Dictionary of National Biography*, eds. H.C.G. Matthew and Brian Harrison (Oxford: Oxford University Press, 2004). 23 June 2006, www.oxforddnb.com/view/article/7463.
144 Allen, *The English Novel*, p. 29; see also C.S. Lewis, *English Literature in the Sixteenth*

Century, Excluding Drama. Vol. 3 in 'The Oxford History of English Literature' (Oxford: Clarendon Press, 1954), p. 429.

145 s.v., 'rogue literature' in *The Oxford Companion to English Literature*, ed. Margaret Drabble, 5th edn (Oxford: Oxford University Press, 1985); on 'rogue literature' more generally, and the work of Deloney, see also Constance C. Relihan, *Fashioning Authority: The Development of Elizabethan Novelistic Discourse* (Kent, Ohio: Kent State University Press, 1994), pp. 1–17.

146 Thomas Deloney, *Thomas of Reading. Or, the sixe worthy yeomen of the West*. Facsimile reprint of 4th edn (London, printed for T[homas] P[avier]: 1612; repr. Menston, Yorkshire: The Scolar Press, 1969), sig. G3v.

147 D.L. Macdonald and Kathleen Scherf, eds., 'Introduction' to Matthew Gregory Lewis, *The Monk: A Romance* (Peterborough, Ontario: Broadview Press, 2004), p. 13.

148 Russell A. Fraser, *Arden of Feversham* in *Drama of the English Renaissance I: The Tudor Period*, eds. Russell A. Fraser and Norman Rabkin (London: Collier Macmillan, 1976), p. 411.

149 George Lillo, *Fatal Curiosity*, ed. William H. McBurney. Regents Restoration Drama Series (Lincoln, Nebraska: University of Nebraska Press, 1966), 12, pp. 55–8; see also William E.A. Saxon, 'The Story of Lillo's ' "Fatal Curiosity"' in *Notes & Queries*, Sixth Series, vol. V (1882), pp. 21–3.

150 Deloney, *Thomas of Reading*, sig. G3v.

151 Ibid.

152 Ibid., H2r.

153 Ibid.

154 Ibid.

155 Percy Bysshe Shelley, *Peter Bell the Third* (1819) in Percy Bysshe Shelley, *Poetical Works* (Oxford: Oxford University Press, 1970), p. 350.

156 David Kynaston, *The City of London. Volume I: A World of its Own, 1815–1890* (London: Chatto & Windus, 1994), *passim*.

157 Peter Ackroyd, *London: The Biography* (London: Vintage, 2001), p. 1.

158 Marjorie Howes, 'Introduction', *Dracula* (London: J.M. Dent/Everyman, 1993), p. viii.

159 See Claire Harman, review of Paul Murray's *From the Shadow of Dracula* (London: Jonathan Cape, 2004) in *Evening Standard*, 'Review' (2 August 2004), p. 66. Harman observes of Stoker's novel: 'Literature it isn't, and no one has ever seriously tried to make it appear so. *Dracula* is possibly the most sublime trash ever written, far more important as a sensory "shocker" than as a text, and massively more successful in the age of film than it was in the author's day, when it didn't make him very much money.'

Chapter 6

1 *Sweeney Todd, The Demon Barber*, anon. (Celebrated Crime Series) (London: Mellifont Press, 1936), p. 3.

2 Correspondence – from Malcolm Morley to Eric Jones Evans, concerning the origin of the Madman's speech in the Pickwick papers as part of an early Sweeney Todd play, with attached press cutting on the writing of a Dickens Concordance (EJE/001191). In the Eric Evans Jones Collection, the University of Bristol.

3 Malcom Morley, 'Dickens's Contribution to *Sweeney Todd*', *Dickensian* 58 (Spring 1962), 92.

4 Ibid., 92–3; the original passages in context appears in Dickens, *The Pickwick Papers*, p. 166.

5 Ibid., 94.

6 Montague Slater, 'Introduction', George Dibdin Pitt, *Sweeney Todd: The Demon Barber of Fleet Street. A Traditional Acting Version* (London: John Lane, 1928).

7 Montague Summers, *A Gothic Bibliography* (London: Fortune Press, 1940), p. 521 (emphasis added).

8 Michael R. Booth, *English Melodrama* (London: Herbert Jenkins, 1965), p. 65.

9 Malcolm Morley, 'Dickens's Contribution', pp. 93–4.

10 Ibid., p. 95.

11 Quoted in Michael Kilgariff, ed., *The Golden Age of Melodrama: Twelve 19th-Century Melodramas* (London: Wolfe Publishing Ltd., 1974), p. 270.

12 For information on the Dibdins and Pitts see *DNB*, s.v. 'Charles Dibdin' and 'Ann Pitt'.

13 Kilgariff, ed., *The Golden Age of Melodrama: Twelve 19th-Century Melodramas*, pp. 238–41.

14 'Affirmation of Sweeney Todd' in *The Times* (Wednesday 26 July 1939), p. 15; Issue 48367; col. E.

15 Ibid.

16 Haining, *Sweeney Todd: The Real Story of the Demon Barber of Fleet Street*, p. 128.

17 Ibid.

18 Ibid.

19 Ibid., pp. 128–9.

20 See Dick Collins, ed., 'Introduction', *The String of Pearls: A Romance* (Ware: Wordsworth Classics, 2005), p. vi.

21 Reprinted in Kilgariff, *The Golden Age of Melodrama*, p. 244.

22 Ibid., p. 248.

23 Ibid., p. 262.

24 Jim Davis, ed., *The Britannia Diaries 1863–1875* (London: Society for Theatre Research, 1992), p. 5.

25 Charles Dickens, 'The Amusements of the People (II)' first published in *Household Words* (13 April 1850); included in Michael Slater, ed., *The Dent Uniform Edition of Dickens's Journalism: The Amusements of the People and Other Papers: Reports, Essays, and Reviews 1834–51* (London: J.M. Dent, 1996), pp. 95–8.

26 Slater, ed., *Dickens's Journalism*, p. 194.

27 Charles Dickens, *Hard Times*, ed. David Craig (Harmondsworth, Middlesex: Penguin, 1969), p. 82.

28 Charles Dickens, *The Dent Uniform Edition of Dickens's Journalism. Vol. IV: The Uncommercial Traveller*, eds. Michael Slater and John Drew (London: J.M. Dent, 2000), Chapter IV.

29 Michael Booth, 'The Social and Literary Context: The Theatre and it Audience' in Michael Booth, Richard Southern, Frederick and Lise-Lane Marks, and Robertson Davies, eds, *The Revels History of Drama in English. Volume VI: 1750–1880* (London: Methuen, 1975), p. 27.

30 Kilgariff, *The Golden Age of Melodrama*, p. 267.

31 Kristen Guest, '"Are You Being Served?"': Cannibalism, Class, and Victorian

Melodrama' in Kristen Guest, ed., *Eating Their Words: Cannibalism and the Boundaries of Cultural Identity* (Albany, New York: State University of New York Press, 2001), pp. 107–27.

32   Ibid., p. 114.

33   Ibid., p. 118.

34   Ibid., p. 119.

35   Turner, *Boys Will Be Boys*, pp. 47–8.

36   'Sweeney Todd, The Barber' by R.P. Weston and Bert Lee (1957) in Michael Marshall, ed., *The Stanley Holloway Monologues* (London: Elm Tree Books/EMI Music Publishing, 1979), p. 79. Note also Stanley Holloway, *Sweeney Todd, The Barber*. New York, 1957. Orchestra conducted by Arthur Liet Phillips, BBL-7237 (33 1/3 LP record).

37   Ibid., pp. 80–1.

38   Ibid.

39   Andrew Sarris, writing in an original review for *The Village Voice* (1965); reprinted in *Halliwell's Film Guide* (7th edn), p. 706.

40   See Michael Marshall, 'Introduction' to *The Stanley Holloway Monologues*, pp. viii–xviii.

41   On the life and career of Stanley Holloway, see Eric Midwinter, 'Stanley Augustus Holloway in *New Oxford Dictionary of National Biography*: www.oxforddnb.com/view/article/31250.

42   Obituary: 'Mr. Stanley Holloway, Rumbustious Cockney actor and singer', in *The Times* (Monday, 1 February 1982), page 10; Issue 61146; col. F.

43   Stanley Holloway, 'Forword' to *The Stanley Holloway Monologues*, p. vi.

44   Stanley Holloway, 'Sweeney Todd the Barber', *'Ere's 'Olloway* (Columbia ML5162), 1957.

Chapter 7

1   Robert Browning, *The Ring and the Book*, eds Richard D. Altick and Thomas J. Collins (Peterborough, Ontario: Broadview Press, 2001), p. 19.

2   *The Times*, 'The "Then and Now" Matinee' (12 April 1927), p. 14; Issue 44554; col. B.

3   On melodramatic acting, as a mode of dramatic performance, see the Appendix to Booth, *English Melodrama*, pp. 190–210.

4   *The Times*, 'The Theatres. New Play for the Globe' (26 April 1928), p. 14; Issue 44877; col. B.

5   Ben Brewster and Lea Jacobs, in their *Theatre to Cinema: Stage Pictorialism and the Early Feature Film* (Oxford: Oxford University Press, 1997), stress, however, that even the earliest such films refrained from merely replicating stage productions on celluloid, and in fact adapted and transformed what they characterize as the 'pictorial' traditions of theatre presentation in the earliest decade of the twentieth century in their efforts to establish a new model for feature film-making.

6   Booth, *English Melodrama*, p. 189 (emphasis added).

7   For basic factual information regarding this version see *The British Film Catalogue,*

1895–1985: A Reference Guide, ed. Denis Gifford (Newton Abbot and London: David & Charles, 1980), Cat. No. 08111.

8   On the dispute and the Brighton conference, see *The Times* (Tuesday, 8 June 1926), p. 14; Issue 44292; col. B.

9   *The British Film Catalogue, 1895–1985: A Reference Guide*, Cat. No. 08400.

10 *The Times* (Tuesday, 6 March 1928), p. 14; Issue 44834; col. B.

11 Jeffrey Richards, ed., *The Unknown '30s: The Alternative History of British Cinema, 1929–39* (London: I.B. Tauris, 1998), p. 147.

12 Haining, *Sweeney Todd*, p. 140. On Fritz Haarmann's activities see Brian Marriner, *Cannibalism: The Last Taboo* (London: Arrow Books, 1992), pp. 103–4; 108–19.

13 On the life and career of Tod Slaughter, see *The Complete Index to British Sound Film since 1928*, ed. Alan Goble (London: Bowker-Saur, 1999), p. 639; *The Encyclopedia of British Film*, ed. Brian McFarland (London: Methuen, 2003), p. 621; Danny Peary, *Cult Movie Stars* (New York: Simon & Schuster, 1991), p. 49; Jonathan Ribby, *English Horror: A Century of Horror Cinema* (London: Reynolds & Hearn, 2000), p. 22; Jeffrey Richards, 'Tod Slaughter and the Cinema of Excess' in *The Unknown 1930s: The Alternative History of British Cinema 1929–39* (London: I.B. Tauris, 1998); 'Sweeney Todd, the Demon Barber of Fleet Street', *The Missing Link*, No. 1 (Spring 1994), www.missinglinkclassichorror.co.uk.

14 *The Times* (20 February 1956), p. 12; Issue 53459; col. C.

15 Stephen Shafer, *Encyclopedia of British Cinema*.

16 *The Times* (20 February 1956), p. 12; Issue 53459; col. C.

17 *The British Film Catalogue*, Cat. No. 09935.

18 Jeffrey Richards, 'Tod Slaughter and the Cinema of Excess', p. 151.

19 Ibid., p. 148.

20 Ibid., p. 152.

21 Ibid., p. 150.

22 Ibid., p. 158.

23 Compare with Jeffrey Richards, 'Tod Slaughter and the Cinema of Excess', pp. 151–2: 'So there are legitimate profits to be made from free enterprise capitalism in the Empire (Mark, Findlay) but illegitimate profits to be made at home by Todd.'

24 Jeffrey Richards, 'Tod Slaughter and the Cinema of Excess', p. 158.

25 Ibid., pp. 158–9.

26 Ibid.

27 Haining, *Sweeney Todd*, p. 143.

28 J.P. Quaine, *Sweeny* [sic] *Todd, The Demon Barber of Fleet Street*, 'an entirely original version for the radio' and set 'in the Reign of George the Second', printed in *The Collector's Miscellany*, N.S. Nos. 11–14 (May–December 1935).

29 'The Case of the Demon Barber' in Ken Greenwald, *The Lost Adventures of Sherlock Holmes: Based on the Original Radio Plays by Denis Green and Anthony Boucher* (New York: Barnes & Noble, 1989), pp. 71–82.

30 Johnstone's adaptation was officially commissioned by Peter Fincham, Controller for BBC1, and Jane Tranter, the Controller for Drama Commissioning in early 2006.

31 The comments of Johnstone, producer Gub Neal and actor Ray Winstone quoted here are taken from the promotional Press Pack issued electronically for the production, available for viewing at: www.bbc.co.uk/pressoffice/pressreleases/stories/2005/12_december/08/todd_synopsis.shtml.

32 Sweeney Todd, BBC Drama Web Page, www.bbc.co.uk/drama/sweeneytodd/.

33   Ibid.

34   Oliver Duff, 'Fact or Fiction? Hair-raising tale of olde London Town' in *Independent*, 'Home Section' (3 January 2006), p. 15.

35   *Sweeney Todd*, dir. David Moore, perf. Ray Winstone, Essie Davis, David Bradley, David Warner, Tom Hardy, Ben Walker. BBC, Size 9 Productions. The synopsis here is based on that issued as part of a Press Pack by the BBC's Press Office in conjunction with the 2006 television production. See: www.bbc.co.uk/pressoffice/ pressreleases/stories/2005/12_december/08/todd_synopsis.shtml.

36   Ray Winstone as quoted on 'Sweeney Todd', BBC Drama Web Page, www.bbc. co.uk/drama/sweeneytodd/.

37   Terry Ramsey, ' "Pick of the Night" ' (*Sweeney Todd*, 9pm, BBC1)' in *Evening Standard* (Tuesday, 3 January 2006), p. 37.

38   Chris Riley, 'Today's TV and Radio Choices' (*Sweeney Todd*, 9 pm, BBC1) in *Daily Telegraph* (Tuesday, 3 January 2006).

39   A.A. Gill in 'Gore blimey; he's such a shocker' in *Sunday Times*, 'Culture' (8 January 2006).

Chapter 8

1   Tony Sarg, *Punch and Judy* (1929; rpt. New York: Arno Press, 1977), p. viii.

2   Hugh Pearman, 'Playing to a grown-up crowd' in *Sunday Times*, 'Culture' (17 December 2006), pp. 18–19.

3   On these see Sarg, *Punch and Judy*; also Michael Byrom, *Punch and Judy: Its Origin and Evolution* (London: Perpetua Press Ltd, 1972), and *Punch in the Italian Puppet Theatre* (Fonthill: Centaur Press, 1983).

4   Sarg, *Punch and Judy*, pp. 66–7.

5   The original play-text, with Cruikshank's incomparable engravings, is reprinted in Sarg's *Punch and Judy*, pp. 87–141.

6   Bill Baird, *The Art of the Puppet* (New York: Macmillan, 1965), p. 156.

7   On Lord Barrymore's purchase of the Fantoccini see George Speaight, *The History of the English Puppet Theatre*, 2nd edn (London: Robert Hale, 1990), p. 136.

8   From an original pamphlet printed in France in 1887, quoted in Jacques Chesnais, *Histoire générale des marionettes* (Paris: 1947); rpt. in George Speaight, *The History of the English Puppet Theatre*, p. 262.

9   George Speaight, *The History of the English Toy Theatre* (London: Studio Vista, 1946), pp. 24–6.

10   Ibid., p. 25.

11   Speaight, *The History of the English Puppet Theatre*, p. 337.

12   Ibid., p. 249.

13   Speaight, *The History of the English Toy Theatre*, p. 179.

14   Mary Saunders, 'Sweeney Todd' in Arthur E. Paterson, ed., *The Puppet Master: The Journal of the British Puppet and Model Theatre Guild* (April 1947), pp. 101–2.

15   'Ebor Marionettes' in *The Times*, 'Arts and Entertainment' (23 January 1937), p. 10; Issue 47590; col. C.

16   Ibid.

17   A.R. Philpott, *Dictionary of Puppetry* (London: Macdonald, 1969): s.v. 'glove puppets'; 'marionettes'.

18 'Sadler's Wells Theatre Ballet', *The Times*, 'Reviews' (Thursday, 1 April 1954), p. 8; Issue 52895; col. E.

19 Nicholas Dromgoole, s.v. 'John Cranko' in *New Oxford Dictionary of National Biography* (2004).

20 'Sadler's Wells Ballet: '"Bonne Bouche"', *The Times* (Saturday, 5 April 1952), p. 3; Issue 52279; col. C.

21 'Cranko's New Ballet: Another Sweeney Todd' in *The Times*, 'Reviews' (11 December 1959), p. 16; Issue 54641; col. C.

22 'The Demon Barber in Bow Street: A Victorian Burlesque' in *The Times*, 'Reviews' (17 August 1960), p. 11; Issue 54852; col. C.

23 Piers Burton-Page, Liner notes, *Symphony No. 6, Fantasy on a theme of John Field, Sweeney Todd Suite, Tam O'Shanter Overture*. Music by Malcolm Arnold. BMG Music, 1993, n.p.

24 'A Musical Version of *Sweeney Todd*' in *The Times*, 'Reviews' (20 July 1959), p. 8; Issue 54517; col. D.

25 'The Demon Barber' in *The Times*, 'Reviews' (10 December 1959), p. 4; Issue 54640; col. E.

26 'Demon Barber with Music: Grimness Becomes Pantomime' in *The Times*, 'Reviews' (11 December 1959), p. 16: Issue 54641; col. D.

27 Herman Melville, *Benito Cereno* in *Melville's Short Novels*, ed. Dan McCall (New York and London: W.W. Norton & Co., 2002), p. 72.

28 Stephen Sondheim, 'Theatre Lyrics' in O.L. Guernsey Jr, ed. *Playwrights, Lyricists, Composers on Theatre*. (New York: Dodd, Mead, 1974), pp. 62–3; quoted in Stephen Banfield, *Sandheim's Broadway Musicals* (Ann Arbor, MI: University of Michigan Press, 1993), pp. 13–14.

29 Frank Rich, 'Conversations with Sondheim' in the *New York Times Magazine* (12 March 2000), p. 38.

30 Ibid., p. 60.

31 Meryle Secrest, *Stephen Sondheim: A Life* (New York: Alfred Knopf, 1998), p. 230.

32 Ibid., p. 230.

33 Ibid., pp. 289–90.

34 Christopher G. Bond, 'Sweeney Todd, by the Author', *Sweeney Todd, The Demon Barber of Fleet Street. A Melodrama* (London: Samuel French Ltd, 1974), p. v.

35 On the Theatre Workshop and its history, see Oscar G. Brockett, *The History of the Theatre*, 7th edn (Boston: Allyn and Bacon, 1995), p. 531. Some of the theatre group's history was recapitulated in the obituary written for one of its most dedicated members, Howard Goorney (1921–2007). See 'Obituaries' in *The Times* (16 April 2007), p. 23; Issue 47233.

36 Irving Wardle, rev. of *Sweeney Todd* (Theatre Workshop) in *The Times* (3 May 1973), p. 7; Issue 58772; col. G.

37 Maxwell Shaw, 'Sweeney Todd, by the Director' in Bond, *Sweeney Todd*, p. iii.

38 Ibid.

39 Ibid.

40 Ibid.

41 Ibid.

42 Christopher G. Bond, 'The Theatre of Pyramids: (And a Camel)' in Daniel Gerould, ed., *Melodrama* (New York: New York Literary Forum, 1980), p. 18.

43 Bond, *Sweeney Todd*, p. 3.

44 Ibid., p. 12.

45 Ibid., p. 21.

46 Ibid.

47 Ibid., pp. 32–3.

48 Wardle, rev. of *Sweeney Todd* (Theatre Workshop), p. 7.

49 Flora Roberts, as quoted in Craig Zadan in *Sondheim and Co*, 2nd edn updated (New York: De Capo Press, 1994), p. 243.

50 Ibid., pp. 243–4.

51 Secrest, *Stephen Sondheim*, p. 291.

52 Roland Penrose, reviewing *Violence in Contemporary Art*, as quoted in Carlos Clarens, *An Illustrated History of Horror and Science-Fiction Films: The Classic Era, 1895–1967* (New York: De Capo Press, 1997), p. v.

53 Sondheim's observation was originally included in an interview given to Sarah Crompton of the *Telegraph*; it was reprinted by the critic Charles Spencer in his own commentary on *Sweeney Todd* in the *Telegraph* 'Arts' section (29 July 2004), p. 20.

54 Secrest, *Stephen Sondheim*, p. 379.

55 Ibid., p. 56. See also *Hangover Square*. Twentieth Century Fox, 1945. Starring Laird Cregar, Linda Darnell, George Sanders. Based on the novel by Patrick Hamilton; screenplay by Barre Lyndon (aka Alfred Edgar). Director, John Brahm; Producer, Robert Bassler; Music, Bernard Herrmann.

56 See Eric Myers, 'Sondheim and the Cinema' in *Playbill* (March 2004), p. 44.

57 Both Mallett and Agate's comments are reprinted in Leslie Halliwell, *Halliwell's Film Guide*, 7th edn (London: Collins Publishing, 1990), p. 442.

58 Myers, p. 44.

59 Philip Lane, Liner notes *Warsaw Concerto and Other Piano Pieces from the Movies* (Hong Kong: LP Naxos, 1997).

60 Secrest, *Stephen Sondheim*, p. 57.

61 Ibid., p. 295.

62 Zadan, *Sondheim & Company*, p. 245.

63 Ibid.

64 Ibid., p. 246.

65 Ibid., p. 245.

66 *New York Times* as cited in Zadan, *Sondheim & Company*, p. 246.

67 See Secrest, *Stephen Sondheim*, p. 291.

68 John Dizikes, *Opera in America: A Cultural History* (London and New Haven: Yale University Press, 1993), p. 509.

69 Zadan, *Sondheim & Company*, pp. 247–8.

70 Ibid., p. 250.

71 Ibid., p. 254.

72 Ibid.

73 Ibid.

74 Martin Gottfried, *Sondheim* (New York: Harry N. Abrams, 1993), p. 125.

75 Stephen Sondheim, 'Larger Than Life: Reflections on Melodrama and Sweeney Todd' in Daniel Gerould, ed., *Melodrama*, p. 8.

76 Gottfried, *Sondheim*, pp. 123–5.

77 Sondheim, 'Larger Than Life', p. 11.

78 Gottfried, *Sondheim*, p. 125.

79 Carol Ilson, *Harold Prince: From 'Pajama Game' to 'Phantom of the Opera'* (New York: Limelight Editions, 1992), p. 391.
80 Jack Kroll as paraphrased in Secrest, *Stephen Sondheim*, p. 296.
81 See Secrest, *Stephen Sondheim*, p. 292.
82 From Robert Kimball, Liner notes to *Sweeney Todd* (RCA, BMG Music, 1979), p. 4.
83 Stephen Sondheim and Hugh Wheeler, *Sweeney Todd, The Demon Barber of Fleet Street. A Musical Thriller* (New York: Dodd, Mead, 1979), pp. 1–2.
84 Ibid., pp. 3–4.
85 Ibid., p. 14.
86 Gottfried, *Sondheim*, p. 135.
87 Sondheim and Wheeler, *Sweeney Todd, The Demon Barber of Fleet Street*, p. 94.
88 Ibid., p. 95.
89 Ibid., pp. 95–6.
90 Ibid., p. 105.
91 Ibid., p. 186.
92 T.E. Kalem as quoted in Zadan, *Sondheim & Company*, p. 258.
93 Gottfried, *Sondheim*, p. 145.
94 Ibid., p. 258.
95 Ibid., pp. 258–60.
96 Douglas Watt as quoted in Ibid., pp. 256–8.
97 Clive Barnes as quoted in Ibid., p. 258.
98 Irving Wardle, '*Sweeney Todd*, Drury Lane' in *The Times* (Wednesday, 12 March 1980), p. 9; Issue 60573; col. G.
99 Ibid.
100 Ibid.
101 Gottfried, *Sondheim*, p. 146.
102 Secrest, *Stephen Sondheim*, p. 301.
103 Sondheim's comments on opera were quoted in John Snelson's 'The Label on the Tin' in the programme for The Royal Opera, Covent Garden, *Sweeney Todd* (2003), p. 27.
104 Sondheim, 'Larger than Life', p. 8.
105 Christopher Hurrell, 'The Time They Did *Sweeney* in Chicago' in *The Sondheim Review* 9 (4) (Spring 2003), 31.
106 John Olsen, 'Terfel Stars in a Rich and Eerie Sweeney' in *The Sondheim Review* 9 (3) (Winter 2000), 12.
107 John Olsen, 'Sondheim Wanted *Sweeney* to be Very Scary' in *The Sondheim Review* 9 (3) (Winter 2003), 13.
108 Snelson, p. 30.
109 Ibid.
110 John Rockwell, 'Urban Popular Song: the Broadway Musical, the Cabaret Revival and the Birth Pangs of American Opera: Stephen Sondheim' in *All American Music: Composition in the Late Twentieth Century* (New York: Knopf, 1983), pp. 209–20; and Carey Blyton, 'Sondheim's *Sweeney Todd* – The Case for the Defence' in *Tempo* 149 (1984), 19–26; both quoted in Banfield, *Sondheim's Broadway Musicals*, p. 287.
111 Fred Plotkin, *Opera 101: A Complete Guide to Learning and Loving Opera* (New York: Hyperion, 1994), p. 94.

112 Donald Jay Grout, with Hermine Weigel Williams, *A Short History of Opera*, 3rd edn. (New York: Columbia University Press, 1988), p. 721.

113 Banfield, *Sondheim's Broadway Musicals*, p. 287.

114 William Wilkie Collins, *No Name*, ed. and intro. Virginia Blain (Oxford: Oxford University Press, 1986), p. 178.

115 See John Roberts Nash, *Dictionary of Crime* (London: Headline Books, 1992), s.v. 'sweeny' [sic]. The reference is in actual fact more probably connected to John Sweeney, the Irishman who first organized the unit. The same slang would of course, in turn, provide the basis for the popular television drama series (1974–8) of the same name.

116 Cliff Edwards, *Hair Raisers 1: Sweeney Todd* (London: Longman, 1981), p. 30.

117 Carey Blyton, *Sweeney Todd, The Barber* (Sevenoaks, Kent: Novello, 1981), n.p.

118 Website www.gillian-cross.com, biography, p. 2.

119 Gillian Cross, *The Dark Behind the Curtain* (Oxford: Oxford University Press, 1982), pp. 97–8.

120 Cross, *The Dark Behind the Curtain*, p. 143.

121 Cozette de Charmoy's volume was originally published in London by the small, independent Gaberbocchus Press; a Canadian 'edition' was printed at the same time by Oberon Press, in Ottawa, and in 1977, De Capo (New York) issued another impression of the work.

122 Cozette de Charmoy, 'Further Adventures of Sweeney Todd Alias Bartolli' in *Melodrama*, p. 19.

123 'My Sweeney is not a Victorian "demon barber" but a romantic hero. And, like other Romantic heroes, he has a sort of immortality.' See Ibid., p. 20.

124 See Debra Kelly, 'The Battlefield in Text and Image: Remains and Relics in the Work of Cozette de Charmoy' in *Forum for Modern Language Studies* 42.1 (January 2006), 53–4. The second critic, quoted in Kelly, above, is N. Wadley, 'Poetic Displacement' in *Cozette de Charmoy* (Catalogue), ed. A. Hémery (Alès: 1995), p. 20.

125 Cozette de Charmoy, *The True Life of Sweeney Todd (A Collage Novel)* (London: Gaberboccus Press, 1973), p. 14.

126 Ibid., p. 29.

127 Ibid., p. 54.

128 Ibid.

129 Ibid., p. 63.

130 Ibid., p. 74.

131 Ibid., pp. 86–7.

132 Ibid., pp. 90–1.

133 Cozette de Charmoy, 'Further Adventures of Sweeney Todd Alias Bartolli' in *Melodrama*, pp. 19–20.

134 Ibid., p. 54.

135 Neil Gaiman maintains an online journal on his official website www. neilgaiman. com. The artist Michael Zulli's log is available for reading on his site, www. michaelzulli. com/.

136 Roger Sabin, *Comics, Comix, & Graphic Novels: The History of Comic Art* (New York: Phaidon, 1996), p. 165.

137 Paul Gravett, as quoted by Bryan Appleyard in *Sunday Times*, 'Culture' (4 March 2007), p. 7.

138 Sabin, *Comics, Comix, & Graphic Novels*, p. 168.

139 Ibid., p. 168.

140 Frank Shanbaker, 'A Piece of Sweeney's Pie' in *Playbill: Sweeney Todd* (December 1979), pp. 84–5.

141 Shanbaker, 'A Piece of Sweeney's Pie', p. 84.

142 Ibid.

143 Zadan, *Sondheim & Co.*, pp. 260–1.

144 Shanbaker, 'A Piece of Sweeney's Pie', p. 85.

145 Reviewed by 'Judge' Bill Gibron, May 2004, and posted on the website forum DVD Verdict: www.dvdverdict.com/reviews/sweeneytodd.php.

146 Ernio Hernandez, reporting for *Playbill* on 26 February 2007 on: www.playbill.com/news/print.asp?id=106058.

147 Kael's comments were reprinted in Halliwell (1989), p. 384.

148 John Harlow, 'Doubts whether Depp can cut it as Sweeney Todd' in *The Times* (13 August 2006): www.timesonline.co.uk /tol/news/world/article607371.ece.

149 See Zadan, *Sondheim & Co.*, pp. 378–80.

150 Harlow, 'Doubts whether Depp can cut it as Sweeney Todd'.

151 Johnny Depp as quoted by John Hiscock, 'I'm not finished with Jack Sparrow', in *Daily Telegraph*, 'Arts' (Monday, 21 May 2007), p. 29.

Appendix

Sweeney Todd: A Genealogy, History and Chronology

The extent to which the story of Sweeney Todd would appear ultimately to be deeply rooted in the rural and urban mythology, the oral history and (more particularly) the emergent literature of crime and criminality in eighteenth- and early-nineteenth-century England is a circumstance that works to preclude any pretensions to a complete and independent historiography of the narrative. The material assembled below, however, takes into account some of those sources that formed the major textual precedents (or 'proto-legends' and 'subtypes') of the barber and the pastry-cook's story as it was first coherently set down in writing within the pages of the publisher and newspaper proprietor Edward Lloyd's *The People's Periodical and Family Library* in 1846–7. A solid black line further sets off the appearance of that same text from such precedents in the chronology below. The list also includes the most significant (though by no means all) of Sweeney Todd's subsequent manifestations in various media in the latter part of the nineteenth century, throughout the twentieth century, and into the earliest years of our own. Certain representations of Todd's narrative (e.g. George Dibdin Pitt and Frederick Hazleton's dramatic adaptations of the story) exist in a number of bewilderingly different and often irreconcilable and even incompatible versions or variants; the chronology looks in such instances merely to indicate the earliest documented appearance of the most significant of such revisions.

1602   Thomas Deloney's (*ca.*1543–*ca.*1602) *Pleasant History of Thomas of Reading* entered in the Stationer's Register; the text survives in later editions ('corrected and enlarged') published in 1612; 1623; 1632; and 1636. Deloney's tale features a 'cunningly carved' bedstead that operates on much the same mechanical and deceptive principles that will eventually distinguish Sweeney

Todd's murderously ingenious barber's chair. Deloney's early narrative is thought by some to be an early source for the oubliette by means of which the barber will similarly dispatch his victims to their death.

1612   Publication of Jacques du Breuil's *Le Théâtre des Antiquités de Paris. Où est traité de la fondation des Eglises et Chapelles de la Cité, Université, Ville, et Diocèse de Paris: comme aussi de l'institution du Parlement, fondation de l'Université et Collèges, et autres choses remarquables* ... (Paris: Claude de La Tour). The first volume of du Breuil's collection contains what is very possibly the earliest published account of the story of a barber who murders his customers, and whose cellar is connected to the premises of a nearby 'patissier' or pastry-cook, who then makes use of the bodies of the victims by turning them into meat pies. The crimes were said to have taken place in a house named Marmousets (the name means, literally, a 'small grotesque figure'); the actual building, which dated from the early thirteenth century (*c.*1206), was subsequently pulled down, and a small monument supposedly erected nearby in memory of the barber's victims. The vacancy created by the destruction of the property itself subsequently made way for the Rue des Marmousets-en-la-Cité.

1691   Swedish artist, cartographer and engineer Peter Mârtensson Lindeström, who had in 1654 travelled from Gothenburg to what was then New Sweden (on the Middle-Atlantic coast of North America), leaves on his death in this year a manuscript account of his journey to the New World. Lindeström's manuscript – although not translated into English or published until 1925, when it appeared under the title *Geographia Americæ. With an Account of the Delaware Indians Based on Surveys and Notes Made 1654–56* – contains a detailed account of a story that he claimed to have been current in (and to have taken place in) Calais, in France, when he passed through that port city on his journey in 1654. The story then being circulated told of the collusion of a resident barber and a pastry-maker of the same town in a series of murders. Lindeström's written version of the tale anticipates the details of Sweeney Todd and Mrs Lovett's narrative in almost every significant respect, including even the use of specially made chair and trap-door that dropped the victims into a secret cellar below the barber's shop. Although, again, Lindeström's account was not published in any form until 1925, the story he recounts – and which he apparently heard from the merchants and residents of the town themselves – suggests that the archetypal tale of a barber who murders people in league with an entrepreneurial pie-maker had already enjoyed a wide circulation in Calais and elsewhere in France since at least the middle of the seventeenth century.

1714   First printing of *A general history of the lives and adventures of the most famous highwaymen, murderers, street-robbers, &c., To which is added, a genuine account of the voyages and plunders of the most notorious pyrates....* by Capt. Charles Johnson (London: printed for and sold by J. Janeway; and by the booksellers of London and Westminster). Capt. Johnson's volume, which was reprinted in London in 1734 and again in Birmingham in 1742, was among the first to include an extended account of 'The Life of Sawney Beane', the legendary 'robber, murderer, and cannibal' who supposedly flourished in 'the desarts [sic] of Galloway' in the reign of King James VI of Scotland. Similar accounts of Sawney Beane – thought by some to have been one of the models for Sweeney Todd – were also to be included in widely circulated and frequently reprinted collections such as (among others) Capt. Alexander Smith's *Memoirs of the life and times, of the famous Jonathan Wild, together with the history and lives of modern rogues, ... that have been executed before and since his death, ...* (London: Samuel Briscoe, 1726), as well as in anonymous anthologies of criminal 'lives' such as *The lives and adventures of the most notorious highway-waymen [sic], street robbers, and murderers, giving a very particular account of the various methods practised by rogues of every class in the execution of their villanies ...* (London: 1759), *The life of Richard Turpin, a notorious highwayman. Containing a particular account of his adventures ... to which is added, the life of Sawney Beane, the Man-Eater* (London: 1800). The story of Sawney Beane was also circulated in a number of undated chapbooks and broadsheets (*The Horrid Life of Sawney Beane. An Atrocious Robber and Assassin ...* (Carlisle: Printed by F. Jollie and Sons); *The History of Sawney Beane and His Family; Robbers and Murderers ...* (Printed and Sold in Aldermary Church Yard, London); *The Life of Sawney Beane, The Man-Eater, Who Inhabited a Cave near the Sea-Side in the Country of Galloway in Scotland* (J. Ferraby, Butchery, Hull) etc.) that were printed and circulated throughout Scotland and England from about 1700. See also 1876, below.

1732   First publication of *Select trials, for murders, robberies, rapes, sodomy, coining, frauds, and other offences. At the Sessions-House in the Old-Bailey. ...* (London: printed for L. Gilliver; and J. Huggonson). Reprinted in expanded editions in 1742 and

1764, these volumes, often referred to simply as *Select Trials at the Old Bailey,* eventually, with other eighteenth-century collections such as the *Newgate Calendar* (see 1779, below), served as hugely influential sources for the writers of the many criminal lives, 'Newgate novels' and penny bloods of the early and mid-nineteenth century.

1779   The story of the barber of the 'Maison des Marmousets' (see 1612, above) was included in Pierre-Thomas-Nicholas Hurtaut's *Dictionnaire historique de la ville de Paris et de ses environs, dans lequel on trouve la description des monuments et curiosités de cette capitale, l'établissement des maisons religieuses, celui des communautés d'artistes et d'artisans, le nombre des rues et leur détail historique, tous les colléges et les bourses qui leur sont affectées ...* (Paris: Moutard).

Earliest, anonymously edited edition of the so-called *Newgate Calendar* (more properly, *The Malefactor's Register; or, the Newgate and Tyburn Calendar. Containing the authentic lives, trials, accounts of executions, and dying speeches, of the most notorious violators of the laws of their country; ... from the year 1700 to Lady-Day 1779... . Embellished with a most elegant and superb set of copper plates, ...*) published in five volumes (London: for Alexander Hogg). Along with the *Select Trials at the Old Bailey* (see 1732, above), the *Newgate Calendar* was an important general source for writers of the earliest, serial versions of Sweeney Todd's narrative; neither publication, however – contrary to the assertions of some writers on the story – contain any explicit references to the barber or Mrs Lovett, nor do their well-known successors in the nineteenth century (e.g. W. Jackson's *The New and Complete Newgate Calendar; or, villainy displayed in all its branches* (London: 1795)).

1784   *The Annual Register* (for December 1784) records a short account of 'a most remarkable murder' committed by a journeyman barber near Hyde Park Corner. The incident, originally reported in the *London Chronicle* (2 December 1784), was later to be incorporated into many of the extended accounts of Sweeney Todd's supposed early career as a barber.

1793   Anthony Pasquin's *The Life of the Late Earl of Barrymore. Including a history of the Wargrave theatricals and original anecdotes of eminent persons. By Anthony Pasquin, esq. A new edition, corrected and much enlarged* (London: printed for H.D. Symonds). Pasquin's life of the 7th Earl of Barrymore includes an anecdotal account, supposed to have been related to Barrymore by the Italian pantomimist

Carlo Antonio Delpini (c.1740–1828), of a true 'Venetian story' wherein a pastry-cook murders a number of small local children and bakes them into pies. Although no barber features in the narrative, the tale stands as a close analogue of its Parisian counterpart.

1814   Two versions of Guilbert de Pixérécourt's enormously popular 'dog-drama' *Le Chien de Montargis* (translated into English as *The Dog of Montargis, or The Forest of Bondy*), by William Barrymore and Thomas Dibdin, respectively, staged for the first time in London. The story very likely served as a primary narrative source for the dog Hector's devotion to Lieutenant Thornhill in the earliest versions of *The String of Pearls* (see 1846–7, below).

1818   (May–June) James Catnach (1792–1841) publishes a broadsheet alleging that the wife of a journeyman tailor, stopping at a butcher's shop near Drury Lane to purchase 'a piece of pork', had witnessed the delivery of a human corpse to the premises. Soon thereafter, the shop of the butcher Thomas Pizzey, in London's Clare Market, was besieged and almost destroyed by an angry mob. Catnach himself avoided being committed at the time, although Pizzey would later successfully sue the ballad and broadsheet publisher for malicious libel.

1824   Earliest appearance in Henry Fisher's monthly magazine, *The Tell-Tale Fireside Companion and Amusing Instructor*, of an item subsequently most often labelled 'Horrid Murder and Shocking Discovery'; the item is about a French barber who murders his customers. Essentially a variation on the 'Marmousets' story (see 1612, above), to which have also been added elements of the traditional French tale of 'Le Chien de Montargis', the tale is again set in Paris, rather than London, although the specific location has unaccountably been shifted from 'Marmousets' to the Rue de la Harpe. The same item, although apparently owing its later circulation to its appearance in Fisher's publication, had already appeared in the *Tickler Magazine* for 1 February 1822 (under 'Correspondence'), and was again to be reprinted in similar such popular magazines as the *Terrific Register; or, Record of Crimes, Judgements, Providences and Calamities*; *The Magazine of Curiosity and Wonder*; and the *New Wonderful and Entertaining Magazine* (under the title 'The Murderous Barber').

1825–6   First publication of Antoine Nicolas Bèraud and Pierre Joseph Spiridon Dufey's *Dictionaire historique de Paris* (Paris: Imprimerie de Casimir, Rue de la Vieille-Monnaie, no. 12) in four volumes. Bèraud and Dufey's *Dictionnaire* – reprinted and expanded in 1828, 1830 and 1832 – contained a brief and widely circulated retelling of the murderous barber of the 'maison, dite des *Marmousets*'.

1835–6   *The Calendar of Horrors! A Weekly Register of The Terrific, Wonderful, Instructive, Legendary, Extraordinary, and Fictitious* published by G. Drake, 12 Houghton Street, Clare Market. *The Calendar of Horrors* (2 April 1835–8 December 1836) famously published a series of tales in the gothic tradition. This sensational periodical has sometimes been mistakenly associated with Edward Lloyd (see *c.*1836–42, below); Thomas Peckett Prest, once credited by many with the authorship of *The String of Pearls*, also contributed to Drake's publication.

*c.*1836–42   London-based printer and newspaper proprietor Edward Lloyd (1815–90) begins publication of the first of a number of periodicals that unapologetically feature sensational literature aimed specifically at the rapidly expanding audience of working class readers. Among Lloyd's earliest publications of this sort was his *History and Lives of the Most Notorious Pirates of all Nations; Narrating a Series of Gallant Sea-Fights, Dreadful Murders, Daring Attacks, Horrid Cruelties and Barbarities; also their Debauched and Profligate Manner of Living, Places of Refuge, &c.* (With Ninety Engravings). The first part of this 72-part work is dated Saturday, 5 March 1836; the last part Saturday, 15 July 1837. Some of Lloyd's subsequent periodicals catering to the same taste in fiction would include *Lloyd's Penny Weekly Miscellany* (1842–7) and *Lloyd's Penny Atlas* (1842–5), and – eventually, from 1846 – *The People's Periodical and Family Library* (see 1846–7, below). Lloyd later in his career attempted to move into more self-consciously 'legitimate' journalism with publications such as *Lloyd's Illustrated London Newspaper* (from September 1842) and, later, the *Daily Chronicle* (starting 1846). Although Lloyd has often been listed in bibliographies as the publisher of *The Calendar of Horrors! A Weekly Register of The Terrific, Wonderful, Instructive, Legendary, Extraordinary, and Fictitious*, this latter title was in fact printed and published not by Lloyd, but by G. Drake, from 2 April 1835 to 8 Dec 8 1836, in 91 numbers.

1840–6   Publication, in serial form, of Charles Dickens's novels *The Old Curiosity Shop* (April 1840–January 1841), *Barnaby Rudge* (January–November 1841) and *Martin Chuzzlewit* (November

1842–July 1844), and – beginning in October 1846 – the earliest numbers of *Dombey and Son* (completed April 1848). Many of the narrative incidents and to some extent even some of the stylistic and thematic aspirations of Sweeney Todd's story as originally told in *The String of Pearls* (see 1846–7, below) would appear to have found their immediate inspiration within this particular series of Dickens's early novels. Chapters 36 and 37 of *Martin Chuzzlewit* (Part XIV, February 1844) make explicit reference to the country legends and urban myths then circulating in England regarding the operations of certain 'preparers of cannibalic pastry' at work in the growing metropolis.

1842   (January) *Blackwood's* magazine, within an article entitled 'Paris – chronicles of the cité', includes an account of the murders at the site of the 'Rue des Marmouzets' [sic], in this instance dating the events narrated therein as simply having occurred before the reign of Francis I (1515–47).

1843   John Nicholson's *Historical and Traditional Tales, in Prose and Verse, connected with the South of Scotland* (Kirkcudbright, Scotland: John Nicholson) offers a timely and particularly popular account of the life of the 'Scottish Cannibal and Man-Eater', Sawney Beane (see 1714, above).

1844   Louis Lurine's *Les Rues de Paris, ancien et moderne* (Paris: G. Kugelmann) again recounts the story of the French barber and patissier, now slightly resituated as having taken place *in* the 'Rue des Marmouzets', and specifically said to have occurred towards the end of the fourteenth century.

        (September–October) *Joddrel, the Barber; or Mystery Unravelled* [sic] published by Edward Lloyd in his *Lloyd's Penny Atlas* (vol. 2, no. 97). The story tells the tale of a French–Irish barber, Lewis Joddrel, whose customers mysteriously disappear from his Bishopsgate shop; it may have served as a possible source for Todd's appearance in *The String of Pearls* just two years later.

1846–7 (21 November–20 March) *The String of Pearls: A Romance* serialized in Edward Lloyd's *The People's Periodical and Family Library*. Published in 18 weekly parts (issues nos. 7–24) and variously attributed to Edward P. Hingston, George Macfarren, Thomas Peckett Prest, James Malcolm Rymer and Albert Richard Smith; the publication of the narrative marks the earliest appearance in

English of the characters of Sweeney Todd, the barber, and his pie-maker accomplice, Mrs Margery Lovett.

1847   (22 February) *The String of Pearls*, written by George Dibdin Pitt, first produced and performed as a drama at the Britannia Theatre, Hoxton. The role of Sweeney Todd was played by Mark Howard; Samuel Sawford, another popular young actor of the day, was featured as Mark Ingestrie. Dibdin Pitt's stage version of the story, significantly, premiered even before publication of Lloyd's original serial has reached its completion. It is through the many later versions and variations of this original dramatic adaptation that the words most often associated with the barber – 'I'll polish him off' – are definitively associated with Todd, and effectively become his 'catchphrase'.

1850   Bound, single-volume edition, running to a total of 732 pages, of an expanded version of the original 1847 tale published by Edward Lloyd. This lengthier (and much inferior) version of *The String of Pearls* (now for the first time subtitled 'The Barber of Fleet Street. A Domestic Romance') appears originally to have been published as a stand-alone penny-part serial, probably beginning some time in 1847–8. The part work ran for 92 eight-page numbers; the earliest chapters are virtually identical to those originally printed by Lloyd three years earlier. As was then typically the practice, numbers 2, 3 and 4 were 'given away' with the first number. This 'penny blood' serial thus ran for a full 89 weeks. The British Library Catalogue suggests that the work was begun by George Macfarren and possibly completed by Thomas Peckett Prest (see 1846–7, above), although such an attribution is now considered unlikely. Includes several illustrations by J. Reading.

*c.*1852–3   *Sweeney Todd: or the Ruffian Barber. A Tale of the Terror of the Seas and the Mysteries of the City* by 'Captain Merry' (pseudonym of American author Harry Hazel (1814–89)) published in New York by H. Long and Brother, Nassau Street. Hazel's work is often a rough and hastily written version (essentially a plagiarism) in 36 chapters of Lloyd's expanded text of 1850.

*c.*1860   Anonymous dramatic adaptation of *The String of Pearls* submitted to the Lord Chamberlain, and performed in the East End at the recently rebuilt (1856) Pavilion Theatre, Whitechapel.

1861   (March) Alfred Rayner's 'popular drama' of *The String of Pearls* performed at London's Victoria Theatre.

(April) London's Marylebone Theatre in the West End (Manager Mr J.H. Cave) announces performance of 'a new Drama, entitled *the String of Pearls; or, Sweeny Tod* [sic], *The Barber of Fleet–street . . . Occurred in London* [sic], *based on fact*'.

(June) Anonymous dramatic adaptation of *The String of Pearls* performed at the Grecian Saloon, City Road, Hoxton (formerly the 'Eagle' Saloon), in London's East End.

1862 (July) *The String of Pearls; or, The Life and Death of Sweeny Todd* [sic] adapted for the stage by 'Mrs. [Henry] Young' performed at the Effingham Saloon, Whitechapel Road. The role of Todd was played by Charles Morton; the role of Mark Ingestrie undertaken by G. Yates.

(July) 'Revival (by desire) of the great Drama' *The String of Pearls* at the City of London Theatre. Sweeney Todd played by Mr R.H. Lingham; Mrs Lovett played by Mrs Ada Dyas, 'assisted by the whole Company'.

*c.*1865 *Sweeney Todd, the Barber of Fleet Street: or, the String of Pearls*, a new dramatic adaptation by Frederick Hazleton (*c.*1825–90) first performed at The Old Bower Saloon, Stangate Street, Lambeth. Hazleton was later alleged by some to have produced an alternative prose version or 'novelisation' of the story at about the same time, although it is highly unlikely that such a prose version by Hazleton ever existed. A fraudulently edited and modernized 'version' of this 'novel' (essentially a redaction of Lloyd's 1846–7 text) was reprinted with an 'Introduction' by Peter Haining in 1980. A version of Hazleton's drama eventually appeared (as vol. 102, in 1875) as one of Lacy's Acting Edition of Plays, a series originally intended to provide reliable acting play-texts of both 'classic' and popular dramas for provincial and amateur theatricals. Throughout the latter half of the nineteenth century, a number of other versions of *Sweeney Todd* – many based to some extent on the texts originally established by Dibdin Pitt and Hazleton – were advertised for performance both in London and in the provinces; these included 'new' versions attributed to Mat Wilkinson, William Latimer, Andrew [sic] Melville, Frank Fortescue, Geoffrey Hewitson, and Fred G. Brooke and Dora Dean.

1865 French novelist Paul Henri Corentin Féval (1816–87) alludes to the French prototype of the Sweeney Todd story in his *La Vampire* ('The Vampire Countess').

1866   First issue of Edward J. Brett's *The Boys of England*, a story paper
               designed to end the dominance of the 'penny bloods' by aiming
               at a distinctly juvenile readership with adventure stories that
               typically featured schoolboy heroes such as the popular 'Jack
               Harkaway', rather than criminal figures.

1873   First appearance of *The Link Boy of Old London* (attributed by
               some to Vane Ireton St John) in *Sons of Britannia*; the narrative,
               which also drew heavily on works such as Dickens's *Oliver Twist*,
               was to be republished in *The Boy's Standard* No. 78 (4 November
               1882) to No. 91 (3 February 1883); Sweeney Todd features as a
               character in the serial, as does Mrs Lovett (under the name of 'the
               Widow Darkman').

1876   Publication of R.S. Crockett's *The Grey Man of Auchinleck*, in
               which the possible Sweeney Todd prototype, Sawney Beane, plays
               a central role.

*c.*1878–80   *Sweeney Todd, the Demon Barber of Fleet Street* published by Charles
               Fox and Co., of 4 Shoe Lane, near Fleet Street. This 48-part
               inferior and repetitive novelization – often based only very
               loosely as an extrapolation on the original 1846–7 text – runs
               in total to 576 double-columned pages. This version of the story
               has plausibly been attributed to Charlton Lea, credited also with
               a version of *Spring-heel'd Jack: The Terror of London*.

*c.*1880   George Dibdin Pitt's adaptation of *Sweeney Todd* published as one
               of 'John Dicks' Standard Plays' in a version substantially different
               from that first submitted to the Lord Chamberlain in 1847. This
               edition asserts that the play was first performed in 1842 – a
               mistake of some consequence, insofar as it has resulted in the
               frequent attribution by later critics of the story itself to Dibdin
               Pitt, rather than to the anonymous author of the 1846–7 *People's
               Periodical* narrative published by Lloyd.

               Puppet versions (typically featuring marionettes) of *Sweeney Todd,
               the Demon Barber of Fleet Street*, using play-texts adapted from the
               original George Dibdin Pitt melodrama, staged in London and
               throughout England by puppet troupes and popular showmen
               including Harry Wilding, Ambrose Tiller, Brown (Hull) and
               Testo (South Wales).

1885   Abridged version entitled *The String of Pearls; or Passages from the
               life of Sweeny* [sic] *Todd, the Demon Barber* published by Charles

345

Fox in six instalments in *The Boy's Standard* (No. 213, n.s. 6 June–No. 218, 11 July).

*c.*1892   *Sweeney Todd the Barber of Fleet Street. A Thrilling Story of the Old City of London. Founded on Facts* published in a shortened version of 13 chapters by A. Ritchie of Red Lion Court, London. The text is based on that originally published by Edward Lloyd in 1846–7.

(November) *The String of Pearls* by Charles A. Clarke and H.R. Silva performed in Birkenhead, in northwest England.

1898   (31 December) The *London Journal* begins to reprint a slightly abridged version of the text of *The String of Pearls* as it had originally appeared in Lloyd's 1846–7 *People's Periodical and Family Library*.

*c.*1907   Volume IV of Paul Sébillot's *Le Folk-Lore de France* (Paris: G.P. Maisonneuve), a French encyclopaedia of folklores and folktales that began publication in 1904, includes a brief recapitulation of the story of the maison 'Marmosets' [sic] (see 1612 etc.).

1910   Publication by the Manchester-based Daisy Bank Press of a short version of the Sweeney Todd story, based on Edward Lloyd's original 1846–7 tale. Between 1910 and 1922 the press brought out some 50 illustrated publications, each of 32 pages, many of which reprinted familiar tales of crime and murder.

1915   Short 'biography' of Todd published by Felix McGlennon.

1925   (21 March) A melodramatic production entitled *Sweeney Todd, the Barbarous Barber* features as the first radio play to be produced and broadcast in Australia (from Melbourne); the text may have been J.P. Quaine's version, published in 1932 (see below).

1926   The earliest film version of *Sweeney Todd* produced by New Era Productions as 'a comedy burlesque stage play' and filmed for the 'Kinematograph Society Garden Party'. The short film – now lost – was directed by British film pioneer George Dewhurst, and starred G.A. Baugham in the title role.

1928   Second (and earliest surviving) film version of *Sweeney Todd*, produced by Harry Rowson (QTS Productions), directed by Walter West, and distributed by Ideal Films Limited. This film

– which advertised itself as having been specifically 'adapted from the famous "Elephant and Castle" melodrama' – featured the well-known actor Moore Marriott as Todd, Iris Derbyshire as Amelia [sic] Lovett, Charles Ashton as Mark Ingestrie, and Zoe Palmer as Johanna.

A self-described 'traditional' version of Dibdin Pitt's *Sweeney Todd* – with an introduction by Montagu Slater – published by John Lane (London).

Sweeney Todd. The Demon Barber, a short version of the barber's story, printed by C.W. Biller (London).

1929   *Sweeney Todd, the Demon Barber* published by C.A. Pearson; the same 'edition' was to be republished by London's Mellifont Press *c.*1936. The text for this version of the story may have been written by Edwin T. Woodhall, a former police constable and agent who eventually contributed a number of other titles to Mellifont's 'Celebrated Crime Series', including *Jack the Ripper, or, When London Walked in Terror* (1937). Other possible authors include Hargrave L. Adam, or William and Leonard Townshend.

1932   Radio play by J.P. Quaine (*Sweeny* [sic] *Todd, The Demon Barber of Fleet Street*, 'an entirely original version for the radio' and set 'in the Reign of George the Second') printed in *The Collector's Miscellany*, N.S. nos. 11–14 (May–December 1935).

1936   Tod Slaughter stars in *Sweeney Todd, The Demon Barber*, directed and produced by George King and released by Ambassador Pictures. Slaughter had already made a speciality of playing such villainous roles to great effect on the stage. The film – a much-simplified version of the story credited to Frederick Hayward and H.F. Maltby and notionally based on the earlier dramatizations of George Dibdin Pitt and Frederick Hazleton – also featured Stelle Rho in the part of Mrs Lovett, Eve Lister as Johanna Oakley and Bruce Seton as Mark Ingestrie.

1946   (28 January) 'The Strange Case of the Demon Barber' – a half-hour-long radio play based in part on an incident included in Arthur Conan Doyle's original Holmes story 'The Yellow Face' (1893), and featuring an encounter between Sherlock Holmes and an actor playing the role of Sweeney Todd who seems to be identifying rather too closely with his stage role – broadcast as part of 'The New Adventures of Sherlock Holmes'. The series was sponsored by the Petri Wine Company of California and broadcast by the Mutual Network. The role of Sherlock Holmes was played by Basil Rathbone, and the production also featured the vocal talents of Nigel Bruce (as Dr Watson) and Luis Hector (as Professor Moriarty). The original radio play was written by Dennis Green and Anthony Boucher, and produced by Russell Seeds. An expanded prose version of the text used for the broadcast (by Ken Greenwald, and based on the original script prepared by Green and Boucher) was included in *The Lost Adventures of Sherlock Holmes*, published in 1989.

*c.*1947   A radio version of George Dibdin Pitt's *Sweeney Todd, the Demon Barber of Fleet Street* broadcast on the Canadian Broadcast Corporation, starring the popular radio and television actor John Drainie and Canadian radio pioneer, Mavor Moore.

Marionettes designed and constructed by John Bickerdike for a new puppet-play production of *Sweeney Todd* featured on the cover of *The Puppet Master*, the journal of the British Puppet and Model Theatre Guild. The marionettes are currently in the collection of the V&A's Museum of Childhood in Bethnal Green, London. Glove puppets of the characters in Todd's story, crafted by Mary Bligh Bond, exist from roughly the same period.

1948   Selections from Edward Lloyd's original version of *The String of Pearls* (1846–7) featured in E.S. Turner's *Boys Will Be Boys: the story of Sweeney Todd, Deadwood Dick, Sexton Blake, Billy Bunter, Dick Barton, et al.* (London: Michael Joseph). Turner's volume was among the first to argue for the value of the 'new mythology' of heroes and villains – e.g. Todd, Jack Sheppard, Spring-heeled Jack, Jack Harkaway, Sexton Blake etc. – contained within the pages of the 'bloods' and 'penny dreadfuls'.

Publication of the short story 'Speciality of the House' by Stanley Ellis (1916–86), an influential tale that owes much to the lingering cultural influence of the Sweeney Todd narrative.

1952   William Kent devotes the final pages of his collection examining some the most popular and persistent beliefs regarding the capital – *London Mystery & Mythology* (London: Staples Press) – to the question: 'Was Sweeney Todd a Fleet Street Barber?'

1956   'Sweeney Todd the Barber' – already a popular comic song by R.P.

Weston (1906–34) in the tradition of the music-hall monologue – recorded by the actor Stanley Holloway, and included on his album *'Ere's Holloway* (Columbia Records, 1956). Holloway's version of Weston's so-called cante fable (which began 'In Fleet Street, that's in London Town / When King Charlie wore the crown, / There lived a man of great renown / 'Twas Sweeney Todd the Barber') continued for some time to feature on the radio as a popular audience request. The number was re-released when it was included on *An Evening at the English Music Hall* (Front Hall Records) in 1984.

1959   (10 December) World premiere of a one-act ballet adaptation – *Sweeney Todd* – with music by the well-known composer Malcolm Arnold (Opus 68a) and choreography by John Cranko at the Shakespeare Memorial Theatre, Stratford. The role of Todd was danced by Donald Britton. The ballet's first London performance was to take place several months later at the Royal Opera House, Covent Garden, on 16 August 1960. The duration of Arnold's score for the piece was just under a half-hour.

        (10 December) Premiere of *The Demon Barber* at the Lyric Theatre, Hammersmith, a musical version of the story with book and lyrics by Donald Cotton and music by Brian Burke; based on George Dibdin Pitt's original play and produced by Colin Graham. The musical starred Roy Godfrey as Sweeney Todd and Barbara Howitt as Mrs Lovett; the role of Jonas Fogg was played by Barry Humphries.

1962   (May) *The World of Sweeney Todd*, book and lyrics by William Scott and Ken Appleby (with additional lyrics by Alan Collins and Mike Burke, and music by Peter Satterfield; arranged by Alan Johnson) staged at the People's Theatre in Newcastle-Upon-Tyne. The production was revived in 1970, and again represented in April 1995 by the Redditch Operatic Society, at the Palace Theatre, Redditch.

        (June) Brian Burton's *Sweeney Todd, The Barber. A Melodrama* adapted 'from George Dibdin Pitt's Victorian version of the legendary drama' first presented at the Crescent Theatre, Birmingham, on 16 June. Featuring Frank Jones as Sweeney Todd, and Frances Bull as Mrs Lovett.

1969   *Sweeney Todd: The Demon Barber of Fleet Street* (subtitled 'A Victorian Melodrama') by Austin Rosser performed at the Dundee Repertory Theatre, Scotland.

Bloodthirsty Butchers, a film directed by Andy Milligan, and written by John Borske and Andy Milligan. An updated and – for its day – exceptionally violent and graphic retelling of the tale, starring the pantomimist Berwick Kaler as Todd, with John Miranda, Jane Helay and Annabella Wood.

'Sweeney Todd' included as the penultimate episode (Season 5, Episode 2) in the British anthology television series *Mystery and Imagination* (1966–70). Directed by Robert Collin, with a teleplay written by Vincent Tilsley based on the original melodrama of George Dibdin Pitt, and starring Freddie Jones in the title role, and Heather Canning as Mrs Lovett. Originally aired on British television 16 February 1970; first shown on American television 12 October 1982.

1973   (5 March) Christopher G. Bond's *Sweeney Todd, The Demon Barber of Fleet Street* opens at the Theatre Workshop, Theatre Royal, Stratford East. Well-known British television actor Brian Murphy starred as Sweeney Todd, and Avis Bunnage as Mrs Lovett. The text of Bond's play would be published by Samuel French (London) in 1974; this version of the story was to serve as the primary source for Stephen Sondheim and Hugh Wheeler's 1979 'musical thriller' of the same name (see 1979, below).

The True Life of Sweeney Todd: A Collage Novel by Cozette de Charmoy published in London by the Gaberbocchus Press. Charmoy's retelling of Todd's narrative expands the barber's life story by means of fragmented illustrations and images, many taken from late nineteenth- and early twentieth-century engravings. Subsequent identical editions of Charmoy's 'sheets' were published by the Oberon Press in Ottawa, Canada, and (in 1977) by De Capo in New York.

1974   Text of an original nineteenth-century version of George Dibdin Pitt's adaptation *The String of Pearls (Sweeney Todd)* included in Michael Kilgarrif's *Golden Age of Melodrama* (pp. 237–72); the volume also includes a valuable descriptive passage from Thomas W. Erle's 1880 *Letters From a Theatrical Scene-Painter* describing an actual nineteenth-century audience at a performance of Dibdin Pitt's drama at the Britannia Theatre, Hoxton.

1975   The French story of the house of 'Marmousets' included in Natalie Bernard and Laurence Guillaume's *Contes Populaires et Legendes de Paris* (Paris: Les Presses de la Renaissance).

1978   Publication of Tim Kelly's *Sweeney Todd, The Demon Barber of the Barbary Coast*, 'freely adapted from the Classic Stage Melodrama of George Pitt and the Novel *The String of Pearls* by Thomas Prest' [sic] (Schulenberg, Texas: I.E. Clark, Inc.).

1979   *Sweeney Todd, The Demon Barber of Fleet Street. A Musical Thriller*, with music and lyrics by Stephen Sondheim and a book by Hugh Wheeler, premieres on 1 March at the Uris Theatre in New York. The cast includes Len Cariou as Sweeney Todd, Angela Lansbury as Mrs Lovett, Victor Garber as the young hero Anthony Hope, Sarah Rice as Johanna, and Merle Louise as the Beggar Woman. Sondheim's musical is subsequently awarded the 1979 Tony and Drama Critics Circle Award for 'Best Musical'. The original cast production was recorded by RCA on 12 and 13 March 1979, and subsequently issued as a two-record set. The work initially attracted less attention when it was first staged at the Theatre Royal, Drury Lane, in London the following year (featuring Denis Quilley and Sheila Hancock). Sondheim's version would, however, be successfully revived by the New York City Opera as soon as October 1984 (having first been staged as an operatic production by the Houston Grand Opera in July of that same year).

1980   Publication of Peter Miller and Randall Lewton's *The Sweeney Todd Shock 'n' Roll Show*, an amateur musical adaptation loosely based on earlier dramatic versions of the story, and originally staged in Liverpool in January 1979.

1981   *Hair Raisers: Part 1: Sweeney Todd* by Cliff Edwards, with illustrations by Michael Strand included in a Longman Publishing series for young adult readers.

        Sweeney Todd, The Barber (Opus 79) by Carey Blyton (1932–2002), nephew to popular children's writer Enid Blyton and Benjamin Britten's personal editor. An audio recording of the piece – 'A Victorian Melodrama for Narrator, unison voices, and piano' – would eventually be released in June 2006. Rather like Edwards's more straightforwardly didactic piece, above, Blyton's work was also aimed at younger audiences, and billed as 'a fun piece for schools'. When performed in full, the song-cycle would run some 17 minutes.

1982   *The Dark Behind the Curtain*, written by Gillian Cross and illustrated by David Parkins. A novel for younger readers, the book takes as its premise the troubled production of a vaguely specified nineteenth-century dramatic version of *Sweeney Todd, the Demon Barber of Fleet Street* by a group of English schoolchildren.

(12 September) Television version of the original Hal Prince, Broadway production of Sondheim and Wheeler's *Sweeney Todd*, directed for the small screen by Terry Hughes and starring George Hearn as Todd and Angela Lansbury as Mrs Lovett aired in America. Hughes won an Emmy Award (1983) for 'Best Direction of a Theatrical-Musical Program'.

1991   The small-scale touring company Pimlico Opera – founded by Wasfi Kani in 1989 – stages Sondheim's 1979 *Sweeney Todd* in London's Wormwood Scrubs prison. The prison collaboration serves as the inspiration for the BBC's TV film (see 2002, below) *Tomorrow La Scala!*, featuring D-wing prisoners, who had been incarcerated for life.

1992   *Taboo 6 – The Sweeney Todd Penny Dreadful* issued as a proposal for a limited edition, collaborative 'work in progress' uniting award-winning graphic novelist Neil Gaiman with Michael Zulli. Although promotional pamphlets for the project featuring 'A Brief Introduction', excerpts from earlier texts, as well as reproductions, pastiches and original sketches and other artwork by Gaiman were published, they did not receive a wide circulation, and neither Gaiman nor Zulli followed through on the project.

1993   Malcolm Arnold's score for John Cranko's 1959 ballet *Sweeney Todd* (Opus 68a) recorded by the Royal Philharmonic Orchestra, conducted by Vernon Handley.

1998   *The Tale of Sweeney Todd*, directed by John Schlesinger and featuring Ben Kingsley, Joanna Lumley and Campbell Scott. The film was written by Peter Buckman with executive producer Peter Shaw (credited specifically with story adaptation). Originally produced for 'Showtime' and Third Row Center Films as a made-for-television movie in America (first aired in the USA on 19 April 1998).

2000   (4–6 May) Performance and recording of Sondheim's *Sweeney Todd 'Live in Concert'* by the New York Philharmonic at Lincoln Center, New York. Featuring George Hearn as Sweeney Todd and Patti LuPone as Mrs Lovett. This successful concert version of Sondheim's *Todd* was subsequently filmed by Ellen M. Krass

Productions (in 2001), as performed by members of the same cast with the San Francisco Symphony. The filmed concert premiered on American television in October 2001.

2002   Director Francesca Joseph's made-for-television film *Tomorrow La Scala!* – in which a small opera company undertakes to mount a production of Sondheim's *Sweeney Todd* in a maximum security prison, the premise of which is the featuring of criminals sentenced to life-imprisonment in the major roles – is premiered at the Cannes Film Festival. Starring Jessica Stevenson and Samantha Spiro, the critically acclaimed film was subsequently nominated for two BAFTA awards.

   Sweeney Todd, credited to John Bilyard and the Basic Skills Agency, published in London by Hodder Murray as part of their 'Livewire' series of remedial books aimed at teenage and adult-age readers with a reading level below age ten.

2003   Sondheim's *Sweeney Todd* – featuring Thomas Allen as Todd and Felicity Palmer as Mrs Lovett – receives its first staging at the Royal Opera House, Covent Garden, London. The production, by Australian director Neil Armfield, with designs by Brian Thomson, had in fact originated at the Lyric Opera in Chicago in 2002–3. (Sondheim's version of *Sweeney Todd* had first been staged in England specifically as an opera by director David McVicar for Opera North, in Leeds, in 1998.)

2004   Sondheim's *Sweeney Todd* – in a revival directed by John Doyle and originally staged as a chamber piece at the Watermill Theatre in Westbury, West Berkshire – transfers to London's West End and eventually (in 2005) to Broadway's Eugene O'Neill Theatre. Director John Doyle would receive a Tony award for the Broadway staging of the production in 2006.

2005   John Doyle's 2004 revival of Sondheim's *Sweeney Todd* recorded in New York, featuring members of the original Broadway cast, including Patti LuPone, Michael Cerveris, Benjamin Magnuson and Lauren Molina (Nonesuch Records, 2005).

   Ray Winstone, Essie Davis and David Warner star in *Sweeney Todd*, an entirely new version of the story written for BBC1 film productions by Joshua St Johnstone and directed by David Moore; originally aired on British television 3 January 2006.

2007   (February) Director Tim Burton begins production at London's Pinewood Studios on the DreamWorks Studios/Warner Bros. film adaptation of the Stephen Sondheim musical *Sweeney Todd, The Demon Barber of Fleet Street*. The film stars actor Johnny Depp in the title role, and Helena Bonham Carter as Mrs Lovett. Also featuring Alan Rickman as Judge Turpin, Timothy Spall as Beadle Bamford, Sacha Baron Cohen as Signor Adolfo Pirelli, Jamie Campbell Bowen as Anthony Hope, Jayne Wisener as Johanna, and veteran actor Christopher Lee as 'The Gentleman Ghost'.

Select Bibliography

Abbott, Geoffrey (2004), *A Macabre Miscellany. One Thousand Grisly and Unusual Facts From Around the World* (London: Virgin Books).

Ackroyd, Peter (2000), *London: The Biography* (London: Vintage).

Acton, Eliza (1847), *Modern Cookery*, 6th edn (London: Longman, Brown, Green, and Longmans).

'Affirmation of Sweeney Todd' in *The Times* (Wednesday, 26 July 1939); p. 15; Issue 48367; col. E.

Altick, Richard D. (1957), *The English Common Reader: A Social History of the Mass Reading Public, 1800–1900* (Chicago: Chicago University Press).

Andrews, William (1904), *At the Sign of the Barber's Pole: Studies in Hirsute History* (Cottingham, Yorkshire: J.R. Tutin).

(1732); (1742); (1764), *Select Trials at the Old Bailey*, 4 vols (London).

(1759), *The Lives and Adventures of the most Notorious Highway-waymen, Street Robbers, and Murders* (London: H. Woodgate and S. Brooks).

(1846); (1847), *The String of Pearls. A Romance*, in *The People's Periodical and Family Library*, ed. E. Lloyd. No. 7, vol. 1 (21 November 1846)–No. 24, vol. 1 (20 March 1847), pp. 97–382.

(*c.*1880), *Sweeney Todd. The Demon Barber of Fleet Street* (London: Charles Fox).

(1936), *Sweeney Todd: The Demon Barber* (Celebrated Crime Series) (London: Mellifont Press).

(*c.*1982), *Sweeney Todd. The Barber of Fleet Street. A Thrilling Story of the Old City of London. Founded on Facts* (London: A. Ritchie).

Arens, William (1979), *The Man-Eating Myth: Anthropology and Anthropophagy* (Oxford: Oxford University Press).

Arnold, Catherine (2006), *Necropolis: London and Its Dead* (London: Simon & Schuster).

Baird, Rosemary (2003), *Mistress of the House: Great Ladies and Grand Houses: 1670–1830* (London: Weidenfeld and Nicolson).

Banfield, Stephen (1993), *Sondheim's Broadway Musicals* (Ann Arbor: University of Michigan Press).

Baring-Gould, Sabine (1913/1993), *A Book of Folklore* (London: Praxis Books).

Baring-Gould, Sabine (1872), *Curious Myths of the Middle Ages* (London: Rivington).

Barker, Francis, Hulme, Peter and Iversen, Margaret, eds (1998), *Cultural Margins: Cannibalism and the Colonial World* (Cambridge: Cambridge University Press).

Bartlett, David W. (1885), *London by Day and Night: or, Men and Things in the Great Metropolis* (New York: Hurst).

Bellenden, John, trans. (1938–41), *The Chronicles of Scotland* compiled by Hector Boece, 1531 (Edinburgh and London: W. Blackwood & Sons, Ltd).

Béraud, Antoine Nicholas and Dufey, Pierre Joseph Spiridion (1828), *Dictionnaire historique de Paris*, 2 vols (Paris: J.N. Barbon).

Besant, Walter (1997), *All Sorts and Conditions of Men*, ed. Helen Small (Oxford: Oxford University Press).

Bettelheim, Bruno (1975/1989), *The Uses of Enchantment: The Meaning and Importance of Fairy Tales* (New York: Vintage Books).

Bishop, William John (1960), *The Early History of Surgery* (London: Hale).

Blyton, Carey (1981), *Sweeney Todd, The Barber: A Victorian Melodrama for narrator, unison voices, and Piano: opus 79* (Borough Green, Kent: Novello).

Bond, Christopher G. (1974), *Sweeney Todd. The Demon Barber of Fleet Street. A Melodrama* (London: Samuel French).

Bondeson, Jan (2003), *The London Monster: Terror in the Streets in 1790* (Stroud, Gloucestershire: Tempus).

Booth, Michael R. (1965), *English Melodrama* (London: Herbert Jenkins).

Booth, Michael R., ed. (1995), *The Lights o' London and Other Victorian Plays* (Oxford: Oxford University Press).

Booth, Michael R. (1975), 'The Social and Literary Context: The Theatre and Its Audience' in Thomas W. Craik and Clifford Leach (eds), *The Revels History of Drama in English (1750–1880)* (London: Methuen), pp. 1–58.

Booth, William (1891), *In Darkest England and the Way Out* (New York: Funk & Wagnalls).

Bordman, Gerald Martin (1981), *American Operetta from H.M.S. Pinafore to Sweeney Todd* (New York: Oxford University Press).

Botting, Fred (1996), *Gothic. The New Critical Idiom* (London and New York: Routledge).

Brandon, Ruth (2004), *The People's Chef: Alexis Soyer, A Life in Seven Courses* (Chichester: Wiley).

Brewster, Ben and Jacobs, Lea (1997), *Theatre to Cinema: Stage Pictorialism and the Early Feature Film* (Oxford: Oxford University Press).

Briggs, Asa (1990), *Victorian Cities* (Harmondsworth, Middlesex: Penguin Books).

Brunel, Pierre, ed. (1992), *Companion to Literary Myths, Heroes and Archetypes*, trans. Wendy Allatson, Judith Hayward and Trista Selous (London and New York: Routledge).

Brunvand, Jan Harold (1984), *The Choking Doberman and Other 'New' Urban Legends* (Harmondsworth, Middlesex: Penguin).

Brunvand, Jan Harold (1981), *The Vanishing Hitchhiker: American Urban Legends and Their Meanings* (New York: W.W. Norton).

Buchanan-Brown, John (1978), *Phiz!: The Book Illustrations of Hablot Knight Brown* (Newton Abbot and London: David Charles).

Burton, Brian (1962), *Sweeney Todd the Barber: A Melodrama* (Birmingham: C. Combridge Ltd).

Butt, John and Tillotson, Kathleen (1957), *Dickens at Work* (London and New York: Methuen).

Byrom, Michael (1972), *Punch and Judy: Its Origins and Evolution* (London: Perpetua Press Ltd).

Byrom, Michael (1983), *Punch in the Italian Puppet Theatre* (Fontwell: Centaur Press).

Campbell, R (1747), *The London Tradesman, being a compendious view of all the trades, professions, arts, both liberal and mechanic, now practised in the cities of London and Westminster* (London: T. Gardner).

Carey, John (1973), *The Violent Effigy: A Study of Dickens's Imagination* (London: Faber & Faber).

Charmoy, Cozette de (1973), *The True Life of Sweeney Todd (A Collage Novel)* (London: Gaberbocchus Press).

Chibnall, Steve and Petley, Julian, eds (2002), *British Horror Cinema* (London and New York: Routledge).

Clery, E.J. (1995), *The Rise of Supernatural Fiction, 1762–1800* (Cambridge: Cambridge University Press).

Cockshut, A.O.J. (1961), *The Imagination of Charles Dickens* (London: Collins).

Collins, Dick, ed. (2005), *The String of Pearls: A Romance. The Original Tale of Sweeney Todd* (Ware: Wordsworth Classics).

Columbus, Christopher (1987), *The Log of Christopher Columbus*, trans. Robert H. Fuson (Southampton: Ashford Press).

Cowan, Ruth (2006), *Relish: The Extraordinary Life of Alexis Soyer, Victorian Celebrity Chef* (London: Weidenfeld and Nicolson).

Critchley, T.A. (1978), *A History of Police in England and Wales* (London: Constable).

Crockett, S.R. (1896), *The Grey Man* (London: Fisher Unwin).

Cross, Gilbert (1977), *Next Week – East Lynne: Domestic Drama in Performance 1820–1874* (London: Associated University Presses).

Cross, Gillian (1982), *The Dark Behind the Curtain* (Oxford: Oxford University Press).

Cross, Nigel (1985), *The Common Writer: Life in Nineteenth-Century Grub Street* (Cambridge: Cambridge University Press).

Danby, Mary, ed. (1981), *65 Great Tales of Horror* (London: Octopus Books Ltd).

Dart, Gregory (2003), 'The Demon Barber and Fleet Street' in *Sweeney Todd: The Demon Barber Fleet Street. A musical thriller*, by Stephen Sondheim, and Royal Opera House, Covent Garden, Programme: 14.

Davis, Jim and Emeljanow, Victor (2001), *Reflecting the Audience: London Theatregoing, 1840–1880* (Hatfield: University of Hertfordshire Press).

De Quincey, Thomas (1987), *Confessions of an English Opium Eater*, ed. Alethea Hayter (Harmondsworth, Middlesex: Penguin Books).

Deloney, Thomas (1612/1969), *Thomas of Reading. Or, the sixe worthy yeomen of the West.* Facsimile reprint of 4th edn: London, printed for T[homas] P[avier] (repr. Menston, Yorkshire: The Scolar Press).

Dickens, Charles (1981), *Charles Dickens's Book of Memoranda: A Photographic and Typographic Facsimile of the Notebook Begun in January 1855,* ed. Fred Kaplan (New York: The New York Public Library).

Dickens, Charles (2000), *The Dent Uniform Edition of Dickens's Journalism,* Volume 4: *The Uncommercial Traveller* and Other Papers, 1859–70, eds Michael Slater and John Drew (London: J.M. Dent).

Dickens, Charles (1998), *'Gone Astray' and Other Papers from* Household Words, *1851–1859'*, ed. Michael Slater (London: J.M. Dent).

Dickens, Charles (1968), *Martin Chuzzlewit*, ed. P.N. Furbank (Harmondsworth, Middlesex: Penguin).

Dickens, Charles (1978), *Nicholas Nickleby*, ed. Michael Slater (Harmonsdworth, Middlesex: Penguin).

Dickens, Charles (1966), *Oliver Twist*, ed. Angus Wilson (Harmondsworth, Middlesex: Penguin).

Dickens, Charles (1986), *Pickwick Papers*, ed. James Kinsley (Oxford: Clarendon Press).

Disher, Maurice Willson (1949), *Blood and Thunder: Mid-Victorian Melodrama and its Origins* (London: Frederick Muller Ltd).

Disher, M. Willson, 'On the Trail of a Legend', *The Times* (Wednesday, 26 July 1939); p. 12; Issue 48367; col. B.

Dizikes, John (1993), *Opera in America: A Cultural History* (London and New Haven: Yale University Press).

Dorson, Richard M. (1976), *Folklore and Fakelore: Essays toward a Discipline of Folk Studies* (Cambridge, Massachusetts, and London: Harvard University Press).

Douglas, John and Mark Olshaker (2000), *The Cases that Haunt Us* (New York: Scribner).

du Breuil, Jacques (1612), *Le Théâtre des Antiquites de Paris* (Paris: Claude de la Tour).

Edwards, Cliff (1981), *Hair Raisers 1: Sweeney Todd* (London: Longman).

Edwards, Philip, ed. (1999), *The Journals of Captain Cook* (London: Penguin Classics).

Fiddes, Nick (1991), *Meat: A Natural Symbol* (London: Routledge).

Fiske, John (1873), *Myths and Myth Makers: Old Tales and Superstitions Interpreted by Comparative Mythology* (Boston: James R. Osgood and Co.).

Frazer, James (1986), *The Golden Bough: A Study in Magic and Religion* (London: Penguin Books).

Frye, Northrop (1957), *Anatomy of Criticism* (Princeton: Princeton University Press).

Gaiman, Neil and Zulli, Michael (1992), *Taboo 6 – The Sweeney Todd Penny Dreadful* (n.p.: SpiderBaby Graphics).

George, M. Dorothy (1925/1984), *London Life in the Eighteenth Century* (Chicago: Academy Chicago Publishers).

Gerould, Daniel, ed. (1980), *Melodrama* (New York: New York Literary Forum).

Gifford, Denis, ed. (1980), *The British Film Catalogue, 1895–1985: A Reference Guide* (Newton Abbot and London: David & Charles).

Goddard, Henry (1956), *Memoirs of a Bow Street Runner* (London: Museum Press Ltd).

Goldman, Laurence, ed. (1999), *The Anthropology of Cannibalism* (London: Bergin & Garvey).

Gordon, Joanne (1990), *Art Isn't Easy: The Achievement of Stephen Sondheim* (Carbondale, Ill: Southern Illinois University Press).

Gottfried, Martin (1993), *Sondheim* (New York: Harry N. Abrams).

Greenwald, Ken (1993), *The Lost Adventures of Sherlock Holmes. Based on the Original Radio Plays by Denis Green and Anthony Boucher* (New York: Barnes and Noble).

Guest, Kristen, ed. (2001), *Eating Their Words: Cannibalism and the Boundaries of Cultural Identity* (Albany, New York: State University of New York Press).

Haining, Peter, ed. (1989), *Dead of Night: Thirteen Stories by the Masters of the Macabre* (New York: Dorset Press).

Haining, Peter, ed. (1973), *Great British Tales of Terror: Gothic Stories of Horror and Romance* (Harmondsworth, Middlesex: Penguin Books).

Haining, Peter (1977), *The Legend and Bizarre Crimes of Spring Heeled Jack* (London: Frederick Muller Ltd).

Haining, Peter, ed. (1975), *The Penny Dreadful, Or, Strange, Horrid & Sensational Tales!* (London: Victor Gollancz).

Haining, Peter (1993), *Sweeney Todd: The Real Story of the Demon Barber of Fleet Street* (London: Boxtree Ltd).

Halliday, Stephen (2006), *Newgate: London's Prototype of Hell* (Stroud, Gloucestershire: Sutton Publishing).

Hamilton, Patrick (1941), *Hangover Square: A Story of Darkest Earl's Court* (London: Constable).

Hayward, Arthur L. (1924), *The Dickens Encyclopedia* (London: George Routledge & Sons Ltd).

[Hazel, Harry] (1865), *Sweeney Todd: Or, The Ruffian Barber. A Tale of the Terrors of the Seas and the Mysteries of the City. By Captain Merry* (New York: H. Long & Brothers).

Herodotus (1954), *The Histories*, trans. Aubrey de Selincourt (Harmondsworth, Middlesex: Penguin).

Hibbert, H.G. (1920), *A Playgoer's Memories* (London: Grant Richards).

Hindley, Charles (1878), *The Life and Times of James Catnach. Late of Seven Dials, Ballad Monger* (London: Reeves and Turner).

Hollingham, Richard (2006), 'Natural Born Cannibals'. *New Scientist*, 2455, 31–3.

Holmes, Ronald (1975), *The Legend of Sawney Bean* (London: Frederick Muller Ltd).

Hough, Richard (1994), *Captain James Cook: A Biography* (London: Hodder & Stoughton).

House, Humphrey (1941), *The Dickens World* (Oxford: Oxford University Press).

Hughes, Kathryn (2005), *The Short Life and Long Times of Mrs Beeton* (London: Fourth Estate).

Hurrell, Christopher (2003), 'The Time They Did *Sweeney* in Chicago'. *The Sondheim Review* 9 (4) (Spring 2003), 31–3.

Ilson, Carol (1992), *Harold Prince: From 'Pajama Game' to 'Phantom of the Opera'* (New York: Limelight Editions).

Jackson, Russell (1989), *Victorian Theatre: A New Mermaid Background Book* (London: A&C Black).

James, Elizabeth and Smith, Helen R. (1998), *Penny Dreadfuls and Boys' Adventures: The Barry Ono Collection of Victorian Popular Literature in the British Library* (London: British Library).

James, Louis (1963), *Fiction for the Working Man* (Oxford: Oxford University Press).

James, Louis (2004), 'Rymer, James Malcolm [*pseuds*. M.J. Errym, Malcolm J. Merry] (1803/4–1884)' in *Oxford Dictionary of National Biography* (Oxford: Oxford University Press), 48, pp. 494–5.

James, Louis and Smith, Helen R. (2004), 'Prest, Thomas Peckett (1809/10–1859)' in *New Oxford Dictionary of National Biography* (Oxford: Oxford University Press), 45, 251–2.

Johnson, Captain C. (1714/1734) *A General History of the Lives and Adventures of the Most Famous Highwaymen, Murderers, Street-Robbers, &c.* (London: J. Janeway).

Johnson, Captain C. (1742), *A General History of the Robberies and Murders of the Most Notorious Pyrates ...* (London: Rivington).

Johnson, Edgar (1952), *Charles Dickens, His Tragedy and Triumph*, 2 vols (New York: Simon & Schuster).

Jones, Max (2004), *The Last Great Quest: Captain Scott's Antarctic Sacrifice* (Oxford: Oxford University Press).

Jones, Steve (1986), *London ... The Sinister Side* (Nottingham: Wicked Publications).

Jones, Steve (1989), *Wicked London* (Nottingham: Wicked Publications).

Jupp, Peter and Howarth, Glannys, eds (1996), *The Changing Face of Death: Historical Accounts of Death and Disposal* (Basingstoke: Macmillan).

Kaye, Marvin, ed. (2002), *Sweeney Todd, the Demon Barber of Fleet Street* (by George Dibdin Pitt) (Holicong, Pennsylvania: Nth Dimension Books).

Keightley, Thomas (1834/1972), *Tales and Popular Fictions: Their Resemblance and Transmission from Country to Country* (London: Whittaker and Co.; rpr. New York: Norwood Editions).

Keller, James (2000), Booklet. 'Notes on Sweeney Todd' in *Sweeney Todd. Live In Concert.* By Stephen Sondheim and Hugh Wheeler (New York Philharmonic), pp. 14–23.

Kent, William (1952), *London Mystery and Mythology* (London: Staples Press Ltd).

Kilgariff, Michael, ed. (1974), *The Golden Age of Melodrama: Twelve 19th-Century Melodramas* (London: Wolfe Publishing Ltd).

King, Stephen (1992), *Danse Macabre* (London: Macdonald and Co.).

Kitson, Peter J. (2004), 'Sustaining the Romantic and Racial Self: Eating People in the 'South Seas'' in *Cultures of Taste/Theories of Appetite – Eating Romanticism*, ed. Timothy Martin (New York: Palgrave-Macmillan), pp. 77–96.

Knapp, A. and Baldwin, W. (1809), *Criminal Chronology; or, the New Newgate Calendar*, 4 vols (London: Nuttall, Fisher, and Dixon).

Korn, Daniel, Radice, Mark and Hawes, Charlie (2001), *Cannibal: The History of the People-Eaters* (London: Macmillan/Channel 4 Books).

Kurlansky, Mark (2002), *Choice Cuts: A Miscellany of Food Writing* (London: Vintage).

Kynaston, David (1994), *The City of London. Volume I: A World of Its Own, 1815–1890* (London: Chatto & Windus).

Lane, Brian (1992), *The Murder Guide to London: Detailed Accounts of the Capital's Most Bizarre Murders* (London: Magpie).

Leach, Maria, ed. (1949), *Funk and Wagnalls Standard Dictionary of Folklore, Mythology, and Legend*, 2 vols (New York: Funk & Wagnalls).

Leslie, Edward (1988), *Desperate Journeys, Abandoned Souls: True Stories of Castaways and Other Survivors* (London: Macmillan).

Lillo, George (1966), *Fatal Curiosity*, ed. William H. McBurney (Regents Restoration Drama Series) (Lincoln, Nebraska: University of Nebraska Press).

Lindeström, Peter Mårtensson (1925/1979), *Geographia Americæ with an Account of the Delaware Indians*, trans. Amandus Johnson (Philadelphia: Swedish Colonial Society; rpr. New York: Arno Press).

Linebaugh, Peter (2003), *The London Hanged: Crime and Civil Society in the Eighteenth Century* (London: Verso).

Linnane, Fergus (2003), *London's Underworld: Three Centuries of Violence and Crime* (London: Robson Books).

Lorie, Peter (1992), *Superstition: A Book of Ancient Lore* (London: Simon & Schuster).

McKechnie, Samuel (1967), *Popular Entertainments Through the Ages* (London: Sampson Low, Marston & Co.).

McWilliam, Rohan (2004), 'Edward Lloyd (1815–1890)' in *Oxford Dictionary of National Biography* (Oxford: Oxford University Press), 34, pp. 118–19.

Martingale, Moira (1993), *Cannibal Killers: The Impossible Monsters* (London: Robert Hale Limited).

Mayhew, Henry (1967), *London Labour and the London Poor*, 4 vols (London: Frank Cass & Co., Ltd).

Midgeley, Mary (1979), *Beast & Man: The Roots of Human Nature* (London: Methuen).

Miller, Peter and Lewton, Randall (1980), *The Sweeney Todd Shock 'n' Roll Show* (London: Samuel French).

Mitchell, R.J. and Leys, M.D.R. (1958), *A History of London Life* (London: Longmans).

Montaigne, Michel de (1957), *The Complete Essays of Montaigne*, trans. Donald M. Frame (Stanford: Stanford University Press).

Moore, Lucy (2000), *Con Men and Cutpurses: Scenes from the Hogarthian Underworld* (London: Penguin).

Moore, Lucy (1997), *The Thieves' Opera* (London: Penguin).

Morley, Malcolm (1962), 'Dickens's Contribution to *Sweeney Todd*'. *Dickensian* 58 (Spring), 92–5.

Morton, James (2004), *The First Detective: The Life and Revolutionary Times of Eugene-Francois Vidocq, Criminal, Spy, and Private Eye* (London: Edbury).

Morton, Timothy, ed. (2004), *Cultures of Taste/Theories of Appetite: Eating Romanticism* (London: Palgrave-Macmillan).

Nash, John Roberts (1992), *Dictionary of Crime* (London: Headline Books).

Newton, H. Chance (1927), *Crime and the Drama; or, Dark Deeds Dramatized* (London: Stanley Paul and Co.).

Nicoll, Allardyce (1959), *History of English Drama, 1600–1900. Volume V: Late Nineteenth Century* (Cambridge: Cambridge University Press).

Nightingale, Moira (1993), *Cannibal Killers* (London: Robert Hale Limited).

Obeyesekere, Gananath (1992), ' "British Cannibals" ': Contemplation of an Event in the Death and Resurrection of James Cook, Explorer'. *Critical Inquiry* 18 (Summer), 630–54.

O'Dell, Sterg (1954/69), *A Chronological List of Prose Fiction in English Printed in England and Other Countries, 1475–1640* (repr. New York: Kraus Reprint Co.).

Olsen, John (2003), 'Sondheim Wanted *Sweeney* to be Very Scary'. *Sondheim Review* 9 (3) (Winter), 13.

Olsen, John (2003), 'Terfel Stars in a Rich and Eerie *Sweeney*'. *Sondheim Review* 9 (3) (Winter), 12.

Opie, Iona and Peter (1959/1967), *The Lore and Language of Schoolchildren* (Oxford: Oxford University Press).

Orsini, Elizabeth (1981), *The Book of Pies* (London: Pan).

Orwell, George (1994), *Essays* (London: Penguin).

Pasquin, Anthony (1793), *The Life of the Late Earl of Barrymore. Including a history of the Wargrave theatricals and original anecdotes of eminent persons. By Anthony Pasquin, esq. A new edition, corrected and much enlarged* (London: H.D. Symonds).

Pate, Janet (1975), *The Black Book of Villains* (London: David & Charles).

Peary, Danny (1991), *Cult Movie Stars* (New York and London: Simon & Schuster).

Pickering, Michael (1999), 'Consuming Doubts: What Some People Ate? Or What Some People Swallowed?' in *The Anthropology of Cannibalism*, ed. Laurence R. Goldman (London: Bergin and Garvey), pp. 52–3.

Porter, Roy (1982), *English Society in the Eighteenth Century* (London: Penguin).

Porter, Roy (2004), *Madmen: A Social History of Madhouses, Mad-Doctors, & Lunatics* (London: Tempus).

Praz, Mario (1986), 'Introductory Essay' in *Three Gothic Novels*, ed. Peter Fairclough (London: Penguin Books), pp. 7–34.

Priestman, Martin, ed. (2003), *The Cambridge Companion to Crime Fiction* (Cambridge: Cambridge University Press), pp. 7–34.

Rahill, Frank (1967), *The World of Melodrama* (University Park and London: Pennsylvania State University Press).

Reidelbach, Maria (1991), *Completely MAD: A History of the Comic Book and Magazine* (New York: Little, Brown, and Company).

Ribby, Jonathan (2000), *English Horror: A Century of Horror Cinema* (London: Reynolds & Hearn).

Richards, Jeffrey, ed. (1998), *The Unknown 1930s: An Alternative History of the British Cinema 1929–39* (London: I.B. Tauris, Publishers).

Rogers, Ben (2003), *Beef and Liberty: Roast Beef, John Bull, and the English Nation* (London: Chatto & Windus).

Rosser, Austin (1971), *Sweeney Todd: The Demon Barber of Fleet Street. A Victorian Melodrama* (Based on the original by George Dibdin Pitt) (London: Samuel French).

Rybczynski, Witold (1996), *City Life* (New York: Touchstone).

Sabin, Roger (1996), *Comics, Comix, & Graphic Novels: The History of Comic Art* (New York: Phaidon).

Saint, Andrew and Darley, Gillian, eds (1994), *The Chronicles of London* (London: Weidenfeld and Nicolson).

Schlicke, Paul, ed. (1999), *The Oxford Reader's Companion to Dickens* (Oxford: Oxford University Press).

Scott, Clement (1899), *The Drama of Yesterday and Today*, 2 vols (London and New York: Macmillan Co.).

Secrest, Meryle (1998), *Stephen Sondheim* (New York: Alfred E. Knopf).

Sharpe, James (2004), *Dick Turpin: The Myth of the English Highwayman* (London: Profile Books).

Shoemaker, Robert (2004), *The London Mob: Violence and Disorder in 18th-century England* (London and New York: London & Hambledon).

Simpson, Jacqueline (1983), 'Urban Legends in *The Pickwick Papers*'. *Journal of American Folklore* 96 (382) (October–December), 462–70.

Smith, Alexander (1726), *Memoirs of the life and times of the famous Jonathan Wild, Together with the History and Lives of Modern Rogues* (London).

Smith, Andrew (2004), *Victorian Demons: Medicine, Masculinity, and the Gothic at the fin-de-siècle* (Manchester: Manchester University Press).

Smith, Helen R. (2002), *New Light on Sweeney Todd, Thomas Peckett Prest, James Malcolm Rymer and Elizabeth Caroline Grey* (London, Bloomsbury: Jarndyce).

Smith, Stephen (2004), *Underground London: Travels Beneath the City Streets* (London: Little Brown).

Sondheim, Stephen (and Hugh Wheeler) (1979), *Sweeney Todd, The Demon Barber of Fleet Street. A Musical Thriller* (New York: Dodd, Mead & Co.).

Sondheim, Stephen (2005), *Sweeney Todd: The Demon Barber of Fleet Street. A Musical Thriller*, Orch. Sarah Travis. Perf. Patti LuPone, Michael Cerveris (Nonesuch).

Sondheim, Stephen (1979), *Sweeney Todd: The Demon Barber of Fleet Street. A Musical Thriller*, Orch. Jonathan Tunick. Perf. Angela Lansbury, Len Cariou and Victor Garber. Cond. Paul Gemignani (RCA Red Seal).

Soyer, Alexis (1855), *A Shilling Cookery for the People* (London: George Routledge and Co.).

Speaight, George (1990), *The History of the English Puppet Theatre*, 2nd edn (London: Robert Hale).

Springhall, John (1994), '"Disseminating Impure Literature": The "Penny Dreadful" Publishing Business Since 1860'. *Economic History Review* New Series 47 (3) (August), 567–84.

Stoker, Bram (1993), *Dracula*, ed. Marjorie Howes (London: J.M. Dent/Everyman).

Stone, Harry (1994), *The Night Side of Dickens: Cannibalism, Passion, Necessity* (Columbus: Ohio State University Press).

Sugden, Philip (1995), *The Complete History of Jack the Ripper* (London: Robinson).

Summers, Montague (1940), *A Gothic Bibliography* (London: Fortune Press).

Summers, Montague (1938), *The Gothic Quest: A History of the Gothic Novel* (London: Fortune Press).

Sutherland, J.A. (1976), *Victorian Novelists and Their Publishers* (London: Athlone Press).

Sweeney Todd (1928), Producer Harry Rowson. Perf. Moore Marriott, Zoe Palmer, Charles Ashton (Stoll Films).

Sweeney Todd (2006), Dir. David Moore. Perf. Roy Winstone, Essie Davis and David Warner (BBC One Film Productions).

Sweeney Todd, The Demon Barber of Fleet Street (1936), Dir. George King. Perf. Tod Slaughter, Stella Rho, Johnny Singer, Eve Lister (Ambassador Pictures).

The Tale of Sweeney Todd (1998), Dir. John Schlesinger. Perf. Ben Kingsley, Joanna Lumley and Campbell Scott (Showtime/Third Row Center Films).

Tannahill, Reay (1975), *Flesh and Blood: A History of the Cannibal Complex* (London: Hamilton).

Tatar, Maria, ed (1999), *The Classic Fairy Tales* (New York and London: W.W. Norton).

Thomas, Joyce (1989), *Inside the Wolf's Belly: Aspects of the Fairy Tale* (Sheffield: Sheffield Academic Press).

Thompson, G. (1840), *Newgate Calendar, containing the lives of the most notorious characters who have violated the laws of their country* (London: Walker & Co.).

Thompson, Philip (1972), *The Grotesque* (London: Methuen & Co.).

Thompson, Stith (1955–8), *Motif-Index of Folk Literature: A Classification of Narrative Elements in Folktales, Ballads, Myths, Fables, Mediaeval Romances, Exempla, Fabliaux, Jest-Books, and Local Legends*, revised edn, 6 vols (Bloomington, Indiana, and London: Indiana University Press).

Tillotson, Kathleen (1954), *Novels of the Eighteen-Forties* (Oxford: Clarendon Press).

Turner, E.S. (1948), *Boys Will Be Boys: the Story of Sweeney Todd, Deadwood Dick, Sexton Blake, Billy Bunter, Dick Barton, et al.* (London: Michael Joseph).

Viagas, Robert (2004), 'Notes on Sweeney Todd' in *Playbill*, The New York City Opera (March), pp. 28–33.

Villette, John (1776), *The Annals of Newgate, or Malefactor's Register. Containing a Particular and Circumstantial account of the lives, transactions, and trials of the most notorious malefactors*, 4 vols (London: J. Wenman).

Visser, Margaret (1991), *Much Depends on Dinner: History and Mythology, Allure and Obsession, Perils and Taboos, of an Ordinary Meal* (London: Viking Penguin).

Visser, Margaret (1991), *The Rituals of Dinner: The Origins, Evolution, Eccentricities, and Meaning of Table Manners* (London: Viking).

Wall, Stephen, ed. (1970), *Charles Dickens: A Critical Anthology* (Penguin Critical Anthologies) (Harmondsworth, Middlesex: Penguin).

Warner, Marina (2000), *No Go the Bogeyman: Scaring, Lulling, and Making Mock* (London: Vintage).

Waugh, Evelyn (1977), *A Handful of Dust* (Boston: Little, Brown and Company).

Wheeler, Michael (1994), *English Fiction of the Victorian Period*, 2nd edn (London: Longman).

Wilkinson, George Theodore (1962), *The Newgate Calendar*, 3 vols (St Albans, Herts.: Granada Publishing).

Wilson, A.N. (2003), *The Victorians* (London: Random House).

Wise, Sarah (2004), *The Italian Boy: Murder and Grave-Robbery in 1830s London* (London: Jonathan Cape).

Witney, Frederick (1947), *Grand Guignol* (London: Constable).

Zadan, Craig (1974/1994), *Sondheim & Company* (New York: De Capo Press).

*

Readers should also be aware of the following online information and internet resources:

Blood and Dime Novels: a forum for collectors to discuss Bloods, Penny Dreadfuls, and Dime Novels. Yahoo Groups. Founded August 2000. Owner and Manager: Justin Gilbert. http://groups.yahoo.com/group/BloodsandDimeNovels.

Crime Library: Criminal Minds and Methods. Serial Killers: Truly Weird or Shocking: Sweeney Todd. Mark Gribben. Courtroom Television Network. 2005. www.crimelibrary.com/serial_killers/weird/todd/index_1.html.

Dime Novels and Penny Dreadfuls. Project Managers: Connie Brooks, Jim Coleman and Eleanore Stewart. Stanford University Dept of Special Collections. December 2006. www-sul.stanford.edu/depts/dp/pennies/home.html.

Sweeney Todd, The Demon Barber of Fleet Street in Concert. Ellen M. Krass Productions and KQED. Public Broadcasting Service. October 2001. www.pbs.org/kqed/demon-barber/index.html.

Index

Fox, George 213
Francatelli, Charles Elmé 6
Frank, Melvin 304
Franklin, Sir John 41, 154
Frazer, James 30–1
  The Golden Bough 31
Frye, Northrop 52, 62, 68–9
  Anatomy of Criticism 68
Fuseli, Henry 253

Gaiman Neil 82–3, 85, 97, 190–1,
  298–300
  American Gods 299
  Neverwhere 300
  Sandman 300
Galt, John 96
  Laurie Todd; or, The Settlers in the Woods 96
Gamble, John 137
Garber, Victor 282
Gaskell, Elizabeth 8, 138
Gay, John 59
Gein, Edward 56
Gesta Romanorum 185
Gibbon, Edward 177
  Decline and Fall of the Roman Empire 177
Gilbert, Frederick 102
Gilbert, W. S. 37
  'Yarn of the Nancy Bell' 37
Gilgamesh 51
Gill, A. A. 245
Gillray, James 233, 253
'Gnomen' 81, 175, 178 (*see also* Notes &
  Queries)
Godfrey, Roy 259
Gog and Magog 92–3, 116
Goldman, Laurence R. 29
Goldoni, Carlo 53–4, 59
  La Favola de' Tre Gobbi ('The Tale of the
  Three Hunchbacks') 53
Goldsmith, Oliver 91, 96, 128, 143, 249
  The Vicar of Wakefield 91, 96, 128
Gordon Riots of 1780 16, 20, 74, 95, 134
Gottfried, Martin 282, 286
Graham, Colin 258–9, 291
Graham, Sir James 184
Grant, C. J. 145
Gravett, Paul 299
Great Exhibition 6

Green, Dennis, 239
Greene, Robert 138, 186
Greenwald, Ken 241
  The Lost Adventures of Sherlock Holmes 241
Grout, Donald Jay 289
  A Short History of Opera 289
Guest, Kristen 212–13
Gulliford, Captain Catherine 4

Haining, Peter 82, 149, 156–8, 175, 202,
  204, 231, 243
Hall, Sir Benjamin 96
Hamilton, Ian 256–7
Hamilton, Maria 204
Hamilton, Patrick 270
Hammerstein, Jimmy 270
Hammerstein, Oscar 260–1, 288
Hancock, Sheila 284
Handley, Vernon 258
Hangover Square 270–2 (*see also* Patrick
  Hamilton)
  George Harvey Bone 270, 272
Hardy, Thomas 138, 221
Hare, William 41, 109, 111, 141
Harmon, Thomas 186
Harris, R. W. 14
Harris, Richard 57
  Hannibal Lecter 57
Harrison, Frederick Valentine 140
Harrison, Harry 57
  Make Room! Make Room! 57
Harrison, John 137
  The Novelist's Magazine 137
Hartman, Fritz 231
Hatter's Castle 238
Haunt of Fear, The 141
Hays, Will 224
Haywood, Eliza 7–8
  The History of Miss Betsy Thoughtless 7
Hazleton, Frederick 78, 107, 197, 213, 220,
  232,
Hazlewood, Colin 201–2
Heaney, Seamus 115
Hearn, George 283, 302–3
Herodotus 29–30, 36
  Histories 29
Herrmann, Bernard 271–2, 275 (*see also*
  Hangover Square)